Social Psychology of Consumer Behavior

Frontiers of Social Psychology

SERIES EDITORS

Arie W. Kruglanski
University of Maryland at College Park

Joseph P. Forgas
University of New South Wales

Frontiers of Social Psychology is a new series of domain-specific handbooks. The purpose of each volume is to provide readers with a cutting-edge overview of the most recent theoretical, methodological, and practical developments in a substantive area of social psychology, in greater depth than is possible in general social psychology handbooks. The editors and contributors are all internationally renowned scholars whose work is at the cutting-edge of research.

Scholarly, yet accessible, the volumes in the *Frontiers* series are an essential resource for senior undergraduates, postgraduates, researchers, and practitioners, and are suitable as texts in advanced courses in specific subareas of social psychology.

PUBLISHED TITLES

Negotiation Theory and Research, Thompson
Close Relationships, Noller and Feeney
Evolution and Social Psychology, Schaller, Simpson, and Kenrick
Social Psychology and the Unconscious, Bargh
Affect in Social Thinking and Behavior, Forgas
The Science of Social Influence, Pratkanis
Social Communication, Fiedler
The Self, Sedikides and Spencer
Personality and Social Behavior, Rhodewalt
Attitudes and Attitude Change, Crano and Prislin
Social Cognition, Strack and Förster
Social Psychology of Consumer Behavior, Wänke

FORTHCOMING TITLES

Exploration in Political Psychology, Krosnick and Chiang
Social Motivation, Dunning
Intergroup Conflicts and Their Resolution, Bar-Tal

For continually updated information about published and forthcoming titles in the *Frontiers of Social Psychology* series, please visit http://www.psypress.com/frontiers

Social Psychology of Consumer Behavior

Edited by
Michaela Wänke

Psychology Press
Taylor & Francis Group

New York   London

Psychology Press
Taylor & Francis Group
270 Madison Avenue
New York, NY 10016

Psychology Press
Taylor & Francis Group
27 Church Road
Hove, East Sussex BN3 2FA

© 2009 by Taylor & Francis Group, LLC
Psychology Press is an imprint of Taylor & Francis Group, an Informa business

10 9 8 7 6 5 4 3 2 1

International Standard Book Number-13: 978-1-84169-498-6 (Hardcover)

Library of Congress Cataloging-in-Publication Data

Social psychology of consumer behavior / editor, Michaela Wanke.
     p. cm. -- (Frontiers of social psychology)
   Includes bibliographical references and index.
     ISBN 978-1-84169-498-6 (hardcover : alk. paper)
     1. Consumer behavior. 2. Consumer behavior--Psychological aspects. 3.
Consumers--Psychology. 4. Social psychology. I. Wänke, Michaela.

HF5415.32.S596 2009
658.8'342--dc22   2008048444

Visit the Taylor & Francis Web site at
http://www.taylorandfrancis.com

and the Psychology Press Web site at
http://www.psypress.com

For my students,
in particular, Sabine, Malte, Florian, Jochim,
Jakub, Stefan, Alice, and Leonie.

Contents

SECTION III AFFECTIVE AND COGNITIVE FEELINGS IN CONSUMER JUDGMENT

SECTION IV SOCIAL AND MEDIA INFLUENCES ON JUDGMENT AND BEHAVIOR

SECTION V GOALS AND SELF-REGULATION

Section *I*

Introduction: A Tale of Two Disciplines

1

What's Social about Consumer Behavior?

MICHAELA WÄNKE
Universität Basel

*T*he topic of consumer psychology typically provokes two sorts of responses. Some people find it fascinating, in particular, the effects of subliminally presented messages in advertising. Others consider consumer psychology to be evil and morally objectionable, in particular, the effects of subliminally presented messages in advertising. Apparently, "The Hidden Persuaders" (Packard, 1957), a best seller in the 1950s and 1960s, has shaped the public's view of consumer psychology for about half a century. Interestingly, in current consumer research we also witness a renewed academic interest in the unconscious (see also Dijksterhuis, this volume). The research snippets that make it into the public arena most often involve unconscious influences in one way or another—although not necessarily subliminal influences. Without doubt, the literature shows many such fascinating—or, depending on perspective, evil, manipulating—effects: People buy more French wine relative to German wine when French rather than German music is played in the supermarket (North, Hargreaves, & McKendrick, 1997); the same wine priced at $45 is not only subjectively rated as better tasting than when priced at $5, but also prompts higher activity in the medial orbitofrontal cortex, the part of the brain that experiences pleasure (Plassmann, O'Doherty, Shiv, & Rangel, 2008); people prefer brands that begin with the first letter of their name (Brendl, Chattopadhyay, Pelham, & Carvallo, 2005); cars depicted as driving from left to right in an ad are perceived as being faster and stronger than cars moving from right to left (Maass, 2007); and, yes, more people chose Lipton Ice Tea over other soft drinks when subliminally primed with Lipton Ice Tea (Karremans, Stroebe, & Claus, 2006).

Whether such findings are fascinating or evil is, of course, in the eye of the beholder, an utterly subjective question, and not suitable for an objective, scientific debate. What is indubitable, however, is that these studies allow researchers to better understand the processes involved in central topics of fundamental social psychology such as priming, self-esteem, embodiment, or (the role of expectation in) attitude formation. The point I want to argue in this introductory chapter, and with this book, *The Social Psychology of Consumer Behavior*, in general, is that consumer behavior is an important, interesting, and fruitful topic for psychology and social psychology in particular. I will illustrate why studying consumer behavior is a genuine social psychological topic. A second goal of the book is to illustrate that psychological research in consumer behavior involves more than a sample of sensational and surprising findings. All chapters in the book document that the research is driven by clearly spelled-out theories embedded in a more inclusive scientific framework, and it delivers important knowledge that is informative for both psychological theory and applied contexts.

SOCIAL PSYCHOLOGY'S ROLE IN STUDYING CONSUMER BEHAVIOR

"Advertising is an essential factor in modern business methods, and to advertise wisely the business man must understand the workings of the minds of his customers. ... he must know how to apply psychology to advertising." Substitute "business person" for "business man," and the statement represents a timely and modern summary of the significance of psychology in explaining consumer behavior. In fact, it was written in 1904 by Walter Dill Scott, a disciple of Wilhelm Wundt, in an article for the *Atlantic Monthly*. Apparently, the notion that psychology can help and advance understanding of consumer behavior is almost as old as psychology as a scientific discipline. Around 1900, Harlow Gale—a psychologist at the University of Minnesota—undertook experimental studies on the effects of advertising and studied such modern phenomena as advertising involvement, attitude toward the ad, and low-involvement learning (Eighmey & Sar, 2007). He also taught a course on the psychology of advertising and influenced many scholars. The first textbooks in consumer psychology soon followed (Scott, 1908; Münsterberg, 1912, 1913), illustrating the fact that the young discipline quickly discovered advertising, marketing, and market research as potential topics of applied research.

A closer look at Scott's essay on "Psychology of Advertising" (1904) reveals quite explicitly one of the major factors in the relationship between psychology and consumer research. He argues that "The time is not far away when the advertising writer will find out the inestimable benefits of knowledge of psychology. ... The mere mention of psychological terms, habit, self, conception, discrimination, association, memory, imagination and perception, reason, emotion, instinct and will, should create a flood of new thought that should appeal to every consumer of advertising space." Scott's call for psychological know-how in order to create better advertising assigns to psychology the role of an auxiliary in understanding, explaining, and modifying consumer behavior. Undoubtedly, social psychological theories and know-how are immensely beneficial in this respect. For example, the question of how advertising affects recipients is hardly distinguishable from the question of how persuasion works in general; social psychologists know under what conditions attitudes correspond to behavior and they can help design conditions so that proenvironmental attitudes translate into recycling habits (see Goldstein & Cialdini, this volume); social psychological know-how suggests that decisions for the more distant future are governed by different concerns than decisions for the near future (see Eyal, Liberman, & Trope, this volume) and therefore the same product claim may be more or less effective depending on the time frame. Not surprisingly, a citation analysis of the *Journal of Consumer Research* (*JCR*) found psychology to be the most influential theoretical base (Leong, 1989). The *Journal of Personality and Social Psychology* was one of the two most important journals in *JCR's* citation network (Phillips, Baumgartner, & Pieters, 1999). The list of recipients of the Distinguished Scientific Contribution Award of the Society for Consumer Psychology contains many whose primary work took place in social psychology.

From this perspective, the prime beneficiary from applying social psychology in a consumer context is consumer research. However, social psychology's engagement in research on consumer behavior is worthwhile for social psychology as well. First, social psychology profits, of course, from validating its theories in a broader context. Applying the more general assumptions to applied questions may help to advance these theories and determine the moderating conditions. Note that according to this view, the stimuli with which theories are tested are interchangeable and consumer stimuli are just one class of many, just as consumer research is just one of many applications. Indeed, this perspective applies to a large part of social psychologists' approach to consumer behavior. For example, Fazio's MODE model postulates the accessibility of an attitude as a moderator of the degree to which the attitude predicts behavior (Fazio, 1990; Fazio & Towles-Schwen, 1999). A seminal study showed that participants' attitudes toward different brands of chocolate bars predicted which chocolate bars they later chose; the effect was greater when the respective attitudes were highly accessible and not so pronounced for less accessible attitudes (Fazio, Powell, & Williams, 1989). The basic assumption is, of course, not restricted to brand attitudes and brand choice but could be (and has been) tested with different stimuli, for example, attitudes toward participating in psychological experiments (Snyder & Kendziersky, 1982), attitudes toward student housing (Regan & Fazio, 1977), and voting behavior (Fazio & Williams, 1986). Applying models and theories in different contexts is central to scientific advancement and is not to be deprecated. But there is a second, and arguably more important, reason for social psychologists to study consumer behavior.

The main argument for social psychology to study consumer behavior is that the consumer domain offers a rich field of topics that are inherently interesting to social psychology. For example, if one wants to understand how persuasion works, one can hardly avoid studying advertising as it is the major field where persuasion occurs. If one wants to understand self-regulation, the behaviors that lend themselves to being studied are often consumption behaviors such as smoking, dieting, substance abuse, and media consumption (see Friese, Hofmann, & Wänke, this volume). In general, studying social behavior often involves studying consumer-related behavior or behavior in a consumer context. As I will elaborate in more detail later, consumer behavior and social behavior overlap to a large extent, and thus studying consumer behavior is a genuine aspect of social psychology.

That consumer behavior is a natural field for studying social behavior is also evident from early work. In the 1920s and 1930s, eminent social psychologists of the University of Vienna—such as Paul Lazarsfeld, Maria Jahoda, and Herta Herzog—explored "Neue Wege der Verkaufspsychologie" (new approaches in the psychology of selling),[1] "Strumpfkauf bei Delka" (buying stockings at Delka), "Wie wirbt man für Schokolade" (how to advertise chocolate), or "Absatzchancen eines fertigen Kaffees auf dem Wiener Markt" (the marketing potential of instant coffee in the Viennese market). In part, their interest was financially motivated: During the Depression, employment at academic institutions was scarce. But clearly their research was also driven by intrinsic interest. They "believed that market research provided social researchers fine opportunities to explore the richness of human behavior" and saw market research as an opportunity to "expand the bounds of social research" (Fullerton, 1994, p. 418). Indeed, the work of the Viennese group, although basically applied and for the most part commercially oriented, is a prime example of how studying consumer behavior can advance knowledge about more general principles. One of their findings was—anticipating persuasion research of the 1980s—that when consumers reflected on their decision, persuasive messages should provide information and compelling arguments in order to be effective. For a product to which little reflection would be devoted, arguments would not be necessary, details should be avoided, and constant repetition of the product name would suffice for producing advertising success (cited from Fullerton, 1999, p. 501). Intriguingly, advice like this bears a remarkable resemblance to what prominent social psychological theories such as the elaboration likelihood model (Petty & Cacioppo, 1986) or the heuristic-systematic model (Chaiken, 1987) would suggest to marketers today. Note that in contrast to applying general social psychological theories to consumer behavior, findings in consumer research could also give rise to social psychological theories.

Of course, the latter could be said about any applied research. What distinguishes the consumer domain from other fields, however, is its pervasiveness. What was true of Vienna in the 1930s is even truer of many societies today: Modern societies are consumer societies. We are constantly surrounded by ads intended to influence our shopping and consumption, and even those of us who do not perceive of shopping as a favorite pastime spend considerable time in evaluating, choosing, or consuming products or services. Being a consumer is a social role almost everybody experiences quite frequently. To the extent that we live in a consumer society, and given that social psychology strives to understand socially relevant behavior, affect, and cognition, social psychology cannot exclude the study of consumer behavior.

SOME SOCIAL ASPECTS OF LIVING
IN A CONSUMER SOCIETY

The following sketches will illustrate that in a consumer society much of the behavior studied by social psychologists relates to consumer stimuli and consumer behavior. Thus, the consumer context provides a rich field for the study of social phenomena and behavior.

Consumer Decisions Are Ubiquitous

Whether we are in the supermarket or not, we are constantly making consumer decisions. We enroll in gyms, use our frequent-flyer miles for a vacation resort, buy health care, choose a restaurant, skip dessert for a healthier lifestyle. In fact, most of our daily decisions do not involve existential decisions such as whom to marry or whether to have children or not, but whether to have tea or coffee, use our credit card or pay cash, or other seemingly trivial decisions. Moreover, many of our daily (consumer) behaviors do not even require intentional decisions. Rather, they may be habitual, such as switching to CNN to get the news or accessing Google when looking up some information. A typical day of a typical person is filled with countless minor consumer decisions or the consequences of previous decisions, starting with the brand of toothpaste in the morning to choosing a movie after work.

Consumer Choices Fulfill a Social-Identity Function

Although for most people being a consumer may not be central to their identity, many of their consumer decisions are nevertheless highly identity-relevant insofar as they correspond to a larger set of values and beliefs and express important aspects of the self. Eating a vegetarian diet because one does not want to endorse cruelty to animals and boycotting clothes potentially made by child laborers are some examples. Some people buy a Prius out of environmental concerns; others boycott Japanese cars—such as the Prius—in order to help the local car industry. In this respect, even the choice between Coke and Pepsi is not necessarily trivial. People who cannot discriminate Coke from Pepsi in a blind test, or who prefer Pepsi, may nevertheless adhere to Coke as a cultural icon. Attempts to change the formula of Coke met with angry protests and opposition. Clearly, consumer products and brands do not only fulfill utilitarian needs (Olson & Mayo, 2000; Shavitt, 1990). In a world of oversupply and differentiating brands, many consumers choose brands in order to express their personality or to affiliate themselves with desired others. They do not simply *use* a Mac; they *are* Mac users, and switching to another brand of PC would be akin to treason. From soft drinks to computers, brands may become an ideology.

People may also perceive of products as extended selves (Belk, 1988); for example, they may identify with their cars just as they do with pets. Likewise, brands may define social groups. The Harley-Davidson Club is a legendary example; an Internet search revealed clubs for almost every car brand and model. In my hometown, I found a Volkswagen New Beetle Club whose stated purpose is to cultivate contacts between New Beetle Drivers by organizing social events (among others, a visit to a car cemetery). On the road, drivers of the same car model often greet each other. Apparently, driving the same model is sufficient to establish social closeness.

Brands, products, and consumption habits not only help to establish social connectivity but also serve as status symbols, defining vertical and horizontal social boundaries. By using particular brands or consuming specific products, people can express a certain lifestyle or attempt to convey a particular social impression. Subscribing to the opera conveys one's social position just as going to a monster truck race does. Whether your choice of drink is wine or beer, cappuccino or herbal tea, your order expresses more than merely your taste in beverages.

Consumer Choices Affect Social Perception

Given that brands and products are part of social expression, it is not surprising that people are judged by the brands and products they use. In particular, products of a social-identity function are used as bases for inferences about a target's personality traits (Shavitt & Nelson, 2000). Likewise, smoking, food choice and amount of food intake have all been shown to affect social impressions. Depending on the subculture of the perceiver (age, country), different personality traits are assumed in smokers compared with nonsmokers (e.g., Cooper & Kohn, 1989; Jones & Carroll, 1998). Various studies found that eaters of a healthier diet are perceived ·as more feminine and in general judged more favorably than eaters of unhealthy foods (for a review see Vartanian, Herman, & Polivy, 2007).

Arguing that a Pepsi drinker is to a Coke drinker what a Capulet was to a Montague is, of course, an exaggeration, but clearly brands may distinguish in-group from out-group members. Possibly this is most extreme among teenagers, where the brand of jeans is perceived to determine coolness and popularity. Nevertheless, the phenomenon is not limited to teen culture, as testified by the previous examples of social communities defined by shared brands.

In sum, from wet versus dry shaving to driving a Porsche versus a Smart, consumer behavior is used as a cue in person perception. Most likely, such cues also manifest in behavior toward these consumers. Physical attacks on women who wear fur are a most extreme example.

Affective Consequences of Consumer Behavior

Obviously, consumption and the use of products and services may give pleasure and satisfaction or displeasure and dissatisfaction. People may experience joy from wearing a new sweater or suffer emotional consequences when products or services fail or cause inconvenience. Product use is only one source of affective consumer experiences. The mere act of choosing and acquisition is another. People enjoy or dislike the experience of shopping. They may take pleasure from the freedom of simply choosing between different options (e.g., Botti & Iyengar, 2004), feel overwhelmed and confused by an abundance of options (e.g., Huffman & Kahn, 1998), or feel frustrated by a limited assortment that does not meet their particular needs (e.g., Chernev, 2003). They may experience gratification and a boost in self-esteem from the fact that they can afford a particular consumer lifestyle or grudge the fact that they cannot. Many daily sources of affective experiences involve consumer behavior in one way or another.

The Consumer Context Provides Unique Social Interactions

Granted, we rarely form deep and meaningful relationships with our hairdressers and waiters. Still, the consumer context affords many social interactions over a day. Again, these interactions—even if brief—may constitute a source of affective experiences. The smile of the barista, the compliment from the shop-assistant, and the friendly help from the concierge are just a few examples of how such consumer-related interactions may make us feel good, worthy, and valued, whereas snappy and rude responses have the opposite effect. Besides, the social roles defined by the consumer context may provide unique opportunities for particular behaviors, interactions, and experiences not inherent in other roles. Being a client or customer makes one expect respect, courtesy, and attendance to one's needs. For some, this may be the only role in their life that gives them a limited sense of being in charge and having others meet their demands. To give another example, complaining is a form of social interaction that mostly takes place within the consumer context. A search for "complaint behavior" in the PsycINFO database found that 34 out of 50 entries were studies from the consumer context. (The rest mostly related to health care, which may to some extent also be viewed as consumer context.) Given the importance of the consumer context to social experiences and interactions, it provides a prime opportunity for studying these social behaviors.

Advertising Exposure Shapes Norms and Values

Every day we are exposed to numerous ads and commercials in magazines and on television, the Internet, and billboards. They may of course affect our attitudes and beliefs about the advertised brands, which in turn may influence our choices and behaviors. But beyond their primary purpose of influencing our product judgments, advertising may have further consequences. Consider an ad that was run several years ago by the car manufacturer Audi. The ad showed an Audi A6 being driven from a luxurious home to work. The caption read "The manager." The ad continued with showing scenes from the life of a manager through the visual perspective of the manager. The captions described the scenes as "works a lot," "keeps fit," "is respected." At the end of the day, the manager drives home, gets out of the car, and is enthusiastically greeted by two children (caption: "has on average two children"). Only then, the perspective shifts and the viewer realizes that the manager is a woman, and the caption reads "and a husband." This ad may not only affect how viewers think of the brand Audi or the model A6, but it may also affect gender stereotypes and may provide a role model for female viewers.

Just like books, movies, or television shows, advertising paints a picture of the world and the society in which we live, and thereby also affects how we perceive social reality. This picture is not necessarily accurate and realistic, but is often biased and distorted (see also Shrum, this volume). Here, many social groups are over- or underrepresented. The same applies to events, personal states, and problems. Imagine a sister planet just like ours with a sister population just like ours—only there is no advertising. Imagine further that the people on the sister planet were to watch Planet Earth commercials. What would they think of those Earthlings? They would probably assume that people on Earth are all very attractive and well groomed, that there are only few old people, but those few old people are all fit and healthy, that poverty is unknown on planet Earth, and that many people are affluent. Although many people seem to suffer from indigestion and headaches, most health problems are rather trivial.

Not only are social groups over- or underrepresented in advertising, a potential bias comes from the way social groups are portrayed and the roles they occupy. For example, studies of the 1970s found that women constituted only 8% of the expert or authority voice-over in U.S. television commercials (O'Donnell & O'Donnell, 1978), and 70% of ads featuring women depicted them in a domestic role or as a sex object (Dominick & Rauch, 1972). Of course, we Earthlings have additional sources of information about the society in which we live, but nevertheless it is reasonable to assume that our constant and ubiquitous exposure to advertising also shapes our perception of social reality (see Shrum, this volume) and that it reinforces stereotypes.

Clearly, advertising does not reflect reality. Nevertheless, it mirrors the aspirations, ideals, and values of a society, even if, as Pollay (1987) argues, the mirror is distorted by reflecting only certain values and lifestyles. In reality not all Earthlings are young and fit, but the overrepresentation of such models indicates that youth and fitness are held in high esteem and represent ideals. An astute observer may decode the values of different societies when traveling between countries merely by watching the ads. The Marlboro man represents the independence and self-actualization that an individualistic society holds dear, whereas social connectivity and harmony are advertising themes and motifs more often found in collectivistic societies (for a more detailed review see Shavitt, Lee, & Torelli, this volume). Similarly, advertising reflects and indicates social change. Although undoubtedly a high gender bias still exists in commercials all over the world, the traditional housewives of the 1950s ads made some room for the career women of the 1990s.[2] Not only have gender roles changed in Western societies, with more women occupying nontraditional roles, but ads, as in the Audi example, also signify that gender equality has become a publicly endorsed ambition.

Whether distortion or accurate reflection, by constituting a significant source of social information and role models, advertising may have an enormous impact on recipients. Social psychology assumes that people learn social norms by observing others' behavior (see also Goldstein & Cialdini, this volume). Given that in a modern society examples of social behavior come not only from our neighbors and colleagues but also, to a considerable extent, from advertising, one would expect that advertising also shapes social norms and standards, in particular in those areas in which advertising recipients lack first-hand knowledge. For instance, simply watching commercials would not only suggest that headaches are apparently a common malady but also that it is normal and socially acceptable to take pills.

Perceiving social groups in particular roles is likely to reinforce stereotypes and affect attitudes and behavior toward those groups. For example, gender-stereotyped radio commercials increased the accessibility of stereotype-related cognitions (Hurtz & Durkin, 2004). Men exposed to ads depicting women as sexual objects were significantly more accepting of rape-supportive attitudes and sex role stereotyping compared with a control group (or to a group viewing ads featuring women in progressive roles) (Lanis & Covell, 1995; McKay & Covell, 1997), and were also more likely to behave in a sexist manner (Rudman & Borgida, 1995). Moreover, advertising affects the self-concepts and behaviors of the stereotyped groups. Women exposed to traditional gender role ads showed lower self-confidence and independence compared with those who saw ads with reversed roles (Jennings, Geis, & Brown, 1980), had less favorable attitudes to the political participation of women compared with a control group (Schwarz, Wagner, Bannert, & Mathes, 1987), and reported fewer aspirations on a subsequent leadership task compared with a control group (Davies, Spencer, & Steele, 2005). In contrast, women exposed to progressive female images were less accepting of rape-myths compared to a control group (Lanis & Covell, 1995).

In view of such findings, one can hardly deny that by being an omnipresent source of social and cultural information, advertising shapes and spreads social and cultural norms. It creates ambitions and ideals, manifests and reinforces values and beliefs. Finally, it forms, strengthens and activates stereotypes.

CONCLUSION

These aspects could, of course, be extended and enlarged, but the aforementioned sketches suffice to illustrate that living in a consumer society has enormous bearings on social cognition, affect, and social behavior. As a social science, social psychology cannot avoid studying these issues. Many daily decisions involve consumer products or services, many daily interactions take place in a consumer context, and both may be a source of affect. Brands and products are used for self-expression as well as for the social perception of others. Advertising may shape and seminate social norms and values beyond shaping brand attitudes. In sum, the answer to the question "What is social about consumer behavior?" is "Almost everything." Consumer behavior represents a natural study ground for many of the phenomena in which social psychologists are interested, and studying consumer behavior is not significantly different from studying social behavior. In addition, studying consumer behavior is not possible without reference to social psychological theories and models. This book attests to both aspects.

OVERVIEW OF THE PRESENT VOLUME

The aim of this volume is twofold. On the one hand, the application of social psychology to consumer behavior is meant to broaden the horizon of social psychologists. On the other hand, students and researchers of consumer behavior will be offered an up-to-date account of relevant theories tailored to their interests. Taken together, the chapters represent three different facets of the relationship between social psychology and research on consumer behavior. First, social psychological research may explain, predict, and modify consumer behavior. Second, social psychology broadens its own spectrum by studying consumer behavior. Most chapters in the present volume reflect both of these aspects. Note that inherent in these two aspects is that social psychology provides the theoretical framework for research in consumer behavior and generously exports ideas to applications in the consumer context. The reverse import of theories, models, and ideas originating from consumer research is rare. Yet, theories developed within the realm of consumer behavior could enrich social psychology's perspective and inspire a more complete understanding of social behavior and information processing (Shavitt & Wänke, 2001; Wyer & Adaval, this volume). The chapter by Kirmani and Campbell and that by Chernev and Hamilton are prime examples of how models and advances genuine to consumer research complement and extend knowledge and theorizing about persuasion and judgment.

In accordance with the overarching theme of the *Frontiers* series, the selection of topics aims at bringing together the most promising and theoretically fruitful research developments by internationally renowned scholars whose work is at the cutting edge of research. But, in contrast with other *Frontiers* volumes, the present selection of chapters is more eclectic due to the diversity and extensiveness of the area. The selection by no means represents a complete and exhaustive picture of social psychology's role in consumer psychology. Nevertheless, in sum, the chapters emphasize and document the mutual relevance of both disciplines.

Introduction: A Tale of Two Disciplines

This first chapter has illustrated some aspects of the reciprocal relationship between social and consumer psychology. The chapter by Wyer and Adaval continues and complements the previous approach and describes the relationship between the two disciplines in a more detailed manner. Interestingly, in exploring their interface, the authors have chosen to focus on the gaps between the two disciplines. On the one hand, they identify instances in which social psychological research has limited applicability to consumer phenomena. On the other hand, they point out some as yet unexplored implications of consumer research for research in social psychology. Convergently, both introductory chapters agree on the reciprocal value of both disciplines and their natural kinship.

The Construal of Consumer Judgments and Decisions

Although the area of choices and judgments is just one of many facets of consumer behavior that are relevant to social psychology, it is certainly a major field. Moreover, it is a field for which social cognition research is of prime relevance. Reflecting this importance, several chapters deal with the construal of consumer judgments. Judgments depend on which building blocks are used and how they are put together. Which building blocks are used depends on what information is accessible and how it is weighted. Two chapters address these two issues. Eyal, Liberman, and Trope argue that psychological distance affects which aspects are taken into account for the mental representation of a target. From a more distant perspective, construals tend to be more abstract and less concrete than from a closer perspective. Thus, with varying temporal, spatial, social, or probabilistic distance, consumers may form different evaluations and may make different choices. Dijksterhuis and colleagues address one of the legendary themes in consumer psychology, albeit from a more modern angle. The "unconscious thought" in their approach is not a representation of repressed motivations but a rational tool for overcoming limited information-processing capacity. Their research suggests that with increasing conscious reflection irrelevant information is overweighted, thereby decreasing the quality of judgment and decisions. Thus, less thought may counterintuitively lead to better judgments.

The chapter by Bless and Greifeneder pertains to how accessible information is used in order to arrive at a judgment, depending on whether the accessible information is included in or excluded from the target assimilation or whether contrast in judgment occurs. The inclusion/exclusion model has been tested in various applications, from stereotyping to survey research. The present chapter shows how the model allows integrating various phenomena of the brand extension literature in one theoretical framework. Vice versa, its application to brand architecture has provided novel insights, which have helped to advance the model.

An important issue in social and consumer judgment is how unobserved information is inferred from observed information. Chernev and Hamilton propose the notion of compensatory reasoning, according to which inferences are drawn from observed strengths and weaknesses in a compensatory manner. Although the assumptions are developed within a consumer context, compensatory inferences could in principle transcend the realm of consumer decisions and find recognition in social judgment research as well.

Affective and Cognitive Feelings in Consumer Judgment

How does evaluation come about? The chapters in the second part seek the answer in the *thoughts* that come to mind when regarding an object. The third part of this book deals with cognitive and affective *feelings*.

Evaluative conditioning shows that stimuli can be evaluated favorably or unfavorably, not because of positive or negative attributes that come to mind, but simply because the targets were paired with a positive or a negative stimulus. To date, the respective literature has been dominated by a debate over the nature of the processes and the boundary conditions, in particular, whether awareness helps or hurts. In a bold strike, De Houwer puts an end to this debate, which may have led the discipline down a blind alley, and allows a fresh and open look at an old phenomenon. He suggests that evaluative conditioning is not tied to one specific process, but that different processes may be responsible depending on circumstances. Elsewhere it has been proposed (Fazio, 2008) that one possible process by which pairing the unconditioned stimulus (UCS) and the conditioned stimulus (CS) elicits transfer is the misattribution of the evaluative response elicited by the UCS to the CS. Misattribution of affective responses elicited by a stimulus to a different stimulus is also at the center of Pham's Generalized Affect-as-Information Model.

His model extends the mood-as-information heuristic originated by Schwarz and Clore (1983) and integrates the various offspring into a broader and more generalized framework. The detailed model not only explains a wide range of judgment phenomena but also allows for the development of novel hypotheses, especially with respect to consumer decision making. Whereas affect is incidental, Schwarz, Song, and Xu investigate subjective experiences that emerge as by-products of information processing itself. The subjectively experienced ease with which information is generated, retrieved, read, or pronounced in turn affects its impact on a subsequent judgment for which it is relevant.

Social and Media Influences on Judgment and Behavior

A central theme in social psychology is that people do not operate in a vacuum but are part of larger social networks and are exposed to direct and indirect influences of others. At the highest level, such social influence is exerted by the social rules and norms of the culture in which the individual operates. Even though they are at the heart of social psychology, the role of culture and cultural differences were long neglected, but now they have become flourishing research topics in social and consumer psychology alike. Shavitt, Lee, and Torelli review some of the implications of culture on consumer judgments, choices, and brand representations. They do so within the areas of self-regulation, risk-taking, and persuasion, and thereby their review also illustrates how topics of social and consumer psychology overlap. In times of globalization, the topic is, of course, also highly relevant for practitioners.

Cultural and social impact is to some extent transported by the media. In a society where watching television replaces social contacts and first-hand experience, social knowledge is often built from vicarious media observations. Bringing the world into one's living room may broaden the mind and serve education. At the same time, media content is often biased and can thus distort a receiver's worldviews. In addition to a review on this so-called cultivation effect, Shrum's chapter focuses on understanding the psychological mechanisms that underlie this effect. His approach is rooted in fundamental social cognition research when he looks at the processes by which judgments are constructed, and how they could possibly be affected by television viewing.

Of course, individuals are also exposed to more direct social influences, such as persuasive appeals. Goldstein and Cialdini illustrate such processes in a domain that also illustrates the wide range of consumer topics: conservation behavior. Based on theories of social influence, they argue that recipients make inferences about social norms from the information presented in persuasive appeals. On the one hand, appeals communicate prescriptive or injunctive norms of what is desired. On the other hand, they communicate descriptive norms by providing information about what is commonly done by others. The authors show how the unintended information about descriptive norms can undermine the persuasive effect, and how such appeals can be phrased more effectively.

However, clearly not all persuasive appeals fall on fertile ground. A most interesting approach to the topic of persuasion resistance has been developed in the consumer context. The Persuasion Knowledge Model assumes that consumers have theories about how marketers try to influence them and contends that consumers use these theories to cope with marketers' persuasion attempts. In their chapter, Kirmani and Campbell describe the basic assumptions of the Persuasion Knowledge Model and review the findings of respective research. Without doubt, the model has valuable implications beyond the consumer context and enriches social psychologists' understanding of persuasion and resistance.

Goals and Self-Regulation

How goals impact on affect, cognition, and behavior and how people juggle their goals are prominent topics in current social psychology (e.g., Forgas, Baumeister, & Tice, in press) as well as in consumer psychology. After all, consumption is goal-driven and depends on self-regulatory mechanisms. Three chapters pertain to this important issue and as a by-product illustrate the considerable overlap between social and consumer psychology in this area.

Regulatory focus theory distinguishes between orienting attention, perception, attitudes, and behaviors toward approaching gains and avoiding nongains (promotion focus) or toward avoiding losses and approaching nonlosses (prevention focus). A person's chronic or temporary regulatory focus plays an important role in the way attributes are weighted in judgments and how information is processed. In the consumer context, regulatory focus influences advertising effectiveness and product choice and evaluation. The chapter by Lee and Higgins reviews recent developments in regulatory focus research and provides an overview of the role of fitting the persuasive message to the regulatory focus (regulatory fit) in consumer judgment and choice.

The two remaining chapters deal with regulating multiple goals. Friese, Hofmann, and Wänke argue that behavior toward a particular object is a function of the net strength of reflective and impulsive responses. After a general review of the findings regarding the use of implicit measures in consumer research, they show for a variety of consumer choices and consumption behaviors that when self-regulatory strength is high, explicit measures, such as product ratings or restraint standards, are good predictors of subsequent choice and consumption. The predictive validity of the explicit measures decreases, and that of implicit measures, in particular, the Implicit Association Test (IAT), increases under conditions of constrained regulatory resources. Thus, the predictive validity of an IAT toward one object depends significantly on the control resources during which the behavior was performed. Fishbach and Zhang also look at the dynamics implied by holding multiple goals. More specifically, their research investigates the simultaneous pursuit of multiple goals in a sequence of actions. They propose a theoretical framework that specifies the conditions under which people highlight a single goal or balance among several goals across actions.

ENDNOTES

1. All examples are cited from Fullerton (1999), and were translated by the present author.

2. It should be emphasized that the amount of change since 1970–1980 is slight and perhaps less than expected (e.g., Bartsch, Burnett, Diller, & Rankin-Williams, 2000; Furnham & Mak, 1999).

REFERENCES

Bartsch, R. A., Burnett, T., Diller, T. R., Rankin-Williams, E. (2000). Gender representation in television commercials: Updating an update. *Sex-Roles, 43*, 735–743.

Belk, R. W. (1988). Possessions and the extended self. *Journal of Consumer Research, 15*, 139–168.

Botti, S., & Iyengar, S. S. (2004). The psychological pleasure and pain of choosing: When people prefer choosing at the cost of subsequent satisfaction. *Journal of Personality and Social Psychology, 87*(3), 312–326.

Brendl, C. M., Chattopadhyay, A., Pelham, B. W., & Carvallo, M. (2005). Name letter branding: Valence transfers when product specific needs are active. *Journal of Consumer Research, 32*, 405–415.

Chaiken, S. (1987). The heuristic model of persuasion. In M. P. Zanna, J. M. Olson, & C. P. Herman (Eds.), *Social influence: The Ontario Symposium* (Vol. 5, pp. 3–39). Hillsdale, NJ: Erlbaum.

Chernev, A. (2003). When more is less and less is more: The role of ideal point availability and assortment in consumer choice. *Journal of Consumer Research, 30*(2), 170–183.

Cooper, W. H., & Kohn, P. M. (1989). The social image of the young female smoker. *British Journal of Addiction, 84*, 935–941.

Davies, P. G., Spencer, S. J., & Steele, C. M. (2005). Clearing the air: Identity safety moderates the effects of stereotype threat on women's leadership aspirations. *Journal of Personality and Social Psychology 88*, 276–287.

Dominick, J. R., & Rauch, G. E. (1972). The image of women in network TV commercials. *Journal of Broadcasting, 16*, 259–265.

Eighmey, J., & Sar, S. (2007). Harlow Gale and the origins of the psychology of advertising. *Journal of Advertising, 36*(4), 147–158.

Fazio, R. H. (1990). Multiple processes by which attitudes guide behavior: The MODE Model as an integrative framework. In M. P. Zanna (Ed.), *Advances in experimental social psychology* (pp. 75–109). San Diego, CA: Academic Press.

Fazio, R. H. (2008). *Evaluative conditioning: The "how" question.* Paper presented at the conference of the Society for Consumer Psychology, New Orleans, LA.

Fazio, R. H., Powell, M. C., & Williams, C. J. (1989). The role of attitude accessibility in the attitude-to-behavior process. *Journal of Consumer Research, 16*(3), 280–288.

Fazio, R. H., & Towles-Schwen, T. (1999). The MODE model of attitude-behavior processes. In S. Chaiken & Y. Trope (Eds.), *Dual-process theories in social psychology* (pp. 97–116). New York: Guilford Press.

Fazio, R. H., & Williams C. J. (1986). Attitude accessibility as a moderator of the attitude-perception and attitude-behavior relations: An investigation of the 1984 presidential election. *Journal of Personality and Social Psychology, 51*, 505–514.

Forgas, J., Baumeister, R., & Tice, D. (Eds.) (in press). The psychology of self regulation. New York: Psychology Press.

Fullerton, R. A. (1994). Tea and the Viennese: A pioneering episode in the analysis of consumer behavior. *Advances in Consumer Research, 21*(1), 418–421.

Fullerton, R. A. (1999). An historic analysis of advertising's role in consumer decision-making: Paul F. Lazarsfeld's European research. *Advances in Consumer Research, 26*(1), 498–503.

Furnham, A. & Mak, T. (1990). Sex-role stereotyping in television commercials: A review and comparison of fourteen studies done on five continents over 25 years. *Sex-Roles, 41*, 413–437.

Huffman, C., & Kahn, B. E. (1998). Variety of sale: Mass customization or mass confusion? *Journal of Retailing, 74*, 491–513.

Hurtz, W., & Durkin, K. (2004). The effects of gender-stereotyped radio commercials. *Journal of Applied Social Psychology, 34*, 1974–1992.

Jennings (Walstedt), J., Geis, R. L., & Brown, V. (1980). The influence of television commercials on women's self-confidence and independent judgment. *Journal of Personality and Social Psychology, 38*, 203–210.

Jones, B., & Caroll, M. (1998). The effect of a video character's smoking status on young females' perceptions of social characteristics. *Adolescence, 33*(131), 657–668.

Karremans, J., Stroebe, W., & Claus, J. (2006). Beyond Vicary's fantasies: The impact of subliminal priming on brand choice. *Journal of Experimental Social Psychology, 42*, 792–798.

Lanis, K., & Covell, K. (1995). Images of women in advertisements: Effects on attitudes related to sexual aggression. *Sex Roles, 32*, 639–649.

Leong, S. M. (1989). A citation analysis of the journal of consumer research. *Journal of Consumer Research, 15*, 492–497.

Maass, A. (2007). Representing people in space: The spatial agency bias. Presented at the European Social Cognition Network Meeting, Brno.

McKay, N. J., & Covell, K. (1997). The impact of women in advertisements on attitudes toward women. *Sex Roles, 36*, 573–583.

Münsterberg, H. (1913). *Psychology and industrial efficiency*. Boston & New York: Houghton Mifflin. [Although not a direct translation, this work was based on Münsterberg, H. (1912). *Psychologie und Wirtschaftsleben. Ein Beitrag zur angewandten Experimental-Psychologie*. Leipzig: Barth].

North, A. C., Hargreaves, D. J., & McKendrick, J. (1997). In-store music affects product choice. *Nature, 390*, 132.

O'Donnell, W. J., & O'Donnell, K. J. (1978). Update: Sex-role messages in TV commercials. *Journal of Communication, 28*, 156–158.

Olson, J. M., & Maio, G. (Eds.). (2000). *Why we evaluate: Functions of attitudes*. Mahwah, NJ: Lawrence Erlbaum.

Packard, V. (1957). *The hidden persuaders*. London: Longmans, Green.

Petty, R. E., & Cacioppo, J. T. (1986). The elaboration likelihood model of persuasion. *Advances in Experimental Social Psychology, 19*, 123–205.

Phillips, D. M., Baumgartner, H., & Pieters, R. (1999). Influence in the evolving citation network of the journal of consumer research. *Advances in Consumer Research, 1999, 26*(1), 203–210.

Plassmann, H., O'Doherty, J., Shiv, B., & Rangel, A. (2008). Marketing actions can modulate neural representations of experienced utility. *Proceedings of the National Academy of Sciences, 105*(3), 1050–1054.

Pollay, R. W. (1987). On the value of reflections on the values in "the distorted mirror." *Journal of Marketing, 51*(3), 104–110.

Regan, D. T., & Fazio, R. H. (1977). On the consistency between attitudes and behavior: Look to the method of attitude formation. *Journal of Experimental Social Psychology, 13*, 28–45.

Rudman, L. A., & Borgida, E. (1995). The afterglow of construct accessibility: The behavioral consequences of priming men to view women as sexual objects. *Journal of Experimental Social Psychology, 31*, 493–517.

Schwarz, N., & Clore, G. L. (1983). Mood, misattribution, and judgments of well-being: Informative and directive functions of affective states. *Journal of Personality and Social Psychology, 45,* 513–523.

Schwarz, N., Wagner, D., Bannert, M., & Mathes, L. (1987). Cognitive accessibility of sex role concepts and attitudes toward political participation: The impact of sexist advertisements. *Sex Roles, 17,* 593–601.

Scott, W. D. (1904). Psychology of advertising. *Atlantic Monthly, 93.*

Scott, W. D. (1908). *The psychology of advertising.* New York: Arno Press.

Shavitt, S. (1990). The role of attitude objects in attitude functions. *Journal of Experimental Social Psychology, 26,* 124–148.

Shavitt, S., & Nelson, M. (2000). The social-identity function in person perception: Communicated meanings of product preferences. In G. Maio & J.M. Olson (Eds.), *Why we evaluate: Function of attitudes* (pp. 37–57). Mahwah, NJ: Lawrence Erlbaum.

Snyder, M., & Kendzierski, D. (1982): Acting on one's attitudes: Procedures for linking attitude and behavior. *Journal of Experimental Social Psychology, 18,* 165–183.

Vartanian, L. R., Herman, C. P., & Polivy, J. (2007). Consumption stereotypes and impression management: How you are what you eat. *Appetite, 48*(3), 265–277.

2

Social Psychology and Consumer Psychology
An Unexplored Interface

ROBERT S. WYER, JR., and RASHMI ADAVAL

Hong Kong University of Science and Technology

*P*urchase decisions often occur in a social context. Furthermore, the communications that influence these decisions frequently refer to people who use the product being evaluated and to social events in which the product is found. It is hardly surprising, therefore, that research and theory in social psychology have had a major impact on research in consumer behavior.

However, this impact is of relatively recent vintage. Marketing research actually developed independently of research in psychology. Early studies of the factors that influence purchase decisions were usually performed by marketing research groups (Fox, 1997). These groups were typically more interested in establishing the effectiveness of a particular advertising strategy in promoting a given line of products than in developing general theoretical principles of consumer behavior. In pursuing this objective, they tended to rely on intuition and to explore phenomena on an ad hoc basis.

Correspondingly, consumer psychology developed independently of the concerns of industry. Early work in this area reflects a desire to understand how consumers respond to advertising. However, it was stimulated by a few pioneering psychologists (e.g., E. W. Scripture, Harlow Gale, and Walter Dill Scott) who chose to study consumer phenomena because they found it inherently interesting (Schumann, Haugtvedt, & Davidson, 2008). As a result, consumer psychology emerged as an academic discipline with few if any a priori theories and concepts of its own to use in characterizing the phenomena with which it was concerned. Rather, it tended to borrow from theory and methodology developed in other areas, notably social psychology.

This tendency is decreasing. As consumer psychology has continued to evolve, researchers have become more sensitive to the idiosyncratic characteristics of the situations to which they wish their research to generalize, and have begun to develop conceptualizations that take these characteristics into account. As a result, they are beginning to ask questions that have not previously been considered in either social psychology or other areas but are nevertheless important in understanding the phenomena of concern in these areas.

Unfortunately, this importance has not yet been fully recognized. Many social psychologists have become aware of the challenge of understanding judgment and decision processes in the consumer domain. However, they have often used theoretical and methodological tools developed in their own discipline that fail to capture the characteristics of a purchase situation.[1] In doing so, they have failed to identify and examine the potential implications of consumer phenomena for research in their own area.

In short, social psychologists have begun to examine consumer phenomena, but their work has often had limited implications for consumer behavior. At the same time, consumer research has begun to examine phenomena that have theoretical and empirical implications for research in social psychology that have not been recognized by social psychologists themselves. In this chapter, we attempt to document these assertions. We review several areas of social psychological research and theorizing, pointing out instances in which this work has limited applicability to consumer phenomena. At the same time, we identify consumer research that has unexplored implications for phenomena of concern in social psychology. To provide a more general context for our discussion, however, we first review the assumptions that traditionally guided marketing and advertising strategies in the many years before consumer research emerged as a major academic discipline. The theoretical and empirical approaches that have been taken in investigating the more specific issues we discuss are often traceable to these assumptions.

A HISTORICAL PERSPECTIVE

A historical review of advertising strategies over the 70 years prior to the advent of academic consumer research reveals that practitioners based their approach on intuitions about the factors that influence the impact of advertisements rather than on evidence that these factors actually had much impact. The success of the ads was often a hit-or-miss proposition. Nevertheless, the intuitions that guided this earlier period in marketing history anticipated, if not dictated, the areas of psychology to which contemporary consumer researchers have paid most attention.

A detailed historical analysis of consumer psychology is provided by Schumann and colleagues (2008). Here, we briefly review the major perspectives that dominated advertising strategies in the years before academic consumer psychology emerged. This history reflects a vacillation between (1) *reason-why* strategies that emphasized the factors that led a product to be useful, and (2) *emotion-based* strategies that focused on consumers' global feelings about a product. The history of these divergent approaches, which are reflected in contemporary consumer research, provides insights into the reasons why certain research paradigms became popular.

Advertising in the Nineteenth Century

The late 1800s marked the beginning of large-scale advertising and gave it the somewhat dubious reputation that it continues to have in many quarters today. As Fox (1997) notes, those were the days of patent medicines when any type of product could be sold and any promise could be made. All that was required was knowledge of the periodicals available in the area and their rates, and an ability to haggle. During this period, products owed their success simply to the fact that they were advertised whereas other products were not. For example, St. Jacob's oil was initially marketed as something that was used by Caesar's legions. When this tactic failed, it was reintroduced as a product made by German monks in the Black Forest. This was more palatable to the public and increased its sales substantially. Once advertising diminished, however, so did sales. Similarly, ads for Lydia Pinkham's vegetable compound appeared around this time and led to the product's popularity. These ads, which may provide the earliest examples of source effects and testimonial advertising, owed their success to the fact that they showed her trustworthy face and were advertised heavily.

Even during these early days of advertising it is possible to track a shift from more direct advertising approaches to more subtle ones. Ivory soap advertised itself as the only soap that floats. The advertisers of Sapolio soap came up with a mysterious ancient saying, "Oilopas Esu," ostensibly found in an Egyptian tomb, to sell their product. The audience found this puzzling until they discovered that it was "Use Sapolio" spelled backwards. Thus, the hard sell gave way to softer appeals with catchy slogans. By the end of the 1800s, this advertising approach was used to introduce several new products, including Kodak cameras, Coca Cola, and Campbell's soup.

Advertising at the Turn of the Century

Advertising in the first decade of the twentieth century was marked by three shifts between soft sell and hard sell. The decade began with a focus on getting people's attention. Thus, unornamented text gave way to delicate, colorful visuals, trade characters such as Aunt Jemima, catchy rhymes and jingles, and humorous appeals. However, advertisers soon realized that although these approaches might help to maintain visibility and sales for established products, they did not sell *new* products. Consequently, reason-why advertising emerged (Fox, 1997). The idea was that advertising should say on paper what a good salesperson would say face-to-face. Although this approach was proclaimed as a new style of advertising, however, it bore a remarkable resemblance to the patent-medicine advertising mentioned earlier.

The second decade of the century, however, saw a return to "atmosphere advertising" or "soft-sell" in which pitches were made by suggestion. This advertising often used pictures to convey a message, and verbal references to the brand were oblique. The objective of this strategy was not to stimulate the consumer to buy per se. Rather, it focused on building an enduring relationship with the consumer (e.g., by developing an image of reliable quality).[2] This return to atmosphere advertising and the techniques used were validated by psychologists such as Walter Dill Scott, who said that reason-why copy was oversold and that consumers had to be persuaded by "suggestion."

The beginning of World War I interestingly created a home for both styles of advertising. Support for the war was drummed up using reason-why advertising. However, atmosphere advertising, which created an image of quality and reputability, helped to keep company names in the public mind as manufacturers switched to war-time production.

Advertising after World War I

The end of the war saw a tremendous increase in advertising budgets as the economy flourished and new products flooded the market. Advertising and marketing flourished in such an environment and this marked the beginning of the period when the ownership of new products ostensibly paved the way to happiness (Fox, 1997). The use of psychology to sell products emerged when John B. Watson (a former academic psychologist) joined the J. Walter Thompson agency. He claimed that the consumer would react only to fundamental or conditioned emotional stimuli that activated basic human drives such as love, fear, and rage. The appeal to basic human drives and emotions soon became pervasive. Woodbury Facial Soap, for example, used a muted sex appeal ("A skin you love to touch"). Ads for products to combat body odor, halitosis, and athlete's foot induced fear of being physically unappealing. At the same time, these feelings stimulated a desire to emulate others who were more attractive. Thus, although testimonials had fallen into disrepute during the "patent medicine" days, they made a comeback through endorsements by famous Hollywood stars for brands such as Lux beauty soap and Lucky Strike cigarettes.

The years after the 1929 stock market crash were dark days for advertising, as consumption decreased. This led advertisers to make extravagant, often ridiculous claims in a desperate attempt to sell their products. Although the credibility of ad agencies was severely damaged as a result of this strategy, it was partly restored by George Gallup, a Northwestern University journalism professor, who performed a systematic study of reader preferences for different appeals, font types, and layouts. This period also marked the emergence of radio as an advertising medium. Radio advertising typically consisted of sponsored shows with the name of the sponsor being inserted into the script as often as possible. Advertising style during this period swung back to a more hard-hitting character and comparative advertising made its appearance. However, a rapid growth of consumerism led to the general sentiment that advertising promotes waste. This sentiment persisted until the advent of World War II, which again led advertising agencies to focus their efforts on selling the war and distracted consumers from the negative effects of advertising.

Advertising after World War II

The fifteen years of prosperity following World War II marked the second boom in advertising, as the demand for products again increased. During this period, a debate emerged between the role of creativity and that of research. To quote Fox,

> Within any given agency, the ascendant researchers found little common ground with the denizens of art and copy. The former thought of advertising as a science and spoke a dense mathematical patois. The latter regarded advertising as an art, or at least a craft, that responded to one's creative muse. Given the tendencies of the day, creatives felt displaced and defensively blamed their problems on "research and other things," as Les Pearl of BBDO put it: "Merchandising men and research men are statistic-ing the creative man to death." (Fox, 1997, p. 182)

Emotion-based research appeared to offer a solution. This research did not treat the consumer as a rational person who knew why he was buying the product, but as a person whose subconscious had to be tapped in order to persuade him. Symbolism in advertising could tap into these unconscious needs. The advent of the Marlboro man image perhaps reflected the zeitgeist of the times. Subliminal advertising also made an appearance when a consultant named James Vicary claimed that sales of cola and popcorn increased when subliminal images were flashed on the screen during a movie.

At the same time, it would be incorrect to say that soft-sell strategies totally dominated this period. The Ted Bates agency, for example, promoted the idea of identifying a "unique selling proposition" for a product and then repeating it continually in ads until consumers got the message. Thus, the focus was not on coming up with new creative approaches but rather on pure repetition of the same message over and over.

Summary

As the preceding discussion testifies the years of advertising that precede the advent of academic consumer research was characterized by cycles of both reason-based and emotion-based advertising. These approaches became more refined with each iterative process. By the middle of the 1960s, however, a need to understand empirically the factors that influenced the effectiveness of these approaches became clear. In investigating these approaches, consumer research used psychology for guidance in understanding both the theoretical basis for the effects and the techniques for investigating them. A general question surrounded the extent to which people's judgments and purchase decisions were influenced by what came to mind and how previously acquired knowledge was brought to bear on the decision. Obvious questions stimulated by hard-sell or reason-based approaches included (1) the procedures that consumers use to extract the evaluative implications of different product features (e.g., brands and attributes) and combine them to form an overall judgment or decision, and (2) the dynamics of communication and persuasion. A consideration of soft-sell or emotion-based approaches, however, gave rise to questions about the role of affect in consumer judgment and the impact of visual imagery.

Many of these questions were all being investigated in social psychology. It was reasonable, therefore, for consumer researchers to turn to social psychology in an attempt to answer them. As we have noted, however, this strategy may have had costs as well as benefits. Methodological tools developed in social psychology may often be of limited applicability to consumer phenomena outside the laboratory. At the same time, they can prevent more central questions from being identified and investigated. Before discussing specific areas of consumer research in which social psychology has had an impact, it may be helpful to review more generally some of the limitations of the paradigms that have been traditionally used in social psychology along with characteristics of the situations they need to consider in order to capture phenomena in consumer judgment.

GENERAL PARADIGMATIC CONCERNS

With few exceptions, theories are constructed to account for a circumscribed range of phenomena that can be identified using a fairly restricted set of procedures and stimulus materials. In such cases, the applicability of the theories may often be limited by the procedures that have been used to evaluate them. Two extensive bodies of research, each of which dominated theorizing in person impression for many years, exemplify these limitations. In both cases, the procedures employed may have *created* a new phenomenon rather than examining a phenomenon that exists independently of the methods used to investigate it.

Two Examples of Paradigmatic Limitations

Impression formation research during the 1960s and 1970s was largely concerned with how the evaluative implications of trait adjective descriptions of a person combine to influence liking for the person. Algebraic models were often quite successful in describing the integration of this information (N. H. Anderson, 1971, 1981). An evaluation of these models, however, required that participants make ratings of persons based on numerous sets of adjectives in a within-subjects design under conditions that were very unlikely to capture the way in which people form impressions of single individuals whom they encounter in daily life. As Wyer and Carlston (1979) pointed out, the early success of simple averaging models in describing the integration of this information was likely to be an artifact of the paradigm used to evaluate them.

In a later phase of impression formation research, which was popular during the 1980s and early 1990s, people were often asked to form impressions on the basis of a randomly ordered list of behaviors, each described out of the social context in which it occurred (for a review, see Srull & Wyer, 1989). By analyzing characteristics of the information that was recalled in these conditions, rigorous models were developed of the processes that underlie the formation of impressions on the basis of such information. However, the type of information conveyed and how it was presented bore little resemblance to the way that people acquire and use information about the persons they encounter outside the laboratory. In fact, when similar information was conveyed in the context of an ostensibly informal conversation, the theories that had successfully captured impression formation processes in the usual paradigm were inapplicable (Wyer, Budesheim, & Lambert, 1990; Wyer, Budesheim, Lambert, & Swan, 1994).

Social psychologists are obviously not alone in their tendency to investigate phenomena that have little generalizability beyond the paradigms they use to examine them. Consumer researchers are guilty of this tendency as well. Because of the difficulty of investigating actual purchasing behavior under conditions that systematically differ with respect to variables that are assumed to influence this behavior, consumer researchers frequently make use of guided scenarios in which participants are asked to imagine themselves in different purchasing situations and to infer what they would do in these imagined situations. Although the use of these procedures can generate interesting results, the similarity of these results to those that might occur in actual purchase situations is sometimes questionable. In fact, the results may reflect differences in participants' implicit theories of shopping behavior, the validity of which is sometimes rather questionable (Ross, 1989; Wyer, 2004).

This is not to say that laboratory research bears no relation to phenomena that occur in the real world. Several studies (see Anderson, Lindsay, & Bushman, 1999) have shown a close correspondence between the implications drawn from laboratory research and those drawn from field studies (see Kardes, Fennis, Hirt, Tormala, & Bullington, in press, for a specific example). Nevertheless, this correspondence is only likely when the paradigms used in the laboratory can capture the factors that potentially influence behavior in daily life. Unfortunately, the situational and informational context of consumer judgments and decisions that typically occur outside the laboratory are rarely taken into account in applying either social psychological research or the theorizing that underlies it.

Representative Concerns of Consumer Research

Several features of consumer situations that are rarely captured by social psychological research may be worth summarizing.

1. Much of the information conveyed in advertisements and television commercials is received under conditions in which people have little interest in either the ad or the product it promotes and, therefore, are unlikely to think about the material in any detail.
2. Product information is often acquired days and even weeks before a purchase decision is made. There can be a long period of time between the transmission of product-related information in an advertisement or television commercial and the decisions on which it bears.
3. Some reason-based purchase decisions might involve a consideration of a single product. More often, however, they require the computation of a preference among several alternatives. (For example, people who wish to buy a television usually do not decide between purchasing a particular model and buying nothing at all. More generally, they decide whether

they should buy a SONY or a Panasonic, or which of two SONY televisions they would prefer.) In principle, consumers could compute their preferences by first estimating the favorableness of each alternative independently and comparing these overall evaluations. When more than one alternative is being considered, however, this may not be the case (but see Posavac, Kardes, Sanbonmatsu, & Fitzsimons, 2004, 2005). Rather, consumers appear to conduct a dimension-by-dimension comparison of the choice alternatives and determine their preference on the basis of these comparisons (Simonson, 1989). This procedure can be performed without making an overall evaluation of any of the alternatives.

4. Product information is usually conveyed both verbally and in pictures. Moreover, the verbal descriptions are sometimes communicated orally as well as in writing. In such cases, the impression that is formed of a product is likely to reflect an integration of the implications of information that is transmitted simultaneously in two or more of these sense modalities.

5. Some of the information presented about a product might consist of a list of attribute descriptions. In other cases, however, the information describes a series of events that are intended to stimulate viewers to imagine themselves using the product in an attractive situation (e.g., driving a Toyota through a scenic mountain pass), independently of any particular features the product may have.

6. At times, purchase decisions are based on purely utilitarian considerations (e.g., the ability of the product to perform a particular function) and are guided by reasons-to-buy. However, other decisions are more likely to be based on affect (i.e., the feelings that a product elicits or that one anticipates to result from using it) independently of any specific features the product might have.

The conditions summarized in the previous list arise in many social judgment and decision situations as well as consumer situations. That is, people often state preferences for the persons with whom they interact; their impressions are often based on visual as well as verbal information about a person (physical appearance, observations of his or her behavior); they do not always think very much about the information they receive, and they are often called upon to make judgments and decisions some time after they receive information to which these responses are relevant. Of the conditions we have outlined, however, only the sixth (concerning the impact of affect and judgments and decisions) has been investigated in any detail in social psychology (see Schwarz & Clore, 1996, for a review). And even in this case, research on product evaluation has identified several ways in which affect can influence the processing of information that were not uncovered in social psychological theory and research (cf. Adaval, 2001, 2003).

The discussion in the remainder of this chapter focuses on several representative areas of social psychology that have guided both reason-based and emotion-based research, thus reflecting the historical variation in these emphases placed on these two advertising strategies. These areas include (1) knowledge accessibility, (2) attitude-behavior relations, (3) communication and persuasion, and (4) the influence of affect and subjective experience. In doing so, we point out limitations on the applicability of this research to consumer judgment and behavior. In several instances, we note research in consumer judgment and behavior that is likely to have implications for social psychological phenomena but have yet to be examined. Although the areas we cover are hardly exhaustive, they are representative of the concerns that existed in the minds of early consumer researchers as well as contemporary ones.

KNOWLEDGE ACCESSIBILITY

Perhaps the most well-established phenomenon to emerge in the past three decades of research on social information processing concerns the impact of knowledge accessibility (for reviews, see Förster & Liberman, 2007; Higgins, 1996; Wyer, 2008). People who are called upon to make a judgment or decision do not normally use all of the relevant information or previously acquired knowledge they have available (Taylor & Fiske, 1978). Rather, they consider only a subset of this information and knowledge that comes to mind most quickly and easily. Consequently, objectively irrelevant experiences that influence the cognitions that are most accessible in memory at the time a judgment or decision is made can influence the nature of this response. Moreover, the experiences that cause these cognitions to be accessible can occur without conscious awareness (Bargh, 1997).

The effect of knowledge accessibility is normally investigated by unobtrusively (often subliminally) stimulating participants to use a selective subset of concepts or knowledge in one situation and observing the impact of these concepts on judgments and behavior in a later, ostensibly unrelated situation. This technique has been successful in demonstrating the impact of accessible trait concepts on the interpretation of ambiguous behavior (Higgins, Rholes, & Jones, 1977; Srull & Wyer, 1979), the effect of describing a stimulus (e.g., a person or event) on both memory for the stimulus (Adaval & Wyer, 2004) and judgments of it (Higgins & Rholes, 1978), the impact of judging a stimulus at one point in time on judgments and decisions at a later time (Carlston, 1980; Higgins & Lurie, 1983; Sherman, Ahlm, Berman, & Lynn, 1978), the effect of beliefs in a proposition on beliefs in other, syllogistically related propositions (Wyer & Hartwick, 1980), the effects of imagining a hypothetical event on predictions of its actual occurrence (Ross, Lepper, Strack, & Steinmetz, 1977; Sherman, Skov, Hervitz, & Stock, 1981), the impact of accessible relational concepts on creative problem solving (Higgins & Chaires, 1980), the selection of standards of comparison for use in assessing a product's expensiveness (Adaval & Monroe, 2002), the use of implicit theories in making causal inferences (Hong, Morris, Chiu, & Benet-Martinez, 2000) and the influence of cultural norms on values and behavioral decisions (Briley, Morris, & Simonson, 2000, 2005; Briley & Wyer, 2001).

A particularly provocative stream of research, initiated by Bargh, Chen, and Burrows (1996), shows that unobtrusively (e.g., subliminally) priming concepts associated with a social stereotype can influence people's own overt behavior. Similarly, subliminally priming a goal can stimulate behavior that is relevant to the attainment of this goal without participants being aware of the goal to which the behavior is relevant (Chartrand & Bargh, 1996, 2002). Several explanations of these phenomena have been proposed (e.g., DeMarree, Wheeler, & Petty, 2005; Dijksterhuis, Smith, van Baaren, & Wigboldus, 2005; Janiszewski & van Osselaer, 2005; Wyer, 2004). One fairly straightforward possibility is suggested by J. R. Anderson's (1982, 1983) conception of *cognitive productions* (see also Smith, 1990). Specifically, people acquire through learning a number of implicit "if [X], then [Y]" rules, where [X] is a configuration of internally or externally generated stimulus features and [Y] is a sequence of behavior that is activated spontaneously when the conditions specified in [X] are experienced. The features that compose [X], which could include a goal sprcification as well as other concepts or percepts, need not all be subject to consc ous awareness. Thus, although a sequence of behavior might lead to the attainment of a general or specific goal, it can often be activated and pursued without consciousness of the goal to which it is relevant.

Note that the eliciting conditions of a production can include not only subliminally primed concepts but features of the immediate situation in which one finds oneself. The sequence of behavior that is elicited is a joint function of both. Thus, although Bargh and colleagues (1996) found that subliminally priming faces of African Americans led White participants to display more anger and irritation upon being asked to repeat a boring task, Colcombe (2001) found that these same primes led White participants to perform less well on a test of mathematical ability and to perform better on a test of rhythm memory.[3] Therefore, different aspects of the primed stereotype came into play, depending on the features of the situational context at hand.

These results emphasize the point that the subliminal priming of behavior-relevant concepts is unlikely to elicit the behavior unless the situational context is one in which the behavior is particularly applicable. Seeing a movie that contains scenes of violence is unlikely to stimulate patrons to walk up to someone spontaneously outside the theater and kick them in the shins. However, it might lead them to react with more anger and irritation if someone steps on their toe while leaving.

Implications for Consumer Behavior

The potential role of knowledge accessibility in consumer judgment and decision making is self-evident. The evidence reported by Bargh and colleagues, for example, could have general implications for the effects of movies and television on consumption and other behavior. They could also account for the effect of unobtrusively using brands as props in television shows. As already noted, however, primed concepts are often insufficient to activate behavior unless the behavior is applicable to the situation at hand. In the case of consumption behavior, the situational cues that determine the applicability of prime-related behavior may be generated internally. Strahan, Spencer, and Zanna (2002; see also Karremans, Stroebe, & Claus, 2006), for example, showed that subliminally priming thirst-related words led participants to drink more of a beverage they were provided in the context of a simulated taste test. However, this was only true of participants who had gone without drinking for several hours before the experiment and were thirsty at the time the primed concepts were activated.

These findings could help to explain the failure to replicate Vicary's unpublished (and, perhaps, bogus; see Pratkanis, 1992) evidence that subliminally flashing "drink Coca Cola" on a movie screen increases sales of the beverage. This should occur only if consumers are thirsty. Moreover, thirsty customers may be primed by the drinks available at the concession stand at the time they enter the theater, and so additional, more subtle priming may be irrelevant.

There is a second possible qualification on the implications of past research on knowledge accessibility for consumer judgment and decision making. In most studies of the effects of activating concepts and knowledge on judgments and behavior, only a short period of time separates the activation of knowledge and the judgments or behavior it influences. As Higgins, Bargh, and Lombardi (1985) found, the effect of recently activated concepts may be quite transitory, whereas the effect of frequently activated concepts, which determines their chronic accessibility in memory, are more enduring. This implies that repeated exposures to a purchase-related stimulus (e.g., a brand name) may have more influence on the likelihood that it comes to mind in a shopping situation than a single encounter with the stimulus in the context of a television show. (This possibility confirms the assumption underlying some of the early advertising strategies devised by Ted Bates where constant repetition of a unique product feature increased its influence in the purchase situation.)

Implications of Consumer Behavior

The theoretical underpinnings of knowledge accessibility are very well established and research in consumer behavior does not call them into serious question. Nevertheless, consumer behavior research has uncovered several phenomena whose potential relevance in social psychology has not yet become fully recognized.

Effects of the Media on Perceptions and Attitudes The assumption that watching television leads viewers to have a distorted perception of reality has had a long history (for a review, see Gerbner, Gross, Morgan, & Signorielli, 1994; Shrum, this volume). In particular, heavy television viewers tend to overestimate the incidence of situations and events that are overrepresented on television. Until fairly recently, however, an explanation of the effect was unclear. For example, people who watch television frequently perceive violent crimes to occur more often than occasional viewers. However, this might not reflect a causal influence of television viewing on perceptions. Rather, it could be the result of socioeconomic factors that independently influence both individuals' viewing behavior and their exposure to crime in their social environment.

Research by Shrum and his colleagues (O'Guinn & Shrum, 1997; Shrum, Wyer, & O'Guinn, 1998; for a review see Shrum, this volume), however, traced heavy viewers' disposition to overestimate the incidence of events that occur frequently on television to the increased accessibility of these events in memory. That is, individuals who are asked to estimate the incidence of a particular event or state of affairs may search memory for instances of the event and base their judgment on the ease with which these instances come to mind (Schwarz, 2004). Memory for the context in which information is received normally decays more rapidly than memory for the information itself and so it often becomes dissociated from the information over time (Pratkanis, Greenwald, Leippe, & Baumgardner, 1988). If the event is shown frequently on television, therefore, heavy viewers are likely to retrieve instances of it more easily than less avid viewers without considering the context in which the event was encountered. Consequently, they may judge it to occur relatively more often. Thus, for example, heavy viewers overestimate the incidence of not only violent crime but also manifestations of an affluent lifestyle (e.g., having a swimming pool in the back yard). Furthermore, they respond in estimating the incidence of these manifestations (O'Guinn & Shrum, 1997).

The tendency for heavy television viewers to overestimate the incidence of affluence seems likely to have a more general impact on attitudes and values associated with materialism. However, this may be true only if viewers actively think about the implications of affluence-related material at the time they encounter it. Shrum, Burroughs, and Rindfleisch (2005) found that this is indeed the case. Data from both a laboratory study and a national survey indicate that although television viewing increased materialistic attitudes and values, this effect was particularly pronounced among viewers with high need for cognition (Cacioppo & Petty, 1982). In short, television viewing influences perceptions of social reality, but these perceptions have an influence on attitudes and values only among viewers who actively think about the shows they see rather than watching them mindlessly. This has obvious implications for the impact of television on consumer behavior. Frequent television viewing can increase familiarity with the products that are advertised, but it is likely to increase liking for these products only if viewers think about the products at the time the advertisements are encountered.

The evidence that the information transmitted on television has little impact on the attitudes and values of individuals who are prone to watch mindlessly without actively thinking about its implications is of considerable importance in understanding media effects on attitude formation and change in social psychology as well as consumer psychology. For example, people may not only differ in the extent to which they think about the information they receive in the media but also may think about it in different ways. Briley, Shrum, and Wyer (2007) provide an example. African American and Caucasian participants viewed a series of clothing ads that varied in the relative proportion of Black and White models that were shown. Caucasian participants paid particular attention to the Black models when the models occurred infrequently. Because these models were highly accessible in memory, they overestimated their incidence when the actual number presented in the ads was low but became more accurate as the number presented increased. African Americans, on the other hand, did not consider individual Black models to be particularly novel but were nevertheless concerned about their representation in the media. Therefore, they did a subjective frequency count of their number that was more accurate when the actual number presented was low than when it was high. Thus, these different processing strategies can lead to different conclusions concerning the representation of minority groups in the media, an issue with clear implications for social psychology.

Pricing   Consumers presumably evaluate the expensiveness of a product with reference to a standard, judging the product to be fairly inexpensive if the price is lower than the standard and as expensive if it is higher. However, the selection of the standard can be influenced by situational factors of which persons are not always aware. Adaval and Monroe (2002) subliminally exposed participants to high or low numbers while they performed an ostensibly irrelevant perceptual task. Then, participants evaluated a target product whose price and other attributes were provided. Participants used a higher standard if they had been primed with high numbers than if they had been primed with low numbers. Consequently, they judged the target to be relatively less expensive in the former condition.

Related phenomena were detected in a field study by Nunes and Boatwright (2004). Individuals in a beachfront shopping area were asked how much they were willing to pay for CDs that were on sale at one of the booths. They were willing to pay more for the CDs if the prices of sweaters on sale at a nearby booth were high than if they were low. Apparently, the high-priced sweaters increased the standard that participants used in evaluating the subjective expensiveness of products in general. Therefore, they subjectively regarded the CDs as less expensive and were willing to pay a higher price for them than they would have been otherwise.

The effects of unobtrusively priming price information are of little direct interest in social psychology. However, social judgments, like consumer judgments, are influenced by the standards that individuals use in computing these judgments (Higgins & Lurie, 1983; Ostrom & Upshaw, 1968). The evidence that the accessibility of these standards can be influenced by factors of which people are unaware and that the effects generalize over both stimulus domains and dimensions of judgment (Adaval & Monroe, 2002) has clear implications for an understanding of the factors underlying judgments of both types.

Effects of Mindsets on Judgments and Decisions

The knowledge that people acquire can include not only simple concepts and descriptive information about persons, objects, and events that are used as a basis for decisions, but also more general strategies that are used in arriving at these decisions. The use of a problem-solving strategy in one situation may increase its accessibility in memory. Consequently, it can produce a *mindset* that, once activated, may be applied in other situations as well. This possibility, which was suggested many years ago by Luchins and Luchins (1959) and more recently by Gollwitzer and Bayer (1999), has been examined in several recent studies of consumer decision making.

For example, Dhar, Huber, and Khan (2007) assumed that a purchase decision is a two-stage process. That is, once individuals have decided that they want to make a purchase, they must consider how they can implement this goal. Thus, a decision to make a purchase activates a second, implemental stage of processing. However, the activities involved at this second stage may induce an implemental mindset that generalizes to later purchase situations, leading consumers to perform this second stage of processing without ever deciding whether they actually wanted to buy something. This means that individuals who have decided to make a purchase at one point in time (thereby activating an implemental mindset) are more likely to make a second, later purchase than they otherwise would be. Dhar and colleagues (2007) found evidence of this shopping momentum. That is, participants who were induced to purchase an inexpensive product early in an experiment were more likely to purchase a second product later than were individuals who had not been confronted with the first purchase decision.

A related finding was reported by Xu and Wyer (2007). They assumed that when consumers are confronted with a choice between two alternatives, they not only must decide whether they want to buy anything at all but also, having done so, must decide which alternative they want. However, computing a preference for one of the alternatives at the outset may activate a "which-to-buy" mindset that presupposes that a decision to purchase something has already been made. Thus, it increases the inclination to make a purchase relative to conditions in which a preference for the alternatives was not computed. Furthermore, once this mindset is activated, it may generalize to future purchase situations. Xu and Wyer found that asking participants to state a preference for two computers in an initial task increased their willingness to purchase a vacation package in a second, imaginary purchase situation. Stating preferences for a series of unrelated consumer activities also increased participants' likelihood of actually purchasing one of two types of candy that were on sale after the experiment.

Xu and Wyer's conceptualization of the processing strategy that underlies a which-to-buy mindset may be too narrow, however. In subsequent research (Xu and Wyer, 2008), some participants were asked to state their relative liking for wild animals, and others were asked to compare them with respect to physical attributes (e.g., "Which is heavier, a hippopotamus or a giraffe?"). In yet another study, they were asked simply to indicate how similar one stimulus was to another (e.g., "How similar is Korea to Japan?"). Performing each task appeared to activate a general comparative-judgment process that influenced participants' willingness to purchase a computer in an unrelated situation that they encountered later. That is, almost any comparative-judgment task was sufficient to activate the which-to-buy mindset that mediated purchase decisions.

Xu and Wyer's (2007) studies indicate that when a goal-directed activity consists of a series of steps, increasing the accessibility of the processes involved in performing an intermediate step in the sequence may stimulate people to apply this step without referring to other steps that normally precede it. This, in turn, may affect the goal-relevant decision that is ultimately made. Analogous situations exist in the social domain. It is interesting to speculate, for example, that people who are offered a choice between two high-calorie deserts at a party are more likely to choose one alternative rather than refusing both if the individuals have been arguing about which of two baseball teams will win the National League pennant. Similarly, they might be more inclined to decide which of two blind dates they will accept rather than declining to accept either.

Hirt, Kardes, and Markman (2004) found that increasing the accessibility of one procedure can induce processing that might not otherwise occur. In their studies (see also Hirt & Markman, 1995), participants who were stimulated to consider alternative courses of action in making a decision in one situation developed a "consider alternatives" mindset that influenced their decision strategies in other, quite unrelated situations. These effects were evident only among individuals with low need for closure. However, participants with high need for closure were generally resistant to considering alternatives, and so attempts to induce a mindset were unsuccessful.

A quite different processing strategy was identified in a series of studies by Briley and his colleagues. Based on Higgins's (1998) conceptualization of promotion and prevention focus (Lee & Higgins, this volume), Briley postulated that individuals often acquire a disposition to focus their attention on either positive consequences of a choice (a promotion mindset) or negative consequences (a prevention mindset) and that once this mindset is activated, it generalizes to situations that are unrelated to the conditions that gave rise to it. In one series of studies (Briley & Wyer, 2002), a "prevention" mindset was activated by leading participants to perceive that they were members of a group (thereby inducing feelings of social responsibility and an unwillingness to take unnecessary risks). Once this mindset was activated, it affected behavior in other, unrelated situations. In a resource allocation task, for example, it increased the tendency to base allocations on equality (thus minimizing the negative feelings that would result if one party's share was less than another's). It also induced participants to choose products that had the least negative features, independently of the favorableness of the positive features they possessed. Finally, it induced a tendency to choose candies of different kinds rather than the same kind when leaving the experiment (thus minimizing the regret that might result from making an incorrect choice).

A prevention mindset can be induced in other ways as well. In a series of studies by Briley, Morris, and Simonson (2005), participants performed a product choice task similar to that employed by Briley and Wyer (2002; see also, Briley, Morris, & Simonson, 2000). The study, which used Hong Kong bilinguals as subjects, was conducted either in English or in Chinese. Conducting the experiment in English activated concepts associated with the promotion orientation typical of Western cultures, whereas conducting it in Chinese activated concepts associated with the prevention motivation typical of Asians. Thus, participants were more likely to choose products that minimized the magnitude of negative attributes in the second case than in the first.

Information Search Strategies   The cognitive procedures that underlie behavior and decisions may often reflect the use of cognitive productions of the sort postulated by J. R. Anderson (1983) and noted earlier. Once activated, these productions are applied automatically with little cognitive deliberation. Evidence that these productions can operate at early stages of processing was obtained by Shen and Wyer (2008b). In a representative study, some participants first rank-ordered a set of stimulus attributes from most to least favorable, leading them to focus their attention on favorable attributes before unfavorable ones. Others ranked the attributes from least to most favorable, which required them to focus on unfavorable attributes first. The search processes activated by this task generalized to an ostensibly unrelated task that required a consideration of several pieces of information. Thus, participants who were unable to consider all of this information made more favorable judgments of the target in the first condition than the second. Similar effects were obtained by simply asking participants to indicate whether they would choose each of a set of products (which induces them to focus on positive features; see Shafir, 1993) or, alternatively, whether they would reject them (which stimulates attention to negative features).

Concluding Remarks

Although the studies described in the preceding section were all stimulated by issues of importance in consumer research, they have implications for social psychological phenomena more generally. In evaluating these implications, it may be worth noting that the concepts and knowledge that have been shown to affect judgments have been activated in the same experimental situation as the judgments they affect. As Smith (1990) points out, these effects are likely to be of very short duration. However, recently activated knowledge and frequently activated knowledge theoretically have similar effects on its accessibility and use (Bargh, Bond, Lombardi, & Tota, 1986). To this extent, laboratory demonstrations of the effects of recently activated concepts and knowledge may indeed provide insight into the effects of chronic individual differences in the accessibility of knowledge that result from learning experiences outside the laboratory.

ATTITUDES AND ATTITUDE-BEHAVIOR RELATIONS

Attitudes were initially conceptualized as a disposition to behave in a positive or negative way toward an object (Allport, 1935). A somewhat later conceptualization (e.g., Rosenberg & Hovland, 1960) defined attitudes as having three components: affective (feelings toward an object), cognitive (beliefs about the object), and conative (behavior toward the object), each of which was an independent manifestation of a single underlying construct.

The adoption of this definition had two related effects. First, it stimulated the construction of measures of attitude along one (e.g., affective) dimension (e.g., Edwards, 1957; Thurstone, 1931) under the implicit assumption that if the measures were valid, they would predict overt behavior. Second, it stimulated the single most heavily researched area in social psychology, concerning the factors that influence attitude formation and change.

A tripartite definition of attitudes is empirically and conceptually unworkable, however, as Zanna and Rempel (1988) pointed out (see also Breckler, 1984). For one thing, it implies that if positive affective or cognitive responses to an object are not accompanied by positive behavior toward the object, they are not, by definition, indicators of an attitude. Contemporary conceptions, therefore, have tended to view an attitude as simply an *evaluation* of an object along a good-bad dimension (cf. Eagly & Chaiken, 1993), leaving its determinants and effects to empirical investigation. Nevertheless, the implicit assumption that attitudes are related to behavior continues to pervade both social psychology and consumer research.

In fact, attitude measures are often very poor predictors of the behavior toward the object to which the attitude pertained. As Fishbein and Ajzen's (1975) Theory of Reasoned Action asserts, a much better predictor of a person's behavior toward an object is the person's attitude toward the *behavior* (for recent extensions of this theory and reviews of its implications, see Ajzen, 1991; Ajzen & Fishbein, 2005). These two attitudes are often not the same. (Weight watchers, for example, may have a positive attitude toward chocolate candy per se but a negative attitude toward buying or eating it.) Although the difference seems self-evident in retrospect, it escaped researchers' attention for generations.

The Fishbein-Ajzen model further specifies the factors that contribute to attitudes toward a behavior and, therefore, intentions to engage in it. In doing so, it formalizes an assumption that implicitly underlies the reason-why advertising strategies used in past advertising. That is, attitudes are an additive function of the evaluations of the possible consequences of the behavior, each weighted by the likelihood that the behavior would actually have this effect. The precise relation among these factors has been questioned (e.g., Miniard & Cohen, 1981: Wyer & Carlston, 1979). Furthermore, the factors that determine the specific subset of consequences that are taken into account are somewhat unclear. If these consequences are simply the ones that happen to be most easily accessible in memory at the time (Higgins, 1996; Wyer, 2008), it would mean that attitudes are inherently unstable. These considerations, of course, do not negate the general implication that situational and individual difference variables influence attitudes toward a behavior through their mediating impact on beliefs that the behavior will have specific favorable and unfavorable consequences. This implication is important in conceptualizing the impact of persuasive communications.

Perhaps a more important constraint on the applicability of the Fishbein-Ajzen conceptualization is reflected in the authors' own description of their theory as concerned with "reasoned action." That is, the theory assumes that attitudes are formed as a result of a deliberative assessment of the likelihood and desirability of its consequences. This may not always be the case. In many instances, attitudes can reflect a conditioned affective response to the object or behavior in question (see De Houwer, this volume) that occurs spontaneously with little cognitive mediation (Zajonc, 1980). Furthermore, individuals are often unable or unmotivated to engage in the cognitive activity required to assess the consequence of a behavior. In this case, their attitudes are likely to be based on other criteria that are easier to apply (e.g., the affect they happen to be experiencing; see Albarracin & Wyer, 2001). We elaborate this possibility presently.

Although attitudes toward a behavior may generally be a stronger determinant of intentions to engage in it than are attitudes toward the object of this behavior, this does not mean that attitudes toward the object play no role at all. However, one's attitude toward an object is not the only basis for a behavioral decision, and the likelihood of applying it depends on how quickly it comes to mind at the time the decision is made (for an elaboration, see Fazio, 1990, 1995). In effect, this suggests that the use of an attitude as a basis for a behavioral decision is governed in part by situational factors that influence its accessibility in memory.

Alternative Conceptualizations

The generalizability of the Fishbein-Ajzen conceptualization is also called into question by evidence that behavior is often the *determinant* of an attitude and not the consequence of it. Cognitive dissonance theory (Festinger, 1957) provides the most formal statement of this effect. That is, if people engage voluntarily in behavior that is inconsistent with their attitude toward a particular referent, they may attempt to rationalize this behavior by convincing themselves that they actually favor the position they have activated. Thus, they change their attitude in the direction implied by their behavior (Cooper, 1998; Cooper & Fazio, 1984; Wicklund & Brehm, 1976). Still other conceptualizations (Bem, 1972; Janis & King, 1954) assert that people use their past behavior to infer their present attitude, and that this can occur without consulting any attitude that they may have formed previously (Albarracin & Wyer, 2000).

In this regard, a refreshing challenge to the assumptions often made by attitude researchers was provided by Schwarz and Bohner (2001). Their conceptualization, which incorporates the possibilities raised by Bem (1972), asserts that all attitudes are *constructed* at the time they are solicited, based on whatever subset of relevant knowledge happens to be accessible in memory at the time. This knowledge could sometimes include a memorial representation of a previously reported attitude as well as other relevant information. However, this is not always the case.[4]

Schwarz and Bohner's conceptualization suggests that although people's attitude toward an object and their decision to engage in behavior toward the object may both be based on a subset of judgment-relevant knowledge that happens to be accessible at the time, the nature of these subsets may differ. Even if each subset necessarily includes a previously formed representation of an attitude, other subsets of knowledge can come into play as well. Viewed in this way, theory and research should be directed toward understanding the factors that determine the subsets of knowledge that people use as a basis for a behavioral decision, and not with the impact of attitudes per se.

Implications for Consumer Behavior

Consumer behavior researchers have long been interested in the effects of situational and informational variables on attitudes toward an ad and the product being advertised under the assumption that these attitudes have something to do with intentions to purchase the product. Thus, early advertising that focused on building an image of reliability through soft-sell and implicit suggestions were based on this assumption (for example, the General Motors ad for Cadillac; see Note 2). However, Fishbein and Ajzen's (1975) observation that behavior is better predicted by attitudes toward the behavior than by attitudes toward the product was often ignored. Although factors that affect attitudes toward the ad, the product, and the behavior may be of theoretical interest, it should not be too surprising if the relations among these effects are low.

Perhaps the most important concern in applying the Fishbein-Ajzen model to consumer judgment and decision processes was noted earlier. Some consumer decisions (e.g., whether to use condoms, to go on a cholesterol-free diet, or to buy a luxury car) undoubtedly involve a careful evaluation of the alternative consequences of the action. Most purchasing decisions, however, are made with very little deliberation at all, and are based on criteria that happen to be salient at the time of purchase. Many such decisions are based on affective reactions toward the product in question, particularly if participants are preoccupied with other thoughts (Shiv & Fedorikhin, 1999). It is clearly of interest to understand when participants are likely to engage in deliberative processing and when they are not (for a review see Friese, Hofmann, & Wänke, this volume). (We discuss this matter more fully in the context of communication and persuasion.) It nevertheless seems likely that the purchase decisions that stimulate the sort of deliberative processing described by the Fishbein-Ajzen model are a very small subset of those that occur in daily life.

As noted earlier, quite different subsets of knowledge may be brought to bear on attitudes toward an ad. A related consideration is made salient by Schwarz and Bohner's (2001) observation that attitudes are constructed at the time one is asked to report them. That is, the subset of knowledge that enters into the construction of an attitude toward a product at one point in time may differ in important ways from the subset that is later retrieved and used as a basis for a decision to purchase it at a later time. These considerations raise questions about the utility of the attitude construct in predicting consumer behavior.

Implications of Consumer Research

A substantial body of research in consumer judgment and decision making raises questions concerning whether attitudes come into play at all. Purchase decisions often involve a choice among attractive alternatives. In principle, these preferences can be determined by assessing one's attitude toward each alternative separately and then comparing these overall evaluations. However, research by Huber, Payne, and Puto (1982), Simonson (1989), and others suggest that consumers often make preference judgments by performing a dimension-by-dimension comparison of the alternatives and basing their choice on the relative number of dimensions on which one product is superior to the other. A particularly provocative series of studies was reported by Simonson (1989) and his colleagues (Shafir, Simonson, & Tversky, 1993; see also Huber et al., 1982). When A is more desirable than B along one dimension but is inferior to B along a second, people's preferences for A and B may not differ. However, if a third option, C, is added, and if A is superior to C but B is not, participants' preference for A over B will increase. Furthermore, this decision might be made without ever computing the overall attitude toward any of the choice alternatives. In fact, when people are asked explicitly to evaluate each choice alternative separately before reporting their preferences, their decision is often quite different (Park & Kim, 2005).

A second series of studies of consumer decision making has identified other effects of comparison processes. For example, when people are asked to choose between two alternatives, A and B, they tend to focus their attention on features of the second product they consider that the first one does not have while ignoring features of the first that the second does not have. Thus, if A and B have unique positive features and people happen to consider A before they consider B, they are more inclined to prefer the second alternative, B. If the alternatives have unique negative features, however, they are more inclined to prefer A (Houston & Sherman, 1995). A by-product of this comparison process is that the features that the alternatives have in common are generally given little weight in computing a preference. The effect of this reduced weight is evident later when the alternatives are evaluated individually (Brunner & Wänke, 2006; Dhar & Sherman, 1996; Wang & Wyer, 2002). Thus, after stating a preference for alternatives with common negative features, people evaluate both the preferred and the rejected alternative more favorably, whereas after choosing between alternatives with common positive features, they evaluate both alternatives less favorably.

The conditions in which comparative judgments of the sort identified by Huber and colleagues (1982) occur outside the laboratory have yet to be circumscribed either theoretically or empirically. Wang and Wyer (2002) found evidence that people make dimension-by-dimension comparisons only if they are explicitly asked to do so. Posavac and colleagues (2004, 2005) also argue that people do not make comparative judgments even if alternatives are available, and that explicitly asking them to do so decreases the favorableness of their ratings. In contrast, Brunner and Wänke (2006) reported that comparison processes *do* occur spontaneously and that cancellation effects can occur even without instructions to consider the alternatives in relation to one another. Whether the choice alternatives are equally salient at the time a decision is made (Posavac et al., 2005) and whether the attributes of the alternatives are described along comparable dimensions are undoubtedly important considerations.

Be that as it may, the evidence that preference judgments and the decisions based on them are made without a prior computation of overall attitudes toward the alternatives raises additional questions about the importance of attitudes or attitude-related judgments as bases for purchase decisions. However, an understanding of preferences and the processes that underlie them are obviously of concern in social psychology as well as consumer behavior. Nevertheless, these processes have received little attention in social psychological research. Investigations of impression formation have normally concentrated on the evaluations of single persons, objects, and events. Yet, many social judgments and decisions obviously require a comparison of persons with one another or with oneself. The processes identified by Simonson, Huber, and their colleagues may be worth considering in conceptualizing these processes and examining them empirically.

COMMUNICATION AND PERSUASION

Although research on attitude formation and change was stimulated by its assumed implications for behavior change, it has normally been conducted in social psychology as an end in itself, without regard for its behavioral implications. In much of this research, participants are asked to read communications that advocate a position with which they initially disagree. The communication is often attributed to a particular source. The factors that potentially influence the impact of such a communication typically concern (1) characteristics of the information itself and how it is presented, (2) characteristics of the information's source, and (3) situational and individual difference factors that influence receptiveness to the information.

Informational Factors

Research on the informational characteristics that influence the impact of a persuasive message, conducted by Carl Hovland and his colleagues many years ago, permitted several conclusions to be drawn concerning these matters. For example, arguments that oppose one's initial position on an issue have greater impact if they are preceded by arguments that support one's position (thereby increasing the perception that the message is unbiased) than if the opposing arguments are presented in isolation. Second, the initial information presented about an issue normally has greater effect than later information (but see Miller & Campbell, 1959, for an exception).

Independently of these more general order effects, a message is often more effective in inducing people to engage in a behavior if it is preceded by a vivid description of the problem that the behavior potentially remedies (Leventhal, 1970). However, this may be true only if individuals feel capable of engaging in the behavior being advocated. If they feel unable to cope with the danger, fear may lead to denial of the problem's seriousness and personal relevance. (For example, a vivid portrayal of the consequences of smoking may be more effective than a mild appeal on smokers who feel capable of quitting, but may have less effect on smokers who feel unable to do so.)

A provocative series of studies by McGuire (1964) concerning the effects of inducing resistance to persuasion suggests that exposing people to a mild attack on their position, which makes them aware of their vulnerability to influence, stimulates them to bolster their defenses. As a result, they are less persuaded by a subsequent counterattitudinal message than participants who were not exposed to the attack. Similarly, persons who are forewarned that a message is intended to influence them are normally more resistant to persuasion than those who receive the message without being forewarned (Jacks & Devine, 2000; Wood & Quinn, 2003).

The effect of forewarning and the "inoculation" effect identified by McGuire may be traceable to the influence of these factors on both the motivation and the ability to counterargue the implications of the message at the time it is received. Situational factors that distract recipients from engaging in this cognitive activity are likely to increase the impact of the message (Festinger & Maccoby, 1964; Osterhouse & Brock, 1970). This, of course, assumes that individuals have received and comprehended the message's implications; people cannot be persuaded by information they have not received. If distraction is so great that individuals do not process the information at all, the impact of the message content is likely to be negligible.

McGuire's (1968, 1972) information-processing model conceptualizes the combined effects of these factors. A simplified version of this model (Wyer, 1974) that conveys the functional relations among influence, reception, and counterarguing is given by the equation

$$P(I) = P(R) [1 - P(CA)]$$

where $P(I)$ is the probability of being influenced by an argument, $P(R)$ is the probability of receiving and comprehending its implications, and $P(CA)$ is the likelihood of counterarguing it effectively. According to this equation, influence is less when comprehension and counterarguing are both low [$P(R) = P(CA) = 0$] or both high [$P(R) = P(CA) = 1$)] than when they are both moderate [$P(R) = P(CA) = .5$]. This means that variables that simultaneously decrease both comprehension and counterarguing (distraction, motivation, intelligence, etc.) will be nonmonotonically related to influence, consistent with McGuire's (1972) conjecture. Thus, in the context of our present discussion, a factor that increases distraction from a low to a moderate level may increase a communication's influence, but a further increase in distraction may decrease its impact. However, distraction will increase a message's influence only if recipients are motivated to counterargue its implications. If $P(CA) = 0$ at the outset, even a small amount of distraction will theoretically decrease its influence.

Individual Differences

Individuals differences in responses to a communication can also be conceptualized in terms of differences in the components of the preceding equation. The most widely applied individual difference measure in social psychology, and among the most successful in capturing differences in responses to information, is the index of *need for cognition* developed by Cacioppo and Petty (1982). This measure purportedly assesses differences in the motivation to engage in effortful cognitive activity and the intrinsic enjoyment of doing so. A second, less well-known but important index, *need for closure* (Webster & Kruglanski, 1994), assesses intolerance of ambiguity, or the desire to reach a definite conclusion or decision. Individuals with high need for cognition may gain pleasure in deliberating over decisions, whereas individuals with high need for closure may find deliberation aversive and try to make a decision without much thought. The relation between these motivational dispositions and the interdependence of their effects are unclear. Perhaps people with low need for cognition *or* high need for closure think less about judgment-irrelevant information they receive and may use criteria that require little thought, albeit for quite different reasons. Whether these differences would be reflected in differences in $P(R)$, $P(CA)$, or both is not clear, however. The responses to information by persons with *both* high need for cognition and high need for closure is also difficult to predict.

Source Effects on Persuasion

The impact of a communication may often depend on characteristics of its source (for recent reviews of source effects in persuasion, see Chaiken and Maheswaran, 1994; Johnson, Maio, & Smith-McLallen, 2005). The source of a message could influence acceptance of the message independently of the arguments contained in it. It could also influence the attention that is given to the message, the interpretation of its content, or the weight that is given to it in relation to other available information. The nature of the influence may depend on the particular source characteristics in question. For example, expertise and trustworthiness, which are among the most commonly investigated source characteristics (Hovland, Janis, & Kelley, 1955; Johnson et al., 2005), may exert their influence in different ways. That is, expertise may influence the weight that is attached to the information presented, whereas trustworthiness may affect the interpretation of the information's implications (Birnbaum & Stegner, 1979).

Other characteristics were identified by Kelman (1958). For example, a message from a source with the power to influence one's personal well being may be endorsed only if the source has access to one's responses. When the same message comes from someone who is used as a standard for social desirability, however, it may be temporarily accepted regardless of whether one reports one's position publicly or privately. However, the magnitude of this influence decreases over time. Only when the message is attributed to someone with expert knowledge about the issue at hand does its influence appear to be fairly enduring.

Kelman's research raises the possibility that the impact of a message's source can be conceptualized independently of the effects of its content. This assumption underlies research on the Sleeper effect (that is, the tendency for a message from a negative source to increase its effect over time; see Gruder et al., 1978; Kumkale & Albarracin, 2004). Attitudes toward the source and implications of the message content may both exert an influence immediately after it is presented. Therefore, if the effects of these factors are in opposite directions, they can partially offset one another. However, memory for contextual features (e.g., the source) decay more rapidly than memory for the message content (Pratkanis et al., 1988). Consequently, the influence of the message content becomes more apparent as time goes on. The assumption that message and source effects are independent also underlies the hypothesis that a message's source is used as a "heuristic" basis for judgments under conditions in which recipients do not have the time or motivation to conduct a detailed analysis of the message content (Chaiken, 1980, 1987; see also Petty & Cacioppo, 1986).

Implications for Consumer Behavior Research

Magazine advertisements and television commercials are essentially persuasive communications that are intended to influence recipients to purchase the product being advertised. It might therefore be reasonable to suppose that the enormous literature on communication and persuasion performed in social psychology (for reviews, see Albarracin, Johnson, & Zanna, 2005) would have clear implications for the effects of these communications. However, the implications may be limited. As noted earlier, research in social psychology has traditionally been concerned with the effectiveness of verbal communications in persuading individuals to change an opinion that they have already formed and are more or less motivated to maintain. Thus, recipients of these messages may often differ in their intrinsic motivation to think about the content of the message, as reflected in differences in need for cognition and need for closure (but see Briñol & Petty, 2005, for qualifications on this assertion).

In contrast, individuals often have little interest in analyzing the content of the advertisements and television commercials and have no strong a priori opinions concerning the products being advertised. Although individuals may generally have a somewhat cynical view of the trustworthiness of advertisements, they are unlikely to devote much cognitive effort to a refutation of the message content. Therefore, the factors that influence communication effectiveness in the consumer domain are likely to have an effect through their influence on the attention to and comprehension of the message [i.e., P(R)] and not through their impact on attempts to refute it [P(CA)].

Individual Differences in Motivation   The role of individual differences in the motivation to er ,age in information processing is also worth considering in this context. When a communication is counterattitudinal, recipients are likely to pay attention to the information conveyed unless they are particularly low in need for cognition. However, people are normally uninterested in advertisements and television commercials. Even recipients with high need for cognition might not think about the content of these messages unless the messages provide some intellectual stimulation. More generally, ads and commercials might not be thought about extensively regardless of individuals' need for cognition. (Indeed, consumers who enjoy challenging intellectual activity might even be *less* attentive to such ads than other consumers are.)

For similar reasons, differences in need for closure seem less likely to influence the processing of information in ads and television commercials. These differences may be more evident in actual purchasing behavior. That is, people with high need for closure are presumably less likely to evaluate choice alternatives carefully and, therefore, may be more inclined to make premature decisions. This possibility is interesting to consider in the context of differences in the disposition to focus on positive vs. negative consequences of a decision outcome (Higgins, 1998). When choice alternatives have both positive and negative features, some individuals may be disposed to focus on positive features before considering negative ones, whereas others may be inclined to focus on negative features at the outset. The effects of these different dispositions should be more evident in individuals with high need for closure.

Source Effects   When individuals are unmotivated and unable to process the message content extensively, characteristics of the source are particularly likely to have an influence (Chaiken, 1980). To this extent, source effects should be particularly evident in advertisements. The assumption that this is true is evident from the widespread use of celebrity endorsers in advertisements both in past and current advertising. Conceptual issues arise in considering the nature of this influence, however. For one thing, it is unclear whether the source of information contained in an ad should be considered to be the ad itself or, if the ad contains an endorsement by a celebrity, the endorser. (In some instances, the source may be considered to be the product's manufacturer; see Goldberg & Hartwick, 1990.) These distinctions could be important. People often consider ads to be untrustworthy and infer that the information they convey is likely to be misleading. Yet, they apparently believe that celebrities like the products they endorse despite the fact that they are being paid vast sums of money to promote these products (Cronley, Kardes, Goddard, & Houghton, 1999). The relative influence of these factors is unclear.

A second question that arises in the case of celebrity endorsers surrounds the reason for their effect. Kelman's (1958) research suggests several source characteristics other than trustworthiness that could come into play, including the endorser's expertise in the domain to which the product pertains, the social prestige of the endorser (and, therefore, the desire to "be like" him or her by using similar products), and the standard set by the celebrity for what is generally socially desirable. In addition, celebrity endorsers may stimulate attention to the ad, leading its content to have more influence. Alternatively, celebrities might draw attention to themselves and, therefore, *distract* viewers from thinking about the ad's implications.

One implication of social psychological research is nonetheless important. Once a stimulus has been evaluated on the basis of information that is available at the time of judgment, this evaluation is stored in memory and may later be retrieved and used as a basis for subsequent judgments independently of the information that gave rise to its construction (Carlston, 1980; Srull & Wyer, 1980; Sherman, Ahlm, Berman, & Lynn, 1978). In the present context, this suggests that if people spontaneously form a favorable impression of a product on the basis of a celebrity endorser's recommendation, the evaluation may later be retrieved and used as a basis for a purchase decisions without considering the conditions that surrounded the construction of this impression.

Implications of Consumer Behavior Research

The impact of advertisements and television commercials on consumers' attitudes and purchase intentions is obviously a central concern of consumer research. A summary of its implications for communication and behavior in general is beyond the scope of this chapter. We focus on only one area in which the implications of consumer research for social psychology are particularly obvious.

Most social psychological research on attitude formation and change has focused almost exclusively on the impact of verbal information, and has rarely considered conditions in which information is conveyed visually as well. In the consumer domain, however, verbal and visual information about a product are frequently presented simultaneously. Although message characteristics (e.g., argument strength) have been studied extensively in social psychology, the manner in which information in different modalities combines to influence attitudes and decisions has rarely been examined. Three series of studies in consumer research exemplify the different roles that pictures can play in a consumer context. These studies, which are interesting to consider in the context of the emotion-based advertising strategies that were applied in the early days of marketing, have implications for contemporary research in social information processing.

Effects of Pictures on Initial Impression Formation   Several studies of the impact of pictures and verbal attribute information on product evaluations were conducted by Yeung and Wyer (2004). They found that when products were described by verbal attribute information alone, participants' evaluations of the product depended on whether they were told to use hedonic (i.e., affective) or utilitarian criteria. When they were shown a picture of the product before receiving the verbal attribute information, however, they formed an initial impression of the product on the basis of the picture alone (and the affect the picture elicited). That is, the attribute information they received later (as well as the criteria they were told to use in making their evaluations) had little effect.

In a quite different study (Sengupta & Fitzsimons, 2000), participants evaluated a product on the basis of an attractive or unattractive picture along with favorable or unfavorable verbal attribute descriptions. Some participants wrote down the reasons for making their evaluations and these reasons, along with the attitude they reported, were determined largely by the verbal attribute descriptions they received. Then, either immediately or five days later, participants were asked to choose which candy they would like to receive as a reward for participating in the study, being shown the pictures of the products they had seen earlier.

When participants had explained their attitude, this attitude was highly correlated with the choice they made immediately after reporting it. However, this correlation decreased substantially after a delay. In the latter case, participants apparently based their candy choices on the attractiveness of the packaging (which was salient at the time their decision was made), and their previously formed reason-based attitude had little impact. In other words, the effects of participants' spontaneous reactions to the pictures overrode any effects of the attitude they had constructed on the basis of the verbal information. Note that this finding indirectly supports the use of emotion-based advertising strategies. More generally, it provides yet another indication that attitudes are often not an important predictor of behavioral decisions in the consumer domain.

Effects of Pictures on Information Processing

The aforementioned studies show that pictures exert an influence on product evaluations independently of the verbal information they accompany. Other research suggests that the nature of their influence depends on how the verbal information is processed. This processing, in turn, may depend on the format in which the verbal information is conveyed. In two series of studies by Adaval and her colleagues, consumers read either a travel brochure describing the events that occurred during a vacation trip (Adaval & Wyer, 1998) or a campaign brochure describing the events that occurred in a political candidate's career (Adaval, Isbell, & Wyer, 2006). In each series of studies, the information was conveyed in either the form of a narrative that conveyed the temporal order in which the events took place or an ostensibly unordered list. Finally, the verbal description of each event was either accompanied by a picture relevant to the event or presented alone.

When the information was conveyed in a narrative, participants appeared to suspend judgment until they had received all of the information available and they could base their impression on the sequence of events as a whole. In this case, pictures increased the vividness of the "story" conveyed by the sequence and increased the extremity of the evaluations. When the information was conveyed in a list, however, participants appeared to engage in an on-line integration of the evaluative implications of each event separately, updating their impression with the implications of each new event as it was presented. In this case, the pictures that accompanied the event descriptions interfered with this piecemeal integration and *decreased* the extremity of the evaluations that participants made.

Other recent studies also show that pictures do not necessarily increase the effectiveness of an advertisement. In a study by Hung and Wyer (2008), for example, participants received advertisements consisting of (1) a description of a problem (e.g., hair loss), (2) a recommendation to use a particular product, and (3) a description of the result (reduction in hair loss). However, the modality of the problem description (picture vs. verbal statement) and that of the solution description were independently varied.

Participants were expected to apply two normative principles in responding to the ads: a general principle that communications are generally intended to be both informative and truthful (Grice, 1975), and a domain-specific principle that advertising claims are likely to be exaggerated. When one component of the ad (either the problem description or the solution description) was pictured and the other was described verbally, participants attempted to interpret the verbal component in a manner that was consistent with the implications of the pictured component, based on their prior knowledge about the type of problem being advertised and the principle that communications are informative and truthful. Having expended this cognitive effort, however, they were not motivated to expend the additional effort required to apply the principle that advertising claims were exaggerated. As a result, they evaluated the product favorably. When both components were pictured, however, the literal implications of the ad could be construed with little effort, and so participants were willing to expect the effort required to apply the principle that ad claims were exaggerated. Consequently, the ad was disparaged and the product was evaluated unfavorably.

The Role of Imagery in Information Processing

Pictures may exert an influence on judgments through their mediating impact on the images they provide of the situations they describe. However, images may be elicited by verbal descriptions of situations as well. The role of imagery in consumer behavior (for a review, see Wyer, Hung, & Jiang, 2008) has been recognized in research by Escalas (2004; see also Green & Brock, 2000, 2004). That is, individuals who read a story may often imagine themselves as a protagonist in the narrative. As a consequence of being "transported" into the situation portrayed in advertisement, they may be more influenced by it.

However, advertisements are often encountered in the context of other information that can also lead recipients to become transported (e.g., a television movie or a magazine story). In this case, the information may intrude on the processing of the ad, depending on when the ad is encountered. Wang and Calder (2006) showed, for example, that when people encounter an ad at the end of a story they are reading, their tendency to be transported into the story increases the impact of the ad on product evaluations. If, on the other hand, the ad is introduced in the middle of the story, thus breaking up the flow of the story, becoming transported into the story has a negative impact on the ad's effectiveness. Although Wang and Calder restricted their consideration to the effects of reading a story, analogous effects seem likely to occur when watching episodes on television that are interrupted constantly by commercials.

The Impact of Visual Imagery on Information Process Is Not Universal

The disposition to form images on the basis of verbal information may be either chronic (Childers, Houston, & Heckler, 1985) or situationally induced. In a series of studies, Jiang, Steinhart, and Wyer (2008) found that when people with a disposition to form visual images (i.e., *visualizers*) receive attribute descriptions of a product that is unfamiliar to them, they often find it difficult to construct an image of it and react unfavorably to the product being described. However, providing a picture of the product can substantially increase their evaluations of it, but the impact of a picture on visualizers' evaluations depends in part on whether the verbal and pictorial information can be integrated into a single image. In contrast, when individuals have a disposition to process information semantically without forming visual images, they are unaffected by these factors.

Concluding Comment   The research summarized in this section concerned the facilitating and disruptive effects of both pictures and visual images on consumer information processing. However, the phenomena identified in these research streams are clearly relevant to an understanding of impression formation more generally. People often read or hear about a person or event in the course of informal conversation under conditions in which a picture of the individuals involved may or may not be available. The impact of this information on the impressions that recipients form may depend on whether they typically form mental images on the basis of such verbal descriptions and, if so, whether a picture or previously formed visual image is available. These contingencies, however, have not been addressed in social psychological research.

AFFECT AND SUBJECTIVE EXPERIENCE

General Considerations

Influences of Affect on Judgments and Behavior   Before the advent of information processing research and theorizing in the mid-1970s, affective reactions were normally viewed as socially conditioned responses to stimulus persons and objects that became associated with these stimuli through learning. The emotion-based advertising strategies employed during the first half of the twentieth century reflect this assumption. For example, if someone experiences positive feelings at the time a person is present or a product is described, these feelings become associated with features of the person or product as well as other features of the situation. Consequently, exposure to these features is likely to elicit similar feelings, providing the basis for liking them (Clore & Byrne, 1974).

However, information processing research and theory has led to the postulation of several additional ways in which affective reactions can potentially influence judgments and behavior. For example, positive or negative affect might activate affect-congruent evaluative concepts in memory that are either brought to bear on the interpretation of new information (Bower, 1981; Forgas, Bower, & Krantz, 1984) or serve as retrieval cues for previously acquired knowledge (Bower, Gilligan, & Monteiro, 1981; Isen, Shalker, Clark, & Karp, 1978). Furthermore, people often base their evaluations of a stimulus on the feelings they happen to be experiencing and attribute to the stimulus they are judging. In such instances, feelings have a direct, informational influence on judgments and decisions (Schwarz & Clore, 1983, 1988, 1996).

Affect can also influence the attention that people pay to the information they receive and use as a basis for judgment (Schwarz, 1990; for a review see Pham, this volume). For example, people who feel happy are inclined to perceive the situation they are in as benign and, therefore, as needing little attention. In contrast, those who feel unhappy are more inclined to judge the situation as problematic and as requiring more detailed consideration. As a result of this difference, people who experience positive affect are less influenced by details of a communication they receive (Bless, Bohner, Schwarz, & Strack, 1990), and are more inclined to use heuristic bases for judgment (Bodenhausen, 1993) than are people who feel sad.

Finally, affect can have a direct, motivational influence. Because positive affect is pleasant, people are often motivated to maintain this affective state and resist engaging in activities that are likely to bring them down. In contrast, negative affect is aversive and people are motivated to eliminate it. (See Isen, 1984, for a discussion of factors that motivate mood-maintenance and mood-repair.) That is, people who feel unhappy may be particularly attracted to activities that permit them to overcome the negative feelings they are experiencing.

Several of the aforementioned conclusions should be qualified. Niedenthal and her colleagues (Niedenthal, Halberstadt, & Setterlund, 1997; Niedenthal & Setterlund, 1994), for example, found that the experience of affect per se increases the accessibility in memory of only those concepts that describe the particular type of affect that people are experiencing (e.g., "happy," "sad," etc.) and do not influence the accessibility of valenced concepts in general. This result raises questions about the influence of affect on memory and comprehension, Furthermore, the impact of affective reactions on the amount of effort expended in activity can depend on the purpose for which the activity is being performed (Martin, Ward, Achee, & Wyer, 1993). That is, people who are motivated to perform well may use their feelings as a basis for evaluating their performance and may persist less long if they are feeling happy (and infer that their performance is satisfactory) than if they are not. If people are performing the same activity for enjoyment, however, they may infer that they are enjoying it more if they are happy and may persevere longer than they would if they were sad.[5]

The Role of Nonaffective Subjective Experience

Affective reactions are only one of several subjective experiences that potentially influence people's judgments and decisions. Stepper and Strack (1993), for example, showed that persons who complete a question while standing upright report being more assertive than persons who complete the questionnaire while slouched at a low table. Proprioceptive cues associated with posture apparently elicited feelings of either assertiveness or lack of it, and these feelings were used as a basis for judgment.

Of greater relevance to the concerns of this chapter is evidence that feelings of ease or difficulty in processing information can have an impact on evaluations of the objects to which the information pertains (Winkielman & Cacioppo, 2001; for reviews, see Schwarz, 1998, 2004; Schwarz, Song & Xu, this volume). For example, people who are asked to generate many instances of assertiveness judge themselves less assertive than people who are asked to generate only a few (Schwarz et al, 1991). Although people generate more instances in the first case, they find it difficult to accomplish and so they infer that they may not have the attribute to which the instances refer. For similar reasons, people who have been asked to generate many reasons why an event occurred predict the event is less inevitable than do people who have been asked to generate just a few (Sanna, Schwarz, & Stocker, 2002).

Implications for Consumer Research

The assumption that happy consumers are more inclined to evaluate products favorably and to make purchases has guided advertising and promotions for many years. This is evidenced by the playing of pleasant music in shopping centers and the use of humor and attractive women in ads and television commercials. That is, the affect elicited by contextual stimuli is assumed to become associated with the product, leading the product to elicit the feelings later and increasing the likelihood of purchasing it (Gorn, 1982; Shimp, 1991).

This process may not be the only one that underlies the impact of affective reactions on consumer judgments and decisions, however. The research on the impact of affect as information (Schwarz & Clore, 1996; Wyer, Clore, & Isbell, 1999; Pham, this volume) suggests that affect is likely to be used as a basis for judgments of a stimulus only if it is likely to be considered a viable basis for evaluating it. This is not always the case. In the product domain, for example, many products may be evaluated on the basis of functional, utilitarian criteria. Consequently, the affect that people are experiencing is unlikely to influence their evaluations of such products (Adaval, 2001; Pham, 1998; Yeung & Wyer, 2004).

When affect is an appropriate criterion for evaluating a stimulus, however, the evaluation of the stimulus may be influenced not only by the feelings that the stimulus actually elicits but also by the affect that people happen to be experiencing for other, objectively irrelevant reasons (Schwarz & Clore, 1983, 1996; for a review see Pham, this volume). People usually cannot distinguish clearly between the various sources of affect they are experiencing at any given time. Consequently, some portion of the affect that they are experiencing for reasons that have nothing to do with the object they are judging may be misattributed to their feelings about the object and, therefore, are likely to influence the evaluation they make.

Much of the research that has been conducted to demonstrate the impact of affect on product evaluations has capitalized on this fact. That is, participants are exposed to feelings that elicit positive or negative affect for reasons that are ostensibly irrelevant to the stimuli they are being asked to judge or the decision they are asked to make. If subjects' judgments of a product are normally based on hedonic, or affective criteria, then extraneous affect, which is likely to become confused with the affect that the object actually elicited, will have an impact as well. If, however, affect is not normally a basis for judgments, either because the stimulus is not affect-eliciting or because affect is considered irrelevant, the extraneous affect that people are experiencing should have no effect (Adaval, 2001; Yeung & Wyer, 2004).

Although the informational influence of affect on product evaluations has been demonstrated in several studies (Pham, 1998, this volume; Yeung & Wyer, 2004, 2005), its motivational influence has been less frequently examined (but see Pham, this volume). It seems reasonable to suppose that people who are feeling unhappy and perceive that a consumption activity (going shopping, treating oneself to a meal at a gourmet restaurant, etc.) will improve their mood are likely to be attracted to it. If, however, they do not believe that the activity will have this effect, they may use the feelings they are experiencing as a basis for evaluating the behavior and, consequently, may be less inclined to engage in the behavior than they otherwise would (Andrade, 2005; Cohen & Andrade, 2004; Shen & Wyer, 2008a).

As noted earlier, affective reactions are not the only subjective experience that can influence individuals' judgments. The subjective ease of processing may be of particular interest (see Schwarz et al., this volume). For example, individuals are less likely to report liking a product if they find it difficult to generate positive attributes of the product than if they find it easy, regardless of the number they actually list (Menon & Raghubir, 2003; Wänke, Bohner, & Jurkowitsch, 1997). Furthermore, when persons receive information about a product, their evaluations may be influenced by their subjective difficulty in processing it. Thus, people evaluate a product less favorably if the information describing it is conveyed in a font that is difficult to read (Novemsky, Dhar, Schwarz, & Simonson, in press). By the same token, difficult-to process information that one encounters before reading product descriptions may make these descriptions seem easier to read and, therefore, lead the product to be evaluated more favorably than it otherwise would be (Shen, Jiang, & Adaval, 2007).

Implications of Consumer Research

As the preceding summary indicates, social psychological research and theory on the impact of subjective experience on judgments are quite applicable to an understanding of consumer behavior. This distinguishes it from the other areas of research we have reviewed. To date, however, the influence has largely been in only one direction. Many important implications of consumer research for the impact of affect on judgments have thus far not been pursued. The role of affect in judgments and behavior has been investigated extensively and new theoretical breakthroughs are rare. Nevertheless, research in consumer behavior and judgment has identified at least three phenomena with general theoretical implications for a more general understanding of affect and information processing.

One concerns the point in time at which affect is likely to exert its influence. Most social psychological research has assumed that the informational influence of affect occurs at the time of judgment (but see Martin et al., 1993). In contrast, Yeung and Wyer (2004) showed that this influence can also occur at earlier stages of processing. When individuals receive an affect-eliciting picture of a product before receiving verbal information, for example, they spontaneously form an impression of the product and the affect they are experiencing influences this impression. Once formed, the impression is retained in memory and is later recalled and used as a basis for evaluating the product independently of the implications of information available about its specific attributes. Pictures have not normally been presented in social psychological research on person impression formation, and so this possibility had not previously been identified. It seems likely, however, that people often form spontaneous impressions of a person on the basis of the person's physical appearance before they receive more specific information about him or her. To this extent, Yeung and Wyer's findings have obvious implications for the role of affect in person judgments outside the laboratory.

Affect-Confirmation Processes   Adaval (2001) found that when judgments are based on specific attributes of a product, attributes that elicit affect similar to the feelings that participants are experiencing for other reasons have greater impact. However, this is not simply a result of selective attention. Rather, when an attribute is evaluated on the basis of the affect it elicits, feelings that consumers are experiencing for other reasons appear to confirm or disconfirm the implications of this affect, thus either increasing or decreasing confidence that these implications have been accurately assessed. This, in turn, leads these attributes to have more or less weight when they are integrated with other information at the time of judgment. (Note that when the attributes are favorable or unfavorable but do not elicit affect, this differential weighting does not occur.) These affect-confirmation processes, which had not been previously identified, are not only important in understanding the impact of affect in impression formation more generally but could also have implications for the differential weighting of arguments presented in a persuasive communication.

Processing of Categorical Information   The impact of affect on the influence of more global, categorical information may differ from its impact on the influence of specific attributes. A second series of studies (Adaval, 2003) provides new theoretical insights into the nature of this impact. People who experience positive affect may pay relatively more attention to global, categorical criteria for judgment (Bless, 2001; Schwarz, 1990). However, the effect of increased attention could be twofold. On one hand, people who experience positive affect may be more inclined to use categorical criteria as a heuristic basis for judgment, thus giving these criteria relatively more weight than other, more detailed information (Schwarz, 1990). Another possibility, however, is suggested by Tesser's (1978) research on the effects of thought on attitude polarization. That is, people who experience positive affect think more extensively about categorical criteria for judgment, with the result that they interpret the implications of this information as more extreme.

Adaval's (2003) research supported the second possibility. That is, inducing positive affect increased the impact of brand name on judgments. Using sophisticated methodology (N. H. Anderson, 1981) to separate differences in the weight attached to information and differences in its scale value (perceptions of its evaluative implications), however, she found that this increase was due to the impact of positive affect on the extremity with which the brand information was interpreted rather than on the weight attached to this information when integrating its implications with those of other product information. If this finding generalizes to the social domain, it might have implications for the impact of affect on the influence of stereotypes and other categorical bases for person impressions.

In summary, social psychological research on the influence of affect on information processing has had a substantial influence on research and theory on advertising effectiveness and on product evaluations more generally. At the same time, research on the role of affect in consumer behavior calls attention to theoretical and empirical issues of particular importance in traditional areas of social psychology that have yet to be examined.

CONCLUDING REMARKS

We have reviewed several areas of social psychology that have had an impact on research in consumer judgment and behavior. Our review is by no means exhaustive. It is nonetheless interesting to note that the main themes of research and theory in consumer behavior are reflections of the implicit theories that guided reason-why and emotion-based advertising strategies in the first half of the twentieth century, before experimental consumer research emerged as an academic discipline. Although research on attitude formation, communication and persuasion, and affect have implications for the factors that influence the effectiveness of each type of strategy, the conditions that determine which strategy is most likely to be effective is less well established.

Although social psychological theory and research has called attention to fundamental issues of relevance to consumer behavior, the paradigms that have been used to investigate these issues have often been inapplicable to the sorts of situations that exist in situations outside the laboratory. At the same time, research and theorizing that has been stimulated by a concern with consumer judgment and decision making has often identified phenomena of importance in developing a more comprehensive theory of judgment and behavior in domains of traditional interest to social psychologists (see also Wänke, this volume).

In short, the influence of social psychology and consumer psychology is (or should be) reciprocal, with each area calling attention to issues of theoretical interest that have not been addressed in the other. This observation is hardly profound, as evident from the increasing frequency with which social psychologists publish in consumer research journals and with which consumer researchers publish in social psychology outlets. The two areas of inquiry have indeed begun to merge. We look forward to a continuation of this trend in the decades to come.

ACKNOWLEDGMENTS

This research was supported in part by grants HKUST6053/01H, HKUST6194/04H, and HKUST6192/04H from the Research Grants Council, Hong Kong. We thank Frank Kardes and L. J. Shrum for valuable comments on an earlier version of the manuscript.

ENDNOTES

1. Our concern with the interface of consumer research and social psychological research should not be confused with a concern about the generalizeability of laboratory research and phenomena that occur in natural settings. In fact, comparisons of the results obtained in laboratory and field experiments suggest that the generalizeability

is very high (Anderson, Lindsay, & Bushman, 1999; see also Kardes, 1996). The comparisons we make concern the applicability of theory and research across disciplines independently of where the research is conducted.

2. For example, General Motors instituted a "The Penalty of Leadership" ad after their Cadillac model with an eight-cylinder engine failed, pointing out that only the very best had to deal with criticisms by the envious few. With no picture and no mention of Cadillac or the V-8, it became one of the most successful campaigns of the period.

3. These effects are likely due to the set of values associated with the African-American stereotype. That is, African Americans are stereotypically uninterested in intellectual achievement whereas they value musical ability. Priming the stereotype may activate these values, leading individuals to exert different amounts of effort, and their performance may reflect this effort.

4. Note that according to this view, a difference between the attitude that a person reports at one point in time and the attitude that the person reports at a later time does not necessarily indicate that the individual consciously changed his or her attitude. Rather, it simply indicates that different subsets of knowledge were used to construct their attitudes at the two times.

5. This result suggests another possible explanation of the influence of positive affect on the impact of persuasive communications. That is, people who are feeling happy may anticipate that careful reading of a counterattitudinal message will be aversive and they may avoid thinking about it carefully. Consequently, the strength of arguments contained in such a message may have little influence on their responses to it. If happy persons anticipate that reading the message will be enjoyable, however, they might pay more attention to it than they otherwise would and might be more sensitive to the quality of arguments contained in it (Wegener, Petty, & Smith, 1995).

REFERENCES

Adaval, R. (2001). Sometimes it just feels right: The differential weighting of affect-consistent and affect-inconsistent product information, *Journal of Consumer Research*, 28, 1–17.

Adaval, R. (2003). How good gets better and bad gets worse: Understanding the impact of affect on evaluations of known brands, *Journal of Consumer Research*, 30, 352–367.

Adaval, R., Isbell, L. M., & Wyer, R. S. (2006). The impact of pictures on narrative- and list-based impression formation: A process interference model. *Journal of Experimental Social Psychology*, 43, 352–364.

Adaval, R., & Monroe, K. B. (2002). Automatic construction and use of contextual information for product and price evaluations, *Journal of Consumer Research*, 28, 572–588.

Adaval, R., & Wyer, R. S. (1998). The role of narratives in consumer information processing. *Journal of Consumer Psychology*, 7, 207–245.

Adaval, R., & Wyer, R. S. (2004). Communicating about a social interaction: Effects on memory for protagonists' statements and nonverbal behaviors. *Journal of Experimental Social Psychology*, 40, 450–465.

Ajzen, I. (1991). The theory of planned behavior. *Organizational Behavior and Human Decision Processes*, 50, 179–211.

Ajzen, I., & Fishbein, M. (2005). The influence of attitudes on behavior. In D. Albarracin, B. T. Johnson, & M. P. Zanna (Eds.) *Handbook of attitudes* (pp. 173–221). Mahwah, NJ: Erlbaum.

Albarracin, D., Johnson, B. T., & Zanna, M. P. (Eds.) (2005). *Handbook of attitudes*. Mahwah, NJ: Erlbaum.

Albarracin, D., & Wyer, R. S. (2000). The cognitive impact of past behavior: Influences on beliefs, attitudes, and future behavioral decisions. *Journal of Personality and Social Psychology, 79*, 5–22.

Albarracin, D., & Wyer, R. S. (2001). Elaborative and nonelaborative processing of a behavior-related persuasive communication. *Personality and Social Psychology Bulletin. 27.* 691–705.

Allport, G. W. (1935). Attitudes. In C. Murchison (Ed.), *Handbook of social psychology* (pp. 798–884). Worcester, MA: Clark University Press.

Anderson, C. A., Lindsay, J. J., & Bushman, B. J. (1999). Research in the psychological laboratory? Truth or triviality. *Current Directions in Psychological Science, 8*, 3–9.

Anderson, J. R. (1982). Acquisition of cognitive skill. *Psychological Review, 89*, 369–406.

Anderson, J. R. (1983). *The architecture of cognition.* Cambridge, MA: Harvard University Press.

Anderson, N. H. (1971). Integration theory and attitude change. *Psychological Review, 78*, 171–206.

Anderson, N. H. (1981). *Foundations of information integration theory.* New York: Academic Press.

Andrade, E. B. (2005). Behavioral consequence of affect: Combining evaluative and regulatory mechanisms. *Journal of Consumer Research, 32*, 355–362.

Bargh, J. A., Bond, R. N., Lombardi, W., & Tota, M. E. (1986). The additive nature of chronic and temporary sources of construct accessibility. *Journal of Personality and Social Psychology, 50*, 869–878.

Bargh, J. A. (1997). The automaticity of everyday life. In R. S. Wyer (Ed.), *Advances in social cognition* (Vol. 10, pp. 1–62). Mahwah, NJ: Erlbaum.

Bargh, J. A., Chen, M., & Burrows, L. (1996). Automaticity of social behavior: Direct effects of trait construct and stereotype activation on action. *Journal of Personality and Social Psychology, 71*, 230–244.

Bem, D. J. (1972). Self-perception theory. In L. Berkowitz (Ed.), *Advances in experimental social psychology* (Vol. 6, pp. 1–62). New York: Academic Press.

Birnbaum, M. H., & Stegner, S. (1979). Source credibility in social judgment: Bias, expertise, and the judge's point of view. *Journal of Personality and Social Psychology, 37*, 48–74.

Bless, H. (2001). Mood and the use of general knowledge structures. In L. L. Martin & G. L. Clore (Eds.), *Theories of mood and cognition: A user's guidebook* (pp. 9–26). Mahwah, NJ: Lawrence Erlbaum Associates.

Bless, H., Bohner, G., Schwarz, H., & Strack, F. (1990). Mood and persuasion: A cognitive response analysis. *Personality and Social Psychology Bulletin, 16*, 331–345.

Bodenhausen, G. V. (1993). Emotions, arousal, and stereotypic judgments: A heuristic model of affect and stereotyping. In D. M. Mackie, & D. L. Hamilton (Eds.), *Affect, cognition, and stereotyping: Interactive processes in group perception* (pp. 13–37). San Diego: Academic Press.

Bower, G. H. (1981). Mood and memory, *American Psychologist, 36*, 129–148.

Bower, G. H., Gilligan, S. G., & Monteiro, K. P. (1981). Selectivity of learning caused by affective states. *Journal of Experimental Psychology: General, 110*, 451–473.

Breckler, S. J. (1984). Empirical validation of affect, behavior and cognition as distinct components of attitude. *Journal of Personality and Social Psychology, 47*, 1191–1205.

Briley, D. A., Morris, M., & Simonson, I. (2000). Reasons as carriers of culture: Dynamic versus dispositional models of cultural influence on decision making. *Journal of Consumer Research, 27*, 157–178.

Briley, D. A., Morris, M. W., & Simonson, I. (2005). Cultural chameleons: Biculturals, conformity motives and decision making. *Journal of Consumer Psychology, 15*, 351–362.

Briley, D. A., Shrum, L. J., & Wyer, R. S. (2007). Subjective impressions of minority group representations in the media: A comparison of majority and minority viewers' judgments and underlying processes. *Journal of Consumer Psychology, 17,* 36–48.

Briley, D. A., & Wyer, R. S. (2001). Transitory determinants of values and decisions: The utility (or nonutility) of individualism and collectivism in understanding cultural differences. *Social Cognition, 19,* 198–229.

Briley, D. A., & Wyer, R. S. (2002). The effect of group membership salience on the avoidance of negative outcomes: Implications for social and consumer decisions. *Journal of Consumer Research, 29,* 400–415.

Briñol, P., & Petty, R. E. (2005). Individual differences in attitude change. In D. Albarracin, B. T. Johnson, & M. P. Zanna (Eds.), *Handbook of attitudes* (pp. 575–615). Mahwah, NJ: Erlbaum.

Brunner, T. A., & Wänke, M. (2006). The reduced and enhanced impact of shared features on individual brand evaluations. *Journal of Consumer Psychology, 16,* 101–111.

Byrne, D. (1971). *The attraction paradigm.* New York: Academic Press.

Cacioppo, J. T., & Petty, R. E. (1982). The need for cognition. *Journal of Personality and Social Psychology, 42,* 116–131.

Carlston, D. E. (1980). Events, inferences and impression formation. In R. Hastie, T. Ostrom, E. Ebbesen, R. Wyer, D. Hamilton, & D. Carlston (Eds.). *Person memory: The cognitive basis of social perception* (pp. 89–119). Hillsdale, NJ: Erlbaum.

Carver, C. S., & Scheier, M. F. (1981). *Attention and self-regulation: A control-theory approach to human behavior.* New York: Springer-Verlag.

Chaiken, S. (1980). Heuristic versus systematic information processing in the use of source versus message cues in persuasion. *Journal of Personality and Social Psychology, 39,* 752–766.

Chaiken, S. (1987). The heuristic model of persuasion. In M. P. Zanna, J. M. Olson, & C. P. Herman (Eds.): *Social influence: The Ontario Symposium* (Vol. 5, pp. 3–39). Hillsdale, NJ: Erlbaum.

Chaiken, S., & Maheswaran, D. (1994). Heuristic processing can bias systematic processing: Effects of source credibility, argument ambiguity and task importance on attitude judgment. *Journal of Personality and Social Psychology, 66,* 460–473.

Chartrand, T. L., & Bargh, J. A. (1996). Automatic activation of impression formation and memorization goals: Nonconscious goal priming reproduces effects of explicit task instructions. *Journal of Personality and Social Psychology, 71,* 464–478.

Chartrand, T. L., & Bargh, J. A. (2002). Nonconscious motivations: Their activation, operation and consequences. In A. Tesser & D. Stapel (Eds.), *Self and motivation: Emerging psychological perspectives* (pp. 13–41). Washington DC: American Psychological Association.

Childers, T. L., Houston, M. J., & Heckler, S. E. (1985). Measurement of individual differences in visual versus verbal information processing. *Journal of Consumer Research, 12,* 125–134.

Clore, G. L., & Byrne, D. (1974). A reinforcement affect model of attraction. In T. L. Huston (Ed.), *Foundations of interpersonal attraction* (pp. 143–170). New York: Academic Press.

Cohen, J. B., & Andrade, E. (2004). Affect intuition and task-contingent affect regulation. *Journal of Consumer Research, 31,* 358–367.

Colcombe, S. J. (2001). Stereotype-consistent and inconsistent behavioral changes after image-based stereotype priming. Unpublished Ph.D. dissertation, University of Illinois at Urbana-Champaign.

Cooper, J. (1998). Unlearning cognitive dissonance: Toward an understanding of the development of cognitive dissonance. *Journal of Experimental Social Psychology, 34,* 562–575.

Cooper, J., & Fazio, R. H. (1984). A new look at dissonance theory. In L. Berkowitz (Ed.), *Advances in experimental social psychology* (Vol.17. pp. 229–266). New York: Academic Press.

Cronley, M. L., Kardes, F. R., Goddard, P., & Houghton, D. C. (1999). Endorsing products for the money: The role of the correspondence bias in celebrity advertising. In E. J. Arnould & L. Scott (Eds.), *Advances in consumer research* (Vol. 25, pp. 627–631). Provo, UT: Association for Consumer Research.

DeMarree, K. G., Wheeler, S. C., & Petty, R. E. (2005). Priming a new identity: Self-monitoring moderates the effects of nonself primes on self-judgment and behavior. *Journal of Personality and Social Psychology, 85,* 657–671.

Dhar, R., Huber, J., & Khan, U. (2007). The shopping momentum effect. *Journal of Marketing Research.*

Dhar, R., & Sherman, S. J. (1996). The effect of common and unique features in consumer choice. *Journal of Consumer Research, 23,* 193–203.

Dijksterhuis, A., Smith, P. K., van Baaren, R. B., & Wigboldus, D. H. J. (2005). The unconscious consumer: Effects of environment on consumer behavior. *Journal of Consumer Psychology, 15,* 193–202.

Eagly, A. H., & Chaiken, S. (1993). *The psychology of attitudes.* Fort Worth, TX: Harcourt Brace Jovanovich.

Edwards, A. L. (1957). *Techniques of attitude scale construction.* East Norwalk, CT: Appleton-Century-Crofts.

Escalas, J. E. (2004). Imagine yourself in the product: Mental simulation, narrative transportation and persuasion. *Journal of Advertising, 33,* 37–48.

Fazio, R. H. (1990). Multiple processes by which attitudes guide behavior: The MODE model as an integrative framework. In M.P. Zanna (Ed.), *Advances in experimental social psychology* (Vol. 23, pp. 75–109). San Diego, CA: Academic Press.

Fazio. R. H. (1995). Attitudes as object-evaluation associations: Determinants, consequences, and correlates of attitude accessibility. In R. E. Petty & J. A. Krosnick (Eds.), *Attitude strength: Antecedents and consequences* (pp. 247–282). Mahwah, NJ: Erlbaum.

Festinger, L. (1957). *A theory of cognitive dissonance.* Stanford, CA: Stanford University Press.

Festinger, L., & Maccoby, E. (1964). On resistance to persuasive communications. *Journal of Abnormal and Social Psychology, 68,* 359–366.

Fishbein, M., & Ajzen, I. (1975). *Belief, attitude, intention, and behavior: An introduction to theory and research.* Reading, MA: Addison-Wesley.

Forgas, J. P., Bower, G. H., & Krantz, S. (1984). The influence of mood on perceptions of social interactions. *Journal of Experimental Social Psychology, 20,* 497–513.

Förster, J., & Liberman, N. (2007). Knowledge activation. In A. W. Kruglanski & E. T. Higgins (Eds.). *Social psychology: Handbook of basic principles* (2nd ed.) New York: Guilford.

Fox, S. (1997). *The mirror makers: History of American Advertising.* Urbana, IL: University of Illinois Press.

Gerbner, G., Gross, L., Morgan, M., & Signorielli, N. (1994). Growing up with television: The cultivation perspective. In J. Bryant & D. Zillmann (Eds.). *Media effects: Advances in theory and research* (pp. 17–41). Hillsdale, NJ: Erlbaum.

Goldberg, M. E., & Hartwick, J. (1990). The effects of advertiser reputation and extremity of advertising claim on advertising effectiveness. *Journal of Consumer Research, 17,* 172–179.

Gollwitzer, P. M., & Bayer, U. (1999). Deliberative versus implemental mindsets in the control of action. In S. Chaiken & Y. Trope (Eds.), *Dual-process theories in social psychology* (pp. 403–422). New York: Guilford Press.

Gorn, G. J. (1982). The effects of music in advertising and choice behavior: A classical conditioning approach. *Journal of Marketing, 46,* 94–101.

Green, M. C., & Brock, T. C. (2000). The role of transportation in the persuasiveness of public narratives. *Journal of Personality and Social Psychology, 79*, 701–721.

Green, M. C., & Brock, T. C. (2004). In the mind's eye: Transportation-imagery model of narrative persuasion. In M. C. Green, J. J. Strange, & T. C. Brock (Eds.) *Narrative impact: Social land cognitive foundations* (pp. 315–341). Mahwah, NJ: Erlbaum.

Grice, H. P. (1975). Logic and conversation. In P. Cole & J. L. Morgan (Eds.), *Syntax and semantics: Speech acts.* (pp. 41–58). New York: Academic Press.

Gruder, C. L., Cook, T. D., Hennigan, K. M., Flay, B. R., Alessis, C., & Halamaj, J. (1978). Empirical tests of the absolute sleeper effect predicted from the discounting cue hypothesis. *Journal of Personality and Social Psychology, 36*, 1061–1074.

Higgins, E. T. (1996). Knowledge activation: Accessibility, applicability, and salience. In E. T. Higgins & A. Kruglanski (Eds.), *Social psychology: Handbook of basic principles* (pp. 133–168). New York: Guilford.

Higgins, E. T. (1998). Promotion and prevention: Regulatory focus as a motivational principle. In M.P. Zanna (Ed.), *Advances in experimental social psychology* (Vol. 30, pp. 1–46). San Diego, CA: Academic Press.

Higgins, E. T., Bargh, J. A., & Lombardi, W. (1985). The nature of priming effects on categorization. *Journal of Experimental Psychology: Learning, Memory, and Cognition, 11*, 59–69.

Higgins, E. T., & Chaires, W. M. (1980). Accessibility of interrelational constructs: Implications for stimulus encoding and creativity. *Journal of Experimental Social Psychology, 16*, 348–361.

Higgins, E. T & Lurie, L. (1983). Context, categorization and recall: The "change-of-standard" effect. *Cognitive Psychology, 15*, 525–547.

Higgins, E. T., & Rholes, W. S. (1978). "Saying is believing": Effects of message modification on memory and liking for the person described. *Journal of Experimental Social Psychology, 14*, 363–378.

Higgins, E. T., Rholes, W. S., & Jones, C. R. (1977). Category accessibility and impression formation. *Journal of Experimental Social Psychology, 13*, 141–154.

Hirt, E. R., Kardes, F. R., & Markman, K. D. (2004). Activating a mental simulation mindset through generation of alternatives: Implications for debiasing in related and unrelated domains. *Journal of Experimental Social Psychology, 40*, 374–383.

Hirt, E. R., & Markman, K. D. (1995). Multiple explanation: A "consider-an-alternative" strategy for debiasing judgments. *Journal of Personality and Social Psychology, 69*, 1069–1086.

Hong, Y., Morris, M. W., Chiu, C., & Benet-Martinez, V. (2000). Multicultural minds: A dynamic constructivist approach to culture and cognition. *American Psychologist, 55*, 709–720.

Houston, D. A., & Sherman, S. J. (1995). Cancellation and focus: The role of shared and unique features in the choice process. *Journal of Experimental Social Psychology, 31*, 357–378.

Hovland, C. I., Janis, I. L., & Kelley, H. H. (1953). *Communication and persuasion: Psychological studies of opinion change.* New Haven, CT: Yale University Press.

Huber, J., Payne, J. W., & Puto, C. (1982). Adding asymmetrically dominated alternatives: Violations of regularity and the similarity hypothesis. *Journal of Consumer Research, 9*, 90–98.

Hung, I. W. P., & Wyer, R. S. (2006). The role of implicit theories in the impact of problem-solving print advertisements. Unpublished manuscript, Hong Kong University of Science and Technology.

Isen, A. M. (1984). Towards understanding the role of affect in cognition, In R. S. Wyer & T. K. Srull (Eds.), *Handbook of Social Cognition* (Vol. 2, pp. 179–236). Hillsdale, NJ; Erlbaum.

Isen, A. M., Shalker, T. E., Clark, M. S., & Karp, L. (1978). Affect, accessibility of material in memory, and behavior: A cognitive loop? *Journal of Personality and Social Psychology, 36*, 1–12.

Jacks, J. Z., & Devine, P. G. (2000). Attitude importance, forewarning of message content, and resistance to persuasion. *Basic and Applied Social Psychology, 22*, 19–29.

Janis, I. L., & King, B. T. (1954). The influence of role playing on opinion change. *Journal of Abnormal & Social Psychology, 49*, 211–218.

Janiszewski, C., & van Osselaer, S. M. J. (2005). Behavior activation is not enough. *Journal of Consumer Psychology, 15*, 218–224.

Jiang, Y., Steinhart, Y., & Wyer, R. S. (2008). The role of visual imagery in consumer information processing. Unpublished manuscript, Hong Kong University of Science and Technology.

Johnson, B. T., Maio, G. R., & Smith-McLallen, A. (2005). Communication and attitude change: Causes, processes and effects. In D. Albarracin, B. T. Johnson, & M. P. Zanna (Eds.), *Handbook of attitudes*. (pp. 617–669). Mahwah, NJ: Erlbaum.

Kardes, F. R. (1996). In defense of experimental consumer psychology. *Journal of Consumer Psychology, 5*, 279–296.

Kardes, F. R., Fennis, B. M., Hirt, E. R., Tormala, Z. L., & Bullington, B. (in press). The role of the need for cognitive closure in the effectiveness of the disrupt-then-reframe influence technique. *Journal of Consumer Research*.

Karremans, J. C., Stroebe, W., & Claus, J. (2006). Beyond Vicary's fantasies: The impact of subliminal priming and brand choice. *Journal of Experimental Social Psychology, 42*, 792–798.

Kelman, H. C. (1958). Compliance, identification, and internalization: Three processes of opinion change. *Journal of Conflict Resolution, 2*, 51–60.

Kumkale, G. T., & Albarracin, D. (2004). The Sleeper effect in persuasion: A meta-analytic review. *Psychological Bulletin, 130*, 143–172.

Leventhal, H. (1970). Findings and theory in the study of fear communications. In L. Berkowitz (Ed.), *Advances in experimental social psychology* (Vol. 5, pp. 119–187). New York: Academic Press.

Luchins, A. S., & Luchins, E. H. (1959). *Rigidity of behavior: A variational approach to the effect of Einstellung*. Oxford, England: University of Oxford Press.

Martin L. L., Ward, D. W., Achee, J. W., & Wyer, R. S. (1993). Mood as input: People have to interpret the motivational implications of their moods. *Journal of Personality and Social Psychology, 64*, 317–326.

McGuire, W. J. (1964). Inducing resistance to persuasion: Some contemporary approaches. In L. Berkowitz (Ed.). *Advances in experimental social psychology* (Vol. 1, pp. 191–229). New York: Academic Press.

McGuire, W. J. (1968). Personality and attitude change: An information-processing theory. In A. G. Greenwald, T. C. Brock, & T. M. Ostrom (Eds.), *Psychological foundations of attitudes* (pp. 171–196). New York: Academic Press.

McGuire, W. J. (1972). Attitude change: An information processing paradigm. In C. G. McClintock (Ed.), *Experimental social psychology* (pp. 108–141). New York: Holt, Rinehart, and Winston.

Menon, G., & Raghubir, P. (2003). Ease of retrieval as an automatic input in judgments: A mere-accessibility framework? *Journal of Consumer Research, 30*, 230–243.

Miller, N. E., & Campbell, D. T. (1959). Recency and primacy in persuasion as a function of the timing of speeches and measurements. *Journal of Abnormal and Social Psychology, 59*, 1–9.

Miniard, P. W., & Cohen, J. B. (1981). An examination of the Fishbein-Ajzen behavioral intentions model's concepts and measures. *Journal of Experimental Social Psychology, 17*, 309–339.

Niedenthal, P. M., Halberstadt, J., & Setterlund, M. B. (1997). Being happy and seeing "happy": Emotional state facilitates visual word recognition. *Cognition and Emotion*, *11*, 594–624.

Niedenthal, P. M., & Setterlund, M. B. (1994). Emotion congruence in perception, *Personality and Social Psychology Bulletin, 20*, 401–411.

Novemksy, N., Dhar, R., Schwarz, N., & Simonson, I. (in press). Preference fluency in consumer choice. *Journal of Marketing Research*.

Nunes, J. C., & Boatwright, P. (2004). Incidental prices and their effect on willingness to pay. *Journal of Marketing Research, 41*, 457–466.

O'Guinn, T. C., & Shrum, L. J. (1997). The role of television in the construction of social reality. *Journal of Consumer Research, 23*, 278–294.

Osterhouse, R. A., & Brock, T. C. (1970). Distraction increases yielding to propaganda by inhibiting counterarguing. *Journal of Personality and Social Psychology, 15*, 344–358.

Ostrom, T. M., & Upshaw, H. S. (1968). Psychological perspective and attitude change. In A. G. Greenwald, T. M. Ostrom, & T. C. Brock (Eds.). *Psychological foundations of attitudes*. New York: Academic Press, 217–242.

Park, J. W., & Kim, J. K. (2005). The effects of decoys on preference shifts: The role of attractiveness and providing justification. *Journal of Consumer Psychology, 15*, 94–107.

Petty, R. E., & Cacioppo, J. T. (1986). *Communication and persuasion: Central and peripheral routes to attitude change*. New York: Springer-Verlag.

Pham, M. T. (1998). Representativeness, relevance and the use of feelings in decision making, *Journal of Consumer Research, 25*, 144–160.

Posavac, S. S., Kardes, F. R., Sanbonmatsu, D. M., & Fitzsimons, G. J. (2005). Blissful insularity: When brands are judged in isolation from competitors. *Marketing Letters, 16*, 87–97.

Posavac, S. S., Sanbonmatsu, D. M., Kardes, F. R., & Fitzsimons, G. J. (2004). The brand positivity effect: When evaluation confers preference. *Journal of Consumer Research, 31*, 643–652.

Pratkanis, A. R. (1992). The cargo-cult science of subliminal persuasion. *Skeptical Inquirer, 16*, 260–272.

Pratkanis, A. R., Greenwald, A. G., Leippe, M. R., & Baumgardner, M. H. (1988). In search of reliable persuasion effects: III. The sleeper effect is dead: Long live the sleeper effect. *Journal of Personality and Social Psychology, 54*, 203–218.

Rosenberg, M., & Hovland, C. I. (1960). Cognitive, affective and behavioral components of attitudes. In. M. Rosenberg, C. Holand, W. McGuire, R. Abelson, & J. Brehm (Eds.), *Attitude organization and change* (pp. 1–14). New Haven, CT: Yale University Press.

Ross, L., Lepper, M. R., Strack, F., & Steinmetz, J. (1977). Social explanation and social expectation: Effects of real and hypothetical explanations on subjective likelihood. *Journal of Personality and Social Psychology, 35*, 817–829.

Ross, M. (1989). Relation of implicit theories to the construction of personal histories. *Psychological Review, 10*, 627–634.

Sanna, L. J., Schwarz, N., & Stocker, S. L. (2002). When debiasing backfires: Accessible content and accessibility experiences in debriefing hindsight. *Journal of Experimental Psychology: Learning, Memory and Cognition, 28*, 497–502.

Schumann, D. W., Haugtvedt, C. P., & Davidson, E. (2008). History of consumer psychology. In C. P. Haugtvedt, P. M. Herr, & F. R. Kardes (Eds.), *Handbook of consumer psychology*. Mahwah, NJ: Erlbaum.

Schwarz, N. (1990). Feelings as information: Informational and motivational functions of affective states. In E. T. Higgins & R. M. Sorrentino (Eds.). *Handbook of motivation and cognition: Foundations of social behavior* (Vol. 2, pp. 527–561). New York: Guilford.

Schwarz, N. (1998). Accessible content and accessibility experiences: The interplay of declarative and experiential information in judgment. *Personality and Social Psychology Review, 2*, 87–99.

Schwarz, N. (2004). Meta-cognitive experiences in consumer judgment and decision making. *Journal of Consumer Psychology, 14*, 332–348.

Schwarz, N., Bless, H., Strack, F., Klumpp, G., Rittenauer-Schatka, H., & Simons, A. (1991). Ease of retrieval as information: Another look at the availability heuristic. *Journal of Personality and Social Psychology, 61*, 195–202.

Schwarz, N., & Bohner, G. (2001). The construction of attitudes. In A. Tesser & N. Schwarz (Eds.), *Blackwell handbook of social psychology: Intraindividual processes* (pp. 436–457). Malden, MA: Blackwell.

Schwarz, N., & Clore, G. L. (1983). Mood, misattribution, and judgments of well-being: Informative and directive functions of affective states. *Journal of Personality and Social Psychology, 45*, 513–523.

Schwarz, N., & Clore, G. L. (1988). How do I feel about it? Informative functions of affective states. In K. Fiedler & J. Forgas (Eds.), *Affect, cognition, and social behavior* (pp. 44–62). Toronto: Hofgrefe International.

Schwarz, N., & Clore, G. L. (1996). Feeling and phenomenal experiences. In E. T. Higgins and A. W. Kruglanski (Eds.). *Social psychology: Handbook of basic principles* (pp. 433–465). New York: Guilford.

Sengupta, J., & Fitzsimons, G. J. (2000). The effects of analyzing reasons for brand preferences: Disruption or reinforcement? *Journal of Marketing Research, 37*, 318–330.

Shafir, E. (1993). Choosing vs. rejecting: Why some options are both better and worse than others. *Memory & Cognition, 21*, 546–556.

Shafir, E., Simonson, I., & Tversky, A. (1993). Reason-based choice. *Cognition, 49*, 11–36.

Shen, H., Jiang, Y., & Adaval, R. (2007). Contrast and assimilation effects of processing fluency. Unpublished manuscript, Hong Kong University of Science and Technology.

Shen, H., & Wyer, R. S. (2008a). The impact of negative affect on anticipated reactions to a new experience. *Journal of Consumer Psychology, 18*, 39–48.

Shen, H., & Wyer, R. S. (2008b). Procedural priming and consumer judgments: Effects on the impact of positively and negatively valenced information. *Journal of Consumer Research, 34*, 727–737.

Sherman, S. J., Ahlm, K., Berman, L., & Lynn, S. J. (1978). Contrast effects and their relationship to subsequent behavior. *Journal of Experimental Social Psychology, 14*, 340–350.

Sherman, S. J., Skov, R. B., Hervitz, E. F., & Stock, C. B. (1981). The effects of explaining hypothetical future events: From possibility to probability to actuality and beyond. *Journal of Experimental Social Psychology, 17*, 142–158.

Shimp, T. A. (1991). Neo-Pavlovian conditioning and its implications for consumer behavior. In T. S. Robertson & H. H. Kassarjian (Eds.), *Handbook of consumer behavior* (pp. 162–187). Englewood Cliffs, NJ: Prentice-Hall.

Shiv, B., & Fedorikhin, A. (1999). Heart and mind in conflict: The interplay of affect and cognition in consumer decision making. *Journal of Consumer Research, 26*, 278–292.

Shrum, L. J., Burroughs, J. E., & Rindfleisch, A. (2005). Television's cultivation of material values. *Journal of Consumer Research, 32*, 473–479.

Shrum, L. J., Wyer, R. S., & O'Guinn, T. (1998). The effects of watching television on perceptions of social reality. *Journal of Consumer Research, 24*, 447–458.

Simonson, I. (1989). Choice based on reasons: The case of attraction and compromise effects. *Journal of Consumer Research, 16*, 158–174.

Srull, T. K., & Wyer, R. S. (1979). The role of category accessibility in the interpretation of information about persons: Some determinants and implications. *Journal of Personality and Social Psychology, 37*, 1660–1672.

Srull, T. K., & Wyer, R. S. (1980). Category accessibility and social perception: Some implications for the study of person memory and interpersonal judgments. *Journal of Personality and Social Psychology, 38*, 841–856.

Srull, T. K., & Wyer, R. S. (1989). Person memory and judgment. *Psychological Review, 96*, 58–63.

Stepper, S., & Strack, F. (1993). Proprioceptive determinants of emotional and nonemotional feelings. *Journal of Personality and Social Psychology, 64*, 211–220.

Strahan, E. J., Spencer, S. J., & Zanna, M. P. (2002). Subliminal priming and persuasion: Striking while the iron is hot. *Journal of Experimental Social Psychology, 38*, 556–568.

Taylor, S. E., & Fiske, S. T. (1978). Salience, attention and attribution: Top of the head phenomena. In L. Berkowitz (Ed.), *Advances in experimental social psychology* (Vol. 11, pp. 249–288). New York: Academic Press.

Tesser, A. (1978). Self-generated attitude change. In L. Berkowitz (Ed.), *Advances in experimental social psychology* (vol. 11). New York: Academic Press, 290–338.

Thurstone, L. L. (1931). Measurement of social attitudes. *Journal of Abnormal and Social Psychology, 26*, 249–269.

Wang, J., & Calder, B. J. (2006). Media transportation and advertising. *Journal of Consumer Research, 33*, 151–162.

Wang, J., & Wyer, R. S. (2002). Comparative judgment processes: The effects of task objectives and time delay on product evaluations. *Journal of Consumer Psychology, 12*, 327–340.

Wänke, M., Bohner, G., & Jurkowitsch, A. (1997). There are many reasons to drive a BMW—Surely you know one: Ease of argument generation influences brand attitudes. *Journal of Consumer Research, 24*, 70–77.

Webster, D. M., & Kruglanski, A. W. (1994). Individual differences in need for cognitive closure. *Journal of Personality and Social Psychology, 67*, 1049–1062.

Wegener, D. T., Petty, R .E., & Smith, S. M. (1995). Positive mood can increase or decrease message scrutiny: The hedonic contingency view of mood and message processing. *Journal of Personality and Social Psychology, 69*, 5–15.

Wicklund, R. A., & Brehm, J. W. (1976). *Perspectives on cognitive dissonance.* Hillsdale, NJ: Erlbaum.

Winkielman, P., & Cacioppo, J. T. (2001). Mind at ease puts a smile on the face: Psychological evidence that processing facilitation elicits positive affect. *Journal of Personality and Social Psychology, 81*, 989–1013.

Wood, W., & Quinn, J. M. (2003). Forewarned and forearmed? Two meta-analysis syntheses of forewarnings of influence appeals. *Psychological Bulletin, 115*, 323–345.

Wyer, R. S. (1974). *Cognitive organization and change: An information processing approach.* Hillsdale, NJ: Erlbaum.

Wyer, R. S. (2004). *Social comprehension and judgment: The role of situation models, narratives, and implicit theories.* Mahwah, NJ; Erlbaum.

Wyer, R. S. (2008). The role of knowledge accessibility in cognition and behavior: Implications for consumer information processing. In C. Haugvedt, F. R. Kardes, and P. M. Herr (Eds.), *Handbook of consumer psychology* (pp. 31–76). Mahwah, NJ: Erlbaum.

Wyer, R. S., Budesheim, T. L., & Lambert, A. J. (1990). Person memory and judgment: The cognitive representation of informal conversations. *Journal of Personality and Social Psychology, 58*, 218–238.

Wyer, R. S., Budesheim, T. L., Lambert, A. J., & Swan, S. (1994). Person memory and judgment: Pragmatic influences on impressions formed in a social context. *Journal of Personality and Social Psychology, 66*, 254–267.

Wyer, R. S., & Carlston, D. E. (1979). *Social cognition, inference and attribution.* Hillsdale, NJ: Erlbaum.

Wyer, R. S., Clore, G. L., & Isbell, L.M. (1999). Affect and information processing. In M. P. Zanna (Ed.), *Advances in Experimental Social Psychology* (Vol. 31, pp. 1–77). San Diego: Academic Press.

Wyer, R. S., & Hartwick, J. (1980). The role of information retrieval and conditional inference processes in belief formation and change. In L. Berkowitz (Ed.), *Advances in experimental social psychology* (Vol. 13, pp. 241–284). New York: Academic Press.

Wyer, R. S., Hung, I. W., & Jiang, Y. (2008). Visual and verbal processing strategies in comprehension and judgment. *Journal of Consumer Psychology.*

Xu, A. J., & Wyer, R. S. (2007) The effect of mindsets on consumer decision strategies. *Journal of Consumer Research, 34,* 556–566.

Xu, A. J., & Wyer, R. S. (2008). The comparative mindset: From animal comparisons to increased purchase intentions. *Psychological Science,* in press.

Yeung, C. W. M., & Wyer, R. S. (2004). Affect, appraisal, and consumer judgment, *Journal of Consumer Research, 31,* 412–424.

Yeung, C. W. M., & Wyer, R.S. (2005). Does loving a brand mean loving its products? The role of brand-elicited affect in brand extension evaluations, *Journal of Marketing Research, 42,* 495–506.

Zajonc, R. B. (1980). Feeling and thinking: Preferences need no inferences. *American Psychologist, 35,* 151–175.

Zanna, M. P., & Rempel, J. K. (1988). Attitudes: A new look at an old concept. In D. Bar-Tal & A. Kruglanski (Eds.), *The social psychology of knowledge* (pp. 315–334). New York: Cambridge University Press.

Section *II*

The Construal of Consumer Judgments and Decisions

3

Psychological Distance and Consumer Behavior
A Construal Level Theory Perspective

TAL EYAL
Ben Gurion University

NIRA LIBERMAN
Tel Aviv University

YAACOV TROPE
New York University

D o we buy products differently when we think of using them in the near future vs. the distant future (e.g., concert tickets for tonight vs. for next month)? Is buying a gift for another different from buying products for our own use? Does Internet shopping affect the way consumers purchase goods? Do consumers evaluate products that they own in a different way than products they may own with some probability? Do consumers treat novel products in a different way than familiar products? We think that these are questions of central importance to the field of consumer psychology. We also think that these questions, although obviously different from each other, have a common theme: They all concern the effect of psychological distance on consumer behavior.

In the present chapter, we approach these and related questions within the framework of construal level theory (CLT) and suggest that psychological distance (i.e., temporal distance, social distance, hypotheticality, and spatial distance) influences people's evaluation and choice in a systematic manner. We first introduce the basic premises of construal level theory and then briefly review empirical findings that applied CLT to evaluation and choice. We also use the CLT framework to raise new questions and make previously untested predictions about consumer behavior. We hope that in doing so, this chapter will inspire further research on the impact of psychological distance on consumer behavior.

CONSTRUAL LEVEL THEORY

Construal level theory (Liberman, Trope, & Stephan, 2007; Trope & Liberman, 2003) rests on two premises: (1) Psychological distance from an object or event increases the tendency to construe it in high-level rather than low-level terms. (2) Evaluations and decisions are formed with respect to the construal of decision alternatives. Together, these two premises suggest that psychological distance systematically influences the way people evaluate alternatives and make choices. In this chapter, we first explain what is high vs. low level of construal, describe what we mean by "psychological distance," and elaborate on why and how psychological distance affects construal. In the main part of the chapter, we discuss the implications of CLT for consumer behavior.

Level of Construal

We distinguish between low-level construals, which are relatively unstructured, contextualized representations that include subordinate and incidental features of objects and events, and high-level construals, which are decontextualized representations that extract the gist from the available information. Thus, whereas low-level representations of events are rich in details, some of which are incidental or peripheral, high-level representations of the same events achieve abstraction by omitting secondary and incidental features. Low-level construal of actions (e.g., going to the gym) addresses the question of how one would perform the action (e.g., wear sneakers, take a towel, etc.), whereas a high-level construal of the same action answers the question why one would perform the action (e.g., prevent heart disease, lose weight).

Note that moving to a higher level of construal of actions, events, or objects involves an implicit decision that some of the features in the lower-level representation are peripheral and less important than others and may be omitted without changing the meaning of the event. For example, representing going to the gym as the means for losing weight omits features such as the location of the activity and retains features such as its effect on one's weight. This representation renders the former less important than the latter. A different high-level representation would involve a different decision as to what is central and what is peripheral and may even reverse the centrality or importance of some of the features. For example, representing going to the gym as the means for getting to know one's neighborhood retains features such as its location and omits features such as its effect on one's weight. In goal-directed actions (e.g., dieting), goal-relevant features (e.g., the calories in a food) are more central than goal-irrelevant features (e.g., color of the food or its crunchiness) and would tend to be omitted from a high-level representation of a goal-relevant object.

Abstraction is a continuum. Representations become more abstract as more unique and incidental features are omitted. Indeed, categories may be thought of as being organized hierarchically (e.g., lollipop, candy, food), with representations that are higher in the hierarchy having less concrete, low-level features (Rosch, 1975). Goals also form hierarchies (Carver & Scheier, 1999; Vallacher & Wegner, 1987), in which each goal-directed action (e.g., studying for an exam) has a super-ordinate "why" level (e.g., get a high grade) and a subordinate "how" level (e.g., reading a textbook), each of which may be further represented on a higher or lower level (e.g., we may ask why get a high grade, or how one reads a textbook). As such, each level in the hierarchy may be defined as low- or high-level, depending on the relation to the other levels of the hierarchy. For example, "reading a text book" is a high-level construal in relation to "flipping the pages" and a low-level construal in relation to "studying for an exam."

Psychological Distance

We refer to an event or object as "psychologically distant" when it is detached from a person's direct experience and as "psychologically near" when it is sensed by him or her. There are different reasons why a stimulus may not be in a person's close proximity (i.e., within the range that is sensed), and these constitute different types of psychological distance: (1) A stimulus may be temporally removed, in the past or the future (e.g., next week vs. next year, last week vs. last year); (2) a stimulus may be only sensed by a different person, that is, socially distant (e.g., self vs. others, friend vs. stranger); (3) a stimulus may be spatially distant (e.g., next door vs. in another building); and finally, (4) a stimulus may be only hypothetical, that is, belong to a counterfactual reality (likely vs. less likely, improbable vs. probable, realistic vs. fantastic). Obviously, moving beyond one's actual experience, beyond what is perceived by the senses, in any of these distance dimensions requires using construals, namely, memories, imaginations, and predictions instead of percepts (for a review, see Liberman, Trope, & Stephan, 2007).

Psychological Distance and Level of Construal

CLT postulates that individuals use higher-level construals to represent more dis-tal events. We think that this tendency evolved as a generalized heuristic, because typically information about concrete, secondary aspects of distant events is lacking, and these details become available only as events draw closer. We typically know less about others than about ourselves, are less certain about the distant future than about the near future, and are less familiar with remote alternatives than about more likely events. Lack of knowledge forces people to use more abstract, high-level construals to represent distant entities. For example, if we hear only faint voices of children in a playground we use our knowledge of what typically happens in playgrounds to construct a picture of what is happening. However, when we see the playground we do not need to resort to such general knowledge in order to get such a representation. An association may thus be formed between psychological distal entities and high-level construals and between psychological proximal entities and low-level construals. We further suggest that this association may be over-generalized, causing people to continue using high-level construals when thinking about distant events and low-level construals when thinking about near events, even when the available information about both events is the same. In the preceding example, this over-generalized heuristic would make us construe on a higher level a videotaped scene of a playground to the extent that we think that it pertained to a distal event, temporally, socially, spatially, or hypothetically.

The effect of distance on level of construal has been supported by research on temporal distance (Liberman & Trope, 1998; Liberman, Sagristano, & Trope, 2002; Förster, Friedman, & Liberman, 2004), spatial distance (Fujita, Henderson, Eng, Trope, & Liberman, 2007; Henderson, Fujita, Trope, & Liberman, 2006), hypotheticality (Todorov, Goren, & Trope, 2006; Wakslak, Trope, Liberman, & Alony, 2006), and social distance (Libby & Eibach, 2002). For example, Liberman and colleagues (2002) showed that the same set of items (e.g., potato chips, boots, hot dogs, blanket) that were used to describe future situations (e.g., a camping trip) were classified into broader, more inclusive categories when the situation was imagined taking place in the distant future than in the near future. With respect to social distance, a large body of social psychological literature demonstrated that individuals make more global, dispositional attributions of others' behavior than their own behavior (Fiedler, Semin, Finkenauer, & Berkel, 1995; Jones, 1979; Jones & Nisbett, 1972; Robins, Spranca, & Mendelsohn, 1996). Although there are many accounts that have been proposed to explain the actor-observer effect, some of which are not related to construal level (e.g., knowledge difference between self and other, self enhancement), it has been demonstrated that the actor-observer effect may reflect different levels of abstraction of action representation (e.g., Fiedler et al., 1995; Semin & Fiedler, 1989). Spatial distance has been investigated by Fujita and colleagues (2006) and Henderson and colleagues (2006). For example, Fujita and colleagues (2006) showed NYU students a video of a conversation between two other NYU students. They found that the interaction was described in more abstract terms when participants believed that the video was filmed at a spatially distant location (Florence) than when it was filmed at a spatially near location (New York City). Finally, hypotheticality has been investigated in Wakslak and colleagues' (2006) research on how the probability of events affects their level of construal. For example, this research found that when reported probability of events was low rather than high, participants were broader in their categorization of the events, segmented ongoing behavioral sequences into fewer units, and were more successful at structuring visual information.

Recently, it has been suggested by Förster (2007) that novelty has an effect on construal that is similar to that of psychological distance. Because we know less about novel events than about familiar events, novelty, like psychological distancing, should promote high-level construal. A series of studies by Förster (2007) corroborated this prediction. In one of the studies (Förster, 2007, Study 4), for example, participants received Vallacher and Wegner's (1989) levels of personal agency questionnaire, which presents 25 activities, each followed by two restatements, one corresponding to the low-level *how* aspect of the activity and the other corresponding to the high-level *why* aspect of the activity. For example, "locking a door" is followed by the alternative restatements (1) "putting a key in the lock" (low-level construal) and (2) "securing the house" (high-level construal). To manipulate novelty, participants were told that the task examines how people think about certain actions in their everyday life and that the task was either newly invented (in the novelty framing condition), not new (in the no-novelty framing condition), or neither (in the control condition). As predicted, the in-the-novelty framing condition participants chose more abstract concepts than those in either the control group or the no-novelty framing group. We think that the question of how novelty affects choice is of special interest for consumer choice, and although it is not a dimension of distance, we discuss it in this chapter.

If, as we argued earlier, the relationship between distance and construal is based on an over-generalized association, then this relationship should be bidirectional. That is, psychological distance may not only affect level of construal, but may also be affected by level of construal. Findings in line with this prediction have been obtained for a variety of distance dimensions. For example, Liberman, Trope, McCrea, and Sherman (2007) examined the effect of construal level on temporal distance. In one of their studies, participants were first asked to indicate either why (i.e., high-level construal) or how (i.e., low-level construal) a person would perform an activity (e.g., "Ron is considering opening a bank account. Why (how) would Ron do that?"), and were then asked to estimate in how much time from now the person would do the activity. As predicted, participants indicated more distant enactment times after a high-level, why construal than after low-level, how construal.

Similar associations were also found between construal and probability judgments (Wakslak, Trope, & Liberman, 2007). For example, in one study, construal level was manipulated by asking participants to think about themselves performing either the main task or a filler task in a described psychology experiment. A focus on central aspects is part of a high-level construal representation, whereas a focus on peripheral aspects constitutes a low-level representation. Participants then indicated how likely they would be to sign up for the experiment. As predicted, participants in the high-level construal condition judged their likelihood of signing up to be lower (i.e., more distant) than those in the low-level construal condition.

In sum, a considerable amount of research has corroborated the hypothesized relationship between level of construal and psychological distance (temporal, spatial, social, and hypothetical). As psychological distance increases, construals become more abstract, and as level of abstraction increases, targets seem more psychologically distant.

We now turn to the implications of this relationship for decision making and choice especially in the context of consumer behavior.

Primary versus Secondary Sources of Value

According to CLT, the attractiveness of an object depends on the value associated with the high-level construal of the object (high-level value) and the value associated with the low-level construal of the object (low-level value). Because psychological distance increases the weight of high-level value and decreases the weight of low-level value, distancing an object should shift the overall attractiveness of that object closer to its high-level value than to its low-level value. When the low-level value of an object is more positive than its high-level value, the object should be more attractive when more proximate. However, when the high-level value of an object is more positive than the low-level value, the object should be more attractive when more remote. For example, a word processor that is old (high-level value) but easy to operate (low-level value) is likely to be perceived as more attractive from temporal proximity than from temporal distance. However, a word processor that is new but difficult to operate is more likely to be perceived as attractive from more temporal distance.

When applied to temporal distance, CLT predicts an effect that may in certain conditions run contrary to time discounting, which is conventionally assumed in economics, decision science, learning, and other disciplines of the behavioral science (Ainslie, 1975; Ainslie & Haslam, 1992; Baumeister & Heatherton, 1996; Elster, 1977; Metcalfe & Mischel, 1999; O'Donoghue & Rabin, 2000; Rachlin, Brown, & Cross, 2000; Read & Loewenstein, 2000; Schelling, 1984). According to time discounting, the value of an outcome is diminished as temporal distance increases. For example, research has shown that individuals often place higher value on a near future reward than on a distant future reward, even when the distant future reward is greater (e.g., Ainslie & Haslam, 1992; Elster & Loewenstein, 1992; Mischel, Grusec, & Masters, 1969; Mischel, Shoda, & Rodriguez, 1989; Read & Loewenstein, 2000). CLT predicts time discounting only when the low-level value is more positive than the high-level value. It predicts the opposite (i.e., time augmentation), however, when the high-level value is more positive than the low-level value.

In what follows, we briefly review applications of this principle to different psychological distances and to different operationalizations of high vs. low value. These operationalizations were identified by CLT research with regard to judgments, decision making, and behavior regulation. Before we elaborate on these applications, let us highlight a few: (1) Desirability concerns are weighed more and feasibility concerns reweighted less with increasing temporal distance; (2) a payoff is weighed more and probability is weighted less with temporal distance; (3) considerations in favor of an option (pros) are weighed more and considerations against an option (cons) are weighted less over temporal distance; (4) adopting a high-level construal for an event produces greater self-control than adopting a low-level construal of the event; (5) central values guide choices more and secondary values guide choices less over temporal distance; (6) high-level affect guides choices more and low-level affect guides choices less with temporal distance.

We examine the effects of four psychological distance dimensions: temporal distance, spatial distance, social distance, and hypotheticality. In addition, we look at the effects of novelty, which, as we argued earlier, has effects similar to psychological distance. We review extant research on those effects and suggest new directions for future research on previously untested predictions derived from CLT. For a more extensive review of CLT (especially with respect to issues other than evaluation and choice) we refer the reader to Liberman, Trope, and Stephan (2007) and Trope and Liberman (2003).

Desirability versus Feasibility

Purchase decisions may involve information on product benefits (e.g., comfort and safety of a car) as well as information on how to purchase it (e.g., terms of payment, location of store). Whereas the former type of information pertains to high-level, desirability concerns, which involve the value of the action's end-state (i.e., the "why" aspect of buying the product), the latter type of information pertains to low-level feasibility concerns, which involve the means used to reach the end-state (i.e., the "how" aspect of buying the product). According to CLT, when information is available on both the desirability and feasibility aspects of the product, desirability concerns should receive greater weight and feasibility concerns should receive lesser weight as distance increases.

Liberman and Trope (1998) tested this prediction as it pertains to temporal distance by asking participants to make decisions about various situations (e.g., whether to attend a guest lecture) that they imagined happening in either the near or the distant future. For each situation, the desirability of the outcome (e.g., how interesting the lecture was) and its feasibility (e.g., how convenient the timing of the lecture was) varied between participants. Consistent with CLT, it was found that the attractiveness of the options increased or decreased as a function of the source of the attractiveness: When outcomes were desirable but hard to obtain, attractiveness increased over time; when outcomes were less desirable but easy to obtain, attractiveness decreased over time.

Todorov, Goren, and Trope (2007) tested a similar prediction with probability as the psychological distance dimension. In one of their studies, participants read about a series of promotional campaigns, constructed so that they were either high in desirability and low in feasibility (e.g., receiving 10 free CDs at an inconvenient location) or low in desirability and high in feasibility (e.g., receiving one free CD at a convenient location). Under high probability (low psychological distance), participants were told that if they signed up for the campaign, they were almost certain to receive a voucher for the company's products. Under low probability (high psychological distance), they were told that they would have about a one in 100 chance of receiving a voucher. As predicted by CLT, it was found that under low probability the high desirability/low feasibility option was preferred over the low desirability/high feasibility option, whereas under high probability the low desirability/high feasibility option was preferred over the high desirability/low feasibility option. Thus, desirability was increasingly weighed over feasibility as psychological distance increased.

Could the same idea apply to persuasive messages? A recent series of studies seems to provide an affirmative answer. For example, Thomas, Chandran, and Trope (2007) expected feasibility related information to have a greater influence on purchase choices for the nearer future, and desirability information to have greater influence over purchase choices for the more distant future. In one study, participants read a promotional offer of a portable USB device for data storage. This information related to either the product's desirability (the addition of a desirable feature at the same price) or the product's feasibility (an in-store coupon lowering the product's final price). Further, participants were told to imagine either deferring the purchase (buying the product at a distant time point instead of now) or expediting the purchase (buying the product at a near future time point instead of sometime later). They then indicated their intention to buy the product at the deferred/expedited time. In line with expectations, when the purchase was moved to the near future, information about the price discount (feasibility) increased purchase intentions, but information about the additional feature (desirability) did not. In contrast, when the purchase was moved to the distant future, desirability information increased purchase intentions but feasibility information did not.

In accordance with this line of thought, Dhar and colleagues (Dhar & Kim, in press; Kim, Dhar, & Novemsky, 2007) have recently suggested that advertisements' claims should be congruent with the distance between the consumer and the message. Specifically, in order to enhance persuasiveness, a message should emphasize higher level aspects, and de-emphasize lower level aspects if it refers to more distal products and sales. For example, ads seen from a distant location, such as highway advertising signs, should refer to higher level, core, and central aspects of a product (e.g., cleaning effectiveness for detergents), while those ads that are typically seen from up close, such as in-store messages, may benefit from emphasizing the product's lower level, secondary, and peripheral aspects (e.g., at a discount, easy to carry, etc.).

In still another line of research on the effect of desirability vs. feasibility on distance-related consumer choices, Agrawal, Trope, and Liberman (2007) predicted that highlighting temporally appropriate aspects of an event at the time that consumers make a decision would lead consumers to associate greater value with their choice. They presented participants with a variety of options, one of which was clearly dominant (i.e., high on both desirability and feasibility dimensions). Choices were made for either the near or the distant future and highlighted either desirability aspects (e.g., "Does the information content on the Web site match your professional interests?", "Would I really enjoy this concert?") or feasibility aspects (e.g., "Is it convenient, easy, and efficient to find information on this Web site?", "How much does this ticket cost?"). As expected, participants were willing to pay more and reported greater value for the distant future option when the choice was framed to make desirability rather than feasibility salient; in contrast, willingness to pay and value were greater for near future choices when feasibility rather than desirability was made salient.

A related finding is the tendency of consumers to choose options based on rebates that they never actually redeem (Soman 1998, see also Lynch & Zauberman, in press). It was recently suggested by Zauberman and Lynch (2005) that CLT logic may account for this tendency. According to this explanation, the weight of feasibility considerations (i.e., time to redeem the rebate) decreases with temporal distance. And because the rebate redemption is generally framed in the distant future, consumers would be better off considering the decision they would make if the rebate had to be redeemed that day. Therefore, to reduce the tendency to be persuaded by rebates, consumers should think about what decision they would make if the rebate had to be redeemed that day.

These findings suggest that temporal distance, hypotheticality, and spatial distance augment the effects of desirability information but discount the effects of feasibility information. The effects of other psychological distance dimensions as well as the effects of novelty on the weight given to feasibility vs. desirability concerns await exploration. For example, based on CLT, it would be predicted that people would weigh desirability aspects of a product more than feasibility aspects when the product is offered in a geographically distant rather than a close location. For example, desirability concerns should play a greater role than feasibility concerns in Internet shopping than in shopping at a local mall. Similarly, people may assign more weight to feasibility aspects than to desirability aspects when making a purchase for themselves rather than for another person, or for a close friend rather than a more remote acquaintance. Finally, with respect to novelty, we would predict that framing a product as novel (rather than an improvement of an old version) would make people's choice more sensitive to desirability aspects of the product and less sensitive to its feasibility aspects. For example, naming a new version of software as "Windows Vista" rather than "Windows 2007" would make people pay more attention to its speed and new features and less attention to the ease of mastering it, or to its convenience of installation.

The reverse direction of influence, from construal level to distance, suggests other interesting hypotheses. For example, people might plan to purchase products high in desirability (but low in feasibility) in the more distant future, or at a distant location (e.g., when traveling) more than products high in feasibility (but low in desirability).

Payoffs versus Probability in Gambles   The distinction between feasibility and desirability may be extended to games of chance in which there is an opportunity of winning a desirable prize. The prize, or payoff, is the superordinate consideration because it determines the desirability of the end state of a gamble. The probability of winning the prize is a subordinate consideration having to do with the properties of the random procedure that determines the feasibility of winning. The subordination of probability to payoffs is evidenced in the asymmetry in the conditional importance of these two types of aspects. Indeed, studies by Sagristano, Trope, and Liberman (2002) demonstrated that the low-level probability consideration being dependent on the value of the high-level payoff consideration is more important than the high-level payoff consideration being dependent on the value of the low-level probability consideration. For example, Sagristano and colleagues (2002; Study 1) presented participants with choices among lotteries that were said to vary in probability of winning and payoff. Participants indicated their interest in receiving information about the probability (payoff), given that the payoff (probability) was either high or low. The results showed that participants' interest in finding out the probability of winning was much lower when they were told that the payoff was low than when they were told that the payoff was high. However, participants' interest in finding out what was the payoff was high regardless of whether the probability was known to be high or low. Thus, interest in probability depended on payoff more than interest in payoff depended on probability, indicating that interest in probability is subordinated to interest in payoff.

The standard expected utility model assumes that probability and payoffs have symmetric weights in determining the attractiveness of gambles. However, according to CLT, because the probability of winning is perceived as subordinated to the payoff and therefore pertains to a lower level of construal than the payoffs, people would assign more weight to payoffs and less weight to probabilities in deciding for more distant gambles. In support of this prediction, Sagristano and colleagues (2002) found that participants rated as more attractive (and were willing to pay higher amounts for) more distant future bets to the extent that they involved higher amounts, but they valued near future bets to the extent that they provided a high probability of winning. As a result, participants took higher risk when they made decisions about the more distant future.

These findings are related to Kahneman and Lovallo's (1993) work on framing decisions as either one in a series of similar decisions or unique, one-time occurrences. For example, when facing a decision on whether to switch to a new telephone provider, one may view the decision as one in a series of decisions about service providers or, alternatively, as a unique, one-time decision in a specific context of time and place about receiving telephone services for a lower price and higher efficiency. In CLT terms, viewing the decision as one in a series of similar decisions constitutes a high-level construal of the situation because it requires ignoring specific contextual features. Kahneman and Lovallo (1993) proposed that risk avoidance in real life often stems from a narrow categorization of the decision situation as a unique, one-time event. For example, if viewed in isolation, a decision to take a new provider that offers lower rates may seem too risky, but when viewed in a broader perspective, the risk may seem less acute. This is because normatively, the value of aggregated outcomes is more likely to be close to its expected utility than the is the value of a single outcome. In other words, risk is reduced with repetition (see Lopes, 1996). In our terms, Kahneman and Lovallo's (1993) analysis suggests that risk aversion may decrease as a result of high level of construal of a risky event as one in an aggregated series of similar events.

Sagristano and colleagues (2002) documented the effect of temporal distance on gambling. Similar results should obtain for other distance dimensions. For example, value might be weighed more than probability when gambling for other people than for oneself or when gambling over the Internet rather than in a real casino. People may also weigh value more than probability when making decisions regarding new situations rather than familiar ones. For example, an innovative medical operation compared to a more conventional and conservative operation might be chosen according to the value of its outcome (e.g., extent of possible health improvement) rather than according to the likelihood of its success.

Moreover, the construal of a risky choice may affect the preferred distance from choice. For example, in promoting a program for weight watching, an advertisement specifying that 30% of their former clients lost 20 lb is likely to persuade people to commit themselves to a program that starts in the distant future rather than immediately. However, an advertisement specifying that 75% of their former clients lost 8 lb is likely to be more persuasive in making people commit to an immediate diet program rather than to a delayed program. In addition, construing a choice (e.g., undergo a medical treatment) as one in a series (e.g., one of the ways to watch one's health) rather than as a unique, one-time event (e.g., a choice whether to receive medication for reducing one's blood pressure) may lead people to take the risk and undergo the treatment in the distant future more than in the near future.

Considerations in Favor versus Against a Choice   When considering a purchase, does the impact of reasons in favor of purchasing the product as compared to reasons against it receive different weight with varying psychological distance? Eyal, Liberman, Trope, and Walther (2004) proposed that reasons in favor of an action (pros) constitute high-level construals whereas reasons against an action (cons) constitute a low-level construals. In support of this proposal, Eyal and colleagues (2004) showed that in the same way that desirability is superordinate to feasibility and payoffs to probabilities (Sagristano et al., 2002, see our discussion earlier in this chapter), pros are superordinate to cons in their conditional importance. Specifically, when considering an action, people see cons as important only if they see enough pros, but they see pros as important irrespective of the existence of cons. For example, participants who chose a tuition loan were interested in learning about the benefits of the plan regardless of whether it had or did not have downsides. However, they were interested in learning about the plan's downsides only when they knew it had some advantages, but not when it lacked any advantages (Eyal et al., 2004, Study 1a). These findings demonstrate that when people consider reasons for and against an action, the subjective importance of con considerations depend on the availability of pro considerations more than the subjective importance of pro considerations depend on the availability of con considerations. Thus, cons are subordinate to pros.

Building on the finding that pros constitute a higher level of construal than cons, it was hypothesized that pros would be more prominent than cons in choices regarding the more distant future. Indeed, Eyal and colleagues (2004) found that participants generated more pros and less cons as temporal distance from the actions increased. Moreover, the tendency to generate more cons produced stronger intentions to adopt the plan under consideration. Importantly, Eyal and colleagues (2004) also found that this was the case only when pros pertained to an action's high-level construal (i.e., high desirability considerations) and cons pertained to an action's low-level construal (i.e., low feasibility considerations). However, when pros pertained to an action's low-level construal (i.e., high feasibility considerations) and cons pertained to an action's high-level construal (i.e., low desirability consideration) no such effect emerged.

Related to this line of research, Herzog, Hansen, and Wänke (2007) suggested that if pros become more salient with temporal distance and cons become more salient with temporal proximity, then participants should experience greater ease when retrieving pros (vs. cons) regarding more distant memories. Participants in their study read about a proposed action that was expected to take place in the near or distant future and were instructed to write down either four pros or four cons regarding the activity. They then rated the ease of generating these arguments, as well as their attitude regarding the described action. As expected, participants found it easier to generate pros and more difficult to generate cons when the issue concerned the distant rather than near future. Participants also had more favorable attitudes toward the action when it was to occur in the distant future. In addition, this latter effect of temporal distance on attitudes was partially mediated by the relative ease of retrieving pros (vs. cons) when considering a more distal action.

The effects of temporal distance on the salience of pros and cons may extend to other distance dimensions. For example, people might generate more pros than cons when considering a highly uncertain event compared to a probable one, making the latter easier to reject. Another interesting prediction is that pros would be more salient than cons in considering a new product rather than an old one, leading to an overall preference for novelty. However, novelty framing would not have a favorable effect on products if the pros concern feasibility (low-level features of the product) and the cons concern desirability (high-level features of the product). Moreover, it is possible that not only does distance lead to differential weighting of pros vs. cons, but also that thinking of pros more than of cons creates a sense of distance and novelty. Thus, framing a product's attributes as advantages (rather than as lack of disadvantages) might make people prefer a new product over an old and familiar one. Such framing may also increase preferences for buying the product as a gift for a friend rather than for one's own use, for ordering a product from a geographically remote location rather than from a local store, or buying a product for a temporally distant use rather than for immediate use.

Self-Control   Like risky choice, resolving a self-control dilemma may also be influenced by the construal of the immediate benefit (temptation) as a unique event that is unrelated to other similar incidents or, instead, as one occurrence in a sequence of multiple similar events (Rachlin, 1997). For example, when attempting to quit smoking, a cigarette may be viewed as just one unique cigarette or, alternatively, as a first in a long string of cigarettes. The former, low-level and concrete construal increases the likelihood of smoking the cigarette, whereas the latter, high-level and more abstract construal increases the likelihood of sticking to one's decision to quit smoking.

Fujita, Trope, Liberman, and Levin-Sagi (2006) have applied CLT to self-control. They proposed that self-control situations involve a conflict between the behavioral implications of high-level construals (i.e., primary, goal-relevant considerations) and the behavioral implications of low-level construals (i.e., secondary, goal-irrelevant considerations). According to Fujita and colleagues (2006), self-control is exerted when a person behaves in accordance with high-level goals, and it fails when a person behaves in accordance with low-level goals. This proposal is aligned with the definition of self-control dilemmas as a choice between two competing goals: A primary, long-term goal (e.g., saving money, eating healthy food, exercising) and a secondary, short-term goal or temptation (e.g., overbuying, eating fatty food, smoking, etc.; Ariely & Wertenbroch, 2002; Baumeister, Heatherton, & Tice, 1994; Loewenstein, 1996; Metcalfe & Mischel, 1999; Rachlin, 1997; Trope & Fishbach, 2000).

This analysis suggests that adopting a psychologically distant perspective as well as a high level of construal would enhance self-control. Indeed, Fujita and colleagues (2006) demonstrated that self-control improved when participants formed higher level construals of the situation. For example, in one study participants were primed with either a high-level or a low-level construal by indicating either why or how they would maintain good physical health (Freitas, Gollwitzer, & Trope, 2004). They then were asked to hold a handgrip while connected to bogus electrodes, which ostensibly assessed psychophysiological indexes related to their personality. They were told that the longer they held the handgrip, the more diagnostic the assessment would be. Thus, participants were presented with a conflict between a desire to get diagnostic, self-relevant information (high-level goal) and the inconvenience of holding the handgrip (low-level goal). As predicted, participants in the high-level construal condition held the handgrip longer than those in the low-level construal condition.

A similar idea has been proposed by Kivetz and Simonson (2002) as an account of hyperopia, which is a reverse self-control, in the context of consumer behavior. Hyperopia is the tendency of consumers to resist luxuries and overemphasize utilitarian necessities. In these situations, consumers must exert self-control and commit long in advance to indulge in luxuries that they would not ordinarily allow themselves. Indeed, results revealed that participants were increasingly likely to choose a luxury promotional option (e.g., a cruise) as opposed to a practical promotional option (e.g., a cash prize) as temporal distance increased. Further, reducing the probability of winning the prize, as another means of enhancing psychological distance, similarly led to an increased selection of the luxury prize alternative.

Related to self-control is the experience of consumer impatience, that is, the preference for smaller, sooner benefits over later, larger ones (Frederick, Loewenstein, & O'Donoghue, 2002; Thaler, 1981). For example, according to Thaler (1981), people prefer one apple today over two apples tomorrow, but they prefer two apples in 31 days over one apple in 30 days. The preferences reverse as one gets closer to the delayed choice. That is, one day away from getting the two delayed apples, one regrets choosing the two apples in 31 days over one apple in 30 days. Recently, Malkoc, Zauberman, and Bettman (2007) have argued that abstract processing should lead consumers to think in a decontextualized manner, which in turn would promote greater consistency in their intertemporal preferences. In one of their studies, participants were primed with abstract or concrete words through a word search task. In an unrelated task, participants imagined receiving a $75 gift certificate from amazon.com and indicated how much money they would require to delay the redemption of this gift certificate by 3 months and by 1 year. As expected, when primed with abstract words, participants' decline in their willingness to pay to avoid a delay in redemption of the gift certificate for 3 months compared to 1 year was lower than when primed with concrete words. Thus, priming high- vs. low-level construals led to a more consistent set of intertemporal preferences.

To summarize, research suggests that adopting a psychological remote perspective as well as more abstract construals increases consumers' ability to exercise self-control. We would further predict that enhancing other psychological distances such as social and spatial distances would also result in more self-control. For example, people may be more successful at advising others (greater social distance) to exert self-control than following this advice themselves. With regard to spatial distance, Internet shopping might be characterized by higher levels of self-control than might shopping on site. Finally, an interesting question is how novelty influences self-control. On the one hand, novelty promotes high-level construal and thus promotes greater self control. On the other hand, in some cases, novelty may make an event seem unique. Therefore, if a product or event is framed as both novel and, at the same time, as nonunique but rather as part of a series of such products or events, self-control might be enhanced. For example, thinking of the first session of a new weight-watch program as the first occasion in a series should subsequently enhance self-control efforts. In contrast, thinking of an action as a new and unique occasion (e.g., smoking a novel brand of cigarettes or smoking a cigarette with a novel social company) would undermine self-control efforts (e.g., refrain from smoking).

Affective Influences on Choice   How do consumers' emotions influence their choices? The literature on self-control has often viewed low-level goals as "affective," that is, as involving representations that are arousing and consummatory ("hot") and high-level goals as being affect-free ("cold") representations (e.g., Loewenstein, 1996; Metcalfe & Mischel, 1999; Mischel & Ayduk, 2004). It is possible, however, that both low-level goals and high-level goals, although experienced differently, are associated with emotions. Specifically, a low-level goal might be a source of low-level emotional experience (Kross, Ayduk, & Mischel, 2005; Metcalfe & Mischel, 1999; Mischel, Shoda, & Rodriguez, 1989) and high-level goals might be a source of a different type of emotional experience—an experience that is high level and more abstract, but nonetheless emotional.

In line with this idea, Eyal and Fishbach (2007) have recently suggested that the positive emotions that accompany the pursuit of high-level versus low-level goals are qualitatively different. Specifically, high-level, self-conscious emotions (e.g., pride and self-worth) are more abstract as they involve inference processes and require adopting a distal perspective (see Liberman, Trope, & Stephan, 2007, for a discussion of level of construal of emotions). Low-level, hedonic emotions (e.g., happiness and joy) do not require elaboration, inference, or psychological distancing. Eyal and Fishbach proposed that high-level emotions are likely to be associated with the pursuit of high-level goals and exertion of self-control (e.g., saving money), whereas low-level emotions are likely to be associated with the pursuit of low-level goals and failures of self-control (e.g., spending money). Therefore, the experience of goal attainment should depend on the level of the goal. For instance, one would feel proud when one fulfills a high-level goal, and happy after fulfilling a low-level, subordinate goal. Further, the duration of the experience might depend on the nature of the goal, such that low-level affect might be short-lived compared to high-level affect. In one study, participants with a salient health goal were offered a choice between a chocolate bar (a low-level temptation of indulging a sweet) and a small bag of baby carrots (a high-level goal of maintaining health). Participants reported their feelings both immediately after eating the snack they had chosen as well as 20 minutes later. As predicted, participants experienced more intense high-level affect (e.g., pride) following the pursuit of a high-level goal than a low-level goal, and this experience remained stable with a temporal delay. Moreover, participants experienced more intense low-level affect (e.g., happiness) following the pursuit of a low-level temptation, and this experience diminished over temporal delay.

Eyal and Fishbach (2007) further suggest that the consideration of high vs. low affective experiences might cue the pursuit of goals at the corresponding level. In one study, participants with a salient health goal were primed with low-level affective concepts (e.g., happy) or high-level affective concepts (e.g., proud) via a lexical decision task. They were then presented with a bowl of 200 Hershey Kisses and offered to take as many as they wished. As predicted, participants consumed less chocolate after being primed with high-level affective concepts than low-level affective concepts. These findings suggest that positive high-level affect concepts, compared to low-level affect concepts, serve as motivational cues for pursuing high-order goals over low-order goals.

Type of affect may be associated with psychological distance not only in the context of self-control. When considering remote actions, people might experience higher level feelings, whereas when considering proximal actions, people might experience lower level feelings. For example, signing a deal for a new car that is delivered in a year may elicit high-level affect such as pride, whereas the deal for a car that is delivered immediately may be associated with low-level feelings of happiness and joy. With respect to spatial distance, buying a gift for a friend who lives abroad (i.e., high spatial distance) would be associated with feelings of pride, whereas buying the same gift for a friend who lives in the same country (i.e., low spatial distance) would be associated with lower-level affect such as happiness. Activation of high-level affective concepts such as pride would lead people to be more open to new experiences and products whereas the activation of low-level affective concepts such as happiness would lead people to stick to old and familiar experiences.

Taking One's Values into Account
How do people's values influence their evaluations and choices? For example, when looking for a new car, to what extent do people consider moral issues such as the impact of the products on the environment or the manufacturers' employment policy rather than more concrete concerns such as the terms of payment and the make of the car?

Personal values, ideologies, and moral principles are abstract, decontextualized, superordinate cognitive structures and as such constitute high-level construals. According to CLT, they would therefore be more readily applied to more psychologically distant decisions. Eyal, Sagristano, Trope, Liberman & Chaiken (2007) used Schwartz's (1992) value questionnaire to measure the importance participants placed on a wide range of values (e.g., hedonism, benevolence, power). They then asked participants to imagine 30 behaviors (e.g., rest as much as I can) and to indicate the likelihood of performing each behavior in either the near future or the distant future. Correlations of the value ratings with the corresponding behavioral intentions revealed that values were more strongly associated with behaviors planned for the distant future than those planned for the near future. Further, a follow-up study found similar results when participants considered actual behavioral opportunities. In a first session, Eyal and colleagues (2007) measured participants' general attitudes toward a variety of activities (e.g., blood donation); in a second session, at a later date, participants were offered an opportunity to commit to doing these activities in either the near future (the next two days) or the distant future (several weeks later). It was found that participants' general attitudes were better predictors of behavioral intentions for the more distant future.

Building on the notion that values and principles are high-level constructs, Fujita, Eyal, Chaiken, Trope, and Liberman (2007) reasoned that values and ideals would be more persuasive when they concern more distant future issues. Participants imagined finding a sale for DVD players either that week (near future condition) or in 3 months (distant future condition). They then viewed a number of arguments endorsing the purchase of a particular DVD player. For half of the participants, the argument list included a value-related argument (the DVD player is made of environmentally friendly materials); for the other half of participants, all of the arguments were value-neutral. As expected, in the distant future condition, evaluations were more positive when the message included a value-related argument than when it consisted only of value-neutral arguments. In contrast, in the near future condition, inclusion of a value-related feature did not enhance persuasion. Thus, persuasive arguments appealing to idealistic values appear to be more persuasive for temporally distant, as opposed to near, attitude objects.

Although values are abstract and trans-situational in their nature and therefore generally pertain to high-level construals, they may still vary in their level of construal due to centrality. Central values are more essential to one's self identity and thus constitute high-level self construals, whereas secondary values constitute lower level self construals. According to CLT, when a situation is related to a number of different values, the individual's central vs. secondary values would be more likely to guide more psychologically distant choices. To test this hypothesis, Eyal, Sagristano, Liberman, and Trope (2007) conducted a two-session study. In the first session, participants rated the extent to which the values of being social and being intellectual are an important part of their self view, and in a second session participants chose between relatively high-brow periodicals (e.g., Newsweek) and low-brow periodicals (e.g., Sports Illustrated). As predicted, in the distant future, but not in the near future, participants for whom intellectual values were more central chose the high-brow magazines, and participants for whom social values were more central chose the low-brow magazines.

These results suggest that consumer choices are based upon one's predominant values when they are made from a distant perspective. However, when the same choices are made from a proximal perspective, consumers' predominant values become less influential. In other words, one's cherished values are expressed in one's plans, but unless committed to in advance, they are not necessarily expressed in one's daily conduct.

Do these time-related shifts in the role of values as internal guides for behavior extend to other distance dimensions? CLT suggests that decisions for the distant future (more than for the near future), for other people (more than for ourselves), for improbable and novel situations (more than for likely and familiar situations) reflect what should be the case "in principle," but decisions for similar situations that are examined in proximity reflect what is the case "in practice." Whenever a discrepancy emerges between the principle and the practice, psychological perspective would yield choice inconsistencies. For example, we would predict that one's cherished values and identities would be more readily applied when giving advice to others than when making personal decisions. Individuals may reason that whereas they, personally, would be willing to compromise their cherished values in specific situations (e.g., choose the lowest price option over the environmentally friendly option), others would not. Primary values may also guide decisions about unlikely uncertain situations more than decisions about likely situations. For example, people with prosocial values may be more willing to donate to charity part of the money they might win in a lottery when the chances of winning that lottery are relatively small.

Satisfaction and Regret

So far, we have discussed the effects of distance on choice. The question we now examine is how distance affects satisfaction with one's choice. On-line decision satisfaction is related to the feeling of fit, the feeling that one is doing something in the right way (for a review, see Higgins, 2006). Retrospective satisfaction with a decision pertains to regret, a phenomenon that has attracted much research attention in the decision-making literature (see Gilovich & Medvec, 1995). What are the implications of CLT for decision satisfaction and regret?

Prediction of Satisfaction   An important domain of inquiry is the calibration between people's predictions of their satisfaction with products and their actual satisfaction. Extensive research on affective forecasting (Gilbert & Wilson, 2000; Gilbert, Pinel, Wilson, Blumberg, & Wheatley, 1998; Gilbert, Morewedge, Risen, & Wilson, 2004; Kahneman & Snell, 1992; Wilson, Meyers & Gilbert, 2003) raises the question of whether people are satisfied with their consumptions as much as they think they would be when making the purchase. For example, are people as happy driving their brand new car as they imagined they would be? This research has demonstrated that both positive and negative emotional reactions tend to be more moderate than initially expected (Gilbert & Wilson, 2000; Mitchell, Thompson, Peterson, & Cronk, 1997). Furthermore, mental construal has been suggested as the underlying mechanism. For example, Gilbert, Wilson, and colleagues (Gilbert et al., 1998; Gilbert & Wilson, 2000; Wilson et al., 2000) proposed that individuals overestimate the intensity and duration of their reactions to future events because they tend to focus on salient consequences of the events (e.g., impressing one's friends with the new shiny car) and underestimate the diluting effect of contextual factors (e.g., standing in traffic jams, getting food stains on the seats).

CLT extends this line of research by proposing that information regarding the event is likely to be represented in a schematic and simplified way when it pertains to distant events more than when it pertains to near events. The same event is more likely to be represented in a way that takes into account situational and peripheral factors when the information pertains to proximal events (see Liberman & Trope, 1998; Nussbaum, Trope, & Liberman, 2003). The emotional forecasting error is thus expected to characterize forecasts of distal events more than forecasts of proximal events. That is, less calibration between people's emotional expectations and their actual experience is expected when predictions are made for the more distant future, when they are made for a more distal individual (e.g., how would your friend vs. a distant person react to a death of a family member?), when they concern geographically remote outcomes (how would I enjoy a vacation in India vs. a vacation in my own country?), and when they concern novel rather than familiar situations.

Regret   Another implication is that people would be more satisfied and make better decisions when distance matches the type of decision problem. For example, making feasibility-related decisions regarding the near future and desirability-related decisions about the distant future should be more satisfactory and yield better outcomes and less regret than making desirability-related decisions about the near future and feasibility-related decisions about the distant future. With respect to regret, it is possible that decisions that are based on high-level value would be regretted less as distance increases. For example, a purchase decision that expresses one's primary core values is likely to be evaluated more positively and produce less regret when evaluated retrospectively from a more distant point in time.

If high-level value is more likely to be expressed in distant future than near future choices, as CLT research shows, then distant future choices may be regretted in the short term but appreciated in the long term. In contrast, near future choices may be appreciated in the short term but regretted in the long term. For example, a person whose egalitarian values lead him to boycott an excellent product of a company that is known for its discrimination of workers may be upset with her decision in the short term but satisfied with the same decision in the long term. In other words, planning the distant future favors long-term postactional satisfaction, whereas making choices for the near future favors short-term postactional satisfaction.

Research on time perspective effects on regret (Gilovich & Medvec, 1994) has shown that temporal distance from past decisions increases regret of inactions but decreases regret of actions. For example, in one study, participants read about two students: One decides to transfer to another prestigious school, and the other decides to stay where he is, resulting in both feeling bad about their decision. The majority of the participants indicated that the student who changed schools would regret his decision more in the present and that the student who did not switch schools would regret more his decision in the long run (Gilovich & Medvec, 1994, Studies 3 and 4). According to Gilovich and Medvec (1994), forces that compel action (justifying regrettable action) are more salient than forces that restrain action (justifying regrettable inaction), and the salience of compelling forces increases with temporal distance, whereas the salience of restraining forces decreases with temporal distance. This analysis is consistent with CLT and the findings reviewed earlier that compelling pro considerations are at a superordinate level relative to restraining con considerations and therefore become more prominent over temporal distance (see Eyal et al., 2004; Herzog et al., 2007).

In line with Gilovich and Medvec's (1995) work, CLT suggests that satisfaction with one's actions depends on distance from these actions. That is, immediate satisfaction with one's actions is likely to be predicted by expectancies formed a relatively short time before performing the actions. However, long-term satisfaction with one's actions is more likely to be predicted by expectancies formed a relatively long time before performing the actions. This also suggests that when we precommit to something a long time in advance, we might regret it as its time of implementation approaches and shortly after that, but then come to appreciate the precommitment choice. For example, when the time of going on a trip approaches, we might regret committing ourselves to the adventure in the first place, but after we return from the journey, we might gradually come to appreciate the precommitment. Similarly, we might first regret but later appreciate decisions that are made for us by others (e.g., a friend's choice of restaurant).

Mental Distancing and Mental Approximation   Another possible way of reducing people's regret is to enhance the congruency, or fit, between one's psychological distance from the decision and the construal of the decision problem (Higgins, 2005). Because an association exists between high-level construal and psychological distant entities and low-level construal and psychologically near entities, a fit between psychological distance and level of construal should make people "feel right" about their decision and thus be more satisfied with it. Thus, based on the logic of CLT, in order to enhance satisfaction with one's purchase, high-level aspects of the product should be emphasized and low-level aspects should be de-emphasized when the temporal, social, or physical distance from one's decision is large. The reverse is true for when the psychological distance is low—in this case high-level aspects of the product should be de-emphasized and low-level aspects should be emphasized.

Initial support for this idea comes from research by Zhao, Hoeffler, and Zauberman (2007), who have shown that asking people to simulate mentally the high-level features of an immediate outcome (i.e., focus on the benefits associated with the outcome) before making a decision causes their immediate decisions to become more consistent with distant future preferences. Moreover, asking people to simulate mentally the low-level features associated with a distant outcome (i.e., focus on the constraints and conveniences associated with the process of reaching the outcome) before making a decision causes their distant decisions to become more consistent with near future preferences. Based on CLT, it may be further predicted that asking people to simulate a distant future event may lead to higher congruency between psychological distance and construal level.

CONCLUSION

Construal level theory proposes that psychological distance changes people's choices by changing the way they mentally represent the choice alternatives. The greater the psychological distance, the more likely are alternatives to be represented in terms of a few central and abstract features (high-level construals) rather than in terms of more concrete and incidental details (low-level construals). Research on the mental construal of near and distant events supports these assumptions, and research on decision and evaluation shows corresponding distance effects on choice. Decisions about distant times, locations, and people and about hypothetical or unlikely situations are based on general strategies and principles. In contrast, decisions about proximal times, locations, and people and about real or likely situations reflect more specific tactics, exceptions, and practical circumstances. The wide range of questions we have considered in this chapter suggests that consumer behavior provides a fertile ground for both theoretical investigation and practical application of construal level theory. Some of these questions have already been answered by empirical research. Other questions await further research.

REFERENCES

Agrawal, N., Trope, Y., & Liberman, N. (2007). Value from highlighting time-appropriate outcomes. Unpublished manuscript, Kellogg School of Management, Northwestern University.

Ainslie, G. (1975). Specious reward: A behavioral theory of impulsiveness and impulse control. *Psychological Bulletin, 82*, 463–496.

Ainslie, G., & Haslam, N. (1992). Hyperbolic discounting. In G. Loewenstein & J. Elster (Eds.), *Choice over time* (pp. 57–92). New York: Russel Sage Foundation.

Ariely, D., & Wertenbroch, K. (2002). Procrastination, deadlines, and performance: Self-control by precommitment. *Psychological Science, 13*, 219–224.

Baumeister, R. F., & Heatherton, T. F. (1996). Self-regulation failure: An overview. *Psychological Inquiry, 7*, 1–15.

Baumeister, R. F., Heatherton, T. F., & Tice, D. M. (1994). *Losing control: How and why people fail at self-regulation.* San Diego: Academic.

Carver, C. S., & Scheier, M. F (1999). Themes and issues in the self-regulation of behavior. In Robert S. Wyer, Jr. (Ed.). *Advances in Social Cognition, Vol. 12* (pp. 1–106).

Dhar, R., & Kim, E. Y. (in press). Seeing the forest or the trees: Implications of construal level theory for consumer choice. *Journal of Consumer Psychology.*

Elster, J. (1977). *Ulysses and the sirens.* Cambridge, England: Cambridge University Press.

Elster, J., & Loewenstein, G. (1992). Utility from memory and anticipation. In G. Loewenstein & J. Elster (Eds.), *Choice over time* (pp. 213–234). New York: Russell Sage Foundation.

Eyal, T., & Fishbach, A. (2007). Two affective systems in self-control. Unpublished manuscript, Ben Gurion University.

Eyal, T., Liberman, N., Trope, Y., & Walther, E. (2004). The pros and cons of temporally near and distant action. *Journal of Personality and Social Psychology, 86*, 781–795.

Eyal, T., Sagristano, M. D., Liberman, N., & Trope, Y. (2007) Resolving value conflicts in planning the future. Unpublished manuscript, Ben Gurion University.

Eyal, T., Sagristano, M. D., Trope, Y., Liberman, N., & Chaiken, S. (2007). When values matter: Expressing values in behavioral intentions for the near vs. distant future. Unpublished manuscript, Ben-Gurion University.

Fiedler, K., Semin, G. R., Finkenauer, C., & Berkel, I. (1995). Actor observer bias in close relationships: The role of self-knowledge and self-related language. *Personality and Social Psychology Bulletin, 21*, 525–538.

Förster, J. (2007). Preparing for novel vs. familiar events: Shifts in global vs. local processing. Unpublished manuscript, International University Bremen.

Förster, J., Friedman, R. S., & Liberman, N. (2004). Temporal construal effects on abstract and concrete thinking: Consequences for insight and creative cognition. *Journal of Personality and Social Psychology, 87*, 177–189.

Frederick, S., Loewenstein, G. F., & O'Donoghue, T. (2002). Time discounting and time preference: A critical review. *Journal of Economic Literature, 40*, 351–401.

Freitas, A. L., Gollwitzer, P. M., & Trope, Y. (2004). The influence of abstract and concrete mindsets on anticipating and guiding others' self-regulatory efforts. *Journal of Experimental Social Psychology*, 40, 739–752.

Fujita, K., Eyal, T., Chaiken, S., Trope, Y., & Liberman, N. (2007). Influencing attitudes toward near and distant objects. Unpublished manuscript, Ohio State University.

Fujita, K., Henderson, M., Eng, J., Trope, Y., & Liberman, N. (2006). Spatial distance and mental construal of social events. *Psychological Science*, 17, 278–282.

Fujita, K., Trope, Y., Liberman, N., & Levin-Sagi, M. (2006). Construal levels and self-control. *Journal of Personality and Social Psychology*, 90, 351–367.

Gilbert, D. T., Pinel, E. C., Wilson, T. D., Blumberg, S. J., & Wheatley, T. P. (1998). Immune neglect: A source of durability bias in affective forecasting. *Journal of Personality and Social Psychology*, 75, 617–638.

Gilbert, D. T., Morewedge, C. K., Risen, J. L., & Wilson, T. D. (2004). Looking forward to looking backward: The misprediction of regret. *Psychological Science*, 15, 346–350.

Gilbert, D. T., & Wilson, T. D. (2000). Miswanting: Some problems in the forecasting of future states. In J. P. Forgas (Ed.), *Feeling and thinking: The role of affect in social cognition* (pp. 178–197). Cambridge: Cambridge University Press.

Gilovich, T., & Medvec, V. H. (1994). The temporal pattern to the experience of regret. *Journal of Personality and Social Psychology*, 37, 357–365.

Gilovich, T., & Medvec, V. H. (1995). The experience of regret: What, when, and why. *Psychological Review*, 102, 379–395.

Henderson, M. D., Fujita, K., Trope, Y., & Liberman, N. (2006). Transcending the "here": The effect of spatial distance on social judgment. *Journal of Personality and Social Psychology*, 91, 845–856.

Herzog, S., Hansen, J., & Wänke, M. (2007). Temporal distance and ease of retrieval. *Journal of Experimental Social Psychology*, 43, 483–488.

Higgins, E. T. (2005). Value from regulatory fit. *Current Directions in Psychological Science*, 14, 209–213.

Higgins, E. T. (2006). Value from hedonic experience and engagement. *Psychological Review*, 113, 439–460.

Jones, E. E. (1979). The rocky road from acts to dispositions. *American Psychologist*, 34, 107–117.

Jones, E. E., & Nisbett, R. E. (1972). The actor and the observer: Divergent perceptions of the causes of behavior. In E. E. Jones, D. E. Kanouse, H. H. Kelley, R. E. Nisbett, S. Valins, & B. Weiner (Eds.), *Attribution: Perceiving the causes of behavior* (pp. 79–94). Morristown, NJ: General Learning Press.

Kahneman, D., & Lovallo, D. (1993). Timid choices and bold forecasts: A cognitive perspective on risk taking. *Management Science*, 39, 17–31.

Kahneman, D., & Snell, J. (1992). Predicting a change in taste: Do people know what they will like? *Journal of Behavioral Decision Making*, 5, 187–200.

Kim, E., Dhar, R., & Novemsky, N. (2007). Consumer receptivity of psychologically near and distant product advertising messages. Manuscript in preparation, Yale University.

Kivetz, R., & Simonson, I. (2002). Self-control for the righteous: Toward a theory of precommitment to indulgence. *Journal of Consumer Research*, 29, 199–217.

Kross, E., Ayduk, O., & Mischel, W. (2005). When asking "why" doesn't hurt: Distinguishing rumination from reflective processing of negative emotions. *Psychological Science*, 16, 709–715.

Libby, L. K., & Eibach, R. P. (2002). Looking back in time: Self-concept change affects visual perspective in autobiographical memory. *Journal of Personality and Social Psychology*, 82, 167–179.

Liberman, N., Trope, Y., Macrae, S., & Sherman, S. (2007). The effect of level of construal on temporal distance. *Journal of Experimental Social Psychology*.

Liberman, N., Sagristano, M., & Trope, Y. (2002). The effect of temporal distance on level of construal. *Journal of Experimental Social Psychology, 38,* 523–535.

Liberman, N., & Trope, Y. (1998). The role of feasibility and desirability considerations in near and distant future decisions: A test of temporal construal theory. *Journal of Personality and Social Psychology, 75,* 5–18.

Liberman, N., Trope, Y., & Stephan, E. (2007). Psychological distance. In A. W. Kruglanski & E. T. Higgins (Eds.), *Social psychology: Handbook of basic principles.* New York: Guilford Press.

Loewenstein, G. (1996). Out of control: Visceral influences on behavior. *Organizational Behavior & Human Decision Processes, 65*(3), 272–292.

Lopes, L. L. (1996). When time is of the essence: Averaging, aspiration, and the short run. *Organizational Behavior & Human Decision Processes, 65,* 179–189.

Lynch, J. G, & Zauberman, G. (in press). Construing consumer decision-making. *Journal of Consumer Psychology.*

Malkoc, S. A., Zauberman, G., & Bettman, J. R. (2007). Impatience is in the mindset: Carryover effects of processing abstractness in sequential tasks. Unpublished manuscript, University of North Carolina, Chapel Hill.

Metcalfe, J., & Mischel, W. (1999). A hot/cool-system analysis of delay of gratification: Dynamics of willpower. *Psychological Review, 106,* 3–19.

Mischel, W., & Ayduk, O. (2004). Willpower in a cognitive-affective processing system: The dynamics of delay of gratification. In R. F. Baumeister & K. D. Vohs (Eds.), *Handbook of self-regulation: Research, theory, and applications* (pp. 99–129). New York: Guilford Press.

Mischel, W., Grusec, J., & Masters, J. C. (1969). Effects of expected delay time on the subjective value of rewards and punishments. *Journal of Personality and Social Psychology, 11,* 363–373.

Mischel, W., Shoda, Y., & Rodriguez, M. L. (1989, May 26). Delay of gratification in children. *Science, 244,* 933–938.

Mitchell, T. R., Thompson, L., Peterson, E., & Cronk, R. (1997). Temporal adjustments in the evaluation of events: The "rosy view." *Journal of Experimental Social Psychology, 33,* 421–448.

Nussbaum, S., Trope, Y., & Liberman, N. (2003). Creeping dispositionism: The temporal dynamics of behavior prediction. *Journal of Personality and Social Psychology, 84,* 485–497.

O'Donoghue, T., & Rabin, M. (2000). The economics of immediate gratification. *Journal of Behavioral Decision Making, 13,* 233–250.

Rachlin, H. (1997). Self and self-control. In J. G. Snodgrass & R. L. Thompson (Eds.), *The self across psychology: Self-recognition, self-awareness, and the self concepts. Annals of the New York Academy of Sciences* (Vol. 818, pp. 85–97). New York: New York Academy of Sciences.

Rachlin, H., Brown, J., & Cross, D. (2000). Discounting in judgments of delay and probability. *Journal of Behavioral Decision Making, 13,* 145–159.

Read, D., & Loewenstein, G. (2000). Time and decision: Introduction to the special issue. *Journal of Behavioral Decision Making, 13,* 141–144.

Robins, R. W., Spranca, M. D., & Mendelsohn, G. A. (1996). The actor-observer effect revisited: Effects of individual differences and repeated social interactions on actor and observer attributions. *Journal of Personality and Social Psychology, 71,* 375–389.

Rosch, E. (1975). Cognitive representations of semantic categories. *Journal of Experimental Psychology: General, 104,* 192–233.

Sagristano, M. D., Eyal, T., Trope, Y., Liberman, N., & Chaiken, S. (2007). When values matter: Expressing values in behavioral intentions for the near vs. distant future. Unpublished manuscript, Florida Atlantic University.

Sagristano, M. D., Trope, Y., & Liberman, N. (2002). Time-dependent gambling: Odds now, money later. *Journal of Experimental Psychology: General, 131,* 364–376.

Schelling, T. (1984). Self command in practice, in theory and in a theory of rational choice. *American Economic Review, 74,* 1–11.

Schwartz, S. H. (1992). Universals in the content and structure of values: Theoretical advances and empirical tests in 20 countries. In M. P. Zanna (Ed.), *Advances in experimental social psychology* (Vol. 25, pp. 1–65). San Diego, CA: Academic Press.

Semin, G. R., & Fiedler, K. (1989). Relocating attributional phenomena within language-cognition interface: The case of actors' and observers' perspectives. *European Journal of Social Psychology, 19,* 491–508.

Soman, D. (1998). The illusion of delayed incentives: Evaluating future effort-money transactions, *Journal of Marketing Research, 35,* 427–438.

Thaler, R. (1981). Some empirical evidence of dynamic inconsistency, *Economic Letters, 8,* 201–207.

Thomas, M., Chandran, S., & Trope, Y. (2007). The effects of temporal distance on purchase construal. Unpublished manuscript, Cornell University.

Todorov, A., Goren, A., & Trope, Y. (2007). Probability as a psychological distance: Construal and preference. *Journal of Experimental Social Psychology, 43,* 473–482.

Trope, Y., & Fishbach, A. (2000). Counteractive self-control in overcoming temptation. *Journal of Personality & Social Psychology, 79*(4), 493–506.

Trope, Y., & Liberman, N. (2003). Temporal construal. *Psychological Review, 110,* 403–421.

Vallacher, R. R., & Wegner, D. M. (1987). What do people think they're doing? Action identification and human behavior. *Psychological Review, 94,* 3–15.

Wakslak, C. J., Trope, Y., & Liberman, N. (2007). The effect of construal level on subjective probability estimates. Unpublished manuscript, New York University.

Wakslak, C. J., Trope, Y., Liberman, N., & Alony, R. (2006). Seeing the forest when entry is unlikely: Probability and the mental representation of events. *Journal of Experimental Psychology: General, 135,* 641–653.

Wilson, T. D., Meyers, J., & Gilbert, D. T. (2003). "How happy was I, anyway?" A retrospective impact bias. *Social Cognition, 21,* 407–432.

Zauberman, G., & Lynch, J. G. (2005). Resource slack and propensity to discount delayed investments of time versus money. *Journal of Experimental Psychology: General, 134,* 23–37.

Zhao, M., Hoeffler, S., & Zauberman, G. (2007). Mental simulation and preference consistency over time: The role of process- versus outcome-focused thoughts. *Journal of Marketing Research, 44,* 379–388.

4

The Rational Unconscious

Conscious versus Unconscious Thought in Complex Consumer Choice

AP DIJKSTERHUIS, RICK B. VAN BAAREN,
KARIN C. A. BONGERS, MAARTEN W. BOS,
MATTHIJS L. VAN LEEUWEN, and
ANDRIES VAN DER LEIJ

Radboud University Nijmegen

TWO WAYS TO LOOK AT RATIONALITY

One of the authors vividly remembers the day he visited a U.S. supermarket for the first time. He was asked to buy, among a few other things, breakfast cereal for his partner. In the Netherlands (where all authors are from), supermarkets are much smaller than in the United States. Moreover, they rarely have more than five or six different alternatives to choose from, whether it is for peanut butter, yogurt, or breakfast cereal. One can imagine the bewilderment the moment he turned the corner and faced the aisle with the cereal. In fact, it was not just "the aisle with the cereal" but simply the "cereal aisle." All six shelves, for their entire 100 or so foot length, contained different versions of this bland, sawdust-based stuff that some people eat for breakfast. Too many alternatives can lead people not to make a choice in the first place (Schwartz, 2004; Iyengar & Lepper, 2000), and indeed, the author's first inclination was to walk on and not buy any cereal at all. However, anticipating that not buying anything would lead to disappointment at home, he chose a different strategy. After taking a deep breath, he just grabbed the first box he saw and quickly left the aisle.

Was this a wise choice? His partner was disappointed by the choice ("no wonder you think cereal tastes like sawdust. This indeed does. But some other brands ... "), but fortunately, choosing poor cereal has only minor consequences. However, other choices are important, sometimes extremely important, and making poor choices in such cases can have very serious consequences.

Because choosing can have such profound consequences, it has received a lot of attention from philosophers and scientists. In most scientific contributions, choosing and decision making was approached from a normative perspective. The emphasis was often less on how we make decisions than on how we, ideally, *should* make decisions. Another way to conceive of it is to conclude that a lot of scientific effort was aimed at how rational (or irrational) our decisions and choices generally are.

Now, how do our choices hold up against the standard of rationality? Obviously, the answer to such a question is dependent on one's definition of rationality. Although most people will have some intuitive sense of what a rational (or an irrational) decision entails, defining the construct is not a trivial matter. There are two distinct ways to look at rationality with diverging consequences for how decision making should be investigated. Broadly stated, one can make the distinction between rationality from a normative viewpoint and rationality from a subjective viewpoint. Evans and Over (1996, 1997; see also Chater, Oaksford, Nakisa, & Redington, 2003) defined the normative version as follows: "Thinking, speaking, reasoning, making a decision, or acting *when one has a reason for what one does sanctioned by a normative theory*" (Evans & Over, 1997, p. 2, italics added). The second definition they offer is more subjective: "Thinking, speaking, reasoning, making a decision, or acting *in a way that is generally reliable and efficient for achieving one's goals*" (Evans & Over, 1997, p. 2, italics added).[1]

For a long time, the first, normative, definition was the one favored by researchers interested in decision making. However, preferences seem to be shifting and various people opt for use of the second, subjective, definition (e.g., Evans & Over, 1997; Gigerenzer & Goldstein, 1996; Stanovich & West, 1999). A big problem with using a normative definition is that it irrevocably leads to the somewhat sobering conclusion that human decision makers are often highly irrational. The number of well-documented phenomena on human decision making that show violations of rationality is humongous (Kahneman & Tversky, 2000; Shafir & LeBoeuf, 2002). This is insightful, but it also strongly suggests it is illuminating (though also more difficult) to pay more attention to people's own goals and standards. It does us more justice. More importantly, it makes more sense from both a psychological and from an evolutionary perspective to use a subjective definition (Cosmides & Tooby, 1996). Evolution cares about whether people achieve their goals (especially the most basic ones such as to find food, to avoid danger, or to procreate) and psychology—to some extent at least—reflects these priorities. Conversely, normative demands such as "logic" or "consistency" are concerns that are at best indirectly related to evolutionary development.

CHOOSING WITHOUT CONSTRAINTS

When we compare decisions people make to standards of subjective rationality, what can we conclude? First, it is important to realize that a subjective definition of rationality does not necessarily imply that the standards we compare people to are less extreme or taxing. Some have argued that normative rational standards are simply too demanding in that they are unrealistic in their level of perfection (e.g., Gigerenzer & Todd, 1999). There is no doubt that this is true, but a subjective definition of rationality in terms of the degree to which a decision or choice fulfills people's goals can be made just as extreme or unrealistic. It simply depends on the goals. If we are willing to assume that people generally make certain choices in the hope that it will increase happiness or satisfaction in the future, one could conclude that the vast majority of choices people make are not very rational because they almost always fail to unleash happiness. Buying a new set of towels or oven mitts will not change happiness or life satisfaction in a significant and enduring way.

That being said, sometimes we do make choices that do impact happiness in pronounced ways, such as when we choose between jobs or houses. The question we want to address here is how we should approach such choices, with the criterion of maximizing subjective rationality. Which decision strategy leads us to fulfill our goals? In other words, when we face a complex, important decision, how should we deal with it in order for the outcome to be highly rewarding, for it to maximize happiness and to minimize negative emotions such as regret?

Let us start with a thought experiment, in which we are allowed to choose without any of the usual psychological constraints. There is no time pressure and there are no computational constraints. Furthermore, we have all the information relevant for the choice at hand. Not only is there no time pressure, but time in itself is not precious. We do not have anything else to do other than to make our choice in the most perfect way possible. That is, we can use all our powers to make the best possible choice. How should we try to achieve this? How should we choose between spending our holiday in Bora Bora, the Seychelles, or the Virgin Islands?

Most people would agree we should engage in what is often called the weighted adding strategy (e.g., Bettman, Luce, & Payne, 1998; Edwards, 1961; Janis & Mann, 1977). In this strategy, the chooser first weights the relative importance of various attributes, such as the water temperature, the size of the balcony of the hotel room, or the availability of cereal for breakfast in the hotel. Subsequently, choice alternatives are assigned values for each of these attributes ("Excellent, no problems on the cereal front. Cereal is banned in the Seychelles."). Finally, these values are, for each choice alternative, multiplied by the relative importance. The resulting scores represent the utility or relative desirability of each alternative.

The problem with the weighted adding strategy is that it is very demanding. After all, we do not live in an ideal world and decision makers *do* face constraints. Our computational abilities are limited, we are often pressured for time and resources, and we often have to choose between alternatives in the absence of (part of) the relevant information. Indeed, most theorists would agree that the weighted adding strategy is nothing more than an interesting ideal, but that it does not constitute a useful tool in real life. Researchers who have investigated the extent to which actual decision makers engage in weighted adding drew sobering conclusions: We rarely do it and even if we try, we are not very good at it (e.g., Dawes, 1979; Swets, Dawes, & Monahan, 2000).

This conclusion notwithstanding, in the present paper our goal is to try to advocate weighted adding as a useful decision-making tool. Too much skepticism may lead us to throw away the baby with the bathwater. Research findings show indeed that people have not been good at successfully using the weighted adding strategy. However, we argue that it is not so much weighted adding itself that is out of reach for people. Instead, poor performance is often caused by the fact that people rely too much on conscious deliberation. Most people believe, explicitly or implicitly, that the more one consciously deliberates about a choice, the closer one can come to the ideal of weighted adding. Our thesis is that this belief is unjustified, and that, ironically, weighted adding becomes more attainable the more we rely on unconscious processes.

In the remainder of this chapter, we first discuss the problems we face when we apply conscious thought or conscious deliberation to complex choice tasks. In doing this, we start out by discussing the relation between conscious thought and the biasing effects of heuristics on choice. Subsequently, we give more direct examples of poor weighting as a consequence of conscious thought. In the second part of this chapter we discuss the potential benefits of employing the unconscious.

THE PITFALLS OF CONSCIOUS DELIBERATION, PART 1: HEURISTICS AND BIASES

A common finding in the literature on decision making is that people are vulnerable to the influence of how decision problems are framed. Tversky and Kahneman (1981; see also Kahneman & Tversky, 1979) discovered that whether choice outcomes are framed in terms of gains or losses has a profound effect on choice. The well-known "Asian disease" problem provides a good example. Assume 600 people are infected with a disease. You have to choose between two intervention programs, both framed in terms of gains: With program A, you save 200 people. With program B, you have a 1/3 chance you save all 600 people, and a 2/3 chance no one will be saved. Faced with this dilemma, most people avoid risk and choose program A. However, one can also frame the choice in terms of losses: With program A, 400 people will die. With program B you have a 1/3 chance no one will die, and a 2/3 chance all will die. In this case, most people choose to be risky and select program B.

There is no rational argument for the influence of framing in such a context. In fact, the two decision problems are exactly the same. Indeed, if framing is studied with a within-participants design whereby participants see both the gain and the loss frame (like the readers of this chapter), the effect is attenuated because most people realize that the choice alternatives amount to the same thing (Stanovich & West, 1999; see also LeBoeuf & Shafir, 2003). Now can one prevent framing effects by asking people to engage in more conscious thought? Can deliberation inhibit this odd bias?

Igou and Bless (in press) tested the relation between amount of conscious thought and framing effects. Interestingly, they found the opposite of what one may have expectedly intuitively. In various experiments, it was shown that more conscious thought led to more pronounced framing effects. In one experiment, for instance, some participants were given the "Asian disease" problem with the cover story that it was just some statistical problem they had to solve. Others were presented with the problem under the guise of an actual medical problem. The people who treated it as a medical problem spent more time thinking about it than the people who merely thought it was a statistical problem, and they showed larger framing effects. In a second study, Igou and Bless demonstrated that the more motivated people are to deliberate about a choice, the bigger framing effects become.

In general, there is strong evidence demonstrating that more motivation to deliberate does not simply lead to better choices. Camerer and Hogarth (1999; see also Shafir & LeBoeuf, 2002) reviewed 74 studies on the relation between motivation (manipulates with incentives) and proneness to heuristics and biases. Although they found that motivation occasionally helps, it can just as well hinder choosing. The problem is that whatever the decision problem is, people always have to apply the right strategy to solve it. More motivation may occasionally help, but often it just leads to more enthusiastic application of a wrong strategy, thereby rendering choices to become inferior (e.g., Arkes, Dawes, & Christensen, 1986).

A nice example of this deleterious effect of motivation was reported by Pelham and Neter (1995). Participants in their experiments were asked to solve various problems. Some problems were transparent and easy to solve, whereas others were difficult and to solve them correctly participants had to avoid certain pitfalls (i.e., they ran the risk of using heuristics that would lead them astray). For instance, some were confronted with the "hospital problem" as used by Kahneman and Tversky (1972, page 443), which reads as follows:

> A certain town is served by two hospitals. In the larger hospital, about 45 babies are born each day, and in the smaller hospital, about 15 babies are born each day. As you know, about 50% of all babies are boys. Sometimes it is higher than 50%, sometimes lower. For a period of one year, each hospital recorded the number of days on which more than 60% of the babies born were boys. Which hospital do you think recorded more such days? (A) the larger hospital, (B) the smaller hospital, or (C) about the same.

As outcomes that deviate from normal (i.e., expected) probabilities are more likely to occur the smaller the sample is, answer B is the right answer. However, 56% of the original Kahneman and Tversky participants chose C. Pelham and Neter gave some of their participants this hospital problem, but gave others an easier, very transparent version. In this transparent version, the smaller hospital had "only 2" babies per day (rather than 15), and each hospital recorded the number of days on which all (100%) of the babies born were boys (rather than 60%).

Importantly, some people were simply asked to solve the problems, whereas others were strongly motivated to solve the problems accurately. As it turned out, this increased motivation helped participants to be more accurate on the easy, transparent problem, but it hindered solving the complex problems. If one is willing to make the rather safe assumption that the motivated participants engaged in more and/or more thorough conscious thinking, it means that conscious thought led to poor decisions. The reason is that more motivation led people to rely even more on the wrong heuristic. If all one is given is a wrong heuristic, more motivation, or more thinking, only leads to more use of that wrong heuristic. As Pelham and Neter put it (1995, p. 583): "If the only tool at a person's disposal is a hammer, convincing the person to work harder can only lead to more vigorous hammering."

Finally, in our own lab we once tested the role of time of conscious thought on the biasing effects of yet another heuristic, the availability heuristic (Tversky & Kahneman, 1973). Our reasoning was based on the logic by Pelham and Neter (1995): When people have to apply a heuristic to solve a problem, and when no alternative strategies are available, harder work can lead to only more use of the heuristic. And when the use of the heuristic leads to errors, greater use leads to greater errors. In the experiment (Dijksterhuis, 2003), participants were asked to estimate how many people die each year—in the Netherlands—as a result of three different causes: AIDS, traffic accidents, and homicide. Participants were asked either to come up with a number for each cause within 12 seconds or to think carefully and were given 45 seconds per cause. Use of the availability heuristic would lead to a relative underestimation of people dying of AIDS and an overestimation of homicide victims, with the traffic deaths falling in between. As expected, people who thought extensively for 45 seconds per cause indeed showed this effect, whereas people who had to estimate within 12 seconds hardly showed signs of the availability heuristic. Again, conscious thought made matters worse.

THE PITFALLS OF CONSCIOUS DELIBERATION PART 2: POOR WEIGHTING

Whereas the work described in the previous section shows the negative effects of conscious thought on various aspects of decision making, there is also evidence that is related even more directly with the theme of this chapter: the human (in)ability to engage in weighted adding. Again, whereas we know that proper weighted adding is difficult, most people also believe that we can come closer to achieving proper weighted adding by more conscious deliberation. However, this is simply not true.

Recently, one of us read a newspaper article that documented an interesting example of what we may call a "weighting error." When buying a house, one trade-off people have to make is between the size of the house and the length of the daily commute to work. Most people (note that the example comes from a Dutch newspaper) work in city centers. As city centers are expensive, a preference for a short commute by necessity means one is forced to buy a small house or apartment. Large houses are affordable, but only for those who are willing to live in the countryside and to face a long commute. It seems that many people think about this trade-off, and many eventually choose the large house. After all, a third bathroom is very important for when grandma and grandpa come over for Christmas, whereas driving two hours each day is really not that bad. Anecdotal evidence has it that a lot of these people come to regret their choice. A third bathroom is a completely superfluous asset for at least 362 or 363 days each year, whereas a long commute *does* become a burden after a while. Recent evidence (Stutzer & Frey, 2007) shows that people with longer commuting time report systematically lower subjective well-being.

Empirical demonstrations of such weighting biases abound. An already classic demonstration was published by Kahneman and colleagues (Kahneman, Frederickson, Schreiber, & Redelmeier, 1993). Their experiment is as simple as it is illuminating. Participants went through two unpleasant experiences: They had to put their hand in very cold water for one minute, and they had to put their hand in the water for 90 seconds, whereby the last half-minute was somewhat less cold, but still unpleasant. If asked which experience they would want to repeat, most participants chose the longer period. Participants neglected the duration and preferred the option with more overall pain, but with less pain on average. Additional research (e.g., Redelmeier & Kahneman, 1996) showed that people use a "peak-end" rule to assess pleasantness of unpleasantness of an experience. The extent to which a past experience is good or bad is based on the most intense part of the experience and on the intensity at the end of the experience.

Gilbert, Wilson, and colleagues (e.g., Gilbert, Pinel, Wilson, Blumberg, & Wheatley, 1998) found that people are generally bad predictors of future emotional experiences. When people are asked to estimate their emotional reactions to important events, they tend to think these reactions are more intense and more enduring than they really are. For example, young professors who were asked how they would feel after having been denied tenure predicted they would be much more devastated than they later really were. This bias in estimating future feelings is important, as anticipated feelings are often taken into account when people make decisions (e.g., Zeelenberg & Beattie, 1997).

Wilson and colleagues (e.g., Wilson & Schooler, 1991; Wilson et al., 1993; see also Levine, Halbertstadt, & Goldstone, 1996) have demonstrated that conscious contemplation disturbs what they called "natural weighting schemes." In one well-known experiment, Wilson and colleagues (1993) compared postchoice satisfaction of people who chose from five different art posters. Some participants had been merely asked to choose, whereas others had been asked to deliberate. More specifically, they had been asked to scrutinize the reasons for their preference carefully. The expectations of the experimenters were confirmed a few weeks later when postchoice satisfaction was assessed. People who engaged in thorough conscious thought were less happy with their choice. Wilson and colleagues (1993, p. 332) attributed this to suboptimal weighing: "Introspection … can change an optimal weighing scheme into a suboptimal one. When people analyze reasons, they might focus on those attributes of the attitude object that seem like plausible causes of the evaluations but were not weighted heavily before." Conscious thought leads people to put disproportionate weight on attributes that are accessible, plausible, and easy to verbalize (see also Schooler, Ohlsson, & Brooks, 1993), and therefore too little weight on other attributes. Recently, we (Dijksterhuis & van Olden, 2006) replicated and extended this experiment (it will be discussed more extensively later in this chapter).

Another problem is that decision makers seem to be often inconsistent in their weighting. They may be inconsistent either over time or between different contexts. The phenomenon of "preference reversal" demonstrates this. What would you prefer, bet A with a 29/36 probability of winning 2 Euros, or bet B with a 7/36 probability of winning 9 Euros? If you are like most people, you prefer Bet A. However, if you ask people what they would be willing to pay for either of these bets, the majority finds bet B to be more valuable (see Tversky, Sattath, & Slovic, 1988; Tversky, Slovic, & Kahneman, 1990, for more information on why this bias occurs). Hsee (1996) showed that such inconsistencies can also be caused by the context. When people compare two dictionaries, a torn one with 20,000 entries and a brand new one with 10,000 entries, most people prefer the torn one. However, when different people judge them separately, the new one with the lower number of entries is generally seen as more valuable.

In experiments by Levine, Halberstadt, and Goldstone (1996), participants had to evaluate a large number of faces that varied along six dimensions (such as the shape of the nose). Participants either merely evaluated these faces or had to think about the reasons for their evaluations before doing so. Of interest to the experimenters was the way people used and weighted the six dimensions to evaluate the faces. The data clearly demonstrated that conscious thought made weighting more varied and inconsistent.

In a series of experiments by Nordgren and Dijksterhuis (2007) participants were asked to make a variety of judgments including the attractiveness of Chinese ideograms or the extraversion of people on the basis of their faces. However, participants judged the exact same stimuli twice, sometimes after a 45-minute delay, in other cases after weeks. Importantly, some participants were asked to judge quickly, whereas others were asked to engage in thorough conscious thought. People who engaged in thorough conscious thought showed more rather than less inconsistency. Quick "gut" judgments were clearly more consistent over time than judgments that were made after conscious reasoning. In addition, conscious reasoning did not lead to better judgments. In one experiment, participants repeatedly judged the quality of various pieces of art. Both what is considered good art (from MOMA, the Museum of Modern Art in New York) and bad art (from MOBA, the Museum of Bad Art in Boston) was included. Conscious thinkers were again less consistent over time but not more accurate. The conclusion was drawn that rather than making judgments more consistent, extensive conscious thought just introduces noise, rendering judgments less consistent. Overall, it seems that conscious thought often disturbs rather than helps weighting.

As the examples in the previous paragraphs demonstrate, human decision making is prone to serious errors and oddities. An intuitive reaction may be to blame such errors on people's lack of motivation to engage in serious conscious thought. Cannot we avoid such errors if we just deliberate a little more? Although it is certainly true that conscious thought can help to prevent some problems, the general rule that conscious thought makes choices and decisions better, intuitive as it may sound, is wrong. Often conscious thought does not help, and sometimes it actually makes matters worse. The bottom-line is that the relation between conscious thought and quality of decision making is complicated, with multiple moderators affecting whether deliberation helps or hinders (e.g., Dijksterhuis & Nordgren, 2006; Lerner & Tetlock, 1999; Wilson & Schooler, 1991).

BOUNDED RATIONALITY OR BOUNDED CONSCIOUSNESS?

As we said before, treating weighted adding as an unrealistic ideal may be like throwing the baby out with the bathwater. The fact that consciousness sometimes does such a poor job does not yet mean people cannot engage in any weighted adding at all, as we have other means than our conscious processes. Our rationality is bounded (Simon, 1955), but this is at least in part caused by the fact that consciousness is bounded. A simple analysis of what is needed for proper weighted adding combined with an analysis of what we know about consciousness makes it transparent why conscious thought is not all that suitable for weighted adding (for a more elaborate discussion, see Dijksterhuis & Nordgren, 2006).

First, in order to engage in weighted adding for a complex choice (e.g., comparing three holiday destinations on a large number of dimensions) one needs quite a bit of processing capacity. One could help capacity by writing attributes on a list, but most people will still spend at least some time thinking about a complex choice in the absence of such a list. This is potentially problematic, because one cannot fit much information in consciousness at the same time. One can think about a single attribute ("The hotel on the Seychelles provides a better breakfast than the hotel on Bora Bora"), but a simultaneous consideration of a lot of information is impossible for consciousness. This incapability of integrating large amounts of information with conscious processing can come at the cost of the quality of decisions because it hinders a full appreciation of complex alternatives (Dijksterhuis, Bos, Nordgren, & Van Baaren, 2006). To quote filmmaker David Lynch, with a "golf-ball-consciousness" one cannot get more than a golf-ball-size appreciation of what was dealt with consciously.

Even more important than capacity is the ability to weight the importance of attributes itself. In a sense, one could argue that for proper weighting, two things are needed. The first is obvious: the capacity to establish proper weights based on diagnostic information. The second is that once such weights are established (or perhaps while establishing these weights), one should refrain from allowing noise to interfere with this process. Like Wilson and colleagues (Wilson & Schooler, 1991), we believe that consciousness does interfere: In popular terms, it often screws things up (Dijksterhuis & Nordgren, 2006).

In the previous sections, we have given some examples of noise introduced by conscious thought. First, Wilson and colleagues showed that we rely more on attributes that are verbalizable, accessible, and plausible and less on attributes that do not qualify as such. Language is consciousness's favorite tool, so it is no wonder that conscious thought leads to a restriction to information that is verbalizable. There are circumstances under which this is not necessarily bad, such as when a decision should be based largely or solely on verbalizable information. For most people, a laptop is a good example, as it really amounts to comparing verbalizable, usually numerical specifications. However, it can also have consequences that are highly problematic, as especially our most important choices (partner, job, house) do and *should* at least in part rely on attributes that are not easy to verbalize. One could ask a friend why she/he loves her/his partner, and of course, cooperative and intelligent as friends go, one will probably get an answer that sounds both sweet and plausible. But does such a verbal description really get anywhere near the psychological "essence" of what love is? Of course it does not. Consciousness does not know anything about such matters.

Second, as we have seen, more conscious thought sometimes leads us to rely even more on (contextual) information that we should really ignore, such as gain/loss frames. In addition, conscious thought can lead us to rely on weird little theories. A nice example is the diversification bias (Simonson, 1990). In an interesting experiment, Simonson asked students to choose one of six snacks they could consume in three future classes. If students choose before each class, they generally choose their same favorite snack over and over again. However, if students have to choose three snacks for three future classes at once, they more often opt for variety. Students base this choice on the generally erroneous theory that it is nicer to have variety rather than to stick to the same snack. Plausible as this may sound, it really makes more sense to choose the same favorite snack. It is your favorite after all, and it is highly likely it will be your favorite tomorrow and next week. Indeed, Simonson showed that students who opted for variety later experienced regret.

To recapitulate, conscious thought is not a good instrument for weighted adding. The capacity of consciousness is low, making it difficult to deal with complex problems. Moreover, conscious thought introduces a number of biases that can lead to very poor assessments of the relative importance of attributes.

UNCONSCIOUS THOUGHT

In recent years, we have conducted research on what we called "unconscious thought." The idea for unconscious thought was partly derived from old work on incubation. The process of incubation is especially relevant for creativity and problem solving. After an initial period during which people gather information, it is at times not fruitful to continue to concentrate on a problem consciously. Instead, a period during which the unconscious can think while conscious attention is directed elsewhere—in other words, a period of incubation—is often helpful.[2]

The key distinction between conscious thought (what we associate with normal thought) and unconscious thought is based on attention. We defined conscious and unconscious thought as such:

> Conscious thought refers to the cognitive and/or affective task-relevant processes one is consciously aware of while attending to a task. For instance, one may compare two holiday destinations and consciously think "The Spanish coast is cheap but I do not want to go there because it is way too crowded." Unconscious thought, on the other hand, refers to cognitive and/or affective

task-relevant processes that take place outside of conscious awareness. One may compare two holiday destinations and not know which one to choose. Subsequently, one does not consciously attend to the problem for a few days, and suddenly the thought "It's going to be Tuscany!" pops into mind. This thought itself is conscious, but the transition from indecision to a preference a few days later is the result of unconscious thought. (Dijksterhuis, 2004, pp. 586–587)[3]

Recently, we formulated a theory called Unconscious Thought Theory (Dijksterhuis & Nordgren, 2006) about the strength and weaknesses of both unconscious and conscious thought. The theory is in part based on recent research from our own laboratory. We started our research by comparing conscious and unconscious thought in the context of decision making. In the first series of experiments, we did the following: First, participants read information pertaining to a choice problem. For instance, they would be presented with information about four different apartments, whereby each apartment was described by 12 different aspects. We rigged the information in such a way that one apartment had much more positive attributes (and therefore less negative) than the others. After participants had read all the information, some were asked to choose between the apartments immediately. Others were given some time to consciously think before they chose, whereas a third group was distracted for a while after which they were asked to choose. Participants in this latter group were hypothesized to engage in unconscious thought. What we generally found with this paradigm is that unconscious thinkers make better decisions than either conscious thinkers or immediate choosers (for more details, see Dijksterhuis, 2004; Dijksterhuis, Bos, Nordgren, & van Baaren, 2006; Dijksterhuis & Nordgren, 2006). Moreover, we have also obtained the effects for participants who chose an actual object (such as a poster) rather than a hypothetical one and whereby quality of choice was operationalized as postchoice satisfaction (Dijksterhuis et al., 2006; Dijksterhuis & van Olden, 2006). We dubbed the effect that unconscious thought improves decisions the "deliberation-without-attention effect" (Dijksterhuis et al., 2006).[4]

In addition, unconscious thought is an active process. Some have argued that the increase in quality of a decision after unconscious thought is merely caused by distraction. That is, an alternative explanation for our effects in the unconscious thought conditions is the process of set-shifting (see e.g., Schooler & Melcher, 1995). According to this alternative explanation, the beneficial effects of a period of distraction from a decision problem do not necessarily result from an active unconscious thought process, but from the disruption of counterproductive conscious thought. For instance, people often approach a problem with wrong cues, wrong heuristics, and/or wrong information. Following a period of distraction, such wrong approaches become less accessible or are forgotten altogether. The effects of distraction on a change of mental set can be both very pronounced (such as when one tries to solve a chess problem and initially gets truly "fixed" in thinking along a wrong path) or more subtle (such as when distraction attenuates the biasing influence of primacy or recency effects). Such processes are often categorized under the umbrella of the "fresh look" explanation: Putting a problem aside for a while allows for a fresh, unbiased new look.

In a recent set of experiments, we refuted this possibility by demonstrating that unconscious thought is a goal-dependent process (Bos, Dijksterhuis & van Baaren, 2007). In our experiments, we again gave participants information about a decision problem. Importantly, we then compared two groups of participants who were both distracted before they made a decision. One group was given the same instructions as in the unconscious thought conditions of our previous work. After having read the decision information but before the distraction period, they were told that we would later ask them some questions about the decision problem. In other words, these participants were given the goal to think unconsciously, or at least the expectation that they had to make a decision later. The other group did not receive this goal. Before the distraction period they were told that they would not have to make a decision later on. Thus, one group had the goal to further process the information, whereas the other group had no such goal. Results showed that the former group made better decisions than the latter. That is, only people with a goal to later make a decision demonstrated superior decision making; the people without a goal did not. This means that unconscious thought is a goal-dependent process and merely distracting people does not help them.

UNCONSCIOUS WEIGHTED ADDING, PART 1: CAPACITY

The fact itself that unconscious thought can facilitate decision making does not yet imply it will bring us closer to the "ideal" of proper weighted adding. However, we think there are reasons to believe that indeed it does.

As we have argued before, weighted adding in the context of relatively complex decisions involving many dimensions requires large processing capacity. In fact, we concluded that this was one of the reasons conscious thought is not really suitable for weighted adding. Unconscious thought, however, has a much larger capacity than conscious thought, which renders it a more suitable candidate for weighted adding. At least capacity constraints will not be in the way.

In another recent set of studies, we (Dijksterhuis, Bos, Nordgren, & van Baaren, 2006) compared choices between simple products and complex products. There are of course many ways in which simple or complex can be operationalized, and we looked at one relevant dimension: the number of relevant attribute dimensions. Examples of simple products with few relevant attributes are CDs (where most people really only care about the music) or a dishwashing brush (where most people do not really care about anything at all). Examples of complex products are cars or houses (where most people want to take into account many different attribute dimensions). As predicted, unconscious thinkers made better decisions about complex products than do conscious thinkers. However, this effect disappeared or was even reversed for simple decisions. In sum, when capacity becomes an issue—that is, for complex products—unconscious thought led to comparatively better choices.

UNCONSCIOUS WEIGHTED ADDING
PART 2: WEIGHTING ITSELF

One of the principles of the Unconscious Thought Theory is the following (and note that it is based on the work by Wilson and colleagues discussed earlier): *The unconscious naturally weights the relative importance of various attributes. Conscious thought often leads to suboptimal weighting because it disturbs this natural process* (Dijksterhuis & Nordgren, 2006, pp. 99–100). The second part of the principle received a lot of attention earlier in this chapter when we discussed the fallacies on conscious thought. It is now time to turn to the first part. Do we engage in weighted adding when we think unconsciously? And if so, how?

We concede that the evidence for superior unconscious weighting is still limited, but we have some hints that we also described in Dijksterhuis and Nordgren (2006, p. 100). One experiment will be discussed again here. Recently, we (Dijksterhuis & van Olden, 2006) replicated and extended the "poster-experiment" by Wilson and colleagues discussed before. Participants chose a poster (out of five) to take home under one of three different conditions. They chose after looking at the posters briefly, after briefly looking at them and then thinking about them for 9 minutes, or after 9 minutes of unconscious thought following a brief look. Participants took their chosen poster home and were called a few weeks later to find out how they felt about their choice. As expected, participants who thought unconsciously were happier with their poster than participants in the other two conditions. In addition, when asked for what amount of money they would be willing to sell their poster, they indicated a sum twice as high as conscious thinkers.

It is possible that conscious thinkers chose poorly because they were indecisive. However, it is also possible that they had a clear preference for the wrong alternative, or, in other words, that they weighted poorly. Right after we asked participants to choose, they were also asked to give their attitude toward each individual poster. By subtracting the average attitude of the four nonchosen posters from the attitude toward the chosen one, we calculated the extremity of their preference. As it turned out, conscious thinkers actually had the clearest preference, whereas unconscious thinkers were relatively indecisive. However, correlations between the attitude toward the chosen poster and later satisfaction revealed that for immediate choosers and for unconscious thinkers, attitudes predicted later satisfaction. This was not the case among conscious thinkers. In other words, unconscious thinkers (and immediate choosers) weighted much better than conscious thinkers.

In a recent set of studies, we (Dijksterhuis, Bos, van Baaren, & van der Leij, 2007a) looked at weighting more closely in experiments in which we compared immediate deciders and unconscious thinkers. We used a paradigm based on work by Alba and Marmorstein (1987). Participants received information about a choice problem. Some objects (in our case, cars) had few positive attributes and many negative ones. However, the positive aspects were highly important (e.g., good gas mileage, excellent safety) whereas the many negative attributes were unimportant (e.g., no cupholders, no sunroof, no logo on the grill, etc.). In contrast to these what we may call "quality-cars," other cars were the exact opposite: They had many positive attributes that were unimportant (cupholders, sunroof, nice logo on the grill, etc.) and few negative but important attributes (poor safety and gas mileage). These we called the "frequency-cars." In our experiments so far, we showed that participants generally chose quality-cars over frequency-cars, which shows they engaged in appropriate weighting. However, the effects differed under different conditions. Whereas immediate choosers indeed weighted to some extent (about 75% chose the quality car), unconscious thinkers showed much stronger weighting effects, up to the point that almost all unconscious thinkers (>90%) chose the quality car.

TOWARD EXPLAINING HOW

As we have seen, when we think unconsciously, we generally have enough capacity to engage in weighted adding, even for relatively complex problems. Moreover, recent evidence shows that we do indeed engage in weighting to at least some extent. The intriguing question is how such an unconscious weighting process ensues. We concede that our current knowledge is both incomplete and speculative, but there are a few avenues that are useful to explore. We briefly discuss two such ideas. The first is based on commonalities between unconscious thought theory and fuzzy trace theory. The second is based on the idea of implicit learning.

To explain what both conscious and unconscious thinkers may do in the paradigm we often use, we can borrow insights from fuzzy trace theory (for a review see Brainerd & Reyna, 1990). Fuzzy trace theory assumes that people encode information in two ways: They distill both the gist of the information and a verbatim representation. It is tempting to believe that a verbatim storage of information is somehow better because it is more precise, but a host of research shows that it is not (e.g., Reyna, Lloyd, & Brainerd, 2003). Verbatim representations are relatively instable and unreliable. Indeed, when people have to judge or decide, they rely more on gist representations and less on verbatim representations the more experienced they are with the decision domain. Reyna, Brainerd, and colleagues have collected an impressive amount of evidence showing that reliance on gist rather than verbatim representations improves performance.

It is likely that unconscious thought works on gist representations whereas conscious thought relies more on verbatim representations. This could explain why conscious thought makes weighting less consistent, as was shown by Levine at al. (1996) and Nordgren and Dijksterhuis (2007). After all, verbatim representations themselves are less stable. Of course, for gist-based decisions to be sound, one needs to be able to infer the correct gists for encoded information in the first place. However, this becomes easier with more practice and it is no wonder that experience leads people to use more gist-based strategies (Reyna, Lloyd, & Brainerd, 2003). This is consistent with recent work in our laboratory in which we show that the quality of decisions correlates with experience for unconscious thinkers. In recent studies (Dijksterhuis, Bos, van Baaren, & van der Leij, 2007b) we have asked participants to predict results of sports events. As expected, unconscious thought is more effective for people with more experience. One would expect the same for conscious thought, but we actually find a surprisingly low correlation between experience and quality of decisions for conscious thinkers. This is fully in line with fuzzy trace theory: Experience helps with gist-based decisions, much less so with verbatim-based decisions.

The fact that unconscious, gist-based processing can be very effective is likely also helped by the fact that we can apply implicit knowledge during unconscious thought that we do not apply during conscious thought. That is, knowledge that is inaccessible to consciousness will probably not be used during conscious thought, but it may well be applied during gist-based, unconscious processing. Recently, Lieberman (2000) made a strong claim for an intimate relation between implicit learning and intuition. Intuitive processes may seem to appear out of nowhere, but they are often based on an impressive amount of implicit knowledge. An anecdote that comes to mind is one used by Malcolm Gladwell in his book *Blink* (2005). A few years ago, a Los Angeles–based museum bought a Kouros, an old Greek statue. Before they acquired it however, they did some tests to check whether it was a forgery or not. Everything seemed fine, until one or two very experienced and knowledgeable art connoisseurs "felt" something was wrong. I emphasize "felt" because these specialists merely sensed something was dodgy without being able to verbalize what was wrong. Their suspicion turned out to be correct, though, when very advanced tests later showed the Kouros was indeed a fake.

What is important here is that these specialists had their suspicion because they could call on an enormous amount of relevant knowledge. That this knowledge was (at least in part) implicit is also obvious, otherwise they would be able to say why the Kouros was a forgery. However, they could not; it just "felt" wrong. A line of research that supports this reasoning is the work on "bootstrapping." The bootstrapping technique (see e.g., Dawes, 1979) neatly shows that we have more knowledge than we often apply. A linear combination of attributes based on a decision maker's past weights does better in decision making than the decision maker on whom the weights are based. This clearly shows that we possess highly useful information that we often fail to apply.

Let us again use a concrete decision example. Let us say you buy a house for the eighth time of your life. The explicit knowledge about what you like and do not like about what is an asset in a house and what is not, about how different attributes will make you feel, is likely only a fraction of your "total" knowledge. Most of this knowledge is implicit, and we hypothesize that such knowledge is applied during unconscious, gist-based thought and not (or at least much less so) during conscious, verbatim-based thought.

CONCLUSIONS

Is giving up weighted adding as an ideal unnecessary? We argue that it is. At least for complex choices, unconscious thought does quite well in approaching weighted adding. One can ask the question whether unconscious thought *does* weighted adding or whether it merely *behaves as if* it does weighted adding. Chater and colleagues (2003) recently published an insightful paper where the distinction is made between rational calculation and rational description. The requirement of rational calculation for weighted adding presupposes that people would "calculate" weighted adding with the exact knowledge of how such things must be calculated.

This seems unrealistic, but it is also an unnecessary requirement. Chater and colleagues (2003, p. 67) use a nice analogy: "The wings of a bird may approximate the results of a calculation of optimal aerodynamic design … but there is, of course, no presumption that the bird conducts any calculations in designing its wing." This analogy may apply to unconscious thought and weighted adding. Perhaps unconscious thought does not quite do it, but it behaves as if it is doing it.

In their paper, Chater and colleagues also show that computer simulations (which are obviously not consciously aware of their own algorithms) can perform rationally on complex decision tasks that require integration of a lot of information. In contrast to current prevailing wisdom, we believe that people can actually do that too. If they are willing to engage in unconscious thought.

ACKNOWLEDGMENTS

This chapter was supported by a VICI-grant from NWO (453-05-004) awarded to the first author.

ENDNOTES

1. Interestingly, the definition of the *Compact Oxford English Dictionary* is broad enough so that it can encompass both the normative and the subjective definition. It says that "rational" means "based on or in accordance with reason or logic." This leans toward a normative definition, but a further search shows that "reason" (at least the noun) can be defined as "good or obvious cause to do something," which creates room for a more subjective take on rationality.
2. Although it needs to be said that whereas the anecdotal evidence for incubation is overwhelming (e.g., Ghiselin, 1952), solid and replicable scientific evidence is fairly scarce (see also Dijksterhuis & Nordgren, 2006).
3. A continuous reliance on sunny holiday destinations as examples of a decision problem is explained by the fact that it always rains in the Netherlands.
4. One may remark that in the paradigm we used conscious thinkers are not given a fair chance. After all, the do not have access to the information (other than through recall from memory) du ng conscious thought. There are different views on this. One can object that cons ious thought during which participants can still read information is also problematic, as one gives conscious thinkers more time to encode information than participants in the other conditions. However, for now it suffices to appreciate that unconscious thought itself is helpful for making decisions, as is demonstrated by the fact the unconscious thinkers always outperform immediate decision makers (the effects have now been independently replicated; see Ham & van den Bos, 2007; Lerouge, Pieters, & Stapel, 2006).

REFERENCES

Alba, J. W., & Marmorstein, H. (1987). The effects if frequency knowledge in consumer decision making. *Journal of Consumer Research, 14*, 14–25.

Arkes, H. R., Dawes, R. M., & Christensen, C. (1986). Factors influencing the use of a decision rule in a probabilistic task. *Organizational Behavior and Human Decision Processing*, 37, 93–110.

Bettman, J. R., Luce, M. F., & Payne, J. W. (1998). Constructive consumer choice processes. *Journal of Consumer Research*, 25, 187–217.

Bos, M. W., Dijksterhuis, A., & van Baaren, R. B. (2007). On the goal-directedness of unconscious thought. Manuscript submitted for publication.

Brainerd, C. J., & Reyna, V. F. (1990). Gist is the grist: Fuzzy-trace theory and the new intuitionism. *Developmental Review*, 10, 3–47.

Camerer, C. F., & Hogarth, R. M. (1999). The effects of financial incentives in experiments: A review and capital-labor-production framework. *Journal of Risk Uncertainty*, 19, 407–441.

Chater, N., Oaksford, M., Nakisa, R., & Redington, M. (2003). Fast, frugal, and rational: How rational norms explain behaviour. *Organizational Behavior and Human Decision Processes*, 90, 63–86.

Cosmides, L., & Tooby, J. (1996). Are humans good intuitive statisticians after all? Rethinking some conclusions from the literature on judgments under uncertainty. *Cognition*, 58, 1–73.

Dawes, R. M. (1979). The robust beauty of improper linear models in decision making. *American Psychologist*, 34, 571–582.

Dijksterhuis, A. (2003). *Conscious thought and the availability heuristic*. Unpublished data set, Radboud University, Nijmegen.

Dijksterhuis, A. (2004). Think different: The merits of unconscious thought in preference development and decision making. *Journal of Personality and Social Psychology*, 87, 586–598.

Dijksterhuis, A., Bos, M. W., Nordgren, L. F., & van Baaren, R. B. (2006). Complex choices better made unconsciously? *Science*, 313, 760–761.

Dijksterhuis, A., Bos, M. W., van Baaren, R. B., & van der Leij, A. R. (2007a). Unconscious thought and the weighting problem in decision making. Manuscript in preparation.

Dijksterhuis, A., Bos, M. W., van Baaren, R. B., & van der Leij, A. R. (2007b). Expertise, conscious thought and unconscious thought. Manuscript in preparation.

Dijksterhuis, A., & Nordgren, L. F. (2006). A theory of unconscious thought. *Perspectives on Psychological Science*, 1, 95–109.

Dijksterhuis, A., & van Olden, Z. (2006). On the benefits of thinking unconsciously: Unconscious thought increases post-choice satisfaction. *Journal of Experimental Social Psychology*, 42, 627–631.

Edwards, W. (1961). Behavioral decision theory. *Annual Review of Psychology*, 12, 473–498.

Evans, J. St. B. T., & Over, D. E. (1996). *Rationality and reasoning*. Hove Sussex, Psychology Press.

Evans, J. St. B. T., & Over, D. E. (1997). Rationality in reasoning: The problem of deductive competence. *Cahiers de Psychologie Cognitive*, 16, 1–35.

Gigerenzer, G., & Goldstein, D. (1996). Reasoning the fast and frugal way: Models of bounded rationality. *Psychological Review*, 103, 650–669.

Gigerenzer, G., Todd, P., & ABC Group (1999). *Simple heuristics that make us smart*. Oxford: Oxford University Press.

Gilbert, D. T., Pinel, E. C., Wilson, T. D., Blumberg, S. J., & Wheatley, T. P. (1998). Immune neglect: A source of durability bias in affective forecasting. *Journal of Personality and Social Psychology*, 75, 617–638.

Gladwell, M. (2004). *Blink: The power of thinking without thinking*. New York: Little, Brown and Company.

Ham, J., & van den Bos, K. (2007). *Unconscious justice judgments: Evidence for better justice judgments without conscious thought.* Poster presented at the Annual Society for Personality and Social Psychology meeting. Memphis, January 25–27, 2007.

Hsee, C. K. (1996). The evaluability hypothesis: An explanation of preference reversals between joint and separate evaluations of alternatives. *Organizational Behavior and Human Decision Processes, 67,* 247–257.

Igou, E. R., & Bless, H. (in press). On undesirable consequences of thinking: Framing effects as a function of substantive processing. *Journal of Behavioral Decision Making.*

Iyengar, S., & Lepper, M. (2000). When choice is demotivating: Can one desire too much of a good thing? *Journal of Personality and Social Psychology, 79,* 995–1006.

Janis, I. L., & Mann, L. (1977). *Decision making: A psychological analysis of conflict, choice, and commitment.* New York: Free Press.

Kahneman, D., Fredrickson, B., Schreiber, C. M., & Redelmeier, D. (1993). When more pain is preferred to less: Adding a better end. *Psychological Science, 4,* 401–405.

Kahneman, D., & Tversky, A. (1972). Subjective probability: A judgment of representativeness. *Cognitive Psychology, 3,* 430–454.

Kahneman, D., & Tversky, A. (1979). Prospect Theory: An analysis of decisions under risk. *Econometrica, 47,* 263–291.

Kahneman, D., & Tversky, A. (2000). *Choices, values, and frames.* New York: Cambridge University Press.

LeBoeuf, R. A., & Shafir, E. (2003). Deep thoughts and shallow frames: On the susceptibility to framing effects. *Journal of Behavioral Decision Making, 16,* 77–92.

Lerner, J. S., & Tetlock, P. E. (1999). Accounting for the effects of accountability. *Psychological Bulletin, 125,* 255–275.

Lerouge, D., Pieters, R., & Stapel, D. A. (2006). *On moderators of unconscious thought.* Paper presented at the Twente Conference on Consumer Psychology, Enschede, November 13 and 14, 2006.

Levine, G. M., Halberstadt, J. B., & Goldstone, R. L. (1996). Reasoning and the weighing of attributes in attitude judgments. *Journal of Personality and Social Psychology, 70,* 230–240.

Lieberman, M. D. (2000). Intuition: A social cognitive neuroscience approach. *Psychological Bulletin, 126,* 109–137.

Nordgren, L. F., & Dijksterhuis, A. (2007). The devil is in the deliberation: Thinking too much reduces judgmental consistency. Manuscript submitted for publication.

Pelham, B. W., & Neter, E. (1995). The effect of motivation on judgment depends on the difficulty of the judgment. *Journal of Personality and Social Psychology, 68,* 581–594.

Redelmeier, D., & Kahneman, D. (1996). Patients' memories of painful medical treatments: Real-time and retrospective evaluations of two minimally invasive procedures. *Pain, 116,* 29–39.

Reyna, V. F., Lloyd, F. J., & Brainerd, C. J. (2003). Memory, development, and rationality: An integrative theory of judgment and decision making. In S. Schneider & J. Shanteau (Eds.), *Emerging perspectives on judgment and decision research* (201–245). New York: Cambridge University Press.

Schooler, J. W., & Melcher, J. (1995). The ineffability of insight. In S. M. Smith, T. B. Ward, & R. A. Finke (Eds.,) *The creative cognition approach* (pp. 97–134). Cambridge, MA: MIT Press.

Schooler, J. W., Ohlsson, S., & Brooks, K. (1993). Thoughts beyond words: When language overshadows insight. *Journal of Experimental Psychology: General, 122,* 166–183.

Schwartz, B. (2004). *The paradox of choice.* New York: Harper Perennial.

Shafir, E., & LeBoeuf, R. (2002). Rationality. *Annual Review of Psychology, 53,* 491–517.

Simon, H. A. (1955). A behavioural model of rational choice. *Quarterly Journal of Economics, 69,* 99–118.

Simonson, I. (1990). The effect of purchase quantity and timing on variety-seeking behavior. *Journal of Marketing Research, 27*, 150–162.

Stanovich, K. E., & West, R. F. (1999). Discrepancies between normative and descriptive models of decision making and the understanding of the acceptance principle. *Cognitive Psychology, 38*, 349–385.

Stutzer, A., & Frey, B. S. (2007). Stress that doesn't pay: The commuting paradox. Manuscript submitted for publication.

Swets, J. A., Dawes, R. M., & Monahan, J. (2000). Psychological science can improve diagnostic decisions. *Psychological Science in the Public Interest, 1*, 1–26.

Tversky, A., & Kahneman, D. (1981, January 30). The framing of decisions and the psychology of choice. *Science, 211*, 453–458.

Tversky, A., Sattath, S., & Slovic, P. (1988). Contingent weighting in judgment and choice. *Psychological Review, 95*, 371–384.

Tversky, A., Slovic, P., & Kahneman, D. (1990). The causes of preference reversal. *American Economic Review, 80*, 204–217.

Wilson, T. D., Lisle, D., Schooler, J. W., Hodges, S. D., Klaaren, K. J., & LaFleur, S. J. (1993). Introspecting about reasons can reduce post-choice satisfaction. *Personality and Social Psychology Bulletin, 19*, 331–339.

Wilson, T. D., & Schooler, J. W. (1991). Thinking too much: Introspection can reduce the quality of preferences and decisions. *Journal of Personality and Social Psychology, 60*, 181–192.

Zeelenberg, M., & Beattie, J. (1997). Consequences of regret aversion 2: Additional evidence for effects of feedback on decision making. *Organizational Behavior and Human Decision Processes, 72*, 63–78.

5

Brands and Successful Brand Extensions

A Social Psychology Perspective on Economic Questions

HERBERT BLESS and RAINER GREIFENEDER

University of Mannheim

*I*n the light of skyrocketing costs for the introduction of new products, brand extensions—the deployment of an existing brand to launch a new product that is not part of the original product family or category—have been a strategic means of increasing popularity (e.g., Aaker, 1991; Loken & John, 1993; see also Rangaswamy, Burke, & Oliva, 1993). Indeed, because of the enormous costs and risks inherent in establishing a new brand, brand managers very often rely on an existing brand image and attempt to transfer the existing beliefs to new products. Even though brand extensions are an attractive way to introduce new products, not every brand extension is successful. Given that about 50 to 60 percent of all brand extensions eventually fail (Vašek, 2002), the determinants of successful brand extensions are a critical economic consideration. In addition, the underlying psychological mechanisms that contribute to a successful or an unsuccessful brand extension constitute a highly interesting domain. In the present chapter, we examine the role of brands and brand extensions from a social psychological perspective. The following is thus not to speculate about the economic promises of brand extensions. Rather, we focus on factors that might explain why some brand extensions are successful, while others fail. In particular, we argue that social psychological research on social judgment can be usefully applied to the domain of brand extensions. In doing so, we will draw especially on research on the emergence of assimilation and contrast effects.

BRANDS AS CATEGORIES

When looking at brands from a (social) psychological perspective, it seems straightforward to consider brands as categories, and the products of a brand as elements of a category (Aaker & Keller, 1990; Aaker, 1991; Boush, 1993). Generally, categories have been defined as a "class of objects that we believe belong together" (Smith, 1990, p. 33), or alternatively as "a number of objects that are considered equivalent" (Rosch, 1978, p. 30). Obviously, both notions ("believe belong together" and "considered equivalent") are rather broad and require additional assumptions about what exactly holds the various elements together. In this respect, different approaches emphasize different aspects. The "classic view" requires that all examples of a category have some necessary defining features that, in aggregate, are sufficient to determine category membership (see Medin, 1989). Often, however, it is not possible to determine which features of a certain product are necessary to allow for its allocation to a brand category. Consider, for example, the case of Porsche: The brand is used to market sports cars, but also sunglasses and pens. In this case, what is the defining feature that allows for determining category membership (unless it is the brand name itself, Porsche)? As this example illustrates, the classic view is limited with respect to the conceptualization of brand extensions.

The "probabilistic view" refrains from assuming necessary features but holds that elements, here products, can be more or less typical and share more or less defining features, thus resulting in more or less typical exemplars. The probabilistic view can be based on two assumptions. The first holds that the exemplars are organized around "general prototypes" (e.g., a classic Mercedes sedan) and are thus context independent. The second assumption holds that exemplars are categorized with respect to situation-specific prototypes. Such situation-specific prototypes are abstracted from a subset of the available exemplars that are retrieved from memory, and are thus context dependent (for a discussion, see Medin, 1989).

Finally, going beyond a pure focus on features and attributes, Medin (1989) proposed a "theory-based" categorization that emphasizes explanatory principles such as naïve theories that are common to category members. For instance, individuals could have the naïve theory that products marketed by the brand Porsche share the attributes "elegance" and "style." In this case, there is neither a sufficient set of defining features (the classic view) nor a prototype (the probabilistic view); rather, what constitutes category membership is derived from naïve theories of what defines a category or brand. Such an approach may provide a fruitful basis for theorizing about brands. Although this more "essentialist" perspective (which focuses somewhat less on product features and similarity) is promising, its implications for the present domain have not been empirically explored. Most noticeably, this approach emphasizes that the categorization of products is not fully determined by product features and similarity. Rather, it suggests that categorization can be influenced also by marketing strategies (see also Wänke, Bless, & Schwarz, 1998).

Independent of how the exact nature of a category is defined, all conceptualizations share the assumption that once an element is assigned to a category (here a product to a brand), this categorization has a very strong impact on subsequent cognitive processes, such as encoding and perception, storage and retrieval, inferences, and the formation of behavioral intentions (see also Shavitt & Wänke, 2001; Loken, 2006). Perhaps most convincingly, the profound consequences of assigning a product to a brand have been demonstrated in studies in which participants tasted a product with different labels (e.g., De Chernatony & McDonald, 1992; McClure et al., 2004; Hoyer & Brown, 1990). In fact, assigning a product to a brand can override objective facts. In an influential study by Hoyer and Brown (1990), for example, participants tasted different varieties of peanut butter. When no brand labels or only unfamiliar ones were provided, participants were highly capable of detecting the best quality product. However, when a familiar brand label was presented, participants preferred the product that was ostensibly produced by the familiar brand. The brand label exerted a very strong influence even if objective information about quality was available. As Smith (1990) points out, once an object (here a product) is assigned to a category (here a brand), this categorization permits a series of inductive inferences. In the study of Hoyer and Brown (1990), the brand presumably led to inferences of product quality, regardless of the objective quality information available through product tasting.

To further understand the impact of brand-label based inferences, one may ask when these inferences are likely to be spontaneously elicited. Interestingly, it appears that their impact is particularly strong in situations in which consumers are unable to directly detect the quality of a product. For example, in contrast to rather tangible characteristics such as taste, a product's durability or attributes such as "chemical free," "environmentally friendly," or "CO_2-neutral" cannot be directly perceived. Such intangible features—or the credibility of pertinent statements, if information is provided by the manufacturer—have to be inferred by the consumers. Given these inferences, it appears likely that the impact of the judgmental context increases the more a judgment pertains to a less "objective" or tangible attribute (e.g., sporty outfit vs. long-lasting battery). It therefore comes as no surprise that research on consumer behavior has often shown that brand labels provide a powerful basis for inferences (see Aaker & Keller, 1990; Loken, 2006; Shavitt & Wänke, 2001).

In addition to influencing inferences, activated brand labels have also been shown to affect basic memory processes. For example, Keller, Heckler, and Houston (1998) reported that activating a product's brand name increased the recall of brand consistent attributes (Morrin, 1999). In line with research on the recall of stereotype-consistent information (e.g., Macrae, Stangor, & Milne, 1994), this effect was particularly pronounced when processing intensity was rather low, that is, in conditions that are comparable to many real-life advertising situations.

In sum, this overview reveals that brands are often conceptualized as categories (e.g., Aaker, 1991) and that the categorization of a product as part of a brand influences a series of subsequent information processes, including inferences (e.g., the quality of peanut butter) and memory processes. Given this pronounced impact, we believe it is helpful to take a closer look at the categorization processes that underlie brand extensions. In particular, we think it is crucial to understand the mechanisms and boundary conditions of categorization. To this aim, the present chapter is guided by the inclusion/exclusion model of social judgment (IEM; Bless, & Schwarz, 1998; Schwarz & Bless, 1992a), which specifies antecedents and consequences of categorization processes. The IEM will be explained subsequently.

Based on the IEM, we address four related issues. First, we discuss how and when a new product is *assimilated* toward the implications of an existing brand. Second, we address the somewhat counter-intuitive notion of *contrast* effects, that is, that a positive evaluated brand may impair evaluations of a new product. *Third*, we explicitly point to the bidirectional relation between influences on brand and product. *Finally*, we turn to product-to-product influences.

It appears important to note that different kinds of extensions have been discussed. On the one hand, extensions may concern products that are quite similar to the previous spectrum of the brand's products (e.g., when a car manufacturer well-known for luxury cars introduces a compact car). On the other hand, such extensions may concern product lines that are only remotely related to earlier products (e.g., when a brand famous for its sports products enters the market with a perfume line). While from a marketing perspective the two sorts of extensions may differ quite substantially and may require very different marketing strategies, from a cognitive perspective the two variants share the basic notion that the implications of a prior category should be transferred to a new product. Given the equivalence from our psychological process-oriented perspective we refrain from further elaborating on this distinction while readily acknowledging its implications for marketing. Independent of the type of the extension, marketers are interested in a successful extension. The emerging questions then pertain to the underlying mediating cognitive processes and to moderators of successful versus unsuccessful extensions.

ASSIMILATION TOWARD THE EXISTING BRAND— THE INTERPLAY OF FEATURES AND PROCESSES

In the following, we discuss how and when a new product is assimilated toward the implications of an existing brand. For this, we first review the notion that a similarity between an extension product and its parent brand determines assimilation. Subsequently, we go beyond the feature aspect and then turn to other factors that influence assimilation (and contrast) embedded in a presentation of the IEM (Schwarz & Bless, 1992a, 2007).

Similarity of Brand and Product Features

The assumption that the successful transfer of a brand image to a new product depends on the similarity between the brand and the product has been the focus of a stellar series of empirical research endeavors (e.g., Aaker, 1991; Aaker & Keller, 1990; Boush & Loken, 1991). This research consistently revealed that the more the accessible features of the existing brand and the extension overlap (i.e., the higher the perceived "fit" between the existing brand and the extension), the more likely it is that beliefs about the brand will be transferred to the new product (for an overview, see also Loken, 2006). For example, Aaker and Keller (1990) reported that an imagined Häagen Dazs candy bar was evaluated more positively than imagined Häagen Dazs popcorn or imagined Häagen Dazs cottage cheese, presumably because the perceived fit between the brand Häagen Dazs and the imagery extension products was higher for the candy bar than for either popcorn or cottage cheese.

Interestingly, recent empirical findings suggest that the perception of brand extension fit varies across cultures (Monga & John, 2007) and individual difference variables (Ahluwalia, forthcoming). For instance, Monga and John (2007) reported that customers in Eastern as compared to Western cultures perceived higher fit between a new product and the extended brand. Thus, whether a fit between a new product and the supposed parent brand is perceived depends on various variables, including typicality of the extension product and cultural variables.

Extending the notion of fit, it has been argued that the perceived similarity between a brand and a new product does not depend only on the pure features of the brand and the product, but also on conceptual dimensions that are similar across otherwise rather diverse product categories. For example, the more prestige-oriented brand Rolex should be more successful in introducing new prestige-oriented products (e.g., bracelet, ring), whereas the more function-oriented brand Timex should be more successful in introducing function-oriented products (e.g., a calculator; Park, Milberg, & Lawson, 1991).

Taken together, prior research has revealed that an evaluative transfer from a brand to an extension product is more likely the higher the perceived fit between the extension product and the parent brand.

Beyond Feature Similarity: The Role of Categorization Processes

Shifting the focus from the features toward the categorization processes, we have previously proposed and empirically demonstrated the enormous flexibility of categorization processes (Schwarz & Bless, 1992a; Wänke, Bless, & Igou, 2001; Wänke et al., 1998). According to this approach, the features provide only the basis for the categorization processes that operate on them. If so, quite comparable sets of brand and product features may result in very different effects depending on the categorization processes that operate on them. That is, not only the features (of the brand and the product, potentially resulting in the perception of fit), but also the processes operating on the features need to be taken into account. Hence, the features of products are not necessarily "destiny" (Wänke et al., 1998) for a successful transfer, but leave sufficient room for marketing operations. For example, the mere manipulation of whether the name of a new product (a car named Milano) reflected a continuation of prior brand products (Firenze, Roma, Siena) or not resulted in a differential transfer of the brand image onto the new product. In particular, the new car was evaluated more in line with the brand when presented as a name continuation rather than a discontinuation. As this research demonstrates, marketing operations may determine whether a brand is included or excluded from the representation of the product, irrespective of the features of the car.

In addressing context effects and the role of categorization processes, Schwarz and Bless have proposed the inclusion/exclusion model of social judgment, IEM (1992a, 2007; see also Bless & Schwarz, 1998; Bless, Schwarz, & Wänke, 2003). The

IEM holds that evaluative judgments require two mental representations, namely a representation of the judgmental target (e.g., the product) and a representation of a standard against which the target is evaluated. It emphasizes the role of information accessibility and assumes that both representations (target and comparison standard) are formed on the spot (see Barsalou, 1987), drawing on information that is chronically or temporarily accessible. Thus, when evaluating a new product, chronically or temporarily accessible brand information may be used to construct the mental representation of the product. Noticeably, information may be used to construct both the target and the comparison standard. If information is used to form a representation of the target, assimilation effects are likely to occur; that is, the inclusion of positive information results in more positive judgments and the inclusion of negative information results in more negative judgments. Assimilation effects are what brand extension strategies are usually launched for. However, if information is excluded from the representation of the judgmental target, it is likely to be used to form the representation of the comparison standard—which in turn results in contrast effects.

In this respect, the IEM holds that three filters channel information use. Individuals will exclude accessible information from the representation of the standard (1) when they believe that this information was brought to mind by some irrelevant influence (Martin, 1986; Strack, Schwarz, Bless, Kübler, & Wänke, 1993), (2) when the information is not considered representative for the target (e.g., driven by typicality, extremity, category width, etc.), and (3) when the use of the information would violate conversational norms (for an overview see Schwarz & Bless, 1992a). Not surprisingly, marketers very heavily aim and hope for assimilation effects so that a positive brand image is transferred to positive product evaluations. As we will argue in the following sections, however, contrast effects need also to be taken into account.

Research on the IEM has revealed substantial support for the previously sketched core assumptions of the IEM and has demonstrated that quite a number of variables may affect the inclusion/exclusion categorization via the three filters (for an overview, see Bless et al., 2003). Given the scope of the present chapter we want to focus on one of these variables, category width.

A successful transfer of beliefs about a category to a new exemplar requires that the exemplar is assigned, that is, included, to the category (for abundant evidence from the stereotype domain, for example, see Fiske & Neuberg, 1990; Fiske, Lin, & Neuberg, 1999). According to the IEM an inclusion of the exemplar is more likely the wider the category (Schwarz & Bless, 1992b).[1] Direct evidence for this assumption is reported by Boush and Loken (1991). Participants in their study were presented with either narrow brands that manufactured one good (e.g., only soups, only condiments, *or* only frozen vegetables) or broad brands that manufactured several goods (e.g., soups, condiments, *and* frozen vegetables). Results indicate that moderately different extension products (e.g., canned food or breakfast cereals) were perceived as more typical of the broad than of the narrow brand, suggesting that a moderately different extension product is more likely to be included the wider the parenting brand.

Given these general assumptions, one may speculate about how variables that have been demonstrated to influence perceived category width in turn increase or decrease the likelihood of successful extensions. For example, a substantial body of research suggests that affective states influence categorization processes, thereby influencing the likelihood that a given exemplar, here the new product, is assigned to an existing category, here the core brand (e.g., Isen & Shalker, 1982). Based on these general ideas about categorization flexibility, research by Barone, Miniard, and Romeo (2000) has addressed the impact of incidental positive affect on the likelihood that a particular extension is categorized into the core brand and is subsequently evaluated more positively. The findings suggest that positive moods, relative to neutral moods, enhance the evaluation of moderately similar brand extensions to a positively evaluated core brand. For very dissimilar or very similar products, however, no bolstering effect of mood was observed (for different positions, see Adaval, 2003; Yeung & Wyer, 2005; for the general role of mood in advertising effectiveness see, for example, Batra & Stayman, 1990).

As illustrated in exemplary form for the case of mood, perceived category width may depend on aspects that are—at least initially—not associated with the features of the brand. In this respect, one may, for example, speculate whether and how level of construal (Liberman, Trope, & Wakslak, 2007; see also Eyal, Liberman, & Trope, this volume) affects category width. In line with construal level theory, one may speculate whether inducing a high level of construal elicits a wider representation of the brand whereas inducing a low level of construal elicits more narrow representations. If so, brand extensions should be more likely to be successful in situations with high rather than low levels of construal.

Processing Intensity

In the preceding section, we have discussed factors that influence the perception of a category, thus having an impact on whether a product is categorized as belonging to a parent brand or not. In the present section we move beyond the perception of categories and ask when knowledge about a category is most likely to be used. We address these issues separately, acknowledging, however, that they are highly inter-twined. With respect to the use of categorical knowledge, most models on social cognition hold that the impact of prior categorical knowledge increases as process-ing intensity decreases. For example, abundant research on impression formation has documented that when either processing capacity (e.g., Bodenhausen, 1990) or processing motivation (e.g., Kruglanski & Webster, 1996; Neuberg & Fiske, 1987) are decreased, the impact of prior categorical knowledge in the form of stereotypes increases (see Fiske & Neuberg, 1990). Similar findings have been observed with respect to categorical knowledge in the form of brands. Sanbonmatsu and Fazio (1990), for example, reported that consumers based their judgments on attributes of the (new) product when they were both sufficiently motivated and capable of processing the relevant information. If, however, consumers were either unable or unwilling to elaborate on the product information, their judgments and deci-sions were based on the implications of the brand (for related evidence see also Maheswaran, Mackie, & Chaiken, 1992). Similarly, product evaluations were also based on the implications of the brand if no individuating product information was available for systematic processing (e.g., Klink & Smith, 2001).

Besides allowing for an elaboration of the product's attributes, processing motivation and processing capacity may also directly influence the categorization processes that operate on the attributes. In this respect, models on social cognition, including the IEM, which is outlined in the previous section, hold that assimilation effects (here the transfer of the brand image to the new product) are generally more likely when processing resources are reduced (e.g., Schwarz & Bless, 1992a; see also Martin & Achee, 1992). Interestingly, research in the domain of stereotyping suggests that this effect persists even when the attributes themselves are sufficiently elaborated (Bless, Schwarz, Bodenhausen, & Thiel, 2001).

The evidence reported in the previous paragraph clearly demonstrates that reliance on categorical information (here the implications of the brand) increases as processing motivation and processing capacity decreases. Interestingly, positive affect, which is seemingly omnipresent in advertising campaigns, has quite similar consequences as decreased processing intensity (e.g., Bless, 2001). In addition to mood influencing the initial categorization processes (as already discussed, Barone et al., 2000), mood may also influence whether or not the implications of a category are used. Although they hold divergent assumptions about the underlying processes, different accounts of the relationship between mood and information processing share the assumption that happy moods increase the likelihood that individuals rely on prior categorical knowledge, whereas sad moods increase the impact of individuating exemplar-specific information (see contributions in Martin & Clore, 2001). In line with this notion, happy individuals were found to base judgments about a target person on the implications of an activated stereotype, whereas sad participants were more likely to account for the implications of a given exemplar (Bodenhausen, Kramer, & Süsser, 1994; see also Bless, Schwarz, & Wieland, 1996; Krauth-Gruber & Ric, 2000). Extending these considerations from the stereotyping domain to the impact of brands, Greifeneder, Bless, and Kuschmann (2007) presented participants with a new product allegedly from either a positively or a negatively evaluated brand. Specifically, participants were asked to evaluate a family van (similar to Dodge Caravan or Renault Espace) that was presented either with Mercedes (positive) or Škoda brand information (less positive). When a happy mood was induced, participants' evaluations of the family van reflected the implications of the alleged parent brand. In contrast, when a neutral or sad mood was induced, no impact of the brand information on the evaluation of the family van was observed (see Figure 5.1).

Expertise

Consumer expertise is, not surprisingly, a central variable that is investigated in the domain of consumer psychology. We suppose that with respect to brand extensions, expertise may exert two different functions, both of them resulting in a decreased likelihood that brand evaluations are transferred to a new product. On the one hand, expertise may influence the capability to elaborate on a product, and on the other hand, expertise is associated with how information is represented in memory.

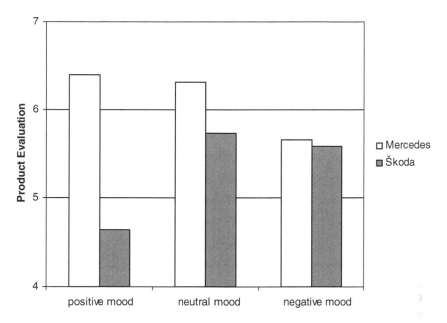

Figure 5.1   Mean Evaluations of the Extension Product as Reported in Greifeneder, Bless, and Kuschmann (2007). Evaluations Range from 1 (Negative) to 9 (Positive), with 5 Being the Neutral Midpoint.

As stated already, the elaboration of individuating features reduces the impact of the brand image. Besides requiring that sufficient resources can be allocated, the elaboration also requires some sort of expertise, that is, prior knowledge that allows for an evaluation of the individuating product attributes. In the absence of such expertise, consumers must rely on their categorical brand knowledge as a heuristic cue to evaluate the product. Thus, compared to novices, experts in a given domain should be *less* likely to reflect the impact of the brand image. In line with this notion, Maheswaran (1994) reported that the country of origin exerted a more pronounced impact on product evaluations when consumers had fairly little knowledge about the product category as compared to consumers holding more expertise. More directly addressing the impact of brands, Wänke and colleagues (1998) demonstrated that when evaluating a new product, context effects in the form of brand membership were dramatically reduced for participants with high expertise in the respective domain. Specifically, the sportive image of a car manu-facturer was more likely to be transferred to a new, more compact-type car for par-ticipants who indicated little rather than much expertise in the domain of cars.

In addition to allowing for an elaboration of the individuating product attri-butes, expertise also influences how brands and products are represented in mem-ory. In this respect it is likely that experts have more finely graded categories than nonexperts. If so, the broader categories of nonexperts more easily allow for an inclusion than the more fine-graded categories of experts. The inclusion in turn should result in an assimilation of the product toward the implication of the exist-ing brand (Schwarz & Bless, 1992a; for a more extended discussion of expertise, see Bless et al., 2003). Hence, both a processing and a memory perspective suggest that judgments of novices as compared to judgments of experts are more likely to reflect assimilation effects.

Regulatory Focus

In addition to cognitive and affective influences on categorization processes, the consequences of brand extensions may also depend on individuals' motivational concerns. According to regulatory focus theory as introduced by Higgins (1998, see also Lee & Higgins, this volume), individuals may form decisions either in a promotion or in a prevention focus (both may be instigated situationally and/ or exist dispositionally). The theory holds that when in a prevention focus, individuals are particularly sensitive to potential losses, while in a promotion focus, individuals are particularly sensitive to potential gains. Linking this theorizing to brand extensions, Yeo and Park (2006) distinguished two components: On the one hand, an extension may be linked to hedonic attainment resulting from a high-quality product. Given their sensitivity to potential gains, individuals in a promotion focus should be guided especially by this first component. On the other hand, purchasing a new product is associated with uncertainty over whether the new product indeed lives up to the assumed quality of the brand's other products. This uncertainty is influenced by the perceived similarity between the product and the brand, with higher similarity implying less risk. Given their sensitivity to potential losses, individuals in a prevention focus should be guided particularly by this second component. In line with these hypotheses, Yeo and Park (2006) observed that participants in a prevention focus evaluated similar extensions more positively than dissimilar ones (because similar extensions constitute less risk), whereas this relation was eliminated when participants were in a promotion focus. In fact, it seems that participants in a promotion focus were guided instead by the potential gains in the respective situations.

Extending Yeo and Park's (2006) considerations, one may speculate that some product category extensions constitute a higher risk than other product category extensions. For example, when buying a newly introduced candy bar, the potential risk seems quite limited relative to when buying a new computer. To the extent that this speculation is true, successful extensions of "less risky" products would require less similarity than "high risk" products. Hence, companies producing "high risk products," in particular, would need to pay close attention to extension strategies in order to prevent the dilution of their brand.

WHEN BRAND EXTENSIONS FAIL: CONTRAST EFFECTS AS THE WORST-CASE SCENARIOS

Given the enormous costs for the introduction of new products, brand extensions have become an increasingly popular strategy (Rangaswamy et al., 1993). Even though brand extensions are attractive avenues for introducing new products, not every brand extension is deemed to be successful. As a matter of fact, many brand extensions fail. For instance, Levi Strauss & Co.'s move to introduce suits with a jeans brand label was a huge and expensive flop. Thus, brand extensions as a seemingly cost-reducing strategy may be associated with certain risks, pertaining both to the new product itself (addressed in this section), as well as to the existing brand (addressed in subsequent sections).

At first glance, one might argue that the "worst-case scenario" of a failed brand extension is chiefly that the invested marketing costs do not result in a transfer of the brand evaluation to the new product. In other words, the evaluation of the new product is unaffected by the evaluation of the brand. However, a growing body of research suggests that the negative effects are likely to go well beyond this seeming worst-case scenario. Indeed, several studies suggest that a failed brand extension may reflect not only the absence of an assimilation effect (product toward brand), but also the presence of a contrast effect. Put differently, a positive brand may not only fail to help the new product (usually assumed to be the worst case), but actually *hurt* the new product by giving rise to boomerang effects. As a matter of fact, instead of being assimilated to it, the evaluations of the new product may shift away from the implications of the brand (a contrast effect).

Direct evidence for the emergence of contrast effects has been observed in the research by Wänke and colleagues (1998) in which participants evaluated a new compact car as *less* sports-car-typical when they had learned about the brand's sportive image than when they had received no information about the brand. In this work, categorization processes were manipulated by varying peripheral attributes. In particular, whether a new car was perceived as belonging to the brand was influenced by the car's name (Milano), which constituted either a continuation (Firenze, Roma, Siena), or a discontinuation (Circle, Square, Triangle) of the products that were already part of the brand. The results demonstrate that superficial dissimilarities, such as a product's name that does not match the naming tradition of the brand, are sufficient to elicit such backfire effects.

How can we account for these, in most cases, unwanted contrast effects? According to the IEM (Schwarz & Bless, 1992a), relevant accessible context information (here the brand image) that does not pass the three filter questions is not used for constructing the representation of the target (exclusion). However, instead of merely being discarded, in many cases this information enters into the construction of the comparison standard and in turn elicits contrast effects. In the studies presented by Wänke and colleagues (1998), the dissimilarity of the new product's name with the prior brand product names caused the participants to exclude the brand membership information (and the respective brand image) from the representation of the new product. Moreover, this information served as a comparison standard: In light of the sports car image of the brand, the new car was considered less sportive than when the brand information had not been provided. Note that merely presenting a name in line with prior brand products eliminated this contrast effect, again suggesting the enormous flexibility and context dependency of the categorization processes. Moreover, as we will discuss, such contrast effects may affect not only the evaluation of the product but also evaluations of the brand (see Romeo, 1991).

Intriguingly, the notion that category membership information may result in contrast effects is not restricted to brands and brand extensions. Such category-based contrast effects have been observed in several other domains of social judgment as well, including the domain of person perception. For example, Bless and colleagues (2001) demonstrated that the evaluation of a target person was contrasted against the implications of the targets' group membership when situational cues implied that the target was atypical for the respective group (see also research by Biernat, Manis, and colleagues, which similarly suggests that category information may create expectancies that subsequently serve as a standard of comparison, thus resulting in contrast effects; Biernat, Manis, & Nelson, 1991; Manis, Biernat, & Nelson, 1991; Manis & Paskewitz, 1984).

Note that such contrast effects may also emerge when a rather unfavorable brand is introducing a new, fairly positive product. If brand membership information is excluded from the mental representation, the negative brand membership information may serve as a standard of comparison and may actually increase the evaluation of the new product (for related evidence see also Brown & Dacin, 1997).

THE BIDIRECTIONAL RELATION BETWEEN BRAND AND BRAND EXTENSION: EFFECTS ON THE BRAND

So far, we have discussed how category information may affect the evaluation of new exemplars—in the present context, how beliefs about a brand may affect a brand extension. Going beyond this aspect, one also needs to consider the reverse perspective; that is, one needs to address how the new product may affect the prior beliefs about the brand. Based on the models on social judgment presented in the previous section, we argue that (1) the impact of brands on extensions and (2) the impact of extensions on brands have to be discussed in combination. The two directions are two sides of the same coin, and one is unlikely to occur without the other. The underlying categorization processes constitute the "coin," that is, the combining element.

According to the IEM (Schwarz & Bless, 1992a, 2007), categorization processes determine whether an exemplar and the category information are included into one mental ad hoc representation or into different representations. Accordingly, a joint representation of brand beliefs and brand extensions leads to an assimilation of the extension to the brand. Importantly, however, the joint representation will also result in an assimilation of brand beliefs toward the new product. Conversely, when brand and extensions are not represented in the same mental construction, the extension is likely to be contrasted against the brand (Wänke et al., 1998). Again, this form of representation should also affect the evaluation of the brand: The brand should be perceived in contrast to the extension.

Evidence supporting these considerations can be obtained from research in person perception and stereotype change. For example, Bless and colleagues (2001) demonstrated that the very same situational contexts that elicited an inclusion of a target person into a social category (and in turn an evaluation of the target on the basis of the stereotype), also led to a change of the stereotype toward the implications of the target person. Thus, the results reflected both sides of the coin, an assimilation of the exemplar evaluation toward the category evaluation, and an assimilation of the category evaluation toward the exemplar evaluation. This linkage was also observed when the situational context elicited an exclusion of the target person from the social category. In this case, the target was contrasted to the implications of the stereotype. Again, this contrast effect also pertained to the stereotype: In light of the exemplar, the category was changed away from the implications of the target person.

When transferring these considerations to the present context of brands, it is necessary to point out that a change of the brand beliefs will not be observed when brand extension and brand are considered similarly favorable or unfavorable (see Schwarz & Bless, 1992a). Thus, one may detect such effects only in situations in which the implications of the brand extension are either superior or inferior relative to the existing brand beliefs. Although we strongly emphasize that the processes that underlie contrast effects of superior and inferior extensions are equivalent, we address these two issues in turn.

Superior Brand Extensions

The notion that with superior brand extension marketers might improve the overall brand evaluation is reflected in strategies in which a high-end product—a so-called top-of-the-line product—is introduced and emphasized in marketing. Empirical evidence with respect to this notion was reported by Wänke and colleagues (2001). When a top-of-the-line-product was added to the existing brand products, the overall brand evaluation increased; that is, the brand was evaluated more positively due to the introduction of the new high-end product. Theoretically, such an assimilation effect should be restricted to situations in which the new exemplar is included into the brand representation. When the top-of-the-line product is excluded from the brand representation (e.g., due to perceived atypicality), the very favorable exemplar should actually hurt the brand. Compared to the new (atypical) product, the existing brand appears less favorable.

Inferior Brand Extensions

The assimilative impact of extensions is unfortunately not restricted to superior brand extensions. Interestingly, as Loken and John noted in 1993, "surprisingly little effort has been directed toward investigating the potential negative effects of brand extensions on family brand names" (p. 71). Up to now, research addressing this question is still rather sparse (for exceptions, see Keller & Aaker, 1992; Milberg, Park, & McCarthy, 1997; Park, McCarthy, & Milberg, 1993; Loken & John, 1993). At first glance, the results of this research seem fairly mixed, with some studies suggesting that unsuccessful extensions do not dilute existing brand beliefs, and others suggesting a negative impact. Again, it would appear that the impact of a negative extension on the brand evaluation depends on how the extension is categorized with respect to the brand. Negative consequences for the brand are likely when the extension is included into the brand representation, for example, due to a perceived similarity.

Though not directly designed to test the implications of the IEM, research reported by Romeo (1991) on the impact of negative extensions is very much in line with this consideration. Presenting negative extensions to an existing brand affected the brand differently depending on the perceived similarity. When the extension (juice) was similar to the brand (Tropicana), the negative extension decreased evaluations of the brand—presumably because the extension was included into the brand category. However, when the extension was dissimilar (sherbet) the negative extension improved brand evaluations—presumably because the dissimilar extension was excluded and in turn served as a comparison standard. In line with these considerations, Milberg and colleagues (1997) did not observe a transfer of the evaluation of a (negative) product on the brand when the product was explicitly labeled as a sub-brand. In fact, one ought to expect contrast effects: The exclusion of the negative brand extension should improve the evaluation of the brand.

Further in line with these considerations, Ahluwalia and Gürhan-Canli (2000) recently suggested that the accessibility of extension information moderates whether a failed extension has a diluting effect on the parent brand. In particular, the authors hypothesized and found that negative extension information led to dilution and positive extension information led to enhancement of the parent brand particularly when extension information was highly accessible. Obviously, the more accessible the extension information is, the more likely it is to be used when forming evaluations of the target or the comparison standard (see Wyer & Srull, 1989; Higgins, 1996). Hence, assimilation and contrast effects should be more likely to occur the more accessible the (positive or negative) extension information is. Note that Ahluwalia and Gürhan-Canli (2000) suggest that their model allows for reconciling the previously inconsistent findings with respect to the diluting impact of failed brand extensions.

It needs to be pointed out that a long-term marketing strategy that is based on contrast effects is not necessarily successful. Whereas a negative product may initially improve the brand perception (if the product does not enter into the representation of the brand), a repetition of such a strategy is likely to eventually harm the brand. Indirect evidence for such delayed effects can be obtained from research on stereotype change. Subtyping, that is, an exclusion of an exemplar from the category, can initially prevent a change of the category representation and even cause contrast effect (see Bless et al., 2001; Kunda & Oleson, 1997). However, repeated subtyping with different exemplars will change the representation of the category and will thus cause assimilation toward the implications of the new, formerly subtyped exemplars (Weber & Crocker, 1983). Thus, even though a marketing strategy based on contrast effects may initially produce desirable effects, the accumulation of contrast effects may in the long-run turn into an assimilation effect.

In one of the previous sections, we have discussed several variables that determine whether and how strongly a new extension is affected by prior brand knowledge. Given our general assumption that the impact of the brand on the extension and the impact of the extension on the brand are two sides of the same coin, we argue that the same processes that influence the impact of the brand are also likely to influence the impact of the extension. Consider, for example, the case of processing intensity. We have argued that decreased processing capacity and/or decreased processing motivation will cause an assimilation of the evaluation of the extension toward the implications of the brand. Complementarily, we argue that decreased processing motivation and/or decreased processing motivation should also cause an assimilation of the brand evaluation toward the implications of the extension. Evidence for this assumption can again be derived from research on stereotype change. For instance, Yzerbyt, Coull, and Rocher (1999) exposed their participants to a target person that was (moderately) inconsistent with their existent stereotype. In reaction to the inconsistent exemplar, participants changed their judgment on stereotype-relevant dimensions. This effect, however, was restricted to situations in which participants' processing capacity was reduced by a secondary task. The authors argue that cognitive resources are necessary for a subtyping of the exemplar, in other words, for the exclusion of the exemplar from the category (see also Kunda & Oleson, 1995, for more details about the assumed subtyping processes).

Similar to the considerations about processing intensity, the "two sides of the same coin" assumption allows for the derivation of hypotheses about the impact of mood and expertise. Given the considerations already mentioned about the impact of the brand on the extension, we argue that an assimilation of the brand toward the implications of the extension is more likely when individuals are in a happy rather than in a neutral or sad mood. Moreover, such assimilation effects should be more likely for individuals with low expertise compared to individuals with high expertise. Note that this relation needs to be qualified if individuals hold high expertise about the brand, but low expertise about the extension product, or vice versa (see Bless et al., 2003, for a more extensive discussion of this issue).

All the considerations noted already are related to a change of the brand evaluation, that is, to a change of the central tendency. Besides altering the central tendency, the inclusion of an extension into the brand category may also influence the perceived distribution (in the sense of homogeneity versus heterogeneity) of the category. Indeed, it has been argued that as more—and more diverse—extensions are included into the brand, the brand may wear out and may no longer be used for a transfer to a new extension (see Loken, 2006). In considering this hypothesis, at least two aspects need to be differentiated: Category width and variability may have an impact on the likelihood that a new extension is included, and they may have an impact on the size of the effect of such an inclusion. With respect to the likelihood of an inclusion, we argue that a new exemplar is more likely to be included into broad rather than narrow categories, that is, categories that comprise numerous exemplars with a considerable variance (see Boush & Loken, 1991). This inclusion may in turn elicit an assimilation of the category toward the implications of the exemplar. While the likelihood of an inclusion should thus increase with category width and variability, the size of the assimilative effect should decrease once the exemplar is included into the mental representation of the brand. Thus, the negative (but also the positive) implications of a brand extension will have more impact on narrow rather than wide brands. These considerations are in line with empirical evidence that pertains to (1) direct manipulations of brand width (Einwiller, Wänke, & Samochowiec, 2006) as well as to (2) the number of product categories associated with a brand as a proxy of perceived category width (Rangaswamy et al., 1993).

PRODUCT-TO-PRODUCT INFLUENCES: HOW AN EXTENSION MAY AFFECT OTHER PRODUCTS

So far, we have addressed (1) how extensions are evaluated in the context of brands, and (2) how brands are evaluated in the context of extensions. The two perspectives reflect either a superordinate or a subordinate relationship between the context (e.g., the brand) and the judgmental target (e.g., the extension product). Besides these two relationships, one may speculate whether an extension product might also influence judgmental targets on the same conceptual level, that is, whether an extension product might have an impact on other products of the brand. In contrast to superordinate or subordinate relationships, such an impact would be a lateral relationship (see Schwarz & Bless, 1992a). According to the IEM—which has guided a substantial part of our discussion—one exemplar cannot be directly included into the representation of another exemplar of the same category (Schwarz & Bless, 1992a). Consequently, the impact of an extension product on other products would be expected to reflect a contrast effect. Evidence in favor of this notion has been observed in various domains, including perceived attractiveness of others (e.g., Kenrick & Gutierres, 1980), perceived own attractiveness (Brown, Novick, Lord, & Richards, 1992), or the trustworthiness of politicians (Schwarz & Bless, 1992b). As Herr, Sherman, and Fazio (1983) pointed out, interexemplar contrast is the most common form of interexemplar influences. Thus, one ought to expect that when extending the brand with a very favorable top-of-the-line product, the evaluation of other, more moderate products would be contrasted against the new "star"—and evaluated more negatively.

However, research suggests that interexemplar assimilation is possible, too. For instance, targets are rated more attractive when they are together with an attractive rather than an unattractive person (Geiselman, Haight, & Kimata, 1984), and a compact car may seem faster and more sporty when presented in the context of other sports cars (Wänke et al., 1998). If this is so, introducing a top-of-the-line product should increase the evaluations of other products of the same brand; the other products should benefit from and assimilate toward the new "star."

Starting out from these considerations, Wänke and colleagues (2001) investigated the impact of a "star" on other members of the same category. They argued that introducing a star will elicit interexemplar contrast, but that additional processes will set in that might counteract this contrast. Among these, the "star" will also increase the overall evaluation of the brand, as detailed in previous paragraphs. When the evaluation of the already existing (moderate) product is—at least in part—derived from its brand membership, this evaluation should benefit from the improved brand evaluation. The counteracting assimilation should be more likely under conditions that increase the likelihood that the moderate product is based on the brand evaluation. (For the specifics of these considerations, see the previous section on assimilation effects.)

To test these hypotheses, Wänke and colleagues (2001) presented participants with ads for several toasters. Two of these toasters were standard models of two different brands (Logan L500; Wellington TA1). For some participants, an additional top-of-the line model for one of the brands was advertised (Logan T5000).

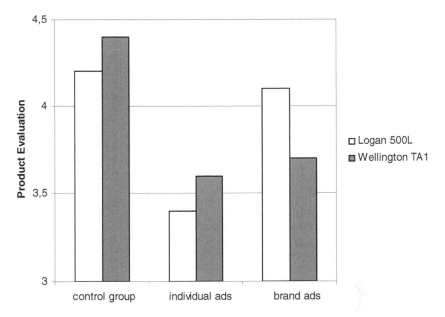

Figure 5.2   Mean Evaluations of the Logan L500 and the Wellington TA1 as Reported in Wänke et al. (2001). Evaluations Range from 1 (Negative) to 7 (Positive).

In one condition (brand ads condition), the ad for the top-of-the-line model shared many peripheral features of the ad for the standard model (e.g., color, logo in same position, same font). In another condition, the ads did not share these features (individual ads condition). As can be seen in Figure 5.2, the results indicate the co-occurrence of assimilation and contrast.

When no top-of-the-line product was introduced, similar evaluations were obtained for the two standard models of the two brands. Introducing the star with the "individual ad" decreased the evaluation of both standard models—independent of whether the standard model belonged to the same or to another brand. However, when the star was introduced with the "brands ad" emphasizing the overlap with the standard model of the same brand, the contrast effect was restricted to the competitor's standard model. As can be seen in Figure 5.2, it would seem that the evaluation of the brand standard model is unaffected by the introduction of the top-of-the-line model, but it is also apparent that the star gives an advantage over the competitor.

Based on these and related findings (see Wänke et al., 2001), we argue that product extensions are likely to exert contrast effects on other products of the same brand, but that such interexemplar contrast can be eliminated by situational conditions that increase the likelihood that product evaluations are derived from the brand. Accordingly, all the variables discussed in the context of whether and how a brand influences a product can be applied here.

CONCLUSION

In the present chapter we have discussed brands and brand extensions from the perspective of social judgment models. We readily acknowledge some shortcomings in our perspective. First, we disregarded the fact that brands may be linked not only to cognitive operations, but also to communicative and self-relevant functions. Indeed, individuals rely on brands not only because brands, for example, indicate the quality of a product, but also because brands allow individuals to define and express themselves (Park, Jaworski, & MacInnis, 1986). Sometimes these latter aspects override the use of the product itself, for example, when individuals intentionally acquire fake brand products. Second, while relying primarily on general models on social judgment, we did not address how brands differ from social categories (in this respect, see Shavitt & Wänke, 2001). Despite these and potential other blind spots of the present perspective, we do believe that research on brand and brand extensions could strongly benefit from social judgments models. In particular, the emphasis on categorization processes and the underlying mechanisms will contribute to a better understanding of the relationship between brand and brand extensions. Such psychological answers will eventually pertain to the economic questions that marketers face when introducing new extensions.

ENDNOTES

1. Note that this assumption pertains to the likelihood of an inclusion but not to the size of the impact. Given an inclusion, the impact on subsequent judgments should increase the smaller the category.

REFERENCES

Aaker, D. A. (1991). *Managing brand equity: Capitalizing on the value of a brand name.* New York: Free Press.

Aaker, D. A., & Keller, K. L. (1990). Consumer evaluations of brand extensions. *Journal of Marketing, 54*(1), 27–41.

Adaval, R. (2003). How good gets better and bad gets worse: Understanding the impact of affect on evaluations of known brands. *Journal of Consumer Research, 30*(3), 352–367.

Ahluwalia, R. (forthcoming). How far can a brand stretch? Understanding the role of self-construal. *Journal of Marketing Research.*

Ahluwalia, R., & Gürhan-Canli, Z. (2000). The effects of extensions on the family brand name: An accessibility-diagnosticity perspective. *Journal of Consumer Research, 27*(3), 371–381.

Barone, M. J., Miniard, P. W., & Romeo, J. B. (2000). The influence of positive mood on brand extension evaluations. *Journal of Consumer Research, 26*(4), 386–400.

Barsalou, L. W. (1987). The instability of graded structure: Implications for the nature of concepts. In U. Neisser (Ed.), *Concepts and conceptual development: Ecological and intellectual factors in categorization* (pp. 101–140). New York, NY: Cambridge University Press.

Batra, R., & Stayman, D. M. (1990). The role of mood in advertising effectiveness. *Journal of Consumer Research, 17*(2), 203–214.

Biernat, M., Manis, M., & Nelson, T. E. (1991). Stereotypes and standards of judgment. *Journal of Personality and Social Psychology, 60*(4), 485–499.

Bless, H. (2001). The consequences of mood on the processing of social information. In A. Tesser & N. Schwarz (Eds.), *Blackwell handbook in social psychology* (pp. 391–412). Oxford, UK: Blackwell Publishers.

Bless, H., & Schwarz, N. (1998). Context effects in political judgement: Assimilation and contrast as a function of categorization processes. *European Journal of Social Psychology, 28*(2), 159–172.

Bless, H., Schwarz, N., Bodenhausen, G. V., & Thiel, L. (2001). Personalized versus generalized benefits of stereotype disconfirmation: Trade-offs in the evaluation of atypical exemplars and their social groups. *Journal of Experimental Social Psychology, 37*(5), 386–397.

Bless, H., Schwarz, N., & Wänke, M. (2003). The size of context effects in social judgment. In J. P. Forgas, K. D. Williams, & W. von Hippel (Eds.), *Social judgments: Implicit and explicit processes* (pp. 180–197). New York, NY: Cambridge University Press.

Bless, H., Schwarz, N., & Wieland, R. (1996). Mood and the impact of category membership and individuating information. *European Journal of Social Psychology, 26*(6), 935–959.

Bodenhausen, G. V. (1990). Stereotypes as judgmental heuristics: Evidence of circadian variations in discrimination. *Psychological Science, 1*(5), 319–322.

Bodenhausen, G. V., Kramer, G. P., & Süsser, K. (1994). Happiness and stereotypic thinking in social judgment. *Journal of Personality and Social Psychology, 66*(4), 621–632.

Boush, D. M. (1993). Brands as categories. In D. A. Aaker & A. Biel (Eds.), *Brand equity and advertising: Advertising's role in building strong brands* (pp. 299–312). Hillsdale, NJ: Erlbaum.

Boush, D. M., & Loken, B. (1991). A process-tracing study of brand extension evaluation. *Journal of Marketing Research, 28*(1), 16–28.

Brown, J. D., Novick, N. J., Lord, K. A., & Richards, J. M. (1992). When Gulliver travels: Social context, psychological closeness, and self-appraisals. *Journal of Personality and Social Psychology, 62*(5), 717–727.

Brown, T. J., & Dacin, P. A. (1997). The company and the product: Corporate associations and consumer product responses. *Journal of Marketing, 61*(1), 68–84.

De Chernatony, L., & McDonald, M. H. (1992). *Creating powerful brands.* Oxford: Butterworth-Heinemann.

Einwiller, S., Wänke, M., & Samochowiec, J. (2006). Unpublished data. FHNW Olten.

Fiske, S. T., Lin, M., & Neuberg, S. L. (1999). The continuum model: Ten years later. In S. Chaiken & Y. Trope (Eds.), *Dual-process theories in social psychology* (pp. 231–254). New York, NY: Guilford Press.

Fiske, S. T., & Neuberg, S. L. (1990). A continuum of impression formation from category-based to individuating processing: Influences of information and motivation on attention and interpretation. In M. P. Zanna (Ed.), *Advances in experimental social psychology* (Vol. 23, pp. 1–74). Orlando, FL: Academic Press.

Geiselman, R. E., Haight, N. A., & Kimata, L. G. (1984). Context effects on the perceived physical attractiveness of faces. *Journal of Experimental Social Psychology, 20*(5), 409–424.

Greifeneder, R., Bless, H., & Kuschmann, T. (2007). Extending the brand image on new products: The facilitative effect of happy mood states. *Journal of Consumer Behavior, 6*, 19–31.

Herr, P. M., Sherman, S. J., & Fazio, R. H. (1983). On the consequences of priming: Assimilation and contrast effects. *Journal of Experimental Social Psychology, 19*(4), 323–340.

Higgins, E. T. (1996). Knowledge activation: Accessibility, applicability, and salience. In E. T. Higgins & A. W. Kruglanski (Eds.), *Social psychology: Handbook of basic principles* (pp. 133–168). New York, NY: Guilford Press.

Higgins, E. T. (1998). Promotion and prevention: Regulatory focus as a motivational principle. In M. P. Zanna (Ed.), *Advances in experimental social psychology* (Vol. 30, pp. 1–46). San Diego, CA: Academic Press.

Hoyer, W. D., & Brown, S. P. (1990). Effects of brand awareness on choice for a common, repeat-purchase product. *Journal of Consumer Research, 17*(2), 141–148.

Isen, A. M., & Shalker, T. E. (1982). The effect of feeling state on evaluation of positive, neutral, and negative stimuli: When you "accentuate the positive," do you "eliminate the negative"? *Social Psychology Quarterly, 45*(1), 58–63.

Keller, K. L., & Aaker, D. A. (1992). The effects of sequential introduction of brand extensions. *Journal of Marketing Research, 29*(1), 35–50.

Keller, K. L., Heckler, S. E., & Houston, M. J. (1998). The effects of brand name suggestiveness on advertising recall. *Journal of Marketing, 62*(1), 48–57.

Kenrick, D. T., & Gutierres, S. E. (1980). Contrast effects and judgments of physical attractiveness: When beauty becomes a social problem. *Journal of Personality and Social Psychology, 38*(1), 131–140.

Klink, R. R., & Smith, D. C. (2001). Threats to the external validity of brand extension research. *Journal of Marketing Research, 38*(3), 326–335.

Krauth-Gruber, S., & Ric, F. (2000). Affect and stereotypic thinking: A test of the mood-and-general-knowledge-model. *Personality and Social Psychology Bulletin, 26*(12), 1587–1597.

Kruglanski, A. W., & Webster, D. M. (1996). Motivated closing of the mind: "Seizing" and "freezing." *Psychological Review, 103*(2), 263–283.

Kunda, Z., & Oleson, K. C. (1995). Maintaining stereotypes in the face of disconfirmation: Constructing grounds for subtyping deviants. *Journal of Personality and Social Psychology, 68*(4), 565–579.

Kunda, Z., & Oleson, K. C. (1997). When exceptions prove the rule: How extremity of deviance determines the impact of deviant examples on stereotypes. *Journal of Personality and Social Psychology, 72*(5), 965–979.

Liberman, N., Trope, Y., & Wakslak, C. (2007). Construal level theory and consumer behavior. *Journal of Consumer Psychology, 17*(2), 113–117.

Loken, B. (2006). Consumer psychology: Categorization, inferences, affect, and persuasion. *Annual Review of Psychology, 57*, 453–485.

Loken, B., & John, D. R. (1993). Diluting brand beliefs: When do brand extensions have a negative impact? *Journal of Marketing, 57*(3), 71–84.

Macrae, C. N., Stangor, C., & Milne, A. B. (1994). Activating social stereotypes: A functional analysis. *Journal of Experimental Social Psychology, 30*(4), 370–389.

Maheswaran, D. (1994). Country of origin as a stereotype: Effects of consumer expertise and attribute strength on product evaluations. *Journal of Consumer Research, 21*(2), 354–365.

Maheswaran, D., Mackie, D. M., & Chaiken, S. (1992). Brand name as a heuristic cue: The effects of task importance and expectancy confirmation on consumer judgments. *Journal of Consumer Psychology, 1*(4), 317–336.

Manis, M., Biernat, M., & Nelson, T. F. (1991). Comparison and expectancy processes in human judgment. *Journal of Personality and Social Psychology, 61*(2), 203–211.

Manis, M., & Paskewitz, J. R. (1984). Specificity in contrast effects: Judgments of psychopathology. Journal *of Experimental Social Psychology, 20*(3), 217–230.

Martin, L. L. (1986). Set/reset: Use and disuse of concepts in impression formation. *Journal of Personality and Social Psychology, 51*(3), 493–504.

Martin, L. L., & Achee, J. W. (1992). Beyond accessibility: The role of processing objectives in judgment. In L. L. Martin & A. Tesser (Eds.), *The construction of social judgments* (pp. 195–216). Hillsdale, NJ, England: Lawrence Erlbaum Associates, Inc.

Martin, L. L., & Clore, G. L. (2001). *Theories of mood and cognition: A user's guidebook.* Mahwah, NJ: Lawrence Erlbaum Associates, Publishers.

McClure, S. M., Li, J., Tomlin, D., Cypert, K. S., Montague, L. M., & Montague, P. R. (2004). Neural correlates of behavioral preference for culturally familiar drinks. *Neuron, 44*, 379–387.

Medin, D. L. (1989). Concepts and conceptual structure. *American Psychologist, 44*(12), 1469–1481.

Milberg, S. J., Park, C. W., & McCarthy, M. S. (1997). Managing negative feedback effects associated with brand extensions: The impact of alternative branding strategies. *Journal of Consumer Psychology, 6*(2), 119–140.

Monga, A. B., & John, D. R. (2007). Cultural differences in brand extension evaluation: The influence of analytic versus holistic thinking. *Journal of Consumer Research, 33*(4), 529–536.

Morrin, M. (1999). The impact of brand extensions on parent brand memory structures and retrieval processes. *Journal of Marketing Research, 36*(4), 517–525.

Neuberg, S. L., & Fiske, S. T. (1987). Motivational influences on impression formation: Outcome dependency, accuracy-driven attention, and individuating processes. *Journal of Personality and Social Psychology, 53*(3), 431–444.

Park, C. W., Jaworski, B. J., & MacInnis, D. J. (1986). Strategic brand concept-image management. *Journal of Marketing, 50*(4), 135–145.

Park, C. W., McCarthy, M., & Milberg, S. (1993). The effects associated with direct and associative brand extension strategies on consumer response to brand extensions. *Advances in Consumer Research, 20*, 28–33.

Park, C. W., Milberg, S., & Lawson, R. (1991). Evaluation of brand extensions: The role of product feature similarity and brand concept consistency. *Journal of Consumer Research, 18*(2), 185–193.

Rangaswamy, A., Burke, R., & Oliva, T. A. (1993). Brand equity and the extendibility of brand names. *International Journal of Research in Marketing, 10*, 61–75.

Romeo, J. B. (1991). The effect of negative information on the evaluations of brand extensions and the family brand. *Advances in Consumer Research, 18*, 399–406.

Rosch, E. (1978). Principles of categorization. In E. Rosch & B. B. Lloyd (Eds.), *Cognition and categorization* (pp. 27–48). Hillsdale, NJ: Lawrence Erlbaum Associates.

Sanbonmatsu, D. M., & Fazio, R. H. (1990). The role of attitudes in memory-based decision making. *Journal of Personality and Social Psychology, 59*(4), 614–622.

Schwarz, N., & Bless, H. (1992a). Constructing reality and its alternatives: An inclusion/exclusion model of assimilation and contrast effects in social judgment. In L. L. Martin & A. Tesser (Eds.), *The construction of social judgments* (pp. 217–245). Hillsdale, NJ, England: Lawrence Erlbaum Associates, Inc.

Schwarz, N., & Bless, H. (1992b). Scandals and the public's trust in politicians: Assimilation and contrast effects. *Personality and Social Psychology Bulletin, 18*(5), 574–579.

Schwarz, N., & Bless, H. (2007). Mental construal processes: The inclusion/exclusion model. In D. A. Stapel & J. Suls (Eds.), *Assimilation and contrast in social psychology* (pp. 119–141). New York: Psychology Press.

Shavitt, S., & Wänke, M. (2001). Consumer behavior. In A. Tesser & N. Schwarz (Eds.), *Blackwell handbook of social psychology* (Vol. 1: Intrapersonal Processes, pp. 569–590). Oxford: Blackwell.

Smith, E. E. (1990). Categorization. In D. N. Osherson & E. E. Smith (Eds.), *Thinking: An invitation to cognitive science*, Vol. 3 (pp. 33–53). Cambridge, MA, U.S.: The MIT Press.

Strack, F., Schwarz, N., Bless, H., Kübler, A., & Wänke, M. (1993). Awareness of the influence as a determinant of assimilation versus contrast. *European Journal of Social Psychology, 23*(1), 53–62.

Vašek, T. (2002). Brand stretching. *McK Wissen, 3,* 72–75.

Wänke, M., Bless, H., & Igou, E. R. (2001). Next to a star: Paling, shining, or both? Turning interexemplar contrast into interexemplar assimilation. *Personality and Social Psychology Bulletin, 27*(1), 14–29.

Wänke, M., Bless, H., & Schwarz, N. (1998). Context effects in product line extensions: Context is not destiny. *Journal of Consumer Psychology, 7*(4), 299–322.

Weber, R., & Crocker, J. (1983). Cognitive processes in the revision of stereotypic beliefs. *Journal of Personality and Social Psychology, 45*(5), 961–977.

Wyer, R. S. J., & Srull, T. K. (1989). *Memory and cognition in its social context.* Hillsdale, NJ, England: Lawrence Erlbaum Associates.

Yeo, J., & Park, J. (2006). Effects of parent-extension similarity and self regulatory focus on evaluations of brand extensions. *Journal of Consumer Psychology, 16*(3), 272–282.

Yeung, C. W. M., & Wyer, R. S., Jr. (2005). Does loving a brand mean loving its products? The role of brand-elicited affect in brand extension evaluations. *Journal of Marketing Research, 42*(4), 495–506.

Yzerbyt, V. Y., Coull, A., & Rocher, S. J. (1999). Fencing off the deviant: The role of cognitive resources in the maintenance of stereotypes. *Journal of Personality and Social Psychology, 77*(3), 449–462.

6

Compensatory Reasoning in Choice

ALEXANDER CHERNEV and RYAN HAMILTON

"Every excess causes a defect; every defect an excess. … For everything you have missed, you have gained something else; and for everything you gain, you lose something."

Ralph Waldo Emerson, Compensation

*T*he term *compensation* is commonly used in reference to the process of offsetting a deficiency or disadvantage in one area by emphasizing a strength or advantage in another. Despite its use in a wide variety of research, compensation as an inference-making mechanism has received surprisingly little attention in the literature. This chapter fills this void by introducing the notion of compensation to inferential reasoning and investigating its antecedents and consequences.

The discussion of compensatory processes in inferential reasoning is organized as follows. We begin by offering an overview of the existing research on compensation in psychology and decision making, underscoring the common pattern of compensation across different domains. We then examine the role of compensatory reasoning in context of the previously identified means of inferential reasoning. In this section, we define the unique properties of compensatory reasoning, outline its underlying processes, and identify the common scenarios in which compensatory reasoning is most likely to occur. We further identify the key domains of compensatory reasoning and document the role of compensatory inferences in consumer decision making and choice. We conclude by identifying the key boundary conditions of compensatory reasoning.

THE CONCEPT OF COMPENSATION

Based on its focus and underlying processes, we distinguish two types of compensation: self-regulatory, which deals with compensation directed toward the self, and evaluative, which deals with compensation that is not directly related to self-regulation. These two types of compensation are discussed in more detail in the following sections.

Self-Regulatory Compensation

Self-regulatory compensation includes the psychological and behavioral mechanisms by which an individual attempts to make up for some negative internal or external event by creating a positive change in the self. Self-regulatory compensation processes can be observed in five distinct domains: physiological compensation, cognitive compensation, affective compensation, self-completion compensation, and behavioral compensation.

Physiological Compensation   Physiological compensation refers to adaptations individuals make in response to physical handicaps. Researchers have found that individuals tend to overcome sensory handicaps by developing extraordinary sensitivity in a different ensory modality (e.g., Adler, 1924; James, 1918). The prototypical example invol s the development of more sensitive hearing by a blind person to compensate for the lack of sight (Witkin, Oltman, Chase, & Freidman, 1971).

Evidence for physiological compensation has also been found within the same sensory modality. Research on neural plasticity in recovery from brain injury includes cases where functionality is restored through a physical "rewiring" of the brain (e.g., Fraser et al., 2002). In this context, the brain of the injured individual compensates for the loss of function caused by the damaged neuronal tissue by blazing new neural pathways through other, undamaged areas of the brain.

Cognitive Compensation   Cognitive compensation involves overcoming deficiencies in cognitive abilities, including attention, perception, and memory. To illustrate, research on aging has shown that aging can negatively impact some of the specific skills associated with a task, such as recall and reaction time, without influencing the overall task performance (Charness, 1981; Salthouse, 1984). In this context, it has been argued that older participants can often compensate for the decline in specific abilities by developing new skills such as better global evaluations or more accurate anticipation, which allow them to maintain overall performance levels.

In addition to cognitive compensation caused by the deterioration of cognitive skills, compensation has also been documented in the area of learning disabilities. It has been shown that individuals with a learning disability in a particular domain can develop extraordinary ability on some other dimension. For instance, individuals with a learning disability impeding written and verbal communications might develop the ability for self-expression using such alternative means as painting and music (Schulman, 1986).

Affective Compensation   Affective compensation involves the self-regulatory processes that enhance positive emotions in the presence of negative emotions. To illustrate, it has been shown that individuals who have suffered a life-altering negative event, such as serious physical handicap, incarceration, or the loss of a loved one, tend to recover their well-being remarkably quickly (Frederick & Loewenstein, 1999). This finding has been attributed to the fact that these individuals often compensate for the traumatic negative events by focusing on other, more positive areas of their lives. In this context, research on bereavement has documented that the loss of a spouse is often accompanied by increased interaction with friends and relatives (Wan & Odell, 1983) and the development of new social networks that might include involvement in religious activities or voluntary associations (Ferraro & Barresi, 1982).

Compensation in Symbolic Self-Completion   Self-completion compensation reflects an individual's attempt to attenuate a discrepancy between a desired and a perceived self-image by displaying external artifacts associated with this self-image. For example, it has been shown that business students with less experience are more likely to compensate for this shortcoming by wearing business attire (Wicklund & Gollwitzer, 1982).

Self-completion compensation can also be observed during mid-life crisis, a time marked by an increased salience of one's age and mortality (Hermans & Oles, 1999). In this case, individuals compensate for the loss of youthfulness and vigor by acquiring conspicuous outward symbols of youth and vitality—sports cars, cosmetic procedures, and much younger romantic partners.

Self-completion compensation can also result from momentary psychological states. For example, it has been shown that when faced with a threat to their self-image, individuals tend to display stronger preferences for self-expressive brands (Chernev & Gal, 2008a). Similarly, it has been documented that psychological states of powerlessness increase consumers' willingness to pay for status-related objects as a means of restoring their lost sense of power (Rucker and Galinsky, 2008).

Behavioral Compensation   Compensation can also involve adjustments to behavior in response to changes in the external environment. To illustrate, it has been shown that individuals respond in compensatory fashion to changes in environmental risk levels (Hedlund, 2000). Thus, people take additional precautions when they perceive their risk to have increased (e.g., walking slower on an icy sidewalk) and engage in riskier behavior when external changes reduce the risk of certain activities (e.g., driving more recklessly in a car known to be equipped with anti-lock brakes).

In addition, individuals have been found to engage in behavioral compensation when faced with choices that involve making a tradeoff between goals. Thus, it has been shown that a decision that favors one goal over another (e.g., ordering a tasty, high-calorie entrée, thereby sacrificing the goal of being healthy in order to satisfy the goal of eating something delicious) is likely to be followed by a decision that restores the goal balance (e.g., opting for a more healthful but less tasty dessert), a behavioral phenomenon referred to as "balancing" (Chernev & Gal, 2008b; Dhar & Simonson, 1999).

Note that behavioral compensation, unlike other types of self-regulatory compensation, can be both positive (compensating for a deficiency) and negative (compensating for an excess). For example, an individual with a certain level of risk tolerance might not only compensate for an excess of risk by engaging in less risky behavior but might also engage in more risky behavior if an activity becomes sufficiently safe. In contrast, other types of self-regulatory compensation tend to be predominantly positive, allowing an individual to overcome a deficiency.

Evaluative Compensation

Research in judgment and decision making has identified other areas of compensation beyond self-regulation. Evaluative compensation involves judgments of external objects or events that are evaluated in a compensatory manner. Two types of evaluative compensation can be identified: compensation in decision processes and compensation in inferential reasoning.

In decision processes, compensation refers to the ability of an option's strength on one attribute to make up for a deficiency on another (Johnson & Meyer, 1984; Payne, Bettman, & Johnson, 1993). Two types of decision strategies can be distinguished: compensatory and noncompensatory. Compensatory strategies, part of most multiattribute utility models (Keeney & Raiffa, 1976), allow an option's strong performance on one attribute to compensate for its poor performance on another. Compensatory processes require explicit tradeoffs among attributes (Bettman, Luce, & Payne, 1998). In contrast, for noncompensatory strategies, such as elimination-by-aspects (Tversky, 1972), a deficiency on a particular attribute eliminates an option from further consideration regardless of its performance on other attributes. Noncompensatory processes allow decision makers to avoid making explicit tradeoffs by simply removing options with poor values from the consideration set.

In inferential reasoning, compensation refers to certain processes used to draw inferences about unavailable or ambiguous information. In this context, the term *compensatory reasoning* refers to a specific inference-making mechanism that is based on individuals' intuition regarding the relative attractiveness of alternatives in a given choice set. The role of compensation in inferential reasoning is discussed in more detail in the following section.

COMPENSATORY PROCESSES IN INFERENTIAL REASONING

This section examines compensation as a specific form of inferential reasoning and outlines the key domains in which compensatory reasoning commonly occurs.

Inferential Reasoning in Individual Decision Making

Building on the existing research on inferential reasoning (Broniarczyk & Alba, 1994; Ford & Smith, 1987; Huber & McCann, 1982), in this section, we focus on two of the most common types of inferential reasoning: evaluative consistency inferences (or the "halo effect") and inferences based on perceived covariation.

Research in social psychology has shown that individuals rarely think of others in mixed terms; instead they tend to see them as consistent across domains. Thus, it has been shown that the first traits individuals recognize in other people influence the interpretation and perception of later ones (e.g., Kelly, 1955; Schneider, 1973)—a phenomenon also referred to as the "halo effect" (Nisbett & Wilson, 1977; Cooper, 1981; see also Ajzen, 1977). For example, it has been shown that attractive people are often judged as having a more desirable personality and a better skill set than people of average appearance (Asch, 1946).

Consistent with findings in social psychology, research in the area of consumer judgment and choice also has shown that individuals may form overall evaluations for each option on the basis of the available information and use these evaluations to infer the unobservable information (Beckwith & Lehmann, 1975; Dick, Chakravarti, & Biehal, 1990). According to this evaluative consistency strategy, the option that is superior on the observable attributes will be inferred to be superior on unobservable attributes as well.

Covariation-based inferences involve assuming that an option's true value on an unavailable or ambiguous attribute is related to its performance on one of the observable attributes. Consistent with this type of inference, the option that is superior on the believed-to-be-correlated attribute will be inferred to be superior on the unobservable attribute. Typical covariation patterns documented in prior research involve pairs of particular factors such as price and quality (Bettman, John, & Scott, 1986), brand name and quality (Janiszewski & Van Osselaer, 2000), and reliability and warranty (Dick, Chakravarti, & Biehal, 1990). To illustrate, individuals might believe that higher quality products are also more expensive (Lichtenstein & Burton, 1989), that higher priced products are likely to perform better on nonprice attributes (Huber & McCann, 1982), and that more reliable products are likely to offer a longer warranty (Broniarczyk & Alba, 1994).

Both evaluative consistency inferences and inferences based on covariation are derived from the assumption that individuals strive for consistency when evaluating missing or ambiguous information. In contrast, the compensatory reasoning approach implies that inferences do not always need to be consistent with the readily available information and that in certain conditions can lead to directionally opposite outcomes. The rationale for these predictions is outlined in more detail in the following sections.

Compensatory Reasoning as an Inferential Process

Recent evidence suggests that in addition to evaluative consistency and covariation of attributes, individuals may also engage in compensatory reasoning to infer incomplete information. In this case, compensatory reasoning is typically driven by a discrepancy between the expected and observed performance of decision alternatives. In particular, compensatory inferences are drawn in scenarios in which individuals who expect options in a given choice set to be balanced in their overall attractiveness are presented with a set in which one option is significantly less (or more) attractive. In this context, compensatory reasoning involves processes used to infer unavailable or ambiguous information, such that an option's deficiency on one dimension is compensated for by high values on another, and vice versa.

To illustrate, imagine the sales listings for two similar houses. The listings reveal some information about each house, such as price and size, but also leave out some information. If one of the listings was clearly superior on the available information (e.g., a bigger house at a lower price), an individual using compensatory reasoning might infer that this house would be inferior on some of the unavailable information (e.g., located in a bad neighborhood or in need of repairs).

Conceptually, the discrepancy between the intuitively expected and actually observed dispersion of options' performance can lead to negative or positive compensation. Negative compensation involves a scenario in which individuals who expect the overall performance to be balanced across all options are presented with a set in which one option dominates the others (e.g., three cars of the same make, model and year, but one is priced significantly lower). In contrast, positive compensation involves a scenario in which individuals who expect the overall performance to be balanced across all options are presented with a set in which one option is inferior to the others (e.g., three similar cars, but one is priced significantly higher). Unlike negative compensation, which involves devaluing the ostensibly more attractive option, positive compensation involves enhancing the performance of an ostensibly unattractive option. Note that despite the difference in direction (enhancement vs. devaluation), both negative and positive compensation aim to resolve the discrepancy between the observed and expected information, thus leading to the same outcome, which involves balancing the overall performance of choice options.

Compensatory reasoning can be better understood when contrasted with evaluative consistency and covariation-based inferences. Recall that evaluative consistency inferences are based on the assumption of imbalance, such that an option that is partially good must be all good and an option that is partially bad must be all bad. The evaluative-consistency strategy is, therefore, directionally opposite to compensatory inferences. Thus, unlike an individual who makes evaluative consistency inferences, an individual who employs a compensatory strategy will infer that an option that is dominant on observable attributes is inferior on unobservable attributes.

Compensatory inferences can also be contrasted with inferences based on observed covariation between attributes. Unlike inferences based on perceived covariation, in which an option's performance on a particular attribute is based on previously observed covariation with other attributes, compensatory inferences derive an option's values from the decision context defined by the other alternatives in the set. These context-based compensatory inferences stem from an individual's belief that options in a given choice set are balanced in a way that advantages on one dimension are compensated for by disadvantages on another, even in the absence of prior attribute-specific covariation beliefs. Thus, an option that excels on a particular attribute can be inferred to be inferior on some of the other attributes simply based on the belief that the overall performance of options in the choice set must be balanced.

Compensatory Decision Processes

There are three common contexts in which individuals are likely to draw compensatory inferences: (1) when evaluating ambiguous information, (2) when inferring missing values of readily identified attributes, and (3) when inferring options' values on attributes that are not identified at the time of the decision. These three types of compensatory reasoning strategies are outlined in more detail below.

Compensatory Reasoning in Evaluating Ambiguous Information

Individuals are often presented with decisions in which options are described on attributes that involve a certain level of ambiguity about their relative performance. For example, descriptors like a PanaBlack screen (Panasonic) and Smart Picture (Magnavox) are used to communicate the quality of a television screen, and ingredients such as Fluoristat (Crest) and Triclene (Aquafresh) are used to differentiate competitive brands of toothpaste. Similarly, many products are described in qualitative terms, such as color protection and stain-removal characteristics of a laundry detergent, which makes evaluating the relative performance of these options difficult. When unfamiliar with the precise meaning of product characteristics, individuals are uncertain about whether choice alternatives in fact vary in their performance on these attributes and which option has higher utility. Faced with a discrepancy between the intuitively expected and the actually observed information, individuals tend to strategically use the ambiguity in product descriptions to draw inferences that compensate for the observed discrepancies (Chernev, 2007). Consider a consumer who is evaluating the (ambiguous) claims of color protection made by two equally priced laundry detergents. If one of these detergents also claims to be superior on some other attribute (e.g., stain removal), consumers might draw compensatory inferences and conclude that this detergent's color protection is not as good.

Compensatory Reasoning in Inferring Missing Values of Readily Identified Attributes

Individuals often must make decisions in situations when some of the relevant information is not readily available for all options (Kivetz & Simonson, 2000). To illustrate, an individual choosing a wireless service provider could have a well-defined list of attributes that are important in making a decision. However, values on each of these attributes might not be readily available for all service providers (e.g., information on coverage area might be easily assessable for some providers but not others). In cases when one of the options is clearly inferior (superior) based on the available information, compensatory reasoning is likely to lead to inferences about the missing attribute values in a way that benefits (detracts from) the option inferior (superior) on the observable attributes, thus balancing the overall performance of the options.

Compensatory Reasoning in Inferring Missing Attribute Dimensions

In addition to making inferences about the performance of options on readily available attributes, individuals often make inferences about the presence of attributes on which option performance will vary in a way that resolves the observed discrepancy. To illustrate, when presented with a choice set in which one option clearly dominates the others, individuals who expect options to be balanced in their overall performance are likely to assume the presence of an unobservable attribute on which this option is deficient (Chernev & Carpenter, 2001). Thus, individuals might resolve the discrepancy between the observed and expected information by making inferences about attributes that are not readily available at the time of the decision. For example, an individual who observes two equally priced wireless service plans, one of which dominates on the observable attributes, may infer the presence of an unobserved attribute—such as customer service, reliability, or nondisclosed fees—on which the apparently dominant plan is inferior.

Domains of Compensatory Reasoning

Individuals rely on compensatory reasoning to make judgments in a variety of domains. Some of the most common scenarios in which compensatory inferences are drawn involve social perception, making probabilistic judgments, and evaluating product performance in consumer choice. These types of inferences are discussed in the following sections.

Compensation in Social Perception   Individuals very often must make inferences about the traits, skills, and abilities of others. Compensation in social inference making is based on the assumption that if a person shows some exceptional skill or ability on one dimension, he or she is likely deficient on some other dimension. These inferences could be based on a naïve capacity theory, which assumes that people have a finite amount of skills, abilities, or talent. The implication is that exceptional ability in one domain must leave less ability to be distributed across other domains. For example, an individual who excels on some easily observable dimension, such as physical attractiveness or athletic prowess, may be assumed to be deficient on some less easily observed dimension, such as intelligence or kindness.

Compensation in social perception is also revealed in inferences based on the inherent belief that the world is ultimately just and fair (Lerner, 1980). As a result of this belief, people are often motivated to infer that observable positive or negative attributes are offset by some counterbalancing factors. Thus, "the poor" may be perceived of as happy and honest, while "the rich" are seen as miserable and dishonest (Kay & Jost, 2003). Likewise, stereotypes that are high in warmth tend to be low in competence, and vice versa (e.g., Fiske, Xu, Cuddy, & Glick, 1999). Other common examples of stereotypes that excel on one dimension while being deficient on another include the "dumb blonde" (high physical attractiveness balanced by low intelligence), the "absent-minded professor" (high intelligence balanced by low common sense or poor memory), and the "shy bookworm" (high intelligence balanced by weak social skills).

Compensation in Probabilistic Judgment   In making judgments about the likelihood of randomly generated events, it is common for people to act as if future outcomes can compensate for past events in the same series. The application of this type of compensatory reasoning to probabilistic judgment can result in a bias known as the "gambler's fallacy." Gambler's fallacy involves the belief that a random event is more likely to occur because it has not happened for a period of time. An example of this fallacy is the commonly held belief that if a series of spins on a roulette wheel has resulted in a string of reds, then black is "due" and hence, a better bet. In this context, future events are viewed as a self-correcting process in which deviation in one direction leads to deviation in the opposite direction to restore the underlying equilibrium (Tversky & Kahneman, 1974).

Compensatory reasoning in probabilistic judgments can be contrasted with the notion of regression toward the mean, introduced by Galton (1886) to describe the general tendency for multiple draws of a random variable to converge on the mean. Although conceptually similar to compensatory reasoning, regression toward the mean describes a naturally occurring phenomenon rather than a pattern in an individual's reasoning processes. Furthermore, unlike compensatory reasoning, which has been used to account for observed inferences that individuals make, regression toward the mean often has been shown *not* to influence individuals' decision making, even when it should (Tversky & Kahneman, 1974).

In addition to social perception and probabilistic judgment, compensatory reasoning also can be applied to inferences made by consumers in the presence of unavailable or missing information. Compensatory reasoning processes in consumer decision making are discussed in more detail in the following section.

COMPENSATORY REASONING IN CONSUMER DECISION MAKING

The discussion of compensatory reasoning in choice revolves around two main issues: the market-efficiency assumption in compensatory reasoning and compensatory reasoning effects in consumer choice.

The Market Efficiency Assumption in Compensatory Reasoning

Compensatory inferences are typically drawn in the presence of a discrepancy between the observed performance of decision alternatives and an individual's belief that options in the choice set should be balanced in their overall performance. In consumer choice, this assumption of balance is often based on the notion of market efficiency. The market-efficiency assumption reflects an individual's belief that offerings are priced at value parity, such that the benefit-cost tradeoffs are constant across options (Chernev & Carpenter, 2001). Thus, in highly efficient markets, the ratio of benefits and costs is constant, such that all offerings are value-equivalent: Higher priced products are also of better quality, and vice versa. In less efficient markets, individuals expect less value parity and a greater dispersion of total benefits at a given price. When presented with scenarios in which options are not at value parity (e.g., one of the options dominates all others), individuals who expect the market to be efficient are likely to draw inferences that compensate for the observed discrepancy and restore the value parity across options.

From a conceptual standpoint, market-efficiency compensatory reasoning can be thought of as two-stage price–quality inferences. Most of the existing research (Huber & McCann, 1982; Johnson & Levin, 1985) has treated the price–quality relationship as a one-stage process in which individuals infer missing quality information on the basis of the observable price, or vice versa. In contrast, inferences based on market efficiency occur in a scenario in which individuals infer relative performance of options on a given nonprice attribute according to options' performance on the other nonprice attributes. In this case, individuals base their inferences not simply on the price–quality relationship but rather on their expectations of the dispersion of the value offered by the options in the choice set. Thus, in a market perceived to be efficient, individuals faced with a set of equally priced options are likely to make an inference that these options should offer equal benefits. Individuals then use this inferred performance parity to make an inference about the unobservable attribute. When one of the options is superior on the observable attributes, individuals are faced with an inconsistency between the observed and the expected information. In an attempt to restore balance to the perceived value of the alternatives, individuals may infer that the observably superior option is inferior on the unobservable attribute (Chernev & Carpenter, 2001).

Compensatory Reasoning Effects

Building on prior research, we identify three types of compensatory effects: (1) compensatory inferences associated with evaluating a single option on a particular attribute, (2) compensatory inferences in evaluating the relative performance of multiple options, and (3) compensatory inferences associated with evaluating all-in-one and specialized options. These three types of compensatory effects are discussed in more detail in the following sections.

Compensatory Reasoning in Evaluating Attribute Performance of a Single Option   Individuals often have to infer a single option's performance on an unobservable or ambiguous attribute based on the information about this option's performance on another attribute. In this case, compensatory inferences are based on the available information about this option's performance, as well as on individuals' beliefs about the typical dispersion of these attributes in different options in the market. Thus, when faced with an option with an extreme value on one attribute, individuals who expect options to be at value parity might infer that this option is likely to be deficient on at least one of the other attributes. These inferences can lead to both negative compensation (when the option is relatively attractive) and positive compensation (when the option is relatively unattractive).

The belief that consumers are likely to use compensatory reasoning to infer overall performance when faced with an option with extreme values is quite common among managers. Thus, a common marketing strategy involves positioning an option as inferior on a particular (typically irrelevant) attribute. To illustrate, Smuckers argues that its awkward-sounding name is, in fact, an indication of the quality of its products: "With a name like Smuckers, it has to be good." In the same vein, Listerine argues that its unattractive taste is an indication of the effectiveness of its mouthwash: "If it did not taste so strong it would not be working. Listerine has the taste people hate." The NO-AD brand of sunscreen implies that because it is not advertised it is able to provide a better product/value to consumers. The rationale for this strategy is the compensatory belief that an option's inferiority on a particular (typically irrelevant) attribute must be compensated by superiority on another (typically more important) attribute. The effectiveness of this strategy has been partially supported by prior research, which has demonstrated that adding an unattractive feature can actually increase an option's purchase likelihood (Simonson, Carmon, & O'Curry, 1994). For example, it has been shown that adding a negligible negative feature (e.g., a scratch on the side panel of a television) can increase the offering's overall attractiveness in cases when a product is priced below the market price.

Compensatory Reasoning in Evaluating the Relative Performance of Multiple Options   Individuals are often faced with multiple decision alternatives that share an unobservable or ambiguous attribute. In this case, they draw inferences about the relative performance of options on the unobservable attribute based on the observed dispersion of their performance and already formed expectations about the relationship between products and/or product attributes. Thus, prior research has shown that when given a decision set in which one of the options dominates the others on all observable attributes, individuals drawing a compensatory inference are likely to infer that this alternative is deficient on an attribute whose values are unknown or ambiguous (Chernev & Carpenter, 2001). It has further been documented that individuals can draw such compensatory inferences even in the absence of well-established beliefs about the likely dispersion of options' performance in the market by implicitly learning the dispersion pattern of performance in sets for which it is readily observable.

Compensatory Reasoning in Evaluating the Relative Performance of Specialized and All-in-One Options   The compensatory reasoning paradigm also can be applied to consumer evaluations of specialized and all-in-one options (Chernev, 2007). Here the term *specialized* is used in reference to options described by a single attribute, whereas the term *all-in-one* is used for options that are described by a combination of attributes. Compensatory reasoning effects in evaluating specialized and all-in-one options can be illustrated as follows. Consider a set of three alternatives, each described on two attributes: Specialized option A is differentiated by the first attribute (e.g., cavity-prevention toothpaste), specialized option B is differentiated by the second attribute (e.g., tartar-protection toothpaste), and the all-in-one option C is differentiated by both attributes (e.g., cavity-prevention and tartar-protection toothpaste).

Consistent with the compensatory reasoning theory, it has been shown that individuals are likely to equate the overall attractiveness of these options, devaluing performance on some of the attributes while enhancing performance on others (Chernev, 2007). In particular, the all-in-one option tends to be devalued, such that the perceived performance of the attributes differentiating this option will decrease in the presence of options specialized on these attributes. In addition to discounting the performance of the all-in-one option, individuals also draw inferences about the specialized options. In particular, the perceived performance of the differentiating attribute of a specialized option (i.e., cavity-prevention functionality of toothpaste A) tends to increase in the presence of an all-in-one option. At the same time, the performance of specialized options on their secondary attributes (i.e., tartar-protection functionality of toothpaste A) tends to be devalued in the presence of an all-in-one option. Thus, compensatory reasoning has been shown to produce two types of effects when evaluating specialized and all-in-one options: compensatory devaluation, which lowers the perceived performance of the all-in-one option, and compensatory polarization, which enhances the perceived performance of the specialized option on the differentiating attribute while detracting from its performance on the secondary attribute(s).

BOUNDARIES OF COMPENSATORY REASONING

So far we have argued that in the presence of a discrepancy between the observed performance of decision alternatives, individuals might draw compensatory inferences that resolve this discrepancy. Not all discrepancies, however, lead to compensatory inferences. Therefore, an important issue involves identifying conditions under which individuals are likely to draw compensatory inferences. In this section we offer a brief overview of four key factors that are likely to influence individuals' reliance on compensatory reasoning in choice.

Assumption of Balance

The key assumption underlying compensatory reasoning is the belief that the overall performance of the objects under consideration is balanced, such that an option's superiority on one attribute is compensated for by inferiority on another. To illustrate, the efficient-market assumption, which implies balance in options' overall attractiveness (i.e., equally priced options should have similar performance) is a common precondition for compensatory inferences to occur in a market setting (Chernev & Carpenter, 2001).

The assumption of balance in compensatory reasoning is referred to as the zero-sum heuristic (Chernev, 2007). The zero-sum heuristic can be related to the zero-sum game assumption in game theory, which implies that the wins and losses in a game will add up to zero for each possible set of strategies (Von Neumann & Morgenstern, 1953). In other words, the zero-sum game assumption implies that one player's winnings should equal the other player's losses. The concept of the zero-sum heuristic is conceptually similar to that of a zero-sum game in that it implies a closed system in which all options are balanced in value, with the relative advantage of each option on one attribute compensated for by a disadvantage on another.

The zero-sum heuristic can also be related to the notion of tradeoff consistency (Simonson & Tversky, 1992). The tradeoff consistency of a given choice set is usually characterized by the rate of exchange between attributes, such that in sets with a constant rate of exchange between attributes the advantages and disadvantages of each option are balanced. In this context, the zero-sum heuristic posits that when evaluating sets comprising options with varying rates of exchange between attributes, individuals who expect a balanced set of options are likely to interpret ambiguous attribute values in a way that decreases the observed tradeoff contrasts and equates the rate of exchange across attributes.

Availability of Other Bases for Inference

It has been shown that when individuals have established beliefs that some of the product attributes are correlated (e.g., the relationship between size and weight, and between reliability and warranty), this correlation tends to supersede individuals' market efficiency beliefs (Chernev & Carpenter, 2001). Given that compensatory inferences involve a rather complex process that requires individuals to form overall evaluations of choice alternatives and contrast these evaluations with their prior beliefs about the dispersion of the overall performance of options in the choice set, inferences with a simpler structure, such as inferences based on simple attribute correlations, are likely to impede the occurrence of compensatory inferences.

Resource Availability

Because compensatory inferences involve a relatively complex evaluation process and require more effort and cognitive resources on the part of the individuals, they are less likely to occur when individuals have constrained resources (e.g., time pressure, parallel decision tasks, and distractions). Indeed, under constrained resources, individuals are more likely to use simplifying decision strategies and noncompensatory rather than compensatory rules (Payne, Bettman, & Johnson, 1993). Likewise, compensatory inferences are less likely to occur when individuals have constrained cognitive resources.

Information-Processing Strategy

Prior research in the area of decision making has identified two distinct information-processing strategies: alternative-based and attribute-based (Payne, Bettman, & Johnson, 1993). Alternative-based (or holistic) information processing involves first forming overall evaluations of choice alternatives, which are then compared to one another. In contrast, attribute-based (or dimensional) information processing involves evaluating options' performance on each of the available attributes without necessarily forming an initial overall impression of each alternative. Because they imply forming an overall evaluation of the choice options, alternative-based strategies tend to be more effortful and resource demanding compared to attribute-based strategies, which often lead to more selective information processing. Given that compensatory inferences typically require overall option evaluations in order to generate value-based comparisons of the alternatives, it can be argued that compensatory inferences are a function of the information-processing strategy used in choice, such that compensatory inferences are less likely to occur in the context of attribute-based than alternative-based evaluations.

CONCLUSION

The concept of compensation has been used in psychology, decision making, and inferential reasoning in different contexts. In psychology, the term *compensation* refers to a mechanism by which an individual makes up for some personal deficiency by developing another ability. In decision research, the term *compensation* has been used in reference to the decision processes underlying an individual's choice, particularly the ability of an option's strength on one attribute to make up for a deficiency on another attribute. Although the idea of compensation has informed research in several diverse areas, it has received relatively little attention in the domain of inference making. In this chapter, we focused on compensatory processes in inferential reasoning and offered a theoretical background for understanding compensatory reasoning processes in individual decision making and choice.

From a conceptual standpoint, compensatory reasoning involves decision processes used to draw inferences about options' performance on dimensions that are ambiguous or unknown. In this context, compensatory inferences stem from the assumption of balance, which implies that in a given choice set, overall performance of options tends to be balanced, such that advantages on one dimension are likely to be compensated for by disadvantages on another. Thus, when faced with a scenario in which decision alternatives vary in their overall performance, individuals who expect options' performance to be balanced, are likely to infer that advantages (disadvantages) on one dimension are likely to be compensated for by disadvantages (advantages) on another.

The zero-sum heuristic highlighted in this chapter contributed to the understanding of a variety of compensatory processes in social psychology and decision making. It can be applied to the relationship across attribute performance of a particular option such that high values on one dimension imply low values on another. It can also be applied to the relationship across options in a given set such that options that dominate others in their overall performance are inferred to be inferior on some of the unobserved/ambiguous dimensions. Finally, the zero-sum heuristic can be applied to phenomena that occur across time when random events are expected to be more likely to occur when they have not happened for a period of time.

Understanding the nature of compensatory reasoning also implies identifying its boundary conditions. Indeed, not every decision in which individuals are presented with a discrepancy between the observed and expected performance of choice alternatives leads to compensatory reasoning. We have identified several factors that are likely to moderate the occurrence and strength of compensatory reasoning—such as the assumption of balance, the availability of other bases for drawing inferences, availability of cognitive resources to draw compensatory inferences, and the degree to which the information-processing involves overall evaluations of decision alternatives. Investigating these factors as well as uncovering new ones offers a promising venue for further research that will shed light on the psychological mechanism underlying compensatory reasoning.

The evidence for compensatory reasoning in consumer choice is just beginning to accumulate. Given the importance of dealing with ambiguous and incomplete information in everyday judgments and evaluations, continued research on compensatory reasoning promises to expand our understanding of the mechanisms by which people make decisions in real-world scenarios.

REFERENCES

Adler, A. (1924). The practice and theory of individual psychology (2nd Ed. Rev.). City: Publisher.

Ajzen, I. (1977). Intuitive theories of events and the effects of base-rate information on prediction. *Journal of Personality and Social Psychology, 35*(5), 303–314.

Asch, S. E. (1946). Forming impressions of personality. *Journal of Abnormal and Social Psychology, 41*, 258–290.

Beckwith, N. E., & Lehmann, D. R. (1975). The importance of halo effects in multi-attribute attitude models. *Journal of Marketing Research, 12*(August), 265–275.

Bettman, J. R., Luce, M. F., & Payne, J. W. (1998). Constructive consumer choice processes. *Journal of Consumer Research, 25*(December), 187–217.

Bettman, J. R., Roedder John, D., & Scott, C. A. (1986). Covariation assessment by consumers. *Journal of Consumer Research, 13*(December), 316–326.

Broniarczyk, S. M., & Alba, J. W. (1994). The role of consumers' intuitions in inference making. *Journal of Consumer Research, 21*(December), 393–407.

Charness, N. (1981). Aging and skilled problem solving. *Journal of Experimental Psychology: General, 110*, 21–38.

Chernev, A. (2007). Jack of all trades or master of one? Product differentiation and compensatory reasoning in consumer choice. *Journal of Consumer Research, 33*(March), 430–444.

Chernev, A., & Carpenter, G. S. (2001). The role of market efficiency intuitions in consumer choice: A case of compensatory inferences. *Journal of Marketing Research, 38*(August), 349–361.

Chernev, A., & Gal, D. (2008a). Boundaries of Self-Expression: Identity Overload and Brand Saturation Consumer Choice, *Working Paper*. Kellogg School of Management, Northwestern University, Evanston, IL.

Chernev, A., & Gal, D. (2008b). When Virtues and Vices Collide: Stereotyping and Calories Estimation in Consumer Choice, *Working Paper*. Kellogg School of Management, Northwestern University, Evanston, IL.

Cooper, W. H. (1981). Ubiquitous halo. *Psychological Bulletin, 90*(2), 218–244.

Dhar, R., & Simonson, I. (1999). Making complementary choices in consumption episodes: Highlighting versus balancing. *Journal of Marketing Research, 36*(February), 29–44.

Dick, A., Chakravarti, D., & Biehal, G. (1990). Memory-based inferences during consumer choice. *Journal of Consumer Research, 17*(June), 82–93.

Emerson, R. W. (1903). *Compensation; an Essay*. Boston: Houghton Mifflin.

Ferraro, K. F., & Barresi, C. M. (1982). The impact of widowhood on the social relations of older persons. *Research on Aging, 4*, 227–247.

Fiske, S. T., Xu, J., Cuddy, A. C., & Glick, P. (1999). (Dis)Respecting versus (dis)liking: Status and interdependence predict ambivalent stereotypes of competence and warmth. *Journal of Social Issues, 55*, 473–489.

Ford, G. T., & Smith, R. A. (1987). Inferential beliefs in consumer evaluations: An assessment of alternative processing strategies. *Journal of Consumer Research, 14*(December), 363–371.

Fraser, C., Power, M., Hamdy, S., Rothwell, J., Hobday, D., Hollander, I., et al. (2002). Driving plasticity in human adult motor cortex is associated with improved motor function after brain injury. *Neuron, 34*, 831–840.

Frederick, S., & Loewenstein, G. (1999). Hedonic adaptation. In D. Kahneman, & E. Diener, & N. Schwarz (Eds.), *Well-being: The foundations of hedonic psychology* (pp. xx–xx). New York: Russell Sage Foundation.

Galton, F. (1886). Regre ,ion towards mediocrity in hereditary stature. *Journal of the Anthropological I ,titute, 15*, 246–263.

Hedlund, J. (2000). P ,ky business: Safety regulations, risk compensation, and individual behavior. *Injury Prevention, 6*, 82–90.

Hermans, H. J. M., & Oles, P. K. (1999). Midlife crisis in men: Affective organization of personal meanings. *Human Relations, 52*(November), 1403–1426.

Huber, J., & McCann, J. (1982). The impact of inferential beliefs on product evaluations. *Journal of Marketing Research, 19*(August), 324–333.

James, W. (1918). *The principles of psychology*. New York: Holt.

Janiszewski, C., & Van Osselaer, S. M. J. (2000). A connectionist model of brand-quality associations. *Journal of Marketing Research, 37*(August), 331–350.

Johnson, E. J., & Meyer, R. J. (1984). Compensatory choice models of noncompensatory processes: The effect of varying context. *Journal of Consumer Research, 11*(June), 528–541.

Johnson, R. D., & Levin, I. P. (1985). More than meets the eye: The effect of missing information on purchase evaluations. *Journal of Consumer Research, 12* (September), 169–77.

Kay, A. C., & Jost, J. T. (2003). Complementary justice: Effects of "poor but happy" and "poor but honest" stereotype exemplars on system justification and implicit activation of the justice motive. *Journal of Personality and Social Psychology, 85*, 823–837.

Keeney, R. L., & Raiffa, H. (1976). *Decisions with multiple objectives: Preferences and value tradeoffs*. New York: Wiley.

Kelly, G. A. (1955). *The psychology of personal constructs* (1st ed.). New York: Norton.

Kivetz, R., & Simonson, I. (2000). The effects of incomplete information on consumer choice. *Journal of Marketing Research, 37*(November), 427–448.

Lerner, M. J. (1980). *The belief in a just world: A fundamental delusion*. New York: Plenum Press.

Lichtenstein, D. R., & Burton, S. (1989). The relationship between perceived and objective price-quality. *Journal of Marketing Research, 26*(November), 429–443.

Nisbett, R. E., & Wilson, T. D. (1977). The halo effect: Evidence for unconscious alteration of judgments. *Journal of Personality & Social Psychology, 35*(April), 450–456.

Payne, J. W., Bettman, J. R., & Johnson, E. J. (1993). *The adaptive decision maker*. New York, NY: Cambridge University Press.

Rucker, D. D., & Galinsky, A. D. (2008). Desire to acquire: Powerlessness and compensatory consumption. *Journal of Consumer Research, 35* (August), 257–267.

Salthouse, T. A. (1984). Effects of age and skill in typing. *Journal of Experimental Psychology: General, 113*, 345–371.

Schneider, D. J. (1973). Implicit personality theory: A review. *Psychological Bulletin, 79*, 294–309.

Schulman, S. (1986). Facing the invisible handicap. *Psychology Today, 20*, 58–64.

Simonson, I., Carmon, Z., & O'Curry, S. (1994). Experimental evidence on the negative effect of product features and sales promotions on brand choice. *Marketing Science, 13*(Winter), 23–40.

Simonson, I., & Tversky, A. (1992). Choice in context: Tradeoff contrast and extremeness aversion. *Journal of Marketing Research, 29*(August), 281–295.

Tversky, A. (1972). Elimination by aspects: A theory of choice. *Psychological Review, 79*(October), 281–299.

Tversky, A., & Kahneman, D. (1974). Judgment under uncertainty: Heuristics and biases. *Science, 185*, 1124–1131.

Von Neumann, J., & Morgenstern, O. (1953). *Theory of games and economic behavior* (3rd ed.). New York, NY: J. Wiley.

Wan, T. T., & Odell, B. G. (1983). Major role losses and social participation of older males. *Research on Aging, 5*, 173–196.

Wicklund, R. A., & Gollwitzer, P. M. (1982). *Symbolic self-completion.* Hillsdale, NJ: L. Erlbaum Associates.

Witkin, H. A., Oltman, P. K., Chase, J. B., & Freidman, F. (1971). Cognitive patterning in the blind. In J. Hellmuth (Ed.), *Cognitive Studies* (pp. xx–xx). New York: Brunner-Mazel.

Section *III*

Affective and Cognitive Feelings in Consumer Judgment

7

Conditioning as a Source of Liking
There Is Nothing Simple about It

JAN DE HOUWER

Ghent University, Ghent, Belgium

A core assumption in marketing research is that consumers tend to buy brands and products that they like. Marketeers are therefore eagerly looking for ways to change the liking of brands and products. Classical conditioning is generally considered to be one of the approaches to influence liking. In learning psychology, the term *evaluative conditioning* is used to refer to classical conditioning of liking. It can be defined as a change in the liking of a stimulus that results from pairing this stimulus with another stimulus. The first stimulus is often called the *conditioned stimulus,* or CS, whereas the second stimulus is often called the *unconditioned stimulus,* or US. Typically, a CS will become more positive when it has been paired with a positive US than when it has been paired with a negative US. A well-known example of evaluative conditioning in advertising is the "have-a-Coke-and-a-smile" ad campaign of the Coca-Cola company. In these ads, the Coke brand name (CS) is repeatedly presented together with images of smiling people having fun (US). It is assumed that this will increase the liking of the brand. Other examples involve the presence of liked celebrities or cute animals in a wide range of ads for products that, as such, have little relation to the celebrities or animals that are featured in the ad. The aim is always the same: By pairing the product with pleasant, liked events, it is hoped that a bit of the liking "rubs off" on the product and that because of this, consumers will afterwards be more likely to buy the product. Given the pervasive impact that liking can have on buying behavior, it is indeed crucial for marketeers to understand when and how liking can be "rubbed off" on products, that is, to understand evaluative conditioning.

Laboratory studies have produced many empirical findings about the conditions under which evaluative conditioning can be found. In the present chapter, I will present a brief overview of this research, focusing on those findings that are relevant for marketing (see De Houwer, Thomas, & Baeyens, 2001, for a more extensive review, and De Houwer, Baeyens, and Field, 2005a, for an update). The existing evidence, however, cannot be interpreted in a meaningful manner without a clear understanding of what the term *evaluative conditioning* means. There is indeed a lot of confusion about what evaluative conditioning is, not only among marketeers, but also among learning and social psychologists. In the present chapter, I will argue that it can be regarded as a procedure, an effect, or as a process (see De Houwer, 2007, for an in depth discussion). To avoid confusion, it is thus important always to specify the sense in which the term *evaluative conditioning* is used. The analysis also has theoretical implications. When defined as an effect, it becomes clear that evaluative conditioning is not necessarily due to the automatic formation of associations but can also be based on other processes such as controlled propositional reasoning (also see De Houwer et al., 2005a). This insight sheds new light on many contradictory findings that have been reported in the literature. It also leads to the conclusion that researchers should focus not only on *whether* a certain condition is crucial for obtaining evaluative conditioning but also on *when* a certain condition is crucial. This next step in research on evaluative conditioning will provide the basis for a much more sophisticated understanding and use of evaluative conditioning in marketing.

A BRIEF OVERVIEW OF THE LITERATURE

A first set of studies showed that evaluative conditioning is a general and ubiquitous phenomenon. It has been demonstrated with a large variety of stimuli, including political slogans presented during a free lunch or in a room with aversive odors (e.g., Razran, 1954), neutral pictures of human faces paired with liked or disliked pictures of human faces (e.g., Levey & Martin, 1975), names of (fictitious) products presented in the context of pleasant or unpleasant pictures or music (e.g., Blair & Shimp, 1992; Gorn, 1982; Stuart, Shimp, & Engle, 1987; Pleyers, Corneille, Luminet, & Yzerbyt, 2007; Walther & Grigoriadis, 2004), and artificial flavorings paired with a bad aftertaste (e.g., Baeyens, Eelen, Van den Bergh, & Crombez, 1990). To take just one example from the context of marketing, Till and Priluck (2000) exposed members of a test group to 15 trials in which the name of a fictitious brand of mouthwash (CS; e.g., Garra) was presented together with a picture of a pleasant visual scene (US; e.g., a boat in tropical waters). These trials were intermixed with filler trials on which other brand names and pictures were presented. A control group was shown the same pictures but in a semirandom order in which CS-US sequences were not permitted. When participants were afterwards asked to indicate their attitudes toward a number of fictitious brands, participants in the test group were found to like the CS brand (i.e., Garra) more than participants in the control group. Interestingly, this effect was not restricted to the original brand but also extended to other fictitious brands with similar names (e.g., Gurra).

Although there have been many successful demonstrations of evaluative conditioning, it is important to note that genuine failures to observe it have also been reported (e.g., Field & Davey, 1999; Rozin, Wrzesniewski, & Byrnes, 1998), including failures in studies involving brands and products as CSs (e.g., Kellaris & Cox,

1989). This suggests that certain (as yet unknown) boundary conditions need to be fulfilled (see De Houwer et al., 2005a, for a discussion).

On the one hand, the available evidence provides good news for marketeers: There is sound evidence that the liking of brands and products can be changed by pairing them with positive or negative stimuli. On the other hand, pairing stimuli does not always seem to work. We therefore need to examine the variables that modulate evaluative conditioning. Two types of variables can be distinguished (De Houwer, 2007): (1) variables related to the manner in which the stimuli are paired, and (2) variables related to the conditions under which the stimuli are paired.

With regard to the manner in which stimuli are paired, a first important variable is the order of the CS (e.g., the brand name) and US (e.g., pleasant pictures). Evidence suggests that conditioned changes in the liking of the CS are typically larger when it is consistently followed by the US (forward conditioning) than when it is preceded by the US (backward conditioning; e.g., Stuart et al., 1987). When translated to an advertising context, this observation implies that pairing a brand name (CS) with positive images or messages (US) will result in a larger increase in liking of the brand when the positive images or messages are always presented after the brand name.

A second important variable is the number of times that the stimuli are paired. Overall, studies have shown that evaluative conditioning becomes stronger when the number of CS-US pairings increases (e.g., Baeyens, Eelen, Crombez, & Van den Bergh, 1992). Those same studies suggest, however, that after a certain number of pairings, additional pairings no longer lead to a strengthening of the effect or might even produce a weakening of the effect. Although more research on this topic is needed, overexposing consumers to ads that are based on the principle of evaluative conditioning might thus have adverse effects.

A third factor concerns (changes in) the statistical contingency between the CS and US. This factor underlies research on a range of phenomena such as the effect of statistical contingency, extinction, CS-preexposure, US pre- and postexposure, cue competition, occasion setting, US-revaluation, and counterconditioning. Although it would take us too far to discuss the research on each of these phenomena (see De Houwer et al., 2001, for a review), I would like to note a few findings that are particularly relevant for marketing research. Most important, although the evidenced is mixed, some studies suggest that evaluative conditioning can be resistant to extinction. That is, once the valence of a CS has been changed by pairing it with a US, the learned valence of the CS cannot be erased by simply presenting the CS on its own (i.e., by removing the CS-US contingency; e.g., Baeyens, Crombez, Van den Bergh, & Eelen, 1988; De Houwer, Baeyens, Vansteenwegen, & Eelen, 2000). This implies that conditioned changes in the liking of brands and products can be long lasting. For instance, when a product is paired with positive images in an ad campaign and if these pairings lead to an increase in the liking of the products, the increased liking of the product can be expected to remain present even after the ad campaign is stopped. This does not imply that conditioned changes in liking can never be erased. One way to change conditioned liking is by counterconditioning, that is, by pairing the CS with a US that has a valence opposite to that of the original US (Baeyens, Eelen, Van den Bergh, & Crombez, 1989). For instance, after brand liking has increased as the result of pairing it with smiling faces, liking can decrease again as the result of pairing the brand with negative stimuli such as frowning faces. Marketeers should also be aware of the phenomenon of US revaluation. This entails that a conditioned change in liking can be reversed by altering the valence of the original US (Baeyens, Eelen, Van den Bergh, & Crombez, 1992; Walther, 2002). For instance, when a liked celebrity endorses a product in an ad, this could increase the popularity of a brand. But when afterwards, the celebrity gets involved in a scandal and becomes disliked, this would also adversely affect the liking of the brand that the celebrity endorsed, even after the ad campaign has been stopped (see Walther, 2002; Walther, Nagengast, & Trasselli, 2005). A similar risk is present when extending a brand to new products. Brand extension can be seen as an instance of evaluative conditioning: The new product (CS) is liked because it is repeatedly paired with a liked brand name (US; see Till & Priluck, 2000; Walther et al., 2005). In this case, the phenomenon of US-revaluation would imply that when the original brand becomes disliked for some reasons, all products that were related with this brand will also become less liked, even if the connection between the brand and the product no longer exists.

Until now we have discussed only variables related to the manner in which stimuli are paired. As mentioned above, there is also a second class of variables that is related to the conditions under which the pairings are presented. The variable that has received most attention in this context is awareness of the CS-US contingencies. Some studies suggest that pairing a CS with a US can change the liking of a CS even when participants are not aware of the fact that the CS and US went together. For instance, some variables seem to have a different effect on contingency awareness than on evaluative conditioning (e.g., Baeyens, Eelen, & Van den Bergh, 1990; Fulcher & Hammerl, 2001). Also, evaluative conditioning has been observed when the CSs or USs were presented so briefly that they could not be detected consciously (e.g., De Houwer, Hendrickx, & Baeyens, 1997; Dijksterhuis, 2004). It should be noted, however, that the evidence regarding unaware evaluative conditioning is mixed. Several well conducted studies strongly suggest that evaluative conditioning occurs only when participants are aware of the CS-US contingencies (e.g., see Field, 2000, and Lovibond & Shanks, 2002, for reviews; see Allen & Janiszewski, 1989, and Pleyers et al., 2007, for evidence in the context of marketing). This debate has important implications for marketeers because its outcome will determine whether marketeers need to draw attention to the fact that the product and US are paired together in order to change the liking of the product.

MISCONCEPTIONS OF (EVALUATIVE) CONDITIONING

Although evaluative conditioning is a potentially important tool for influencing consumer behavior, many marketeers and consumer psychologists seem to have an outdated view on (evaluative) conditioning. For instance, in textbooks of consumer behavior (e.g., Arnould, Price, & Zinkhan, 2004; Evans, Jamal, & Foxall, 2006), conditioning is most often described as a very simple, noncognitive learning process that involves changes in involuntary responses to stimuli as the result of the contiguity-driven, unconscious formation of associations. In fact, this view corresponds largely to the behaviorist theories that dominated (learning) psychology more than 40 years ago. During the past 40 years, views on conditioning have changed dramatically. An abundance of evidence has shown that cognitive processes such as expectancy, attention, memory, awareness, and even reasoning play a crucial role in conditioning (e.g., Dawson & Schell, 1987; De Houwer, Vandorpe, & Beckers, 2005). But also many learning psychologists to some extent still carry with them the behavioristic stereotype of conditioning. Most importantly, even though they generally acknowledge the importance of mental representations and cognitive processes, many still cling to the assumption that conditioning is a process that involves the automatic, bottom-up formation of associations between mental representations (see De Houwer et al., 2005a, for a discussion). This is perhaps even more so for evaluative conditioning than for other types of conditioning because evaluative conditioning involves changes in a seemingly very primitive response, namely liking.

In my opinion, this view of evaluative conditioning hampers research not only because it is outdated, but most crucially because it defines evaluative conditioning in terms of a process rather than a procedure. I will argue that real progress in understanding evaluative conditioning can be made only if evaluative conditioning is defined as an effect and if one allows for the possibility that different kinds of processes can underlie evaluative conditioning effects (see De Houwer, 2007, for a more detailed discussion). As I will explain in the next sections, evaluative conditioning is an effect that undeniably occurs in human and nonhuman animals: It is beyond dispute that pairing stimuli can result in changes in the liking of those stimuli and for that reason, evaluative conditioning deserves much attention. What can be disputed, however, are theories about the processes that might underlie evaluative conditioning effects. It is even likely that different types of processes can produce evaluative conditioning effects. This insight sheds new light on the many conflicting findings that have been reported in the literature on evaluative conditioning and opens the way for new research. If evaluative conditioning effects can be due to different processes, then not all manifestations of evaluative conditioning will have the same properties (i.e., occur under the same conditions). Hence, one should adopt a metaconditional approach (De Houwer, 2007): Research should focus not only on whether evaluative conditioning effects have certain properties but also on the conditions that determine when evaluative conditioning has those properties. For instance, when studying extinction, the crucial question should not be *whether* evaluative conditioning effects show extinction (i.e., are no longer present when CS-US pairings are followed by repeated presentations of the CS in isolation) but *when* evaluative conditioning shows extinction and when not. Likewise, marketeers should not only decide whether they will implement an evaluative conditioning procedure, but also take into account the conditions under which the evaluative conditioning procedure will be implemented because this could determine what effects the procedure will have (e.g., a change in liking that is or is not resistant to extinction). In sum, in order for psychologists and marketeers to truly understand and utilize the potential of evaluative conditioning, they need be more precise in their definition of evaluative conditioning and need to wake up to the fact that conditioning is not nearly as simple as commonly assumed.

In the next section, I will first try to clarify what it means to define evaluative conditioning as a procedure, an effect, or a theory. Afterwards, I will discuss possible processes that could underlie evaluative conditioning effects and use this to provide a starting point for metaconditional research.

A CONCEPTUAL ANALYSIS

Let us return to the example of the "have-a-Coke-and-a-smile" ads. To say that this is an example of evaluative conditioning can mean several things. First, it could imply that the marketeers behind the ad campaign use a *procedure* that is in essence identical to the procedure used in evaluative conditioning studies. Both in the ads and in lab studies, stimuli (e.g., a brand name and pictures of smiling people) are presented together in a certain manner and it is assessed whether this leads to changes in liking.[1] In this sense, evaluative conditioning simply refers to what a marketeer does. Because it refers to objective facts, there can be little discussion about whether a certain ad or study involves evaluative conditioning in the sense of a procedure.

Saying that the Coke ads provide an example of evaluative conditioning can also be understood in the sense that the pairing of the brand name and the smiling faces actually produces a change in the liking of the Coke brand. Evaluative conditioning is now understood to be an *effect* of the procedure rather than the procedure itself. It refers to the effect of the ads, not to the ads as such. More generally, evaluative conditioning as an effect refers to an actual change in the liking of stimuli that is due to the fact that stimuli were paired in a certain manner. It is important to note that observing a change in liking is not enough to claim that evaluative conditioning as an effect has occurred. A change in liking can be regarded as an evaluative conditioning effect only if the change is due to the pairing of stimuli. Assume, for instance, that the Coke ads result in an increased liking of Coke. It is possible that this increase in liking is due not to the fact that the Coke brand was paired with positive images but to the fact that the brand name was repeatedly presented to the consumers. From research on the mere exposure effect (for a review, see Bornstein, 1989), we know that the repeated presentation of a stimulus can result in an increased liking of that stimulus. If the increase in liking for the brand is due to the repeated stimulus exposures, it would be wrong to label the change in liking as an evaluative conditioning effect.

Unlike evaluative conditioning as a procedure, evaluative conditioning as an effect thus entails more than a simple observation. Not only is it necessary to observe an objective change in liking, but one also needs to be confident that the observed change can be attributed to the pairing of stimuli, that is, to an evaluative conditioning procedure. In the lab, one can check whether a change in liking is due to the pairing of stimuli by adding control conditions to the design of the study. For instance, one can compare the changes in liking for experimental stimuli that have been paired with positive stimuli with changes in liking for control stimuli that have been presented equally often as the experimental stimuli but that have not been paired with positive stimuli (see De Houwer et al., 2001, for a discussion of appropriate control conditions). If the liking of the experimental stimuli changes in a different way than that of the control stimuli, one can infer with a high degree of confidence that the change in liking of the experimental stimuli was due to the pairing with the positive stimuli and thus a case of evaluative conditioning as an effect. Outside of the lab, for instance, in the context of real-life advertising, it will often be difficult to implement the appropriate control conditions. In such cases, one should be aware that labeling a change in liking as an evaluative conditioning effect is actually based on a hypothetical causal attribution rather than on pure observation.

The third and final way in which the concept *evaluative conditioning* can be used is in terms of a theoretical mechanism or process. As indicated above, many marketeers and psychologists explicitly or implicitly regard evaluative conditioning as an automatic, bottom-up, and low-level process that involves the formation and updating of associations between representations in memory. Regardless of the validity or merits of this particular view, one should realize that it is very difficult to demonstrate that a change in valence is due to a particular process. Theoretical constructs such as processes cannot be observed directly. For instance, nobody has ever seen a representation or an association between representations. The problem would be solved if evaluative conditioning effects could be due to only one type of process. In that case, observing an evaluative conditioning effect would allow one to infer that the evaluative conditioning process has taken place. But it is impossible to determine on an a priori basis that there is only one process that can lead to evaluative conditioning effects. Evaluative conditioning effects could, at least in principle, be due to a variety of processes. Therefore, in order to conclude that *the* evaluative conditioning process has taken place, it is not sufficient to observe an evaluative conditioning effect. Hence, defining *evaluative conditioning* as a process has the important disadvantage that it becomes extremely difficult to determine when "real" evaluative conditioning has taken place (see De Houwer, 2007, for a more extensive discussion of this issue).

This analysis of the concept *evaluative conditioning* has important implications. First, given that there are three ways to define the concept *evaluative conditioning* (i.e., as a procedure, effect, or theory), it is crucial to always clearly specify the meaning that one is referring to.[2] Otherwise, conceptual confusion could lead to important misunderstandings. For instance, assume that future studies would demonstrate convincingly that evaluative conditioning effects can occur only when participants are aware of the presented pairings (see Pleyers et al., 2007, for recent evidence supporting that position). If evaluative conditioning is defined as changes in liking that are due to the automatic (in the sense of unconscious) formation of associations, such evidence will lead to the conclusion that evaluative conditioning does not exist. But this conclusion does not change the fact that the pairing of stimuli does lead to changes in liking. In other words, evidence against evaluative conditioning defined as a particular process does not constitute evidence against evaluative conditioning defined as an effect.[3]

Second, the distinction between evaluative conditioning as an effect and evaluative conditioning as a process highlights the fact that several processes can be responsible for evaluative conditioning effects. Because of this, it could be that under certain conditions, evaluative conditioning effects have certain properties (e.g., resistant to extinction, no need for awareness), whereas under other conditions, they have other properties (e.g., no resistance to extinction, need for awareness). If this is true, learning psychologists *and* marketeers are faced with an important problem. Learning psychologists will fail in their aim to describe the properties of evaluative conditioning. For instance, sometimes researchers might find that evaluative conditioning is resistant to extinction and other times they might find that it does show extinction. Marketeers will therefore not know whether they can expect long-lasting effects of their ads. In fact, the current literature on evaluative conditioning shows this kind of confusion. There now is general agreement about the fact that evaluative conditioning is a genuine phenomenon (an agreement that has been reached only recently; see De Houwer et al., 2005a). But there is little else that evaluative conditioning researchers agree about. For instance, in a recent special issue on this issue (De Houwer, Baeyens, & Field, 2005b), some researchers claimed that evaluative conditioning effects depend on contingency awareness, require attention, and do show extinction (e.g., Lipp & Purkis, 2005), whereas others argued that it does not depend on awareness, does not require attention, and is resistant to extinction (e.g., Walther et al., 2005). Such disputes render it impossible for marketeers to use evaluative conditioning in a scientifically informed manner.

The analysis presented in this chapter (also see De Houwer, 2007) sheds new light on these conflicting findings: It is possible that the effects observed in the different studies were due to different processes. In the next paragraph, I will discuss two possible processes that could underlie evaluative conditioning effects, describe how this could explain some of the existing conflicting findings, and generate a number of new hypotheses that can be tested in future metaconditional research.

TOWARD A METACONDITIONAL APPROACH

A Dual Process Model

As mentioned above, many researchers have one particular kind of process in mind when they think about evaluative conditioning: the automatic formation and updating of associative links between representations. Let us return to the example of the "have-a-Coke-and-a-smile" ads. Because the Coke brand is paired with images of smiling people, it is assumed that the representation of the Coke brand in memory will become associated with the representation of smiling people or with the positive affect that is evoked by these smiling people. When people see the Coke brand after being exposed to the ads, this will activate the representation of smiling people or positive affect, leading to positive feelings. These positive feelings are then automatically misattributed to the brand. Different associative models differ in their assumptions about the type of representations that are associated (e.g., stimulus or response representations), the rules that govern the formation of associations (e.g., reduction of prediction error), and the conditions under which associations influence behavior (e.g., direct translation or comparison of different associations). But all are based on the idea that conditioning effects are based on the automatic formation and updating of associations in memory.

The current dominance of associative models in research on evaluative conditioning is perhaps not surprising given that such models have always been prominent in conditioning research. However, there is no a priori reason why evaluative conditioning effects can be due only to association formation. Evaluative conditioning effects are by definition associative in nature (i.e., by definition due to procedure of the pairing of stimuli), but they are not necessarily due to the automatic formation of associations in memory. The pairing of stimuli can result in effects that are driven by processes other than the automatic formation of associations in memory. For instance, De Houwer and colleagues (2005a) pointed out that people might intentionally use conscious propositional knowledge about contingencies between stimuli as a basis for their evaluation of those stimuli. Assume that you receive an electric shock every time you see a picture of a triangle but never after seeing a picture of a circle. Afterwards you are asked to indicate how much you like the triangle and how much you like the circle. Probably you will say that you like the triangle less than the circle. When asked why, you can point to the fact that the triangle signals the shock as a justifiable reason for disliking the triangle. In a similar manner, consumers might justify their liking for the Versace brand by pointing out that their musical hero Madonna endorses Versace in ads. In these cases, the change in liking is due to the pairing of stimuli (i.e., the triangle and the shock or Versace and Madonna). Therefore, it is an evaluative conditioning effect. However, the change in liking is not produced by automatic associative processes. Rather, it is a genuine change in liking that is based on the fact that people have acquired conscious propositional knowledge about the relation between the triangle and the shock (or Versace and Madonna) and that they used this knowledge as a basis for evaluating the triangle (or Versace).[4]

The proposal that evaluative conditioning effects can be based either on the automatic formation of associations in memory or the controlled use of conscious propositional knowledge boils down to a dual process model of evaluative conditioning. Similar dual process models have been proposed in many areas of psychology (e.g., Gawronski & Bodenhausen, 2006; Sloman, 1996; Strack & Deutsch, 2004) and it is clear that these models are not without problems (e.g., Kruglanski, Erb, Pierro, Mannetti, & Chun, 2006; Moors & De Houwer, 2006). Nevertheless, they can be used as a source of inspiration for trying to understand when evaluative conditioning will have certain properties. Most importantly, these dual process models include assumptions about the conditions under which the two processes are likely to operate. For instance, the formation of conscious propositional knowledge about contingencies by definition implies awareness of the contingencies. Also, such knowledge is likely to reflect changes in contingencies such as those that occur during an extinction procedure. Hence, evaluative conditioning effects that are due to the use of conscious propositional knowledge about contingencies should depend on contingency awareness and be sensitive to extinction. Referring to the example given above, if people start liking Versace because they consciously learn that Versace is endorsed by Madonna, then there will be a strong relation between liking of Versace and conscious knowledge about the fact Madonna endorses Versace. Also, liking of Versace can be expected to disappear after people learn that Madonna no longer endorses Versace.

With regard to the automatic formation of associations, it is often assumed that associations can be formed independently of contingency awareness and reflect only the spatiotemporal contiguity between stimuli rather than the statistical contingency (e.g., De Houwer et al., 2001; Gawronski & Bodenhausen, 2006; Walther et al., 2005). Hence, evaluative conditioning effects that are due to the automatic formation of associations should not depend on contingency awareness and might not be sensitive to extinction. Returning to our example, if the liking of Versace is due to the automatic formation of an association in memory between the representations of Madonna and Versace, then it would be present even if people do not consciously know that Madonna endorses Versace (i.e., unaware evaluative conditioning) and might remain present after Madonna stops endorsing Versace (i.e., resistance to extinction). Which process is responsible for evaluative conditioning effects might thus have important implications for the properties of the effect.

Based on dual process models one could thus explain why the existing evidence regarding the role of extinction and contingency awareness in evaluative conditioning is mixed: In studies that provided evidence for extinction and against unaware evaluative conditioning, the conditioning effects might have been due to the acquisition of conscious propositional knowledge. Evidence supporting unaware evaluative conditioning and questioning the impact of extinction might have originated in studies where effects were due to the automatic formation of associations.

Implications for Future Research

Although this explanation of past conflicting results clearly is post-hoc, it does lead to interesting new predictions. Most importantly, it can be predicted that different properties might tend to co-occur. For instance, from the previous paragraph, it can be inferred that evaluative conditioning effects that do not depend on contingency awareness might typically also be resistant to extinction. The reverse could also hold (i.e., evaluative conditioning that does depend on contingency awareness would show extinction). To the best of my knowledge, these predictions have not yet been tested in the literature. The reason probably is that researchers have until now regarded evaluative conditioning as a unitary process that has one fixed set of properties. From the viewpoint that two or more processes can produce evaluative conditioning effects, research should examine not only whether but also when evaluative conditioning has a certain property. The multiple process view thus implies a metaconditional approach that attempts to identify clusters of properties that tend to co-occur (also see De Houwer, 2007).

Implementing such a metaconditioning approach will not be easy. There are several potential pitfalls that should be taken into consideration. First, past research has shown that it is not easy to establish whether evaluative conditioning has a certain property, that is, whether a certain condition (e.g., contingency awareness or absence of extinction trials) is important for observing evaluative conditioning effects. However, in the metaconditional approach, the emphasis is not on how to establish that a certain condition is crucial but on whether the impact of different conditions is related. For instance, rather than trying to find a paradigm in which participants are completely unaware of the contingencies, it might be more useful to compare the properties of evaluative conditioning in situations where contingency awareness is poor (and propositional knowledge about stimulus properties can thus have little effect) with the same features in situations when contingency awareness is good (and propositional knowledge could have a strong effect). It might well be that extinction is more likely to occur in the latter situations. Also, it is striking that in some experimental set-ups, there is a strong relation between contingency awareness and evaluative conditioning (e.g., Pleyers et al., 2007), whereas in other set-ups the relation is absent or even negative (e.g., Baeyens et al., 1990; Fulcher & Hammerl, 2001; Walther & Nagengast, 2006). Although such correlations do not allow for definite conclusions about unaware evaluative conditioning (e.g., De Houwer, 2001; Field, 2000; Shanks & St. John, 1994), it would be interesting to examine whether the conditioning effects in these set-ups also differ with regard to other properties (e.g., extinction). If one can consistently observe that, for instance, extinction occurs when evaluative conditioning is strongly related to contingency awareness but not when evaluative conditioning is independent of contingency awareness, this would be a valuable observation regardless of whether one agrees that the criterion used for establishing the effect of extinction or the role of contingency awareness is the ultimate criterion. Moreover, if one can observe such a systematic link between the effect of different conditions, this could actually be taken as evidence for the validity of the criteria that were used to establish the impact of the conditions (also see De Houwer, 2007).

A second potential pitfall of the metaconditional approach is that specific predictions about clusters of conditions depend on multiple, often ill-specified theoretical assumptions. The value of (the predictions of) the approach thus depends on the validity and specificity of the theoretical assumptions. For instance, it is often assumed that associative knowledge can be expressed automatically whereas propositional knowledge can influence behavior only in an intentional, controlled manner (e.g., Gawronski & Bodenhausen, 2006; Strack & Deutsch, 2004). Researchers have therefore looked for measures of stimulus valence that do not give participants the opportunity to take into account propositional knowledge about stimulus contingencies. In recent years, a number of tasks have been introduced that can be used to measure automatic affective reactions. These so-called implicit measures (see also Friese, Hofmann, & Wänke, this volume) have attracted attention because they promise to provide a way of eliminating the impact of propositional knowledge on evaluative conditioning (e.g., De Houwer, Hermans, & Eelen, 1998; Hermans, Baeyens, & Eelen, 2003; Mitchell, Anderson, & Lovibond, 2003). This would imply that evaluative conditioning effects as registered by implicit measures provide an undistorted view on how associations are formed automatically.

Although the use of implicit measures in evaluative conditioning research could indeed provide an important step forward, researchers should be aware of the possibility that implicit measures can be influenced also by propositional knowledge. Recent research indeed suggests that at least certain implicit measures are not immune to propositional knowledge and are therefore not suitable as a pure index of association formation (De Houwer, 2006; also see De Houwer, Beckers, & Moors, in press). This example illustrates that one should always be aware that theoretical assumptions underlying (metaconditional) research might well be invalid. Such assumptions thus need to be tested empirically.

SUMMARY AND CONCLUSIONS

Humans and other organisms tend to want, do, and buy more often the things they like than the things they do not like. To understand and control human (consumer) behavior, it is therefore imperative that we understand how likes and dislikes are acquired. Evaluative conditioning research has shown that the preference for a stimulus can be influenced by pairing that stimulus with another stimulus. Understanding evaluative conditioning can thus provide many insights into human behavior. Unfortunately, we still do not know much about this important phenomenon. We know that it can work and that it can be successfully applied to change attitudes toward brands and products, but we also know that it does not always work. To make matters worse, the current literature on evaluative conditioning contains many conflicting results that have not been reconciled in a satisfactory manner. This makes it difficult for marketeers to decide whether or how to use evaluative conditioning in their practice.

In the present chapter, I have argued that progress in our understanding of evaluative conditioning is hampered by confusion regarding the meaning of the concept *evaluative conditioning*. It can be used to refer to a procedure (i.e., pairing stimuli and checking whether this produces changes in liking), an effect (i.e., an actual change in liking as the result of pairing stimuli), or a theoretical process (i.e., the process by which pairing stimuli results in changes in liking). Problems arise when evaluative conditioning is defined in terms of a particular process. Not only is it difficult to determine whether a particular change in liking is due to a particular process (and thus to determine whether evaluative conditioning has occurred), but such a view also tends to narrow theoretical thinking about evaluative conditioning in general. Most importantly, it detracts attention away from the possibility that several processes can be responsible for evaluative conditioning effects, that is, for a change in liking that is due to the pairing of stimuli. It is therefore advisable to define evaluative conditioning in terms of an effect and to allow for the possibility that such effects can be due to different processes.

In the final part of this chapter, I put forward the hypothesis that evaluative conditioning effects could be due to at least two types of processes: the automatic formation of associations in memory and the controlled use of propositional knowledge about stimulus contingencies. I proposed this dual process hypothesis for two reasons. First, it sheds new light on the many conflicting results that have been reported in the literature: It might well be that the observed conditioning effects were in some cases due to one process and in other cases due to the other process. Second, the dual process hypothesis provides inspiration for metaconditional research: Given certain assumptions, hypotheses can be generated about clusters of properties that might co-occur. For marketeers, such metaconditional research could provide valuable knowledge about what to expect from evaluative conditioning.

Future empirical research will determine whether the dual process hypothesis has any merits. But regardless of the outcome of this research, the conceptual analysis presented in this chapter makes clear that researchers should be open to the possibility that evaluative conditioning is not the simple phenomenon it appears to be. This should not discourage researchers from using or examining evaluative conditioning. There can be no doubt about the basic effect: The liking of a stimulus can be changed by pairing it with another stimulus. Evaluative conditioning procedures thus remain a powerful tool in the hands of marketeers and others who want to influence the liking of stimuli. But the usefulness of this tool will increase once we know more about when certain properties are important. The main message of this chapter is that these properties might well differ from situation to situation and that researchers should try to uncover the variables that modulate the properties of evaluative conditioning.

ACKNOWLEDGMENT

Jan De Houwer, Ghent University. The preparation of this chapter was made possible by Grant BOF/GOA2006/001 of Ghent University. I thank Klaus Fiedler and Bertram Gawronski for comments on a first draft of the chapter.

ENDNOTES

1. As a procedure, evaluative conditioning is thus a form of classical conditioning: It is examined whether the pairing of stimuli influences reactions to those stimuli. What distinguishes an evaluative conditioning procedure from other classical conditioning procedures is that changes in evaluative reactions are examined.
2. Note that the same holds for many other concepts in psychology. For instance, *priming* can be used to refer to a procedure of presenting a prime stimulus before a related target stimulus, to the observed effect of presenting a prime before a related stimulus, or to the processes responsible for the priming effect (e.g., spreading of activation).
3. History teaches us that conceptual confusion can have serious consequences. For instance, in a highly influential chapter, Brewer (1974) reviewed evidence showing that classical conditioning in humans depends on awareness of stimulus contingencies. Based on this evidence, he titled his chapter "There Is No Evidence for Classical Conditioning in Humans." Many researchers concluded on the basis of the title that conditioning *effects* are restricted to nonhuman animals and thus lost interest in the phenomenon. What Brewer really wanted to say, however, was that the behavioristic (S-R) theory of classical conditioning was incorrect. The conditioning effect as such (i.e., pairing stimuli can influence the responses of humans) was never in doubt.
4. Note that these changes are not due to demand compliance. Demand compliance also entails that people have conscious propositional knowledge about the stimulus contingencies, but in the case of demand compliance, they use this knowledge because they believe that this is what the experimenter or marketeer wants them to do. Both types of effect thus depend on the use of propositional knowledge about stimulus contingencies, but the knowledge is used for different reasons (i.e., to arrive at a genuine evaluation of the stimuli vs. to comply with the expectations of the experimenter or marketeer; see Meersmans, De Houwer, Baeyens, Thomas, & Eelen, 2005).

REFERENCES

Allen, C. T., & Janiszewski, C. A. (1989). Assessing the role of contingency awareness in attitudinal conditioning with implications for advertising research. *Journal of Marketing
Research, 26,* 30–43.

Arnould, E., Price, L., & Zinkhan, G. (2004). *Consumers* (2nd ed.). New York, NY:
McGraw-Hill/Irwin.

Baeyens, F., Crombez, G., Van den Bergh, O., & Eelen, P. (1988). Once in contact, always
in contact: Evaluative conditioning is resistant to extinction. *Advances in Behaviour
Research and Therapy, 10,* 179–199.

Baeyens, F., Eelen, P., Crombez, G., & Van den Bergh, O. (1992). Human evaluative conditioning: Acquisition trials, presentation schedule, evaluative style and contingency
awareness. *Behaviour Research and Therapy, 30,* 133–142.

Baeyens, F., Eelen, P., & Van den Bergh, O. (1990). Contingency awareness in evaluative conditioning: A case for unaware affective-evaluative learning. *Cognition and
Emotion, 4,* 3–18.

Baeyens, F., Eelen, P., Van den Bergh, O., & Crombez, G. (1989). Acquired affective-evaluative value: Conservative but not unchangeable. *Behaviour Research and Therapy,
27,* 279–287.

Baeyens, F., Eelen, P., Van den Bergh, O., & Crombez, G. (1990). Flavor-flavor and color-
flavor conditioning in humans. *Learning and Motivation, 21,* 434–455.

Baeyens, F., Eelen, P., Van den Bergh, O., & Crombez, G. (1992). The content of learning
in human evaluative conditioning: Acquired valence is sensitive to US-revaluation.
Learning and Motivation, 23, 200–224.

Blair, M. E., & Shimp, T. A. (1992). Consequences of an unpleasant experience with music:
A second-order negative conditioning perspective. *Journal of Advertising, 21,* 35–44.

Bornstein, R. F. (1989). Exposure and affect. Overview and meta-analysis of research 1968–
1987. *Psychological Bulletin, 106,* 265–289.

Brewer, W. F. (1974). There is no convincing evidence of conditioning in adult humans.
In W. B. Weimer & D. S. Palermo (Eds.), *Cognition and the symbolic processes* (pp.
1–42). Hillsdale, NJ: Erlbaum.

Dawson, M. E., & Schell, A. M. (1987). Human autonomic and skeletal classical conditioning: The role of conscious cognitive factors. In G. Davey (Ed.) *Cognitive processes
and Pavlovian conditioning in humans* (pp. 27–56). Chichester, UK: Wiley.

De Houwer, J. (2001). Contingency awareness and evaluative conditioning: When will it be
enough? *Consciousness and Cognition, 10,* 550–558.

De Houwer, J. (2006). Using the implicit association test does not rule out an impact of conscious propositional knowledge on evaluative conditioning. *Learning and Motivation,
37,* 176–187.

De Houwer, J. (2007). A conceptual and theoretical analysis of evaluative conditioning. *The
Spanish Journal of Psychology, 10,* 230–241.

De Houwer, J., Baeyens, F., & Field, A. P. (2005a). Associative learning of likes and dislikes:
Some current controversies and possible ways forward. *Cognition and Emotion, 19,*
161–174.

De Houwer, J., Baeyens, F., & Field, A. P. (2005b). Associative learning of likes and dislikes
[Special Issue]. *Cognition and Emotion, 19*(2).

De Houwer, J., Baeyens, F., Vansteenwegen, D., & Eelen, P. (2000). Evaluative conditioning in the picture-picture paradigm with random assignment of conditioned stimuli
to unconditioned stimuli. *Journal of Experimental Psychology: Animal Behaviour
Processes, 26,* 237–242.

De Houwer, J., Beckers, T., & Moors, A. (2007). Novel attitudes can be faked on the implicit association test. *Journal of Experimental Social Psychology, 43,* 972–978.

De Houwer, J., Hendrickx, H., & Baeyens, F. (1997). Evaluative learning with "subliminally" presented stimuli. *Consciousness and Cognition, 6,* 87–107.

De Houwer, J., Hermans, D., & Eelen, P. (1998). Affective and identity priming with episodically associated stimuli. *Cognition and Emotion, 12,* 145–169.

De Houwer, J., Thomas, S., & Baeyens, F. (2001) Associative learning of likes and dislikes: A review of 25 years of research on human evaluative conditioning. *Psychological Bulletin, 127,* 853–869.

De Houwer, J., Vandorpe, S., & Beckers, T. (2005). On the role of controlled cognitive processes in human associative learning. In A. Wills (Ed.), *New directions in human associative learning* (pp. 41–63). Mahwah, NJ: Lawrence Erlbaum.

Dijksterhuis, A. (2004). I like myself but I don't know why: Enhancing implicit self-esteem by subliminal evaluative conditioning. *Journal of Personality and Social Psychology, 86,* 345–355.

Evans, M., Jamal, A., & Foxall, G. R. (2006). *Consumer behaviour.* Chichester, UK: Wiley.

Field, A. P. (2000). I like it, but I'm not sure why: Can evaluative conditioning occur without conscious awareness? *Consciousness and Cognition, 9,* 13–36.

Field, A. P., & Davey, G. C. L. (1999). Reevaluating evaluative conditioning: A nonassociative explanation of conditioning effects in the visual evaluative conditioning paradigm. *Journal of Experimental Psychology: Animal Behaviour Processes, 25,* 211–224.

Fulcher, E. P., & Hammerl, M. (2001). When all is revealed: A dissociation between evaluative learning and contingency awareness. *Consciousness and Cognition, 10,* 524–549.

Gawronski, B., & Bodenhausen, G. V. (2006). Associative and propositional processes in evaluation: An integrative review of implicit and explicit attitude change. *Psychological Bulletin, 132,* 692–731.

Gorn, G. J. (1982). The effects of music in advertising on choice behaviour: A classical conditioning approach. *Journal of Marketing, 46,* 94–101.

Hermans, D., Baeyens, F., & Eelen, P. (2003). On the acquisition and activation of evaluative information in memory: The study of evaluative learning and affective priming combined. In J. Musch & K. C. Klauer (Eds.), *The psychology of evaluation: Affective processes in cognition and emotion* (pp. 139–168). Mahwah, NJ: Erlbaum.

Kellaris, J. J., & Cox, A. D. (1989). The effects of background music in advertising: A reassessment. *Journal of Consumer Research, 16,* 113–118.

Kruglanski, A. W., Erb, H. P., Pierro A., Mannetti, L., & Chun, W. Y. (2006). On parametric continuities in the world of binary either ors. *Psychological Inquiry, 17,* 153–165.

Levey, A. B., & Martin, I. (1975). Classical conditioning of human "evaluative" responses. *Behaviour Research and Therapy, 13,* 222–226.

Lipp, O. V., & Purkis, H. M. (2005). The effects of assessment type on verbal ratings of conditional stimulus valence and contingency judgement: Implications for the extinction of evaluative learning. *Journal of Experimental Psychology: Animal Behavior Processes, 32,* 431–440.

Lovibond, P. F., & Shanks, D. R. (2002). The role of awareness in Pavlovian conditioning: Empirical evidence and theoretical implications. *Journal of Experimental Psychology: Animal Behavior Processes, 28,* 3–26.

Meersmans, T., De Houwer, J., Baeyens, F., Randell, T., & Eelen, P. (2005). Beyond evaluative conditioning: Searching for associative transfer of non-evaluative stimulus properties. *Cognition and Emotion, 19,* 283–306.

Mitchell, C. J., Anderson, N. E., & Lovibond, P. F. (2003). Measuring evaluative conditioning using the implicit association test. *Learning and Motivation, 34,* 203–217.

Moors, A., & De Houwer, J. (2006). Problems with dividing the realm of cognitive processes. *Psychological Inquiry, 17,* 199–204.

Lipp, O. V., & Purkis, H. M. (2005). No support for dual process accounts of human affective learning in simple Parlovian condition. *Cognition and Emotion, 19*, 269–282.

Pleyers, G., Corneille, O., Luminet, O., & Yzerbyt, V. (2007). Aware and (dis)liking: Item-based analyses reveal that valence acquisition via evaluative conditioning emerges only when there is contingency awareness. *Journal of Experimental Psychology: Learning, Memory & Cognition, 33*, 130–144.

Razran, G. (1954). The conditioned evocation of attitudes (cognitive conditioning?). *Journal of Experimental Psychology, 48*, 278–282.

Rozin, P., Wrzesniewski, A., & Byrnes, D. (1998). The elusiveness of evaluative conditioning. *Learning and Motivation, 29*, 397–415.

Shanks, D. R., & St. John, M. F. (1994). Characteristics of dissociable human learning systems. *Behavioural and Brain Sciences, 17*, 367–447.

Sloman, S. A. (1996). The empirical case for two systems of reasoning. *Psychological Bulletin, 119*, 3–22.

Strack, F., & Deutsch, R. (2004). Reflective and impulsive determinants of social behavior. *Personality and Social Psychology Review, 8*, 220–247.

Stuart, E. W., Shimp, T. A., & Engle, R. W. (1987). Classical conditioning of consumer attitudes: Four experiments in an advertising context. *Journal of Consumer Research, 14*, 334–351.

Till, B. D., & Priluck, R. L. (2000). Stimulus generalization in classical conditioning: An initial investigation. *Psychology & Marketing, 17*, 55–72.

Walther, E. (2002). Guilty by mere association: Evaluative conditioning and the spreading attitude effect. *Journal of Personality and Social Psychology, 82*, 919–934.

Walther, E., & Grigoriadis, S. (2004). Why sad people like shoes better: The influence of mood on the evaluative conditioning of consumer attitudes. *Psychology & Marketing, 21*, 755–773.

Walther, E., & Nagengast, B. (2006). Evaluative conditioning and the awareness issue: Assessing contingency awareness with the four-picture recognition test. *Journal of Experimental Psychology: Animal Behavior Processes, 32*, 454–459.

Walther, E., Nagengast, B., & Trasselli, C. (2005). Evaluative conditioning in social psychology: Facts and speculations. *Cognition and Emotion, 19*, 175–196.

8

The Lexicon and Grammar of Affect as Information in Consumer Decision Making
The GAIM

MICHEL TUAN PHAM

Columbia University

A s epitomized by Blaise Pascal's famous quote, "The heart has its reason of which reason knows nothing," emotions have historically been conceived as psychobiological forces that energize and channel people's behavior, sometimes at the expense of their better judgment. In advancing the "affect-as-information" hypothesis that moods, feelings, and emotions serve as sources of information, Schwarz and Clore (1983, 1996) introduced a radical departure from this historical way of thinking about affect. Rather than viewing affect as some kind of force that is separate from people's thoughts, Schwarz and Clore (1983, 1996) conceptualized affective feelings as informational inputs to people's judgment. Building on previous suggestions by Wyer and Carlston (1979), they theorized that people often draw inferences from their momentary feelings toward objects and situations (Schwarz, 1990; Schwarz & Clore, 1996). The most documented inference—the one that Schwarz and Clore (1983, 1988) originally focused on—is an evaluative inference based on the valence of the momentary feelings. People generally interpret pleasant feelings as evidence of liking, satisfaction, or well-being, and unpleasant feelings as evidence of disliking, dissatisfaction, or misery. Schwarz and Clore (1988) called this type of inference the "How do I feel about it?" heuristic (hereafter, HDIF heuristic). In early affect-as-information research (Schwarz & Clore, 1983; Schwarz, Strack, Kommer, & Wagner, 1987), the HDIF heuristic was discussed primarily as an explanation for the pervasive assimilative influence that mood states exert on evaluative judgments—a phenomenon known as mood-congruent judgment (see Mayer, Gaschke, Braverman, & Evans, 1992). However, the affect-as-information hypothesis has much broader implications. As is discussed in this chapter, the affect-as-information hypothesis, as a metaphor, has enormous explanatory power beyond the HDIF heuristic and the mood-congruent-judgment phenomenon.

This chapter evaluates the progress that has been made on the affect-as-information hypothesis since Schwarz and Clore's (1983, 1996) seminal contribution. The primary purpose of the chapter is to examine how the original tenets of the affect-as-information hypothesis can be extended to explain a wide range of judgment phenomena, especially with respect to consumer decision making. To this end, research within social psychology as well as research from other fields such as consumer behavior and behavioral decision making will be reviewed. However, only research that is amenable to an affect-as-information interpretation will be discussed. For example, the extensive literature on mood effects on information processing and memory will not be examined (see Cohen, Pham, & Andrade, 2007, for a review). Also, this review focuses on the information value of *affective* feelings only; cognitive feelings such as feelings of familiarity or feelings of fluency are not discussed. (See Clore, 1992; Schwarz, 2004; Schwarz & Clore, 2007; and Schwarz, Song, and Xu, this volume, for detailed discussions of cognitive feelings.)

The chapter is organized into three main sections. The first section identifies distinct types of information that people seem to derive from their feelings. In a sense, these different types of information constitute the *lexicon* of feelings as information. The second section identifies the basic principles that guide the processes by which feelings provide these various types of information. These principles can be thought of as rules that govern and structure the ways in which feelings acquire and convey judgment-relevant meaning. In a sense, these principles collectively define the *grammar* of feelings as information. In the concluding section the state of our knowledge and the chapter's main theoretical propositions are summarized in a generalized model of affect as information in judgment and decision making, the GAIM (for Generalized Affect-as-Information Model of judgment).

THE LEXICON OF FEELINGS AS INFORMATION

If affective feelings are seen as sources of information, what types of information do they provide? Feelings seem to provide at least six distinct types of information: (1) information about value, (2) information about the strength of preference, (3) information about risk, (4) information about conviction, (5) information about situational demands, and (6) information about motives and wants. Each type of information can be seen as an answer to a prototypical question such as "How do I feel about it?" or "What do I feel like doing?" It is these questions and their answers that collectively define the lexicon of feelings as information.

"How Do I Feel about It?"—Feelings as Information about Value

By far, the most widely documented affect-as-information inference is that of a target object's value from the pleasantness of the feelings that it elicits. According to

Schwarz and Clore (1983, 1988), people often evaluate target objects by inspecting "how they feel" while they think about these objects. Any feeling recorded while the person is thinking about an object is generally assumed to be telling something *about* the object of attention—an assumption known as the aboutness principle (Higgins, 1998). As a result, the experience of positive feelings while thinking about a target object is generally interpreted to mean that the target is desirable, attractive, valuable, etc., whereas the experience of negative feelings is interpreted to mean that the target is undesirable, unattractive, not valuable, etc. Schwarz and Clore (1988) called this process the "How do I feel about it?" (HDIF) heuristic. In Schwarz and Clore's (1983) original studies, the target object was the respondents' lives, and the dimension on which it was evaluated was their satisfaction with their lives. Judgments of life satisfaction were found to be more positive among respondents who were induced to be in a good mood than among those who were induced to be in a bad mood. According to the proposed affect-as-information explanation, when asked to evaluate their satisfaction with their lives, many respondents asked themselves "How do I feel about it?"; those who "felt good" concluded that they must be happy and satisfied with their lives, and those who "felt bad" concluded that they must be unhappy and dissatisfied with their lives. In relying on the HDIF heuristic, however, respondents failed to realize that some of their feelings were not integral responses to their lives but incidental feelings resulting from their experimentally manipulated mood states. Consistent with this explanation, Schwarz and Clore (1983) further found that, when it was made salient to the respondents that their feelings were caused by factors *other* than their lives, the effect of mood on reported life satisfaction largely disappeared.

This basic finding has since been replicated in dozens of studies (Albarracin & Kumkale, 2003; Gorn, Goldberg, & Basu, 1993; Ottati & Isbell, 1996; Pham, 1998; Siemer & Reisenzein, 1998). For example, Gorn, Goldberg, and Basu (1993) found that participants evaluated stereo speakers more favorably when pleasant music was played through the speakers than when unpleasant music was played through them. However, when participants were asked to evaluate the music *before* they rated the speakers—that is, when it was made salient that the source of the feelings was the music itself, not the speakers—the effect disappeared.

Pham (1998) offered that the HDIF heuristic plays a central role in consumer decision making. Whereas consumer decision making is generally conceptualized as a process of integration and comparison of the evaluative implications of the options' main attributes (Bettman, 1979; Wilkie & Pessemier, 1973), Pham (1998) argued instead that consumers often picture the options in their minds and compare how they feel. He also proposed that reliance on the HDIF heuristic is more likely when consumers have experiential motives (e.g., choosing a novel to read on a vacation) than when consumers have instrumental motives (e.g., comparing different tax preparation manuals). Consistent with these propositions, Pham (1998) observed that incidentally induced mood states had stronger assimilative influences on intentions to see a new movie when the decision was framed in experiential terms (to see the movie to have a good time) than when it was framed in instrumental terms (to see the movie to qualify for a subsequent study). Consistent with the proposition that the reliance on the HDIF heuristic in consumer decision making often entails a concrete picturing of the options, it was also found that the effects of mood under experiential motives were more pronounced among respondents with a more visual processing style than among respondents with a more verbal processing style. (The role of imagery in affect as information is discussed further later in this chapter.)

The idea that decisions are often based on subjective affective responses to the options has also been gaining acceptance in behavioral decision research, where this idea is generically known as the "affect heuristic" (Slovic, Finucane, Peters, & MacGregor, 2002). However, the emphasis in the behavioral-decision literature has been somewhat different. Whereas affect-as-information research in social psychology and consumer behavior has typically focused on the processes by which feelings, once elicited, enter evaluative judgments, behavioral decision research on affect has focused more on how features of the options influence the feelings that are elicited (e.g., Hsee & Rottenstreich, 2004; Hsee, Zhang, Yu, & Xi, 2003; Mellers, Schwartz, Ho, & Ritov, 1997). Conceptualizing choices as guided by subjective affective responses to the options helps explain a variety of findings that are difficult to explain with standard models of choices. For example, Slovic and his colleagues (2002) observed that people asked to evaluate simple gambles by assigning a price to them assigned greater dollar value to bets with a lower probability of a larger payoff (e.g., average price of a 7/36 probability to win $9 = $2.11) than to bets with a higher probability of a smaller payoff (e.g., average price of a 29/36 probability to win $2 = $1.25). In contrast, people asked to evaluate the same gambles by rating their attractiveness on a 0–20 scale assigned greater ratings to bets with a higher probability of a smaller payoff (e.g., average rating of a 29/36 probability to win $2 = 13.2) than to bets with a lower probability of a larger payoff (e.g., average rating of a 7/36 probability to win $9 = 7.5). The authors hypothesized that these preference reversals occurred because a pricing mode of value assessment increases the weight attached to the payoffs, which are also expressed in dollar terms, whereas an attractiveness-rating mode of value assessment increases the weight attached to the probabilities, which are more easily translated into affective assessments: A high probability of winning "feels good" and a low probability of winning "feels bad." To further test this explanation, Slovic and his colleagues (2002) devised an ingenious way of making a bet such as "a 7/36 probability to win $9"—a bet that normally "feels bad" as a low probability of winning—"feel good": They associated this bet with a complementary probability of incurring a very small loss (e.g., a 29/36 probability to lose 5¢). Counter-intuitively, adding this probability of a small loss to the bet in fact *increased* its attractiveness rating. This is presumably because subjective affective responses to the gamble were now driven by the appealing contrast between the large gain ($9) and the very small loss (5¢).

"How Strongly Do I Feel about It?"—Feelings as Information about the Strength of Preference

When monitoring their feelings to make evaluative inferences as in the HDIF heuristic, people appear to monitor not only the valence of their feelings but also the *intensity* of these feelings (i.e., the physiological arousal that accompanies the feelings). Support for this proposition can be seen in the finding that incidental arousal is often misattributed to target objects, thus polarizing their evaluations. For example, residual arousal from a scary event (e.g., following a roller-coaster ride or while crossing a high suspension bridge) usually increases people's attraction to good-looking strangers of the opposite sex and decreases their attraction to not-so-good-looking strangers or strangers of the same sex (Dienstbier, 1979; Dutton & Aron, 1974; White, Fishbein, & Rutsein, 1981). Although other interpretations have been proposed (e.g., J. B. Allen, Kenrick, Linder, & McCall, 1989; Foster, Witcher, Campbell, & Green, 1998), this effect can be interpreted from a feelings-as-information perspective. In judging their attraction to another person, it is natural for people to ask themselves, "How do I feel about him (her)?" In doing so, they record not only the valence of their feelings (which, in these studies, was typically dictated by the gender and physical attractiveness of the other person) but also the intensity of their feelings (which in these studies was influenced by incidental arousal). Consistent with an affect-as-information interpretation, the amplifying effect of incidental arousal on target evaluation is generally weakened when the actual source of the arousal is salient or when people are led to attribute the arousal to factors that are unrelated to the target (Foster, Witcher, Campbell, & Green, 1998; Reisenzein & Gattinger, 1982; Schwarz, Servay, & Kumpf, 1985).

Similar effects were obtained in a recent study of advertising evaluation by Gorn, Pham, and Sin (2001). In this study, music was used to manipulate participants' incidental mood both in term of valence and in terms of arousal. Then, in a supposedly unrelated study, participants were asked to evaluate an ad whose affective tone was either pleasant or unpleasant. As predicted, the arousal of participants' preexisting mood magnified the effect of the ad's affective tone on participants' evaluations: Under high arousal, evaluations became even more favorable when the ad's tone was pleasant and more unfavorable when the ad's tone was unpleasant. (The valence of the mood did not have any effect.) This result is again consistent with the idea that people monitor the intensity of their feelings when making target evaluations and sometimes fail to realize that the intensity of these feelings may be inflated by residual incidental arousal. Thus, whereas people often use the valence of their feelings to infer the *direction* of their attitudes and preferences, they additionally use the intensity of these feelings to infer the *strength* of these attitudes and preferences—as if asking themselves, "How *strongly* do I feel about it?"[1]

"How Scary Does It Feel?"—Feelings as Information about Risk

Closely related to the HDIF heuristic, in which value is inferred from the valence of one's momentary feelings, is the inference of risk from feelings of fear, dread, and anxiety elicited by a target. This inference might be called a "How scary does it feel?" heuristic. A large body of evidence shows that people's perceptions of risk and danger are not determined solely by beliefs about potential negative consequences of objects and situations; they are also driven by feelings of fear, dread, or anxiety elicited by these objects and situations (Loewenstein, Weber, Hsee,

& Welch, 2001). Loewenstein and his colleagues (2001) call this proposition the "risk-as-feelings" hypothesis. Early support for this hypothesis was obtained by Johnson and Tversky (1983), who observed that respondents made anxious by vivid stories about the death of a person provided higher occurrence estimates for variety of risks (e.g., leukemia, fire, homicides) than control respondents who were not made anxious. One possible explanation—other than the affect-as-information explanation—is that participants' state of anxiety primed mood-consistent material in memory (e.g., memories of a relative who died of a terrible disease), thereby distorting their perceptions and beliefs about the risks (Bower, 1981; Forgas, 1995; Isen, Shalker, Clark, & Karp, 1978). However, if this explanation were correct, the anxiety-mood effect on risk estimates should be stronger if there is a direct relation between the content of the story and the risk to be estimated than if there is no relation. Instead, Johnson and Tversky (1983) found that the effect was *the same* whether or not there was a direct relation between the content of the story and the risk to be estimated. This lack of contingency suggests that it was the *feelings* elicited by the stories, not the *content* of these stories, that influenced respondents' risk perceptions, which is consistent with an affect-as-information explanation.

Additional support for the risk-as-feeling hypothesis comes from the well-documented phenomenon that risks and threats are generally taken more seriously when communicated in concrete and vivid terms (i.e., in an emotionally engaging manner) than when communicated in more abstract or pallid terms (Hendrickx, Vlek, & Oppewal, 1989; Sinaceur, Heath, & Cole, 2005). For example, it was observed in France that newspaper articles using the emotional label "Mad Cow disease" resulted in more dramatic decreases in beef consumption than comparable articles using the scientific label "Creutzfeldt-Jakob disease" (Sinaceur et al., 2005). As shall be discussed later, the images that threats bring to mind play an important role in feelings-based inferences of risks (as the images of the options do in the HDIF heuristic). Further evidence for the risk-as-feelings hypothesis comes from the finding that the behavioral consequences of fear are typically more pronounced as one gets temporally closer to the threat, even though, objectively, the level of risk remains the same (Loewenstein, Weber, Hsee, & Welch, 2001). For example, students who had volunteered to tell a joke in front of the class the following week for a small compensation were highly likely to "chicken out" at the last minute when given an opportunity to do so (Welch, 1999, as cited in Loewenstein et al., 2001). Even though, theoretically, the threat of embarrassment was the same when the students initially made the decision to volunteer a joke and immediately before the joke was due, the fear of embarrassment was presumably more acute immediately before the joke was due.

Note that in the "How scary does it feel?" heuristic, it is feelings related to fear in particular (e.g., anxiety, dread, terror, etc.), not negative feelings in general, that are used to infer risk and danger. For example, whereas experimentally induced fear leads to more pessimistic risk estimates and more risk-averse choices, experimentally induced anger has the opposite effects of lowering risk estimates and encouraging risk-seeking (Lerner, Gonzalez, Small, & Fischhoff, 2003; Lerner & Keltner, 2001). The preceding caveat illustrates a more general point about affect-as-information: The information conveyed by feelings goes beyond their valence and intensity (Lerner & Keltner, 2000; Raghunathan & Pham, 1999). As illustrated by the differential effects of anger and fear, even feelings of the same valence and intensity can convey very different types of information. A growing body of research indeed shows that people tend to draw different inferences from feelings with distinct emotional qualities (e.g., feelings of fear vs. anger vs. sadness; feelings of happiness vs. pride vs. gratitude). In particular, people generally draw inferences that are consistent with the typical appraisal antecedents of the associated emotions (Lerner & Keltner, 2000; Raghunathan & Pham, 1999). For instance, Keltner, Ellsworth, and Edwards (1993) found that individuals incidentally made to feel sad tended to attribute events to situational factors (e.g., "I missed the flight because the traffic was bad"), whereas individuals incidentally made to feel angry tended to attribute the same events to human factors (e.g., "I missed the flight because the cab driver was terrible"). This is presumably because anger is typically caused by the actions of people, whereas sadness is typically caused by factors that are more situational. Appraisal-consistent inferences and judgments from distinct emotional feelings have been observed in many other studies (Bodenhausen, Sheppard, & Kramer, 1994; Gallagher & Clore, 1985; Keltner, Ellsworth, & Edwards, 1993; Lerner & Keltner, 2000, 2001; Raghunathan & Pham, 1999; Tiedens & Linton, 2001). Moreover, consistent with an affect-as-information explanation, these effects tend to be eliminated when people are led to attribute their feelings to a source unrelated to the target (DeSteno, Petty, Wegener, & Rucker, 2000; Dunn & Schweitzer, 2005; Raghunathan, Pham, & Corfman, 2006). Therefore, the emotional quality of the feelings is a critical determinant of the specific information being conveyed, as illustrated both by the "How scary does it feel?" heuristic and by the heuristic discussed next.

"How Certain Do I Feel about It?"—Feelings as Information about Conviction

Somewhat related to the inference of strength of preference from the arousal intensity of emotional responses is the inference of strength of conviction from emotional feelings varying in certainty appraisal. Some emotions such as anger, disgust, and joy are typically experienced in response to situations appraised as certain, whereas other emotions such as fear, surprise, and hope are typically experienced in response to situations appraised as uncertain (Frijda, Kuipers, & Terschure, 1989; Roseman, 1991; Smith & Ellsworth, 1985). Feelings associated with either type of emotions seem to influence people's general sense of confidence, as if they were inferring the certainty of their beliefs and actions from the certainty of the felt emotion's characteristic appraisal. As a result, judgments made when people are feeling angry, disgusted, or joyful are typically made with a greater sense of certainty, confidence, or conviction than judgments made when people are not experiencing these particular emotional feelings (Bodenhausen, Sheppard, & Kramer, 1994; Tiedens & Linton, 2001). For example, Tiedens and Linton (2001) observed that participants who were induced in high-certainty emotional states of disgust or happiness had higher confidence in their predictions than participants who were induced in low-certainty emotional states of fear or hope. Consistent with previous findings by Bodenhausen, Sheppard, and Kramer (1994), Tiedens and Linton (2001) also found that, compared to participants induced in low-certainty emotional states (e.g., hope, surprise, sadness), participants induced in high-certainty emotional states (e.g., disgust, anger, joy) were more likely to make judgments based on stereotypes and heuristic processing, suggesting that they had higher confidence in their prior knowledge. Similarly, Briñol, Petty, and Barden (2007) recently observed that participants induced in a high-certainty state of happiness reported greater confidence in their thoughts about a previously read message than participants induced in a low-certainty state of sadness.

Therefore, when making judgments and decisions, people sometimes appear to ask themselves, "How certain do I feel about it?"—thereby making more confident and cursory judgments when their feelings suggest high certainty. This proposition may explain why feelings of anger (a high-certainty emotion) are often associated with higher risk taking (Fessler, Pillsworth, & Flamson, 2004; Leith & Baumeister, 1996; Lerner, Gonzalez, Small, & Fischhoff, 2003; Lerner & Keltner, 2001). This may be because angry individuals may have particularly strong convictions in their beliefs.

"How Serious Does It Feel?"—Feelings as Information about Situational Demands

Related to the previous heuristic, feelings also seem to be used to infer the level of vigilance and effort required by a task or situation—a phenomenon that Schwarz (2002) called cognitive tuning. In general, negative affective states are interpreted as calling for increased vigilance and effort, whereas positive affective states are interpreted as allowing more nonchalance and less effort. According to Schwarz (2002), this is because negative affective states signal that the environment is potentially threatening, whereas positive affective states signal that the environment is safe. Consistent with this idea, it is typically found in persuasion studies that negative incidental moods increase people's processing of the substance of the message and decrease their reliance on heuristic cues, whereas positive incidental moods have the opposite effect (Bless, Bohner, Schwarz, & Strack, 1990; Bless, Mackie, & Schwarz, 1992; Mackie & Worth, 1989). Similar effects are also found with other types of judgments (Bodenhausen, Kramer, & Suesser, 1994); and even subtle affective cues such as the color of the paper on which the information is provided can produce similar effects (Soldat, Sinclair, & Mark, 1997). Moreover, consistent with an affect-as-information explanation, these effects tend to disappear when people are led to attribute their feelings to external factors (Sinclair, Mark, & Clore, 1994).

Therefore, when faced with new tasks and situations, people appear to ask themselves, "How serious does it feel?" When their feelings are negative, they infer that the task or situation is serious and therefore demands more careful, data-driven processing; when their feelings are positive, they infer that the task or situation is more benign and therefore allows more heuristic, internal-knowledge-based processing. Note that while the "How-serious-does-it-feel?" heuristic also has an evaluation component ("the situation is good/bad"), it is quite different from the HDIF heuristic. Whereas in the HDIF heuristic the valence of the feelings is mapped onto an attitudinal dimension of liking (approach) or disliking (avoidance), in the "How serious does it feel?" heuristic the valence of the feelings is mapped onto a mental-set dimension of seriousness (vigilance) or benign-ness (nonchalance).

Note also that the cognitive-tuning phenomenon relates to inferences of situational demands from positive versus negative mood states that are diffuse and relatively undifferentiated. Affective states that have a more distinct emotional quality need not lead to similar inferences. For example, as mentioned in the preceding subsection, negative emotional states associated with high certainty (e.g., anger, disgust) tend to *decrease* the depth of processing in judgment, and positive emotional states associated with high uncertainty (e.g., hope) tend to *increase* the depth of processing in judgment (Bodenhausen, Sheppard, & Kramer, 1994; Tiedens & Linton, 2001). Pham (2007) recently theorized that, among the various negative states with a distinct emotional quality, it is those associated with sadness in particular that are most likely to activate the type of increased vigilance described. This is because sadness may have originally functioned as a signal for situational-reappraisal, especially when aspirations were not met. In contrast, positive feelings may have served as a signal to engage in more contemplative thoughts and explorative behaviors; hence, the greater nonchalance triggered by positive mood states.

"What Would I Feel Better about?" and "What Do I Feel Like Doing?"—Feelings as Motivational Information

People also seem to infer from their feelings the priorities that they should set and the goals that they should pursue in a given situation. That is, feelings can convey motivational information. For example, Raghunathan and Pham (1999) found that, in choices between a high-risk/high-reward option and a low-risk/low-reward option, sad individuals consistently favor the former, whereas anxious individuals consistently favor the latter. (Neutral-mood individuals exhibit preferences that are in between; see also Raghunathan, Pham, and Corfman, 2006.) These researchers interpreted this finding as follows: Sad individuals tend to infer that they have lost something of value, a typical cause of sadness. This inference in turn seems to activate a goal of reward acquisition that shifts preferences toward high-reward options. In contrast, anxious individuals tend to infer that the situation is uncertain and beyond control, a typical cause of anxiety. This inference activates a goal of risk avoidance that shifts preferences toward low-risk options. Therefore, feelings seem to convey information not only about essential characteristics of the situation, but also about the priorities and goals that the situation calls for. This chain of inferences need not be conscious. According to Raghunathan and Pham (1999), it may be performed intuitively by asking "What would I feel better about?"—with sadness leading to the conclusion that one would feel better about higher-reward (but higher-risk) options, and anxiety leading to the conclusion that one would feel better about lower-risk (but lower-reward) options.

Conceptually related results were observed by Lerner, Small, and Loewenstein (2004), who found that incidental states of disgust reduce both the price that people are willing to pay to purchase a small item and the price that they are willing to accept to sell the same item. This finding can be explained as follows: Disgust is usually experienced in reaction to the ingestion of or proximity to things that our body finds noxious (Rozin & Fallon, 1987). This emotional state is thus closely associated with a motivation to expel or avoid the noxious item. Therefore, when experiencing feelings of disgust, people tend to infer that that they should "get rid of" or avoid certain items, which reduces both the price that disgusted participants are willing to accept to sell an item and the price that they are willing to pay to buy a similar item. Note again that this chain of inference need not be conscious. Rather, it may take the form of asking oneself "What do I feel like doing?" and reaching the conclusion that "I feel like selling it" or "I don't feel like buying it" when feeling disgusted. Lerner and her colleagues (2004) also found that incidental states of sadness increase the price that people are willing to pay to purchase the small item and decrease the price that people are willing to accept to sell the item. This finding can be explained as follows: As illustrated by the Raghunathan and Pham (1999) findings, sadness triggers a motivation of reward acquisition. To the extent that acquiring a new item can be seen as a reward, this motivation increases the price that sad participants are willing to pay to buy this new item. However, consistent with the notion that sadness is a signal for situation-reappraisal (Pham, 2007), sadness also triggers a motivation to change one's circumstances (Lerner, Small, & Loewenstein, 2004). To the extent that selling a possession can be seen as a change of circumstances, this motivation decreases the price that sad participants are willing to accept to sell the item. Again, this chain of inference may take the form of asking oneself "What do I feel like doing?" and reaching the conclusion that "I feel like buying it" or "I feel like selling it" when experiencing sadness.

The "What would I feel better about?" and "What do I feel like doing?" heuristics are similar to the HDIF heuristic in that decision makers are trying to project how the options would make them feel. However, unlike in the HDIF heuristic, in these motivational heuristics the anticipatory feelings are conditional on the current affective state. Options that address the core motivational implications of the initial affective state (e.g., sadness, anxiety, disgust) will "feel better" than options that do not address the core motivational implications. In other words, it is the trajectory or direction of movement suggested by the feelings that is informative.

In summary, the lexicon of feelings as information goes beyond the inference of value from the HDIF heuristic. People seem to make at least six major types of inferences from their feelings: (1) inferences about the value of target objects ("How do I feel about it?"), (2) inferences about the strength of their preferences ("How strongly do I feel about it?"), (3) inferences about the level of risk and threat ("How scary does it feel?"), (4) inferences about their level of conviction ("How certain do I feel?"), (5) inferences about situational demands ("How serious does it feel?"), and (6) inferences about their motivations and priorities ("What do I feel like?" and "What would I feel better about?"). Let us now proceed to the processing rules that govern these major types of inferences and define the grammar of feelings as information.

THE GRAMMAR OF FEELINGS AS INFORMATION

Now that the range of information provided by feelings has been reviewed, let us turn to the principles that govern the information value of feelings in judgment. Six principles can be identified: (1) the principle of necessity and sufficiency of feelings, (2) the principle of relative accessibility, (3) the principle of relative diagnosticity, (4) the principle of imagery boundedness, (5) the principle of query and response-mapping dependency, and (6) the principle of situational engagement. Much like grammatical rules that dictate how words convey meaning in a given language, these principles structure the way in which feelings acquire and convey information in judgment. In this sense, these six principles collectively define the grammar of feelings as information.

The Necessity and Sufficiency of Feelings

Because the experience of feelings is generally associated with certain cognitions (e.g., appraisals, beliefs, and thoughts), one could question whether the information conveyed by feelings lies in the feelings themselves or instead in the cognitions that typically accompany these feelings (Fishbein & Middlestadt, 1995). Several findings suggest that the experience of genuine feelings is both necessary and sufficient to convey information. Evidence of the sufficiency of feelings in conveying information comes from the findings that even somatomotor inductions of affect produce judgmental inferences that are consistent with the lexicon of feeling described in the previous section. For example, in one study (Keltner, Ellsworth, et al., 1993, Experiment 4), participants were instructed to assume physical poses that, unbeknownst to them, were characteristic of anger (e.g., eyebrows down with hands and teeth clenched) or sadness (e.g., inner corners of the eyebrows raised while gazing down). Although no higher-level cognition was involved, participants unknowingly modeling anger made causal attributions consistent with anger, whereas participants modeling sadness made attributions consistent with sadness. Similarly, Martin, Harlow, and Strack (1992) asked participants to make evaluations while either (1) holding a pen lightly between their teeth, which resulted in the unknowing mimicking of a smile, or (2) biting strongly on a paper towel, which activated facial muscles associated with anger. Participants who unknowingly mimicked smiling reported more favorable evaluations than those who mimicked anger. It appears therefore that even these low-level affective responses are sufficient for meaningful feelings-as-information inferences.

Other studies suggest that the experience of feelings may also be necessary for their informational and motivational signals to be conveyed. For instance, in a recent study, respondents were exposed to the same anxiety- or sadness-producing scenarios as those used by Raghunathan and Pham (1999) and again asked to make a choice that involved a risk-versus-reward trade-off (Pham & Raghunathan, 2007). Using a manipulation inspired by Strack, Schwarz, and Gschneidinger

(1985), respondents in the "hot" condition were asked to empathize with the situation described in the scenario, whereas respondents in the "cold" condition were asked to analyze the situation described in the scenario. A pretest had shown that even though both groups of respondents were exposed to the same descriptive scenario content, genuine feelings of anxiety or sadness were more likely to be experienced in the hot condition than in the cold condition. As expected, respondents in the hot condition exhibited similar choice tendencies as those uncovered by Raghunathan and Pham (1999). Sad participants were again more likely to prefer the high-risk/high-reward option, whereas anxious participants were more likely to prefer the low-risk/low-reward option. (Neutral mood participants exhibited preferences that were in between.) In contrast, respondents in the cold condition were *not* influenced by the affective content of the scenarios. That is, cold exposure to the same descriptive sadness- or anxiety-related information did not activate the motivational orientations observed in previous studies. This finding suggests that genuine feelings of anxiety and sadness may be necessary for people to shift their preferences toward lower risks or toward greater rewards (for similar results, see Keltner, Ellsworth, et al., 1993, Experiment 3).

The necessity and sufficiency of feelings as information has important methodological implications. A popular methodology in behavioral decision research involves the analysis of responses to hypothetical decision scenarios presented in the form of short vignettes (e.g., "Imagine that you are at the beach and very thirsty [...] how much would you be willing to pay for a beer?"). Some researchers have used similar vignettes to study the role of affect in judgment and decision making. However, it is not clear that such vignettes are suitable for the study of real affective phenomena. This is because genuinely experienced feelings (e.g., experienced anger), including those experienced anticipatorily at the thought of the object, may function very differently from mere affective beliefs (e.g., anticipated anger), which these hypothetical vignettes are more likely to capture (Pham, 2004). The difference between these affective beliefs and genuine affective feelings is illustrated by another study by Pham and Raghunathan (2007). Participants were again asked to make a choice involving a risk-versus-reward trade-off. Before they made this choice, participants in the "experiencing" condition were induced in genuine states of sadness, anxiety, or neutral affect using the same manipulation as in previous studies. In contrast, participants in the "projection" condition were asked to imagine the state of someone who was experiencing sadness, anxiety, or neutral affect and predict which choice they would make. Whereas participants in the experiencing condition once again replicated the sadness > neutral > anxiety pattern observed in previous studies, participants in the projection condition did not. Therefore, affective beliefs (here, projected affective states) need not have the same informational value as genuinely experienced feelings.[2]

The contrast between mere affective beliefs and genuinely experienced feelings is also problematic for studies that rely on retrospective or projective self-reports of affective responses as predictors of attitudes and behaviors toward target objects (e.g., C. T. Allen, Machleit, & Kleine, 1992; Bagozzi, Baumgartner, & Pieters, 1998). Again, such self-reports may be more likely to tap into affective beliefs whose effects are not necessarily representative of those of genuine feelings.

If feelings are indeed sources of information, their influence on judgments and decisions should depend on the same types of factors as those known to moderate the influence of other types of inputs on judgments and decisions. According to Feldman and Lynch (1988), the influence of inputs on judgments depends on two broad classes of factors: (1) the relative accessibility of these inputs compared to alternative inputs, and (2) the relative diagnosticity of these inputs compared to alternative inputs. A substantial body of evidence indicates that these two general principles apply to feelings as information as well. (Although here these two principles are treated as conceptually distinct for clarity of exposition, the diagnosticity and accessibility of input can be related empirically. For example, a highly accessible input can be perceived subjectively as more diagnostic.)

The Relative Accessibility of Feelings

A number of studies suggest that feelings have greater influence on judgment when they are more accessible (Albarracin & Kumkale, 2003; Siemer & Reisenzein, 1998). An obvious determinant of the relative accessibility of feelings is their sheer intensity. Another is their salience. For example, Siemer and Reisenzein (1998) observed that mood-congruent effects on judgments were more pronounced when participants were encouraged to pay attention to their feelings than when they were not.[3] In addition, because the relative accessibility of an input is a function of its own accessibility and the accessibility of competing inputs (Feldman & Lynch, 1988), the relative accessibility of feelings—hence, their influence on judgment— should also increase when alternative bases of judgments become less accessible. A number of studies indeed show that the influence of feelings on judgment is stronger when alternative bases of judgment are relatively inaccessible than when they are more accessible (Bakamitsos, 2006; Gorn, Pham, & Sin, 2001; Isen & Shalker, 1982; Levine, Wyer, & Schwarz, 1994; Miniard, Bhatla, & Sirdeshmukh, 1992). One determinant of the relative accessibility of feelings is the mere availability (or lack thereof) of alternative bases of judgments. For example, Bakamitsos (2006) observed that mood-congruency effects on product evaluations were more pronounced when no information about the product's attributes was provided than when this information was provided. Therefore, consistent with Feldman and Lynch's (1988) relative accessibility principle, the availability of alternative bases of judgment decreases the influence of feelings on evaluations. Another determinant of the relative accessibility of feelings is the evaluative clarity or ambiguity of alternative bases of judgment. For example, Gorn, Pham, and Sin (2001) observed that a positive incidental mood (induced through a musical manipulation) had a stronger mood-congruent influence on participants' evaluations of an ad when the ad's affective tone was neutral than when it was clearly positive or clearly negative. Similarly, Miniard, Bhatla, and Sirdeshmukh (1992) found that incidental mood states had a stronger mood-congruent influence on postconsumption ratings of a brand of peanut butter whose taste was neutral than on similar ratings of a brand of peanut butter whose taste was clearly good or clearly bad (see also Isen & Shalker, 1982).

Consistent with Zajonc's (1980) well-known hypothesis about the primacy of affect in judgment, a number of studies indicate that feelings tend to be relatively more accessible than more descriptive bases of judgment. For example, using a real-time assessment instrument, Pham, Cohen, Pracejus, and Hughes (2001) observed that stimulus-based feeling responses to moderately complex everyday stimuli such as magazine pictures and television commercials were registered more rapidly than were cognitive assessments of the same stimuli. Verplanken, Hofstee, and Janssen (1998) obtained similar findings in memory-based judgments of well-known brands and countries. Because feelings are generally more accessible than more descriptive inputs, situations that constrain people's processing capacity usually increase the weight that people attach to feelings in judgments and decisions (Pham, Cohen, Pracejus, & Hughes, 2001; Rottenstreich, Sood, & Brenner, 2007; Shiv & Fedorikhin, 1999; Siemer & Reisenzein, 1998). For example, Shiv and Fedorikhin (1999) observed that in choices between an affectively attractive option (a tempting piece of chocolate cake) and a descriptively attractive option (a healthier fruit salad), reducing processing resources increases preferences for the affectively attractive option. Similarly, Rottenstreich, Sood, and Brenner (2007) found that, because memory-based choices place greater demands on processing resources than do stimulus-based choices, the former increase the weight attached to affective inputs compared to the latter.

The Relative Diagnosticity of Feelings

The very notion of affect as information implies that people should rely on their feelings only to the extent that these feelings are perceived to be informative or diagnostic. Consistent with this proposition, numerous studies show that the reliance on feelings in judgment is proportional to their perceived diagnosticity. Different dimensions of the perceived diagnosticity of feelings in judgment and decisions can be distinguished: (1) their perceived representativeness, (2) their perceived relevance, (3) their perceived predictive validity, and (4) their perceived convergent validity. Although the distinction among these four dimensions of perceived diagnosticity of feelings is mostly conceptual, there are also some empirical differences among these dimensions, as discussed further.

Diagnosticity as Representativeness   The most widely documented determinant of the perceived diagnosticity of feelings is their representativeness, that is, the degree to which the feelings are perceived to emanate from and reflect essential properties of the target (Pham, 1998; Strack, 1992). As mentioned before, numerous studies have shown that the influence of feelings on judgment is stronger when people attribute their feelings to the target than when they attribute them to an unrelated source (Gorn, Goldberg, & Basu, 1993; Schwarz & Clore, 1983; Siemer & Reisenzein, 1998). For example, Schwarz and Clore (1983) originally observed that respondents who were in a good mood as a result of being interviewed on a sunny day reported higher life satisfaction than those who were in a bad mood as a result of being interviewed on a rainy day. However, if respondents' attention was directed to the weather as an explanation for their feelings, the effect disappeared. This finding suggests that respondents were influenced by their feelings only to the extent that they believed these feelings to be representative of how they felt about their lives. When it was made salient to them that their feelings were not representative of their lives, respondents refrained from using these feelings in their judgments. This basic contingency is a hallmark of the affect-as-information framework. The perceived representativeness of feelings has been shown to moderate not only the reliance on the HDIF heuristic (Gorn, Goldberg, & Basu, 1993; Pham, 1998; Siemer & Reisenzein, 1998), but also the reliance on other feelings-as-information heuristics (Keltner, Locke, & Audrain, 1993; Raghunathan, Pham, & Corfman, 2006; Schwarz, Servay, & Kumpf, 1985; Soldat, Sinclair, & Mark, 1997). Note that, by default, people tend to assume that their feelings *are* representative of the target, even when the actual source of the feelings is incidental (Schwarz, 1990). It is only when an alternative explanation for their feelings is made salient that they question the representativeness of their feelings, or when they have a high motivation and ability to identify and correct for unwanted feeling influences on judgment (Albarracin & Kumkale, 2003; Ottati & Isbell, 1996).

In typical affect-as-information studies, feelings are manipulated through incidental mood inductions, and therefore are *not* representative of the target. However, the effects of representativeness can also be observed when feelings *are* in fact representative of the target, that is, when the feelings are genuine integral affective responses to the target. For example, Pham (1998, Experiment 3) observed that intentions to attend a high school reunion—an event likely to elicit positive anticipatory feelings when relying on the HDIF heuristic—were lower when participants were led to attribute their feelings to a piece of music that was being played softly in the background than when no music was being played. (A pretest had shown that the music did not affect people's mood when played at such a low volume.) Apparently, participants attributed part of their integral feelings toward the high school reunion to the piece of music, resulting in a "subtraction effect" (see Martin, Seta, & Crelia, 1990) caused by the discounting of these integral feelings from the judgment.

Although the representativeness of feelings is often treated as a dichotomy—echoing the often-used distinction between "integral" versus "incidental" feelings (Bodenhausen, 1993), it should rather be conceived as a continuum. Rather than being either representative ("integral") or nonrepresentative of the target ("incidental"), feelings may sometimes be somewhat representative of the target.[4] In such cases, inferences from the feelings appear to be commensurate with the degree of overlap between the attributed source of the feelings and the target. For example, Raghunathan, Pham, and Corfman (2006) observed that when their source was *not* salient, incidentally induced feelings of sadness or anxiety influenced participants' risk-reward trade-offs even when the trade-offs were totally unrelated to the source of sadness or anxiety. However, when the source of anxiety or sadness *was* salient, feelings of sadness or anxiety influenced participants' risk-reward trade-offs *only* in domains that were thematically related to the source of anxiety or sadness. This suggests that participants who were aware of the source of their anxiety or sadness drew inferences from their feelings only to the extent that they perceived some degree of relatedness between the source of their feelings and the target decision (see Shen & Wyer, 2008, for related results). The fact that perceived representativeness is a matter of degree rather than an all-or-nothing attribute of feelings is also illustrated in a series of studies by Keltner, Locke, and Audrain (1993), who found, for instance, that students' negative feelings following an exam (1) depressed their judgments of life satisfaction when the feelings were attributed to things in general but not when the feelings were attributed to the exam in particular, and (2) depressed their judgments of academic satisfaction when the feelings were attributed to the exam but not when the feelings were attributed to things in general.

Diagnosticity as Relevance   Pham (1998) proposed that, holding the representativeness of the feelings constant, the reliance on feelings as information additionally depends on their perceived relevance to the judgment or decision at hand. Consistent with this proposition, he observed that people are more influenced by their mood when making decisions guided by experiential motives than when making decisions guided by instrumental motives—an effect that has been replicated in multiple studies (Adaval, 2001; Yeung & Wyer, 2004). Presumably, this is because feelings are perceived to be more relevant for assessing the potential fulfillment of experiential goals (e.g., "Would I have fun at this movie?") than for assessing the potential fulfillment of instrumental goals (e.g., "Would seeing this movie help me achieve X?"). Similarly, it has been found that achievement-related emotions (cheerfulness vs. dejection) have stronger influence on product evaluations when consumers have achievement goals than when they have protection goals, whereas protection-related emotions (quiescence vs. agitation) have stronger influence when consumers have protection goals than when they have achievement goals (Bosmans & Baumgartner, 2005). Therefore, the more relevant the emotional feelings to the goal being pursued, the more influence they have on judgment. In general, feelings will also be perceived as more relevant when the dimension of judgment is primarily affective (e.g., physical attractiveness, enjoyment) than when it is more cognitive (e.g., intelligence, usefulness; see R. S. Wyer, Clore, & Isbell, 1999). For example, Schwarz and colleagues (1987) found that mood states have greater influence on judgments of well-being—presumably a more affective judgment—than on reported satisfaction with one's work or current housing—presumably more cognitive judgments.

Diagnosticity as Predictive Validity   Holding the perceived representativeness of the feelings constant, the reliance on feelings in judgments also appears to depend on their perceived predictive validity. For example, Avnet and Pham (2007) used a procedure adapted from Schwarz and colleagues (1991) to manipulate participants' momentary trust in their feelings while holding the perceived representativeness and relevance of these feelings constant. Schwarz and colleagues (1991) had found that when material is easy to retrieve from memory, the experience of ease of retrieval reinforces the judgmental implications of the retrieved material, whereas when the material is difficult to retrieve, the experience of difficulty of retrieval reverses the judgmental implications of the retrieved material. Building on this finding, Avnet and Pham (2007) asked participants to recollect either two instances of successful reliance on feelings in judgments or decisions, which is subjectively easy, or 10 instances, which is subjectively difficult. It was predicted that participants in the two-instance condition would have higher momentary trust in their feelings than participants in the 10-instance condition. As predicted, it was found that participants' evaluations of a book were more strongly affected by their incidental mood state when they had high momentary trust in their feelings than when they had low momentary trust. Similarly, participants' attitudes toward an advertised message were more affected by the pleasantness of the commercial's soundtrack when they had high momentary trust in their feelings than when they had low momentary trust. According to Avnet and Pham (2007), these findings suggest that the reliance on feelings as information may involve a metacognitive assessment of the predictive validity of the feelings. The notion of predictive validity as a dimension of the perceived diagnosticity of the feelings in judgment also transpires in Raghunathan and Pham's (1999) finding that anxiety and sadness have more influence on individuals making decisions for themselves than on individuals making decisions for someone else. This is presumably because people perceived their feelings to be more predictive of their own preferences than of someone else's.

Diagnosticity as Convergent Validity   Some studies suggest that the perceived diagnosticity of feelings increases when the feeling experience seems to converge across multiple sources (Adaval, 2001; Gasper & Clore, 1998). For example, Adaval (2001) found that consumers place greater weight on product attribute information when this information is evaluatively consistent with the consumer's mood than when it is evaluatively inconsistent. According to Adaval (2001), when there is evaluative convergence between the attribute information and the mood state, the information "just feels right," which increases its perceived validity (see Lee and Higgins's chapter in this volume for a discussion of the related notion of regulatory fit). Similarly, Gasper and Clore (1998) observed that incidental states of anxiety had stronger influence on judgments of personal risk—consistent with a "How scary does it feel?" heuristic—among participants with high trait anxiety than among participants with low trait anxiety. Among participants with high trait anxiety, incidental feelings of anxiety influenced judgments of personal risk even when the actual source of the incidental feelings of anxiety was made salient (i.e., even when their representativeness was decreased). Apparently, the consistency between the incidental feeling experience of anxiety and the person's chronic tendency to experience such feelings increases the perceived validity of these feelings.

The proposed distinction among these four dimensions of perceived diagnosticity of feelings is primarily meant to be conceptual and taxonomic. However, empirical differences among these dimensions can also be identified. As mentioned above, there is evidence that feelings are generally assumed to be representative of the target by default (Schwarz, 1990; Albarracin & Kumkale, 2003). In contrast, the relevance of the feelings to the judgment or decision to be made appears to be assessed with much greater flexibility. For example, the finding that feelings are used more when the decision makers have experiential motives than when they have instrumental motives (Pham, 1998) is too robust to be compatible with the notion that feelings are assumed to be relevant by default. Rather, it appears that the relevance of feelings is assessed with great efficiency and flexibility. This efficiency and flexibility also transpires in a recent unpublished analysis of consumer responses to a thousand Belgian television commercials (Geuens, Pham, and De Pelsmaker, 2007). In this study, a large sample of Belgian consumers was asked to watch a large number of television commercials and rate their attitudes toward each advertised brand. Separate groups of coders were used to code (1) the emotional content of each ad and (2) the hedonic-versus-utilitarian nature of each advertised product or service. Aggregate analyses across ads show that consumers' brand attitudes were more influenced by the emotional content of the ad when the advertised product or service was hedonic than when it was utilitarian. This interaction between the emotional content of the ad and the product's or service's category is quite remarkable considering that respondents who reported their brand attitudes saw 40 to 50 commercials in a row and were not explicitly asked to pay attention to the emotional content of the ad or to the hedonic/utilitarian nature of each advertised product or service. In other words, despite viewing many commercials in a row, respondents appear to spontaneously adjust their brand attitude judgments online for the relevance of their feelings. This type of efficient adjustment for the relevance of feelings is very different from the type of default value that is assumed with respect to the representativeness of feelings. Additional research may reveal further differences among the four dimensions of diagnosticity identified above.

Note that the four dimensions of perceived diagnosticity of feelings discussed here—perceived representativeness, perceived relevance, predictive validity, and convergent validity—all have a logical basis. It seems logical to rely more on one's feelings if they are perceived to be representative of the target, if they are relevant to the judgment or decision at hand, if they are perceived to have predictive validity, and if they are perceived to have convergent validity. In other words, these four dimensions of the subjective diagnosticity of feelings all have some *objective* grounding. However, it appears that certain factors that do *not* have a logical basis of diagnosticity—namely, the person's regulatory focus and the person's temporal perspective—also influence the reliance on feelings through their influence on subjective diagnosticity. These factors are discussed independently under the separate notion of situational engagement.

On the Imagery Boundedness of Seeing How It Feels

Decision making often involves an assessment of options that are not present in the decision maker's environment (e.g., deciding from home which restaurant to go to) or whose evaluative consequences need to be projected (e.g., assessing whether a trip to the beach would be fun). Building on previous theoretical suggestions (Kahneman & Snell, 1990), Pham (1998) proposed that consumers often make such decisions by accessing or constructing mental pictures of the options and "seeing how they feel," especially when the consumers have experiential motives. Consistent with this proposition, he found (1) that reliance on the HDIF heuristic is more pronounced among consumers with a visual as opposed to propositional style of processing, and (2) that anticipatory feeling responses are indeed instantiated when consumers evaluate options with experiential motives. The proposition that decision making is often based on anticipatory feeling responses to mental pictures of the options has been echoed by other researchers (Gilbert, Gill, & Wilson, 2002; Hsee & Rottenstreich, 2004; Loewenstein, Weber, Hsee, & Welch, 2001; Rottenstreich & Hsee, 2001). For example, Slovic and his colleagues observed that affective ratings of mental pictures elicited by various cities were strongly correlated with people's intention to visit or live in these cities (Finucane, Alhakami, Slovic, & Johnson, 2000).

The characteristics of the mental pictures involved in feeling-based judgments and decisions have important consequences on the nature of these judgments and decisions. According to Kahneman and his colleagues (Kahneman, Ritov, & Schkade, 1999; Kahneman & Snell, 1990), the pictures involved in affective valuations tend to be discrete, prototypical representations of the target and have a fixed-time, snapshot-like quality as opposed to a continuous-time, film-like quality. As a result, affective judgments involving such mental pictures tend to have distinct properties (see Pham, 2007 for a review).

One of these properties is an insensitivity to the scale of the target. For example, in a study by Hsee and Rottenstreich (2004), respondents were asked how much they would be willing to donate to save either one or four pandas. When the number of pandas saved was represented in an abstract fashion (one or four dots), donations were much higher in the four-panda condition than in the one-panda condition, as would logically be expected. However, when the number of pandas saved was represented in an affectively rich fashion (one or four pictures of cute pandas), donations were not different in the four- and one-panda conditions, suggesting that affective judgments of value tend to be insensitive to quantitative information about the target. This result echoes other findings showing that when assessing the value of programs designed to save a large number of human lives—an emotionally charged judgment—people exhibit substantial insensitivity to the absolute number of lives saved (Fetherstonhaugh, Slovic, Johnson, & Friedrich, 1997). The insensitivity of affective judgments to the quantitative scale of the target seems to arise from the fact that such judgments are typically based on a concrete prototypical picture of the target that captures its identity (e.g., panda) but not quantitative information beyond this identity.

A second, related property is an insensitivity to probability beyond the presence or absence of uncertainty (Loewenstein, Weber, Hsee, & Welch, 2001; Monat, Averill, & Lazarus, 1972; Rottenstreich & Hsee, 2001; Sunstein, 2003). For example, awareness of the timing of an imminent threat produces the same level of stress and physiological arousal whether the threat has a 5%, 50%, or 100% probability of occurrence (Monat, Averill, & Lazarus, 1972). Similarly, people are not willing to pay much more to avoid a high probability of receiving an electric shock—a prospect rich in negative affect—than to avoid a low probability of receiving the same shock, even though they are willing to pay much more to avoid a high probability of losing $20—a prospect less rich in affect—than to avoid a low probability of losing $20 (Rottenstreich & Hsee, 2001). These findings can also be explained by the discrete nature of the mental images of threats that people invoke in affective assessments of risk. For example, when assessing the risk of dying in a plane crash, a prospect presumably rich in affect, people typically conjure vivid images of planes crashing. Such images typically do not incorporate probability information beyond the nature of the threat itself (Loewenstein, Weber, Hsee, & Welch, 2001). In contrast, prospects that are poorer in affect appear to bring to mind representations that do include the prospect's probabilistic information (e.g., "a 20% chance of X" rather than simply the image of X). According to Slovic and his colleagues, affective valuations are sensitive to possibility (i.e., deviations from certainty) rather than to probability (Slovic, Finucane, Peters, & MacGregor, 2002).

A third property of affective valuations is an insensitivity to the temporal context of the options (Gilbert, Gill, & Wilson, 2002). That is, affective valuations of options are less sensitive to the temporal element surrounding the options than are cognitive valuations of the same options. Again, this is because the mental pictures of the targets that are accessed in affective valuations are less likely to incorporate temporal information. For example, the prospect of having a nice dinner at a fancy restaurant tends to bring the same image to mind whether the dinner is at 6:00 pm on a Sunday or at 11:00 pm on a Friday. Gilbert and his colleagues (2002) observed, for instance, that participants who are hungry tended to judge the idea of eating spaghetti as very attractive, whether the meal was set to take place in the evening or in the morning. In contrast, participants who were not hungry rated the idea of eating spaghetti as significantly more attractive in the evening than in the morning. The authors propose that this is because hungry participants tend to over-project how they feel toward the meal, which they represent in an atemporal fashion ("spaghetti" rather than "spaghetti in the morning"), whereas participants who are not hungry are able to correct this tendency and adjust their judgment for the fact that spaghetti is generally more appropriate as an evening meal than as a morning meal.

Query and Response-Mapping Dependency

A growing body of research suggests that feelings are subject to contingent behavioral interpretation. In other words, the same feelings may have different behavioral consequences depending on how they are interpreted by the decision maker. Two sources of interpretational differences can be distinguished: (1) the first lies in the *question* that the decision makers are trying to answer privately while monitoring their feelings; (2) the second lies in the *mapping* of the privately interpreted feelings onto overt behavioral or judgment responses.

Query Dependency   Depending on the question privately being asked (i.e., query being made), the same feelings may have different interpretations and therefore different behavioral consequences.[5] For example, in a series of studies by Martin, Ward, Achee, and Wyer (1993), respondents who were either in a positive mood or in a negative mood were asked to perform various tasks under one of two sets of instructions. One group was asked to keep working until they were satisfied with their performance. The other group was asked to keep working until they no longer enjoyed the task. When instructed to keep working until they were satisfied with their performance, respondents in a negative mood worked longer than those in a positive mood, a result consistent with the finding discussed earlier that negative mood typically leads to more careful processing compared to positive mood. However, when instructed to keep working until they no longer enjoyed the task, the effect reversed: Respondents in a negative mood stopped *sooner* than those in a positive mood. This interaction may be understood in terms of query dependency. When the instruction was to keep working until satisfied with the performance, participants likely asked themselves something like "How happy am I with my performance?" In light of this query, a negative mood was construed as dissatisfaction with one's effort, producing greater perseverance, whereas a positive mood was construed as satisfaction with one's effort, triggering an early stop. In contrast, when the instruction was to keep working until the task was no longer enjoyed, participants likely asked themselves "How much fun am I having?" In light of this question, a negative mood was construed as the task being not fun, producing an early stop, whereas a positive mood was construed as the task being fun, producing perseverance. Therefore, the same feelings, positive or negative, can have very different interpretations and behavioral implications depending on the question that people are privately asking themselves (e.g., "Am I happy with my performance?" vs. "Am I having fun?").

The principle of query dependency can also account for recent results by Andrade (2005) and similar results by Kivetz and Kivetz (2007). Andrade (2005) recently found that positive-mood participants expressed higher willingness to consume a new brand of chocolate than neutral-mood participants. This mood-congruency finding is consistent with multiple explanations, including different affect-as-information inferences. For example, if participants asked themselves "How do I feel about this chocolate?," positive-mood participants would presumably reach more favorable judgments than would neutral-mood participants. More interesting, however, was the effect of negative mood. Unlike the effect of positive mood, this effect was different for men and women. Whereas men in a negative mood expressed lower willingness to consume the chocolate than men in a neutral mood did, consistent with mood-congruency, women in a negative mood expressed *higher* willingness to consume the chocolate than women in a neutral mood did, reversing the mood-congruency effect. According to Andrade (2005), this is because women are more likely to view chocolate as having mood-lifting properties. As a result, women in a negative mood find eating chocolate more attractive than women in a neutral mood do. This finding can also be interpreted in terms of differences in queries. Whereas men facing chocolates tend to ask themselves "How do I feel about it?", women facing the same options are more likely to ask themselves an affect-regulation question such as "Would it make me feel better or worse?" As a result, men exhibit classic mood-congruency: reaching more favorable evaluations under positive mood than under neutral mood, and more unfavorable evaluations under negative mood than under neutral mood. In contrast, women reach more favorable evaluations both under positive mood ("I would feel worse not eating chocolate") and under negative mood ("I would feel better eating chocolate") compared to a neutral mood.

Very similar results by Kivetz and Kivetz (2007) can be reinterpreted in the same way. These researchers found that when given an ostensibly real choice between a soothing massage and a grocery-store credit, negative-mood participants were more likely to choose the massage than neutral-mood participants. However, when the choice was described as only hypothetical, negative-mood participants were less likely to choose the massage than neutral-mood participants. A query-dependency interpretation of the results would propose that description of the choice as being real versus only hypothetical changed the nature of the question that respondents spontaneously asked themselves. When the choice was described as real, respondents were more likely to view the options in affect-regulation terms and privately ask themselves a question such as "Which one would make me feel better?" As a result, negative-mood participants exhibited stronger preferences for the more hedonically rewarding massage than neutral-mood participants did. In contrast, when the choice was described as only hypothetical, respondents were more inclined to view it in more abstract terms and ask themselves instead "How do I feel about it?" As a result, negative-mood participants exhibited lower preferences for the massage than neutral-mood participants, presumably because the massage did not feel attractive (assuming that the massage was the more salient of the two options).

Response-Mapping Dependency

The second source of differences in the interpretation of feelings lies in the *mapping* of privately interpreted feelings onto an overt response. Even if the question addressed by the feelings is held constant, behavioral response may still be different. For example, Martin, Abend, Sedikides, and Green (1997) found that, when asked to evaluate a story that was meant to be happy, participants in a happy mood reported more favorable evaluations than participants in a sad mood, consistent with typical mood congruency. However, when asked to evaluate a story that was meant to be sad, participants in a sad mood reported more favorable evaluations than participants in a happy mood. These results can be interpreted in terms of differences not in query, but in response mapping. In both conditions, participants likely asked themselves the same question (made the same query): "How does this story make me feel?" A pre-existing happy mood skewed participants' private responses toward "It makes me feel happy," and a pre-existing sad mood skewed their private responses toward "It makes me feel sad." The main difference across conditions was in the *translation* of these private responses onto overt judgmental responses. When participants were asked to assess whether it was "a good happy story," private subjective responses that "It makes me feel happy" meant "Yes," and private subjective responses that "It makes me feel sad" meant "No." In contrast, when participants were asked to assess whether it was "a good sad story," private subjective responses that "It makes me feel happy" meant "No," and private subjective responses that "It makes me feel sad" meant "Yes."

Overall, these results demonstrate that the information value of the feelings lies not so much in the feelings themselves as in the *interaction* between these feelings and (1) the questions that people are trying to answer privately when consulting their feelings (query dependency) and (2) the task they are trying to complete with these private answers (response-mapping dependency). These private questions and the mapping of their private answers will be dictated by situational demands, the nature of the judgments or choices to be made, and more generally the person's currently active goals (Pham, 2004).

Situational Engagement of the Affective System

An emerging body of findings suggests that certain motivational and situational factors encourage the reliance on feelings as information in judgment and decision making even if, from a logical standpoint, the objective (as opposed to subjective) diagnosticity of the feelings is held constant. Two of these factors have recently been identified: the person's regulatory focus and the person's temporal perspective. These factors seem to influence the engagement of the overall affective system of judgment and decision making independent of the logical diagnosticity of the feelings (i.e., independent of their representativeness, relevance, predictive validity, and convergent validity).

According to regulatory focus theory (Higgins, 1997), human self-regulation involves two separate systems: a promotion system, whose strategic orientation is approach-oriented, and a prevention system, whose strategic orientation is avoidance-oriented. For example, in the pursuit of a goal such as "becoming an excellent tennis player," the promotion system will favor approach strategies that seek matches to the desired end-state (e.g., attending tennis camps, practicing every day), whereas the prevention system will favor avoidance strategies that prevent mismatches to the desired end-state (e.g., refraining from smoking) (see also Pham & Higgins, 2005). Pham and Avnet (2004) observed that in persuasion settings, a promotion focus increases the reliance on one's feeling response to the advertisement and decreases the reliance on the substance of the message, whereas a prevention focus has opposite effects. They additionally found that these changes in the reliance on feelings versus substantive information were driven by an increase in the perceived diagnosticity of feelings among promotion-focused individuals compared to prevention-focused individuals, even though there is no real logical basis for the difference in perceived diagnosticity across the two orientations (unlike in studies where the representativeness, relevance, predictive validity, or convergent validity of feelings was varied). In subsequent studies (Pham & Avnet, 2007), these researchers found similar effects in other judgment settings. For example, compared to chronically prevention-focused individuals, chronically promotion-focused individuals (1) put more weight on affective information in forming impressions of other people and (2) are more influenced by their mood state in evaluating products.

Pham (2004, 2007) recently theorized that the affective system of judgment and decision making is a system of the present. As a likely remnant of our evolutionary past, the affective system was most probably meant to guide our ancestors through choices that they faced in their immediate environment. Consequently, it can be hypothesized that feelings are more likely to serve as sources of information in judgment and decisions set in the present or in the immediate future than in judgment and decisions set in a more distant future, even if, logically, feelings should be equally diagnostic across time frames. Consistent with this hypothesis, Chang and Pham (2007) recently found that, given a choice between two apartments—one that is more attractive on affective dimensions and one that is more attractive on cognitive dimensions—consumers deciding for the immediate future tend to choose the affectively superior option, whereas consumers deciding for a more distant future tend to choose the cognitively superior option. To further document that it is the weight of affective information in particular that varies with the temporal perspective, they show in another experiment that consumers' mood also exerts more influence on their decision to rent a given apartment for the coming month than on the decision to rent the same apartment one year from now. In additional experiments, they further show that the scope insensitivity bias mentioned earlier as being characteristic of affect-based evaluations (Hsee & Rottenstreich, 2004) is more pronounced in decisions set in the immediate future than in decisions set in a more distant future. This bias is also more pronounced when consumers are primed to think about a recent past than when they are primed to think about a more distant past. These findings collectively suggest that a present orientation skews judgment and decision making toward a more affective mode of thinking and a greater reliance on feelings as information. Note again that there is no clear logical reason why feelings would objectively be more diagnostic for decisions set in the present than for decisions set in the future because the criteria would remain the same across time frame. Therefore, some factors such as the person's regulatory focus or temporal perspective trigger a greater or lower engagement of the entire affective system of judgment independently of the objective diagnosticity of the feelings.

GAIM: A GENERALIZED AFFECT-AS-INFORMATION MODEL OF JUDGMENT

It should be clear from this chapter that the affect-as-information framework has much to offer to our understanding of consumer judgment and decision making. This framework has enormous explanatory power beyond its traditional applications in social psychology. The framework can be generalized into a broader model of informational influences of affect in judgment and decision making that accounts for a wide range of phenomena: the GAIM (pronounced "game"), for Generalized Affect-as-Information Model of judgment (see Figure 8.1).

According to the GAIM, the reliance on feelings in judgment is conditional on the interaction of three set of factors: (1) the target to be evaluated, (2) the person's goals, and (3) various situational factors. Mental access to the target is achieved either through direct perception if the target is present in the immediate environment, or through an intermediary mental representation or "mental picture" if the target is not present in the immediate environment. A combination of perception and mental representation is possible (e.g., a consumer reviewing a BMW 3-series brochure and imagining driving the featured vehicle).

The mental representation of the target that is typically accessed when feelings are sought as information tends to be concrete, prototypical, and discrete (i.e., picture-like rather than movie-like). Although this mental representation may provide a clear picture of the target's imagined identity, it typically does not fully capture

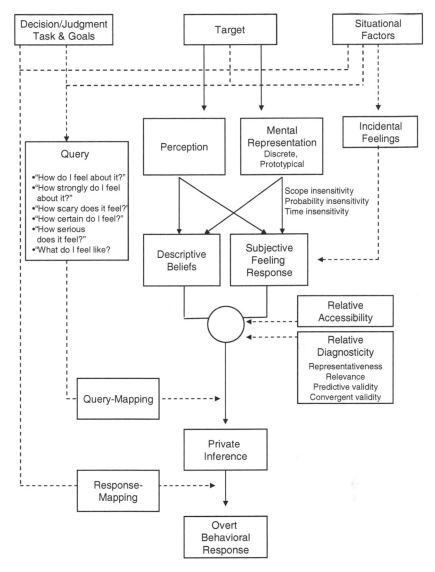

Figure 8.1   GAIM: A Generalized Affect-as-Information Model of Judgment.

the target's quantitative scope, its probability, and its temporal context. As a result, judgments based on affect tend to be scope-insensitive, probability-insensitive, and temporal-context-insensitive, but they are very sensitive to the identity of the target (Pham, 2007).

Perception of the target and/or its mental representation triggers two types of informational inputs: descriptive beliefs about the target's major attributes and subjective feelings. These subjective feelings are characterized not only by their valence and intensity, but also by their emotional quality (e.g., sadness vs. anxiety; joy vs. pride), which is dictated by a cognitive appraisal of the target that is partially automatic (Buck, 1985; Hoffmann, 1986). Due to pervasive misattribution, a person's subjective feelings toward a target can easily be contaminated by incidental feelings such as those arising from a contextually induced mood state. The subjective affective response to a mental representation of the target (as opposed to a direct perception of the target) can be called an "anticipatory affective response" (e.g., "Thinking about it makes me excited"). It is a genuine feeling response that is not to be confused with a descriptive belief about affective consequences of the target (e.g., "It would be fun"), which might rather be called an "anticipated affect" or an "affective expectation."

It is probable that, upon perception or mental representation of the target, descriptive beliefs about the target and subjective feelings toward the target are activated in parallel rather than strictly sequentially. However, because subjective feelings tend to be elicited and registered faster than descriptive beliefs (Pham, Cohen, Pracejus, & Hughes, 2001; Verplanken, Hofstee, & Janssen, 1998; Zajonc, 1980), descriptive beliefs toward the target often tend to be steered in the direction of the initial feelings (Pham, Cohen, Pracejus, & Hughes, 2001; Yeung & Wyer, 2004). That is, spontaneous "cognitive responses" toward the target tend to be correlates of initial affective responses to the target rather than truly independent inputs.[6]

The relative weight that subjective feelings and descriptive beliefs receive in the formation of a private inference about the target depends on standard accessibility-diagnosticity principles (Feldman & Lynch, 1988). Everything else being equal, subjective feelings are weighted more heavily (relative to descriptive beliefs) if they are more accessible and perceived to be more diagnostic. An obvious determinant of the relative accessibility of the feelings is their sheer intensity; another is the degree to which the person is attending to his or her feelings. Other indirect determinants include factors that influence the relative accessibility of descriptive beliefs. The perceived diagnosticity of feeling is a function of several factors: (1) their perceived representativeness—that is, the degree to which the feelings are perceived to emanate from and reflect essential properties of the target; (2) their perceived relevance for the judgment or decision at hand, which depends on the person's motives; (3) their perceived predictive validity, which depends, among other things, on whether the judgment is done for the self or for someone else; and (4) their perceived convergence with other judgment inputs. Each of these types of determinants seems to have a logical basis in shaping the perceived diagnosticity of feelings. However, other factors that do *not* seem logically related to the objective diagnosticity of feelings also seem to influence the subjective diagnosticity of feelings by triggering the situational engagement of the entire affective system of judgment. Everything else being equal, subjective feelings are relied upon more under a promotion focus than under a prevention focus (Pham & Avnet, 2004, 2007) and under a present time orientation than under a past or future time orientation (Chang & Pham, 2007).

If subjective feelings are relatively accessible and perceived to be diagnostic, they are used as inputs for the formation of a private inference such as how attractive the target is or how serious the situation is. The nature of the particular inference drawn from the subjective feelings depends on the person's judgmental query when assessing his or her feelings. These queries can be thought of as a set of pro-totypical questions such as (1) "How do I feel about it?"—the most common query, (2) "How strongly do I feel about it?", (3) "How scary does it feel?", (4) "How certain do I feel?", (5) "How serious does it feel?", and (6) "What do I feel like?" or "What would I feel better about?" Although feelings are probably also used to answer other queries beyond the ones discussed here, it is conjectured that the number of queries that are commonly answered through the monitoring of one's feelings is fairly lim-ited. In other words, the lexicon of affect as information is restricted. The particular query being addressed should depend on (1) the person's goals, (2) the target(s) being evaluated, and (3) various situational factors. For example, a person facing a single salient option (e.g., a single job offer) is likely to submit a noncomparative query such as "How do I feel about it?" In contrast, a person facing a choice between two options involving a trade-off between two important attributes (e.g., high salary with low job security vs. lower salary with high job security) is more likely to sub-mit a comparative query such as "What do I feel better about?", which would help clarify the relative importance of the competing motives. Thus, the same feelings may lead to different private inferences, and therefore different overt behavioral responses, depending on the decision maker's goals, the target(s), and the situation. For example, as shown by Martin and colleagues (1993), depending on the task instructions, a negative feeling may be interpreted as indicating dissatisfaction with one's task performance—thus increasing task perseverance—or as indicating a lack of enjoyment of the task—thus decreasing task perseverance. Similarly, as observed by Andrade (2005), a negative mood may be interpreted as dislike of a piece of chocolate if the chocolate's mood-lifting properties are not salient ("How do I feel about it?"), but as a craving for chocolate if the chocolate's mood-lifting properties are salient ("Would it make me feel better?"). Even if the person's private inference is held constant, the goals, the target(s), and the situation may additionally influence this person's overt behavioral response by altering the mapping of the private infer-ence onto the overt response. For example, as observed by Martin and colleagues (1997), a given private inference that "this story is sad" will be mapped onto an evaluative scale differently if the story is meant to be sad ("It is a good [sad] story") than if the story is meant to be funny ("It is a bad [funny] story").

To conclude, a great deal has been learned since Schwarz and Clore's (1983) seminal article. The reliance on feelings as information is pervasive and clearly not limited to the "How do I feel about it?" heuristic. This reliance appears to be part of an overall affective system of judgment and decision making with its own logic, principles, and rules. One can think of the reliance on feelings as informa-tion in judgment as a somewhat elaborate metacognitive dialogue with oneself—a dialogue with its own language: the language of feeling.

ENDNOTES

1. Note that, theoretically, the intensity of affective responses should also make their source more salient. Therefore, the intensity of affective responses may have different effects on judgment extremity, depending on whether the responses emanate from

the target itself or from a source unrelated to the target (e.g., a contextually induced mood state). When affective responses emanate integrally from the target, their intensity should monotonically increase the extremity of judgment about this target through the "How strongly do I feel about it?" heuristic. When affective responses are only incidental to the target, their intensity may instead have an inverted-U influence on the extremity of judgment about this target. That is, compared to target judgments based on mild incidental affective responses, target judgments based on moderately intense incidental affective responses may be more extreme or polarized (as observed, for instance, by Gorn, Pham, and Sin, 2001) due to the "How strongly do I feel about it?" heuristic. However, compared to target judgments based on moderately intense incidental affective responses, target judgment based on *very intense* incidental affective responses may be *less* extreme or polarized because the actual source of these very intense incidental affective responses may be quite salient, reducing their perceived informativeness for judging the target.

2. Although I believe there are qualitative differences between the types of feelings that are elicited by "experience" modes of processing and the type of affective beliefs that are elicited by "projection" modes of processing (see also Robinson & Clore, 2002), it is also possible that the difference between the two modes of processing is quantitative rather than qualitative in that projection modes of processing may simply elicit feelings of lower intensity.

3. Note, however, that while attention to incidental feelings may increase their influence on judgment, attention to the actual source of these feelings may decrease their influence on judgment, as discussed in subsection on the perceived diagnosticity of feelings.

4. The distinction between integral and incidental affect refers to the objective source of feelings. Integral feelings are "elicited by features of the target object, whether these features are real, perceived, or only imagined," whereas incidental feelings are "those whose source is clearly unconnected to the object to be evaluated" (Cohen, Pham, & Andrade, 2007). In contrast, the notion of representativeness refers to the subjective cause of the feelings, more specifically, the degree to which the feelings are perceived to emanate from or reflect essential properties of the target.

5. The use of the term *query* was inspired by an interesting program of research called "query theory," by Eric Johnson, Elke Weber, and their colleagues (Weber et al., 2007).

6. The phrase *cognitive responses* in reference to the spontaneous thoughts elicited by a target may thus be a misnomer in that it conveys the impression that affective and cognitive responses are truly independent judgment inputs, whereas the former often shape the latter (Pham, Cohen, Pracejus, & Hughes, 2001).

REFERENCES

Adaval, R. (2001). Sometimes it just feels right: The differential weighting of affect-consistent and affect-inconsistent product information. *Journal of Consumer Research, 28*(1), 1–17.

Albarracin, D., & Kumkale, G. T. (2003). Affect as information in persuasion: A model of affect identification and discounting. *Journal of Personality and Social Psychology, 84*(3), 453–469.

Allen, C. T., Machleit, K. A., & Kleine, S. S. (1992). A comparison of attitudes and emotions as predictors of behavior at diverse levels of behavioral experience. *Journal of Consumer Research, 18*(4), 493–504.

Allen, J. B., Kenrick, D. T., Linder, D. E., & McCall, M. A. (1989). Arousal and attraction: A response-facilitation alternative to misattribution and negative-reinforcement models. *Journal of Personality and Social Psychology, 57*(2), 261.

Andrade, E. B. (2005). Behavioral consequences of affect: Combining evaluative and regulatory mechanisms. *Journal of Consumer Research, 32*(3), 355–362.

Avnet, T., & Pham, M. T. (2007). *Metacognitive and non-metacognitive reliance on affect-as-information.* New York: Yeshiva University.

Bagozzi, R. P., Baumgartner, H., & Pieters, R. (1998). Goal-directed emotions. *Cognition & Emotion, 12*(1), 1–26.

Bakamitsos, G. A. (2006). A Cue alone or a probe to think? The dual role of affect in product evaluations. *Journal of Consumer Research, 33*(3).

Bettman, J. R. (1979). Decision processes: Choice among alternatives. In J. R. Bettman (Ed.), *An information processing theory of consumer choice.* Reading, MA: Addison-Wesley.

Bless, H., Bohner, G., Schwarz, N., & Strack, F. (1990). Mood and persuasion—A cognitive response analysis. *Personality and Social Psychology Bulletin, 16*(2), 331–345.

Bless, H., Mackie, D. M., & Schwarz, N. (1992). Mood effects on attitude judgments—Independent effects of mood before and after message elaboration. *Journal of Personality and Social Psychology, 63*(4), 585–595.

Bodenhausen, G. V. (1993). Emotions, arousal, and stereotype-based discrimination: A heuristic model of affect and stereotyping. In D. M. Mackie & D. L. Hamilton (Eds.), *Affect, cognition, and stereotyping* (pp. 13–37). San Diego, CA: Academic Press.

Bodenhausen, G. V., Kramer, G. P., & Suesser, K. (1994). Happiness and stereotypic thinking in social judgment. *Journal of Personality & Social Psychology, 66*(4), 621–632.

Bodenhausen, G. V., Sheppard, L. A., & Kramer, G. P. (1994). Negative affect and social judgment—The differential impact of anger and sadness. *European Journal of Social Psychology, 24*(1), 45–62.

Bosmans, A., & Baumgartner, H. (2005). Goal-relevant emotional information: When extraneous affect leads to persuasion and when it does not. *Journal of Consumer Research, 32*(3), 424–434.

Bower, G. H. (1981). Mood and memory. *American Psychologist, 36*(2), 129–148.

Briñol, P., Petty, R. E., & Barden, J. (2007). Happiness versus sadness as a determinant of thought confidence in persuasion: A self-validation analysis. *Journal of Personality and Social Psychology, 93*(5), 711–727.

Buck, R. (1985). Prime theory—An integrated view of motivation and emotion. *Psychological Review, 92*(3), 389–413.

Chang, H., & Pham, M. T. (2007). *Affect as a decision making system of the present.* Unpublishsed working paper, New York: Columbia University.

Clore, G. L. (1992). Cognitive phenomenology: Feelings and the construction of judgement. In L. L. M. A. Tesser (Ed.), *The construction of social judgements* (pp. 133–163). Hillsdale, NJ: Lawrence Erlbawm Associates.

Cohen, J. B., Pham, M. T., & Andrade, E. B. (2007). The nature and role of affect in consumer behavior. In C. P. Haugtvedt, P. M. Herr, & F. R. Kardes (Eds.), *Handbook of consumer psychology.* Mahwah, NJ: Lawrence Erlbaum.

DeSteno, D., Petty, R. E., Wegener, D. T., & Rucker, D. D. (2000). Beyond valence in the perception of likelihood: The role of emotion specificity. *Journal of Personality and Social Psychology, 78*(3), 397–416.

Dienstbier, R. A. (1979). Attraction increases and decreases as a function of emotion-attribution and appropriate social cues. In *Motivation and emotion* (Vol. 3, pp. 201–218). Lincoln: University of Nebraska Press.

Dunn, J. R., & Schweitzer, M. E. (2005). Feeling and believing: The influence of emotion on trust. *Journal of Personality and Social Psychology, 88*(5), 736–748.

Dutton, D. G., & Aron, A. P. (1974). Some evidence for heightened sexual attraction under conditions of high anxiety. *Journal of Personality and Social Psychology, 30*(4), 510–517.

Feldman, J. M., & Lynch, J. G. (1988). Self-generated validity and other effects of measurement on belief, attitude, intention, and behavior. *Journal of Applied Psychology, 73*(3), 421–435.

Fessler, D. M. T., Pillsworth, E. G., & Flamson, T. J. (2004). Angry men and disgusted women: An evolutionary approach to the influence of emotions on risk taking. *Organizational Behavior and Human Decision Processes, 95*(1), 107–123.

Fetherstonhaugh, D., Slovic, P., Johnson, S. M., & Friedrich, J. (1997). Insensitivity to the value of human life: A study of psychophysical numbing. *Journal of Risk and Uncertainty, 14*(3), 283–300.

Finucane, M. L., Alhakami, A., Slovic, P., & Johnson, S. M. (2000). The affect heuristic in judgments of risks and benefits. *Journal of Behavioral Decision Making, 13*(1), 1–17.

Fishbein, M., & Middlestadt, S. (1995). Noncognitive effects on attitude formation and change: Fact or artifact? *Journal of Consumer Psychology, 4*(2), 181–202.

Forgas, J. P. (1995). Mood and judgement: The affect infusion model (AIM). *Psychological Bulletin, 117*(1), 39.

Foster, C. A., Witcher, B. S., Campbell, W. K., & Green, J. D. (1998). Arousal and attraction: Evidence for automatic and controlled processes. *Journal of Personality and Social Psychology, 74*(1), 86–101.

Frijda, N. H., Kuipers, P., & Terschure, E. (1989). Relations among emotion, appraisal, and emotional action readiness. *Journal of Personality and Social Psychology, 57*(2), 212–228.

Gallagher, D., & Clore, G. L. (1985). *Effects of fear and anger on judgments of risk and evaluations of blame.* Paper presented at the meetings of the Midwestern Psychological Association, Chicago, IL.

Gasper, K., & Clore, G. L. (1998). The persistent use of negative affect by anxious individuals to estimate risk. *Journal of Personality and Social Psychology, 74*(5), 1350–1363.

Gilbert, D. T., Gill, M. J., & Wilson, T. D. (2002). The future is now: Temporal correction in affective forecasting. *Organizational Behavior and Human Decision Processes, 88*(1), 430–444.

Gorn, G. J., Goldberg, M. E., & Basu, K. (1993). Mood, awareness and product evaluation. *Journal of Consumer Psychology, 2*(3), 237–256.

Gorn, G. J., Pham, M. T., & Sin, L. Y. (2001). When arousal influences ad evaluation and valence does not (and vice versa). *Journal of Consumer Psychology, 11*(1), 43–55.

Hendrickx, L., Vlek, C., & Oppewal, H. (1989). Relative importance of scenario information and frequency information in the judgment of risk. *Acta Psychologica, 72*(1), 41–63.

Higgins, E. T. (1997). Beyond pleasure and pain. *American Psychologist, 52*(12), 1280–1300.

Higgins, E. T. (1998). The aboutness principle: A pervasive influence on human inference. *Social Cognition, 16*(1), 173–198.

Hoffmann, M. L. (1986). Affect, cognition, and motivation. In R. M. Sorrentino & E. T. Higgins (Eds.), *The handbook of motivation and cognition.* New York: Guilford Press.

Hsee, C. K., & Rottenstreich, Y. (2004). Music, pandas, and muggers: On the affective psychology of value. *Journal of Experimental Psychology-General, 133*(1), 23–30.

Hsee, C. K., Zhang, J., Yu, F., & Xi, Y. (2003). Lay rationalism and inconsistency between predicted experience and decision. *Journal of Behavioral Decision Making, 16*(4), 257–272.

Isen, A. M., & Shalker, T. E. (1982). The effect of feeling state on evaluation of positive, neutral, and negative stimuli—When you accentuate the positive, do you eliminate the negative. *Social Psychology Quarterly, 45*(1), 58–63.

Isen, A. M., Shalker, T. E., Clark, M., & Karp, L. (1978). Affect, accessibility of material in memory, and behavior—Cognitive loop. *Journal of Personality and Social Psychology, 36*(1), 1–12.

Johnson, E. J., & Tversky, A. (1983). Affect, generalization, and the perception of risk. *Journal of Personality and Social Psychology, 45*(1), 20–31.

Kahneman, D., Ritov, I., & Schkade, D. (1999). Economic preferences or attitude expressions? An analysis of dollar responses to public issues. *Journal of Risk and Uncertainty, 19*(1–3), 203–235.

Kahneman, D., & Snell, J. (1990). Predicting utility. In R. M. Hogarth (Ed.), *Insights in decision making—A tribute to Hillel. J. Einhorn* (pp. 295–342). Chicago: The University of Chicago Press.

Keltner, D., Ellsworth, P. C., & Edwards, K. (1993). Beyond simple pessimism: Effects of sadness and anger on social perception. *Journal of Personality and Social Psychology, 64*(5), 740.

Keltner, D., Locke, K. D., & Audrain, P. C. (1993). The influence of attributions on the relevance of negative feelings to personal satisfaction. *Personality and Social Psychology Bulletin, 19*(1), 21–29.

Kivetz, R., & Kivetz, Y. (2007). *Reconciling mood congruency and mood regulation: The role of psychological distance.* Unpublished working paper, New York: Columbia University.

Leith, K. P., & Baumeister, R. F. (1996). Why do bad moods increase self-defeating behavior? Emotion, risk taking, and self-regulation. *Journal of Personality and Social Psychology, 71*(6), 1250–1267.

Lerner, J. S., Gonzalez, R. M., Small, D. A., & Fischhoff, B. (2003). Effects of fear and anger on perceived risks of terrorism: A national field experiment. *Psychological Science, 14*(2), 144–150.

Lerner, J. S., & Keltner, D. (2000). Beyond valence: Toward a model of emotion-specific influences on judgement and choice. *Cognition & Emotion, 14*(4), 473–493.

Lerner, J. S., & Keltner, D. (2001). Fear, anger, and risk. *Journal of Personality & Social Psychology, 81*(1), 146–159.

Lerner, J. S., Small, D. A., & Loewenstein, G. (2004). Heart strings and purse strings—Carryover effects of emotions on economic decisions. *Psychological Science, 15*(5), 337–341.

Levine, S. R., Wyer, R. S., & Schwarz, N. (1994). Are you what you feel—The affective and cognitive determinants of self-judgments. *European Journal of Social Psychology, 24*(1), 63–77.

Loewenstein, G., Weber, E. U., Hsee, C. K., & Welch, N. (2001). Risk as feelings. *Psychological Bulletin, 127*(2), 267–286.

Mackie, D. M., & Worth, L. T. (1989). Processing deficits and the mediation of positive affect in persuasion. *Journal of Personality and Social Psychology, 57*(1), 27–40.

Martin, L. L., Abend, T., Sedikides, C., & Green, J. D. (1997). How would it feel if … ? Mood as input to a role fulfillment evaluation process. *Journal of Personality & Social Psychology, 73*(2), 242–253.

Martin, L. L., Harlow, T. F., & Strack, F. (1992). The role of bodily sensations in the evaluation of social events. *Personality and Social Psychology Bulletin, 18*(4), 412–419.

Martin, L. L., Seta, J. J., & Crelia, R. A. (1990). Assimilation and contrast as a function of people's willingness and ability to expend effort in forming an impression. *Journal of Personality and Social Psychology, 59*(1), 27–37.

Martin, L. L., Ward, D. W., Achee, J. W., & Wyer, R. S. (1993). Mood as input—People have to interpret the motivational implications of their moods. *Journal of Personality and Social Psychology, 64*(3), 317–326.

Mayer, J. D., Gaschke, Y. N., Braverman, D. L., & Evans, T. W. (1992). Mood-congruent judgment is a general effect. *Journal of Personality and Social Psychology, 63*(1), 119–132.

Mellers, B. A., Schwartz, A., Ho, K., & Ritov, I. (1997). Decision affect theory: Emotional reactions to the outcomes of risky options. *Psychological Science, 8*(6), 423–429.

Miniard, P. W., Bhatla, S., & Sirdeshmukh, D. (1992). Mood as a determinant of postconsumption product evaluations. *Journal of Consumer Psychology, 1*(2), 173–195.

Monat, A., Averill, J. R., & Lazarus, R. S. (1972). Anticipatory stress and coping reactions under various conditions of uncertainty. *Journal of Personality and Social Psychology, 24*(2), 237–253.

Ottati, V. C., & Isbell, L. M. (1996). Effects of mood during exposure to target information on subsequently reported judgments: An on-line model of misattribution and correction. *Journal of Personality and Social Psychology, 71*(1), 39–53.

Pham, M. T. (1998). Representativeness, relevance, and the use of feelings in decision making. *Journal of Consumer Research, 25*(2), 144–159.

Pham, M. T. (2004). The Logic of Feeling. *Journal of Consumer Psychology, 14*(4), 360–369.

Pham, M. T. (2007). Emotion and rationality: A critical review and interpretation of empirical evidence. *Review of General Psychology, 11*(2), 155–178.

Pham, M. T., & Avnet, T. (2004). Ideals and oughts and the reliance on affect versus substance in persuasion. *Journal of Consumer Research, 30*(4), 503–518.

Pham, M. T., & Avnet, T. (2007). *Regulatory focus as a moderator of the affect heuristic.* Unpublished manuscript, Columbia University, New York.

Pham, M. T., Cohen, J. B., Pracejus, J. W., & Hughes, G. D. (2001). Affect monitoring and the primacy of feelings in judgment. *Journal of Consumer Research, 28*(2), 167–188.

Pham, M. T., & Higgins, E. T. (2005). Promotion and prevention in consumer decision making: The state of the art and theoretical propositions. In S. Ratneshwar & D. G. Mick (Eds.), *Inside consumption: Consumer motives, goals, and desires* (pp. 8–43). New York, NY: Routledge.

Pham, M. T., & Raghunathan, R. (2007). *On the distinction between feelings and thinking about feelings: The case of anxiety vs. sadness.* Unpublished working paper, New York: Columbia University.

Raghunathan, R., & Pham, M. T. (1999). All negative moods are not equal: Motivational influences of anxiety and sadness on decision making. *Organizational Behavior and Human Decision Processes, 79*(1), 56–77.

Raghunathan, R., Pham, M. T., & Corfman, K. P. (2006). Informational properties of anxiety and sadness, and displaced coping. *Journal of Consumer Research, 32*(4).

Reisenzein, R., & Gattinger, E. (1982). Salience of arousal as a mediator of misattribution of transferred excitation. *Motivation and Emotion, 6*(4), 315–328.

Robinson, M. D., & Clore, G. L. (2002). Belief and feeling: Evidence for an accessibility model of emotional self-report. *Psychological Bulletin, 128*(6), 934–960.

Roseman, I. J. (1991). Appraisal determinants of discrete emotions. *Cognition & Emotion, 5*(3), 161–200.

Rottenstreich, Y., & Hsee, C. K. (2001). Money, kisses, and electric shocks: On the affective psychology of risk. *Psychological Science, 12*(3), 185–190.

Rottenstreich, Y., Sood, S., & Brenner, L. (2007). Feeling and thinking in memory-based versus stimulus-based choices. *Journal of Consumer Research, 33*(4), 461–469.

Rozin, P., & Fallon, A. E. (1987). A perspective on disgust. *Psychological Review, 94*(1), 23–41.

Schwarz, N. (1990). Feelings as information: Informational and motivational functions of affective states. In R. M. Sorrentino & E. T. Higgins (Eds.), *Handbook of motivation and cognition* (Vol. 2, pp. 521–561). New York: Guilford Press.

Schwarz, N. (2002). Situated cognition and the wisdom of feelings: Cognitive tuning. In L. F. Barrett & P. Salovey (Eds.), *The wisdom in feelings: Psychological processes in emotional intelligence* (pp. 144–166). New York: The Guilford Press.

Schwarz, N. (2004). Metacognitive experiences in consumer judgment and decision making. *Journal of Consumer Psychology, 14*(4), 332–348.

Schwarz, N., Bless, H., Strack, F., Klumpp, G., Rittenauer Schatka, H., & Simons, A. (1991). Ease of retrieval as information—Another look at the availability heuristic. *Journal of Personality and Social Psychology, 61*(2), 195–202.

Schwarz, N., & Clore, G. L. (1983). Mood, misattribution, and judgments of well-being— Informative and directive functions of affective states. *Journal of Personality and Social Psychology, 45*(3), 513–523.

Schwarz, N., & Clore, G. L. (1996). Feelings and phenomenal experiences. In E. T. Higgins & A. W. Kruglanski (Eds.), *Social psychology: Handbook of basic principles* (pp. 433–465). New York: The Guilford Press.

Schwarz, N., & Clore, G. L. (2007). Feelings and emotional experiences. In A. W. Kruglanski & E. T. Higgins (Eds.), *Social psychology: Handbook of basic principles* (2nd ed., pp. 385–407): New York: The Guilford Press.

Schwarz, N., Servay, W., & Kumpf, M. (1985). Attribution of arousal as a mediator of the effectiveness of fear-arousing communications. *Journal of Applied Social Psychology, 15*(2), 178–188.

Schwarz, N., Strack, F., Kommer, D., & Wagner, D. (1987). Soccer, rooms, and the quality of your life—Mood effects on judgments of satisfaction with life in general and with specific domains. *European Journal of Social Psychology, 17*(1), 69–79.

Shen, H., & Wyer, R. S. (2008). The impact of negative affect on responses to affect regulating experiences. *Journal of Consumer Psychology, 18*(9), 39–48.

Shiv, B., & Fedorikhin, A. (1999). Heart and mind in conflict: The interplay of affect and cognition in consumer decision making. *Journal of Consumer Research, 26*(3), 278–292.

Siemer, M., & Reisenzein, R. (1998). Effects of mood on evaluative judgements: Influence of reduced processing capacity and mood salience. *Cognition & Emotion, 12*(6), 783–805.

Sinaceur, M., Heath, C., & Cole, S. (2005). Emotional and deliberative reactions to a public crisis—Mad Cow disease in France. *Psychological Science, 16*(3), 247–254.

Sinclair, R. C., Mark, M. M., & Clore, G. L. (1994). Mood-related persuasion depends on (mis)attributions. *Social Cognition, 12*(4), 309–326.

Slovic, P., Finucane, M., Peters, E., & MacGregor, D. G. (2002). The affect heuristic. In T. Gilovich, D. Griffin, & D. Kahneman (Eds.), *Heuristics and biases: The psychology of intuitive judgment* (pp. 397–420). New York: Cambridge University Press.

Smith, C. A., & Ellsworth, P. C. (1985). Patterns of cognitive appraisal in emotion. *Journal of Personality and Social Psychology, 48*(4), 813–838.

Soldat, A. S., Sinclair, R. C., & Mark, M. M. (1997). Color as an environmental processing cue: External affective cues can directly affect processing strategy without affecting mood. *Social Cognition, 15*(1), 55–71.

Strack, F. (1992). The different routes to social judgements: Experiential versus informational strategies. In L. L. M. A. Tesser (Ed.), *The construction of social judgements* (pp. 249–275). Hillsdale, NJ: Lawrence Erlbawm Associates.

Strack, F., Schwarz, N., & Gschneidinger, E. (1985). Happiness and reminiscing—The role of time perspective, affect, and mode of thinking. *Journal of Personality and Social Psychology, 49*(6), 1460–1469.

Sunstein, C. R. (2003). Terrorism and probability neglect. *Journal of Risk and Uncertainty, 26*(2–3), 121–136.

Tiedens, L. Z., & Linton, S. (2001). Judgment under emotional certainty and uncertainty: The effects of specific emotions on information processing. *Journal of Personality and Social Psychology, 81*(6), 973–988.

Verplanken, B., Hofstee, G., & Janssen, H. J. W. (1998). Accessibility of effective versus cognitive components of attitudes. *European Journal of Social Psychology, 28*(1), 23–35.

Weber, E. U., Johnson, E. J., Milch, K. F., Chang, H., Brodscholl, J. C., & Goldstein, D. G. (2007). Asymmetric discounting in intertemporal choice—A query-theory account. *Psychological Science, 18*(6), 516–523.

Welch, E. (1999). *The heat of the moment.* Unpublished Doctoral Dissertation, Carnegie Mellon University, Pittsburg.

White, G. L., Fishbein, S., & Rutsein, J. (1981). Passionate love and the misattribution of arousal. *Journal of Personality and Social Psychology, 41*(1), 56–62.

Wilkie, W. L., & Pessemier, E. A. (1973). Issues in marketing's use of multi-attribute attitude models. *Journal of Marketing Research, 10*(4), 428–441.

Wyer, J., Robert S., & Carlston, D. E. (1979). Indirect effects of information on judgements. In *Social cognition, inference, and attribution* (pp. 191–220). Hillsdale, NJ: Lawrence Erlbaum Associates.

Wyer, R. S., Clore, G. L., & Isbell, L. M. (1999). Affect and information processing. In M. P. Zanna (Ed.), *Advances in experimental social psychology* (Vol. 31; pp. 1–77). San Diego, CA: Academic Press.

Yeung, C. W. M., & Wyer, R. S. (2004). Affect, appraisal, and consumer judgment. *Journal of Consumer Research, 31*(2), 412–424.

Zajonc, R. B. (1980). Feeling and thinking—Preferences need no inferences. *American Psychologist, 35*(2), 151–175.

9

When Thinking Is Difficult
Metacognitive Experiences as Information

NORBERT SCHWARZ AND HYUNJIN SONG

University of Michigan

JING XU

Peking University

D ifferent approaches to consumer decision making paint dramatically different pictures of how consumers arrive at a choice. From the perspective of microeconomics, consumers know what they like and want and reveal their preferences in the choices they make (Samuelson, 1938; Savage, 1954). Decision problems arise mostly because consumers cannot satisfy all preferences simultaneously and face trade-offs and market constraints. In the words of Daniel McFadden (1999, p. 75), a Nobel laureate in economics, "The standard model in economics is that consumers behave as if (…) preferences are primitive, consistent and immutable (preference-rationality), and the cognitive process is simply preference maximization, given market constraints (process-rationality)." In contrast, psychologists commonly assume that consumers' preferences are often constructed on the spot (e.g., Bettman, Luce, & Payne, 1998; see Griffin, Liu, & Kahn, 2005 for a recent review). Presumably, consumers consider the attributes of a product, elaborate on them, and compare them with the attributes of competing products to arrive at an informed judgment. This process is malleable and can lead to different outcomes, depending on which of many attributes a consumer focuses on and which thoughts come to mind in a given context (for reviews see Bless & Greifeneder, this volume; Griffin et al., 2005; Schwarz, 2007, in press).

However, neither of these approaches can account for a rapidly growing body of findings that apparently challenge common sense and basic assumptions of rational decision making. One of these assumptions is that only relevant attributes of the choice object matter. When making an investment, for example, investors presumably consider the quality of the company and its growth and earnings potential. Yet an analysis of initial public offerings on the New York Stock Exchange indicates that investors are more likely to part from their money when the name of the company, or the ticker symbol of its stock, is easy rather than difficult to pronounce (Alter & Oppenheimer, 2006). Similarly, people looking for a suitable exercise routine presumably consider the nature of the exercise and its likely fitness benefits in deciding which routine to follow. Yet the same exercise routine is less likely to be chosen when its description is printed in a font that is difficult rather than easy to read (Song & Schwarz, in press (a)). Another basic assumption of models of rational decision making holds that the more positive attributes we identify in a product, the more likely we are, ceteris paribus, to choose it. Yet consumers are more likely to prefer a Mercedes over a BMW the more positive attributes of the BMW they brought to mind (Wänke, Bohner, & Jurkowitsch, 1997). Similarly, we should be less likely to defer choice, waiting for another opportunity, the more reasons we see for making a choice. Yet again, consumers are more likely to walk away from a choice opportunity the more reasons they generated for a choice (Novemsky, Dhar, Schwarz, & Simonson, 2007). In these examples, consumers' decisions are not only incompatible with the assumptions of microeconomics, but also incompatible with core assumptions of standard psychological models of judgment and choice.

To understand these phenomena, we must move beyond the emphasis on accessible declarative information about the choice alternatives that is central to most psychological models. People's reasoning is always accompanied by subjective experiences, such as their apparent affective response to what they are thinking about or the experience that information is easy or difficult to bring to mind. In many situations, these feelings provide valid information about the object of judgment. If thinking about a vacation destination puts us into a good mood, chances are that we may really enjoy this destination more than one that elicits less positive feelings. Similarly, if it is hard to think of good reasons for a choice, chances are that there actually may be few good reasons. In these cases, our subjective experiences are a response to what we are thinking about and provide meaningful information about the choice alternatives. But, unfortunately, we are more sensitive to our subjective experiences than to their source. We generally consider any of the thoughts that come to mind and any feelings we experience as being "about" whatever is in the focus of our attention (see Higgins, 1998, for a discussion). Hence, we may misread a pre-existing positive or negative mood as our affective response to what we are thinking about, resulting in more positive evaluations of the same target when a sunny day left us in a good mood than when a rainy day left us in a bad one (e.g., Schwarz & Clore, 1983; see Pham, this volume, for a review). Similarly, we may miss that the difficulty we encounter in generating reasons for a choice is merely due to an unrealistically demanding task, for example, the request to list ten good reasons rather than merely two (e.g., Novemsky et al., 2007). In these cases, our subjective experiences are a function of incidental variables that are unrelated to any "relevant" attributes of the choice objects. Whenever people become aware that their subjective experiences are due to such incidental influences, the informational value of their experiences is undermined and they turn to other sources of information to arrive at a judgment (e.g., Schwarz & Clore, 1983; Novemsky et al., 2007). What people learn from their subjective experiences and how they assess their informational value has been conceptualized in the feelings-as-information model (Schwarz, 1990; see also Pham, this volume) that provides a general account of the interplay of feeling and thinking (see Schwarz & Clore, 2007, for a comprehensive review).

The present chapter focuses on one particular type of experiential information, namely the ease or difficulty with which information can be recalled from memory, thoughts can be generated, and new information can be processed. These experiences are summarily referred to as metacognitive experiences. Like moods, emotions, and bodily sensations they can serve as a source of information in their own right. Unlike other types of experiential information, however, they can also qualify the implications of accessible declarative information. In general, people's judgments are consistent with *what* comes to mind (declarative information) when recall or thought generation is easy, but opposite to the implications of declarative information when recall or thought generation is difficult. As a result, we cannot predict consumer judgment and choice by knowing solely *what* is on a consumer's mind, i.e., by focusing on accessible declarative information. Instead, judgment and choice are always a *joint* function of declarative and experiential information; hence, we need to consider the interplay of feeling and thinking to make sense of consumer behavior.

EASE OF RECALL AND THOUGHT GENERATION: ACCESSIBILITY EXPERIENCES

Psychological models of judgment and decision making commonly focus on *what* comes to mind. When asked to make a judgment, people presumably retrieve relevant information about the target and base their judgment on the attributes that come to mind.

Hence, we should find, for example, that people who were just asked to recall many examples of their own assertive behavior judge themselves as more assertive than people who had to recall only a few examples. Similarly, people who just thought of many good reasons to drive a BMW should be more likely to prefer the BMW over another brand than people who thought of only a few reasons. Empirically, this is not the case.

For example, Schwarz and colleagues (1991) asked participants to recall either six or 12 examples of their own assertive or unassertive behavior. Subsequently, participants rated their own assertiveness. As shown in Figure 9.1, participants rated themselves as more assertive after recalling six examples of assertive behavior than after recalling six examples of unassertive behavior. Yet increasing the number of recalled examples not only failed to increase the difference but reversed the observed pattern: Participants who successfully recalled 12 examples of assertive behavior rated themselves as *less* assertive than participants who recalled

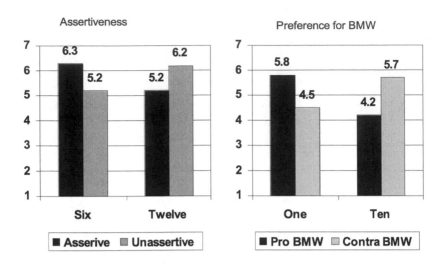

Figure 9.1   Assertiveness Judgments and Product Preferencs as a Function of Thought Content and Accessibility Experiences. *Note*: Higher values indicate higher ratings of assertiveness (left-hand panel) and higher preference for a BMW over a Mercedes (right hand panel). The left-hand panel is adapted from Schwarz, Bless, Strack, Klumpp, Rittenauer-Schatka, and Simons (1991) and the right-hand panel from Wänke, Bahner, and Jurowitsch, A. (1997). Reprinted by permission.

12 examples of unassertive behavior. Moreover, those who recalled 12 assertive (unassertive, respectively) behaviors rated themselves as less (more, respectively) assertive than those who recalled only six examples. Similarly, Wänke and her colleagues (1997) asked participants to imagine how easy it would be for them to list either one reason or 10 reasons for or against choosing a BMW over a Mercedes. Presumably, participants assessed the ease or difficulty of their task by thinking of a few reasons. Paralleling the assertiveness findings, those who imagined listing ten reasons for choosing a BMW found the task more difficult than those who imagined listing only one reason and hence evaluated the BMW less favorably. Conversely, those who imagined listing 10 reasons against choosing a BMW evaluated the BMW more favorably than those who imagined listing only one.

In both studies, participants' judgments were consistent with the thoughts they had just listed or imagined when only a few thoughts were requested, but inconsistent with these thoughts when many thoughts were requested. This pattern of results may reflect two different processes. On the one hand, participants may have been able to recall a few good reasons or examples early on, but later reasons and examples may have become less and less compelling. If so, the results would be consistent with a content-focused judgment process. On the other hand, participants also reported that it was easy to recall a few good reasons or examples, but difficult to recall many. This difficulty, in turn, may have suggested that there cannot be that many reasons or examples, or why else would it be so difficult to bring them to mind? If so, their judgments would be based on their metacognitive experience rather than on the content of their thoughts per se. A solid body of research supports the latter interpretation.

Content or Experience?

Most importantly, the logic of the feelings-as-information approach (Schwarz, 1990; for a review see Pham, this volume) predicts that the influence of subjective experiences is eliminated when people attribute their experience to an irrelevant source, thus undermining its informational value for the judgment at hand. Applying this logic to the experienced difficulty of recall, Schwarz and colleagues (1991, Experiment 3) induced some of their participants to attribute their recall experience to the influence of background music played to them. In this case, participants reported higher assertiveness the more assertive behaviors they had recalled, and lower assertiveness the more unassertive behaviors they had recalled. This reversal of the otherwise obtained pattern indicates that participants drew on the content of their thoughts once the informational value of their recall experience was called into question. The reversal further implies that participants who listed many examples did not find their examples specious—once their recall difficulty was explained away, they were happy to rely on them. Indeed, content analyses provided no evidence that the quality of the examples deteriorated the more examples participants had to recall. Later studies replicated this misattribution effect and consistently showed that people rely on their metacognitive experiences when they seem relevant to the task at hand, but turn to the content of their thoughts once the informational value of the subjective experience is undermined (e.g., Haddock, Rothman, Reber, & Schwarz, 1999; Novemsky et al., 2007; Sanna & Schwarz, 2003; Sanna, Schwarz, & Small, 2002).

Other studies manipulated participants' metacognitive experience in ways that are independent of the number of thoughts generated. For example, Stepper and Strack (1993; see also Sanna, Schwarz, & Small, 2002) asked all participants to recall six examples of assertive or unassertive behavior, thus holding actual recall demands constant. To manipulate the experienced ease of recall, they induced participants to contract either their corrugator muscle or their zygomaticus muscle during the recall task. Contraction of the corrugator muscle produces a furrowed brow, an expression commonly associated with a feeling of effort. Contraction of the zygomaticus muscle produces a light smile, an expression commonly associated with a feeling of ease. As expected, participants who recalled six examples of assertive behavior while adopting a light smile judged themselves as more assertive than participants who adopted a furrowed brow. Conversely, participants who recalled six examples of unassertive behavior while adopting a light smile judged themselves as less assertive than participants who adopted a furrowed brow.

These two lines of research also bear on a recent proposal by Tormala, Falces, Brinol, and Petty (2007), who noted that participants who have to list many thoughts may also have more unrequested thoughts; for example, those asked to list many thoughts in favor of a position may also find a larger number of unfavorable thoughts coming to mind than those who have to list only a few favorable thoughts. They suggested that these unrequested thoughts, rather than the experience of difficulty per se, may drive the effects shown in Figure 9.1, reflecting a content-baseu judgment strategy. But if so, the pattern of participants' judgments should not reverse when the diagnostic value of the subjective experience is called into question—attributing one's difficulty to background music (Schwarz et al., 1991), for example, does nothing to discredit the substantive relevance of any unrequested thoughts one might have had. Similarly, the observation that bodily feedback in form of a furrowed brow parallels the effects of difficult recall difficulty (Sanna, Schwarz, & Small, 2002; Stepper & Strack, 1993) argues against a crucial role of unrequested thoughts. In these studies, the number of thoughts listed was held constant, suggesting that the number of any unrequested thoughts that may have come to mind was similar across conditions as well. In short, unrequested thoughts do not provide a coherent account of the available findings, although they are probably part and parcel of the experience of difficulty.

As a third approach to disentangling the role of thought content and subjective experience, Wänke, Bl ss, and Biller (1996) asked participants to generate either a few or many argur ents and subsequently presented these arguments to other, yoked participants As expected, participants who actively generated arguments drew on their accessibility experiences and were less persuaded by their own arguments, the more they had to generate. In contrast, yoked participants, who merely read the examples generated by others and were hence deprived of any thought-generation experience, were more influenced the more examples they read.

In combination, these studies illustrate that judgments are a *joint* function of declarative and experiential information. People's judgments are consistent with the implications of accessible thought content when recall or thought generation is experienced as easy, but opposite to the implications of accessible thought content when recall or thought generation is experienced as difficult. However, people do not draw on their accessibility experiences when their informational value for the judgment at hand is called into question, paralleling earlier observations about the informational functions of moods (e.g., Schwarz & Clore, 1983; for a review see Schwarz & Clore, 2007).

Beyond Judgment: Implications for Choice

Decision researchers repeatedly observed that consumers are more likely to defer choice, or to select a compromise alternative, when they find it difficult to form a preference for one of the options offered to them (e.g., Dhar & Simonson, 2003; see Novemsky et al., 2007, for a review). In these studies, decision difficulty is typically manipulated by changing the relevant attributes of the choice alternatives in ways that require difficult trade-offs between desirable features. If the subjective experience of difficulty is at the heart of these effects, similar outcomes should be observed when difficulty is manipulated through other means, holding the actual attributes of the choice alternatives constant. Empirically, this is the case.

For example, Novemsky and colleagues (2007, Experiment 2) provided participants with descriptions of two digital cameras and asked them how difficult it would be for them to come up with two or 10 reasons for selecting one of them. Next, participants could either make a choice or defer choice, waiting for another opportunity to make a selection. As predicted, participants were more likely to defer choice when asked to think of 10 reasons for making a choice, which they rated as difficult, than when asked to think of merely two, which they rated as easy. Specifically, 61% of the participants deferred choice in the former condition, whereas only 49% did so in the latter condition. Additional experiments showed that thinking of many reasons for a choice increased the size of compromise effects (Simonson, 1989), unless participants were made aware that their difficulty was due to the nature of the thought request rather than the nature of the choice alternatives (see Novemsky et al., 2007, for more detail).

In combination, these findings illustrate that the ease or difficulty with which consumers can generate reasons for a choice is an important determinant of decision behavior. Whereas content-focused models predict that consumers should be more likely to make a choice the more reasons they see for doing so, the subjective experience of difficulty produces the opposite effect. Presumably, this subjective experience is also at the heart of choice deferral and compromise effects when the difficulty arises from the actual trade-offs required by the choice set. If so, consumers may be more willing to make such difficult choices when they can attribute the experienced difficulty to another source, thus undermining its informational value for the choice at hand. This possibility awaits further research.

Naïve Theories as Inference Rules

In the above studies, participants presumably inferred from the difficulty of generating many reasons or examples that there are not many, or else it would not be so difficult to bring them to mind. This inference is consistent with a (usually correct) naïve theory of memory that underlies Tversky and Kahneman's (1973) availability heuristic: It is easier to recall exemplars from high- rather than low-frequency categories. However, people hold many different naïve theories about their own mental processes (for reviews see Schwarz, 2004; Skurnik, Schwarz, & Winkielman, 2000). For example, they also (correctly) assume that it is easier to recall examples when they know a lot about the respective domain than when they do not. Accordingly, what they infer from a given accessibility experience depends on which of many applicable naïve theories they bring to bear on their task, as an example may illustrate.

Xu (reported in Schwarz, Cho, and Xu, 2005) asked students to list two or six "fine Italian restaurants" in town. When first asked how many fine Italian restaurants the city has, they inferred from the difficulty of listing six that there cannot be many. This inference is consistent with Tversky and Kahneman's (1973) availability heuristic. However, when first asked how much they know about town, they inferred from the same difficulty that they know little about their college town. Note, however, that each of these judgments entails an attribution of the recall experience, either to the number of restaurants in town or to one's own expertise. Once this implicit attribution is made, the experience is uninformative for the next judgment that requires a different theory, making it likely that people turn to accessible thought content instead. Confirming this prediction, participants who first concluded that their difficulty reflects a lack of knowledge subsequently inferred that there are many fine Italian restaurants in town—after all, they listed quite a few and they do not even know much about town. Conversely, those who first concluded that there are not many restaurants in town subsequently reported high expertise—after all, there are not many such restaurants and they nevertheless listed quite a few, so they must know a lot about town (for a conceptual replication with different naïve theories, see Xu & Schwarz, 2005).

In sum, what people conclude from their accessibility experiences depends on which of many naïve theories of memory and cognition they bring to bear. Applicable theories are recruited by the judgment task and the same experience can result in different substantive conclusions (see Schwarz, 2004, for a review). Moreover, every theory-based judgment entails a causal attribution of the experience to the source specified in the naïve theory, e.g., that there are few fine Italian restaurants in town or that one knows little about town. Accordingly, the first judgment can undermine the informational value of the experience for later judgments that require the application of a different theory, much as has been observed for other (mis)attribution manipulations. Once the informational value of the experience is called into question, people turn to the content of their thoughts as an alternative source of information. Hence, subsequent judgments are content rather than experience based, resulting in a reversal of the observed effects (see Schwarz, 2004, for a more detailed discussion of the role of naïve theories).

Processing Motivation

Social cognition researchers commonly assume that people's processing style depends on the motivation and cognitive resources they bring to the task. When either cognitive capacity or processing motivation are low, people tend to rely on heuristic shortcuts; when both cognitive capacity and processing motivation are high, people are likely to engage in more systematic processing, with increased attention to detail (for reviews see the contributions in Chaiken & Trope, 1999). Both of these variables have also been found to influence whether people rely on their accessibility experiences or on accessible thought content in forming a judgment.

For example, Rothman and Schwarz (1998) asked male participants to recall either a few or many behaviors that increase or decrease their risk for heart disease. To manipulate processing motivation, participants were first asked to report on their family history of heart disease. Presumably, this recall task has higher personal relevance for those with a family history than for those without, once this history is rendered salient. As expected, men *with* a family history of heart disease drew on the relevant behavioral information they recalled. They reported higher vulnerability after recalling eight rather than three risk-increasing behaviors, and lower vulnerability after recalling eight rather than three risk-decreasing behaviors. In contrast, men *without* a family history of heart disease drew on their accessibility experiences, resulting in the opposite pattern. They reported lower vulnerability after recalling eight rather than three risk-increasing behaviors, and higher vulnerability after recalling eight rather than three risk-decreasing behaviors. These findings (and a conceptual replication by Grayson & Schwarz, 1999) suggest that people are likely to draw on their subjective accessibility experiences under low processing motivation, but on accessible content under high processing motivation.

Research into the interplay of mood and accessibility experiences provides converging support. As numerous studies demonstrated, being in a happy mood fosters heuristic processing strategies, whereas being in a sad mood fosters systematic processing strategies (for reviews see Schwarz & Clore, 2007). Drawing on this work, Ruder and Bless (2003) predicted that people in an induced happy mood would rely on their accessibility experiences, whereas people in an induced sad mood would rely on recalled content. Their four experiments consistently supported these predictions. Finally, Florack and Zoabi (2003) observed that people high in need for cognition, a dispositional variable associated with high processing motivation, were less likely to rely on their accessibility experiences than were people low in need for cognition.

Testing the role of processing capacity, Greifeneder and Bless (2007) asked participants to list few or many arguments in favor of a position and instructed them to work carefully on all tasks, thus increasing their processing motivation. Following the argument listing task, they manipulated participants' processing capacity by asking half of them to hold an eight-digit number in mind while forming a judgment. As expected under high processing motivation, participants drew on the content of their thoughts when their processing capacity was not restrained and reported more favorable judgments after generating many rather than few supporting arguments. In contrast, participants who had to hold an eight-digit number in mind relied on their accessibility experiences and reported less favorable judgments after generating many rather than few supporting arguments. Additional experiments replicated this pattern and provided further support for the underlying process assumptions.

In combination, the reviewed findings consistently indicate that low processing motivation or capacity increase reliance on metacognitive experiences as a heuristically relevant source of information. This observation does not imply, however, that these are the *only* conditions under which people rely on metacognitive experiences as a source of information. As numerous persuasion studies demonstrated, when other sources of information are ambiguous or insufficient, people base their judgments on heuristic inputs even under conditions of high motivation and capacity (for a review, see Eagly & Chaiken, 1993). The same has been observed for accessibility experiences. For example, Wänke and Bless (2000) presented participants with persuasive arguments and manipulated how easily they could recall these arguments later on, by providing differentially helpful contextual cues. They observed that participants were more persuaded by the same arguments when this manipulation facilitated their recall. Presumably, the easily recalled arguments were perceived as more familiar and compelling, for reasons discussed in the next section. More important, this effect was more pronounced under high than under low processing motivation, reiterating the general observation that argument quality is more likely to influence attitude judgments when recipients are motivated to process the arguments (for a review, see Eagly & Chaiken, 1993). Exploring the specific conditions under which high processing motivation facilitates rather than impairs reliance on metacognitive experiences provides a promising avenue for future research.

Summary

In sum, the reviewed studies illustrate that there is more to thinking than thought content. Whenever people recall information from memory or generate new thoughts, they can draw on two distinct sources of information: the content they brought to mind (declarative information) and the subjective experiences they had while doing so (experiential information). These experiences include their apparent affective reactions to what they are thinking about (addressed by Pham, this volume) as well as the ease or difficulty of the thought process. What people conclude from their metacognitive experience depends on which of many naïve theories of memory and cognition they bring to bear. The most broadly applicable one holds that it is easier to recall some examples or to generate some arguments when many rather than few of them exist. Application of this theory results in an ironic effect: The more examples people try to recall, the more difficult the recall process becomes and the more they convince themselves that there are not many, resulting in judgments that are opposite to the implications of recalled content. Hence, people evaluate a BMW less favorably the more reasons they considered recalling for driving one (Wänke et al., 1997), see themselves as less assertive the more examples of their own assertive behavior they listed (Schwarz et al., 1991), and conclude that they ride their bicycle less often the more instances of bicycling they recalled (Aarts & Dijksterhuis, 1999). Accordingly, their judgments are consistent with the implications of thought content when recall or thought generation was easy, but opposite to these implications when it was difficult (see Figure 9.1).

This ironic effect often thwarts good intentions. Concerned that people may rely on the first thing that comes to mind, many decision researchers recommend that deciders should make an effort to counterargue their initial thoughts by asking themselves, "What are some reasons that my initial judgment might be wrong?" (Larrick, 2004, p. 323). Ironically, the more people try to do so, the more difficult it is—and the more likely they are to convince themselves that their initial judgment was right on target, as Sanna and Schwarz (2004) observed for a variety of different biases (for a review see Schwarz, Sanna, Skurnik, & Yoon, 2007).

As is the case for any other source of information, people do not rely on their accessibility experiences when their informational value for the judgment at hand is called into question. This is the case when they attribute the experience to an irrelevant source, either due to a (mis)attribution manipulation (e.g., Schwarz et al., 1991) or through the attribution entailed by a preceding judgment (e.g., Schwarz et al., 2005). Finally, they are more likely to rely on their accessibility experiences when processing motivation or capacity is low rather than high (e.g., Greifeneder & Bless, 2007; Rothman & Schwarz, 1998).

THE EASE OF PROCESSING NEW INFORMATION: FLUENCY EXPERIENCES

Much like retrieving information from memory can feel easy or difficult, so can the acquisition of new information. When consumers encounter an advertisement or see a new product on the shelves of their supermarket, the information may be easy or difficult to perceive and process. Numerous variables can influence this experience (for a review see Reber, Schwarz, & Winkielman, 2004). Some variables affect the speed and accuracy of low-level processes concerned with the identification of a stimulus' physical identity and form; they influence *perceptual fluency* (e.g., Jacoby, Kelley, and Dywan 1989). Relevant examples include figure-ground contrast, the clarity with which a stimulus is presented, the duration of its presentation, or the amount of previous exposure to the stimulus. Other variables influence the speed and accuracy of high-level processes concerned with the identification of stimulus meaning and its relation to semantic knowledge structures; these variables influence *conceptual fluency* (e.g., Whittlesea, 1993). Relevant examples include semantic predictability, the consistency between the stimulus and its context, and the availability of appropriate mental concepts for stimulus classification. Empirically, perceptual and conceptual fluency have similar effects on judgment and we refer to them with the general term *processing fluency*. Processing fluency can be assessed with objective measures, such as processing speed and accuracy, as well as subjective measures, such as subjective impressions of effort, speed, and accuracy.

Fluency experiences can influence consumer judgment and decision making in several ways. First, consumers may misread the ease or difficulty with which they process information about a product as bearing on other aspects of product use or decision making. Second, consumers may draw on naïve theories of mental processing to infer the likely meaning of any encountered difficulty, paralleling the use of naïve theories in inferences from accessibility experiences. Finally, fluent processing is experienced as pleasant and elicits positive affect, which, in turn, can feed into other judgments. Next, we address these different possibilities. As will become apparent, processing fluency plays an important role in key consumer judgments, from choice deferral to the assessment of risk and from the perceived truth value of advertisement claims to the appreciation of a product's aesthetic appeal.

When It Is Hard to Read, It Is Hard to Do

When considering a new product, consumers often wonder how easy it is to use. Does the new gadget for my laptop require a crash course in computer science or is it truly plug-and-play? Does the new exercise equipment provide a smooth experience or is it difficult and awkward to use? One way to find out is to read the instructions and to run a mental simulation. When we find the instructions difficult to follow, the product may indeed require a level of skill that exceeds our expertise and we may be well advised to look for a simpler alternative. But as we have already seen, people are usually more sensitive to their metacognitive experiences than to where those experiences come from. Hence, they may misread processing experiences that arise from an irrelevant source as bearing on features of the product, concluding, for example, that the product is difficult to use merely because a poor print font makes the instructions hard to read. Several studies support this conjecture.

For example, Song and Schwarz (in press (a)) asked participants to read a one-page description of an exercise routine, printed in one of the fonts shown in

EASY TO READ CONDITION

- Tuck your chin into your chest, and then lift your chin upward as far as possible. 6-10 repetitions

- Lower your left ear toward your left shoulder and then your right ear toward your right shoulder. 6-10 repetitions

Hard to read condition

- *Tuck your chin into your chest, and then lift your chin upward as far as possible. 6-10 repetitions*

- *Lower your left ear toward your left shoulder and then your right ear toward your right shoulder. 6-10 repetitions*

Figure 9.2   Exercise Instructions in Easy vs. Difficult-to-Read Print Font.

Figure 9.2. As expected, participants inferred that the exercise routine would flow less naturally and take more time when the font was difficult to read, resulting in a lower reported willingness to make the exercise part of their daily routine. Similarly, participants of a second study inferred that preparing a Japanese lunch roll would require more effort and skill when the print font made the recipe hard to read, and were less inclined to prepare that dish at home. In both cases, participants misread the difficulty of reading the instructions as indicative of the difficulty of performing the described behaviors. Importantly, these effects were obtained even though participants correctly understood the instructions in both print font conditions as indicated by their performance on a subsequent knowledge test. It is therefore important that marketers ensure that instructions are easy to read. When printed in a small font to fit small packaging, even straightforward instructions may convey that the product is difficult to use, dissuading consumers from a purchase.

Just as people mistake the difficulty of reading instructions as indicative of the difficulty of performing the behavior, they mistake the difficulty of processing product information as indicative of the difficulty of making a choice. In the preceding section, we already saw that consumers defer choice when they find it difficult to generate many reasons for a choice (Novemsky et al., 2007). They also do so when the product descriptions are difficult to read. For example, Novemsky and colleagues (2007) presented participants with descriptions of two cordless telephones. When the font was easy to read, 17% of the participants deferred choice, whereas 41% did so when it was hard to read. For other participants, the instructions included a sentence that made them aware of the obvious: "This information may be difficult to read because of the font." In this case, the print font no longer exerted an influence and 16% of the participants deferred choice in both font conditions.

As these findings illustrate, consumers may draw on the ease with which they can process product information when asking themselves consumption-relevant questions: Will this product be difficult to use? Am I confident enough to make a choice or does the decision still feel too difficult? In many cases, their processing experience will indeed be due to substantive aspects of the product description and will hence provide useful information. In other cases, however, their experience may merely be due to the print font or other contextual variables. Unfortunately, consumers are unlikely to notice the irrelevant source, unless their attention is drawn to it.

Seems Like I Heard It Before: Fluency, Familiarity, and the Consequences

Other inferences from processing fluency involve naïve theories of mental processing (for a review see Schwarz, 2004), as already seen in the discussion of accessibility experiences. The most broadly applicable naïve theory holds that familiar material is easier to process than novel material. While this belief is correct, the reverse inference does not hold: Not everything that is easy to process is also familiar. Instead, the experienced processing fluency may merely derive from favorable presentation variables, such as the print font or good figure-ground contrast. Yet people are unlikely to notice such incidental sources of fluency and erroneously conclude that novel material is familiar whenever it is easy to process. For example, Whittlesea, Jacoby, and Girard (1990) exposed participants to a study list of rapidly presented words. Subsequently, participants completed a recognition test that manipulated the fluency with which test words could be processed through differential visual clarity. As expected, test words shown with higher clarity seemed more familiar and were hence more likely to be erroneously "recognized" as having appeared on the previous list. This effect was eliminated when participants were aware that the clarity of the visual presentation was manipulated and hence discounted the informational value of the fluency experience (see Kelley & Rhodes, 2002, for a review of related studies).

This fluency-familiarity link has important implications for consumer judgment and public opinion (see Schwarz et al., 2007, for a review). Here we address its influence on judgments of social consensus, truth, and risk.

Social Consensus and Truth   As Festinger (1954) noted, people often draw on social consensus to assess the validity of an opinion when its objective truth is difficult to determine—if many people believe it, there is probably something to it. To determine social consensus, people may attend to the apparent familiarity of the opinion, assuming that they would have heard it a few times if many people share it. Given that fluently processed information seems more familiar than less fluently processed information, variables that influence processing fluency may therefore also influence judgments of social consensus and truth. Empirically, this is the case.

Not surprisingly, one relevant variable is actual exposure frequency. For example, Weaver, Garcia, Schwarz, and Miller (2007) exposed participants to multiple repetitions of the same statement. For some participants, each repetition came from a different communicator, whereas for others, all repetitions came from the same communicator. When later asked to estimate how widely the conveyed opinion is shared, participants estimated higher social consensus the more often they had read the identical statement—even when each repetition came from the same single source. Apparently, participants drew on the familiarity of the opinion in assessing its popularity, but were insufficiently sensitive to where this familiarity came from. As a result, a single repetitive voice sounded like a chorus.

This inferred social consensus contributes to the observation that repeated exposure to a statement increases its acceptance as true. In a classic study of rumor transmission, Allport and Lepkin (1945) observed that the strongest predictor of belief in wartime rumors was simple repetition. Numerous subsequent studies demonstrated that a given statement is more likely to be judged "true" the more often it is repeated. This illusion of truth effect (Begg, Anas, & Farinacci, 1992) has been obtained with trivia statements or words from a foreign language (e.g., Hasher, Goldstein, & Toppino, 1977) as well as advertising materials (e.g., Hawkins & Hoch, 1992). Illusions of truth are even observed when participants are explicitly told at the time of exposure that the information is false, as a study by Skurnik, Yoon, Park, and Schwarz (2005) illustrates. They exposed older and younger adults once or thrice to product statements such as "Shark cartilage is good for your arthritis," and these statements were explicitly marked as "true" or "false." Not surprisingly, all participants were less likely to accept a statement as true the more often they were told that it is false—but only when they were tested immediately. After a three-day delay, repeated warnings backfired for older adults: They were now more likely to assume that a statement is true, the more often they were exposed to it and were explicitly told that it is false. This finding is consistent with the observation that explicit memory declines with age, whereas implicit memory remains largely intact (see Park, 2000). Hence, after three days, older adults could not recall whether the statement was originally marked as true or false, but still experienced its content as highly familiar, leading them to accept it as true. Ironically, this mechanism turns warnings into recommendations. This finding has important implications for public information campaigns and suggests that false information is best left alone—repeating it in order to debunk it only increases its familiarity and later acceptance as true. Hence, information campaigns should focus on what is true, taking advantage of high repetition and favorable presentation variables (addressed below) to render the truth as fluent and familiar as possible (see Schwarz et al., 2007, for a discussion).

If the influence of message repetition is indeed due to increased processing fluency, any other variable that increases fluency should have parallel effects. Empirically, this is again the case. For example, Reber and Schwarz (1999) found that participants were more likely to accept statements like "Osorno is a city in Chile" as true when the statements were presented in colors that made them easy (e.g., dark blue) rather than difficult (e.g., light blue) to read against the background. Similarly, McGlone and Tofighbakhsh (2000) manipulated processing fluency by presenting substantively equivalent novel aphorisms in a rhyming (e.g., "woes unite foes") or nonrhyming form (e.g., "woes unite enemies"). As expected, participants judged substantively equivalent aphorisms as more true when they rhymed than when they did not. This familiarity-truth link may also contribute to the observation that a previously presented persuasive argument is more influential when contextual cues facilitate its easy recall later on (Wänke & Bless, 2000).

In combination, the reviewed findings indicate that processing fluency can serve as an experiential basis of truth judgments. In the absence of more diagnostic information, people draw on the apparent familiarity of the statement to infer its likely truth value. This inference is based on the (usually correct) naïve theory that widely shared opinions are both more likely to be familiar and more likely to be correct than more idiosyncratic ones. Hence, if it seems like they heard it before, there is probably something to it (Festinger, 1954). By the same token, people should infer that apparently familiar information is likely to be false when they have reason to believe that false information is more common in the given context. Empirically, this is the case. For example, Skurnik (1998; see also Skurnik et al., 2000) presented participants with a list of statements, most of which were either marked as true or marked as false, thus inducing the expectation that either truth or falseness is more common in this context. Next, participants saw a second list of statements and subsequently had to recall whether a given statement from the second list was marked true or false. The results showed the expected impact of expectations: When the first list induced an expectation of falseness, participants inferred falseness rather than truth from familiarity. In a later series of elegant studies, Unkelbach (2007) confirmed that fluency can result in inferences of truth or falseness, depending on people's assumptions about their prevalence in the environment.

In sum, which inference people draw from high processing fluency depends on the naïve theory they apply. In most cases, they are likely to believe that familiar information is true. This belief is supported by the logic of social consensus (Festinger, 1954) as well as by the tacit assumptions that underlie the conduct of conversation in daily life (Grice, 1975), which require speakers to say the truth— believing otherwise would imply that most people are either wrong or habitual liars. Nevertheless, when situational cues suggest that false information is more frequent in the given context than true information, people will infer from high fluency that the information is probably false. Future research may fruitfully address which natural contexts give rise to this belief.

Perceived Risk   In many situations, familiarity information is also likely to inform risk assessments: A mushroom we have eaten many times before is less likely to hurt us than a novel and unfamiliar one. Because fluently processed information seems more familiar than disfluently processed information, incidental variables that affect consumers' processing experience may also affect their risk judgments. Song and Schwarz (in press (b)) tested this conjecture by asking participants to evaluate the likely risk posed by various ostensible food additives. To manipulate processing fluency, they named these food additives with labels that were easy (e.g., Ecotrin) or difficult (e.g., Fluthractnip) to pronounce. As predicted, participants judged the additives as more likely to be hazardous when their names were difficult rather than easy to pronounce. A follow-up study replicated this finding and showed that difficult-to-pronounce additives were also perceived as more novel than the easy-to-pronounce ones. More important, participants' novelty ratings fully mediated the effect of name difficulty on risk ratings, as theoretically predicted.

Similar effects were obtained when participants made risk judgments in a domain where risk has a positive connotation, namely when evaluating the excitement provided by adventurous amusement park rides. As expected, participants rated amusement park rides as more "exciting and adventurous" when their names were difficult (e.g., Vaiveahtoishi Train) rather than easy (e.g., Ohanzee Train) to pronounce. That processing fluency affects risk judgments when risk has either a negative connotation (as in the hazardousness of food additives) or a positive one (as in the adventurousness of amusement park rides) suggests that the effect is primarily driven by perceived familiarity, consistent with the results of the mediation analysis. Nevertheless, participants' differential affective reactions to fluent and disfluent material, addressed in the next section, may further contribute to the obtained results. Future research may fruitfully apply affective misattribution manipulations to address this issue.

The same fluency-risk link is also apparent in an important set of findings reported by Alter and Oppenheimer (2006), who studied fluency effects in the stock market. Drawing on records of the New York Stock Exchange, they identified companies who were newly traded on the stock market and followed the fate of these initial public offerings over the first year. They observed that stocks with an easy-to-pronounce ticker symbol (e.g., KAR) did better in the market than stocks with a difficult-to-pronounce symbol (e.g., RDO); this effect was most pronounced on the first day of trading and diminished over time, as more information about the companies became available. Specifically, investing $1000 in a basket of stocks with fluent ticker symbols would have yielded an excess profit of $85.35 over a basket with disfluent ticker symbols on the first day of trading; this advantage was reduced to a still impressive $20.25 by the end of the first year of trading. Similar effects were observed in an independent data set when fluency of the stock names, rather than the fluency of ticker symbols, was used as a predictor. Presumably, stocks with an easy-to-pronounce name or ticker symbol seemed more familiar and less risky than stocks with a difficult-to-pronounce name or symbol, enticing more investors to buy them. Moreover, the positive affective response to fluently processed stimuli, addressed below, may have given these stocks an additional advantage, consistent with the observation that stock markets are more likely to go up on sunny than on rainy days (Hirshleifer & Shumway, 2003; Saunders, 1993).

To date, Alter and Oppenheimer's (2006) findings provide the most compelling evidence for the real-world impact of processing fluency. They are all the more impressive in light of the widely shared assumption that markets are efficient and trades are based on relevant company attributes, which legions of analysts attempt to assess. Quite clearly, name fluency is an important aspect of marketing decisions.

Affect, Preference, and Beauty

The experience of processing fluency is hedonically marked and high fluency gives rise to a positive affective reaction that can itself serve as a basis of judgment (Winkielman, Schwarz, Fazendeiro, & Reber, 2003). This affective impact of fluency can be captured with psychophysiological as well as self-report measures. For example, Winkielman and Cacioppo (2001) assessed participants' affective responses to fluent stimuli with facial electromyography (EMG). This methodology takes advantage of the observation that positive affective responses increase activity over the region of the zygomaticus major ("smiling muscle"), whereas negative affective responses increase activity over the region of the corrugator supercilli ("frowning muscle"; e.g., Cacioppo, Petty, Losch, & Kim 1986). They observed that high fluency was associated with stronger activity over the zygomaticus region (indicative of positive affect), but was not associated with activity of the corrugator region (indicative of negative affect). Similarly, Monahan, Murphy, and Zajonc (2000) reported that repeated exposure to initially neutral stimuli improved participants' self-reported mood, again reflecting positive affective reactions to fluently processed stimuli.

These positive affective responses, in turn, may serve as a basis for evaluative judgments, consistent with the feelings-as-information logic (Schwarz & Clore, 1983; see Pham, this volume). Empirically, this is the case. In a classic and highly influential study, Zajonc (1968) observed that participants evaluated stimuli more positively the more often they were exposed to them. This observation became known as the mere exposure effect (for a review see Bornstein, 1989). From the present perspective, the mere exposure effect is a function of the increased processing fluency that results from repeated exposure (Jacoby et al., 1989; Seamon, Brody, & Kauff, 1983). If so, *any* variable that facilitates fluent processing should also facilitate positive evaluations, even with a single exposure. Numerous studies support this prediction.

For example, Reber, Winkielman, and Schwarz (1998) presented participants with slightly degraded pictures of everyday objects and manipulated processing fluency through a visual priming procedure. Depending on conditions, the target picture was preceded by a subliminally presented, highly degraded contour of either the target picture or a different picture. As predicted, pictures preceded by matched contours were recognized faster, indicating higher fluency, and were liked more than pictures preceded by mismatched contours. Extending this work, Winkielman and Fazendeiro (reported in Winkielman et al., 2003) showed participants unambiguous pictures of common objects and manipulated processing fluency through semantic primes. In the high-fluency condition, the picture (e.g., of a lock) was preceded by a matching word (e.g., "lock"), in the moderate-fluency condition by an associatively related word (e.g., "key"), and in the low-fluency condition by an unrelated word (e.g., "snow"). As predicted, pictures preceded by matching words were liked more than pictures preceded by related words, which, in turn, were liked more than pictures preceded by unrelated words. Follow-up studies indicated that these fluency effects do not require that the concept primes immediately precede the target pictures. Instead, the same pattern of effects was obtained when participants studied a list of concept primes well before they were exposed to the pictures. Lee and Labroo (2004; see also Labroo, Dhar, & Schwarz, 2008) obtained similar findings in the consumer domain. They found, for example, that consumers reported more positive attitudes toward ketchup when they were previously exposed to a closely related product (mayonnaise) rather than an unrelated one. Presumably, the closely related product facilitated processing of the target product, much as related semantic primes facilitated processing of the target pictures in the study by Winkielman et al. (2003).

Numerous other variables that affect processing fluency produce parallel effects, from figure-ground contrast and presentation duration (e.g., Reber et al., 1998) to the prototypicality of the stimulus (e.g., Halberstadt & Rhodes, 2000; Langlois & Roggman, 1990). Moreover, the influence of many variables addressed in the psychology of aesthetics (see Arnheim, 1974; Tatarkiewicz, 1970), such as figural goodness, symmetry, and information density, can be traced to the mediating role of processing fluency: All of these variables facilitate stimulus identification and elicit more positive evaluations.

Fluency Theory of Aesthetic Pleasure   Based on these and related findings, Reber, Schwarz, and Winkielman (2004) proposed a fluency theory of aesthetic pleasure that assigns a central role to the perceiver's processing dynamics: The more fluently perceivers can process a stimulus, the more positive is their aesthetic response. This proposal provides an integrative account of diverse variables and traces their influence to the same underlying process. First, *image variables* that have long been known to influence aesthetic judgments, such as figural goodness, figure-ground contrast, symmetry, and prototypicality, exert their influence by facilitating or impairing fluent processing of the stimulus. Second, *perceiver variables*, such as a history of previous exposure or a motivational state to which the stimulus is relevant, similarly exert their influence through processing fluency. Third, previously unidentified *contextual variables*, such as visual or semantic priming, operate in the same fashion and also affect aesthetic appreciation through their influence on processing fluency. Such contextual variables play no role in traditional theories of aesthetics or in lay intuitions about aesthetic appeal and are uniquely identified as determinants of aesthetic pleasure by Reber and colleagues' (2004) fluency theory.

This theory has important implications for marketing. Most obviously, it suggests that marketers are well advised to design images that allow for fluent processing. Traditional design variables, such as figural goodness, symmetry, and figure-ground contrast, are relevant in this regard and usually observed. In addition, repeated exposure to an image will increase the fluency with which it can be processed, resulting in more favorable evaluations, as known since Zajonc's (1968) identification of the mere exposure effect. Less obvious, fluent processing can also be facilitated by the context in which an image is presented, as illustrated by the observation that previous exposure to related visual material (Reber et al., 1998), semantic concepts (Labroo et al., 2008), or related products on a supermarket shelf (Lee & Labroo, 2004) can increase processing fluency and the favorable evaluation of products. These contextual variables provide new and promising marketing avenues that have so far not been systematically exploited.

CODA

We began this chapter by contrasting the assumptions of microeconomics with psychological models (e.g., Bettman et al., 1998) that emphasize the context dependency of constructed preferences. Informed by theories of information processing (Lachman, Lachman, & Butterfield, 1979), these models share cognitive psychology's traditional focus on *what* comes to mind. As our review indicates, however, *what* comes to mind is not sufficient to understand consumer judgment and choice. Reasoning and decision making is always accompanied by subjective experiences in the form of affective reactions and metacognitive experiences. Consumers draw on these experiences as a source of information, resulting in many counterintuitive effects, such as the observation that investors' prefer stocks with easy-to-pronounce ticker symbols or the finding that consumers like a product less, the more reasons they generated that speak in its favor. As the reviewed research illustrates, any comprehensive model of consumer judgment needs to pay close attention to the interplay of experiential and declarative information in judgment and choice.

REFERENCES

Aarts, H., & Dijksterhuis, A. (1999). How often did I do it? Experienced ease of retrieval and frequency estimates of past behavior. *Acta Psychologica, 103*, 77–89.

Allport, F. H., & Lepkin, M. (1945). Wartime rumors of waste and special privilege: Why some people believe them. *Journal of Abnormal and Social Psychology, 40*, 3–36.

Alter, A. L., & Oppenheimer, D. M. (2006). Predicting short-term stock fluctuations by using processing fluency. *Proceedings of the National Academy of Science, 103*, 9369–9372.

Arnheim, R. (1974). *Art and visual perception: A psychology of the creative eye*. Berkeley, CA: University of California Press.

Begg, I. M., Anas, A., & Farinacci, S. (1992). Dissociation of processes in belief: Source recollection, statement familiarity, and the illusion of truth. *Journal of Experimental Psychology: General, 121*, 446–458.

Bettman, J., Luce, M. F., & Payne, J. (1998). Constructive consumer choice processes. *Journal of Consumer Research, 25*, 187–217.

Bornstein, R. F. (1989). Exposure and affect: Overview and meta-analysis of research 1968–1987. *Psychological Bulletin, 106*, 265–289.

Cacioppo, J. T., Petty, R. E., Losch, M. E., & Kim, H. S. (1986). Electromyographic activity over facial muscle regions can differentiate the valence and intensity of affective reactions. *Journal of Personality and Social Psychology, 50*, 260–268.

Chaiken, S., & Trope, Y. (Eds.) (1999). *Dual process theories in social psychology*. New York: Guilford.

Dhar, R., & Simonson, I. (2003). The effect of forced choice on choice. *Journal of Marketing Research, 40*, 146–160.

Eagly, A. H., & Chaiken, S. (1993). *The psychology of attitudes*. Fort Worth, TX: Harcourt Brace Jovanovich.

Festinger, L. (1954). A theory of social comparison processes. *Human Relations, 7*, 123–146.

Florack, A., & Zoabi, H. (2003). Risikoverhalten bei Aktiengeschäften: Wenn Anleger nach-denklich werden. [Risk behavior in share transactions: When investors think about reasons.] *Zeitschrift für Sozialpsychologie, 34,* 65–78.

Grayson, C.E., & Schwarz, N. (1999). Beliefs influence information processing strategies: Declarative and experiential information in risk assessment. *Social Cognition, 17,* 1–18.

Greifeneder, R., & Bless, ˙˙. (2007). Relying on accessible content vs. accessibility experiences: The case of rocessing capacity. *Social Cognition, 25,* 853–881.

Grice, H. P. (1975). L˙ ˙ic and conversation. In P. Cole,& J. L. Morgan (Eds.), *Syntax and semantics, Vol. ˙: Speech acts* (pp. 41–58). New York: Academic Press.

Griffin, D., Liu, W., & Kahn, U. (2005). A new look at constructed choice processes. *Marketing Letters, 16,* 321–333.

Haddock, G., Rothman, A. J., Reber, R., & Schwarz, N. (1999). Forming judgments of attitude certainty, importance, and intensity: The role of subjective experiences. *Personality and Social Psychology Bulletin, 25,* 771–782.

Halberstadt, J., & Rhodes, G. (2000). The attractiveness of nonface average: Implications for an evolutionary explanation of the attractiveness of average faces. *Psychological Science, 11,* 285–289.

Hasher, L., Goldstein, D., & Toppino, T. (1977). Frequency and the conference of referential validity. *Journal of Verbal Learning and Verbal Behavior, 16,* 107–112.

Hawkins, S. A., & Hoch, S. J. (1992). Low-involvement learning: Memory without evaluation. *Journal of Consumer Research, 19,* 212–225.

Higgins, E. T. (1998). The aboutness principle: A pervasive influence on human inference. *Social Cognition, 16,* 173–198.

Hirshleifer, D., & Shumway, T. (2003). Good day sunshine: Stock returns and the weather. *Journal of Finance,58,* 1009–1032.

Jacoby, L. L., Kelley, C. M., & Dywan, J. (1989). Memory attributions. In H. L. Roediger & F. I. M. Craik (Eds.), *Varieties of memory and consciousness: Essays in honour of Endel Tulving* (pp. 391–422). Hillsdale, NJ: Erlbaum.

Kelley, C. M., & Rhodes, M. G. (2002). Making sense and nonsense of experience: Attributions in memory and judgment. *The Psychology of Learning and Motivation, 41,* 293–320.

Labroo, A. A., Dhar, R., & Schwarz, N. (in press). Of frog wines and smiling watches: Semantic priming of perceptual features and brand evaluation. *Journal of Consumer Research.*

Lachman, R., Lachman, J. T., & Butterfield, E. C. (1979). *Cognitive psychology and information processing.* Hillsdale, NJ: Erlbaum.

Langlois, J. H., & Roggman, L. A. (1990). Attractive faces are only average. *Psychological Science, 1,* 115–121.

Larrick, R. P. (2004). Debiasing. In D. J. Koehler & N. Harvey (Eds.), *Blackwell handbook of judgment and decision making* (pp. 316–337). Oxford, UK: Blackwell Publishing.

Lee, A. Y., & Labroo, A. A. (2004). The effect of conceptual and perceptual fluency on brand evaluation. *Journal of Marketing Research, 41,* 151–165.

McFadden, D. (1999). Rationality for economists? *Journal of Risk and Uncertainty, 19,* 73–105.

McGlone, M. S., & Tofighbakhsh, J. (2000). Birds of a feather flock conjointly(?): Rhyme as reason in aphorisms. *Psychological Science, 11,* 424–428.

Monahan, J. L., Murphy, S. T., & Zajonc, R. B. (2000). Subliminal mere exposure: Specific, general, and diffuse effects. *Psychological Science, 11,* 462–466.

Novemsky, N., Dhar, R., Schwarz, N., & Simonson, I. (2007). Preference fluency in choice. *Journal of Marketing Research, 44,* 347–356.

Park, D. C. (2000). The basic mechanisms accounting for age-related decline in cognitive function. In D. C. Park & N. Schwarz (Eds.). *Cognitive aging: A primer* (pp 3–22). Philadelphia, PA: Psychology Press.

Reber, R., & Schwarz, N. (1999). Effects of perceptual fluency on judgments of truth. *Consciousness and Cognition, 8*, 338–342.

Reber, R., Schwarz, N., & Winkielman, P. (2004). Processing fluency and aesthetic pleasure: Is beauty in the perceiver's processing experience? *Personality and Social Psychology Review, 8*, 364–382.

Reber, R., Winkielman P., & Schwarz N. (1998). Effects of perceptual fluency on affective judgments. *Psychological Science, 9*, 45–48.

Rothman, A. J., & Schwarz, N. (1998). Constructing perceptions of vulnerability: Personal relevance and the use of experiential information in health judgments. *Personality and Social Psychology Bulletin, 24*, 1053–1064.

Ruder, M., & Bless, H. (2003). Mood and the reliance on the ease of retrieval heuristic. *Journal of Personality and Social Psychology, 85*, 20–32.

Samuelson, P. A. (1938). A note on the pure theory of consumer's behavior. *Economica, 5*, 61–71.

Sanna, L. J., & Schwarz, N. (2003). Debiasing hindsight: The role of accessibility experiences and attributions. *Journal of Experimental Social Psychology, 39*, 287–295.

Sanna, L., & Schwarz, N. (2004). Integrating temporal biases: The interplay of focal thoughts and accessibility experiences. *Psychological Science, 17*, 474–481.

Sanna, L., Schwarz, N., & Small, E. (2002). Accessibility experiences and the hindsight bias: I-knew-it-all-along versus It-could-never-have-happened. *Memory & Cognition, 30*, 1288–1296.

Saunders, E. M. (1993). Stock prices and Wall Street weather. *American Economic Review, 83*, 1337–1345.

Savage, L. J. (1954/1972). *The foundations of statistics*. New York, NY: Dover.

Schwarz, N. (1990). Feelings as information: Informational and motivational functions of affective states. In E. T. Higgins & R. Sorrentino (Eds.), *Handbook of motivation and cognition: Foundations of social behavior* (Vol. 2, pp. 527–561). New York: Guilford Press.

Schwarz, N. (2004). Meta-cognitive experiences in consumer judgment and decision making. *Journal of Consumer Psychology, 14*, 332–348.

Schwarz, N. (2007). Attitude construction: Evaluation in context. *Social Cognition, 25*, 638–656.

Schwarz, N. (in press). Mental construal in social judgment. In F. Strack & J. Förster (Eds.), *Social cognition: The basis of human interaction*. Philadelphia: Psychology Press.

Schwarz, N., Bless, H., Strack, F., Klumpp, G., Rittenauer-Schatka, H., & Simons, A. (1991). Ease of retrieval as information: Another look at the availability heuristic. *Journal of Personality and Social Psychology, 61*, 195–202.

Schwarz, N., Cho, H., & Xu, J. (2005, July). *Diverging inferences from identical inputs: The role of naive theories*. Paper presented at the meetings of the European Association of Experimental Social Psychology, Würzburg, Germany.

Schwarz, N., & Clore, G. L. (1983). Mood, misattribution, and judgments of well-being: Informative and directive functions of affective states. *Journal of Personality and Social Psychology, 45*, 513–523.

Schwarz, N., & Clore, G. L. (2007). Feelings and phenomenal experiences. In A. Kruglanski & E. T. Higgins (Eds.), *Social psychology. Handbook of basic principles* (2nd ed.; pp. 385–407). New York: Guilford.

Schwarz, N., Sanna, L., Skurnik, I., & Yoon, C. (2007). Metacognitive experiences and the intricacies of setting people straight: Implications for debiasing and public information campaigns. *Advances in Experimental Social Psychology, 39*, 127–161.

Seamon, J. G., Brody, N., & Kauff, D. M. (1983). Affective discrimination of stimuli that are not recognized: Effects of shadowing, masking, and central laterality. *Journal of Experimental Psychology: Learning, Memory and Cognition, 9*, 544–555.

Simonson, I. (1989). Choice based on reasons: The case of attraction and compromise effects. *Journal of Consumer Research, 16*, 158–174.

Skurnik, I. (1998). *Metacognition and the illusion of truth*. Dissertation, Princeton University.

Skurnik, I., Schwarz, N., & Winkielman, P. (2000). Drawing inferences from feelings: The role of naive beliefs. In H. Bless & J. Forgas (Eds.), *The message within: The role of subjective experience in social cognition and behavior* (pp. 162–175). Philadelphia, PA: Psychology Press.

Skurnik, I., Yoon, C., Park, D. C., & Schwarz, N. (2005). How warnings about false claims become recommendations. *Journal of Consumer Research, 31*, 713–724.

Song, H., & Schwarz, N. (in press (a)). If it's easy to read, it's easy to do: Processing fluency affects the prediction of time and effort. *Psychological Science*.

Song, H., & Schwarz, N. (in press (b)). If it's difficult-to-pronounce, it must be risky: Processing fluency and risk perception. *Psychological Science*.

Stepper, S., & Strack F. (1993). Proprioceptive determinants of emotional and nonemotional feelings. *Journal of Personality and Social Psychology, 64*, 211–220.

Tatarkiewicz, W. (1970). *History of aesthetics*. The Hague: Mouton.

Tormala, Z. L., Falces, C., Brinol, P., & Petty, R. E. (2007). Ease of retrieval effects in social judgment: The role of unrequested cognitions. *Journal of Personality and Social Psychology, 93*,143–157.

Tversky, A., & Kahneman, D. (1973). Availability: A heuristic for judging frequency and probability. *Cognitive Psychology, 5*, 207–232.

Unkelbach, C. (2007). Reversing the truth effect: Learning the interpretation of processing fluency in judgments of truth. *Journal of Experimental Psychology: Learning, Memory, and Cognition, 33*, 219–230.

Wänke, M., & Bless, H. (2000). The effects of subjective ease of retrieval on attitudinal judgments: The moderating role of processing motivation. In H. Bless & J. P. Forgas (Eds.), *The message within: The role of subjective experience in social cognition and behavior* (pp. 143–161). Philadelphia: Psychology Press.

Wänke, M., Bless, H., & Biller, B. (1996). Subjective experience versus content of information in the construction of attitude judgments. *Personality and Social Psychology Bulletin, 22*, 1105–1113.

Wänke, M., Bohner, G., & Jurkowitsch, A. (1997). There are many reasons to drive a BMW—Surely you know one: Ease of argument generation influences brand attitudes. *Journal of Consumer Research, 24*, 70–77

Weaver, K., Garcia, S. M., Schwarz, N., & Miller, D. T. (2007). Inferring the popularity of an opinion from its familiarity: A repetitive voice can sound like a chorus. *Journal of Personality and Social Psychology, 92*, 821–833.

Whittlesea, B. W. A. (1993). Illusions of familiarity. *Journal of Experimental Psychology: Learning, Memory, and Cognition, 19*, 1235–1253.

Whittlesea, B. W. A., Jacoby, L. L., & Girard, K. (1990). Illusions of immediate memory: Evidence of an attributional basis for feelings of familiarity and perceptual quality. *Journal of Memory and Language, 29*, 716–732.

Winkielman, P., & Cacioppo, J. T. (2001). Mind at ease puts a smile on the face: Psychophysiological evidence that processing facilitation leads to positive affect. *Journal of Personality and Social Psychology, 81*, 989–1000.

Winkielman, P., Schwarz, N., Fazendeiro, T., & Reber, R. (2003). The hedonic marking of processing fluency: Implications for evaluative judgment. In J. Musch & K. C. Klauer (Eds.), *The psychology of evaluation: Affective processes in cognition and emotion* (pp. 189–217). Mahwah, NJ: Erlbaum.

Xu, J., & Schwarz, N. (2005, February). *Was it long ago or unimportant? Diverging inferences from difficulty of recall*. Society for Consumer Psychology, St. Petersburg Beach, FL

Zajonc, R. B. (1968). Attitudinal effects of mere exposure. *Journal of Personality and Social Psychology: Monograph Supplement, 9,* 1–27.

Section *IV*

Social and Media Influences on Judgment and Behavior

10

Cross-Cultural Issues in Consumer Behavior

SHARON SHAVITT

University of Illinois—Urbana-Champaign

ANGELA Y. LEE

Northwestern University

CARLOS J. TORELLI

University of Minnesota

O ne of the most difficult choices that multinational corporations face is deciding whether to run the same marketing campaign globally or to customize it to the local taste in different countries. In many cases, companies develop their marketing strategy in one country and then do "disaster checking" as they launch the same strategy in other countries instead of trying to discover what would work best in each market (Clegg, 2005). This often leads to ineffective marketing campaigns and damaged reputations. As new global markets emerge, and existing markets become increasingly segmented along ethnic or subcultural lines, the need to market effectively to consumers who have different cultural values has never been more important. Thus, it is no surprise that in the last decade or so, culture has rapidly emerged as a central focus of research in consumer behavior.

What Is Culture?

Culture consists of shared elements that provide the standards for perceiving, believing, evaluating, communicating, and acting among those who share a language, a historical period, and a geographic location. As a psychological construct, culture can be studied in multiple ways—across nations, across ethnic groups within nations, across individuals within nations (focusing on cultural orientation), and even across situations within individuals through the priming of cultural values. As will be discussed presently, regardless of how culture is studied, cultural distinctions have been demonstrated to have important implications for advertising content, persuasiveness of appeals, consumer motivation, consumer judgment processes, and consumer response styles.

Coverage and Scope

The present chapter reviews these topics. Our coverage is necessarily selective, focusing on findings specific to the consumer domain rather than a more general review of cultural differences (for excellent general reviews, see Chiu & Hong, 2006; Smith, Bond, & Kagitcibasi, 2006). Our content is organized around the theoretical implications of cultural differences in consumer judgments, choices, and brand representations. We focus our coverage on the areas of self-regulation, risk taking, and persuasion because these represent domains that have received particularly significant research attention, and because this research has uncovered underlying psychological processes connecting cultural variables to consumer behavior. For each of these areas, we review implications for information processing, brand evaluations and preferences, and choices.

In our coverage, the cultural constructs of individualism/collectivism and the independent/interdependent self-construals associated with them are given special attention because extensive research has demonstrated the implications of these distinctions for processes and outcomes relevant to consumer behavior. The most recent refinements to these constructs are briefly reviewed in an attempt to identify additional cultural variables likely to enhance the understanding of cross-cultural consumer behavior. We close with a discussion of the role of consumer brands as cultural symbols in the era of globalization and multiculturalism.

KEY CONSTRUCTS AND DIMENSIONS OF CULTURE

The constructs of *individualism* and *collectivism* represent the most broadly used dimensions of cultural variability for cross-cultural comparison (Gudykunst & Ting-Toomey, 1988). In individualistic cultures, people value independence from others and subordinate the goals of their in-groups to their own personal goals. In collectivistic cultures, in contrast, individuals value interdependent relationships to others and subordinate their personal goals to those of their in-groups (Hofstede, 1980, 2001; Triandis, 1989). The key distinction involves the extent to which one defines the self in relation to others. In individualistic cultural contexts, people tend to have an independent self-construal (Markus & Kitayama, 1991) whereby the self is defined as autonomous and unique. In collectivistic cultural contexts, people tend to have an interdependent self-construal (Markus & Kitayama, 1991) whereby the self is seen as inextricably and fundamentally embedded within a larger social network of roles and relationships. This distinction has also been referred to as egocentric vs. sociocentric selves (Shweder & Bourne, 1982).

National cultures that celebrate the values of independence, as in the United States, Canada, Germany, and Denmark, are typically categorized as individualistic societies in which an independent self-construal is common. In contrast, cultures that nurture the values of fulfilling one's obligations and responsibilities over one's own personal wishes or desires, including most East Asian and Latin American countries, such as China, Korea, Japan, and Mexico, are categorized as collectivistic societies in which an interdependent self-construal is common (Hofstede, 1980, 2001; Markus & Kitayama, 1991; Triandis, 1989).

A very large body of research in psychology has demonstrated the many implications of individualism/collectivism and independent/interdependent self-construals for social perception and social behavior (see Markus & Kitayama, 1991; Triandis, 1989, 1995). In general terms, these findings indicate consistently that individualists and people with an independent self-construal are oriented toward products and experiences that promote achievement and autonomy, offer personal benefits, and enable expression of one's distinctive qualities. They tend to be *promotion focused*, regulating their attitudes and behaviors in pursuit of positive outcomes and aspirations. Collectivists and people with an interdependent self-construal are oriented toward products and experiences that allow one to avoid negative outcomes, maintain harmony and strong social connections with others, and dutifully fulfill social roles. They tend to be *prevention focused*, regulating their attitudes and behaviors in pursuit of security and the avoidance of negative outcomes (Higgins, 1997).

Numerous studies have pointed to important differences between individualistic and collectivistic societies in the kind of information that is featured and seen as important or persuasive in consumer messages. Individualists and people with an independent self-construal are persuaded by information that addresses their promotion regulatory concerns, including messages about personal achievement, individuality, uniqueness, and self-improvement. Collectivists and people with an interdependent self-construal are persuaded by information that addresses their prevention regulatory concerns, including messages about harmony, group goals, conformity, and security. These types of differences emerge in the prevalence of different types of advertising appeals (e.g., Alden, Hoyer, & Lee, 1993; S. M. Choi, Lee, & Kim, 2005; Han & Shavitt, 1994; J. W. Hong, Muderrisoglu, & Zinkhan, 1987; Kim & Markus, 1999; Lin, 2001), the processing and persuasiveness of advertising messages (Aaker & Maheswaran, 1997; Aaker & Williams, 1998; Han & Shavitt, 1994; Y. Zhang & Gelb, 1996), the perceived importance of product information (Aaker & Lee, 2001; A. Y. Lee, Aaker, & Gardner, 2000), and the determinants of consumers' purchase intentions (C. Lee & Green, 1991), among other outcomes.

Although a given self-construal can be more chronically accessible in a particular culture, all cultures provide sufficient experiences with independent and interdependent views of the self to allow either self-construal to be primed (see Oyserman, Coon, & Kemmelmeier, 2002; Oyserman & Lee, 2007). Indeed, people in general, and especially bicultural people, can readily switch back and forth between independent and interdependent cultural frames in response to their contexts (Briley, Morris, & Simonson, 2005; Fu, Chiu, Morris, & Young, 2007;

Lau-Gesk, 2003). For instance, Lau-Gesk (2003) found that independent (interdependent) self-construals were temporarily activated when bicultural consumers were exposed to individually focused (interpersonally focused) appeals. When activated, these situationally accessible self-views appear to alter social perception and consumer judgments in ways that are highly consistent with cross-cultural findings (e.g., Brewer & Gardner, 1996; Gardner, Gabriel, & Lee, 1999; Y.-y. Hong, Ip, A. Y. Lee et al., 2000; Chiu, Morris, & Menon, 2001; Mandel, 2003; Torelli, 2006; Trafimow, Triandis, & Goto, 1991; Lalwani & Shavitt, in press).

In sum, the distinctions between individualistic and collectivistic societies, and independent and interdependent self-construals, are crucial to the cross-cultural understanding of consumer behavior. Indeed, whereas the 1980s were labeled the decade of individualism/collectivism in cross-cultural psychology (Kagitcibasi, 1994), similar distinctions represent the dominant structural approach in cross-cultural consumer research in the 1990s and 2000s. As noted, the studies to be reviewed in this chapter offer a wealth of evidence that these cultural classifications have fundamental implications for consumption-related outcomes.

Emerging Cultural Dimensions

The conceptualizations of individualism and collectivism, and independence and interdependence, have historically been broad and multidimensional, summarizing a host of differences in focus of attention, self-definitions, motivations, emotional connections to in-groups, and belief systems and behavioral patterns (Bond, 2002; Ho & Chiu, 1994; Hofstede, 1980; Oyserman et al., 2002; Triandis, 1995; Triandis, Bontempo, Villareal, Asai, & Lucca, 1988; Triandis, Leung, Villareal, & Clack, 1985). Nevertheless, recent studies have proposed useful refinements to the broader individualism/collectivism or independent/interdependent cultural categories. For instance, Rhee, Uleman, and Lee (1996) distinguished between versions of individualism and collectivism referencing family (kin) and nonfamily (nonkin) in-groups, and showed that Asians and European Americans manifested distinct patterns of relations between kin and nonkin individualism. Gelfand, Bhawuk, Nishii, and Bechtold (2004) distinguished between institutional and in-group collectivism, and showed that there can be substantial differences in the degree to which a society encourages institutional collective action versus interpersonal interdependence (e.g., Scandinavian societies emphasize the former but not the latter).

More recently, Brewer and Chen (2007) have distinguished between a *relational* form of collectivism (dominant in East Asian cultures) that emphasizes relationships between the self and particular close others, and a *group-focused* form of collectivism (more common in Western cultures) that emphasizes relationships with others by virtue of common membership in a symbolic group (see also Gaines et al., 1997). This group/relational distinction in interdependence is congruent with gender differences in cultural orientations indicating that women are more relational but less group-oriented than men in their patterns of interdependent judgments and behaviors (Gabriel & Gardner, 1999; see also Kashima et al., 1995).

In sum, the nature and meaning of individualism and collectivism (or of independent and interdependent self-construals) appear to vary across cultural, institutional, gender, and ethnic lines. Although the breadth of the individualism/collectivism constructs lends integrative strengths, more recent research suggests that further refinements of these categories enhance the prediction of consumer behavior.

The Horizontal/Vertical Distinction   Within the individualism/collectivism framework, Triandis and his colleagues (Singelis, Triandis, Bhawuk, & Gelfand, 1995; Triandis, 1995; Triandis & Gelfand, 1998) have recently introduced a further distinction between societies that are *horizontal* (valuing equality) and those that are *vertical* (emphasizing hierarchy). The horizontal/vertical distinction emerges from the observation that American or British individualism differs from, say, Norwegian or Danish individualism in much the same way that Japanese or Korean collectivism differs from the collectivism of the Israeli kibbutz. Specifically, in vertical individualist (VI) societies (e.g., the United States and Great Britain), people strive to become distinguished and acquire status via competition, whereas in horizontal individualist (HI) cultural contexts (e.g., Sweden and Norway), people value uniqueness but are not especially interested in becoming distinguished and achieving high status. In vertical collectivistic (VC) societies (e.g., Korea and Japan), people emphasize the subordination of their goals to those of their in-groups, submit to the will of authority, and support competitions between their in-groups and out-groups. Finally, in horizontal collectivist (HC) cultural contexts (e.g., exemplified historically by the Israeli kibbutz), people see themselves as similar to others and emphasize common goals with others, interdependence, and sociability, but they do not submit to authority.

When such distinctions are taken into account, it becomes apparent that the societies chosen to represent individualistic and collectivistic cultural syndromes in consumer research have almost exclusively been vertically oriented. Specifically, the modal comparisons are between the United States (VI) and any of a number of Pacific Rim countries (VC). It may be argued, therefore, that much of what is known about consumer behavior in individualistic and collectivistic societies reflects vertical forms of these syndromes and may not generalize, for example, to comparisons between Sweden (HI) and Israel (HC) or other sets of horizontal cultures. As an example, conformity in product choice, as examined by Kim and Markus (1999), may be a tendency specific to VC cultures, in which deference to authority and to in-group wishes is stressed. Much lower levels of conformity may be observed in HC cultures, which emphasize sociability but not deference (Triandis & Gelfand, 1998). Thus, it may be inappropriate to ascribe differences in consumers' conformity between Korea (VC) and the United States (VI) solely to the role of individualism/collectivism or independence/interdependence, because such conformity might not be prevalent in horizontal societies. In particular, levels of product conformity in an HC culture might not exceed those in an HI culture.

Indeed, several recent studies of this horizontal/vertical cultural distinction have provided evidence for its value as a predictor of new consumer psychology phenomena and as a basis for refining the understanding of known phenomena (Shavitt, Lalwani, Zhang, & Torelli, 2006). For instance, Lalwani, Shavitt, and Johnson (2006) showed that differences in the self-presentational responses observed for individualists and collectivists are mediated at the individual level by the horizontal but not the vertical versions of these cultural orientations. This suggests that culturally linked self-presentational efforts reflect distinct goals of being seen as self-reliant and capable (valued in HI contexts) versus sociable and benevolent (valued in HC contexts).

In a study about country-of-origin effects, Gürhan-Canli and Maheswaran (2000) demonstrated that the tendency to favor products from one's own country over foreign products emerged more strongly in Japan (a VC culture) than in the United States (a VI culture). This fits well with a conceptualization of collectivists as being oriented toward their in-groups. However, mediational analyses using individual consumers' self-rated cultural values indicated that only the vertical aspect of individualism and collectivism accounted for the country-of-origin effects in Japan. In other words, the collectivistic tendency to favor one's own country's products appeared to be driven by cultural values that stress hierarchy, competition, and deference to in-group wishes, not by values that stress interdependence more generally.

In line with this, research suggests that advertising messages with themes that emphasize status, prestige, hierarchy, and distinction may be more prevalent and persuasive in vertical cultural contexts (Shavitt, Lalwani et al., 2006). Such advertisements also appear to be generally more persuasive for those with a vertical cultural orientation, and may be inappropriate for those with a horizontal one. Shavitt, Zhang, and Johnson (2006) asked U.S. respondents to write advertisements that they personally would find persuasive. The extent to which the ad appeals that they wrote emphasized status themes was positively correlated with respondents' vertical cultural orientation and negatively correlated with their horizontal cultural orientation. Moreover, content analyses of magazine advertisements in several countries suggested that status-oriented themes of hierarchy, luxury, prominence, and distinction were generally more prevalent in societies presumed to have vertical cultural profiles (e.g., Korea, Russia) than a horizontal cultural profile (Denmark).

Additional Dimensions Numerous other cultural distinctions deserve further attention in consumer research. A focus upon these relatively under-researched constructs as antecedents may allow for broadening the range of cultural differences beyond those currently investigated. For instance, Schwartz's (1992) circumplex structure of values, which has emerged as highly robust cross-nationally, appears largely consistent with the HI/VI/HC/VC typology and offers a particularly detailed and comprehensive basis for classification. In his large-scale studies of work values, Hofstede (Hofstede, 1980, 2001) derived three other dimensions of cultural variation in addition to individualism: *power distance* (acceptance of power inequality in organizations, a construct conceptually relevant to the vertical/horizontal distinction), *uncertainty avoidance* (the degree of tolerance for ambiguity or uncertainty about the future), and *masculinity/femininity* (preference for achievement and assertiveness versus modesty and nurturing relationships). Indeed, individualism was the second dimension identified by Hofstede (1980), whereas power distance emerged as the first dimension. Oyserman (2006) suggests that a separate power dimension (high vs. low power) may help to advance our understanding of the effects of (not) having power in different cultures. A few marketing-oriented studies have employed Hofstede's nation-level classifications (e.g., Blodgett, Lu, Rose, & Vitell, 2001; Dwyer, Mesak, & Hsu, 2005; Earley, 1999; Johnson, Kulesa, Cho, & Shavitt, 2005; Nelson, Brunel, Supphellen, & Manchanda, 2006; Spencer-Oatey, 1997), but more potential remains for identifying consequences for consumer judgments and behaviors. For instance, uncertainty avoidance has been conceptualized as a syndrome related to anxiety, rule orientation, need for security, and deference to experts (Hofstede, 1980). As such, one might speculate that the level of uncertainty avoidance in a culture will predict the tendency for advertisements to use fear appeals or appeals that emphasize safety and security, and the tendency for advertisements to employ expert spokespersons. Differences along this cultural dimension may also predict patterns in the diffusion of product innovations, particularly innovations whose purchase entails a degree of risk.

CULTURE AND SELF-REGULATORY GOALS

Closely linked to the individualism/collectivism distinction is the independent goal of distinguishing oneself from others through success and achievement and the interdependent goal of maintaining harmony with respect to others through the fulfillment of obligations and responsibilities. These two goals serve as important self-regulatory guides that direct consumers' attention, attitudes, and behaviors (Higgins, 1997; see also Lee & Higgins, this volume).

The independent goal of being positively distinct, with its emphasis on achievement and autonomy, is more consistent with a promotion focus, whereas the interdependent goal of harmoniously fitting in with others, with its emphasis on fulfilling social roles and maintaining connections with others, is more consistent with a prevention focus. Thus, people from Western individualistic cultures (whose independent self-construal is more accessible) tend to be promotion focused, whereas people from Eastern collectivistic cultures (whose interdependent self-construal is more accessible) tend to be prevention focused. People with a promotion focus regulate their attitudes and behaviors toward the pursuit of growth and the achievement of hopes and aspirations to satisfy their needs for nurturance. They pursue their goals with eagerness and are sensitive to the presence and absence of positive outcomes. In contrast, those with a prevention focus regulate their attitudes and behaviors toward the pursuit of safety and the fulfillment of duties and obligations to satisfy their needs for security. They pursue their goals with vigilance and are sensitive to the presence and absence of negative outcomes.

That distinct self-construals are associated with distinct types of self-regulatory focus has important implications for consumer research. First, consumers consider information that is compatible with the dominant self-view to be more important (A. Y. Lee et al., 2000). Specifically, promotion-focused information that addresses the concerns of growth and achievement is more relevant and hence deemed more important to those individuals with a dominant independent (compared to interdependent) self-construal. On the other hand, prevention-focused information that addresses the concerns of safety and security is more relevant and hence deemed more important to those individuals with a dominant interdependent (compared to independent) self-construal (Aaker & Lee, 2001; A. Y. Lee et al., 2000).

Using different operationalizations of self-construal that include cultural orientation (North American vs. East Asian), individual disposition (Singelis, 1994), and situational prime, Lee and her colleagues (A. Y. Lee et al., 2000) demonstrate that individuals with a more accessible independent self-view perceive a scenario that emphasizes gains or nongains to be more important than one that emphasizes losses or nonlosses. They also experience more intense promotion-focused emotions such as cheerfulness and dejection. In contrast, those with a more dominant interdependent self-view perceive a scenario that emphasizes losses or nonlosses to be more important than one that emphasizes gains or nongains. They also experience more intense prevention-focused emotions such as peacefulness and agitation. Thus, consumers with distinct self-construals are more persuaded by information that addresses their regulatory concerns when argument quality is strong (Aaker & Lee, 2001; Agrawal & Maheswaran, 2005; J. Wang & Lee, 2006), but less persuaded when argument quality is weak, as compared to when the information does not address their regulatory concerns.

Chen, Ng, and Rao (2005) also found that consumers with a dominant independent self-construal are more willing to pay for expedited delivery when presented with a promotion framed message (i.e., to enjoy a product early), whereas those with a dominant interdependent self-construal are more willing to pay for expedited delivery when presented with a prevention framed message (i.e., avoid delay in receiving a product). These matching effects between self-construal and regulatory focus are observed regardless of whether self-construal is situationally made more accessible or is culturally nurtured (Aaker & Lee, 2001; Agrawal & Maheswaran, 2005; Chen et al., 2005).

Interestingly, brand commitment (defined as consumers' public attachment or pledging to the brand) seems to moderate the effectiveness of the chronic versus situational regulatory relevance effects (Agrawal & Maheswaran, 2005). In particular, Agrawal and Maheswaran (2005) found that appeals consistent with the chronic self-construal are more persuasive under high brand commitment, whereas appeals consistent with the primed (independent or interdependent) self-construal are more effective under low brand commitment. According to the authors, consumers who are committed to the brand have a readily accessible knowledge structure related to the brand. To these consumers, not only is brand information highly accessible, it is also linked to other chronically accessible knowledge in memory. Exposure to brand information that is highly relevant to the self is likely to activate consumers' chronic self-construal. Thus, their attention and attitudes will tend to be guided more by their chronic self-construal than by the primed self-construal. However, for low commitment consumers, exposure to brand information is less likely to activate any chronic self knowledge. Thus, their preferences will tend to be guided more by their currently accessible self-construal (i.e., the primed self-construal) than by their chronic self-construal.

More recent research suggests that regulatory relevance effects may be moderated by involvement such that people are more likely to rely on their regulatory focus as a filter to selectively process information when they are not expending cognitive resources to process information (Briley & Aaker, 2006; J. Wang & Lee, 2006). For example, Briley and Aaker (2006) demonstrated that participants who are culturally inclined to have a promotion or prevention focus hold more favorable attitudes toward those products that address their regulatory concerns—but only when they are asked to provide their initial reactions or when their evaluation is made under cognitive load or under time pressure. The culturally induced regulatory relevance effects disappear when participants are asked to make deliberated evaluations or when they are able to expend cognitive resources on the task. For a more detailed discussion on effects of regulatory focus on persuasion, please see the chapter on regulatory fit by Lee and Higgins in this volume.

Distinct self-construals with their corresponding regulatory goals also appear to be the basis of different temporal perspectives across members of different cultures such that those with a dominant independent self-construal are more likely to construe events at a more distant future than those with a dominant interdependent self-construal (S. Lee & Lee, 2007). For the independents, their regulatory goal that emphasizes growth and achievement takes time to attain. Further, their sensitivity to gains and nongains prompts them to focus on positives (vs. negatives) that are more salient in the distant future (Eyal, Liberman, Trope, & Walther, 2004). In contrast, for the interdependents, their regulatory orientation that emphasizes safety and security necessitates their keeping a close watch on their surrounding environment and on the immediate future. Further, their sensitivity to losses and nonlosses prompts them to focus on negatives (vs. positives) that are more salient in the near future. Interdependents' close attention to the self in relationship with others also requires their construing the self and others in contexts that are concrete and specific (vs. abstract and general; I. Choi, Dalal, Kim-Prieto, & Park, 2003), which are more characteristic of near versus far temporal distance. Indeed, Lee and Lee (2007) observed that those with a dominant interdependent self-construal (e.g., Koreans) are likely to construe a future event to be temporally more proximal than those with a dominant independent self-construal (e.g., Americans); interdependents also respond more positively to events scheduled in the near future than do independents. The implication is that persuasive appeals that make salient the temporal distance that corresponds with consumers' self-view would be more persuasive than appeals that make salient a mismatched temporal distance. For example, a political campaign that focuses on the future long-term outlook should be more persuasive among those with an independent self-construal, whereas a campaign message that draws people's attention to the current situation should be more persuasive among those with an interdependent self-construal.

This section highlights the importance of understanding the regulatory orientation of the two distinct self-views. However, efforts to generalize this relationship should proceed with caution. As discussed earlier, cultures differ not only in their levels of individualism and collectivism, but also in the extent to which they are vertical (emphasizing hierarchy) or horizontal (emphasizing equality or openness; Triandis, 1995; Triandis & Gelfand, 1998). It is possible that construal-induced shifts in regulatory focus are limited to cultures that are vertical in structure. For instance, to the extent that competing to distinguish oneself positively is more prevalent in vertical than horizontal individualist cultures, an independent promotion focus is more likely among members of a vertical individualist culture (e.g., United States) than among a horizontal individualist culture (e.g., Norway, Sweden). And to the extent that conformity and obedience are more normative in a vertical collectivist culture with its emphasis on fulfilling duties than in a horizontal collectivist culture, an interdependent prevention focus should be more prevalent among members of a vertical collectivist culture (e.g., Japan, Korea) than among a horizontal collectivist culture (e.g., an Israeli kibbutz). More research is needed to investigate whether the relationship between self-construal and regulatory focus may be generalized across both horizontal and vertical types of individualism and collectivism.

CULTURE, RISK TAKING, AND IMPULSIVITY

Another area of interest related to goals and self-regulation is how culture influences people's attitudes toward risk and the way they make risky choices. Based on the literature reviewed in the previous section, one would expect that members of collectivist cultures, who tend to be prevention-focused, would be more risk averse than members of individualist cultures, who tend to be promotion-focused (A. Y. Lee et al., 2000). In particular, individuals who are promotion-focused are inclined to adopt an eagerness strategy, which translates into greater openness to risk, whereas those who are prevention-focused are inclined to adopt a vigilant strategy, which usually translates into more conservative behaviors (Crowe & Higgins, 1997). Consider an array of options: Options that have greater potential upsides are likely to also come with greater potential downsides, whereas options with smaller potential downsides are often those with smaller potential upsides. Thus, when choosing between a risky alternative with greater upsides and downsides and a conservative alternative with smaller downsides and upsides, individuals who pay more attention to positive outcomes (i.e., the promotion-focused) would favor the risky option, whereas those who focus more on negative outcomes (i.e., the prevention-focused) would favor the conservative option. These different attitudes toward risk are consistent with findings that promotion-focused participants emphasize speed at the expense of accuracy in different drawing and proofreading tasks and that the reverse is true for those with a prevention focus (Förster, Higgins, & Bianco, 2003).

However, empirical investigations examining how people with distinct cultural self-construals make decisions involving risks have produced mixed results. For instance, Mandel (2003) observed that participants primed with an interdependent versus independent self-construal were more likely to choose a safe versus a risky option when choosing a shirt to wear to a family gathering or when playing truth or dare. However, these same participants were more likely to choose the risky option when making a decision regarding a lottery ticket or a parking ticket. Along similar lines, Hsee and Weber (1999) presented Chinese and Americans with safe versus risky options in three decision domains—financial (to invest money in a savings account or in stocks), academic (to write a term paper on a conservative topic so that the grade would be predictable or to write the paper on a provocative topic so the grade could vary), and medical (to take a pain reliever with a moderate but sure effectiveness or one with a high variance of effectiveness). They found that Chinese were more risk-seeking in the financial domain than their American counterparts, but not in the academic and medical domains. Taken together, these results suggest that while individuals with a dominant interdependent self-construal are more risk averse than those with a dominant independent self-construal in general, they are less risk averse when their decision involves financial risks.

To account for the findings that Chinese were more risk-seeking in the financial domain, Weber and Hsee (Weber & Hsee, 1998, 2000) proposed that members of collectivist cultures can afford to take greater financial risks because their social network buffers them from financial downfalls. That is, individuals' social networks serve as a cushion that could protect them should they take risks and fall; and the wider their social network, the larger the cushion. Because people in collectivist cultures have larger social networks to fall back on relative to those in individualist cultures, they are more likely to choose seemingly riskier options because their perceived risks for those options are smaller than the perceived risks for people in individualist cultures. In one study, Weber and Hsee (1998) surveyed American, German, Polish, and Chinese respondents about their perception of the riskiness of a set of financial investment options and their willingness to pay for these options. They found that their Chinese respondents perceived the risks to be the lowest and paid the highest prices for the investments, whereas American respondents perceived the investments to be most risky and paid the lowest prices for them. Once risk perception was accounted for, the cross-cultural difference in risk aversion disappeared. Consistent with this cushion hypothesis, Mandel (2003) showed that the difference between independent and interdependent participants' risky financial choices is mediated by the size of their social network—the larger their social network, the more risk-taking participants were.

Hamilton and Biehal (2005) suggest that this social network cushioning effect among the interdependents may be offset by their self-regulatory goals. They find that those primed with an independent self-construal tend to prefer mutual funds that are more risky (i.e., more volatile) than do those primed with an interdependent self-construal; and this difference is mediated by the strength of their regulatory goal in that risky preferences are fostered by promotion goals and discouraged by prevention goals.

It is worth noting that both Mandel (2003) and Hamilton and Biehal (2005) manipulated self-construal but found opposite effects of self-construal on risky financial decisions. Whereas an interdependent self-construal may bring to mind a larger social network that serves as a safety net and hence changes risk perceptions, the associated prevention focus also prompts people to be more vigilant and hence lowers the threshold for risk tolerance.

Interestingly, Briley and Wyer (2002) found that both Chinese and American participants whose cultural identity was made salient (vs. not) were more likely to choose a compromise alternative (i.e., an option with moderate values on two different attributes) over more extreme options (i.e., options with a high value on one attribute and a low value along a second attribute) when choosing between such products as cameras, stereo sets, or computers. When presented with the task of picking two pieces of candy, cultural identity-primed participants were also more likely to pick two different candies than two pieces of the same candy. To the extent that choosing the compromise alternative or picking one of each candy reduces the risk of social embarrassment and postchoice regret, the authors presented the results as evidence that individuals who think of themselves as part of a larger collective (i.e., those with an interdependent mindset) are more risk averse, independent of national culture. More systematic investigations of how culture and self-construal affect consumers' risky decision making await future research.

Besides having an influence on the individual's attitude toward risks, culture also plays an important role in the individual's self-regulation of emotions and behaviors. Because the maintenance of harmony within the group often relies on members' ability to manage their emotions and behaviors, collectivist cultures tend to emphasize the control and moderation of one's feelings and actions more so than do individualistic cultures (Potter, 1988; Russell & Yik, 1996; Tsai & Levenson, 1997). Indeed, it has been reported that members of collectivist cultures often control their negative emotions and display positive emotions only to acquaintances (Gudykunst, 1993). Children in these societies are also socialized to control their impulses at an early age (Ho, 1994).

It follows that culture would play an important role in consumers' purchase behavior by imposing norms on the appropriateness of impulse-buying activities (Kacen & Lee, 2002). When consumers believe that impulse buying is socially unacceptable, they are more likely to refrain from acting on their impulsive tendencies (Rook & Fisher, 1995). Whereas members of individualist cultures are more motivated by their own preferences and personal goals, members of collectivist cultures are often motivated by norms and duties imposed by society. Thus, people with a dominant interdependent self-construal who tend to focus on relationship harmony and group preferences should be better at monitoring and adjusting their behavior based on "what is right" rather than on "what I want." Along these lines, Chen, Ng, and Rao (2005) found that consumers with a dominant independent self-construal are less patient in that they are willing to pay more to expedite the delivery of an online book purchase than those with a dominant interdependent self-construal.

Kacen and Lee (2002) surveyed respondents from Australia, the United States, Singapore, Malaysia, and Hong Kong and found that the relationship between trait buying impulsiveness and actual impulsive buying behavior is stronger for individualists (respondents from Australia, the United States) than for collectivists (respondents from Hong Kong, Malaysia, Singapore). Further, they reported a positive relationship between respondents' independent self-construal and impulsivity among the individualists, but not among the collectivists. These results suggest that impulsivity in buying behavior in individualistic societies is more a function of personality than normative constraints, and are consistent with findings that attitude-behavior correlations are stronger in individualistic than collectivistic cultures (Bagozzi, Wong, Abe, & Bergami, 2000; Kashima, Siegal, Tanaka, & Kashima, 1992; J. A. Lee, 2000).

CULTURE AND PERSUASIVE APPEALS

Most research on cultural influences on judgment and persuasion has examined the implications of individualism/collectivism or independent/interdependent self-construals. In general, the findings suggest that the prevalence or the persuasiveness of a given type of appeal matches the cultural value orientation of the society. For instance, appeals to individuality, personal benefits, and achievement tend to be more prevalent and persuasive in individualistic compared to collectivistic cultures, whereas appeals to group benefits, harmony, and conformity tend to be more prevalent and persuasive in collectivistic compared to individualistic cultures. Such evidence for "cultural matching" in the nature of appeals has since been followed by studies examining the distinct psychological processes driving persuasion across cultures. These studies suggest that culture can affect how people process and organize in memory product-related information. It can determine the type of information that is weighed more heavily for making judgments (e.g., product attributes versus other consumers' opinions). It can also influence thinking styles and the mental representations of brand information.

Cultural Differences in the Content of Message Appeals

Cross-cultural content analyses of advertisements can yield valuable evidence about distinctions in cultural values. For instance, American advertisers are often exhorted to focus on the advertised brand's attributes and advantages (e.g., Ogilvy, 1985), based on the assumption that consumer learning about the brand precedes other marketing effects, such as liking and buying the brand (Lavidge & Steiner, 1961), at least under high-involvement conditions (Vaughn, 1980). Thus, advertisements that attempt to "teach" the consumer about the advertised brand are typical in the United States, although other types of advertisements are also used.

In contrast, as Miracle (1987) has suggested, the typical goal of advertisements in Japan appears very different. There, advertisements tend to focus on "making friends" with the audience and showing that the company understands their feelings (Javalgi, Cutler, & Malhotra, 1995). The assumption is that consumers will buy once they feel familiar with and have a sense of trust in the company. Because Japan, Korea, and other Pacific Rim countries are collectivist, "high context" cultures that tend toward implicit and indirect communication practices (Hall, 1976), Miracle suggested that the mood and tone of commercials in these countries will be particularly important in establishing good feelings about the advertiser (see also Taylor, Miracle, & Wilson, 1997). Indeed, studies have shown that advertisements in Japan and Korea rely more on symbolism, mood, and aesthetics and less on direct approaches such as brand comparisons than do advertisements in the United States (B. Cho, Kwon, Gentry, Jun, & Kropp, 1999; di Benedetto, Tamate, & Chandran, 1992; J. W. Hong et al., 1987; Javalgi et al., 1995).

This is not to argue that advertisements in collectivist societies use more of a "soft sell" approach in contrast to a "hard sell," information-driven approach in the West. Information content in the advertisements of collectivist cultures can be very high (Tse, Belk, & Zhou, 1989), sometimes even higher than in the United States

(J. W. Hong et al., 1987; Rice & Lu, 1988; for a review see Taylor et al., 1997). It is generally more an issue of the type of appeal that the information is supporting.

For instance, a content analysis of magazine advertisements revealed that in Korea, compared to the United States, advertisements are more focused on family well-being, interdependence, group goals, and harmony, whereas they are less focused on self-improvement, ambition, personal goals, independence, and individuality (Han & Shavitt, 1994). However, as one might expect, the nature of the advertised product moderated these effects. Cultural differences emerged strongly only for products that tend to be purchased and used along with other persons (e.g., groceries, cars). Products that do not tend to be shared (e.g., health and beauty aids, clothing) are promoted more in terms of personal, individualistic benefits in both countries.

Paralleling the overall cross-national differences, a content analysis by Kim and Markus (1999) indicated that Korean advertisements, compared to U.S. advertisements, were characterized by more conformity themes (e.g., respect for collective values and beliefs) and fewer uniqueness themes (e.g., rebelling against collective values and beliefs). (For other ad comparisons relevant to individualism/collectivism, see B. Cho et al., 1999; S. M. Choi et al., 2005; Javalgi et al., 1995; Tak, Kaid, & Lee, 1997.)

Recently, studies have extended these cultural conclusions into analyses of Web site content (C.-H. Cho & Cheon, 2005; Singh & Matsuo, 2004). For instance, Cho and Cheon (2005) found that corporate Web sites in the United States and United Kingdom tend to emphasize consumer-message and consumer-marketer interactivity. In contrast, those in Japan and Korea tended to emphasize consumer-consumer interactivity, a pattern consistent with cultural values stressing collectivistic activities that foster interdependence and sociability.

Finally, in studying humorous appeals, Alden, Hoyer, and Lee (1993) found that advertisements from both Korea and Thailand contain more group-oriented situations than those from Germany and the United States. However, it is worth noting that in these studies, evidence also emerged for the value of the vertical/horizontal distinction previously discussed. Specifically, relationships between the central characters in advertisements that used humor were more often unequal in cultures characterized as having higher power distance (i.e., relatively vertical cultures, such as Korea) than in those labeled as lower in power distance (such as Germany), in which these relationships were more often equal. Such unequal relationships portrayed in the advertisements may reflect the hierarchical interpersonal relationships that are more likely to exist in vertical societies.

Cultural Differences in Judgment and Persuasion

The persuasiveness of appeals appears to mirror the cultural differences in their prevalence. An experiment by Han and Shavitt (1994) showed that appeals to individualistic values (e.g., "Solo cleans with a softness that you will love") are more persuasive in the United States and appeals to collectivistic values (e.g., "Solo cleans with a softness that your family will love") are more persuasive in Korea. Again, however, this effect was much more evident for products that are shared (laundry detergent, clothes iron) than for those that are not (chewing gum, running shoes).

Zhang and Gelb (1996) found a similar pattern in the persuasiveness of individualistic versus collectivistic appeals in an experiment conducted in the United States and China. Moreover, this effect appeared to be moderated by whether the advertised product is socially visible (camera) versus privately used (toothbrush). Finally, Wang and Mowen (1997) showed in a U.S. sample that individual differences in separateness/connectedness self-schema (i.e., the degree to which one views the self as independent of or interconnected with important others) predicts attitudes toward individualistic versus collectivistic ad appeals for a credit card. Thus, cultural orientation and national culture have implications for the effectiveness of appeals. However, such cultural differences are anticipated only for those products or uses that are relevant to both personal and group goals.

Wang, Bristol, Mowen, and Chakraborty (2000) further demonstrated that individual differences in separateness/connectedness self-schema mediate both the effects of culture and of gender on the persuasiveness of individualistic versus collectivistic appeals. Their analysis demonstrated that this mediating role is played by distinct dimensions of separateness/connectedness self-schema for cultural as opposed to gender-based effects.

Cultural differences in persuasion are also revealed in the diagnosticity of certain types of information. For instance, Aaker and Maheswaran (1997) showed that consensus information regarding other consumers' opinions is not treated as a heuristic cue by Hong Kong Chinese (as it is in the United States, Maheswaran & Chaiken, 1991) but is instead perceived and processed as diagnostic information. Thus, collectivists resolve incongruity in favor of consensus information, not brand attributes. This would be expected in a culture that stresses conformity and responsiveness to others' views. However, cues whose (low) diagnosticity is not expected to vary cross-culturally (e.g., number of attributes presented) elicit similar heuristic processing in the United States and Hong Kong.

Further research indicates that, whereas members of both U.S. and Chinese cultures resolve incongruities in the product information they receive, they tend to do so in different ways (Aaker & Sengupta, 2000). Specifically, U.S. consumers tend to resolve incongruity with an attenuation strategy in which one piece of information is favored over another, inconsistent piece of information. In contrast, Hong Kong Chinese consumers tend to follow an additive strategy in which both pieces of information are combined to influence judgments. This is consistent with the view that East Asians think holistically and take more information into account when making judgments (I. Choi et al., 2003; Nisbett, Peng, Choi, & Norenzayan, 2001).

Cultural Differences in Brand Representations

Recent research points to cultural differences in the mental representation of brand information. Ng and Houston (2006) found that an interdependent view of the self facilitates the accessibility of brand exemplars (i.e., specific products or subcategories), whereas an independent view of the self facilitates the retrieval of brand beliefs (i.e., general descriptive or evaluative thoughts). The authors argue that these results are driven by a tendency by independent consumers to focus on "global beliefs" abstracted from prior product experiences and a tendency by interdependent consumers to focus on contextual and incidental details about the product. The focus of interdependent consumers on contextual variables also led to more favorable evaluations (compared to those of independent consumers) of brand extensions perceived to be used in the same usage occasion as an existing product mix.

Monga and John (2007) provide further insights into the cognitive processes underlying cross-cultural differences in the representation of brand information. They found that priming an interdependent (vs. an independent) self-construal led consumers to perceive a higher degree of fit between a brand extension and the parent brand and to evaluate more positively the brand extension. These findings are attributed to more holistic thinking style, which is oriented toward object-field relationships and is associated with an interdependent view of the self (see Kühnen, Hannover, & Schubert, 2001).

BRANDS AS SYMBOLS OF SELF AND OF CULTURE

Consumers use certain products or brands to express to others their personal values (Richins, 1994). Although the self-expressive function of products may reflect a universal goal, recent research suggests that certain cultures value self-expression more than others do. Moreover, brands and products vary in their likelihood of playing a self-expressive role (see Shavitt, 1990)—that is, some brands are more iconic than others. As a result, such brands may be more likely to carry and activate cultural meanings.

One important aspect of individualism is the expression of inner thoughts and feelings in order to realize one's individuality (Bellah, Madsen, Sullivan, Swidler, & Tipton, 1985). In contrast, in collectivistic cultures expression of one's thoughts is not particularly encouraged. Accordingly, Kim and Sherman (2007) showed that culturally shared assumptions about the function and importance of self-expression impact consumers' judgments. In their studies, European Americans instructed (vs. not) to express their choice of a pen evaluated an unchosen pen more negatively, indicating that they became more attached to the pen they chose. These effects were absent among East Asian Americans. In sum, cultural differences in how people self-expressed through their preferences apparently led to differences in how people felt about their preferences once they were expressed.

Certain brands become consensus expressions of a set of ideas or values held dear by individuals in a given society (Holt, 2004). Consumers associate these brands with the values that are characteristic of the culture (Aaker, Benet-Martinez, & Garolera, 2001). For example, some brands in the United States are associated with ruggedness (e.g., the Marlboro man) and some brands in Japan are associated with peacefulness, and ruggedness and peacefulness are dimensions characteristic of American and East Asian cultures, respectively. To the extent that these brands are associated with knowledge about the culture, they can reach an iconic status and act as cultural reminders (see Betsky, 1997; Ortner, 1973). Encountering such iconic brands can serve as subtle cultural primes that can lead to culturally congruent judgments and behaviors. In line with this reasoning, in a study about the effects of the exposure to American icons on consumers' judgments, Torelli, Chiu, & Keh (2007) found that exposure to iconic brands (e.g., Kellogg's Corn Flakes) led American participants to organize material in memory around cultural themes and to evaluate foreign competitors more negatively.

To the extent that iconic brands can be used to communicate their associated values, consumers can rely on these brands for fulfilling important identity goals. With the advancement of globalization, the marketplace is suffused with images of various iconic brands and products. Continued exposure to iconic products and brands can serve as a cognitive socialization process whereby different cultural values and beliefs are repeatedly activated in consumers' working memory. As Lau-Gesk (2003) pointed out, as the world becomes more culturally diverse and mobile, it is more common for consumers to possess knowledge about the symbols and values of multiple cultures. Thus, J. Zhang (in press) shows that the responses to persuasive appeals by young Chinese consumers resemble those found among bicultural individuals (e.g., East Asians born and raised in the United States). This state of affairs may help to explain why, in rapidly transitioning economies, Westernized appeals are increasingly common. For example, appeals to youth/modernity, individuality/independence, and technology are rather salient in Chinese advertisements (J. Zhang & Shavitt, 2003) as well as frequently employed by current Taiwanese advertising agencies (Shao, Raymond, & Taylor, 1999).

In addition, consumers in developing countries tend to respond favorably to markedly Western products. For instance, in one study of Indian consumers (Batra, Ramaswamy, Alden, Steenkamp, & Ramachander, 2000), brands perceived as having a nonlocal (Western) country of origin were favored over brands perceived to be local. This effect was stronger for consumers with a greater admiration for the lifestyle in economically developed countries. These cultural-incongruity findings are meaningful because they suggest the important role that advertising can play in reshaping cultural values in countries experiencing rapid economic growth (J. Zhang & Shavitt, 2003). Rather than reflecting existing cultural values, advertising content in those countries promotes new aspirational values, such as individuality and modernity, hence these new values become acceptable and desirable among consumers. Understanding the cognitive implications of multicultural environments for consumers is likely to be a key research topic in cross-cultural consumer psychology for years to come.

CONCLUSIONS

As marketing efforts become increasingly globalized, understanding cross-cultural consumer behavior has become a mainstream goal of consumer research. In recent years, research in consumer behavior has addressed a broadening set of cross-cultural issues and dimensions. However, the need for a deeper understanding of the psychological mechanisms underlying cross-cultural differences continues to grow. Significant progress has come on several fronts, including an enhanced understanding of the relations between culture and self-construal, motivation, self-regulation, and consumer persuasion. As societies become more globalized, cultural boundaries will become more blurred and new hybrids of cultural values will emerge, along with an increased need to understand these phenomena better.

ACKNOWLEDGMENTS

Preparation of this chapter was supported by Grant #1R01HD053636-01A1 from the National Institutes of Health and Grant #0648539 from the National Science Foundation to Sharon Shavitt, and Grant #63842 from the Robert Wood Johnson Foundation to Sharon Shavitt and Carlos J. Torelli, and also by the ACR/Sheth Cross-Cultural Dissertation Proposal Award to Carlos J. Torelli.

REFERENCES

Aaker, J. L., Benet-Martinez, V., & Garolera, J. (2001). Consumption symbols as carriers of culture: A study of Japanese and Spanish brand personality constructs. *Journal of Personality and Social Psychology, 81*(3), 492–508.

Aaker, J. L., & Lee, A. Y. (2001). "I" seek pleasures and "we" avoid pains: The role of self-regulatory goals in information processing and persuasion. *Journal of Consumer Research, 28*(1), 33–49.

Aaker, J. L., & Maheswaran, D. (1997). The effect of cultural orientation on persuasion. *Journal of Consumer Research, 24*(3), 315–328.

Aaker, J. L., & Sengupta, J. (2000). Addivity versus attenuation: The role of culture in the resolution of information incongruity. *Journal of Consumer Psychology, 9*(2), 67–82.

Aaker, J. L., & Williams, P. (1998). Empathy versus pride: The influence of emotional appeals across cultures. *Journal of Consumer Research, 25*(3), 241–261.

Agrawal, N., & Maheswaran, D. (2005). The effects of self-construal and commitment on persuasion. *Journal of Consumer Research, 31*(March), 841–849.

Alden, D. L., Hoyer, W. D., & Lee, C. (1993). Identifying global and culture-specific dimensions of humor in advertising: A multinational analysis. *Journal of Marketing, 57*(2), 64–75.

Bagozzi, R. P., Wong, N., Abe, S., & Bergami, M. (2000). Cultural and situational contingencies and the theory of reasoned action: Application to fast food restaurant consumption. *Journal of Consumer Psychology, 9*(2), 97–106.

Batra, R., Ramaswamy, V., Alden, D. L., Steenkamp, J.-B. E. M., & Ramachander, S. (2000). Effects of brand local and nonlocal origin on consumer attitudes in developing countries. *Journal of Consumer Psychology, 9*(2), 83–95.

Bellah, R. N., Madsen, R., Sullivan, W. M., Swidler, A., & Tipton, S. M. (1985). *Habits of the heart: Individualism and commitment in American life.* New York: Harper & Row.

Betsky, A. (1997). *Icons: Magnets of meaning.* San Francisco: Chronicle Books.

Blodgett, J. G., Lu, L.-C., Rose, G. M., & Vitell, S. J. (2001). Ethical sensitivity to stakeholder interests: A cross-cultural comparison. *Journal of the Academy of Marketing Science, 29*(2), 190–202.

Bond, M. H. (2002). Reclaiming the individual from Hofstede's ecological analysis—A 20-year odyssey: Comment on Oyserman et al. *Psychological Bulletin, 128*(1), 73–77.

Brewer, M. B., & Chen, Y.-R. (2007). Where (who) are collectives in collectivism? Toward conceptual clarification of individualism and collectivism. *Psychological Review, 114*(1), 133–151.

Brewer, M. B., & Gardner, W. (1996). Who is this "we"? Levels of collective identity and self representations. *Journal of Personality & Social Psychology, 71*(1), 83–93.

Briley, D. A., & Aaker, J. L. (2006). When does culture matter? Effects of personal knowledge on the correction of culture-based judgments. *Journal of Marketing Research, 43*(3), 395–408.

Briley, D. A., Morris, M. W., & Simonson, I. (2005). Cultural chameleons: Biculturals, conformity motives, and decision making. *Journal of Consumer Psychology, 15*(4), 351–362.

Briley, D. A., & Wyer, R. S., Jr. (2002). The effect of group membership salience on the avoidance of negative outcomes: Implications for social and consumer decisions. *Journal of Consumer Research, 29*(3), 400–415.

Chen, H., Ng, S., & Rao, A. R. (2005). Cultural differences in consumer impatience. *Journal of Marketing Research, 42*(3), 291–301.

Chiu, C.-y., & Hong, Y.-y. (2006). *Social psychology of culture*. New York: Psychology Press.

Cho, B., Kwon, U., Gentry, J. W., Jun, S., & Kropp, F. (1999). Cultural values reflected in theme and execution: A comparative study of U.S. and Korean television commercials. *Journal of Advertising, 28*(4), 59–73.

Cho, C.-H., & Cheon, H. J. (2005). Cross-cultural comparisons of interactivity on corporate websites. *Journal of Advertising, 34*(2), 99–115.

Choi, I., Dalal, R., Kim-Prieto, C., & Park, H. (2003). Culture and judgement of causal relevance. *Journal of Personality and Social Psychology, 84*(1), 46–59.

Choi, S. M., Lee, W.-N., & Kim, H.-J. (2005). Lessons from the rich and famous: A cross-cultural comparison of celebrity endorsement in advertising. *Journal of Advertising, 34*(2), 85–98.

Clegg, A. (2005). A word to the worldly-wise. *Marketing Week, 28*(42), 43–48.

Crowe, E., & Higgins, E. (1997). Regulatory focus and strategic inclinations: Promotion and prevention in decision-making. *Organizational Behavior and Human Decision Processes, 69*(2), 117–132.

di Benedetto, C. A., Tamate, M., & Chandran, R. (1992). Developing creative advertising strategy for the Japanese marketplace. *Journal of Advertising Research, 32*, 39–48.

Dwyer, S., Mesak, H., & Hsu, M. (2005). An exploratory examination of the influence of national culture on cross-national product diffusion. *Journal of International Marketing, 13*(2), 1–27.

Earley, P. C. (1999). Playing follow the leader: Status-determining traits in relation to collective efficacy across cultures. *Organizational Behavior and Human Decision Processes, 80*(3), 192–212.

Eyal, T., Liberman, N., Trope, Y., & Walther, E. (2004). The pros and cons of temporally near and distant action. *Journal of Personality & Social Psychology, 86*(6), 781–795.

Förster, J., Higgins, T. E., & Bianco, A. T. (2003). Speed/accuracy decisions in task performance: Built-in trade-off or separate strategic concerns? *Organizational Behavior and Human Decision Processes, 90*(1), 148–164.

Fu, J. H.-y., Chiu, C.-y., Morris, M. W., & Young, M. J. (2007). Spontaneous inferences from cultural cues: Varying responses of cultural insiders and outsiders. *Journal of Cross-Cultural Psychology, 38*(1), 58–75.

Gabriel, S., & Gardner, W. L. (1999). Are there "his" and "hers" types of interdependence? The implications of gender differences in collective versus relational interdependence for affect, behavior, and cognition. *Journal of Personality and Social Psychology, 77*(3), 642–655.

Gaines, S. O., Jr., Marelich, W. D., Bledsoe, K. L., Steers, W., Henderson, M. C., Granrose, C. S., et al. (1997). Links between race/ethnicity and cultural values as mediated by racial/ethnic identity and moderated by gender. *Journal of Personality and Social Psychology, 72*(6), 1460–1476.

Gardner, W. L., Gabriel, S., & Lee, A. Y. (1999). "I" value freedom, but "we" value relationships: Self-construal priming mirrors cultural differences in judgment. *Psychological Science, 10*(4), 321–326.

Gelfand, M. J., Bhawuk, D., Nishii, L. H., & Bechtold, D. J. (2004). Individualism and collectivism. In R. J. House, P. J. Hanges, M. Javidan, P. W. Dorfman, & V. Gupta (Eds.), *Culture, leadership, and organizations: The GLOBE study of 62 societies* (pp. 437–512). Thousand Oaks, CA: Sage.

Gudykunst, W. B. (1993). *Communication in Japan and the United States*. NY: State University of New York Press.

Gudykunst, W. B., & Ting-Toomey, S. (1988). *Culture and interpersonal communication*. Newbury Park, CA: Sage.

Gürhan-Canli, Z., & Maheswaran, D. (2000). Cultural variations in country of origin effects. *Journal of Marketing Research, 37*(3), 309–317.

Hall, E. T. (1976). *Beyond culture*. Oxford: Anchor.

Hamilton, R. W., & Biehal, G. J. (2005). Achieving your goals or protecting their future? The effects of self-view on goals and choices. *Journal of Consumer Research, 32*(2), 277–283.

Han, S.-P., & Shavitt, S. (1994). Persuasion and culture: Advertising appeals in individualistic and collectivistic societies. *Journal of Experimental Social Psychology, 30*(4), 326.

Higgins, E. T. (1997). Beyond pleasure and pain. *American Psychologist, 52*(12), 1280.

Ho, D. Y.-F. (1994). Cognitive socialization in Confucian heritage cultures. In P. M. Greenfield & R. R. Cocking (Eds.), *Cross-cultural roots of minority child development* (pp. 285–313). NJ: Lawrence Erlbaum Associates, Inc.

Ho, D. Y.-F., & Chiu, C.-Y. (1994). Component ideas of individualism, collectivism, and social organization: An application in the study of Chinese culture. In U. Kim, H. C. Triandis, C. Kagitcibasi, S.-C. Choi, & G. Yoon (Eds.), *Individualism and collectivism: Theory and applications* (pp. 137–156). Thousand Oaks, CA: Sage Publications, Inc.

Hofstede, G. H. (1980). *Culture's consequences: International differences in work-related values*. Newbury Park: Sage.

Hofstede, G. H. (2001). *Culture's consequences: Comparing values, behaviors, institutions and organizations across nations*. Thousand Oaks, CA: Sage.

Holt, D. B. (2004). *How brands become icons: The principles of cultural branding*. Cambridge, MA: Harvard Business School Press.

Hong, J. W., Muderrisoglu, A., & Zinkhan, G. M. (1987). Cultural differences and advertising expression: A comparative content analysis of Japanese and U.S. magazine advertising. *Journal of Advertising, 16*(1), 55–62.

Hong, Y.-y., Ip, G., Chiu, C.-y., Morris, M. W., & Menon, T. (2001). Cultural identity and dynamic construction of the self: collective duties and individual rights in Chinese and American cultures. *Social Cognition, 19*(3), 251–268.

Hsee, C. K., & Weber, E. U. (1999). Cross-national differences in risk preference and lay predictions. *Journal of Behavioral Decision Making, 12*(2), 165–179.

Javalgi, R. G., Cutler, B. D., & Malhotra, N. K. (1995). Print advertising at the component level: A cross-cultural comparison of the United States and Japan. *Journal of Business Research, 34*(2), 117–124.

Johnson, T. P., Kulesa, P., Cho, Y. I., & Shavitt, S. (2005). The relation between culture and response styles: Evidence from 19 countries. *Journal of Cross-Cultural Psychology, 36*(2), 264–277.

Kacen, J. J., & Lee, J. A. (2002). The influence of culture on consumer impulsive buying behavior. *Journal of Consumer Psychology, 12*(2), 163–176.

Kagitcibasi, C. (1994). A critical appraisal of individualism and collectivism: Toward a new formulation. In U. Kim, H. C. Triandis, C. Kagitcibasi, S.-C. Choi, & G. Yoon (Eds.), *Individualism and collectivism: Theory, method, and applications* (pp. 52–65). Thousand Oaks, CA: Sage.

Kashima, Y., Siegal, M., Tanaka, K., & Kashima, E. S. (1992). Do people believe behaviours are consistent with attitudes? Towards a cultural psychology of attribution processes. *British Journal of Social Psychology, 31*(2), 111–124.

Kashima, Y., Yamaguchi, S., Kim, U., Choi, S.-C., Gelfand, M. J., & Yuki, M. (1995). Culture, gender, and self: A perspective from individualism-collectivism research. *Journal of Personality and Social Psychology, 69*(5), 925–937.

Kim, H. S., & Markus, H. R. (1999). Deviance or uniqueness, harmony or conformity? A cultural analysis. *Journal of Personality & Social Psychology, 77*(4), 785–800.

Kim, H. S., & Sherman, D. K. (2007). "Express yourself": Culture and the effect of self-expression on choice. *Journal of Personality & Social Psychology, 92*(1), 1–11.

Kühnen, U., Hannover, B., & Schubert, B. (2001). The semantic-procedural interface model of the self: The role of self-knowledge for context-dependent versus context-independent modes of thinking. *Journal of Personality and Social Psychology, 80*(3), 397–409.

Lalwani, A. K., & Shavitt, S. (in press). The "me" I claim to be: Cultural self-construal elicits self-presentational goal pursuit. *Journal of Personality and Social Psychology*.

Lalwani, A. K., & Shavitt, S., & Johnson, T. (2006). What is the relation beween cultural orientation and socially desirable responding? *Journal of Personality and Social Psychology, 90*(1), 165–178.

Lau-Gesk, L. G. (2003). Activating culture through persuasion appeals: An examination of the bicultural consumer. *Journal of Consumer Psychology, 13*(3), 301–315.

Lavidge, R. J., & Steiner, G. A. (1961). A model for predictive measurements of advertising effectiveness. *Journal of Marketing, 25*(6), 59–62.

Lee, A. Y., Aaker, J. L., & Gardner, W. L. (2000). The pleasures and pains of distinct self-construals: The role of interdependence in regulatory focus. *Journal of Personality and Social Psychology, 78*(6), 1122–1134.

Lee, C., & Green, R. T. (1991). Cross-cultural examination of the Fishbein behavioral intentions model. *Journal of International Business Studies, 22*(2), 289–305.

Lee, J. A. (2000). Adapting Triandis's model of subjective culture and social behavior relations to consumer behavior. *Journal of Consumer Psychology, 9*(2), 117–126.

Lee, S., & Lee, A. Y. (2007). The far and near of self views: Self-construal and temporal perspective. Manuscript under review.

Lin, C. A. (2001). Cultural values reflected in Chinese and American television advertising. *Journal of Advertising, 30*(4), 83–94.

Maheswaran, D., & Chaiken, S. (1991). Promoting systematic processing in low-motivation settings: Effect of incongruent information on processing and judgment. *Journal of Personality & Social Psychology, 61*(1), 13–25.

Mandel, N. (2003). Shifting selves and decision making: The effects of self-construal priming on consumer risk-taking. *Journal of Consumer Research, 30*(1), 30–40.

Markus, H. R., & Kitayama, S. (1991). Culture and the self: Implications for cognition, emotion, and motivation. *Psychological Review, 98*(2), 224–253.

Miracle, G. E. (1987). Feel-do-learn: An alternative sequence underlying Japanese consumer response to television commercials. In F. G. Feasley (Ed.), *Proceedings of the L.A. Conference of the American Academy of Advertising*. Columbia, SC: The University of South Carolina.

Monga, A. B., & John, D. R. (2007). Cultural differences in brand extension evaluation: The influence of analytic versus holistic thinking. *Journal of Consumer Research, 33*(4), 529–536.

Nelson, M. R., Brunel, F. F., Supphellen, M., & Manchanda, R. V. (2006). Effects of culture, gender, and moral obligations on responses to charity advertising across masculine and feminine cultures. *Journal of Consumer Psychology, 16*(1), 45–56.

Ng, S., & Houston, M. J. (2006). Exemplars or beliefs? The impact of self-view on the nature and relative influence of brand associations. *Journal of Consumer Research, 32*(4), 519–529.

Nisbett, R. E., Peng, K., Choi, I., & Norenzayan, A. (2001). Culture and systems of thought: Holistic versus analytic cognition. *Psychological Review, 108*(2), 291–310.

Ogilvy, D. (1985). *Ogilvy on advertising.* New York: Vintage Books.

Ortner, S. B. (1973). On key symbols. *American Anthropologist, 75*(5), 1338–1346.

Oyserman, D. (2006). High power, low power, and equality: Culture beyond individualism and collectivism. *Journal of Consumer Psychology, 16*(4), 352–256.

Oyserman, D., Coon, H. M., & Kemmelmeier, M. (2002). Rethinking individualism and collectivism: Evaluation of theoretical assumptions and meta-analyses. *Psychological Bulletin, 128*(1), 3–72.

Oyserman, D., & Lee, S. W.-S. (2007). Priming 'culture': Culture as situated cognition. In S. Kitayama & D. Cohen (Eds.), *Handbook of cultural psychology* (pp. 255–282). New York: Guilford Press.

Potter, S. H. (1988). The cultural construction of emotion in rural Chinese social life. *Ethos, 16*(2), 181–208.

Rhee, E., Uleman, J. S., & Lee, H. K. (1996). Variations in collectivism and individualism by ingroup and culture: Confirmatory factor analysis. *Journal of Personality and Social Psychology, 71*(5), 1037–1054.

Rice, M. D., & Lu, Z. (1988). A content analysis of Chinese magazine advertisements. *Journal of Advertising, 17*(4), 43–48.

Richins, M. L. (1994). Special possessions and the expression of material values. *Journal of Consumer Research, 21*(3), 522–531.

Rook, D. W., & Fisher, R. J. (1995). Normative influences on impulsive buying behavior. *Journal of Consumer Research, 22*(3), 305–313.

Russell, J. A., & Yik, M. S. (1996). Emotion among the Chinese. In M. H. Bond (Ed.), *The handbook of Chinese psychology* (pp. 166–188). Hong Kong, China: Oxford University Press.

Schwartz, S. H. (1992). Universals in the content and structure of values: Theoretical advances and empirical tests in 20 countries. In M. P. Zanna (Ed.), *Advances in experimental social psychology* (Vol. 25, pp. 1–65). San Diego, CA: Academic Press.

Shao, A. T., Raymond, M. A., & Taylor, C. (1999). Shifting advertising appeals in Taiwan. *Journal of Advertising Research, 39*(6), 61–69.

Shavitt, S. (1990). The role of attitude objects in attitude functions. *Journal of Experimental Social Psychology, 26*(2), 124–148.

Shavitt, S., Lalwani, A. K., Zhang, J., & Torelli, C. J. (2006). The horizontal/vertical distinction in cross-cultural consumer research. *Journal of Consumer Psychology, 16*(4), 325–356.

Shavitt, S., Zhang, J., & Johnson, T. P. (2006). Horizontal and vertical cultural differences in advertising and consumer persuasion. Unpublished data, University of Illinois.

Shweder, R. A., & Bourne, E. J. (1982). Does the concept of person vary cross-culturally? In A. J. Marsella & G. M. White (Eds.), *Cultural conceptions of mental health and therapy* (pp. 130–204). London: Reidel.

Singelis, T. M. (1994). The measurement of independent and interdependent self-construals. *Personality and Social Psychology Bulletin, 20*(5), 580–591.

Singelis, T. M., Triandis, H. C., Bhawuk, D., & Gelfand, M. J. (1995). Horizontal and vertical dimensions of individualism and collectivism: A theoretical and measurement refinement. *Cross-Cultural Research: The Journal of Comparative Social Science, 29*(3), 240–275.

Singh, N., & Matsuo, H. (2004). Measuring cultural adaptation on the Web: a content analytic study of U.S. and Japanese web sites. *Journal of Business Research, 57*(8), 864–872.

Smith, P. B., Bond, M. H., & Kagitcibasi, C. (2006). *Understanding social psychology across cultures: Living and working in a changing world.* Thousand Oaks, CA: Sage Publications.

Spencer-Oatey, H. (1997). Unequal relationships in high and low power distance societies: A comparative study of tutor-student role relations in Britain and China. *Journal of Cross-Cultural Psychology, 28*(3), 284–302.

Tak, J., Kaid, L. L., & Lee, S. (1997). A cross-cultural study of political advertising in the United States and Korea. *Communication Research, 24,* 413–430.

Taylor, C. R., Miracle, G. E., & Wilson, R. D. (1997). The impact of information level on the effectiveness of U.S. and Korean television commercials. *Journal of Advertising, 26*(1), 1–18.

Torelli, C. J. (2006). Individuality or conformity? The effect of independent and interdependent self-concepts on public judgments. *Journal of Consumer Psychology, 16*(3), 240–248.

Torelli, C. J., Chiu, C.-y., & Keh, H. T. (2007). Psychological reactions to foreign cultures in globalized economy: Effects of simultaneous activation of ingroup and outgroup cultures. Manuscript under review.

Trafimow, D., Triandis, H. C., & Goto, S. G. (1991). Some tests of the distinction between the private self and the collective self. *Journal of Personality & Social Psychology, 60*(5), 649–655.

Triandis, H. C. (1989). The self and social behavior in differing cultural contexts. *Psychological Review, 96*(3), 506–520.

Triandis, H. C. (1995). *Individualism & collectivism.* CO: Westview Press.

Triandis, H. C., Bontempo, R., Villareal, M. J., Asai, M., & Lucca, N. (1988). Individualism and collectivism: Cross-cultural perspectives on self-group relationships. *Journal of Personality and Social Psychology, 54*(2), 323–338.

Triandis, H. C., & Gelfand, M. J. (1998). Converging measurement of horizontal and vertical individualism and collectivism. *Journal of Personality and Social Psychology, 74*(1), 118–128.

Triandis, H. C., Leung, K., Villareal, M. J., & Clack, F. L. (1985). Allocentric versus idiocentric tendencies: Convergent and discriminant validation. *Journal of Research in Personality, 19*(4), 395–415.

Tsai, J. L., & Levenson, R. W. (1997). Cultural influences of emotional responding: Chinese American and European American dating couples during interpersonal conflict. *Journal of Cross-Cultural Psychology, 28*(5), 600–625.

Tse, D. K., Belk, R. W., & Zhou, N. (1989). Becoming a consumer society: A longitudinal and cross-cultural content analysis of print ads from Hong Kong, the People's Republic of China, and Taiwan. *Journal of Consumer Research, 15*(4), 457–472.

Vaughn, R. (1980). How advertising works: A planning model. *Journal of Advertising Research, 20*(5), 27–33.

Wang, C. L., Bristol, T., Mowen, J. C., & Chakraborty, G. (2000). Alternative modes of self-construal: Dimensions of connectedness-separateness and advertising appeals to the cultural and gender-specific self. *Journal of Consumer Psychology, 9*(2), 107–115.

Wang, C. L., & Mowen, J. C. (1997). The separateness-connectedness self-schema: Scale development and application to message construction. *Psychology & Marketing, 14*(2), 185–207.

Wang, J., & Lee, A. Y. (2006). The role of regulatory focus in preference construction. *Journal of Marketing Research, 43*(1), 28–38.

Weber, E. U., & Hsee, C. K. (1998). Cross-cultural differences in risk perception, but cross-cultural similarities in attitudes towards perceived risk. *Management Science, 44*(9), 1205–1217.

Weber, E. U., & Hsee, C. K. (2000). Culture and individual judgment and decision making. *Applied Psychology: An International Review, 49*(1), 32–61.

Zhang, J. (in press). The effect of advertising appeals in activating self-construals: A case of 'bicultural' Chinese X-generation consumers. *Journal of Advertising*, in press.

Zhang, J., & Shavitt, S. (2003). Cultural values in advertisements to the Chinese X-generation: Promoting modernity and individualism. *Journal of Advertising, 32*(1), 23–33.

Zhang, Y., & Gelb, B. D. (1996). Matching advertising appeals to culture: The influence of products' use conditions. *Journal of Advertising, 25*(3), 29–46.

11

Television Viewing and Social Reality
Effects and Underlying Processes

L. J. SHRUM

University of Texas at San Antonio

M ention the subject of television effects to consumer psychologists and they would likely assume you are referring to advertising. With only a few exceptions (e.g., Russell, Norman, & Heckler, 2004), most consumer research on television effects has focused on understanding how advertising works and what makes it effective. However, these are intended effects. What have gone relatively unnoticed in consumer research are the unintended effects of television viewing, particularly the effects of the programs between the ads. Certainly, social psychologists are well aware of these types of effects, particularly for the effects of media violence (Bushman & Anderson, 2001; Wood, Wong, & Chachere, 1991) and explicit sexual portrayals (Donnerstein & Berkowitz, 1981; Malamuth & Impett, 2001). However, what have for the most part escaped attention are the more subtle effects of the narrative or "storytelling" aspect of television programs.

In this chapter, I discuss research that investigates the effects of television viewing on a range of judgments, including social perceptions, attitudes, values, and beliefs. This research looks at how television often portrays a very distorted and circumscribed view of reality and the consequent effects of frequent viewing of these distortions. In addition, the chapter provides a particular focus on understanding the psychological mechanisms that underlie this effect. Although the notion that frequent television viewing would affect the attitudes and social perceptions of viewers may seem intuitively obvious, demonstrating this effect has been remarkably difficult (McGuire, 1986). Much like the research on media violence and aggression, it has been plagued by relatively small effect sizes, some inconsistencies across studies, and until recently a general lack of a clear theoretical model that can explain the underlying psychological mechanisms. The goal of this chapter is to elaborate on these explanatory mechanisms, and in doing so to reconcile some of the disparate findings from previous research.

CULTIVATION THEORY AND RESEARCH

The vast amount of research that is the focus of this chapter is often referred to as "cultivation research." Cultivation theory is probably best understood as a sociological theory. Developed by George Gerbner and colleagues (see Gerbner, 1969; Gerbner & Gross, 1976; Gerbner, Gross, Morgan, & Signorielli, 1980), the general notion is that television is the dominant socializing force in American society and thus has a profound influence on audiences' perceptions of social reality. The theory is premised on two related propositions: (1) that television programs present a consistent but dramatically distorted view of the real world, and (2) that frequent viewing of these consistent and very formulaic representations results in the internalization of these distortions into viewers' worldviews. Put differently, cultivation theory posits that television dominates the symbolic environment of its viewers to such a degree that the distorted images and messages in television programs are "cultivated" by viewers and come to replace worldviews that are developed through daily experience, and this effect occurs in proportion to the frequency of viewing. These distorted portrayals are posited to affect a wide variety of judgments, including perceptions of what others have and do (descriptive norms), judgments about what others should have and do (injunctive norms; see Goldstein & Cialdini, this volume), and the development of attitudes and values that form viewers' belief systems.

The first premise—that television presents systematic distortions of reality—has received substantial support and little challenge (but see Newcomb, 1978). Numerous content analyses have shown that the world of television is clearly different from the real world.[1] The world of television is remarkably violent, with estimates of five overt acts of crime or violence per hour in an average program, 75% of programs airing in prime time showing some sort of violence, and the rate of crime and violence in programs occurring 10 times more often than real-world violence (Gerbner, Gross, Morgan, & Signorielli, 1986; Lichter, Lichter, & Rothman, 1994). Relative to the real world, the television world is also more affluent and materialistic (O'Guinn & Shrum, 1997), doctors, lawyers, and police officers make up a much larger proportion of the work force (DeFleur, 1964; Smythe, 1954), and television characters tend to be more dishonest and maritally unfaithful (Lichter et al., 1994), relative to the real world. Moreover, these findings have remained relatively stable over time (Signorielli, 1990).

Perhaps more important, television distorts more than simple demographics; it also distorts underlying messages. Perhaps Howard Beale, Paddy Chayefsky's (1976) character in the movie *Network*, put it best:

> Don't come to television for the truth. TV's a goddamned amusement park.
> We'll tell you the good guys always win. We'll tell you nobody ever gets cancer
> at Archie Bunker's house. We'll tell you any shit you want to hear.

Research has provided supportive evidence that the messages portrayed in television programs may be related to viewer attitudes. For example, television viewing has been shown to correlate negatively with support for civil liberties (Carlson, 1983) and positively with more permissive attitudes toward sex (Ward & Rivadeneyra, 1999), and be related to attitudes toward criminal justice that are consistent with television portrayals (Haney & Manzolati, 1980). Even more problematic is when some of these distortions are consistently paired with certain characteristics (e.g., good guy = white male; villain = ethnic minority). Research suggests that in fact minorities are more likely to be portrayed as criminals on prime time (U.S.) television programs (including news; Dixon & Linz, 2000; Lichter et al., 1994).

The second premise—that frequent viewing of these distortions biases viewers' beliefs toward these distortions—has also received frequent support. The premise is generally tested by measuring the amount of television people watch and correlating this measure with various measures of attitudes, beliefs, and perceptions. The measures that are chosen correspond directly to the constructs that are prevalent and overrepresented in the television world (e.g., as in the examples just noted, constructs such as crime and violence, affluence, marital discord, and occupational prevalence). In support of the premise, studies have shown that the more people watch television, the higher are their estimates of real-world violence (Gerbner et al., 1980; Hawkins, Pingree, & Adler, 1987; Shrum, Wyer, & O'Guinn, 1998), personal crime risk (Shrum & Bischak, 2001), perceived danger (Gerbner et al., 1980), and anxiety and fearfulness (Bryant, Carveth, & Brown, 1981). Studies have also shown that frequency of viewing is positively correlated with interpersonal mistrust (Gerbner et al., 1980), greater pessimism about marriage (Shrum, 1999a), estimates of the prevalence of doctors, lawyers, and police officers in the work force (Shrum, 1996, 2001), greater faith in doctors (Volgy & Schwarz, 1980), estimates of societal affluence and ownership of expensive products (Potter, 1991; O'Guinn & Shrum, 1997), and materialism (Shrum, Burroughs, & Rindfleisch, 2005).

Although support for the influence of frequent consumption of the television message has received impressive support, this research has also been subject to frequent criticism. The primary criticism is that the vast amount of it is survey research that reports correlational data, making it vulnerable to alternative explanations such as reverse causality or spuriousness. Some of the criticism is justified. For example, several critiques and re-analyses of Gerbner and colleagues' data have shown that not only did Gerbner and colleagues often do a poor job of addressing obvious third-variable explanations by failing to statistically control for such variables age, education, sex, and hours worked outside the home, but when these control variables are controlled simultaneously, the cultivation effect is reduced to nonsignificance (cf. Hirsch, 1980; Hughes, 1980).

A second criticism of cultivation research is that the results have not always been consistent. As just noted, careful statistical control of other possible causal variables can eliminate the cultivation effect. In an exhaustive review of the early studies on the cultivation effect, Hawkins and Pingree (1982) observed that the effects appeared to be more consistent and stable for certain types of criterion variables than for others. They noted that when the dependent variables pertain to percentage estimates (e.g., % of Americans involved in some kind of violence in an average year, % chances of being involved in a violent crime), the cultivation effect is consistently positive. However, when the dependent variables pertain more to attitudes and beliefs (e.g., fear of walking home alone at night, alienation, interpersonal mistrust), the results are mixed. Although research subsequent to that review has shown consistent and robust effects for both types of dependent measures, the lack of consistency of the early work was nevertheless damaging.

Finally, a third criticism of cultivation theory is its lack of explanatory mechanisms at the individual level (Hawkins & Pingree, 1990; Shrum, 1995). Other than predicting a general main effect for television viewing, the theoretical formulations offered no hypotheses regarding boundary conditions, nor did they specify any type of psychological mechanism (perhaps other than general learning) for how television was integrated into real-world beliefs. Although the theory was introduced in more sociological terms (for a review, see Shanahan & Morgan, 1999), the variables are measured at the individual level, and thus the lack of a psychological explanation for the effect is clearly limiting.

A SOCIAL COGNITION EXPLANATION OF CULTIVATION EFFECTS

Although the need for a psychological explanation of cultivation effects was recognized early on, early attempts to generate and validate such explanations were generally unsuccessful (for a review, see Shrum, 2007a). These early models viewed cultivation effects in terms of social learning theory (Bandura, 1977) in which viewers learned appropriate responses to situations by observing the behavior of television actors, or by a general observation of what values, attitudes, and beliefs are normative due to their pervasive portrayals on television programs. Consequently, the focus was primarily on the nature of the independent variable (frequency and content of viewing) and what variables might impede learning, such as viewers' cognitive processing abilities, perceived reality of television programs, and inference making processes (Hawkins & Pingree, 1982).

An alternative approach to explaining cultivation effects, and one that has informed the research to be reviewed here, is somewhat opposite of the approach just described. That is, instead of focusing on the independent variable and its properties, it may be useful to focus on the dependent variables (judgments) and how they are constructed, and then construct plausible explanations for how information learned through television viewing might plausibly influence those judgments. This approach seems particularly appealing given that the consistency of the cultivation effect has been shown to differ across dependent variables. Thus, it may be that television viewing affects different judgments in different ways.

A close examination of the types of dependent variables typically used in cultivation research bolsters this reasoning. Consider the following two constructs and their typical operationalizations for measuring cultivation effects:

Crime/Violence
    What percentage of Americans have been involved in a violent crime?

What percentage of women are raped in their lifetime?
I am afraid to walk alone at night.
The world is a mean and violent place.

Affluence
What percentage of Americans have a private swimming pool?
What percentage of Americans are millionaires?
I admire people who own expensive homes, cars, and clothes.
The things I own say a lot about how well I'm doing in life.

Although the common method of categorizing these dependent variables is by topic, it is likely apparent to most social psychologists that the variables can be categorized by type of judgment. Specifically, the first two judgments in each category are frequency or probability judgments, whereas the second two are attitude or belief judgments. Moreover, not only are the judgments quite different in nature, but the processes through which these judgments are constructed are also frequently different. Given this, it seems plausible that the manner in which television information may be used in their construction may also differ.

The possibility that television viewing influences the two types of judgments in different ways forms the basis of the research that is reported in the remainder of this chapter. Models are presented for each type of judgment, along with empirical research that provides support for the models. As the subsequent discussion details, not only does television viewing affect the judgments differently, but the underlying factors often exert their effects in opposite ways.

Frequency and Probability Judgments

The types of frequency and probability judgments used to measure cultivation effects have a number of important characteristics that have implications for how television may influence those judgments. For one, the judgments are for the most part memory-based (Hastie & Park, 1986). That is, precise judgments of the likelihood of being a victim of a violent crime or the prevalence of private swimming pools in American households are ones that people would not make spontaneously, but only when asked to do so (usually by a researcher). Thus, people are unlikely to have such estimates stored in memory. Instead, to provide their estimate, they would need to recall information from memory and construct their estimates at the time the judgment is requested.

A second characteristic of the frequency and probability judgments is that they are set-size judgments. Set-size judgments reflect estimates of the frequency of occurrence of a category (e.g., millionaires) within a larger, superordinate category (Americans). One important characteristic of set-size judgments is that they have been shown to be precisely the ones that tend to be influenced by judgmental heuristics such as availability (Manis, Shedler, Jonides, & Nelson, 1993). That is, in constructing set-size judgments, rather than going through an exhaustive count of instances in memory and using this information to construct an estimate, people instead employ a cognitive shortcut and base their estimates on the subjective ease with which an instance can be recalled (Schwarz et al., 1991; Schwarz & Wänke, 2002; Tversky & Kahneman, 1973).

These various characteristics of the types of frequency and probability judgments used to test for cultivation effects have implications for possible scenarios for how television information may influence those judgments. First, the memory-based nature of the judgments suggests that if television information has an effect on them, this effect occurs via the recall of television-influenced information at the time the judgment is required (and not during the viewing process). Second, the set-size nature of the judgments, coupled with the relative difficulty of constructing them, suggests that they are constructed through heuristic processing, and specifically, through the use of heuristics such as availability and simulation.

Television Viewing and Accessibility Bias

From these two general propositions, more specific and testable propositions can be derived. The first pertains to the use of the availability heuristic in constructing the judgments. One possible explanation for the positive relation between the frequency of viewing and the magnitude of the estimates is that frequent viewing increases the accessibility of exemplars relevant to the judgment (e.g., violence, police officer, unfaithful spouse, house with a pool). Thus, heavy viewers should have information relative to the judgment more accessible from memory than should light viewers, and if people base their judgments on this accessibility, it should produce higher estimates for heavy than for light viewers, precisely as cultivation theory predicts. Moreover, this accessibility bias should mediate the relation between viewing frequency and judgment.

A series of studies has provided support for this proposition. Busselle and Shrum (2003) reported evidence that relevant exemplars are more accessible for heavy than for light viewers. Participants were prompted to recall or imagine an instance of particular events, some of which are frequently portrayed on television, and to indicate the ease with which they could recall the examples and their source. Media examples were more likely to be recalled for events that are portrayed often in the media but infrequently experienced directly (e.g., murder, trial), whereas personal experiences were more likely to be recalled for events with which participants had high direct experience, regardless of frequency of media portrayals (e.g., highway accidents, dates). These results are consistent with research showing that direct experience enhances accessibility (Fazio, Chen, McDonel, & Sherman, 1982). More important, ease of retrieving the exemplars was positively correlated with frequency of television viewing, but only for the viewing of programs that frequently portrayed the events and when direct experience was low. Thus, television exemplars appear to be more accessible for heavy than for light viewers in expected ways.

Other studies have also provided evidence of an accessibility bias resulting from television viewing, as well as its mediating function. Shrum and O'Guinn (1993) had participants indicate their various frequency and probability judgments and measured the speed with which the participants reported their judgments. If the accessibility of relevant exemplars is a function of television viewing frequency, then not only should heavier viewers report higher estimates than lighter viewers (consistent with a cultivation effect), but they should make their judgments faster. As expected, heavy viewers estimated higher and faster than light viewers, and controlling for speed of response eliminated the cultivation effect. Other studies have replicated this effect across a variety of dependent variables and provided more stringent tests of the mediating role of accessibility (cf. Busselle, 2001; Shrum, 1996; Shrum, O'Guinn, Semenik, & Faber, 1991).

Television Viewing and Source Discounting

Although the notion that television viewing enhances accessibility, which in turn influences judgments, is intuitive, it also raises some ambiguities. For one, it suggests that people willingly use examples from television programs as a basis for their judgments. Yet, this seems counterintuitive. Why would people use information from presumably nonveridical sources (e.g., fictional television) to construct their estimates of real-world incidence?[2] In other words, it seems unlikely that people would construct their estimates of the prevalence of American millionaires on the ease with which they can recall a television character who is a millionaire. However, one way in which this process could take place is if the source of the memory (i.e., television) is not discounted (Johnson, Hashtroudi, & Lindsay, 1993). That is, if participants do not routinely pay attention to the source of their memories in the process of constructing their judgments, then they would not source-discount.[3] Such lack of discounting might take place under conditions in which participants are not concerned about the accuracy of their answers, conditions that are likely present in anonymous surveys.

Shrum and colleagues (1998) tested the proposition that people do not normally discount television-based exemplars when constructing their frequency and probability estimates by priming television as a possible source of information. Priming source was expected to make salient the lack of veridicality of the information (and thus its lack of diagnosticity). In source-priming conditions, source was made salient by simply asking participants to report their television viewing frequency prior to providing their judgments of the prevalence of crime and certain occupations. In relation-priming conditions, participants were forewarned of the possible influence of television information on their judgments, thus increasing both the salience of television and its effects. In no-priming conditions, participants provided their estimates of crime and occupations before they reported their television viewing behavior. Because the primes were salient rather than unobtrusive, we expected that participants would correct for the influence of television by discounting nonveridical (and thus inapplicable) information such as television exemplars, similar to the effects noted by Martin (1986; Martin, Seta, & Crelia, 1990; see also Higgins, Rholes, & Jones, 1977 for the lack of effects of inapplicable primes). However, we also expected that this discounting effect would be greater for heavier viewers than for lighter viewers. Because heavy viewers should be more likely to retrieve television-based exemplars than should light viewers, they should have more to discount.

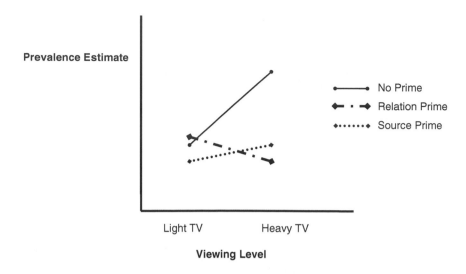

Figure 11.1   Television viewing effects as a function of priming conditions.

This viewing by priming conditions interaction was in fact what we found. As can be seen in Figure 11.1 (for simplicity, the effects are averaged across dependent variables), the expected cultivation effect was obtained in no-priming conditions but was eliminated in both source- and relation-priming conditions (neither of the slopes are significant). Most important, as expected, the priming conditions affected only the heavy viewers, as there were no significant differences in estimates between any priming conditions for light viewers. These results are similar to those obtained by Wänke, Schwarz, & Bless (1995), who found that perceived diagnosticity of the recall experience itself (rather than the diagnosticity of the recalled exemplars) influenced the use of the availability heuristic in judgment construction.

One possible explanation for the adjustments noted is a demand effect in which participants adjusted because they perceived they were expected to do so. Yet if this were the case, we would expect that both light and heavy viewers would show adjustment effects. As Figure 11.1 shows, this was not the case for light viewers. However, it is possible that viewers adjusted based on their perceptions of themselves as heavier or lighter viewers. That is, heavy viewers may have adjusted more because they were aware that they were heavy viewers and thus understood their estimates should be more affected by viewing than should those of light viewers. Light viewers, realizing that they watch little television and thus should not be affected much by it, adjusted relatively less. This possibility was tested in a second study that manipulated participants' perceptions of whether they were heavy or light viewers by manipulating the scale values that participants used to report their television viewing frequency (see Schwarz, Hippler, Deutsch, & Strack, 1985). Although the manipulation was successful, the discounting in the priming conditions held regardless of the manipulated perceptions of viewing frequency.

Heuristic versus Systematic Processing

The findings of Shrum and colleagues (1998) are consistent with the proposition that the judgments of frequency and probability used to test for cultivation effects are memory-based ones that rely on the recall of information at the time the judgment is required. If this is so, then additional propositions can be derived that pertain to the conditions under which heuristics should (or should not) be used. Heuristics tend to be used most when involvement with or the importance of the judgment construction task is low. At these times, because the estimates are relatively difficult to accurately construct, people rely on cognitive shortcuts to simplify the task (for a review, see Sherman & Corty, 1984). However, suppose that it is important for people to be accurate in their judgments, thus making them more involved in the judgment construction task. Under these conditions, it is likely that people will think more carefully about their judgments, use information from a variety of sources, and scrutinize more carefully the source of the information they retrieve. If so, then television information should have relatively little impact on their judgments.

Shrum (2001) tested the proposition that task involvement would moderate the cultivation effect. Participants were induced to process either systematically or heuristically, or given no inducement. In systematic processing conditions, participants were prompted to think carefully about their answers prior to reporting them by using an accuracy motivation/task importance manipulation (Chaiken & Maheswaran, 1994; Maheswaran & Chaiken, 1991). They were instructed to be as accurate as possible, were told that their answers would be graded by the experimenter and that the experimenter would discuss their answers with them after the study and expect them to justify their answers. In contract, in heuristic processing conditions, participants were instructed to answer quickly and spontaneously by giving the first answer that came to them "off the top of their head." In control conditions, participants were simply asked to provide their answers to the questions that followed. The questions pertained to four constructs typically used in cultivation research: prevalence of crime, certain occupations, marital discord, and societal affluence. After providing their estimates, participants reported their television viewing frequency.

If typical cultivation effects involving judgments of frequency and probability are normally made through the use of cognitive heuristics, then inducing participants to use them (heuristic conditions) should have no effect relative to control conditions. Thus, the positive relation between television viewing frequency and magnitude of the estimates should not differ between the heuristic and control conditions. However, inducing participants to avoid the use of heuristics (systematic condition) should reduce the magnitude of the cultivation effect relative to the other two conditions. The results (averaged across the four dependent variables) can be seen in Figure 11.2. As expected, both the heuristic and control groups produced robust cultivation effects that did not differ from each other. In contrast, the cultivation effect was eliminated (nonsignificantly negative) in the systematic condition. Note also that, just as with the results from Shrum and colleagues (1998) shown in Figure 11.1, the processing manipulation affected only

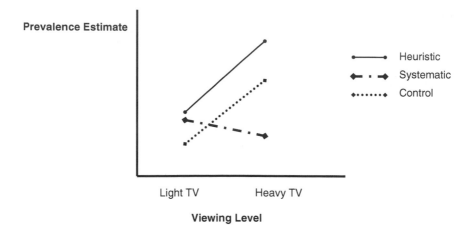

Figure 11.2   Television viewing effects as a function of processing conditions.

the heavy viewers; the estimates did not differ among light viewers as a function of experimental condition. Moreover, this exact pattern held for all four dependent variables. These results are similar to those observed by Greifeneder and Bless (2007), who showed that heuristics are used under capacity constraint conditions but not under full resources conditions.

The results of Shrum (2001) provide support for the notion that the use of cognitive heuristics can explain the cultivation effect. When systematic processing was induced, the cultivation effect was eliminated. In that study, task involvement was used to induce systematic processing and thus (presumably) more careful scrutiny of information used to construct judgments. However, low involvement (at the time of judgment) is not the only process that is likely to induce heuristic processing. People are also more likely to use heuristics when ability to process information is low. If this is the case, then similar to the effects just noted, low ability to process information should also result in heuristic processing.

Shrum (2007b) conducted a field experiment to test the notion that low ability to process information should enhance the cultivation effect. A general population, random-sample survey was administered to assess the relation between television viewing frequency and seven different dependent variables: estimates of societal crime prevalence, personal crime risk in ones' own neighborhood, personal crime risk in New York City (outside own neighborhood), vice behaviors such as drug use and prostitution, societal affluence, marital discord, and prevalence of particular occupations, all overrepresented on television relative to their real-world incidence. Ability to process information was manipulated by varying whether participants completed their surveys via a telephone or mail. Because telephone surveys tend to result in more time pressure and "satisficing" (choosing the easiest answer) than most other forms of surveys (Holbrook, Green, & Krosnick, 2003), the telephone surveys were expected to produce a greater tendency to use heuristics than were mail surveys. If so, and the cultivation effect is the result of the use of these heuristics, the telephone survey conditions should show a larger cultivation effect than the mail survey conditions. Moreover, this effect should hold for all of the dependent variables except personal crime risk in one's own neighborhood. Judgments of this kind have been shown to be influenced primarily by direct experience and not by media information (Shrum & Bischak, 2001; Tyler, 1980; Tyler & Cook, 1984).

As expected, method of survey administration affected judgments. Estimates were uniformly higher in the telephone than in the mail survey conditions, consistent with heuristic processing conditions and confirming Holbrook and colleagues' (2003) observation that survey method can impact descriptive judgments. More germane to the cultivation effect and its underlying processes, the magnitude of the cultivation effect was greater in telephone than in mail survey conditions for all of the dependent variables except estimates of personal crime risk in one's own neighborhood, which as predicted did not differ as a function of survey method.

Summary   The research just reviewed tested the proposition that the frequency and probability judgments that are typically used as indicators of a cultivation effect are memory-based judgments that can be explained through the use of judgmental heuristics such as availability. If the judgments are made through the use of the availability heuristic, then accessibility differences should be discernable as a function of frequency of viewing. Moreover, conditions that facilitate or inhibit the use of heuristics during judgment construction should correspondingly facilitate or inhibit the cultivation effect. Consistent with these propositions, research has provided reliable evidence that television viewing increases the accessibility of exemplars relevant to the judgment and that this accessibility mediates the relation between viewing frequency and the magnitude of the judgments. In addition, conditions that inhibit the use of heuristics, such as high motivation for accurate judgments or reminders about the source of the information recalled, significantly reduce the magnitude of the cultivation effect, whereas conditions that facilitate the use of heuristics, such as time pressure, increase the magnitude of the cultivation effect.

Note that the facilitating and inhibiting conditions refer to conditions at the time the judgment is required, and thus not during the actual viewing experience. This finding runs counter to a typical learning model in which the television lessons are integrated into social perceptions through an online process during viewing. Thus, at least for the frequency and probability judgments, the lessons get "learned" at the time of judgment through the recall of television-based information stored in memory during the viewing process. However, people are generally unaware that television is the source of the information they recall and thus unaware of the influence of television viewing on their judgments.

The frequency and probability judgments of the types just described have formed a significant part of research on the cultivation effect. Cultivation effects for these judgments have generally been larger and more consistent than effects for other types of judgments such as values, attitudes, and beliefs. For these reasons, along with the general success in providing a psychological process explanation for the effects, research on the effects of television viewing on values, attitudes, and beliefs have been comparatively sparse. This is unfortunate for at least two reasons. One is that the question of how television information gets processed and integrated into evaluative belief systems seems to better capture the notion of cultivation. It seems safe to assume that television's impact on whether people condone violence, are less trustful of their citizens, or lust after wealth and status are more important societal issues than its impact on beliefs about how many doctors and lawyers there are in the workforce. The second reason that a focus on the memory-based frequency and probability judgments is unfortunate is that they are relatively rare. Not only are they infrequently made, but they are actually difficult to produce at all, even in the lab (Hastie & Park, 1986). Instead, most judgments made in everyday life tend to be online judgments that are spontaneously generated as information is encountered. Such judgments include impression formation, stereotyping, and attitude construction, and in fact preventing people from making these spontaneous, online judgments is remarkably difficult. The next section addresses whether and how television may influence these types of judgments.

Values, Attitudes, and Beliefs

Judgments such as values, attitudes, and beliefs are quite different from the frequency and probability judgments just discussed. One difference is that they are for the most part online judgments. That is, as information is encountered in everyday life, it is used to either construct new evaluative judgments or update old ones. This notion has important implications for understanding how television might impact those judgments. For one, it suggests that the effect of television viewing on values and attitudes should occur during the viewing process rather than at the time the judgment is requested by the researcher. People spontaneously use the information from a television program to form or update attitudes and then simply recall those attitudes and report them when requested to do so. For another, it suggests that television's cultivation of attitudes and values can be thought of as a process of online persuasion. As noted earlier, television programs are not sterile and value-free, but instead often convey the dominant norms and values of society. In turn, these television messages may be viewed as persuasive communications (whether intended or not) that may potentially impact the attitudes, values, and beliefs of viewers. If so, then factors that facilitate or inhibit persuasion, such as motivation and ability to process information (Petty & Cacioppo, 1986), should likewise facilitate or inhibit the cultivation effect.

Television Viewing and Materialism

Shrum and colleagues (2005) tested this notion by investigating whether motivation and ability to process information during viewing moderates the effect of television viewing frequency on material values. A survey was sent to a randomly selected sample of U.S. residents. Motivation to process information was operationalized as need for cognition (Cacioppo, Petty, & Kao, 1984), attention was operationalized as individual differences in the extent to which viewers regularly pay close attention while viewing (Rubin, Perse, & Taylor, 1988), and materialism was measured with the Richins and Dawson (1992) Material Values Scale. If television viewing influences material values through a persuasion process, then the relation between viewing frequency and materialism should be greater for those higher in motivation to process information compared to those lower in motivation to process, and greater for those higher in ability to process information compared to those lower in ability to process.

The results were according to predictions. Both need for cognition and attention while viewing (which were uncorrelated with each other) interacted significantly with the relation between television viewing and materialism in the expected ways. Although both the high- and low-need-for-cognition groups showed positive relations between viewing frequency and level of materialism, the effect was greater for the high-need-for-cognition group. In a similar manner, the high-attention group showed stronger cultivation effects than did the low-attention group, although the cultivation effects were again significant for both groups. Moreover, the patterns were again similar to those found for the frequency and probability judgments (see Figures 11.1 and 11.2) in that the effects of need for cognition and attention were noted primarily for heavy viewers.

Although consistent with a persuasion explanation for cultivation effects for material values, the notion that high-need-for-cognition viewers would show stronger cultivation effects than would low-need-for-cognition viewers runs somewhat counter to the stereotypes of high-need-for-cognition people. Those high in need for cognition might be expected to avoid television because it is not cognitively challenging (Kubey & Csikszentmihalyi, 1990). Indeed, in Study 1 of Shrum and colleagues (2005), need for cognition was negatively correlated with frequency of viewing, but the effect was relatively small ($r = -.15$). Moreover, although those high in need for cognition tend to elaborate more on information presented in a communication than those low in need for cognition, those high in need for cognition are also known to scrutinize arguments more carefully and counterargue weak messages to a greater degree than those low in need for cognition. Because it is plausible that television messages might be considered weak arguments because they come from a nonveridical source, the precise nature of the elaborations of high-need-for-cognition viewers is unclear.

There is an alternative explanation, however, for the noted effects, one consistent with the pattern of effects observed by Shrum and colleagues (2005, Study 1). As just noted, the correlation between need for cognition and television-viewing frequency is actually relatively small. Thus, despite the negative correlation, there are nevertheless many heavy viewers who are high in need for cognition. Moreover, they are heavy viewers presumably because they enjoy watching television, and constantly counterarguing television messages is likely to be inconsistent with that enjoyment. Instead, it seems more likely that heavy viewers will suspend disbelief in order to become engrossed in the program.

This proposition was also tested by Shrum and colleagues (2005, Study 2). Participants viewed a 20-minute film segment that was either high (*Wall Street*) or low (*Gorillas in the Mist*) in materialism. Afterward, they completed a thought-listing task, followed by need for cognition and narrative transportation scales. *Narrative transportation* refers to the extent to which viewers (or readers) become absorbed in a story and feel they are actually part of the experience (Green & Brock, 2000; Green, Garst, & Brock, 2004). As expected, high-need-for-cognition

participants listed more favorable thoughts than low-need-for-cognition participants, but this was true only for heavy viewers. Moreover, consistent with the
notion that high-need-for-cognition viewers would suspend disbelief rather than
counterargue in an effort to become absorbed in the program, high-need-for-cognition participants who were heavy viewers were more transported than light viewers who were high in need for cognition. The role of transportation in the online
persuasion process was further confirmed in study that manipulated whether participants saw a high- or low-materialism program (Shrum, 2006). Participants who
saw the high materialism program reported more materialistic values (Richins &
Dawson, 1992) and greater financial aspirations (Kasser & Ryan, 1993) than those
who saw the low-materialism program, but the effect was greater for those who
reported being more transported during the program.

The online nature of attitude activation also has implications for attitude accessibility. If attitudes are activated spontaneously during viewing, the attitudes may
be affected in ways other than simply attitude valence or extremity (for a review
see Petty & Krosnick, 1995). In particular, frequent activation of attitudes should
make them more accessible, and thus more predictive of behavior, than attitudes
that are less frequently activated (Fazio et al., 1982). Thus, it may be that frequent
viewing of certain messages may not affect attitude extremity, but may affect attitude accessibility. For example, if viewers watch a program that conveys a theme
or message with which they agree (e.g., tough on crime, materialism signals success), viewing may not necessarily make the attitude more positive, but may simply
reinforce the existing positive attitude.

Shrum (1999a) investigated this proposition by asking participants to indicate
their attitudes toward concepts that a content analysis revealed were frequently
portrayed on soap operas (marital discord, distrust of people, owning expensive
products) and recorded both their attitude extremity and attitude accessibility (via
reaction times). As expected, heavier soap-opera viewers had more accessible attitudes than lighter soap-opera viewers, and this effect held over and above the
effects of attitude extremity.

Summary   The research just reviewed provides support for the proposition that
television viewing influences values and attitudes through an online persuasion
process in which those who are higher in motivation and ability to process information are more influenced by the messages contained in the television programs
than those lower in motivation and ability, similar to the processes proposed by
Petty and Cacioppo (1986). Moreover, this general process appears to be enhanced
by the degree to which viewers can suspend disbelief and become absorbed or
transported into the program, a process which tends to reduce counterarguing of
the television message.

Note that the moderating effects of motivation and ability to process information for values and attitudes operate quite differently, if not in an opposite manner, from viewing effects for frequency and probability judgments. Recall that for
these latter judgments, which are memory-based and occur through the recall of
television information at the time the judgment is elicited, motivation and ability
to process information *decreases* the cultivation effect, and this process occurs at

the time of recall when the judgment is elicited. The effects occur through greater scrutiny of the information that is recalled, more attention to unreliable information, and consideration of information from a variety of sources, rather than simply relying on the (television) information that comes most easily to mind. Conversely, for the values and attitude judgments, which are online and occur spontaneously during viewing, motivation and ability to process information *increases* the effects of the television message. This pattern of effects is part and parcel of maximizing the enjoyment of viewing entertainment television. Rather than motivation and ability factors increasing the scrutiny of the message, such scrutiny is suspended in order for the viewer to be absorbed into the program (which maximizes enjoyment), and thus motivation and ability factors increase the extent to which the television message itself is absorbed and integrated into existing belief structures.

Qualifications and Limitations

Although the research just reviewed tends to support the general framework that is proposed for the processes underlying cultivation effects, a few observations are worth noting with regard to limitations of some of the assumptions. One of the most problematic is the notion of causality. As noted earlier, one of the criticisms of early research on television effects was its almost exclusive reliance on correlational data. However, it is also obvious that most of the studies that have been reported in support of the process models I have proposed have also measured rather than manipulated television viewing. The key difference is that within the context of the studies that measure television viewing, other variables that represented proposed process variables were manipulated (accuracy motivation, heuristic processing, source discounting, time pressure). Given both the pattern and consistency of the data, alternative hypotheses of reverse causality or other variable influence have difficulty in accounting for these findings. The choice to measure rather than manipulate television viewing was made in order to capture more naturalistic effects. That said, the more recent studies on the relation between television and materialism have required that viewing be manipulated in order to better determine the processes that are occurring during viewing, and these studies have also provided results consistent with theory.

A second issue worth noting is the assumption that attitudes are for the most part online judgments. Of course, not all attitudes are formed in this fashion. In some instances, particularly when current attitudes are not that accessible or do not exist, or when individuals are not that confident in the veracity of their current attitude, then they may be motivated to search memory for information to compute or recompute their attitude. However, this would likely occur when attitude objects are not that common. Given that most of the attitudes that are measured are common ones frequently addressed not only on television but in everyday life, it seems reasonable to think that at least the attitudes addressed in this research are constructed in an online fashion. Moreover, this is particularly true for personal values, which by definition are stable, closely held abstractions that form the basis of people's belief systems (Rokeach, 1973).

Finally, the separate models that were offered for frequency and probability judgments, and attitudes, values, and belief judgments suggest that these two types of judgments are independent. Obviously, this does not have to be so. It seems intuitive that judgments about, say, the frequency of violent crime might cause one to be more fearful of crime. In fact, this was the early assumption in cultivation research, and the frequency/probability and attitudes/values judgments were termed first-order and second-order judgments, respectively (Hawkins & Pingree, 1982), with the assumption that the former influenced the latter. However, research that tested this proposition has shown little consistency and support (cf. Hawkins et al., 1987; Potter, 1991). Such lack of effects makes sense if indeed first-order, frequency judgments are seldom spontaneous and made in a memory-based fashion at the time the judgment is requested. If so, then they could logically have little effect on the attitudes and values that are currently held (although the reverse might be true: Judgments of prevalence of crime may be inferred from one's own fear of crime).

IMPLICATIONS OF THE PROCESSES UNDERLYING TELEVISION-VIEWING EFFECTS

The purpose of this chapter was not only to show that television program content has a demonstrable effect on those who view it, but also to explicate the processes underlying these effects. The latter purpose is particularly important because the validity of these effects has been controversial. On the one hand, the effects may seem relatively obvious to social scientists familiar with the processes underlying concepts such as perception, impression formation, and attitude construction. On the other hand, the effects often seem counterintuitive to those who believe that attitudes and beliefs are always constructed or performed through conscious, controlled processes and that behaviors are always chosen through a rational and generally thoughtful process that is under the control of "free will." Hence, most people think they are relatively unaffected by such things as viewing film and television violence because they realize that much of this violence is fiction meant to entertain, and thus should logically have little or no effect on their real-world decisions. Of course, the last 30 years (at least) of social cognition research points to just the opposite, that people are generally unaware of the true influences on their attitudes and behavior and that a vast majority of these influences occur outside of conscious awareness (Hassin, Uleman, & Bargh, 2005; see Dijksterhuis, this volume).

One way of increasing confidence in the validity of television effects is through the development and testing of the processes that underlie these effects. Toward this end, I have reviewed research that has focused on the processes underlying a particular type of television effect, the cultivation effect. Like many media effects, it has been the subject of substantial criticism, in large part because the research has been predominantly correlational and the effects have been both small and inconsistent. The models I have proposed for how these effects operate help explain why the effects may at times be small or even nonexistent. As the models indicate, there are a number of factors or situations that may either facilitate or inhibit the extent to which information garnered through television viewing may ultimately impact judgments. Moreover, the nature of these effects depends on whether the judgments are online or memory-based.

Understanding the underlying processes of television viewing effects has implications for developing methods to reduce these effects. Because many of the effects that have been discussed are widely considered to be harmful or detrimental to viewers, educational efforts to reduce these effects have been developed. Generally termed "media literacy" programs (Kubey, 1997), they attempt to educate viewers about the potentially harmful effects of television viewing, particularly in terms of making viewers aware of television's distorted portrayal of reality, whether this distortion is purposeful (with advertisements) or not (with programs). Thus, for example, programs might inform viewers that the overall content of television is overly violent and that viewing such violence may have certain deleterious effects, or that the content of news is not always representative but instead is selective, such that the crimes that are chosen for inclusion on the news are more likely to depict minorities as perpetrators than baseline statistics would predict (Dixon & Linz, 2000). Thus, the media literacy efforts generally teach viewers to "read the media" (Shrum et al., 2005). However, the research just reviewed has additional implications. For one, it suggests that such tactics may work well for non-narrative programs such as news, which people tend to process critically and with some skepticism, but not so well for fictional narratives in which viewers suspend disbelief and critical viewing in order to experience maximum enjoyment from the program. In addition, for memory-based judgments, reading the media should have little effect. Instead, viewers should be encouraged to also "read the judgment" by learning how frequent viewing of distorted portrayals influences certain types of judgments, so that when such a judgment is elicited, people may have a greater chance of discounting television-based information. Ideally, such a comprehensive approach to media literacy will have optimum success in combating the ill effects of television's influence on viewers' perceptions, attitudes, and values.

CONCLUSION

The research reviewed here answers questions that have plagued cultivation research for some time, particularly with respect to understanding the possible underlying mechanisms of the effect. However, there are clearly many questions that have been left unanswered. For one, although the various mechanisms that have been proposed and tested have received empirical support, there are likely a number of other mechanisms that may also contribute to the overall effect. For example, cultivation effects of frequency and probability judgments may occur through the applications of heuristics other than availability, such as simulation and representativeness. Cultivation effects for attitudes and values might be explained through mere exposure in which liking and condoning violence results from repeated exposure to violent stimuli (portrayals). Alternatively, socialization through observational learning may occur when viewers conclude that certain attitudes and values are normative because they occur so frequently and consistently in television programs. Another possible mechanism is that television viewing influences values such as materialism, not through repeated exposure to materialistic content, but through content that makes viewers insecure. Terror Management Theory (Greenberg, Pyszczynski, & Solomon, 1986) posits that when people are made to feel insecure, particularly due to thoughts of their own death (mortality salience), they react by bolstering self-esteem. In materialistic societies in which money is used to gauge self-worth (such as the United States), people may attempt to bolster self-esteem through materialistic pursuits. Thus, to the extent to which television programs induce thoughts of one's own death (and surely the various thrillers, action-adventures, and horror flicks do so often), it may move viewers toward greater materialism (Arndt, Solomon, Kasser, & Sheldon, 2004; Kasser, 2002). Needless to say, there are still a host of questions about how, and how much, television affects its viewers.

ENDNOTES

1. These content analyses, as well as most of the research to be discussed, pertain to American television. Although a number of studies have investigated the effects of television viewing in countries other than the United States (e.g., Van den Bulck, 2002; Weimann, 1984), the bulk of the research has been done with American audiences, perhaps because the frequency of viewing of American viewers is so high (about 30 hours per week; Nielsen, 2006).
2. It is possible that people may make the assumption that television is in fact reflective of real life. However, when participants have been asked to provide their beliefs about the reality of television portrayals, they invariably fall well below the mid-point on scales that measure perceived reality of television (for a review, see Shrum, 1999b).
3. Note that a lack of attention to specific aspects of the exemplars is consistent with Tversky and Kahneman's (1973) conceptualization of the availability heuristic and the use of subjective ease of recall in constructing frequency estimates. (See also Schwarz et al., 1991, for further development of this notion.)

REFERENCES

Arndt, J., Solomon, S., Kasser, T., & Sheldon, K. M. (2004). The urge to splurge: A terror management account of materialism and consumer behavior. *Journal of Consumer Psychology*, *14*, 198–212.

Bandura, A. (1977). *Social learning theory*. New York: General Learning Press.

Bryant, J., Carveth, R. A., & Brown, D. (1981). Television viewing and anxiety: An experimental investigation. *Journal of Communication*, *31*(2), 106–119.

Bushman, B. J., & Anderson, C. A. (2001). Media violence and the American public: Scientific facts versus media misinformation. *American Psychologist*, *56*, 477–489.

Busselle, R. W. (2001). The role of exemplar accessibility in social reality judgments. *Media Psychology*, *3*, 43–67.

Busselle, R. W., & Shrum, L. J. (2003). Media exposure and the accessibility of social information. *Media Psychology*, *5*, 255–282.

Cacioppo, J. T., Petty, R. E & Kao, C. F. (1984). The efficient assessment of need for cognition. *Journal of Per nality Assessment*, *48*, 306–307.

Carlson, J. M. (1983). Crime show viewing by preadults: The impact on attitudes toward civil liberties. *Communication Research*, *10*, 529–552.

Chaiken, S., & Maheswaran, D. (1994). Heuristic processing can bias systematic processing: Effects of source credibility, argument ambiguity, and task importance on attitude judgment. *Journal of Personality and Social Psychology*, *66*, 460–473.

Chayefsky, P. (writer). (1976) *Network* [Motion Picture]. United States: Metro-Goldwyn-Mayer, Inc.

DeFleur, M. L. (1964). Occupational roles as portrayed on television. *Public Opinion Quarterly*, *28*, 57–74.

Dixon, T. L., & Linz, D. (2000). Overrepresentation and underrepresentation of African Americans and Latinos as lawbreakers on television news. *Journal of Communication*, *50*(2), 131–154.

Donnerstein, E., & Berkowitz, L. (1981). Victim reactions in aggressive erotic films as a factor in violence against women. *Journal of Personality and Social Psychology*, *41*, 710–724.

Fazio, R. H., Chen, J., McDonel, E. C., & Sherman, S. J. (1982). Attitude accessibility, attitude-behavior consistency, and strength of the object-evaluation association. *Journal of Experimental Social Psychology*, *18*, 339–357.

Gerbner, G. (1969). Toward 'cultural indicators': The analysis of mass mediated message systems. *AV Communication Review*, *6*, 85–108.

Gerbner, G., & Gross, L. (1976). Living with television: The violence profile. *Journal of Communication*, *26* (2), 182–190.

Gerbner, G., Gross, L., Morgan, M., & Signorielli, N. (1980). The 'mainstreaming' of America: Violence profile no. 11. *Journal of Communication*, *30*(3), 10–29.

Gerbner, G., Gross, L., Morgan, M., & Signorielli, N. (1986). Living with television: The dynamics of the cultivation process. In J. Bryant & D. Zillmann (Eds.), *Perspectives on media effects* (pp. 17–40). Hillsdale, NJ: Lawrence Erlbaum.

Gerbner, G., Gross, L., Morgan, M., Signorielli, N., & Shanahan, J. (2002). Growing up with television: Cultivation processes. In J. Bryant & D. Zillmann (Eds.), *Media effects: Advances in theory and research* (2nd ed., pp. 43–67). Mahwah, NJ: Lawrence Erlbaum.

Green, M. C., & Brock, T. C. (2000). The role of transportation in the persuasiveness of public narratives. *Journal of Personality and Social Psychology*, *79*, 701–721.

Green, M. C., Garst, J., & Brock, T. C. (2004). The power of fiction: Determinants and boundaries. In L. J. Shrum (Ed.), *The psychology of entertainment media: Blurring the lines between entertainment and persuasion* (pp. 161–176). Mahwah, NJ: Lawrence Erlbaum.

Greenberg, J., Pyszczynski, T., & Solomon, S. (1986). The causes and consequences of a need for self-esteem: A terror management theory. In R. F. Baumeister (Ed.), *Public self and private self* (pp. 189–212). New York: Springer-Verlag.

Greifeneder, R., & Bless, H. (2007). Relying on accessible content vs. accessibility experiences: The case of processing capacity. *Social Cognition*, *25*, 853–881.

Haney, C., & Manzolati, J. (1980). Television criminology: Network illusions of criminal justice realities. In E. Aronson (Ed.), *Readings about the social animal*. San Francisco: Freeman.

Hassin, R. R., Uleman, J. S., & Bargh, J. A. (Eds.). (2005). *The new unconscious*. New York: Oxford University Press.

Hastie, R., & Park, B. (1986). The relationship between memory and judgment depends on whether the judgment task is memory-based or on-line. *Psychological Review*, *93*, 258–268.

Hawkins, R. P., & Pingree, S. (1982). Television's influence on constructions of social reality. In D. Pearl, L. Bouthilet, & J. Lazar (Eds.), *Television and behavior: Ten years of scientific progress and implications for the eighties* (Vol. 2, pp. 224–247). Washington, DC: Government Printing Office.

Hawkins, R. P., & Pingree, S. (1990). Divergent psychological processes in constructing social reality from mass media content. In N. Signorielli & M. Morgan (Eds.), *Cultivation analysis: New directions in media effects research* (pp. 33–50). Newbury Park, CA: Sage.

Hawkins, R. P., Pingree, S., & Adler, I. (1987). Searching for cognitive processes in the cultivation effect. *Human Communication Research, 13*, 553–577.

Higgins, E. T., Rholes, W. S., & Jones, C. R. (1977). Category accessibility and impression formation. *Journal of Experimental Social Psychology, 13*, 141–154.

Hirsch, P. (1980). The scary world of the nonviewer and other anomalies: A reanalysis of Gerbner et al.'s findings on cultivation analysis. *Communication Research, 7*, 403–456.

Holbrook, A. L., Green, M. C., & Krosnick, J. A. (2003). Telephone versus face-to-face interviewing of national probability samples with long questionnaires: Comparison of respondent satisficing and social desirability response bias. *Public Opinion Quarterly, 67*, 79–125.

Hughes, M. (1980). The fruits of cultivation analysis: A reexamination of some effects of television watching. *Public Opinion Quarterly, 44*, 287–302.

Johnson, M. K., Hashtroudi, S., & Lindsay, D. S. (1993). Source monitoring. *Psychological Bulletin, 114*, 3–28.

Kasser, T. (2002). *The high price of materialism.* Cambridge, MA: MIT Press.

Kasser, T., & Ryan, R. M. (1993). A dark side of the American dream: Correlates of financial success as a central life aspiration. *Journal of Personality and Social Psychology, 65*, 410–422.

Kubey, R. (Ed.). (1997). *Media literacy in the information age: Current perspectives.* New Brunswick, NJ: Transaction Publishers.

Kubey, R., & Csikszentmihalyi, M. (1990). *Television viewing and the quality of life: How viewing shapes everyday experience.* Hillsdale, NJ: Lawrence Erlbaum.

Lichter, S. R., Lichter, L. S., & Rothman, S. (1994). *Prime time: How TV portrays American culture.* Washington, DC: Regnery.

Maheswaran, D., & Chaiken, S. (1991). Promoting systematic processing in low-motivation settings: Effect of incongruent information on processing and judgment. *Journal of Personality and Social Psychology, 61*, 13–25.

Malamuth, N. M., & Impett, E. A. (2001). Research on sex in the media: What do we know about effects on children and adolescents? In D. Singer & J. Singer (Eds.), *Handbook of children in the media* (pp. 269–287): Newbury Park: Sage.

Manis, M., Shedler, J., Jonides, J., & Nelson, T. E. (1993). Availability heuristic in judgments of set size and frequency of occurrence. *Journal of Personality and Social Psychology, 65*, 448–457.

Martin, L. L. (1986). Set/reset: Use and disuse of concepts in impression formation. *Journal of Personality and Social Psychology, 51*, 493–504.

Martin, L. L., Seta, J. J., & Crelia, R. A. (1990). Assimilation and contrast as a function of people's willingness and ability to expend effort in forming an impression. *Journal of Personality and Social Psychology, 59*, 27–37.

McGuire, W. J. (1986). The myth of massive media impact: Savagings and salvagings. In G. Comstock (Ed.), *Public communication and behavior* (Vol. 1, pp. 173–257). New York: Academic Press.

Newcomb, H. (1978). Assessing the violence profile studies of Gerbner and Gross: A humanistic critique and suggestion. *Communication Research, 5*, 264–282.

Nielsen, A. C. (2006). *Nielsen report on television.* Northbrook, IL: Author.

O'Guinn, T. C., & Shrum, L. J. (1997). The role of television in the construction of consumer reality. *Journal of Consumer Research, 23*, 278–294.

Petty, R. E., & Cacioppo, J. T. (1986). *Communication and persuasion: Central and peripheral routes to attitude change.* New York: Springer-Verlag.

Petty, R. E., & Krosnick, J. A. (Eds.). (1995). *Attitude strength: Antecedents and consequences.* Mahwah, NJ: Lawrence Erlbaum.

Potter, W. J. (1991). Examining cultivation from a psychological perspective. *Communication Research, 18,* 92–113.

Richins, M. L. (2004). The material values scale: Measurement properties and development of a short form. *Journal of Consumer Research, 31,* 209–219.

Richins, M. L., & Dawson, S. (1992). A consumer values orientation for materialism and its measurement: Scale development and validation. *Journal of Consumer Research, 19,* 303–316.

Rokeach, M. (1973). *The nature of human values.* New York: The Free Press.

Rubin, A. M., Perse, E. M., & Taylor, D. S. (1988). A methodological examination of cultivation. *Communication Research, 15,* 107–134.

Russell, C. A., Norman, A. T., & Heckler, S. E. (2004). The consumption of television programming: Development and validation of the connectedness scale. *Journal of Consumer Research, 31,* 150–161.

Schwarz, N., Bless, H., Strack, F., Klumpp, G., Rittenauer-Schatka, H., & Simons, A. (1991). Ease of retrieval as information: Another look at the availability heuristic. *Journal of Personality and Social Psychology, 61,* 195–202.

Schwarz, N., Hippler, H. J., Deutsch, B., & Strack, F. (1985). Response categories: Effects on behavioral reports and comparative judgments. *Public Opinion Quarterly, 49,* 388–395.

Schwarz, N., & Wänke, M. (2002). Experiential and contextual heuristics in frequency judgment: Ease of recall and response scales. In P. Sedlmeier & T. Betsch (Eds.), *Etc.: Frequency processing and cognition* (pp. 89–108). Oxford, UK: Oxford University Press.

Shanahan, J., & Morgan, M. (1999). *Television and its viewers: Cultivation theory and research.* Cambridge, UK: Cambridge University Press.

Sherman, S. J., & Corty, E. (1984). Cognitive heuristics. In R. S. Wyer & T. K. Srull (Eds.), *Handbook of social cognition* (Vol. 1, pp. 189–286). Hillsdale, NJ: Lawrence Erlbaum.

Shrum, L. J. (1995). Assessing the social influence of television: A social cognition perspective on cultivation effects. *Communication Research, 22,* 402–429.

Shrum, L. J. (1996). Psychological processes underlying cultivation effects: Further tests of construct accessibility. *Human Communication Research, 22,* 482–509.

Shrum, L. J. (1999a). The relationship of television viewing with attitude strength and extremity: Implications for the cultivation effect. *Media Psychology, 1,* 3–25.

Shrum, L. J. (1999b). Television and persuasion: Effects of the programs between the ads. *Psychology & Marketing, 16,* 119–140.

Shrum, L. J. (2001). Processing strategy moderates the cultivation effect. *Human Communication Research, 27,* 94–120.

Shrum, L. J. (2006). *Narrative transportation moderates the influence of television viewing on material values.* Unpublished manuscript.

Shrum, L. J. (2007a). Cultivation and social cognition. In D. R. Roskos-Ewoldsen & J. L. Monahan (Eds.), *Communication and social cognition: Theories and methods* (pp. 245–272). Mahwah, NJ: Lawrence Erlbaum.

Shrum, L. J. (2007b). The implications of survey method for measuring cultivation effects. *Human Communication Research, 33* 64–80.

Shrum, L. J., & Bischak, V. D. (2001). Mainstreaming, resonance, and impersonal impact: Testing moderators of the cultivation effect for estimates of crime risk. *Human Communication Research, 27,* 187–215.

Shrum, L. J., Burroughs, J. E., & Rindfleisch, A. (2005). Television's cultivation of material values. *Journal of Consumer Research, 32,* 473–479.

Shrum, L. J., & O'Guinn, T. C. (1993). Processes and effects in the construction of social reality: Construct accessibility as an explanatory variable. *Communication Research*, 20, 436–471.

Shrum, L. J., O'Guinn, T. C., Semenik, R. J., & Faber, R. J. (1991). Process and effects in the construction of normative consumer beliefs: The role of television. In R. H. Holman & M. R. Solomon (Eds.), *Advances in consumer research* (Vol. 18, pp. 755–763). Provo, UT: Association for Consumer Research.

Shrum, L. J., Wyer, R. S., & O'Guinn, T. C. (1998). The effects of television consumption on social perceptions: The use of priming procedures to investigate psychological processes. *Journal of Consumer Research, 24*, 447–458.

Signorielli, N. (1990). Television's mean and dangerous world: A continuation of the cultural indicators perspective. In N. Signorielli & M. Morgan (Eds.), *Cultivation analysis: New directions in media effects research* (pp. 85–106). Newbury Park, CA: Sage.

Smythe, D. W. (1954). Reality as presented by television. *Public Opinion Quarterly, 18*, 143–156.

Tversky, A., & Kahneman, D. (1973). Availability: A heuristic for judging frequency and probability. *Cognitive Psychology, 5*, 207–232.

Tyler, T. R. (1980). Impact of directly and indirectly experienced events: The origin of crime-related judgments and behaviors. *Journal of Personality and Social Psychology, 39*, 13–28.

Tyler, T. R., & Cook, F. L. (1984). The mass media and judgments of risk: Distinguishing impact on personal and societal level judgments. *Journal of Personality and Social Psychology, 47*, 693–708.

Van den Bulck, J. (2002). The impact of television fiction on public expectations of survival following inhospital cardiopulmonary resuscitation by medical professionals. *European Journal of Emergency Medicine, 9*, 325–329.

Volgy, T., & Schwarz, J. (1980). Television entertainment programming and sociopolitical attitudes. *Journalism Quarterly, 57*(Spring), 150–155.

Wänke, M., Schwarz, N., & Bless, H. (1995). The availability heuristic revisited: Experienced ease of retrieval in mundane frequency estimates. *Acta Psychologica, 89*, 83–90.

Ward, L. M., & Rivadeneyra, R. (1999). Contributions of entertainment television to adolescents' sexual attitudes and expectations: The role of viewing amount versus viewer involvement. *The Journal of Sex Research, 36*, 237–249.

Weimann, G. (1984). Images of life in America: The impact of American T.V. in Israel. *International Journal of Intercultural Relations, 8*, 185–197.

Wood, W., Wong, F. Y., & Chachere, J. G. (1991). Effects of media violence on viewers' aggression in unconstrained social interaction. *Psychological Bulletin, 109*, 371–383.

12

Normative Influences on Consumption and Conservation Behaviors

NOAH J. GOLDSTEIN

University of California-Los Angeles

ROBERT B. CIALDINI

Arizona State University

OVERVIEW OF THIS CHAPTER

*A*fter decades of debate regarding the role of normative perceptions in people's everyday actions (e.g., Berkowitz, 1972; Darley & Latané, 1970; Fishbein & Ajzen, 1975; Sherif, 1936), it is now clear that social norms direct people's behaviors in predictable ways (Aarts & Dijksterhuis, 2003; Kerr, 1995; Schultz, 1999; Terry & Hogg, 2000; Turner, 1991). Having reached somewhat of a consensus on *what* norms are capable of doing, researchers have turned their attention to issues such as *when* their causal impact is likely to be greatest and *how* different kinds of social norms influence behavior via different mediating mechanisms.

Several theoretical perspectives have emerged to address these issues. Although our coverage of the normative literature in this chapter concentrates primarily on one of these perspectives—namely, the Focus Theory of Normative Conduct (Cialdini, Kallgren, & Reno, 1991; Cialdini, Reno, & Kallgren, 1990)—we will also discuss this literature from the perspective of social identity and self-categorization theories (e.g., Abrams & Hogg, 1990). In addition, we will examine the implications of social psychological research on social norms for how consumers behave.

However, rather than focusing on how social norms influence individuals' *consumption* behaviors, we will focus on a severely understudied area of consumer behavior—that is, how social norms influence individuals' *conservation* behaviors. Specifically, we will emphasize the role of social norms in motivating people to conserve environment resources—such as electricity, water, and raw materials, to name a few—rather than consume them.

Finally, toward the end of the chapter, we will show how consumer behavior research in this domain calls into question one of the fundamental assumptions of social psychological theories—particularly social identity and self-categorization theories.

SOCIAL IDENTITY AND SELF-CATEGORIZATION THEORIES

Although it is certainly the case that deviating from normative attitudes and behaviors often provides individuals with a sense of uniqueness and personal identity (Blanton & Christie, 2003; Kim & Markus, 1999; Nail, MacDonald, & Levy, 2000), there is perhaps an even stronger drive for people to also maintain positive self-evaluations by identifying with and conforming to valued groups (Brewer & Roccas, 2001; Cialdini & Goldstein, 2004; Pool, Wood, & Leck, 1998). The majority of the research conducted in this area over the past two decades has come from the perspective of social identity (Tajfel, 1978; Tajfel & Turner, 1979; see also Hogg & Abrams, 1988) and self-categorization theories (Turner, 1987, 1999).

The concept of social identity has taken on a variety of different meanings in various disciplines within social psychology (Brewer, 2001). However, social identity is often defined broadly as an expansion of the self-concept involving a shift in the level of self-conception from the individual self to the collective self, typically based on perceived membership in a social category (Brewer, 2003; Hogg, 2003).

Categorization can occur at different levels of abstraction, from a concrete group of people (e.g., people in my Mac online user forum) to broader concepts (e.g., citizen, American, environmentalist) (Turner, 1991). Self-categorization theory is an extension of social identity theory that focuses more on the mechanisms and influences of the categorization process (Terry, Hogg, & White, 2000; Turner, Hogg, Oakes, Reicher, & Wetherell, 1987), but the two are usually discussed together because of their shared theoretical underpinnings and the similar predictions that are derived from their common perspective.

The social identity and self-categorization perspective contends that behavioral outcomes are influenced by reference group norms, but only for those who consider group membership to be a salient basis for self-representation (e.g., Ellemers, Spears, & Doosje, 2002; Hogg, 2003; White, Hogg, & Terry, 2002). Notably, one of the primary factors that appears to influence whether group membership is seen as a salient basis for self-conceptualization is the meaningfulness and level of identification that one has for the group (e.g., Deshpande, Hoyer, & Donthu, 1986; Kleine, Kleine, & Kernan, 1993; Reed, 2004; Stayman & Deshpande, 1989; Terry, Hogg, & White, 1999). For instance, researchers have found that the perceived norms of participants' reference group of peers and friends was a significant predictor of the participants' intentions to engage in healthy behaviors (Terry & Hogg, 1996) and household recycling (Terry et al., 1999) only for those who strongly identified with the group. We will return to the social identity/self-categorization perspective later in the chapter.

FOCUS THEORY OF NORMATIVE CONDUCT

Before we continue any further with a discussion of the role norms play in influencing behavior, it is important to take a step back for a moment and ask, Just what exactly *are* social norms, anyway? The meaning of social norms has been somewhat amorphous over the decades (for a brief history, see Cialdini & Trost, 1998). Looking both to clarify the definitional confusion that had clouded researchers' ability to understand the roles of social norms (see Shaffer, 1983) and to better predict when social norms will influence behavior, Cialdini and colleagues (Cialdini, Reno, & Kallgren, 1990; Cialdini et al., 1991) developed the Focus Theory of Normative Conduct. Focus Theory has two central propositions. The first is that there are two different types of norms, descriptive and injunctive, which can have considerably different effects on behavior. The second is that any given norm is likely to influence behavior directly to the extent that is it salient. We will consider the evidence for each of these propositions in turn.

Differentiating Descriptive and Injunctive Norms

Similar to the distinction that Deutsch and Gerard (1955) made between informational and normative influences, Cialdini and colleagues (1990) suggested that descriptive and injunctive norms influence conduct through separate sources of motivation. Akin to what Cialdini (2001) has called "social proof," *descriptive norms* refer to what is commonly done in a given situation, and they motivate human action by informing individuals of what is likely to be effective or adaptive behavior in that situation. A wide variety of research shows that the behavior of others in the social environment shapes individuals' interpretations of and responses to the situation (Bearden & Etzel, 1982; Burnkrant & Cousineau, 1975; Moschis, 1976), especially in novel, ambiguous, or uncertain situations (Hochbaum, 1954; Park & Lessig, 1977). Injunctive norms, on the other hand, refer to what is commonly approved or disapproved within the culture, and they motivate behavior through informal social sanctions. In brief, descriptive norms refer to perceptions of what *is* done, whereas injunctive norms refer to perceptions of what *ought to be* done. The two are often confused as a single construct because what is commonly approved within a culture is also what is commonly done in a culture. However, this is not always the case. For example, although most people probably believe that a person *should* turn the lights off every time he or she leaves the room (injunctive norm), it may very well be that most people do not actually engage in this behavior (descriptive norm).

The mechanisms through which descriptive and injunctive norms spur and guide people's actions have remained relatively unexplored. However, Cialdini and colleagues (Cialdini, 2003; Cialdini, Barrett, et al., 2007) recently suggested that injunctive and descriptive norms influence behavior via different routes. They posited that individuals focusing on descriptive norms need not engage in elaborate cognitive processing of the relevant information because applying the heuristic rule "I should do what most others do" is based primarily on the simple observations of others' situation-specific behaviors. In contrast, acting on information provided by injunctive norms proves a more cognitively demanding route because it is based on an understanding of the culture's moral rules—that is, what others are likely to approve. To test whether these two types of norms are mediated through these different mechanisms, the researchers had participants watch public service announcements (PSAs) that featured both injunctive and descriptive norms in favor of recycling. Immediately after viewing the ads, participants completed a number of items that assessed their beliefs about recycling norms, their perceptions of the ads, and their recycling intentions. In support of the contention that descriptive and injunctive norms influence behavior through different levels of cognitive analysis, the relationship between recycling intentions and participants' perceptions that the ads conveyed approval for recycling (injunctive norm) was mediated by their cognitive evaluations of the ads' persuasiveness, whereas the effect of descriptive normative information on intentions was direct (i.e., unmediated by considerations of ad persuasiveness).

If the mechanism through which descriptive norms affect conduct is rooted more in perception than in cognition, perhaps its power to motivate behavior might be limited to the setting in which it was originally perceived. Reno, Cialdini, and Kallgren (1993) contended that descriptive norms are more situation-specific in the information they convey, as these norms communicate what others have felt is an effective course of action in that particular setting or situation. Thus, they suggested that the effect of the descriptive norm is less likely to transfer across situations than is the effect of injunctive norms. This is because injunctive norms more generally convey the kind of behavior that is approved or disapproved within a culture, which is subject to less variation across situations. Therefore, the influence of injunctive norms should transfer across a wide variety of environments. Reno and colleagues (1993) found that descriptive and injunctive norms against littering were equally successful at reducing littering when the opportunity for their participants to litter occurred in the same setting in which the norm was made salient. However, only the injunctive norm reduced littering rates when the opportunity to litter occurred in an environment that was different from the one in which the norm was made salient.

It is important to note that we are not arguing that descriptive norms never transfer across situations or environments, but rather that they are simply less likely to do so than are injunctive norms. Both types of norms are particularly likely to generalize to other situations and settings when they are associated with mnemonic cues that are also present in these other situations and settings, a hypothesis that we will return to later in the chapter.

Aligning and Misaligning Norms

Communicators who are attempting to create maximally effective normative messages must decide whether to activate injunctive norms, descriptive norms, or both. Recall that two central postulates of Focus Theory are that norms direct behavior only when they are salient (Kallgren, Reno, & Cialdini, 2000) and that the activation of the injunctive norm or the descriptive norm may elicit considerably different behavioral responses (Reno et al., 1993). Unfortunately, many communicators fail to be mindful that they must focus the target audience on the type of norm that is aligned with the end objective. For example, officials attempting to combat detrimental behavior (and raise public awareness of this behavior) often make the mistake of characterizing it as regrettably prevalent, which unintentionally focuses their audience on the unfavorable descriptive norm.

One notable example of a subtle misalignment of injunctive and descriptive norms comes from a commercial produced in the early 1970s by the Keep America Beautiful organization. Designed to reduce littering nationwide, the spot begins with a stately and serious-looking Native American dressed in traditional garb canoeing across a river. As he paddles through the waterway, the river is clearly effluent-filled and debris-ridden, and the air is replete with industrial pollutants spewing from smokestacks. After pulling his craft along a soiled shore, a driver zooming down an adjacent street tosses a bag of trash out of his car, splattering its contents across the Native American's feet. As a lone teardrop tracks slowly down his previously stoic countenance, a voiceover intones, "People start pollution. People can stop it."

Several years ago, the Keep American Beautiful organization brought the teary-eyed Native American back in another antilittering commercial that in our view retains, if not amplifies, the potentially problematic feature of the original ad. The camera features several people waiting at a bus stop, engaging in everyday activities such as drinking coffee, reading the newspaper, and smoking cigarettes. After the bus arrives and they all climb aboard, the camera cuts to the empty bus stop waiting area, now completely covered with cups, newspapers, and cigarette butts that are strewn about. The camera slowly zooms in to a poster of the Native American overlooking the garbage, still with a tear in his eye. As the screen fades to black, the text of the spot's take-home message appears: "Back by *popular neglect*" [emphasis added].

What sort of message is conveyed by this phrase and by the litter-filled environments featured in both of these ads? Although the injunctive norm against littering is obvious and powerful, both of the ads present a descriptive norm for littering that indicates that, despite strong disapproval of the behavior, many people do in fact engage in that behavior. Thus, it is possible that the descriptive norm depicting the prevalence of littering behavior may have actually undermined the potency of the antilittering injunctive norm.

Other examples are abundant. In a long-running print ad titled "Gross National Product," Woodsy proclaims, "This year Americans will produce more litter and pollution than ever before." As another example, visitors at Arizona's Petrified Forest National Park quickly learn from prominent signage that the park's existence is threatened because so many past visitors have been taking pieces of petrified wood from the grounds: "Your heritage is being vandalized every day by theft losses of petrified wood of 14 tons a year, mostly a small piece at a time." Furthermore, a commercial intended to discourage minors from using marijuana depicts a lone middle school student resisting the pressures of a whole busload of her peers. Similarly, to call attention to the need for government intervention against cigarette smoking among children, Federal Drug Administration Commissioner David Kessler publicized the fact that "more than 3 million youths in the U.S. smoke and that 3,000 become regular smokers each day" (Scott, 1995).

Although these communications may in fact reflect reality and are clearly motivated by good intentions, the influence agents behind these campaigns may fail to realize that by using a negative descriptive norm as part of a rallying cry, they might be inadvertently focusing the message recipients on the prevalence, rather than the undesirability, of that behavior. To test this hypothesis, Cialdini and colleagues (Cialdini, 2003; Cialdini, Demaine, et al., 2006) created two signs designed to deter wood theft at Petrified Forest National Park: One was injunctive in nature and the other was descriptive in nature. The researchers secretly placed marked pieces of petrified wood along visitor pathways, and alternated which of the two signs were posted at the entrance of each pathway. The injunctive normative sign stated, "Please don't remove the petrified wood from the park, in order to preserve the natural state of the Petrified Forest," and was accompanied by a picture of a visitor stealing a piece of wood, with a red circle-and-bar (i.e., the universal "No" symbol) superimposed over his hand. The descriptive normative sign emphasizing the prevalence of theft informed visitors, "Many past visitors have removed the petrified wood from the park, changing the natural state of the Petrified Forest," and was accompanied by a picture of several park visitors taking pieces of wood.

Compared to a no-sign control condition in which 2.92% of the pieces were stolen, the descriptive norm message resulted in significantly more theft (7.92%). The injunctive norm message, in contrast, resulted in marginally less theft (1.67%) than the control condition. These results are in line with the suggestion that when a descriptive norm for a situation indicates that an undesirable behavior occurs with great frequency, a communicator might indeed cause unintentional damage by publicizing this information. Thus, rather than conveying the descriptive norm, communicators in such circumstances should focus the audience on what kind of behavior is approved or disapproved in that setting.

Considering the importance of norm salience in directing behavior, norm-based persuasive approaches are likely to be most effective when the descriptive and injunctive norms are presented in concert and aligned with one another (Cialdini & Goldstein, 2004). To examine the influence of an information campaign that combined the motivational prowess of injunctive and descriptive norms, Cialdini and colleagues (Cialdini, 2003; Cialdini et al., 2007) created a set of three PSAs designed to increase recycling activity in Arizona. Each PSA featured a scene in which the majority of individuals in the ad engaged in recycling, spoke approvingly of it, and spoke disapprovingly of a single person in the scene who did not recycle. Thus, the act of recycling material was linked to images indicating that recycling activity is both widely performed and almost unanimously approved. The PSAs also included humorous dialogue, information about how to recycle, and the benefits of doing so. For instance, one purposely campy PSA featured a set of neighbors in a "Leave It to Beaver" type of scene, with several people standing on a driveway:

> Child: Over here Mrs. Rodriguez, it's our week to take the recycling down to the center.
> [Child hands a paper bag filled with newspapers to his mother, who places it onto the flatbed of a truck. Mrs. Rodriguez does the same.]
> Child: Gee Dad, where's Mr. Jenkins?
> [Mrs. Rodriguez rolls her eyes.]
> Dad [disappointed]: Well son, you see, Mr. Jenkins doesn't recycle.
> [The camera cuts to a slovenly, unkempt Mr. Jenkins snoozing on a lawn chair in his backyard, old newspapers lying all around him. The camera then cuts to the child, who has a single tear rolling down his cheek. A picture of the geographical outline of the state of Arizona then appears on the screen, filled with the faces of scores of different people. The words "Arizona Recycles" accompany the picture.]

In a field test, this PSA and two others like it were played on local TV and radio stations of four Arizona communities. The results revealed a 25.35% net advantage in recycling tonnage over a pair of control communities not exposed to the PSAs.

A Focus on Focus: The Importance of Focus

By now, it should be evident that descriptive and injunctive norms are orthogonal constructs that are capable of eliciting considerably different behaviors. However, given that countless social norms have the potential to operate in almost any setting or social situation, what determines which norm or norms will have a direct influence on behavior? Recall that the second postulate of Focus Theory is that a norm will directly affect conduct to the extent that it is focal (i.e., salient) in consciousness.

Cialdini and colleagues (1990) tested this assertion within the context of littering behavior. Dormitory residents who found a flier in their mailboxes encountered an environment that was prearranged to contain no litter (the control condition), one piece of very conspicuous litter (a hollowed-out, end piece of watermelon rind), or an assortment of different kinds of litter, including the watermelon rind. The purpose of the large, eye-catching watermelon rind was to ensure that participants would focus on the descriptive norm in that setting regarding the typicality of littering behavior. Thus, when the environment's only blemish was the watermelon rind, participants would focus on the fact that, with the exception of the rind, littering is uncommon in that setting. On the other hand, when the environment was filled with rubbish in addition to the rind, participants would focus on the fact that littering is common in that setting. Consistent with predictions, the authors found that compared to the littering rate in the clean environment (10.7%), participants in the fully littered environment littered at a significantly higher rate (26.7%), whereas participants who encountered the watermelon rind in the otherwise spotless area littered at a significantly lower rate (3.6%). The finding that the completely litter-free environment actually yielded higher littering rates than the environment containing the lone rind is especially noteworthy because the data cannot be accounted for by other perspectives, such as social learning theory (e.g., Bandura, 1977). That is, if this were simply a modeling effect, participants who observed the discarded rind would have been more likely, not less, to litter than participants in the completely unadulterated environment.

Researchers have also demonstrated the importance of focus when the injunctive and descriptive norms of a setting are not in line with one another. For example, in an experiment conducted by Reno and colleagues (1993, Study 1), library-goers returning to their parked cars passed by a confederate who littered a piece of trash, picked up a piece of trash, or simply walked by. To manipulate the descriptive norm for littering in that setting, the environment was altered to be either completely devoid or completely full of litter. Much like the presence of the rind in the previously described experiment, the littering of the rubbish by the confederate was meant to *focus* participants on that descriptive norm. The picking up of the litter, however, was meant to focus participants on the widely held injunctive norm—that is, people, and society at large, roundly disapprove of people who litter. The researchers found that compared to those in the control conditions, the library-goers in the descriptive-norm focus condition littered less only when the environment was litter-free (see Figure 12.1). However, those in the injunctive-norm condition littered less than their control counterparts regardless of the state of the surrounding environment, demonstrating that by focusing the participants' attention on the injunctive norm, the information conveyed by the descriptive norm was rendered uninfluential.

The evidence from the normative literature makes it clear that one's behaviors seem to be relatively unaffected by normative information—even one's own—unless the information is in focus (Cialdini & Goldstein, 2004). Given that relevant norms must be salient to trigger the appropriate norm-congruent behavior, those attempting to persuade others to engage in a particular behavior face the dual challenge of making the norm focal not only immediately following message reception, but also in the future. Cialdini and colleagues (2007) argue that the long-term effectiveness of persuasive communications such as public service announcements

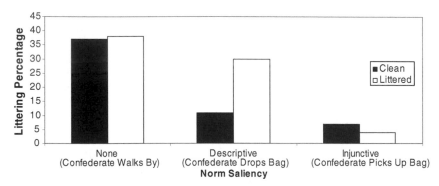

Figure 12.1   Littering Rates as a Function of Norm Saliency and Condition of the Environment.

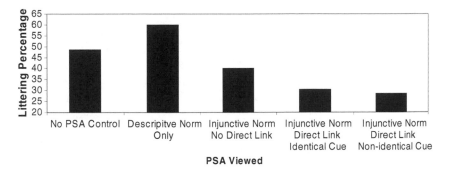

Figure 12.2   Littering Rates as a Function of Public Service Announcement Viewed.

is threatened because normative information becomes less accessible over time. They hypothesized that linking an injunctive normative message to a functional mnemonic cue (see Tulving, 1983) would increase norm accessibility at later times when the norm would not have been focal otherwise. Consistent with their predictions, they found that participants who viewed a PSA in which the wording of an injunctive norm ("You know, people who litter are real jerks") was superimposed directly over a piece of litter (retrieval cue) were significantly less likely to litter a paper towel in a stairwell several hours later than were those who saw the same wording placed elsewhere on the screen (see Figure 12.2). This was the case regardless of whether the retrieval cue featured in the PSA was a paper towel or a newspaper, suggesting that linking social disapproval to the basic category of litter was enough to elicit the desired change (Cialdini et al., 2007). Moreover, participants who saw the phrase "Americans will produce more litter than ever" superimposed on the litter were most likely to litter, demonstrating once again the potential harm caused by characterizing a behavior as regrettably common.

SOCIAL NORMS: INFLUENCES ON CONSUMPTION AND CONSERVATION BEHAVIORS

The Effect of Social Norms Marketing Campaigns

Should one conclude from the last finding that highlighting descriptive norms is always likely to be a counterproductive tactic in information campaigns? Not at all. In contrast to situations in which destructive behavior is prevalent, highlighting descriptive norms should be effective for those action domains in which less harmful or even beneficial behavior is prevalent. In keeping with this idea, more and more colleges each year have harnessed a concept called social norms marketing (Frauenfelder, 2001). In utilizing social norms marketing, a college campus might advertise results from a survey revealing that over 70% of students on campus have fewer than three drinks when they party.

Social norms marketing campaigns seek to reduce the occurrence of damaging behavior by correcting people's overestimations of the prevalence of that behavior. These campaigns are particularly popular on college campuses because students tend to overestimate the extent to which their peers abuse drugs and alcohol (Baer, Stacy, & Larimer, 1991; Borsari & Carey, 2003; Perkins & Berkowitz, 1986; Perkins & Wechsler, 1996; Prentice & Miller, 1993). Researchers consider this widespread misperception important because of the link between normative beliefs and the student's attitudes and behaviors (e.g., Clapp & McDonnell, 2000; Nagoshi, 1999; Perkins & Wechsler, 1996). Proponents of the plan have argued that if students learn that drug or alcohol abuse is less common than they had thought, they will be less likely to engage in that behavior themselves (Perkins, 2002).

Despite the wide adoption of social norms marketing campaigns, evidence for the success of these programs has been surprisingly mixed. Although many studies appear to confirm the effectiveness of the social marketing approach (e.g., Agostinelli, Brown, & Miller, 1995; Haines & Spear, 1996; Neighbors, Larimer, Lewis, 2004), other studies have failed to produce substantial changes in behavior (e.g., Clapp, Lange, Russell, Shillington, & Voas, 2003; Granfield, 2005; Peeler, Far, Miller, & Brigham, 2000; Russell, Clapp, DeJong, 2005; Werch, et al., 2000). In fact, some studies indicate that social norms marketing campaigns have actually *increased* the undesirable behaviors and misperceptions they set out to decrease (e.g., Perkins, Haines, & Rice, 2005; Wechsler, et al., 2003; Werch et al., 2000).

Unfortunately, very few studies that have investigated the effects of social norms have used control groups (Campo et al., 2003), and often it is impossible to isolate the effects of the social norms campaign from other concurrent programs and campaigns (Neighbors et al., 2004). A number of studies have found that these campaigns do correct the misperceptions but do not influence actual drinking behavior (e.g., Barnett, Far, Mauss, & Miller, 1996; Werch, et al., 2000).

Perhaps one reason that some studies examining the effectiveness of social norms campaigns report changes in perceptions but not parallel changes in behavior is that students are focused on the normative information when they are responding to the items on the questionnaire, but not when they are in settings that typically elicit that behavior. The results of the retrieval cue study described earlier suggest that if the descriptive norm is not in focus in settings in which these behaviors typically occur, the norms may be less effective or not effective at all at curbing the undesirable conduct. Posters, signs, and other forms of media conveying the campaign's normative message are commonly placed in libraries, classrooms, student unions, health centers, and in areas of residence halls other than the dorm rooms themselves. Although t¹ ᵢ accurate descriptive norm is quite likely to be in focus for the small minority ɔf individuals who consider getting inebriated during a visit to the university he ᵢth center or library, the remote voice of the normative appeal may be inaudible, drowned out by the loud music and the crowded drinking areas of bars, clubs, fraternity and sorority parties, and dorm rooms. Although difficult to arrange from a pragmatic standpoint, the foregoing analysis suggests that students' likelihood of focusing on the correct normative information in the appropriate settings could be strengthened by placing the campaign's logo on objects native to those settings (e.g., coasters, entrance bracelets, hand stamps).

The Constructive, Destructive, and Reconstructive Power of Social Norms

We noted earlier that several studies have shown that social norms marketing campaigns designed to curb college student alcohol consumption may have actually increased the undesirable perceptions and behaviors they set out to decrease in some cases. Why might this be? A close analysis of social norms theory and research provides a potential explanation for the lack of effects and affords for the possibility of backfire effects. As we have already discussed, descriptive norms provide a standard that people are motivated to follow. Because people tend to measure the appropriateness of their behavior by how far away they are from the norm or average, being deviant is being above *or* below the norm. Although it is the case that the majority of college students do overestimate the prevalence of alcohol consumption on campus (see Berkowitz, 2004, for a review), a substantial proportion of them actually *underestimate* its prevalence—as high as one-fifth by some estimates (e.g., Perkins et al., 2005) and nearly one-half by others (e.g., Wechsler & Kuo, 2000). Because these campaigns provide specific descriptive normative information that can serve as a comparison to an individual's own behavior, the descriptive norm may act as a magnet for behavior for those who consume above *and* below the average, whereby those who previously consumed less alcohol than the norm may be motivated to consume more. Thus, although providing descriptive normative information may decrease undesirable behaviors for individuals who perform such behavior at a rate above the norm, the same message may actually serve to *increase* the same undesirable behaviors for individuals who perform such behaviors at a rate below the norm.

This analysis raises an important question: If descriptive normative information can elicit such an undesirable and inadvertent backfire effect, is there a way to eliminate this problematic effect? As we discussed earlier, according to Focus Theory, if only one of the two types of norms is prominent in consciousness for individuals, it will direct their behavior accordingly (for a review, see Cialdini & Goldstein, 2004). Therefore, in situations in which descriptive normative information might normally produce an undesirable backfire effect, it is possible that adding an injunctive element to the message—in this case, one indicating that energy conservation is approved—might prevent the occurrence of the backfire effect.

Schultz, Nolan, Cialdini, Goldstein, and Griskevicius (2007) conducted a field experiment to investigate these hypotheses in the context of household residential energy consumption and conservation. In that study, the authors obtained permission from participating residents to read their energy meters at various times before, during, and after the intervention took place. After obtaining baseline energy usage measures, households were divided by examining whether their energy consumption level was either above or below that of the average household in the community at baseline. Next, all households received feedback about how much energy they had consumed in the prior week. However, half of the households were randomly assigned to receive information about the energy consumption of the average household in their neighborhood over the same period (the descriptive norm). In contrast, the other half of the households received the same descriptive normative information *and* an injunctive message conveying that their energy consumption level behavior was either approved or disapproved. Specifically, households that were consuming less than the average received a positively valenced emoticon (☺), whereas those that were consuming more than the average received a negatively valenced emoticon (☹). The dependent measure was residents' actual household energy consumption after the intervention.

The researchers had three major predictions, all of which were confirmed. First, for households consuming *more* energy than their neighborhood average, descriptive normative information alone *decreased* energy consumption—a result indicative of the constructive power of social norms, whereby descriptive normative information facilitated conservation rather than consumption behavior. Second, for households consuming *less* energy than their neighborhood average, descriptive normative information *increased* energy consumption—that is, actually produced an undesirable backfire effect. This result is indicative of the destructive power of social norms, whereby a well-intended application of normative information actually served to decrease conservation behaviors and increase consumption behaviors. Third, for the households consuming *less* energy than their neighborhood average, providing both descriptive normative information *and* an injunctive message that others approve of this low consumption behavior prevented the undesirable backfire effect from occurring; these households continued to consume energy at low rates. Such a result is indicative of the reconstructive power of the injunctive message to eliminate the untoward effects of the descriptive norm.

Rooms for Improvement: Using Normative Messages in a Hotel Setting

The investigation conducted by Schultz and colleagues (2007) is an example of how field research on consumer behavior can inform our understanding of basic social psychological processes. In a related line of research, Goldstein, Cialdini, & Griskevicius (2007; in press) set out to examine how field research in a different consumer setting—hotel rooms—might not only give us insight into basic social psychological processes, but perhaps also challenge aspects of an established theoretical perspective. We will return to this last point toward the end of this section. In the meantime, we will begin by focusing on some of the basic and applied aspects of that research.

Consistent with the theme of this chapter, the work conducted by Goldstein and colleagues focused on how to optimally motivate people to engage in energy and environmental conservation behaviors. Nearly everyone who has stayed in a hotel in the last few years has seen signs in their hotel rooms that urge guests to reuse their towels to help conserve environmental resources by saving energy and reducing the amount of detergent-related pollutants released into the environment. According to the company that supplies such cards to hoteliers, most guests will recycle at least one towel sometime during their stay, provided that they are asked to do so.

An informal survey of the messages conveyed by dozens of request cards from a wide variety of hotels revealed that the cards most frequently attempt to boost recycling efforts by focusing guests on either basic environmental protection or environmental cooperation (Cialdini & Goldstein, 2002). That is, guests are almost invariably informed that reusing one's towels will conserve energy and help save the environment. In addition, they are frequently told that towel reuse will allow them to become cooperating partners with the hotel in furthering its conservation efforts. To encourage such cooperation, guests may be told that the hotel will donate some of the savings from its towel reuse program to environmental causes. The hotels presumably expect this kind of appeal to increase recycling above the simple environmental protection appeal. Two other common but less pervasive types of messages are those appealing to guests' sense of social responsibility to future generations and those informing the guests of the substantial potential savings to the hotel, which implicitly might be interpreted as passing the savings onto its clientele in the long run.

Notable in its absence from these persuasive appeals was one based on social norms, particularly descriptive norms. One of the simplest (and most applied) hypotheses that Goldstein and colleagues (2007; in press) set out to test was that simply informing guests that the majority of their counterparts do reuse their towels when requested might enhance compliance rates. To examine that question, they placed cards with five conceptually different towel-recycling appeals in a large hotel in Arizona, where the room attendants were trained to record the relevant reuse data. All of the cards were identical in two respects. First, on the front, they informed guests that they could participate in the program by placing their used towels on the bathroom towel rack or curtain rod. Second, on the back, they provided information regarding the extent to which the environment would benefit and energy would be conserved if most guests participated in the program.

The cards differed, however, in the persuasive appeals designed to stimulate towel recycling. The five messages were chosen to reflect the purest forms of the four most common types of appeals the authors had observed in their informal survey, plus one message explicitly conveying the descriptive norm for towel recycling at that hotel. Each of the five signs communicated its message using a short headline in boldface and capital letters; additional text was located underneath that further explicated the appeal:

- One appeal focused guests on *environmental protection*: "HELP SAVE THE ENVIRONMENT. You can show your respect for nature and help save the environment by reusing your towels during your stay."
- A second type of card focused guests on *environmental cooperation*: "PARTNER WITH US TO HELP SAVE THE ENVIRONMENT. In exchange for your participation in this program, we at the hotel will donate a percentage of the energy savings to a nonprofit environmental protection organization. The environment deserves our combined efforts. You can join us by reusing your towels during your stay."
- A third type focused guests on the *benefit to the hotel*: "HELP THE HOTEL SAVE ENERGY. The hotel management is concerned about the

rising expense to the hotel of energy, labor, and other resources. You can help the hotel save energy by reusing your towels during your stay."

- A fourth type focused guests on *future generations*: "HELP SAVE RESOURCES FOR FUTURE GENERATIONS. Future generations deserve our concern. Please do your part to protect the environment and conserve dwindling resources for future generations to enjoy. You can help preserve these precious resources for all of us by reusing your towels during your stay."

- Finally, a fifth type of card focused guests on the *descriptive norms* of the situation: "JOIN YOUR FELLOW CITIZENS IN HELPING TO SAVE THE ENVIRONMENT. Almost 75% of guests who are asked to participate in our new resource savings program do help by using their towels more than once. You can join your fellow citizens in this program to help save the environment by reusing your towels during your stay."

The data revealed that the *benefit to the hotel* condition (15.6%), which contained neither an injunctive nor a descriptive component in its message, was least effective in stimulating towel reuse (see Figure 12.3). Compared to this message, the three messages containing an injunctive but no descriptive component (*environmental focus*, *cooperation focus*, and *future generations focus* conditions), which did not differ from one another, yielded enhanced compliance (an average of 30.2%). Most notably, the *descriptive norm focus* condition, which contained both an injunctive and descriptive component, fared best of all (34.8%). The authors noted two interesting aspects of the data. First, the most successful of the communications was one they had never seen employed in the wide range of such messages they had observed, which highlights the utility of employing social science research and theory rather than communicator hunches or best guesses in crafting persuasive appeals.

Second, in the *cooperation focus* condition, the hotel's pledge to donate to an environmental cause when its guests participated in the program did not increase recycling at all. Why not? Although there were several feasible explanations, the researchers posited that this condition failed to augment compliance rates because there is no injunctive norm obligating an influence target to cooperate with individuals who offer the target something only on the condition that the target performs a

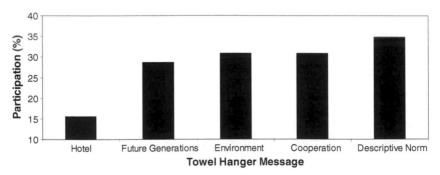

Figure 12.3   Towel Reuse Rates as Function of Sign in Room.

favor first. However, there is a powerful sense of social obligation in all societies—embodied in the injunctive norm of reciprocation (see Cialdini, 2001; Gouldner, 1960)—to cooperate with individuals who do something for the target first and then ask for a favor in return. This analysis suggests that the *cooperation focus* condition got the concept of cooperation right but the sequence wrong. Based on the literature, a better way to induce the desired response would be for the hotel to give the donation first and then ask guests to cooperate in this effort by conserving resources (see Berry & Kanouse, 1987; Church, 1993; James & Bolstein, 1992). To test this idea, Goldstein and colleagues (2007) conducted a second study, this time at a different local hotel. In addition to the *environmental* focus and *cooperation focus* appeals, the researchers included a *reciprocation norm* focus appeal. It stated, "WE'RE DOING OUR PART FOR THE ENVIRONMENT. CAN WE COUNT ON YOU? Because we are committed to preserving the environment, we have made a financial contribution to a nonprofit environmental protection organization on behalf of the hotel and its guests. If you would like to help us in recovering the expense, while conserving natural resources, please reuse your towels during your stay." The data revealed a significant advantage for the *reciprocation focus* condition (45.2%) over the *environmental focus* condition (35.1%) and more important, the *cooperation focus* (30.7%) condition (see Figure 12.4). This finding serves as a reminder that a relatively minor change, informed by social psychological theory, can serve as a corrective to existing practices that are misguided.

Let us return to the results of the first hotel study with an eye toward how well they fit with the social identity/self-categorization perspective. Goldstein and colleagues (2007) found the highest participation rate with the message informing the guests that the overwhelming majority of others do in fact participate in the program when given the opportunity. But recall that the message asked them to join their "fellow citizens" in this act of environmental protection. Because the wording of the sign in the descriptive norm focus condition may have caused participants to spontaneously categorize themselves as either citizens in general or American citizens in particular (both are categories that seem meaningful and likely to engender strong identification), the extent to which self-categorization processes contributed to the enhanced compliance rates is not clear. If self-categorization processes did in fact contribute to the more favorable compliance rates, the authors reasoned that it

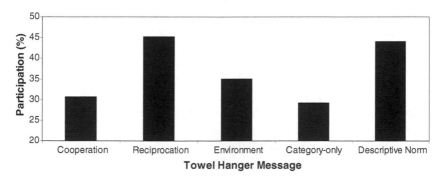

Figure 12.4   Towel Reuse Rates as Function of Sign in Room.

could have done so via two separate mechanisms. First, it is possible that once the category of *citizen* was made salient to the participants, they were more likely to follow the externally supplied descriptive norm of that category. Second, it is possible that once the category of citizen was made salient to the participants, they were more likely to reuse their towels because they were following the norms implicit to being a good citizen (e.g., social roles). In this second scenario, the enhanced compliance rates could have occurred even if the descriptive normative information provided by the message had no effect whatsoever on the participants.

To address some of these questions, Goldstein and colleagues (2007) added two conditions to the three (*environmental focus, cooperative focus, reciprocation norm focus*) already described for the second study:

- The *category-only focus* condition was an appeal that was designed to activate the category of American citizen, but did not provide any descriptive normative information: "HELP SAVE OUR COUNTRY'S NATURAL RESOURCES. We think it is important for American citizens to act to preserve this country's environment. You can help save America's natural resources by reusing your towels during your stay."
- The *descriptive norm focus* condition used the exact same wording as in Study 1, except that references to the term *citizen* were removed and replaced with the term *guest*: "JOIN YOUR FELLOW GUESTS IN HELPING TO SAVE THE ENVIRONMENT. Almost 75% of guests who are asked to participate in our new resource savings program do help by using their towels more than once. You can join your fellow guests in this program to help save the environment by reusing your towels during your stay."

Two findings are notable (see Figure 12.4). First, similar to the findings of Study 1, the *descriptive norm focus* condition yielded a significantly higher towel reuse rate (44.1%) than both of the two most common types of appeals, the *environmental focus* (35.1%) and the *cooperation focus* (30.7%) appeals.[1] Second, the towel reuse rates were significantly higher in the *descriptive norm focus* condition than in the *category-only focus* condition (29.2%). Because the message conveying the descriptive norm did not reference a particularly meaningful group or category, yet was still successful, the authors concluded that there was little evidence to suggest that the relative success achieved by the *descriptive norm focus* condition in Study 1 was due to self-categorization processes. Furthermore, the relative failure of the *category-only focus* condition to boost compliance rates beyond the standard signs indicated to the authors that making a meaningful social identity salient without additional descriptive normative information appeared to be ineffective. Thus, compared to the more traditional messages, the *descriptive norm focus* condition that did not use a meaningful social category (from Study 2) appeared to be as effective as the descriptive norm focus condition that used a meaningful social category (from Study 1). However, the two could not be directly compared to one another because they were not employed concurrently within the same study.

The researchers were also interested in investigating whether such normative effects might be mediated by the extent to which the hotel visitors perceived that they shared a unit relationship with members of the salient reference group (Heider, 1958). Heider (1958) suggested that meaningful similarities engender strong feelings of association between a person and another entity, but that minor and irrelevant similarities can create an effect of similar magnitude (see Burger, Messian, Patel, del Prado, & Anderson, 2004). Moreover, to keep in a state of balance, individuals might be driven to change their attitudes or behavior in accordance with the entity with which they share a unit relationship. In their study of intergroup relations, Henri Tajfel, who was one of the founders of social identity theory, and his colleagues (e.g., Tajfel, Billig, Bundy, & Flament, 1971) demonstrated in the minimal group paradigm that arbitrary similarities foster ingroup cohesion. Yet, Ellemers and colleagues (2002) noted that individuals' commitments to these minimal groups are low estimates of people's real-world commitments to and identification with real groups because these groups are less meaningful than real groups. Similarly, social identity and self-categorization researchers often emphasize that the more meaningful a reference group is, the more an individual's behavior is likely to be in line with the behavioral norms of that group (e.g., Ellemers et al., 2002; Terry et al., 1999).

Goldstein and colleagues (2007) sought to examine whether hotel guests might be more likely to follow the norms of personally meaningless groups than those of personally meaningful groups under one particular circumstance: when the norms of the meaningless group provide a much closer connection to their immediate surroundings than the norms of the more meaningful group. To explore this issue, they conducted a third hotel study that used five different messages. One was the standard *environmental focus* condition. The second and third conditions were the two *descriptive norm focus* conditions used in Study 1 and Study 2; that is, one used the *citizen* terminology and the other used the *guest* terminology. The fourth condition allowed the researchers to pair the descriptive norm with a meaningful category more commonly utilized in social identity and self-categorization research—gender (e.g., Bardach & Park, 1996; Maccoby, 1988; Swan & Wyer, 1997; White et al., 2002). The message for the *gender-based descriptive norm focus* condition stated, "JOIN THE MEN AND WOMEN WHO ARE HELPING TO SAVE THE ENVIRONMENT. In a study conducted in Fall 2003, 76% of the women and 74% of the men participated in our new resource savings program by using their towels more than once. You can join the other men and women in this program to help save the environment by reusing your towels during your stay." The message in the fifth condition was designed to use a completely arbitrary and meaningless similarity between the reference group and the participants to create the feeling of a shared unit relationship: those who had previously stayed in the same room as the participant. The message for the *unit-based descriptive norm focus* condition stated, "JOIN YOUR FELLOW GUESTS IN HELPING TO SAVE THE ENVIRONMENT. In a study conducted in Fall 2003, 75% of the guests who stayed in this room (#xxx) participated in our new resource savings program by using their towels more than once. You can join your fellow guests in this

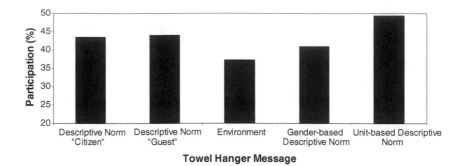

Figure 12.5 Towel Reuse Rates as Function of Sign in Room.

program to help save the environment by reusing your towers during your stay."
(Note, for example, that "#xxx" would read "#313" for Room 313.)

In addition to showing once again that the signs conveying the descriptive norm were more effective than the standard environmental appeal, the researchers found that the sign characterizing the norms of the least personally meaningful reference group elicited greater participation in the conservation program (49.3%) than the signs characterizing the norms of the much more personally meaningful reference groups (the other three descriptive norm conditions yielded 42.8%; see Figure 12.5).[2]

These findings are not entirely consistent with a key prediction of social identity and self-categorization theories—that people should be more likely to follow group norms when the reference group is personally meaningful to them.[3] These results also suggest that researchers going forward should consider focusing greater attention on the role that *situational* similarities (e.g., the same immediate environment), rather than *personal* similarities (e.g., belonging to the same social category), play in influencing adherence to social norms. A close inspection of the normative social identity literature and of the body of research examining the role of similarity on norm adherence reveals that both research areas have focused almost exclusively on the importance of commonalities between personal, rather than contextual, characteristics of individuals and the groups whose behaviors they observe (Goldstein et al., in press). That is, these literatures examine how personal similarities (e.g., in attitudes, gender, ethnicity, age, values) between a target individual and a group of people influence the target's adherence to the group's social norms. Future research further investigating the largely ignored role of *situational* similarities in norm adherence would be welcome.

SUMMARY AND CONCLUSION

In this chapter, we reviewed the social psychological literature on how social norms motivate and guide human action, concentrating primarily on how the results of field experiments inform and are informed by the focus theory of normative conduct and by the social identity literature. We then shifted to how social psychological theories and findings in the domain of social norms contribute to the understanding of consumer behavior, focusing primarily on descriptive norms (what most people do) and injunctive norms (what most people approve or disapprove). Specifically, we detailed how the proper use of such norms, including the norm of reciprocity, can motivate consumers to behave in ways that conserve, rather than consume, environmental resources. Finally, we pointed to the ways in which the study of normative influences on consumer behavior can help advance social psychological theory in the process.

In sum, we have shown how consumer research and basic social psychological research can inform and challenge each other, and we fully expect that the influence that the two fields have on one another will continue to grow.

ENDNOTES

1. We hasten to note that at first glance, there appears to be an important shortcoming to the descriptive normative approach. Specifically, we informed participants that a large majority (75%) of the hotel's guests participated in the towel reuse program—a number provided by the company that supplies such cards to hoteliers—yet the best-performing message yielded a towel reuse rate that did not even reach 50%. There are two reasons for this discrepancy that render this a less worrisome problem. First, in keeping with the data reported by the towel hanger suppliers, the signs in our study informed the guests that the majority of individuals recycled at least one towel sometime during their stay. Because we examined towel reuse data only for participants' first eligible day, the compliance rate we observed is likely an underestimation of the number of individuals who recycle their towels at least once during their stay. Second, we used the most conservative standards for counting compliance; that is, we did not count as a reuse effort a towel that was hung on a door hook or doorknob—a very common practice for towel recyclers who misunderstand or do not thoroughly read the instructions—as we wanted to eliminate the likelihood of guests complying unintentionally with the request. Thus, the overall percentage of towel reuse was artificially suppressed.
2. In a separate test, we found that individuals reported that their identity as a hotel guest in a particular room was significantly less important to them than their identity as a citizen, a male or female, or a hotel guest in general.
3. We should note, however, that it is possible that had we used reference groups that are even more meaningful to hotel guests than those based on citizenship or gender, the results might have turned out more in favor of the social identity and self-categorization perspectives.

REFERENCES

Aarts, H., & Dijksterhuis, A. (2003). The silence of the library: Environment, situational norm and social behavior. *Journal of Personality and Social Psychology, 84*, 18–28.

Abrams, D., & Hogg, M. A. (1990). Social identification, self-categorization, and social influence. *European Review of Social Psychology, 1*, 195–228.

Agostinelli, G., Brown, J. M., & Miller, W. R. (1995). Effects of normative feedback on consumption among heavy drinking college students. *Journal of Drug Education, 25*, 31–40.

Baer, J. S., Stacy, A., & Larimer, M. (1991). Biases in the perception of drinking norms among college students. *Journal of Studies on Alcohol, 52*, 580–586.

Bandura, A. (1977). *Social learning theory*. New York: General Learning Press.

Bardach, L., & Park, B. (1996). The effect of in-group/out-group status on memory for consistent and inconsistent behavior of an individual. *Personality and Social Psychology Bulletin, 22*, 169–178.

Barnett, L. A., Far, J. M., Mauss, A. L., & Miller, J. A. (1996). Changing perceptions of peer norms as a drinking reduction program for college students. *Journal of Alcohol and Drug Education, 41*, 39–62.

Bearden, W. O., & Etzel, M. J. (1982). Reference group influence on product and brand purchase decisions. *Journal of Consumer Research, 9*, 183–194.

Berkowitz, L. (1972). Social norms, feelings, and other factors affecting helping and altruism. In L. Berkowitz (Ed.), *Advances in experimental social psychology* (Vol. 6, 63–108). San Diego, CA: Academic Press.

Berkowitz, A.D. (2004). An overview of the social norms approach. In L. Lederman & L. Stewart (Eds.), Changing the culture of college drinking (pp. 193–214). Cresskill, NJ: Hampton Press.

Berry, S. H., & Kanouse, D. E. (1987). Physician response to a mailed survey: An experiment in timing of payment. *Public Opinion Quarterly, 51*, 102–114.

Blanton, H., & Christie, C. (2003). Deviance regulation: A theory of action and identity. *Review of General Psychology, 7*, 115–149.

Blanton, H., Stuart, A. E., & VandenEijnden, R. J. J. M. (2001). An introduction to deviance-regulation theory: The effect of behavioral norms on message framing. *Personality and Social Psychology Bulletin, 27*, 848–858.

Blanton, H., VandenEijnden, R. J. J. M., Buunk, B. P., Gibbons, F. X., Gerrard, M., & Bakker, A. (2001). Accentuate the negative: Social images in the prediction and promotion of condom use. *Journal of Applied Social Psychology, 31*, 274–295.

Borsari, B., & Carey, K. B. (2003). Descriptive and injunctive norms in college drinking: A meta-analytic integration. *Journal of Studies on Alcohol, 64*, 331–341.

Brewer, M. (2003). Optimal distinctiveness, social identity, and the self. In M. R. Leary & J. P. Tangney (Eds.) *Handbook of self and identity* (pp. 480–491). New York: Guilford Press.

Brewer, M. B. (2001). The many faces of social identity: Implications for political psychology: *Political Psychology, 22*, 115–125.

Brewer, M. B., & Roccas, S. (2001). Individual values, social identity, and optimal distinctiveness. In C. Sedikides & M. Brewer (Eds.), *Individual self, relational self, collective self* (pp. 219–237). Philadelphia: Psychology Press.

Burger, J. M., Messian, N., Patel, S., del Prado, A., & Anderson, C. (2004). What a coincidence! The effects of incidental similarity on compliance. *Personality and Social Psychology Bulletin, 30*, 35–43.

Burnkrant, R. E., & Cousineau, A. (1975). Informational and normative social influence in buyer behavior. *Journal of Consumer Research, 2*, 206–215.

Campo, S., Brossard, D., Frazer, M. S., Marchell, T., Lewis, D., & Talbot, J. (2003). Are social norms campaigns really magic bullets? Assessing the effects of students' misperceptions on drinking behavior. *Health Communication, 15*, 481–497.

Carver, C. S., & Scheier, M. F. (1978). Self-focusing effects of dispositional self-consciousness, mirror presence, and audience presence. *Journal of Personality and Social Psychology, 36*, 324–332.

Church, A. H. (1993). Estimating the effects of incentives on mail survey response rates: A meta-analysis. *Public Opinion Quarterly, 57*, 62–79.

Cialdini, R. B. (2001). *Influence: Science and practice* (4th ed.) Needham Heights, MA: Allyn & Bacon.

Cialdini, R. B. (2003). Crafting normative messages to protect the environment. *Current Directions in Psychological Science, 12*, 105–109.

Cialdini, R. B., Barrett, D. W., Bator, R., Demaine, L., Sagarin, B. J., Rhoads, K. v. L., & Winter, P. L. (2007). *Activating and aligning social norms for persuasive impact.* Manuscript in preparation.

Cialdini, R. B., Demaine, L. J., Sagarin, B. J., Barrett, D. W., Rhoads, K. v. K., & Winter, P. L. (2006). Managing social norms for persuasive impact. *Social Influence, 1*, 3–15.

Cialdini, R. B., & Goldstein, N. J. (2004). Social influence: Compliance and conformity. *Annual Review of Psychology, 55*, 591–622.

Cialdini, R. B., & Goldstein, N. J. (2002). The science and practice of persuasion. *Cornell Hotel and Restaurant Administration Quarterly, 43*, 40–50.

Cialdini, R. B., Kallgren, C. A., & Reno, R. R. (1991). A focus theory of normative conduct: A theoretical refinement and reevaluation of the role of norms in human behavior. In L. Berkowitz (Ed.), *Advances in experimental social psychology* (Vol. 24, pp. 201–234). San Diego, CA: Academic Press.

Cialdini, R. B., Reno, R. R., & Kallgren, C. A. (1990). A focus theory of normative conduct: Recycling the concept of norms to reduce littering in public places. *Journal of Personality and Social Psychology, 58*, 1015–1026.

Cialdini, R. B., & Trost, M. R. (1998). Social influence: Social norms, conformity, and compliance. In D. T. Gilbert, S. T. Fiske, & G. Lindzey (Eds.), *The handbook of social psychology* (Vol II, pp. 151–192). Boston, MA: McGraw-Hill.

Clapp, J. D., Lange, J. E., Russell, C., Shillington, A., & Voas, R. (2003). A failed norms social marketing campaign. *Journal of Studies on Alcohol, 64*, 409–414.

Clapp, J. D., & McDonnell, A. L. (2000). The relationship of perceptions of alcohol promotion and peer drinking norms to alcohol problems reported by college students. *Journal of College Student Development, 41*, 19–26.

Collins, S. E., Carey, K. B., & Sliwinski, M. J. (2002). Mailed personalized normative feedback as a brief intervention for at-risk college drinkers. *Journal of Studies on Alcohol, 63*, 559–567.

Darley, J. M., & Latané, B. (1970). Norms and normative behavior: Field studies of social interdependence. In J. Macaulay & L. Berkowitz (Eds.), *Altruism and helping behavior* (pp. 83–102). New York: Academic Press.

DeJong, W., & Linkenbach, J. (1999). Telling it like it is: Using social norms marketing campaigns to reduce student drinking. *American Association of Higher Education Bulletin, 32*, 11–16.

Deshpande, R., Hoyer, W. D., & Donthu, N. (1986). The intensity of ethnic affiliation: A study of the sociology of Hispanic consumption. *Journal of Consumer Research, 13*, 214–220.

Deutsch, M., & Gerard, H. B. (1955). A study of normative and informational social influences upon individual judgment. *Journal of Abnormal and Social Psychology, 51*, 629–636.

Ditto, P. H., & Griffin, J. (1993). The value of uniqueness: Self-evaluation and the perceived prevalence of valenced characteristics. *Journal of Social Behavior and Personality, 8*, 221–240.

Duval, S., & Wicklund, R. A. (1972). *A theory of objective self-awareness.* New York: Academic Press.

Ellemers, N., Spears, R., & Doosje, B. (2002). Self and social identity. *Annual Review of Psychology, 53*, 161–186.

Fishbein, M. & Ajzen, I. (1975). *Belief, attitude, intention, and behavior.* Reading, MA: Addison-Wesley.

Frauenfelder, M. (2001, December 9). Social-norms marketing. *New York Times Magazine*, p. 100.

Goldstein, N. J., Cialdini, R. B., & Griskevicius, V. (2007). Unpublished data.

Goldstein, N. J., Cialdini, R. B., & Griskevicius, V. (in press). A room with a viewpoint: Using social norms to motivate environmental conservation in hotels. *Journal of Consumer Research*.

Gouldner, A. W. (1960). The norm of reciprocity: A preliminary statement. *American Sociological Review, 25*, 161–178.

Granfield, R. (2005). Alcohol use in college: Limitations on the transformation of social norms. *Addiction Research and Theory, 13*, 281–292.

Haines, M. P., & Spear, S. F. (1996). Changing the perception of the norm: A strategy to decrease binge drinking among college students. *Journal of American College Health, 45*, 134–140.

Heider, F. (1958). *The psychology of interpersonal relations*. New York: Wiley.

Hochbaum, G. M. (1954). The relation between group members' self-confidence and their reactions to group pressures to uniformity. *American Sociological Review, 19*, 678–687.

Hogg, M. A. (2003). Social identity. In M. R. Leary & J. P. Tangney (Eds.), *Handbook of self and identity* (pp. 462–479). New York, The Guilford Press.

Hogg, M. A., & Abrams, D. (1988). *Social identifications. A social psychology of intergroup relations and group processes*. London: Routledge.

James, J. M., & Bolstein, R. (1992). Large monetary incentives and their effect on mail survey response rates. *Public Opinion Quarterly, 56*, 442–453.

Kallgren, C. A., Reno, R. R., & Cialdini, R. B. (2000). A focus theory of normative conduct: When norms do and do not affect behavior. *Personality and Social Psychology Bulletin, 26*, 1002–1012.

Kerr, N. L. (1995). Norms in social dilemmas. In D. Schroeder (Ed.), *Social dilemmas: Perspectives on individuals and groups* (pp. 31–48). Westport, CT: Praeger.

Kim H. S., & Markus H. R. (1999). Deviance or uniqueness, harmony or conformity? A cultural analysis. *Journal of Personality and Social Psychology, 77*, 785–800.

Kleine, R. E., Klein, S. S., & Kernan, J. B. (1993). Mundane consumption and the self: A social identity perspective. *Journal of Consumer Psychology, 2*, 209–235.

Maccoby, E. M. (1988). Gender as a social category. *Developmental Psychology, 24*, 755–765.

McGuire, W. J., McGuire, C. V., Child, P., & Fujioka, T. (1978). Salience of ethnicity in the spontaneous self-concept as a function of one's ethnic distinctiveness in the social environment. *Journal of Personality and Social Psychology, 36*, 511–520.

Moschis, G. P. (1976). Social comparison and informal group influence. *Journal of Marketing Research, 13*, 237–244.

Nagoshi, C. T. (1999). Perceived control of drinking and other predictors of alcohol use and problems in a college student sample. *Addiction Research, 7*, 291–306.

Nail P. R., MacDonald G., & Levy D. A. (2000). Proposal of a four-dimensional model of social response. *Psychological Bulletin, 126*, 454–470.

Neighbors, C., Larimer, M. E., & Lewis, M. A. (2004). Targeting misperceptions of descriptive drinking norms: Efficacy of a computer delivered personalized normative feedback intervention. *Journal of Consulting and Clinical Psychology, 72*, 434–447.

Nelson, L. J., & Miller, D. T. (1995). The distinctiveness effect in social categorization: You are what makes you unusual. *Psychological Science, 6*, 246–249.

Park, C. W., & Lessig, P. V. (1977). Students and housewives: Differences in susceptibility to reference group influence. *Journal of Consumer Research, 4*, 102–110.

Peeler, C.M., Far, J., Miller, J., & Brigham, T.A. (2000). An analysis of the effects of a program to reduce heavy drinking among college students. *Journal of Alcohol and Drug Education, 45*, 39–54.

Perkins, H. W. (2002). Social norms and the prevention of alcohol misuse in collegiate contexts. *Journal of Studies on Alcohol, Supplement 14*, 164–172.

Perkins, H. W. (Ed.) (2003). *The social norms approach to preventing school and college age substance abuse: A handbook for educators, counselors, and clinicians.* San Francisco: Jossey-Bass.

Perkins, H. W., & Berkowitz, A. D. (1986). Perceiving the community norms of alcohol use among students: Some research implications for campus alcohol education programming. *The International Journal of the Addictions, 21*, 961–976.

Perkins, H. W., Haines, M. P., & Rice, R. (2005). Misperceiving the college drinking norm and related problems: A nationwide study of exposure to prevention information, perceived norms and student alcohol misuse. *Journal of Studies on Alcohol, 66*, 470–478.

Perkins, H. W., & Wechsler, H. (1996). Variation in perceived college drinking norms and its impact on alcohol abuse: A nationwide study. *Journal of Drug Issues, 26*, 961–974.

Pool G. J., Wood W., & Leck K. (1998). The self-esteem motive in social influence: Agreement with valued majorities and disagreement with derogated minorities. *Journal of Personality and Social Psychology, 75*, 967–975.

Prentice, D. A., & Miller, D. T. (1993). Pluralistic ignorance and alcohol use on campus: Some consequences of misperceiving the social norm. *Journal of Personality and Social Psychology, 64*, 243–256.

Reed, A. (2004). Activating the self-importance of consumer selves: Exploring identity salience effects on judgments. *Journal of Consumer Research, 31*, 286–295.

Reno, R. R., Cialdini, R. B., & Kallgren, C. A. (1993). The transsituational influence of social norms. *Journal of Personality and Social Psychology, 64*, 104–112.

Russell, C., Clapp, J. D., & DeJong, W. (2005). "Done 4": Analysis of a failed social norms marketing campaign. *Health Communication, 17*, 57–65.

Schultz, P. W. (1999). Changing behavior with normative feedback interventions: A field experiment on curbside recycling. *Basic and Applied Social Psychology, 21*, 25–38.

Schultz, P. W., Nolan, J. M., Cialdini, R. B., Goldstein, N. J., & Griskevicius, V. (2007). The constructive, destructive, and reconstructive power of social norms. *Psychological Science, 18*, 429–434.

Schwartz, S. H. (1973). Normative explanations of helping behavior: A critique, proposal, and empirical test. *Journal of Experimental Social Psychology, 9*, 349–364.

Schwartz, S. H. (1977). Normative influences in altruism. In L. Berkowitz (Ed.), *Advances in experimental social psychology* (Vol. 10, pp. 221–279). San Diego, CA: Academic Press.

Scott, W. (1995, December 24). Personality parade. *Parade Magazine*, p. 2.

Shaffer, L. S. (1983). Toward Pepitone's vision of a normative social psychology: What is a social norm? *Journal of Mind and Behavior, 4*, 275–294.

Sherif, M. (1936). *The psychology of social norms.* New York: Harper.

Stayman, D. M., & Deshpande, R. (1989). Situational ethnicity and consumer behavior. *Journal of Consumer Research, 16*, 361–371.

Swan, S., & Wyer, R. S. (1997). Gender stereotypes and social identity: How being in the minority affects judgment of self and others. *Personality and Social Psychology Bulletin, 23*, 1265–1276.

Tajfel, H. (1978). *Differentiation between social groups: Studies in the social psychology of intergroup relations.* New York: Academic.

Tajfel, H., Billig, M. G., Bundy, R. P., & Flament, C. (1971). Social categorization and intergroup behavior. *European Journal of Social Psychology, 1*, 149–178.

Tajfel H., & Turner J. (1979). An integrative theory of intergroup conflict. In W. G. Austin & S. Worchel (Eds.), *The social psychology of intergroup relations* (pp. 33–48). Monterey, CA: Brooks-Cole.

Terry, D. J., & Hogg, M. A. (1996). Group norms and the attitude-behaviour relationship: A role for group identification. *Personality and Social Psychology Bulletin, 22,* 776–793.

Terry, D. J., & Hogg. M. A. (2000). *Attitudes, behavior, and social context: The role of norms and group membership.* Mahwah, NJ: Lawrence Erlbaum Associates.

Terry, D. J., Hogg, M. A., & White, K. M. (1999). The theory of planned behaviour: Self-identity, social identity, and group norms. *British Journal of Social Psychology, 38,* 225–244.

Terry, D. J., Hogg, M. A., & White, K. M. (2000). Attitude-behavior relations: Social identity and group membership. In D. J. Terry & M. A. Hogg (Eds.), *Attitudes, behavior, and social context: The role of norms and group membership* (pp. 67–93). Mahwah, NJ: Erlbaum.

The fifty greatest TV commercials of all time. (1999, July 3–9). *TV Guide,* pp. 2–34.

Tulving, E. (1983). *Elements of episodic memory.* New York: Oxford University Press.

Turner, J. C. (1987). A self-categorization theory. In J. C. Turner, M. A. Hogg, P. H. Oakes, S. D. Reicher, & M. S. Wetherell (Eds.), *Rediscovering the social group: A self-categorization theory* (pp. 42–67). Oxford: Blackwell.

Turner, J. C. (1991). *Social influence.* Milton Keynes: Open University Press.

Turner, J. C. (1999). Some current issues in research on social identity and self-categorization theories. In N. Ellemers, R. Spears, & B. Doosje (Eds.), *Social identity: Context, commitment, content* (pp. 6–34). Oxford, UK: Blackwell.

Turner J. C., Hogg, M. A., Oakes P. J., Reicher, S. D., & Wetherell M. S. (Eds.) (1987). *Rediscovering the social group: A self-categorization theory.* Oxford: Blackwell.

Wechsler, H., & Kuo, M. (2000). College students define binge drinking and estimate its prevalence: Results of a national survey. *Journal of American College Health, 49,* 57–60.

Wechsler, H., Nelson, T., Lee, J. E., Seiberg, M., Lewis, C., & Keeling, R. (2003). Perception and reality: A national evaluation of social norms marketing interventions to reduce college students' heavy alcohol use. *Quarterly Journal of Studies on Alcohol, 64,* 484–494.

Werch, C. E., Pappas, D. M., Carlson, J. M., DiClemente, C. C., Chally, P. S., & Sinder, J. A. (2000). Results of a social intervention to prevent binge drinking among first-year residential college students. *Journal of American College Health, 49,* 85–92.

White, K. M., Hogg, M. A & Terry, D. J. (2002). Improving attitude-behavior correspondence through exposure to normative support from a salient ingroup. *Basic and Applied Social Psychology, 24,* 91–103.

13

Taking the Target's Perspective
The Persuasion Knowledge Model

AMNA KIRMANI

University of Maryland

MARGARET C. CAMPBELL

University of Colorado

*I*n 1994, Friestad and Wright coined the term *persuasion knowledge* to refer to people's intuitive theories about how marketers try to persuade consumers. The Persuasion Knowledge Model (PKM) depicts the persuasion target as an active participant in a dyadic interaction with a persuasion agent, in which both target and agent are attempting to achieve their own goals. The PKM views marketplace interaction as a game between buyer and seller, assumes that consumers have intuitive theories about the game, and asserts that these theories are used to evaluate and cope with marketers' persuasion attempts.

The strong emphasis on the perspective of the target of persuasion distinguishes the PKM from many other models of persuasion. Research on persuasion in both consumer and social psychology has historically focused on the perspective of the persuader. The emphasis has been on how to gain compliance from a target, how to design messages that induce attitude change in the direction of the message sender, and how to use opinion leaders and reference groups to effect change (See, for example, Goldstein & Cialdini, this volume, as well as the volume *The Science of Social Influence* in the *Frontiers* series). Even the literature on resistance to persuasion primarily follows the influencer's perspective, with an emphasis on how to overcome resistance (Knowles & Linn, 2004a).

More recently, however, social psychologists have begun to pay greater attention to the target of persuasion. Researchers in a variety of resistance contexts (e.g., forewarning, Wood & Quinn, 2003; metacognitions, Tormala & Petty, 2002;

Tormala, Clarkson, & Petty, 2006; and illusion of vulnerability, Sagarin, Cialdini, Rice, & Serna, 2002) have begun to ask questions about the goals, cognitions, and behaviors of targets of persuasion. These questions and their underlying perspective are consistent with the PKM.

In this chapter, we describe the Persuasion Knowledge Model, present the findings of research based on persuasion knowledge, and suggest ways in which the PKM may be applied to other psychological contexts. The basic thesis of the chapter is that the perspective of the target advocated by the PKM allows important insights into the study of persuasion in both consumer behavior and social psychology. Although the PKM was developed within the context of consumers, it is a general framework that can be applied to any persuasion interaction. Therefore, it may benefit social psychologists to understand the concept of persuasion knowledge as well as the research stream that it has generated to provide an alternative view that may provide new insights.

THE PERSUASION KNOWLEDGE MODEL

Figure 13.1 shows the persuasion knowledge model. The PKM stresses that influence is a dyadic interaction between the persuasion agent and target in which the participants have three types of knowledge: topic knowledge (i.e., the issue or content), agent knowledge (i.e., of the other party), and persuasion knowledge (i.e., how persuasion occurs). The agent's persuasion knowledge is combined with topic and target knowledge to attempt to influence the persuasion target. Similarly, the target's persuasion knowledge is combined with agent and content knowledge to enable targets to "cope with" persuasion attempts. The PKM points out that consumers' persuasion knowledge is critical to how consumers make sense of and respond to marketing efforts and can be used in a variety of ways to help consumers achieve their own goals within the situation.

Persuasion knowledge consists of theories and beliefs about how persuasion agents attempt to persuade, including beliefs about marketers' motives, strategies, and tactics; beliefs about the effects of persuasion tactics and the appropriateness of tactics; beliefs about psychological mediators of persuasion; and strategies to respond to others' influence attempts. Persuasion knowledge may be either a chronic, individual difference variable (Bearden, Hardesty, & Rose, 2001) or a situationally induced variable that can be accessed in a variety of persuasion interactions.

Agent knowledge has to do with the consumer's thoughts and beliefs about the persuasion agent, e.g., the agent's traits, abilities, motives, and goals. This can include general stereotype knowledge, for example, "car salespeople are pushy" (Sujan, Bettman, & Sujan, 1986), or specific knowledge about a particular agent, for example, "Suzie knows a lot about gourmet food and can be trusted to give me a good recommendation." Topic knowledge is composed of the beliefs that the consumer has about a particular topic, e.g., "this digital camera is outdated," or "this brand is known for its toughness." Consumers' persuasion knowledge is expected to interact with their (nonpersuasion) agent knowledge and topic knowledge to shape persuasion interactions and influence responses to persuasion attempts. Although earlier models of persuasion include some components of agent and topic knowledge (e.g.,

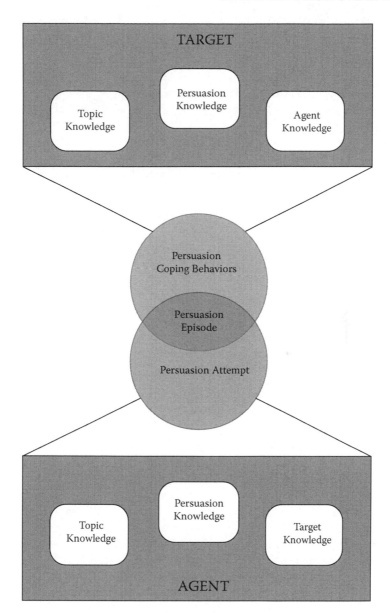

Figure 13.1   The Persuasion Knowledge Model.

consideration of source characteristics, such as credibility and trustworthiness, as well as consideration of issue familiarity or expertise; Petty & Cacioppo, 1986; Eagly & Chaiken, 1993; Kruglanski & Thompson, 1999), the existence and role of persuasion knowledge had not been much considered prior to the PKM (see Friestad & Wright, 1994, for further discussion). Thus, most of the research in the PKM stream has focused on understanding consumers' persuasion knowledge and theories and beliefs about how persuasion agents attempt to influence consumers' responses.

A few aspects of the PKM are important to note. First, the PKM examines a persuasion attempt from the consumer target's point of view, and the consumer's perception that something is an attempt to persuade is central to the theory. Second, the theory is neutral as to whether a consumer's persuasion knowledge is accurate. It does not matter whether a consumer has correctly identified an attempt to persuade, nor does it matter whether the consumer's beliefs about how the marketer is trying to persuade are correct. Rather, the focus of research is on understanding how the consumer's beliefs about persuasion influence the ways in which the consumer responds. Finally, the PKM proposes that consumers have their own goals within persuasion interactions and that they "cope" with persuasion in order to attempt to maintain control and achieve their goals.

In the next section, we describe the content of persuasion knowledge in more detail. We focus on some major areas that have been researched in consumer behavior: inferring a persuasion agent's motives, understanding persuasion tactics, consideration of persuasion effectiveness, consideration of appropriateness, consideration of marketing effort, coping responses, and persuasion knowledge as an individual difference variable.

Inferring a Persuasion Agent's Motives

A consumer must draw upon his or her persuasion knowledge in order to decide whether something is a persuasion attempt (e.g., Friestad & Wright, 1994). When a consumer notices something in his/her environment, she/he needs to compare it to knowledge stored in memory to determine whether someone is trying to exert influence. Thus, one of the fundamental uses of persuasion knowledge is to make inferences of motive (Campbell & Kirmani, 2000). Consumers will sometimes infer whether there is a persuasion motive behind an action (e.g., is this person offering to buy me a drink because she is friendly or because she is being paid by the drinks company?). Under certain conditions, a consumer will try to infer finer level motives (e.g., is the salesperson telling me I look good in the dress because she really thinks this dress is better on me or because she wants me to buy the more expensive dress?).

Research shows that inferences of motive involve some level of cognitive effort. For example, consumers are more likely to make inferences of persuasion motive when they have cognitive capacity and accessibility of motives is high (Campbell & Kirmani, 2000). The flip side of this is that consumers are relatively unlikely to consider the motives for the marketer's behaviors when cognitive capacity is constrained (e.g., the consumer is cognitively busy) or when the concept of persuasion motive is inaccessible (e.g., a persuasion tactic is not recognized). Campbell and Kirmani (2000) demonstrated that activation and use of persuasion knowledge requires higher order, attributional thinking. The research indicates that consumers appear to need both ability and motivation to make inferences about another's persuasion and are less likely to use persuasion knowledge in cognitively busy interactions.

Because an inference of motive is considered an indicator of activation or use of persuasion knowledge, a large proportion of research focuses on motives. Research has identified a number of variables that increase the likelihood of an inference of ulterior motive. These include sources that are biased (Williams, Fitzsimons, & Block, 2004); the use of rhetorical questions (Ahluwalia & Burnkrant, 2004); negative advertising comparisons, e.g., their brand is worse than ours (Jain & Posavac, 2004); incongruent product placement, e.g., a product that is not tied into the story line (Russell, 2002); the use of flattery (Campbell & Kirmani, 2000); expensive default options, such as highlighting a base computer that has many upgraded features (Brown & Krishna, 2004); incomplete comparisons, e.g., comparing your store's prices to those of other stores for only some brands (Barone, Manning, & Miniard, 2004; Kirmani & Zhu 2007); advocacy advertising, e.g., an issue- rather than product-oriented corporate ad, such as one urging people to quit smoking (Menon & Kahn, 2003); borrowed-interest tactics, e.g., attaching the persuasive topic to something in which the audience has an inherent interest, such as a baby or puppy (Campbell, 1995); cause-related marketing, e.g., the corporation promises to donate some portion of its proceeds to charity (Szykman, Bloom, & Blazing, 2004); and a prevention regulatory focus (Kirmani & Zhu, 2007). Some of this research finds that suspicion of firms' ulterior motives can lead to resistance to persuasion, resulting in less favorable attitudes toward the brand or marketer (Campbell, 1995; Campbell & Kirmani, 2000; Jain & Posavac, 2004; Kirmani & Zhu, 2007).

Understanding the Persuasion Agent's Tactics

Another important component of persuasion knowledge is consumers' beliefs or naïve theories about the tactics that marketing agents use to persuade. Research indicates that consumers have theories about how marketers persuade and how persuasion tactics could work to achieve influence (e.g., Friestad & Wright, 1995). For instance, Friestad and Wright (1995) showed that consumers believe that psychological events (e.g., attention, feeling emotion, connecting, etc.) are important to the persuasion process and that different events play different roles in the persuasion process. Consumers indicated that a marketer could persuade by getting a consumer to feel more connected to the product or by getting the consumer to feel positive emotions through advertising, etc. Moreover, consumers evinced ideas about the relative difficulty of eliciting a variety of psychological events, as well as of the importance of these psychological events to advertising effectiveness. For example, consumers indicated that eliciting connection between consumers and advertising is more difficult than gaining attention, but that connection is more important for successful persuasion (Friestad & Wright, 1995).

An interesting outgrowth of consumer psychology's focus on the consumer as persuasion target is the focus on how people "learn" that certain actions are influence tactics (e.g., Friestad & Wright, 1994). As children, people are likely to take actions at face value, without thinking about whether there is an underlying persuasion motive (e.g., Bousch, Friestad, & Rose, 1994). However, around age 11, consumers begin to consider underlying motive. Adults can continue to learn as they are exposed to actions that they come to believe are intended to influence. For example, after a consumer comes into contact with several different salespeople, all of whom emphasize their similarity to the consumer, the consumer may come to believe that emphasizing similarity is a tactic of persuasion. The realization that a particular action is a persuasion tactic has been termed a *change of meaning* (Friestad & Wright, 1994, p. 13). *Change of meaning* refers to when a consumer decides that an agent engages in a particular behavior in order to try to persuade and then thinks of the behavior as a persuasion tactic.

Some research examines whether consumers can be taught to interpret certain actions as persuasion tactics. Research indicates that there are conditions under which outside information on persuasion tactics, such as an article describing an action as a persuasion tactic, can result in learning such that consumers then think of those actions as persuasion tactics (Williams, Fitzsimons, & Bloch, 2004). However, it appears that consumers tend to think of themselves as more resistant to persuasion tactics than are their peers; thus, learning that something can persuade others is not necessarily applied to the self (Sagarin, Cialdini, Rice, & Serna, 2002). Because a consumer does not apply the learned understanding of an action as a persuasion tactic to believing that the tactic can effectively persuade him or her, the consumer is less likely to use the tactic beliefs or increase resistance to the persuasion tactic (e.g., Sagarin, et al., 2002). Ironically, consumers' "illusion of invulnerability" makes them more susceptible to persuasion. Dispelling this illusion is likely enhance their abilities to resist persuasion.

Although research is beginning to shed light onto some actions that are commonly identified as persuasion tactics, there is still much we do not know. A promising area for future research is to identify conditions that give rise to changes of meaning, as well as to gain better understanding of the process by which people learn about how others persuade.

Consideration of Persuasion Effectiveness

As noted above, consumers' persuasion knowledge can include ideas that certain actions are persuasion tactics and ideas about what makes persuasion tactics effective. Clearly, then, it is important to examine consumers' thoughts about persuasion tactics and how these thoughts influence responses. In the 1980s, consumer researchers began to consider that consumers might have responses to marketers' actions (e.g., advertisements) that differed from their responses to brands (Mitchell & Olson, 1981). The construct of "attitude toward the ad" was developed, referring to the thoughts and feelings that consumers had about an ad. Research demonstrated that attitude toward the ad could influence consumers' brand attitudes, either because of simple affect transfer (i.e., I like the ad, so I like the brand) or because of a more complex thought process (e.g., the tactics that are being used are effective or believable; therefore, I like this brand) (MacKenzie, Lutz, & Belch, 1986).

Since this time, a great deal of research has focused on the construct of attitude toward the ad (see Brown & Stayman, 1992). It is now widely accepted that feelings elicited by advertising and other forms of marketing communications play an important role in consumers' response to products. An important component of this is the idea that consumers think about the marketer's action (i.e., the ad itself), and not just about the topic of persuasion or brand. However, there is room for additional research into how consumers think about persuasive effectiveness, both of ads and of other forms of persuasion. Further, there is much to be understood about the conditions that give rise to consideration of actions as tactics of persuasion and of tactic effectiveness. While research clearly suggests that people use their persuasion knowledge to respond to others, we still need further understanding of when, how, and with what effect.

Consideration of Appropriateness

Another important component of persuasion knowledge is beliefs about the appropriateness of different persuasion tactics. Whereas beliefs about effectiveness have to do with the likely influence of a persuasion tactic (e.g., is this tactic likely to persuade the target?), beliefs about appropriateness have to do with the consumer's judgment of acceptable ways to influence consumer targets (e.g., is it "fair" to use this tactic?). Consumers are likely to respond more negatively to marketing efforts that they deem inappropriate (Campbell, 1995). For instance, Shiv, Edell, and Payne (1997) find that under high elaboration, consumers may view negatively framed ads (e.g., "MCI had over twice as many network outages as AT&T") as inappropriate, leading to lower brand choice.

Perceptions of appropriateness may be related to inferences of the marketer's intent. For example, the consumer's perception that the marketer's tactics are inappropriate (e.g., borrowed interest advertising appeals such as using sexually suggestive ads to sell clothing) leads to inferences of manipulative intent and negative responses to the product and marketer (Campbell, 1995). Likewise, consumers attempt to understand why a marketer has put extra effort into a product display. When the marketer's effort is attributed purely to a desire to persuade, the consumer is likely to respond more negatively to the effort (Morales, 2005). An interesting aspect of judgments of inappropriateness is that these judgments are often influenced by the context, e.g., the type of influence agent, the timing of the tactic, or the goals of the target. Part of persuasion knowledge seems to be intuitive theories about appropriateness that are conditioned on the specific details of the persuasion episode. The conditions under which different persuasion tactics are perceived as (in)appropriate would be a fruitful avenue for future research.

Inferences of Marketers' Effort

Besides making inferences about motives, consumers may draw inferences about the amount of effort the marketer expends on a persuasion effort. Research suggests a curvilinear relationship between perceived effort and consumer response. When consumers believe that marketers are expending effort to try to persuade them, they infer that the marketer must have a good (high-quality) product. For instance, expenditures on expensive advertising (e.g., the use of celebrity endorsers, frequent repetition, and longer ads; Kirmani, 1990; Kirmani & Wright, 1989) and above-average warranties (Boulding & Kirmani, 1993) have been shown to lead to higher perceptions of marketer effort; higher effort translates into perceptions of a high-quality product. Similarly, effort in making and displaying products appears to increase consumers' overall evaluations and willingness to pay for products (Morales, 2005). Up to a point, consumers appear to think that if the marketer is putting so much effort into promoting the product, the product must be good.

However, when consumers perceive that a marketer is putting "too much" effort into promoting or selling a product, they are likely to respond negatively. For instance, a level of advertising expenditure that is deemed inappropriately high leads to lower perceptions of product quality (Kirmani, 1997). Consumers appear to think, "if they're trying so hard to influence me, something must be wrong" (Kirmani, 1997). Thus, too strong a persuasion effort leads to suspicion and lower perceptions of product quality.

The notion that effort leads to positive evaluations has appeared recently in the social psychology literature (Kruger, Wirtz, Van Boven, & Altermatt, 2004). Kruger and colleagues (2004) discuss the role of effort as a heuristic for quality in a nonmarketing context. For instance, they demonstrate that when an artist spends higher effort (i.e., time) on a painting, individuals may infer that the painting is good. The underlying process depicted in this chapter is the same as the one described in Kirmani and Wright (1989). However, Kruger and colleagues (2004) do not explore limits to this heuristic, i.e., when effort may be perceived as too much or inappropriate.

At this point, there is evidence that perception of others' effort influences responses and evaluations. However, the relative role of perceptions of marketers' effort remains unclear. Additional research is needed to gain insight into how often consumers think about marketers' effort level and the relative importance and interplay of this variable with others in the consumer's environment. Similarly, more could be done in terms of investigating the role of effort in nonmarketing contexts.

Consumers' Coping Responses

Because social psychological research has primarily focused on the agent of social influence, targets' responses to influence attempts have been given little attention. Typically, any attention to targets' responses has focused on whether the target complies with the agent's request. Recently, however, resistance has been conceptualized as a process rather than just an outcome. For instance, Knowles and Linn (2004b) describe resistance as more than just noncompliance; they conceptualize resistance as involving reactance, distrust, scrutiny, and inertia.

The PKM's focus on the target allows an even broader view of coping responses. This conceptualization suggests that consumers can have both resistance and non-resistance cognitions and behaviors in response to persuasion. In particular, focusing on the target's perspective alters the conceptualization of the "end game" of the persuasion episode. From the agent's perspective—the traditional perspective of social psychology—the end game is whether the target complies with the agent's persuasion. From the target's point of view, however, achievement of his/her own salient goal(s) is more important than either complying or not complying with the agent's request. Thus, the target's coping behavior is often geared toward goal achievement and draws upon persuasion knowledge in order to further progress toward the salient goal. Because of this, coping responses may draw upon memory of prior events, include evaluations of persuasion attempts, and involve forecasting the agent's responses. For example, targets may anticipate an upcoming persuasion attempt and outline their responses to it; or they may evaluate the interaction or outcome or continue thinking about it after the compliance outcome has been reached. In sum, coping may involve a response process that includes components before, during, and after the compliance outcome.

Given the centrality of coping to the PKM, it is somewhat surprising that little research specifically studies consumers' coping strategies. We are aware of only one published paper that focuses on strategies that consumers use in responding to marketing persuasion (Kirmani & Campbell, 2004). In this research, we used both qualitative and experimental methods to gain insight into consumer "response behaviors." The research identified 15 different strategies that consumers use to respond to persuasion attempts, showing that consumers both resist and manage marketers' persuasion attempts. As in the persuasion-resistance literature, consumers appear to sometimes act as "persuasion sentries," guarding against and resisting unwanted marketing persuasion. Additionally, as proposed by the conceptualization of consumers as goal-seeking, consumers sometimes act as "persuasion seekers," using and managing marketing persuasion agents in attempting to achieve their own consumption goals. Consumers revealed a variety of strategies for each role. We discuss these strategies in more detail in a later section.

A useful area for future research is to examine persuasion coping responses more deeply. In addition to more research on response tactics, there is need for research on other types of coping. For example, research on stress shows both cognitive and emotional coping (e.g., Carver, Scheier, & Weintraub, 1989). We know little about the role that emotional coping plays in persuasion contexts, so it would be interesting to examine the range people have for coping with persuasion as well as the potential outcomes that could result from different types of coping. For instance, Vohs, Baumeister, and Chin (2007) suggest that feeling duped by another's persuasion attempt is an emotion that may be similar to other self-blame emotions, such as guilt and shame. However, there is little research on the emotional aspects of feeling duped.

Persuasion Knowledge as an Individual Difference Variable

Persuasion knowledge has been conceptualized as both a situational and an individual difference variable. The notion that persuasion knowledge may be an individual variable led to the development of a scale that measures persuasion knowledge as a subcomponent of consumer self-confidence (Bearden, Hardesty, & Rose, 2001). The scale includes six items that assess the consumer's recognition of persuasion tactics (I know when an offer is "too good to be true"; I can tell when an offer has strings attached; I have no trouble understanding the bargaining tactics used by salespersons; I know when a marketer is pressuring me to buy; I can see through sales gimmicks used to get consumers to buy; I can separate fact from fantasy in advertising). This scale has been used to divide people into high and low PKs, with clear behavioral differences between the two groups (Ahluwalia & Burnkrant, 2004; Brown & Krishna, 2004). For instance, Ahluwalia and Burnkrant (2004) show that when rhetorical questions become salient, consumers with high persuasion tactic knowledge may focus on why the persuasion agent is using a rhetorical question. When individuals have high persuasion tactic knowledge, positive prior attitudes toward the agent enhance message persuasion, while negative prior attitudes toward the agent diminish message persuasion. However, low-PK individuals are not sensitive to the source of the rhetorical questions and thus do not show this difference. This research highlights the notion that the level of persuasion knowledge influences persuasion outcomes.

Social psychologists have also begun to examine individual differences in specific types of persuasion knowledge. Individual difference measures of persuasion knowledge include beliefs about one's own persuasability (Tormala & Petty, 2002) and resistance to persuasion (Briñol, Rucker, Tormala, & Petty, 2004). For instance, Tormala and Petty (2002) investigate people's metacognitions about the ease with which they can be persuaded. Under low elaboration, individuals may use beliefs about their own vulnerability to persuasion as a persuasion cue. Under high elaboration, beliefs about one's own persuasability did not have an impact on attitude change. Interestingly, the result for high levels of persuasion knowledge in this research is opposite that of Ahluwalia and Burnkrant (2004) discussed earlier. These different patterns of results suggest that beliefs about one's own persuasability are different from beliefs about one's understanding of persuasion tactics. This shows that persuasion knowledge encompasses a variety of types of knowledge about persuasion and persuasion interactions and that it is important to gain understanding of the range of such knowledge and implications of different types of persuasion knowledge.

Examining individuals' experience with persuasion may reveal important insights into targets' behavior, whether in marketing or nonmarketing situations. Moreover, experience with persuasion is likely to interact with other types of knowledge (agent knowledge and topic knowledge) to affect outcomes. One area of interest would be in examining the extent to which persuasion knowledge is domain specific and whether knowledge learned in one domain is transferred to another. For instance, is a persuasion expert in one domain likely to be an expert in a different domain? As a related question, how specific is the learning of tactics encapsulated as a change of meaning? If a consumer comes to believe that salespeople emphasize their similarity to the consumer as a tactic of persuasion, would she/he be likely to then believe that the same tactic is used in advertising or that it is specific to the persuasion context?

Another interesting area that has yet to be examined is the relationship between persuasion knowledge in commercial domains and persuasion knowledge in interpersonal domains. For example, it would be important to understand how and when persuasion knowledge about marketing interactions affects responses in nonmarketing contexts. For example, is a consumer likely to translate a change of meaning from marketplace persuasion to noncommercial interactions?

As stated at the beginning of this chapter, although the Persuasion Knowledge Model was developed in the context of marketing persuasion, it may be applied to nonmarketing contexts as well. In the next section, we turn to consideration of the ways in which research in the Persuasion Knowledge Model stream contributes to social psychology.

THE PKM AND SOCIAL PSYCHOLOGY

We consider some of the differences between the PKM perspective and perspectives taken in the social psychological literature, highlighting ways in which the PKM's consumer psychology perspective can suggest useful direction for more general psychological insight. In order to do this, we draw both from published literature and from two unpublished sources of data. The first data set is a recall study in which 94 undergraduate business students were asked to detail a time when a family member, friend, instructor, or salesperson tried to get them to do something, and their responses to that influence attempt. Each participant provided two descriptions, for a total of 181 complete descriptions of persuasion attempts (five were incomplete). The second data set is a diary study described in Kirmani and Campbell (2004), in which 36 undergraduate business students logged onto a Web site at least three times a week for a six-week period to describe a situation in which someone attempted to persuade them and their response to the attempt. Respondents reported the basic persuasion attempt, when the persuasion episode occurred, who tried to persuade them, when they realized it was a persuasion attempt, and the compliance outcome. In both data sets, participants provided examples of persuasion efforts from a variety of different types of people; some were in professional persuader roles (e.g., salespeople, advertisers, managers) while others were in personal roles (e.g., friends, parents, siblings). Important issues arise from consideration of the target's perspective and the target-agent relationship.

The Target's Perspective

First, we consider how the target's perspective affects responses to marketing persuasion and extend some of these findings to nonmarketing situations. We focus on the following aspects of the target's perspective: the target's view of persuasion as the primary role of marketing agents, the agent's role as helper, the target as active participant, and the target's metacognitions.

Persuasion as Agent's Primary Role   From the target's perspective, marketing agents serve two basic roles: persuader and helper. Consumers believe that persuasion is usually the primary role of marketing agents; thus, interactions with marketing agents typically are based on an expectation of a persuasion attempt. The fact that persuasion is likely to be the primary purpose of a consumer's interaction with a marketing agent adds a level of wariness and distrust that may pervade the interaction (Darke & Ritchie, 2007). For example, many consumers perceive the salesperson's simple question, "May I help you?" as the beginning of a potential sales pitch. Similarly, the beginning of an ad may be interpreted as a persuasion attempt, leading to some level of distrust (Darke & Ritchie, 2007). Accordingly, the target may act as a persuasion sentry, guarding against unwanted influence from an agent (Kirmani & Campbell, 2004). As mentioned earlier, Kirmani and Campbell (2004) identified several sentry strategies used by consumer targets. Besides using several strategies that appear in the compliance-resistance literature (e.g., forestall, deceive, resist assertively, confront, punish, withdraw), the target may also plan for coping with persuasion by using the strategies of *prepare*, and *enlist a companion*. These two anticipatory strategies reflect the target's recognition that a persuasion attempt is forthcoming. *Prepare* involves entering the interaction armed with information that the target has collected prior to the interaction in order to defend against a marketing agent's persuasion. For instance, a consumer can go more confidently into a car dealership after having done extensive research on cars on the Internet. This will ensure that he has the tools to counterargue the salesperson's pitch or otherwise resist unwanted persuasion. *Enlisting a companion* is a tactic that involves bringing a third party along to help the target deal with the persuasion attempt. By enlisting a companion, the target makes sure that he will have someone on his side in the upcoming battle with the marketing agent. The companion may be a friend, spouse, parent, etc., who (1) may be a better negotiator, (2) may be more knowledgeable about the product, or (3) may serve to provide the additional cognitive capacity to identify unwanted persuasion. These target coping strategies do not appear in the persuasion-resistance literature.

The Agent's Role as Helper The dual role of marketing agents as persuaders and helpers makes interactions with marketing agents somewhat complex. The target recognizes that while the agent is primarily there to move the target toward purchase, the agent can also help the target achieve the target's goals. For instance, advertisements may contain valuable information about product benefits, and salespeople may be able to facilitate the buying process by searching for products and finding options that the target could not easily identify himself. One consumer in our data described a service agent as follows: " … she is providing a service, I mean so she does that, the fact that we are ultimately paying for it, it seems like a valid transaction in my mind." Another mentioned the tension between the agent's role as persuader and helper: "Her goal clearly is to get me to make a purchase, but the way that she approached it was by being helpful, and that is what I would expect someone like that to be."

Thus, besides approaching an interaction warily, the target may also approach it with the idea that she/he would like, or in some cases, may need to use the agent to achieve his goals. Accordingly, Kirmani and Campbell (2004) identify several "seeker strategies" used by targets to try to gain or maximize the benefit of agent help. Interestingly, some of these strategies (e.g., ask, establish personal connection, and reward) have been identified as *influence* strategies but have not previously been associated with targets. Their inclusion as response strategies reinforces the idea that consumers are active participants within the persuasion interaction and are trying to influence the persuaders.

Other strategies, such as *test, direct*, and *accept assistance*, do not appear in the psychology literature. *Test* involves the target's active assessment of whether the agent has the necessary expertise to help the target's goal pursuit. For instance, the target may ask questions to determine whether a computer salesperson is truly knowledgeable about computers. Another seeker strategy, *direct*, is used to get the agent to help with the target's goal achievement. This strategy involves getting the agent to understand the target's needs so that the agent will work toward the target's goals. For instance, the target can tell a computer salesperson about capabilities that are needed and the price range of interest. The purpose is to focus the agent's attention on the relevant models and stop the agent from showing the target models that are unsuitable. Finally, *accept assistance* is another strategy that recognizes the role of salespeople as helpers; it involves going along with an agent because the agent's suggestions are compatible with the target's goals. All of these strategies are ways the target gets the agent to work for the target.

This dual role of the agent as persuader and helper means that targets may have to trade off the agent's role as persuader with the role as helper. Depending on characteristics of the target, the agent, and the situation, one of these roles may be more dominant. Research is needed to better understand the dynamics of marketer and nonmarketer interactions and how people value and influence the roles that a persuader may play.

The Target as Active Participant

As the foregoing discussion indicates, the target is an active participant in a persuasion interaction, using both seeker and sentry strategies to achieve the target's own goals. Within a single interaction, and across multiple interactions, the target may act as recipient, resistor, influencer, or anticipator. He may move fluidly across these different roles, blurring the line between "target" and "agent." Further, the target can gain more persuasion knowledge from each persuasion interaction that he or she can use in later interactions.

The active target may approach a persuasion interaction with a variety of goals, and these goals will shape the target's response to persuasion. There is extensive research on how agents' goals affect the tactics used by influence agents (e.g., Rule, Bisanz, & Kohn, 1985; Schrader & Dillard, 1998). Similarly, there is some work suggesting that targets' goals or motives affect selection of resistance tactics (McLaughlin, Cody, & Robey, 1980; Wood & Quinn, 2003). For instance, a meta-analysis of the forewarning literature reveals that the target's defense motivations (i.e., bolstering current attitudes or enhancing self-image) affected whether targets resisted or accepted a message (Wood & Quinn, 2003). At this point, however, the role of targets' goals in the persuasion response process remains primarily unexplored.

In the diary study described earlier, we asked respondents to describe their goals in the persuasion interactions. A variety of target goals surfaced in the data, some centered on the self, some on the relationship, and some on the persuasion interaction. Not surprisingly, there were a variety of self-centered goals that included doing well or succeeding (e.g., getting a good grade, getting a raise); managing one's self-concept (e.g., behaving in line with personal ethics or standards); managing one's hedonic state (e.g., having a good time); and maintaining prior course (i.e., what the target was doing prior to the persuasion attempt, such as studying). Perhaps more interesting were target goals that focused on the relationship, including trying to change or maintain the relationship; managing the agent's impressions of the target (including getting the agent to understand the target's point of view); managing the agent's self impressions and feelings; and managing others' impressions of the target or of the agent. Targets also identified goals that focused on the persuasion interaction itself, such as managing future interactions with the agent, "winning" the exchange, resisting persuasion, and ending the interaction. This last set of goals is particularly interesting because it directly relates to persuasion. The idea that targets may enter a persuasion episode with the idea of winning is interesting, and is likely to occur in both marketing and nonmarketing interactions. At this point, there is need for research that examines targets' goals more fully (e.g., Friestad & Wright, 1994).

The Target's Metacognitions   The target is also likely to have metacognitions about the marketplace, defined as "everyday individuals' thinking about market-related thinking" (Wright, 2002, p. 677). Marketplace metacognition includes people's beliefs about their own mental states and about the states of others, as well as about processes, strategies, and intentions as these relate to the social domain of marketplace interactions.

The PKM's focus on consumers' intuitive theories about what marketers are trying to do is consistent with recent research on metacognition in psychology (e.g., Schwarz, 1994; Tormala & Petty, 2002). Jost, Kruglanski, and Nelson (1998) argue that metacognition includes individuals' folk theories about how people (they and others) think. These include folk theories about intentional behavior (Malle & Knobe, 1997) and naïve theories about the sources of bias in persuasion (Wegener & Petty, 1997). Tormala and Petty (2002) find that successful resistance of persuasion increases attitude certainty when consumers realize that they resisted a strong message. This increase in attitude certainty suggests a thinking process along the lines of, "if I successfully resisted such a strong message, I must really believe my original view," which leads the person to become more certain of his attitude. In contrast, when the consumer perceives that he or she is doing a poor job resisting persuasion, attitude certainty may decrease (Tormala, Clarkson, & Petty, 2006).

In addition, inferences of motives ascribe intentionality to marketing agents, and consideration of others' intentionality is thought to be a central form of metacognition. When thinking about the marketer's intentions, a consumer tries to guess the marketer's thinking and motives and to respond accordingly. Thus, it is clear that research on metacognition both contributes to and gains from the current research on persuasion knowledge.

Metacognitions also show up in terms of people's intuitive theories about persuasion, such as the belief that if a marketer is expending so much effort, he must think he has a good product. The personal interviews reported in Kirmani and Campbell (2004) reveal some other theories consumers have about the persuasion process. These include that avoiding eye contact and being uncommunicative are ways to avoid a salesperson because he will think that you're not interested; that small talk or chatting are ways to establish a relationship and therefore get good deals from a serviceman because he will think of you as a friend; that salespeople expect you to be unprepared, and that being prepared can give you a relative advantage against the salesperson. Brown and Krishna (2004) show that consumers believe that a default option (e.g., a base computer that comes with certain options) is one that the marketer wants people to buy, and this belief affects how consumers respond to the default option.

Although some research on persuasion knowledge speaks to issues of metacognition, more could be done both on specific consumer theories and, more importantly, at a higher level of interaction. For instance, it is possible that consumers may play mind games with marketers. We have uncovered consumers' cognitions at the level of "the ad includes a celebrity endorser because the marketer thinks that this will get me to buy the product." Can consumers think at a higher level of abstraction? For instance, might consumers reason as follows: "the ad includes a celebrity endorser because the marketer thinks that this will get me to buy the product *because he thinks that I think that celebrity endorsers are cool?*" More remains to be done to uncover the metacognitions that consumers may have about the persuasion process.

The Target-Agent Relationship

The relationship between a target and a persuasion agent is likely to influence persuasion interactions as well as outcomes. Our own experiences with salespeople or advertisements versus children, friends, etc., suggest that people's approach and response to persuasion is impacted by these relationships. Some literature makes the distinction between communal versus exchange relationships (e.g., Clark & Mills, 1979). Marketing relationships are typically classified as exchange relationships, defined as those based upon reciprocal exchange, or quid pro quo (Clark et al., 1979). Within these relationships, typified by people one does business with, individuals are concerned about their own gain. In contrast, many nonmarketing relationships are considered to be communal, conceptualized as those based upon concern for the welfare of the other. Within these relationships, typified by friends and family, individuals are concerned with the needs and preferences of the other.

Persuasion is likely to be differentially salient across exchange and communal relationships. Whereas persuasion is likely to be fairly accessible in exchange relationships, it is less salient in communal relationships because persuasion typically plays a secondary role within the relationship. Thus, individuals' interactions with friends, family, romantic partners, teachers, etc., are not necessarily defined by persuasion. While persuasion sometimes becomes important or expected in these relationships, it is not the *raison d'etre* of the relationship. Consequently, the point at which the target recognizes the persuasive intent of the agent may differ across relationships. Whereas recognition of persuasive intent tends to occur early in a marketing interaction, in most nonmarketing relationships, recognition of persuasive intent may be delayed (unless individuals have been explicitly forewarned; Wood & Quinn, 2003). In these cases, the target engages in the interchange without initially thinking that the agent is attempting to persuade him or her. Then, at some point in the interaction, a change of meaning occurs and the interaction is transformed into a persuasive encounter. In our data, quite a few respondents said things along the lines of "I just thought he was being nice, but then I realized … " when describing interactions within communal relationships. For example, one diary respondent described the following encounter in which a change of meaning occurred late:

> When I was in eighth grade my sister was a senior in high school. My parents went out of town for two weeks, and my sister was having parties at home. (Boy

did I think I was cool—seniors in high school at my home—wow!) She told me to come downstairs and she would give me a cigarette and a beer. Of course I went down there. Afterwards, she told me that since I had done it too, and had participated in the party, I couldn't tell mom and dad or I would get caught, too. She tricked me.

We speculate that compared to early recognition, delayed recognition of persuasion intent is likely to generate more negative perceptions of the agent. The target has been lulled into a sense of security about the interaction, and then realizes that she/he is being sold to. Therefore, the target experiences a change of meaning and negative emotion. This would suggest that recognition of persuasion intent may be more damaging in nonmarketing relationships (where it is unexpected) than in marketing relationships (where it is expected).

Related to this is the concept of mixed motive situations. For instance, a tutor may be a helper (adding to an individual's knowledge in a specific area) or a persuader (someone who tries to convince the individual to buy more tutoring sessions). Similarly, mixed motive situations may occur when friends try to sell something (e.g., magazines) to friends. In our data, we found that these mixed motive situations were some of the most difficult interactions for targets because of the ambiguity about whether, at any given time, the agent was a helper or a persuader. In these cases, the target indicated difficulty coping with the interaction, in part because it involved components of both communal and exchange relationships. The issues of persuasion within nonpersuasion environments and exchange elements within communal relationships (or vice versa) offer interesting avenues for future research.

One interesting idea that is beginning to emerge from consumer research is that marketing relationships are much more nuanced than the exchange-versus-communal dichotomy would suggest. For example, marketing relationships may be expanded beyond this dichotomy to include authority ranking, equality matching, communal sharing, and market pricing (Fiske, 1992); research shows that these characteristics of relationships influence reactions to market pricing (McGraw, Tetlock, & Kristel, 2003). Similarly, relationships with marketing agents can be characterized by several dimensions, such as cooperative vs. competitive, task oriented vs. socio-emotional, and high vs. low dependency (Kirmani & Campbell, 2004). This research showed that consumers may develop long-term relationships with salespeople in stores that they visit frequently, e.g., department stores and specialty stores. Familiar agents (e.g., a personal shopper from Nordstrom) often transform the buying experience from a utilitarian one to an experiential one, with an emphasis on relationship goals, commitment, and trust. As a result, the use of strategies that could build the relationship, such as establish personal connection and reward, is likely to be higher in socio-emotional relationships, and the use of strategies that might harm the relationship, such as confront, punish, and withdraw, is likely to be lower.

The complexity of marketing relationships is demonstrated in research that shows that consumers can have relationships with brands that reflect the types of relationships that they have with other people (Fournier, 1998). Importantly, this research shows that some marketplace relationships involve psychosocial and emotional meanings, bonds, and needs. Additional research suggests that there are conditions under which marketplace relationships have a communal, rather than purely exchange-based, nature and that the extent to which a marketplace relationship is more communal influences consumer response to market actions (Aggarwal & Law, 2005; Aggarwal & Zhang, 2006).

Thus, some of the learning about communal relationships may be relevant to marketing relationships, and vice versa. One important element of such research must be the recognition that not all persuasion agents and forms of persuasion are the same. Researchers must move away from the assumption that what is learned from experiments in which an advertisement is the method of persuasion is the same as one in which a statement from the participant's university, or a newspaper article, etc., is used. The persuasion knowledge that a target applies to understanding, interpreting and coping with persuasion is dependent upon the channel of persuasion.

CONCLUSION

By emphasizing the role of the target, the Persuasion Knowledge Model (Friestad & Wright, 1994) provides a distinctive and important perspective on persuasion. The PKM views the target of persuasion as an active participant in a dynamic persuasion process. The target may draw inferences about agents' motives and effort, recognize some of the tactics used by persuasion agents, examine the effectiveness and appropriateness of persuasion tactics, form metacognitions about the persuasion process, and cope with persuasion cognitively, emotionally, and behaviorally. Persuasion knowledge, along with topic and agent knowledge, allows the target to pursue his or her goals in a given persuasion encounter and across persuasion encounters.

We suggest that this perspective on persuasion may be useful across a variety of domains, not just consumer psychology. The perspective is already being used in a variety of contexts within and outside persuasion, representing a shift in research in persuasion. This focus on the target is similar to the shift to the target's perspective in research on social stigmas (e.g., Swim & Stangor, 1998; Levin & van Laar, 2006). In that research stream, the target's perspective has allowed much new learning, including learning about the emotions, motivations, and coping strategies of stigma targets. This research has moved from viewing the target as a passive recipient of stigmas to someone who is actively coping with the effects of stigmas. Persuasion research may go through a similar phase, leading to new insights into the persuasion process and the persuasion target's cognitive, emotional, and behavioral coping strategies.

REFERENCES

Aggarwal, P., & Law, S. (2005). Role of relationship norms in processing brand information. *Journal of Consumer Research, 32*, 453–464.

Aggarwal, P., & Zhang, M. (2006). The moderating effect of relationship norm salience on consumers' loss aversion. *Journal of Consumer Research, 33,* 413–419.

Ahluwalia, R., & Burnkrant, R. E. (2004). Answering questions about questions: A persuasion knowledge perspective for understanding the effects of rhetorical questions. *Journal of Consumer Research, 31,* 26–42.

Barone, M. J., Manning, K. C., & Miniard, P. W. (2004). Consumer response to retailers' use of partially comparative pricing. *Journal of Marketing, 68,* 37–47.

Bearden, W. O., Hardesty, D. M., & Rose, R. L. (2001). Consumer self-confidence: Refinements in conceptualization and measurement. *Journal of Consumer Research, 28,* 121–134.

Boulding, W., & Kirmani, A. (1993). A consumer-side experimental examination of signalling theory. *Journal of Consumer Research, 20,* 111–123.

Bousch, D. M., Friestad, M., & Rose, G. M. (1994). Adolescent skepticism toward TV advertising and knowledge of advertiser tactics. *Journal of Consumer Research, 21,* 165–175.

Briñol, P., Rucker, D. D., Tormala, Z. L., & Petty, R. E. (2004). Individual differences in resistance to persuasion: The role of beliefs and meta-beliefs. In E. S. Knowles and J. A. Linn (Eds.), *Resistance and persuasion* (pp. 83–104). Mahwah, NJ: Lawrence Erlbaum Associates Publishers.

Brown, C. L., & Krishna, A. (2004). The skeptical shopper: A metacognitive account for the effects of default options on choice. *Journal of Consumer Research, 31,* 529–539.

Brown, S. P., & Stayman, D. M. (1992). Antecedents and consequences of attitude toward the ad: A meta-analysis. *Journal of Consumer Research, 19,* 34–51.

Campbell, M. C. (1995). When attention-getting advertising tactics elicit consumer inferences of manipulative intent: The importance of balancing benefits and investments. *Journal of Consumer Psychology, 4,* 225–254.

Campbell, M. C., & Kirmani, A. (2000). Consumers' use of persuasion knowledge: The effects of accessibility and cognitive capacity on perceptions of an influence agent. *Journal of Consumer Research, 27,* 69–83.

Carver, C. S., Scheier, M. F., & Weintraub, J. K. (1989). Assessing coping strategies: A theoretically based approach. *Journal of Personality and Social Psychology, 56,* 267–283.

Clark, M., & Mills, J. (1979).Interpersonal attraction in exchange and communal relationships. *Journal of Personality and Social Psychology, 37,* 12–24.

Darke, P. R., & Ritchie, J. B. (2007). The defensive consumer: Advertising deception, defensive processing, and distrust. *Journal of Marketing Research, 44,* 114–127.

Eagly, A. H., & Chaiken, S. (1993). *The psychology of attitudes.* Fort Worth, TX: Harcourt Brace Jovanovich.

Fiske, A. P. (1992). The four elementary forms of sociality: Framework for a unified theory of social relations. *Psychological Review, 99*(4), 689–723

Fournier, S. (1998). Consumers and their brands: Developing relationship theory in consumer research. *Journal of Consumer Research, 24,* 343–373.

Friedstad, M., & Wright, P. (1994). The persuasion knowledge model: How people cope with persuasion attempts. *Journal of Consumer Research, 21,* 1–31.

Friestad, M., & Wright, P. (1995). Persuasion knowledge: Lay people's and researchers' beliefs about the psychology of advertising. *Journal of Consumer Research, 21,* 1–31.

Hamilton, R. W. (2003). Why do people suggest what they do not want? Using context effects to influence others' choices. *Journal of Consumer Research, 29,* 492–506.

Jain, S. P., & Posavac, S. S. (2004). Valenced comparisons. *Journal of Marketing Research, 41,* 46–58.

Jost J. T., Kruglanski A. W., & Nelson T. O. (1998). Social metacognition: An expansionist review. *Personality and Social Psychology Review, 2,* 137–154.

Kirmani, A. (1990). The effect of perceived advertising costs on brand perceptions. *Journal of Consumer Research, 17*, 160–171.

Kirmani, A. (1997). Advertising repetition as a signal of quality: If it's advertised so often, something must be wrong. *Journal of Advertising, 26*, 77–86.

Kirmani, A., & Campbell, M. C. (2004). Goal seeker and persuasion sentry: How consumer targets respond to interpersonal marketing persuasion. *Journal of Consumer Research, 31*, 573–582.

Kirmani, A., & Wright, P. (1989). Money talks: Perceived advertising expense and expected product quality. *Journal of Consumer Research, 16*, 344–353.

Kirmani, A., & Zhu, R. (2007). Vigilant against manipulation: The effects of regulatory focus on the use of persuasion knowledge. *Journal of Marketing Research, 44*.

Knowles, E. S., & Linn, J. A. (2004a). *Resistance and persuasion.* Mahwah, NJ: Lawrence Erlbaum Associates.

Knowles, E. S. & Linn, J. A. (2004b). Approach-avoidance model of persuasion: Alpha and Omega strategies for change. In E. S. Knowles & J. A. Linn (Eds.), *Resistance and persuasion* (pp.117–148). Mahwah, NJ: Lawrence Erlbaum Associates Publishers.

Kruger, J., Wirtz, D., Van Boven, L., & Altermatt, T. W. (2004). The effort heuristic. *Journal of Experimental Social Psychology, 40*, 91–98.

Kruglanski, A., & E. P. Thompson (1999). Persuasion by a single route: A view from the unimodel. *Psychological Inquiry, 10*, 83–109.

Levin, S., & van Laar, C. (2006). *Stigma and group inequality: Social psychological perspectives* (Vol. xiii). Mahwah, NJ: Lawrence Erlbaum Associates Publishers.

MacKenzie, S. B., Lutz, R. J., & Belch, G. E. (1986). The role of attitude toward the ad as a mediator of advertising effectiveness: A test of competing explanations. *Journal of Marketing Research, 23*, 130–143.

Malle, B. F., & Knobe, J. (1997). The folk concept of intentionality. *Journal of Experimental Social Psychology, 33*, 101–121.

McGraw, A. P., Tetlock, P. E., & Kristel, O. V. (2003). The limits of fungibility: Relational schemata and the value of things. *Journal of Consumer Research, 30*, 219–229.

McLaughlin, M. L., Cody, M. J., & Robey, C. S. (1980). Situational influences on the selection of strategies to resist compliance-gaining attempts. *Human Communication Research, 7*, 14–36.

Menon, S., & Kahn, B. (2003). Corporate sponsorships of philanthropic activities: When do they impact perception of sponsor brand? *Journal of Consumer Psychology, 13*, 316–327.

Mitchell, A. A., & Olson, J. C. (1981). Are product attribute beliefs the only mediator of advertising effects on brand attitude? *Journal of Marketing Research, 18*, 318–332.

Morales, A. C. (2005). Giving firms an 'E' for effort: Consumer responses to high-effort firms. *Journal of Consumer Research, 31*, 806–812.

Rule, B. G., Bisanz, G. L., & Kohn, M. (1985). Anatomy of a persuasion schema: Targets, goals, and strategies. *Journal of Personality and Social Psychology, 48*, 1127–1140.

Russell, C. (2002). Investigating the effectiveness of product placements in television shows: The role of modality and plot connection congruence on brand memory and attitude. *Journal of Consumer Research, 29*, 306–318.

Sagarin, B. J., Cialdini, R. B., Rice, W. E., & Serna, S. B. (2002). Dispelling the illusion of invulnerability: The motivations and mechanisms of resistance to persuasion. *Journal of Personality and Social Psychology, 83*, 526–541.

Schrader D. C., & Dillard J. P. (1998). Goal structures and interpersonal influence. *Communication Studies, 49*, 276–293.

Schwarz, N. (1994). Judgment in a social context: Biases, shortcomings, and the logic of conversation. In M. P. Zanna (Ed.), *Advances in experimental social psychology* (Vol. 26, pp.123–162). San Diego, CA: Academic Press.

Shiv, B., Edell, J. A., & Payne, J. W. (1997). Factors affecting the impact of negatively and positively framed ad messages. *Journal of Consumer Research, 24,* 285–294.

Sujan, M., Bettman, J., & Sujan, H. (1986). Effects of consumer expectations on information processing in selling encounters. *Journal of Marketing Research, 23,* 346–353.

Swim, J. K., & Stangor, C. (1998). *Prejudice: The target's perspective* (Vol. xiv, pp. 332). San Diego, CA: Academic Press.

Szykman, L. R., Bloom, P. N., & Blazing, J. (2004). Does corporate sponsorship of a socially-oriented message make a difference? An investigation of the effects of sponsorship identity on responses to an anti-drinking and driving message. *Journal of Consumer Psychology, 14,* 13–20.

Tormala Z. L., Clarkson J. J., & Petty R. E. (2006). Resisting persuasion by the skin of one's teeth: The hidden success of resisted persuasive messages. *Journal of Personality and Social Psychology, 91,* 423–435.

Tormala Z. L., & Petty R. E. (2002). What doesn't kill me makes me stronger: The effects of resisting persuasion on attitude certainty. *Journal of Personality and Social Psychology, 83,* 1298–1313.

Vohs, K. D., Baumeister, R. F., & Chin, J. (2007). Feeling duped: Emotional, motivational, and cognitive aspects of being exploited by others. *Review of General Psychology, 11,* 127–141.

Wegener, D. T., & Petty, R. E. (1997). The flexible correction model: The role of naive theories of bias in bias correction. In M. P. Zanna (Ed.), *Advances in experimental social psychology* (Vol. 29, pp.141–208). Mahwah, NJ: Lawrence Erlbaum Associates.

Williams, P., Fitzimons, G. J., & Block, L. G. (2004). When consumers do not recognize 'benign' intention questions as persuasion attempts. *Journal of Consumer Research, 31,* 540–550.

Wood, W., & Quinn, J. M. (2003). Forewarned and forearmed? Two meta-analysis syntheses of forewarnings of influence appeals. *Psychological Bulletin, 129,* 119–138.

Wright, P. (2002). Marketplace metacognition and social intelligence. *Journal of Consumer Research, 28,* 667–682.

Section V

Goals and Self-Regulation

14

The Persuasive Power of Regulatory Fit

ANGELA Y. LEE
Northwestern University

E. TORY HIGGINS
Columbia University

*C*onsumers are goal-driven. How they process information and make decisions is driven by their consumption goals (e.g., I need a cup of coffee) as well as by their self-regulatory goals, which service more fundamental needs. Research in the last decade has shown how people's fundamental needs for nurturance and security have influenced their judgment and behavior. According to regulatory focus theory (Higgins, 1997, 1998), people with a salient nurturance need regulate their attention, perception, attitudes, and behaviors toward approaching gains and avoiding nongains (i.e., they are promotion-oriented), whereas those with a salient security need regulate their attention, perception, attitudes, and behaviors toward avoiding losses and approaching nonlosses (i.e., they are prevention-oriented). And it is not unusual for the same consumption goal to be motivated by different regulatory focus orientations. For instance, as seen in some television advertising campaigns promoting Starbucks coffee, Glen and Stacy may both be loyal customers of Starbucks. However, Glen is drinking his DoubleShot espresso "to bring on the day," whereas Stacy is enjoying her Frappuccino moment to help ward off demanding bosses and colleagues.

Consumers' regulatory focus plays an important role in determining the kind of products and services they consume; their promotion or prevention orientation also influences the persuasiveness of advertising messages or the attractiveness of product offerings they encounter. This chapter reviews the recent developments in regulatory focus research and provides an overview of the persuasive nature of regulatory fit on consumer judgment and choice. It should be noted that regulatory fit effects are not restricted to the case of regulatory focus orientations (e.g., Avnet & Higgins, 2003; Bianco, Higgins, & Klem, 2003). For example, regulatory mode theory distinguishes between locomotion and assessment as two different components of self-regulation (Kruglanski et al., 2000). Whereas the nature of locomotion as a regulatory orientation involves the initiating of movement away from a current state to a new state, the nature of assessment as a regulatory orientation is to measure, interpret, and evaluate. And people experience regulatory fit when they make decisions in a way that matches their locomotion or assessment orientation (Avnet & Higgins, 2003). However, the bulk of the regulatory fit research relating to consumer behavior has examined fit effects involving promotion and prevention orientations; thus, this will be the emphasis for this chapter.

In the next sections, we will first define regulatory fit and then review the different ways in which people may experience regulatory fit and the effects of regulatory fit on attitudes and behaviors. We then propose different mechanisms that may underlie the effects of regulatory fit on persuasion and identify potential boundary conditions. We close by discussing broader implications of regulatory fit on people's welfare and suggesting directions for future research.

WHAT IS REGULATORY FIT?

People are guided by their regulatory orientations in their goal pursuit activities. These guiding orientations may be chronically stable and reflect differences in cultural orientation (Lee, Aaker, & Gardner, 2000) or childhood experience with caretakers (Higgins, 1998); or they may be situationally primed, as when people are prompted to think about their hopes and aspirations versus their duties and obligations (Freitas & Higgins, 2002), or about their financial investments in terms of stocks versus bonds (Zhou & Pham, 2004), or when their independent versus interdependent self-construal is made salient (Aaker & Lee, 2001). Regardless of whether their regulatory orientation is chronically accessible or temporarily primed, individuals with a promotion orientation strive toward growth and accomplishments. They focus on achieving their hopes and aspirations and are sensitive to the presence and absence of positive outcomes. They pursue their goals with eagerness, preferring strategies that ensure matches to their desired end-state; that is, they aim to approach gains and avoid nongains. On the other hand, individuals with a prevention orientation strive toward safety and security. They focus on fulfilling their duties and responsibilities and are sensitive to the presence and absence of negative outcomes. They pursue their goals with vigilance, preferring strategies that ensure against mismatches to their desired end-states; that is, they aim to avoid losses and approach nonlosses. Because of the different needs the two regulatory orientations service, certain goal-pursuit strategies may sustain one orientation (resulting in fit) but disrupt the other (resulting in nonfit). For example, an eager strategy that focuses on means of advancement (to attain gains and avoid nongains) would represent a regulatory fit for those with a promotion orientation but a regulatory nonfit for those with a prevention orientation. In contrast, a vigilant strategy that focuses on means of being careful (to avoid losses and maintain nonlosses) would represent a regulatory fit for those with a prevention orientation but a nonfit for those with a promotion orientation.

When people experience regulatory fit, their goal pursuit activity feels right. They become more strongly engaged in whatever they are doing and develop more intense reactions toward the goal enabling (or disabling) objects (Higgins, 2000, 2005). In the context of consumer judgment and choice, regulatory fit has been shown to impact attitudes, willingness to pay, and brand choice.

THE PERSUASIVENESS OF REGULATORY FIT

People experience regulatory fit when they process information or make trade-off decisions in a manner that aligns with their regulatory orientation. Decisions made under fit (vs. nonfit) conditions feel more right (Camacho, Higgins, & Luger, 2003), and the processing of fit (vs. nonfit) information is more fluent (Lee & Aaker, 2004; Labroo & Lee, 2006). When people's general reaction to a persuasive message or product is positive, the subjective experiences of feeling right and fluent processing can increase their willingness to pay, enhance the favorability of their attitudes, and facilitate their brand choice.

A review of the literature suggests there are at least three ways in which regulatory fit may be experienced. First, people may experience regulatory fit when they employ goal pursuit strategies that fit (vs. disrupt) their regulatory orientation. For example, Pham and Avnet (2004) showed that, when making a decision, individuals with a promotion orientation tend to rely more on their affect whereas those with a prevention orientation tend to rely more on reasons. Based on these findings, Avnet and Higgins (2006) asked research participants to choose between two brands of correction fluids either based on feelings or on reasons, and then indicate how much they would be willing to pay for the correction fluid. They found that promotion-oriented participants who evaluated the correction fluids based on their feelings were willing to pay 50% more for the product of their choice as compared to those who evaluated the correction fluids based on reasons; and prevention-oriented participants were willing to pay almost 40% more for the product when they evaluated the products based on reasons than on their feelings.

In another series of studies, research participants were asked to choose between a coffee mug and a pen by thinking what they would gain if they were to make each choice (i.e., an eager strategy favored by those with a promotion orientation) or what they would lose if they were not to make each choice (i.e., a vigilant strategy favored by those with a prevention orientation; Higgins, Idson, Freitas, Spiegel, & Molden, 2003). The results showed that promotion-oriented participants who focused on potential gains were willing to pay much more for the mug than were those who focused on potential losses. In contrast, prevention-oriented participants who focused on potential losses were willing to pay much more for the mug than were those who focused on potential gains.

A second way in which regulatory fit may be effected is when people process information that fits (vs. disrupts) their regulatory orientation. For example, in a study that examined the effectiveness of antismoking campaigns among teenagers, Zhao and Pechmann (2007) first measured the chronic regulatory orientation of

1200 ninth-graders and then exposed them to one of four different 30-second anti-smoking advertising messages. Each ad depicted an indoor gathering of a group of young college students and showed either a smoker lighting up a cigarette or a smoker putting out a cigarette. More specifically, one ad emphasized gains and showed people giving approving looks to a smoker after he put out the cigarette, and the smoker looking happy. Another ad emphasized nongains and showed people stop talking and smiling as the smoker lit up a cigarette, and the smoker looked sad when that happened. A third ad emphasized losses and showed people getting angry and giving disapproving looks to the smoker, and the smoker looking nervous; and the fourth ad emphasized nonlosses and showed people stop giving disapproving looks to the smoker after he put out the cigarette, and the smoker looked relieved. The authors found that promotion-oriented teenagers were most persuaded by the gain-framed ad to not smoke, whereas prevention-oriented teenagers were most persuaded by the loss-framed ad. These results showing that a gain (vs. nongain) frame is more persuasive for those with a promotion orientation and a loss (vs. nonloss) frame is more persuasive for those with a prevention orientation are consistent with the fit notion that striving toward gains involves more eagerness than does avoiding nongains, and avoiding losses involves more vigilance than does striving toward nonlosses (Idson, Liberman, & Higgins, 2000).

Keller (2006) demonstrated the regulatory fit effect by first priming participants with either a promotion or a prevention orientation, and then presenting them with a message advocating the use of sunscreen that highlights either an eager strategy that involves self-efficacy appraisals (e.g., how easy it is to use sunscreen) or a vigilant strategy that involves response efficacy appraisals (e.g., how effective the sunscreen is). Consistent with the regulatory fit hypothesis, promotion-oriented participants were more persuaded by the self-efficacy than by the response efficacy message whereas prevention-oriented participants were more persuaded by the response efficacy than by the self-efficacy message. Along similar lines, Cesario, Grant, and Higgins presented participants with a message advocating an after-school program (Cesario et al., 2004, Study 2). The program was described in either eager terms (e.g., advance, support, succeed) or vigilant terms (e.g., secure, prevent, failing). Their results showed that participants with a chronic promotion orientation were more persuaded by the eager (vs. vigilant) message, and the reverse was observed among those with a chronic prevention orientation. In another study, Werth and Förster (2007, Study 1) found that promotion-oriented participants were more persuaded by product information that emphasized comfort versus safety, and the reverse was observed among the prevention-oriented participants (see also Wang & Lee, 2006).

Similar effects of regulatory fit on persuasion are documented elsewhere. In striving for growth and accomplishments, individuals with a promotion orientation are more likely to represent their desired end-states at a more abstract, global level to ensure against missing any hits. And in striving for safety and security, those with a prevention orientation are more likely to represent their desired end-states at a more concrete, local level to avoid any mishaps. Thus, information construed at an abstract, high level should fit with a promotion orientation, whereas information construed at a concrete, low level should fit with a prevention orientation. Indeed,

Semin, Higgins, Gil de Montes, Estourget, & Valencia (Study 3, 2005) showed that promotion-oriented individuals were more persuaded by messages constructed with abstract predicates involving adjectives, whereas prevention-oriented individuals were more persuaded by messages constructed with concrete predicates involving action verbs. Keller, Lee, and Sternthal (2006) also found that advertising messages that address high-level desirability concerns lead to more favorable attitudes among those with a promotion orientation, whereas messages that address low-level feasibility concerns lead to more favorable attitudes among those with a prevention orientation. Conversely, Förster and Higgins (2005) manipulated whether participants first processed information globally or locally prior to choosing between two objects. More specifically, participants were presented with a series of global letters that were each made up of rows of closely spaced local letters, and were asked to identify either the global letter or the local letter. Then participants were instructed to choose between a mug and a pen by thinking about either what they would gain by choosing the pen or the mug (an eager strategy) or what they would lose by not choosing the pen or the mug (a vigilant strategy). The authors found that those who had just performed the global task assigned a higher price to their chosen object if they used eager means to make their decision rather than vigilant means, whereas the reverse was true for those who had just completed the local task. These results offer convergent evidence for a fit relationship between one's regulatory orientation and construal level. For an excellent discussion of high- versus low-level processing, please see the chapter on construal level theory by Eyal, Liberman, and Trope in this volume.

More recent research showed that regulatory fit may also be created by nonverbal behaviors of the source of the message. More specifically, Cesario and Higgins (2007) showed that gestures, speech rate, and body position and movements that convey a sense of eagerness versus vigilance during message delivery resulted in a more effective message for recipients with distinct regulatory orientations. Recipients' "feeling right" experience was thought to underlie the regulatory fit effect on message effectiveness.

Finally, regulatory fit may be operationalized within a message that renders the message more persuasive, independent of the regulatory orientation of the message recipients (e.g., Cesario et al., 2004, Study 1; Lee & Aaker, 2004). The idea is that a message advocating an end-state may be represented in the recipient's mind as a servicing promotion or prevention goal, and fit (vs. nonfit) is effected when the message prompts the recipient also to think about fulfilling that goal using either eager or vigilant means. For example, Lee and Aaker (2004) presented participants with advertising messages that address either promotion concerns that emphasized growth (e.g., get energized) or prevention concerns that emphasized safety (e.g., prevent clogged arteries). Their results showed that promotion messages are more persuasive when they focus on gains (e.g., get energized) than on nongains (e.g., miss out on getting energized); and prevention messages are more persuasive when they focus on losses (e.g., miss out on preventing clogged arteries) than on nonlosses (e.g., prevent clogged arteries).

Thus, the evidence is clear that fit messages can be more persuasive than nonfit messages. It is important to note that these regulatory fit effects observed are reflective of a self-regulatory goal system that is distinct from a simple approach-avoidance system. In particular, regulatory focus theory distinguishes between two separate approach-avoidance systems: a promotion system that approaches gains and avoids nongains, and a prevention system that approaches nonlosses and avoids losses (see Higgins, 1997). This distinction was highlighted by Labroo and Lee (2006), who tested whether the fit effect conforms to the hedonic principles of approach and avoidance (i.e., greater persuasion occurs when there is a valence match of positive vs. negative outcomes), or to the regulatory orientations of promotion and prevention (i.e., greater persuasion occurs when there is a regulatory focus match of promotion vs. prevention). In their study, they first presented participants with either a gain-framed (e.g., "feeling confident") or a loss-framed (e.g., "feeling humiliated") prime, and then asked them to evaluate a nongain-framed (e.g., "not feeling great") or a nonloss-framed ("freedom from embarrassment") targe . If the fit effect relies on a valence match of approach and avoidance, then gair primed participants should evaluate the nonloss target more favorably than the nongain target, and loss-primed participants should evaluate the nongain target more favorably than the nonloss target. On the other hand, if the fit effect relies on a regulatory focus match of promotion and prevention, then gain-primed participants should evaluate the nongain target more favorably than the nonloss target, and the reverse should hold for the loss-primed participants. The results were consistent with a regulatory focus match and provided clear evidence that the regulatory fit effect on persuasion is *not* a hedonic matching effect.

What is also becoming clear is that the two distinct regulatory focus orientations represent two complex motivational systems. Table 14.1 provides a summary of what we currently know about these two complex systems. The implication is that any combination of the elements within each system can potentially be used to create fit and in turn affect judgment and choice. Further, each of these elements may potentially moderate established regulatory fit effects by introducing nonfit. Empirical evidence of these effects awaits future research.

MECHANISMS UNDERLYING THE REGULATORY FIT EFFECTS

What drives the regulatory fit effect on persuasion?

Regulatory fit makes people "feel right" about what they are doing and makes them engage more strongly in what they are doing (Higgins, 2000). These two factors are obviously related given that engaging strongly and fluently in what one is doing is likely to make what one is doing "feel right"; and "feeling right" about what one is doing is likely to make one engage more strongly in it. Although related in these ways, it is still possible for each of these factors to have its own separate influence on persuasion. How these two factors may have separate, conjoined, or interactive effects on persuasion is a central question for future research on regulatory fit and persuasion. Given that any answer to this question would be mostly speculative at this point, we will not address these issues in this chapter, except to recognize that regulatory fit can influence persuasion through either the "feeling

TABLE 14.1   Potential Matches within the Promotion and Prevention Systems

Promotion System	Prevention System	Source
Nurturance Needs	Security Needs	Higgins, 1997
Ideal Self-Standards	Ought Self-Standards	Higgins, 1997
Independent Self-Construal	Interdependent Self-Construal	Lee et al., 2000
Cheerfulness/Dejection	Calmness/Agitation	Higgins, 1997
Gain/Nongain Incentives	Loss/Nonloss Incentives	Higgins, 1997
Eagerness Strategies	Vigilance Strategies	Higgins et al., 2003
Abstract, Global Construal	Concrete, Local Construal	Semin et al., 2005 Förster & Higgins, 2005
Distant Temporal Distance	Proximal Temporal Distance	Pennington & Roese, 2003
Creative	Analytical	Crowe & Higgins, 1997 Friedman & Förster, 2001 Zhu & Meyers-Levy, 2007
Affect-Based Processing	Reason-Based Processing	Pham & Avnet, 2004 Avnet & Higgins, 2006
Change, Attainment	Stability, Maintenance	Liberman et al., 1999 Brodscholl et al., 2007
Speed, Quantity	Accuracy, Quality	Förster et al., 2003
Additive Counterfactuals	Subtractive Counterfactuals	Roese et al., 1999

right" or engagement strength mechanism and that the psychological processes underlying the effects of these two mechanisms need not be the same. Because most previous research testing regulatory fit effects on persuasion have been more concerned with the "feeling right" experience than with engagement strength per se, we will emphasize here the regulatory fit factor of "feeling right."

When people experience regulatory fit, the goal pursuit activity "feels right." One way that this "feeling right" experience could influence persuasion is that it informs the individual about something, just as other kinds of feelings can be informative (Schwarz, 1990; Schwarz & Clore, 1983, 1988; for a review see Pham, this volume). In this way, for example, "feeling right" while processing a message could persuade people to eat more fruits and vegetables (Cesario et al., 2004), make an after-school program more worthy of supporting (Camacho et al., 2003), or render certain products more attractive (Higgins et al., 2003; Labroo & Lee, 2006).

There are different ways in which "feeling right" could be informative and potentially influence persuasion. For example, the message recipients may "feel right" about the goal advocated in the message (e.g., implementing an after-school program), resulting in more favorable attitudes toward the goal. Alternatively, they may "feel right" about the message and consider the arguments put forth to be more persuasive, which in turn leads to more favorable attitudes toward the target. It is also possible that message recipients "feel right" about their reaction to the message, in which case, their reaction will be intensified—positive attitudes become more positive, and negative attitudes become more negative (e.g., Cesario et al., 2004).

That greater persuasion can come from people "feeling right" about their reactions receives some support from the research by Higgins and colleagues (2003). In particular, their results showed that the higher value of some chosen products for those who "feel right" from regulatory fit is *not* due to some simple inference process, such as the following: (1) My decision to choose this product must be good if I feel right about it; and (2) if I made a good decision in choosing this product, then the product must be good. Higgins and colleagues (2003) report that regulatory fit does not make people believe that their decision-making process was better or more effective. Rather, regulatory fit seems to involve a general state of feeling right that can create value by intensifying people's evaluative response to something. Further, the effect of regulatory fit can go beyond the task at hand to influence subsequent evaluations. In other words, the influence of regulatory fit on value creation and persuasion can be an incidental, ambient effect and need not be task-specific or integral to the target. Higgins and colleagues (2003, Study 4) demonstrated this ambient effect of regulatory fit by asking people to first think about their hopes and aspirations (a promotion induction) or their duties and obligations (a prevention induction), and then write down either five eagerness-related (a promotion strategy) or five vigilance-related (a prevention strategy) action plans. Later, all participants were asked to rate how good-natured some dogs are in an allegedly unrelated study. Participants who experienced fit (i.e., those who generated eagerness action plans to fulfill hopes and aspirations and those who generated vigilance action plans to fulfill duties and obligations) rated the dogs as more good-natured than did those who experienced nonfit (i.e., those who generated vigilance action plans to fulfill hopes and aspirations and those who generated eagerness action plans to fulfill duties and obligations).

The ambient effect of regulatory fit was also demonstrated by Hong and Lee (2008, Study 4). Participants in their study were first presented with a message about getting tested for hepatitis C and were asked to evaluate the persuasiveness of the message. Then the regulatory fit manipulation was introduced, followed by participants indicating their intention to get tested for hepatitis C. Because regulatory fit was manipulated using an induction that was unrelated to hepatitis C *after* participants read the message, results showing no difference in participants' evaluation of the message prior to the fit manipulation but greater intention to get tested for hepatitis C among those who experienced fit (vs. nonfit) provide further support for the notion that regulatory fit creates value through intensifying reactions rather than through inferential reasoning involving message persuasiveness.

If the regulatory fit effect on persuasion can occur because people attribute their "feeling right" experience from regulatory fit to feeling right about their response to something else, then alerting people to the true source of their feeling should eliminate the regulatory fit effect. To test this, Cesario and colleagues (2004, Study 3) directed half of their participants' attention to the correct source of their feeling right experience by telling them that "sometimes thinking about using the right means to attain each goal can make people 'feel right' about their goal pursuit" and asking them to indicate the extent to which they "felt right." As predicted, this manipulation eliminated the regulatory fit effect on judgment. The effects of "feeling right" are in many ways similar to those observed when people experience positive mood (e.g., Schwarz & Clore, 1983; see also the review on mood by Pham in this volume). However, the "feeling right" experience is distinct from hedonic positive mood. In particular, Cesario and colleagues (2004, Studies 3 and 4) found that regulatory fit and hedonic positive mood each had significant independent effects on attitudes; the effect of regulatory fit remained significant when participants' mood was controlled for in the model.

The findings from these studies suggest that people "feel right" when they adopt strategies that fit with their regulatory orientations. When people are not aware of the source of their "feeling right" experience, this fit experience can intensify their evaluative response to something else. However, "feeling right" is not the only mechanism through which regulatory fit can influence judgment. Regulatory fit also enhances engagement strength, as demonstrated by Hong and Lee (2008), who showed that participants experiencing regulatory fit relative to a control group were able to squeeze a handgrip longer and solve more anagrams, and had more willpower to resist temptation. In contrast, participants who experienced regulatory nonfit showed weakened engagement strength relative to those in the control group.

It is notable that the mechanism of increased engagement strength from regulatory fit could also contribute to people's evaluative response being intensified (see Higgins, 2006). That is, both "feeling right" from fit and increased engagement strength from fit can contribute to the same regulatory fit effect—intensified reactions to something. Further, both mechanisms can also contribute to another regulatory fit effect documented in the literature—increased fluency of message processing (Labroo & Lee, 2006; Lee & Aaker, 2004). Such a fluency effect of fit was first documented in Lee and Aaker's (2004) research, where regulatory fit was operationalized not by a match between people's regulatory orientation and their decision-making strategies, but by a match between different elements of the message. Lee and Aaker (2004) reported that a fit message is easier to process than a nonfit message. More specifically, participants read either a promotion or prevention message advocating the benefits of Welch's grape juice, and the message was framed either positively or negatively. Some participants subsequently completed a perceptual identification task whereby they were asked to identify target words presented very briefly on the computer screen (50 ms). The results showed that participants could more readily identify words that came from fit versus nonfit messages (Study 4b). In another study, participants indicated that the fit messages were easier to process and to understand than nonfit messages. Mediation analysis shows that the regulatory fit effect on persuasion was mediated by participants' perceived processing fluency of the message (Study 4a). Interestingly, participants were also asked to generate reasons why one would drink Welch's grape juice. Although participants exposed to the fit messages generated more support reasons than did those exposed to the nonfit messages, the number of reasons did not mediate the regulatory fit effect observed (Study 5). Once again, these findings suggest that regulatory fit effects on persuasion are not driven by inferential reasoning but by mechanisms—the "feeling right" experience and increased engagement strength—that can intensify people's reactions. (For a more thorough discussion of the effects of processing fluency and retrieval ease, please see the chapter on ease by Schwarz, Song, & Xu in this volume.)

Considering that the regulatory fit experience involves both "feeling right" and engagement strength, the question of how these two constructs relate naturally follows. It is possible that fluent processing of the fit message may be the result of stronger engagement from fit, and fluent processing of the fit message may offer a "feel right" experience for the message recipient that can lead to more favorable attitudes. Further investigations of the relationship between engagement, processing fluency, and "feeling right" within the nomological network of regulatory fit effects should provide a fruitful avenue of future research.

BOUNDARY CONDITIONS OF THE REGULATORY FIT EFFECT

Most the studies reviewed so far suggest that regulatory fit has a positive effect on value generation and persuasion. However, it is important to note that there are at least two conditions under which a more positive outcome may not be observed. The first boundary condition involves the valence of people's response. When people experience regulatory fit, they "feel right" about the goal-pursuit activity and become more strongly engaged in the activity. However, this heightened engagement or "feeling right" experience does not necessarily lead to more favorable evaluations. As discussed earlier, regulatory fit intensifies, rather than enhances, reactions. Thus, if people's evaluation of a target is positive, their assessment becomes more positive when they experience regulatory fit; but if their evaluation is negative, their assessment becomes more negative when they experience regulatory fit.

To illustrate, Cesario and colleagues (2004, Study 4) first induced the experience of regulatory fit or nonfit among their participants, and then presented them with a proposal for an after-school program. Participants were asked to evaluate the proposal and also to list their thoughts about the possible consequences of the proposal. The results showed that when participants felt right about their positive thoughts, they developed more favorable attitudes toward the proposal, whereas when they felt right about their negative thoughts, they developed *less* favorable attitudes toward the proposal. Further evidence that regulatory fit intensifies reaction is presented by Aaker and Lee (2001, Study 3). In their study, the authors manipulated argument strength and regulatory fit in an advertising message about tennis racquets. Regulatory fit was operationalized by priming participants' independent or interdependent self-construal, which has been shown to be associated with distinct regulatory orientation (Lee et al., 2000), and by making salient either eager means (to win the tennis tournament) or vigilant means (to not lose the tennis tournament) of goal pursuit in the message. They found that participants evaluated the tennis racquet more positively when they were presented with the fit than the nonfit message, but only when the arguments were strong. Participants evaluated the tennis racquet in the fit (vs. nonfit) message less positively when the arguments were weak.

A second boundary condition of the regulatory fit effect on persuasion involves motivation. Lee and Aaker (2004) showed that the regulatory fit effect on participants' evaluations of the product was *not* mediated by the number of support reasons they generated; rather, the effect was mediated by processing fluency. Thus, the regulatory fit effect seems to reflect people relying on their "it feels right" experience rather than on the strength of their arguments for judgment and decision making. When they are alerted to the source of this feeling, the regulatory fit effect disappears (Cesario et al., 2004), presumably because people are motivated to make good, unbiased decisions. The implication is that when people are explicitly motivated to process information by way of reasoned action, the regulatory fit experience has less influence over their judgment. Of course, this moderating effect of involvement should depend on whether the regulatory fit effect on persuasion derives from the "feeling right" mechanism or from the strength of engagement mechanism. A bias from "feeling right" may be more easily controlled when people are motivated, but a bias from engagement strength may be more difficult to detect and in turn control.

Recent research by Wang and Lee (2006) further illustrates the importance of taking into account people's initial motivation to process information in studying the regulatory fit effect on persuasion. The authors manipulated involvement in their studies by telling participants that they were part of either a small select group of respondents whose opinion really mattered (high involvement) or a large sample of respondents whose evaluation would be averaged for consideration (low involvement). Their results showed that the regulatory fit effect on information search, judgment, and choice was observed only in the low-involvement condition. When participants were motivated to process information, the regulatory fit effect disappeared. Hong and Lee (2008) also showed that people who experienced regulatory fit were more likely to get tested for hepatitis C, but only when they did not perceive themselves to be at high risk. Participants who thought they were vulnerable to the disease were equally likely to get tested in the fit and nonfit conditions. One explanation for such findings is that high personal or issue involvement creates high engagement strength by itself, without the need for regulatory fit. The implication is that only when engagement strength is relatively low or moderate, as when personal or issue involvement is not high, will regulatory fit effects from increasing engagement strength (or from "feeling right") be observed.

In summary, the regulatory fit effect is observed when people are not highly motivated to process information (Hong & Lee, 2008; Wang & Lee, 2006), or when they are not aware of the source of their "feeling right" experience (Cesario et al., 2004). Further, the regulatory fit experience—both "feeling right" and engagement strength—is better conceptualized as a magnifier than as an enhancer of attitudes. Generally speaking, when people experience regulatory fit, their reactions are intensified—positive reactions become more positive, and negative reactions become more negative.

Finally, it should be noted that regulatory nonfit, which is an interesting psychological experience in its own right, has been shown to dampen willingness to pay (e.g., Avnet & Higgins, 2006), foster less favorable attitudes (e.g., Aaker & Lee, 2001; Lee & Aaker, 2004), and lower probability of brand choice (e.g., Wang

& Lee, 2006). However, the general feeling that something does not feel right (feels wrong, is problematic) may signal that more scrutiny is necessary. And this increased scrutiny may lead to more positive response if the initial incongruity can be resolved and/or if systematic or elaborated processing reveals that a product's attributes or a message's arguments are of high quality. In this light, regulatory nonfit effects on persuasion also merit more research attention in the future.

BEYOND PERSUASION

The effects of regulatory fit and nonfit are not limited to persuasion effects (see Higgins, 2005). As just one example, recent research by Hong and Lee (2008) suggests that the experience of regulatory fit strengthens self-regulation (which underlies successful goal attainment), whereas the experience of regulatory nonfit undermines self-regulation. In a series of studies, they examined the effects of regulatory fit and nonfit using a variety of self-regulation tasks. The results showed that participants who experienced regulatory fit could squeeze a handgrip longer and were more likely to get tested for hepatitis relative to those who experienced regulatory nonfit. Further, relative to a control group, participants who experienced regulatory fit were less likely to yield to temptation; in particular, these participants were more likely to choose an apple versus a chocolate bar for a snack relative to a control group, whereas those who experienced regulatory nonfit were more likely to choose the chocolate bar versus the apple relative to the control.

There is also evidence that the "feeling right" experience from regulatory fit can increase one's well-being because it involves experiencing oneself as behaving in a suitable and appropriate manner. This experience of responding in the right way to objects and events in the world has been shown to produce beneficial effects on physical health, as evidenced from a daily diary study on emotional well-being that using strategies that fit one's dominant regulatory focus when coping with life hassles is beneficial (Grant, Higgins, Baer, & Bolger, 2005).

These findings have important implications for people's welfare in general, and consumers in particular, especially in the health domain. First, regulatory fit may enhance subjective well-being by invoking an "it feels right" experience. The regulatory fit effect on persuasion may enhance compliance with various health-related initiatives by rendering the arguments more valid or the advocated cause more worthy of pursuit. Further, the "feeling right" experience and increased engagement strength may promote confidence and heighten motivation, both of which may serve to buffer the anticipatory anxiety that so often prevents people from taking diagnostic tests or discourages them from seeking treatment for different medical conditions. Finally, the regulatory fit effect on self-regulation may help tackle the many health-related problems such as obesity, substance abuse, and impulsive behaviors that require significant self-control.

CONCLUSION

Consumers are goal-driven. Regardless of whether their needs for nurturance and security are chronically accessible or temporarily made salient situationally, consumers' regulatory focus orientation has a significant influence on how they process information, evaluate products, and make brand choice decisions. In this chapter, we have limited our review of the literature to the persuasion effects of regulatory fit from regulatory focus (see also Cesario, Higgins, & Scholer, 2007). We have offered only a glimpse into the role of two complex motivational systems in regulatory fit and the resultant effects of fit on persuasion. There is a lot more to learn about the effects of regulatory fit and nonfit.

For example, we have identified two possible mediators of the regulatory fit effect on persuasion: the "feeling right" experience and engagement strength. What are the conditions under which each of these mediators may account for the regulatory fit effect? Do these constructs interact, and if so, how? We have also identified three ways in which regulatory fit may be operationalized: (1) when individuals use goal-pursuit strategies that match (vs. disrupt) their regulatory orientations, (2) individuals process information that makes salient certain goal pursuit strategies that match (vs. disrupt) their regulatory orientation, and (3) when elements within a message are represented as fit (vs. nonfit) in the recipients' mind. Do different mechanisms underlie the regulatory fit effect depending on how regulatory fit is operationalized? We have discussed regulatory fit as exerting an ambient, incidental effect versus an integral, task-specific effect on judgment. Are these effects different or similar? Many questions remain unanswered, and more are yet to surface.

REFERENCES

Aaker, J. L., & Lee, A. Y. (2001). I seek pleasures and we avoid pains: The role of self regulatory goals in information processing and persuasion. *Journal of Consumer Research, 28*, 33–49.

Avnet, T., & Higgins, E. T. (2003). Locomotion, assessment, and regulatory fit: Value transfer from "how" to "what." *Journal of Experimental Social Psychology, 39*, 525–530.

Avnet, T., & Higgins, E. T. (2006). How regulatory fit affects value in consumer choices and opinions. *Journal of Marketing Research, 43*, 1–10.

Bianco, A. T., Higgins, E. T., & Klem, A. (2003). How "fun/importance" fit impacts performance: Relating implicit theories to instructions. *Personality and Social Psychology Bulletin, 29*, 1091–1103.

Brodscholl, J. C., Kober, H., & Higgins, E. T. (2007). Strategies of self-regulation in goal attainment versus goal maintenance. *European Journal of Social Psychology, 37*, 628–648.

Camacho, C. J., Higgins, E. T., & Luger, L. (2003). Moral value transfer from regulatory fit: What feels right is right and what feels wrong is wrong. *Journal of Personality & Social Psychology, 84*, 498–510.

Cesario, J., Grant, H., & Higgins, E. T. (2004). Regulatory fit and persuasion: Transfer from "feeling right." *Journal of Personality and Social Psychology, 86*, 388–404.

Cesario, J., & Higgins, E. T. (2007). How nonverbal behaviors can increase persuasion by making message recipients "feel right." Manuscript submitted for publication.

Cesario, J., Higgins, E. T., & Scholer, A. A. (2007). Regulatory fit and persuasion: Basic principles and remaining questions. Unpublished manuscript, Michigan State University.

Crowe, E., & Higgins, E. T. (1997). Regulatory focus and strategic inclinations: Promotion and prevention in decision-making. *Organizational Behavior and Human Decision Processes, 69,* 117–132.

Förster, J., & Higgins, E. T. (2005). How global vs. local perception fits regulatory focus. *Psychological Science, 16,* 631–636.

Förster, J., Higgins, E. T., & Bianco, A. T. (2003). Speed/accuracy decisions in task performance: Built-in trade-off or separate strategic concerns? *Organizational Behavior and Human Decision Processes, 90,* 148–164.

Freitas, A. L., & Higgins, E. T. (2002). Enjoying goal-directed actions: The role of regulatory fit. *Psychological Science, 13,* 1–6.

Friedman, R. S., & Förster, J. (2001). The effects of promotion and prevention cues on creativity. *Journal of Personality and Social Psychology, 81,* 1001–1013.

Grant, H., Higgins, E. T., Baer, A., & Bolger, N. (2005). Coping style and regulatory fit: Emotional ups and downs in daily life. Unpublished manuscript, Columbia University.

Higgins, E. T. (1997). Beyond pleasure and pain. *American Psychologist, 52,* 1280–1300.

Higgins, E. T. (1998). Promotion and prevention: Regulatory focus as a motivational principle. In M. P. Zanna (Ed.), *Advances in experimental social psychology* (Vol. 30, pp. 1–46). New York: Academic Press.

Higgins, E. T. (2000). Making a good decision: Value from fit. *American Psychologist, 55,* 1217–1230.

Higgins, E. T. (2005). Value from regulatory fit. *Current Directions in Psychological Science, 14,* 208–213.

Higgins, E. T. (2006). Value from hedonic experience *and* engagement. *Psychological Review, 113,* 439–460.

Higgins, E. T., Idson, L. C., Freitas, A. L., Spiegel, S., & Molden, D. C. (2003). Transfer of value from fit. *Journal of Personality and Social Psychology, 84,* 1140–1153.

Hong, J., & Lee, A. Y. (2008). Be fit and be strong: Mastering self-regulation with regulatory fit. *Journal of Consumer Research, 36,* 682–695.

Idson, L. C., Liberman, N., & Higgins, E. T. (2000). Distinguishing gains from nonlosses and losses from nongains: A regulatory focus perspective on hedonic intensity. *Journal of Experimental Social Psychology, 36,* 252–274.

Keller, A. P. (2006). Regulatory focus and efficacy of health messages. *Journal of Consumer Research, 33,* 109–114.

Keller, P., Lee, A. Y., & Sternthal, B. (2006). Construing fit to judgment: The effects of regulatory focus and level of construal. Working paper, Kellogg School of Management, Northwestern University.

Kruglanski, A. W., Thompson, E. P., Higgins, E. T., Atash, M. N., Pierro, A., Shah, J. Y., & Spiegel, S. (2000). To "do the right thing" or to "just do it": Locomotion and assessment as distinct self-regulatory imperatives. *Journal of Personality and Social Psychology, 79,* 793–815.

Labroo, A., & Lee, A. Y. (2006). Between two brands: A goal fluency account of brand evaluation. *Journal of Marketing Research, 18,* 374–385.

Lee, A. Y., & Aaker, J. L. (2004). Bringing the frame into focus: The influence of regulatory fit on processing fluency and persuasion. *Journal of Personality and Social Psychology, 86,* 205–218.

Lee, A. Y., Aaker, J. L., & Gardner, W. L. (2000). The pleasures and pains of distinct self-construals: The role of interdependence in regulatory focus. *Journal of Personality and Social Psychology, 78,* 1122–1134.

Liberman, N., Idson, L. C., Camacho, C. J., & Higgins, E. T. (1999). Promotion and prevention choices between stability and change. *Journal of Personality and Social Psychology, 77,* 1135–1145.

Pennington, G. L., & Roese, N. J. (2003). Regulatory focus and temporal perspective. *Journal of Experimental Social Psychology, 39*, 563–576.

Pham, M., & Avnet, T. (2004). Ideals and oughts and the reliance on affect versus substance in persuasion. *Journal of Consumer Research, 30*, 503–518.

Roese, N. J., Hur, T., & Pennington, G. (1999). Counterfactual thinking and regulatory focus: Implications for action versus inaction and sufficiency versus necessity. *Journal of Personality and Social Psychology, 77*, 1109–1120.

Schwarz, N. (1990). Feelings as information: Informational and motivational functions of affective states. In E. T. Higgins & R. M. Sorrentino (Eds.), *Handbook of motivation and cognition: Foundations of social behavior* (Vol. 2, pp. 527–561). New York: Guilford Press.

Schwarz, N., & Clore, G. L. (1983). Mood, misattribution, and judgments of well-being: Informative and directive functions of affective states. *Journal of Personality and Social Psychology, 45*, 513–523.

Schwarz, N., & Clore, G. L. (1988). How do I feel about it? The informative function of affective states. In K. Fiedler and J. Forgas (Eds.), *Affect, cognition and social behavior* (pp. 44–62). Toronto: C. J. Hogrefe.

Semin, G. R., Higgins, E. T., Gil de Montes, L., Estourget, Y., & Valencia, J. (2005). Linguistic signatures of regulatory focus: How abstraction fits promotion more than prevention. *Journal of Personality and Social Psychology, 89*, 36–45

Wang, J., & Lee, A. Y. (2006). The role of regulatory focus in preference construction. *Journal of Marketing Research, 43*, 28–38.

Werth, L., and Förster, J. (2007). The effects of regulatory focus on braking speed. *Journal of Applied Social Psychology, 44*, 671–687.

Zhao, G., & Pechmann, C. (in press). The impact of regulatory focus on adolescents' response to antismoking advertising campaigns. *Journal of Marketing Research*.

Zhou, R., & Pham, M. (2004). Promotion and prevention across mental accounts: When financial products dictate consumers' investment goals. *Journal of Consumer Research, 31*, 125–135.

Zhu, R., & Meyers-Levy, J. (2007). Exploring the cognitive mechanism that underlies regulatory focus effects. *Journal of Consumer Research, 34*, 89–96.

15

The Impulsive Consumer
Predicting Consumer Behavior with Implicit Reaction Time Measures

MALTE FRIESE

University of Basel, Switzerland

WILHELM HOFMANN

University of Würzburg, Germany

MICHAELA WÄNKE

University of Basel, Switzerland

An examination of contemporary textbooks on consumer behavior reveals that research in this area has been dominated by the use of explicit self-report measures to uncover what consumers think and feel about products, advertisements, or consumption-related behaviors (e.g., Blackwell, Miniard, & Engel, 2001; Kardes, 2002). In fact, social psychology in general has relied heavily on these measures, such as feeling thermometers and Likert-type or semantic differential scales (Kihlstrom, 2004). There is no doubt that self-report measures have helped further our understanding of consumer behavior, and they indeed predict behavior quite well if used appropriately (Ajzen & Fishbein, 1977; Glasman & Albarracín, 2006; Vargas, 2004). Yet despite their popularity there is also some discontent with self-report measures: For instance, they are subject to self-presentational distortions; they require respondents to have conscious access to their attitudes and to be willing to retrieve or construe them (Cacioppo & Sandman, 1981); they are subject to cognitive and communicative biases that occur during question comprehension and judgment formation (Sudman, Bradburn, & Schwarz, 1996);

and perhaps most importantly, self-reports tap into more elaborated thoughts rather than spontaneous reactions (Fazio & Olson, 2003). All of these limitations of course restrict the predictive validity of self-reported attitudes. The recent redis-covery that human behavior in general and consumer behavior in particular is partly influenced by spontaneous or impulsive processes that can occur outside of people's conscious awareness (see Dijksterhuis, this volume; De Houwer, this volume) renders self-reports less useful for the prediction of such behaviors. Indirect measures and especially measures based on reaction times—often referred to as implicit measures—seem a promising alternative. To the extent that consumer behavior is influenced by impulsive processes, and to the extent that implicit mea-sures tap into these processes, implicit measures may prove to be a valuable supple-ment to researchers' toolboxes (Fazio & Olson, 2003). This chapter focuses on the prediction of consumer behavior with such implicit reaction time measures.

In the first part of this chapter we will give a very brief overview of the use of indirect measures in consumer research and of the most prominent implicit reaction time measures in current use. After this rather technical introduction we will review studies that explored whether and to what extent implicit measures contribute to the prediction of consumer behavior over and above explicit self-report measures on a general level. In a third section, we will review a series of studies that investigated under what specific circumstances implicit measures are especially likely to contribute to the prediction of consumer behavior. We argue that any sophisticated attempt to predict consumer behavior needs to consider multiple and interacting influences in order to unscramble the dynamics of behav-ior regulation.

IMPLICIT MEASURES

Researchers have long recognized the reactivity of explicit self-report measures, prompting them to find ways to assess attitudes and other constructs indirectly (e.g., Webb, Campbell, Schwartz, & Sechrest, 1966). Indirect measures do not ask respondents directly for a self-assessment of (for example) an attitude. Rather, the attitude is assumed to influence some kind of other behavior and the inten-sity of the influence is considered to be indicative of the underlying attitude (De Houwer, 2006). Haire's shopping list procedure is a widely celebrated example of how indirect measures can contribute relevant information where self-reports fail (Haire, 1950). When instant coffee was introduced in 1949, sales were disappoint-ing. Consumers reported disliking the taste—a clear contradiction of the results of previously conducted blind taste tests in which consumers had not noticed a difference between instant and drip coffee. Instead of asking consumers directly for their opinion of instant coffee, Haire gave them a shopping list and asked them to describe the person who had allegedly written the list. Among other items the list contained Nescafé instant coffee in one condition or Maxwell drip coffee in the other condition. When consumers described the instant coffee buyer as lazy and an inadequate mother and housewife, it became clear that poor taste was probably not the reason that kept consumers from buying instant coffee, despite what they claimed overtly.

Free-association procedures are also used in market research. They are based on the assumption that people have more positive associations toward objects they like than toward objects they dislike. The numbers of positive and negative associations that are reported by respondents serve as indirect indicators of their attitudes (Salcher, 1995). The error-choice technique introduced by Hammond (1948) works in a similar manner. The task is described as a knowledge test. Respondents choose between two alternative answers to a question, both of which are, in fact, wrong. One is favorably biased for the product in question, the other unfavorably. The assumption is that underlying attitudes toward the product influence the answers to the questions. For example, say a manufacturer of potato chips has reduced the fat content of the product by 10%. If consumers are asked, "How much has the fat content of these potato chips been reduced?" and the possible answers are "5%" and "15%," a more positive attitude toward the product would be assumed if respondents chose the higher percentage, because low fat content is generally regarded as a positive product feature.

Thanks to the development of personal computers over the last 25 years or so, which enabled the reliable measurement of reaction times, a number of techniques based on reaction times have been developed (for reviews, see Fazio & Olson, 2003; Wittenbrink & Schwarz, 2007). Borrowing from memory research, where implicit measures do not require conscious recollection of the material (Roediger, 1990), these new reaction-time measures have been referred to as implicit measures, emphasizing their difference from explicit self-reports. De Houwer (2006) proposed several characteristics that define the implicitness of an implicit measure. Among the assumptions most often brought forward by many researchers are that respondents are not aware of what is being assessed with the procedure and that the assessed content is not available for introspection, even if respondents might have the motivation to report it. Also, implicit measures are assumed to be more difficult to fake than traditional self-report measures (e.g., Steffens, 2004). Of course, this last property is of special importance in sensitive domains in which explicit measures may lack adequate validity.

However, the extent to which the techniques commonly used today meet all or any of these criteria is open to debate (De Houwer, 2006). Although such measures are not necessarily covert or nonreactive, nor is the content necessarily unavailable for introspection, it is safe to assume that implicit attitude measures capture a good deal of rather spontaneously available evaluative reactions (Conrey, Sherman, Gawronski, Hugenberg, & Groom, 2005; Payne, 2005).[1] Therefore, in line with Fazio and Olson (2003), and supported by its wide acceptance in the literature, we will continue to use the term *implicit measures*.

Among implicit measures based on reaction time are evaluative (Fazio, Jackson, Dunton, & Williams, 1995; Fazio, Sanbonmatsu, Powell, & Kardes, 1986) and semantic (Wittenbrink, Judd, & Park, 1997) priming procedures, the Extrinsic Affective Simon Task (EAST; De Houwer, 2003), and the Go/No-Go Association Task (GNAT; Nosek & Banaji, 2001), to name just a few. Most prominently, the Implicit Association Test (IAT; Greenwald, McGhee, & Schwartz, 1998) has provoked a vast amount of research in social psychology and many other subdisciplines (for reviews, see Lane, Banaji, Nosek, & Greenwald, 2007; Nosek, Greenwald, &

Banaji, 2006). The IAT has attracted much attention in part because of the large effect sizes it delivers, the usually high reliability estimates compared with other implicit measures, and encouraging construct and predictive validity (Friese, Hofmann, & Schmitt, 2008; Greenwald, Poehlman, Uhlmann, & Banaji, in press; Nosek et al., 2006). Besides, it is easy to administer.

The IAT is intended to measure the strength of associations between concepts (Greenwald et al., 1998). In a typical IAT, stimuli of two target categories and two attribute categories have to be sorted on just two response keys. For example, in one critical block, the categories *Mercedes* and *pleasant* may share a response key and the categories *BMW* and *unpleasant* share another response key. In another critical block the assignment for *Mercedes* and *BMW* is reversed. If participants are faster in categorizing *Mercedes* and *pleasant* (and *BMW* and *unpleasant*) than in categorizing *Mercedes* and *unpleasant* (vs. *BMW* and *pleasant*) on the same response key, a positive spontaneous reaction toward Mercedes relative to BMW is inferred. This difference in average response latencies of these two critical blocks is termed the IAT effect (see Greenwald, Nosek, & Banaji, 2003, for details on the scoring algorithm). As becomes clear from this description, the IAT delivers an index of a person's *relative* preference. It is thus particularly valuable when researchers are interested in such a relative preference and where a natural or reasonable counter-category exists (e.g., Coke vs. Pepsi, women vs. men). However, in many circumstances researchers may be interested in assessing absolute rather than relative preferences for a single target category in focus (e.g., only Mercedes). Several measures have been developed for this very purpose (e.g., the EAST or the GNAT). A close relative of the original IAT seems to be especially promising, due to its comparatively encouraging psychometric properties, the Single Category Implicit Association Test (SC-IAT; Karpinski & Steinman, 2006; see Bluemke & Friese, in press, for an investigation of the psychometric properties). For example, in the SC-IAT a target category (e.g., Mercedes) is paired with pleasant stimuli in one critical block and with unpleasant stimuli in the other block. The difference in average reaction times of these blocks provides an estimate for whether the spontaneous reaction of a person toward Mercedes is rather positive or negative, irrespective of any other related target objects (e.g., BMW).

It should be noted that research has revealed how IAT effects can be influenced by other factors besides attitudes or other constructs of interest. Hence, the absolute interpretation of IAT effects as an attitude measure may be difficult (Bluemke & Friese, 2006; Fiedler, Messner, & Bluemke, 2006; Mierke & Klauer, 2003; Rothermund & Wentura, 2004). Research relying on correlations instead of mean effects may be better suited to demonstrate validity that emerges despite these unwanted influences. Both IAT and SC-IAT measures as well as other implicit measures have been used this way in the study of consumer behavior, as we will see shortly.

DO IMPLICIT MEASURES PREDICT CONSUMER BEHAVIOR?

Contemporary dual-process and dual-system theories in social psychology assume that behavior is driven by a joint function of reflective and impulsive processes (e.g., Epstein, 1994; Fazio & Towles-Schwen, 1999; Strack & Deutsch, 2004; Wilson, Lindsey, & Schooler, 2000). Thus, no behavior can be assumed to be "process pure," that is, driven entirely by reflective or impulsive processes. Rather, both kinds of processes contribute to varying degrees.[2]

Everyday experiences and scientific evidence from different lines of research converge in the idea that in many instances, in addition to reflective intentions, uncontrolled processes influence consumer behavior as well. Effects of such impulsive processes on behavior are evident in diverse ways. For example, people often end up buying things they did not intend to buy when they entered a store (Cobb & Hoyer, 1986; Puri, 1996; Rook, 1987). The extra bag of potato chips or the tasty chocolate bar may be especially likely to "tumble" into one's shopping cart if one is absent-mindedly thinking about other things or talking to a friend while walking through the aisles.

In principle, momentarily unmonitored internal cues such as desires and need states, or external cues such as hearing a particular type of music in the store or seeing a specific brand, may unintentionally activate behavioral schemata (Bargh, 2002; Dijksterhuis, Smith, van Baaren, & Wigboldus, 2005). For example, sales of French wine increased when a supermarket played French music and German music did the same for German wine (North, Hargreaves, & McKendrick, 1997). Shoppers may have been aware of the music that was played in the supermarket, but they probably did not expect or notice that this music influenced their shopping behavior (Chartrand, 2005).

Other research has shown that consumers are more likely to pick a brand with a name that starts with letters from their own names than with other letters, but respondents were unaware of this influence on their preferences (name letter branding; Brendl, Chattopadhyay, Pelham, & Carvallo, 2005). In a study by Tanner and colleagues (Tanner, Ferraro, Chartrand, Bettman, & van Baaren, 2008), participants consumed more of a supposedly new drink when they were mimicked by a confederate during the alleged product test. Presumably, the positive affect evoked by the mimicry (Chartrand & Bargh, 1999) transferred to the tested product and resulted in increased consumption compared to a control group.

As is evident from these examples, there is abundant support for the notion that uncontrolled processes can influence consumer behavior in several different ways, influencing brand choice and consumption. Given these influences, researchers should try to identify these processes and use them for the prediction of behavior. While explicit measures are chiefly influenced by deliberate responding, implicit measures as introduced in the previous examples aim at tapping primarily spontaneous, or automatic processes. Thus, if consumer behavior is at least partly influenced by automatic processes, implicit measures in general should explain unique variance over and above explicit measures, resulting in an additive pattern of predictive validity (Perugini, 2005). Several studies have tested this hypothesis, predominantly with regard to the predictive validity of attitudes.

In a study on brand preferences, Maison, Greenwald, and Bruin (2004, Study 1) implicitly and explicitly assessed attitudes toward two brands of yogurt. In a multiple regression analysis of participants' preferred brands, the implicit measure (an IAT) was a marginally significant predictor beyond the explicit attitude measure (the difference between the average evaluation of each brand). The explicit measure predicted the self-reported brand preferences very reliably and the implicit and explicit attitude measures were highly correlated. As a consequence, the IAT could not much improve the overall prediction of behavior. In a second study, the authors used a similar approach to predict the preferred of two fast-food restaurants. The IAT clearly failed to explain incremental variance. However, in a third study, an IAT significantly enhanced the prediction of the self-reported behavioral preference for Coke versus Pepsi beyond an explicit attitude measure. The same pattern occurred when predicting participants' ability to discriminate the two soft drinks in a blind taste test.

Further evidence comes from the domain of fair-trade buying behavior. Fair-trade products enjoy a high degree of acceptance and support in opinion surveys. However, these positive attitudes rarely translate into behavior (e.g., Boulstridge & Carrigan, 2000; Carrigan & Attalla, 2001). In their study, Vantomme, Geuens, De Houwer, and De Pelsmacker (2006) reasoned that this attitude–behavior gap could partly be due to explicit measures' susceptibility to social desirability concerns. After all, it may be hard to argue that it is a good idea *not* to give producers a fair price for their products. An implicit measure should be less influenced by such social desirability concerns. Participants filled in explicit attitude measures and completed an IAT regarding fair-trade versus conventional products. Corroborating Vantomme and colleagues' hypothesis, the two attitude measures contributed independently to the prediction of whether participants regularly did or did not buy fair-trade products.

Finally, although only remotely related to consumer behavior, results from a political voting study show that SC-IAT measures of political parties improved the prediction of subsequent voting behavior beyond explicit measures of party attitude (Friese, Bluemke, & Wänke, 2007).

The studies presented so far featured self-reported behavior as their criterion for predictive validity. This allows for the prediction of those behaviors that are otherwise difficult to observe in the laboratory, such as regular consumption or buying preferences. On the other hand, directly observed behavior allows for more experimental control than do reported behaviors and represents an even more rigorous criterion by which to measure the usefulness of implicit measures. A handful of studies have investigated how the two kinds of measures relate to behavior observed in the laboratory.

Again in the domain of fair-trade products, one study was concerned with choice behavior regarding fair-trade coffee versus coffee of a conventional brand (Wänke, Plessner, De Houwer, Richter, & Gärtner, 2006). After reading some information on the fair-trade concept, participants completed an explicit attitude measure and an IAT on fair-trade coffee versus conventional coffee. At the end of the session they could choose a total of 10 sachets of instant cappuccino as a reward for their participation, including any number of fair-trade or conventional sachets as long as the total number did not exceed 10. Although explicitly measured attitudes were strongly related to choice behavior, the IAT independently improved the prediction.

Several studies have investigated the IAT's predictive validity with regard to the choice between fruit and sweets. Researchers reasoned that both categories are positively valenced, but for different reasons. Although fruit is very healthy, it may be less tempting than sweets that are comparatively unhealthy. Because implicit measures are believed to assess primarily affective aspects of an attitude (Gawronski & Bodenhausen, 2006; Hofmann, Gawronski, Gschwendner, Le, & Schmitt, 2005), the hope was that this setup would allow for comparatively low implicit–explicit correlations and therefore a higher chance of incremental validity for the implicit measure. The results of these studies are mixed.

Karpinski and Hilton (2001) failed to find evidence for an IAT predicting the choice between an apple and a candy bar even when entered as the only predictor in a regression analysis. In a replication of this study, an IAT that was closely modeled after the one used by Karpinski and Hilton again showed no incremental validity over explicit measures (Spruyt, Hermans, De Houwer, Vandekerckhove, & Eelen, 2007). In this study, the authors compared the predictive validity of an IAT, a standard affective priming task (Fazio et al., 1995), and a variant of this procedure, the picture–picture naming task (Spruyt, Hermans, De Houwer, & Eelen, 2002). The standard affective priming task did not relate to behavior either. However, the naming task predicted participants' choices between the apple and the candy bar beyond explicit attitude measures.

More encouraging results come from Richetin, Perugini, Prestwich, and O'Gorman (2007). These authors analyzed the collective data of four very similar studies. All of them, again, were concerned with the prediction of choices between fruit and sweets. Unlike previous research (Karpinski & Hilton, 2001; Spruyt et al., 2007), Richetin and colleagues' study included several control variables in the multiple regression analysis, such as gender and the order of critical blocks in the IAT. Also, they offered participants not just one specific fruit and one specific snack, but a variety of options from each category. In this analysis both explicit attitude measures and an IAT were highly significant and independent predictors of choice behavior.

Taken together, there is mixed evidence for an additive model of the predictive validity of implicit and explicit measures (Perugini, 2005) for the prediction of consumer behavior. As summarized in Table 15.1, in some studies the implicit measure contributed independently to the prediction of behavior; in others it failed to do so. In any case, in almost every study presented in this section the explicit measure was clearly the dominant predictor and the implicit measure explained comparatively little variance.

At first glance, this outcome may strike one as disappointing. After all, what is all the hype on implicit measures about? Can it be that implicit measures do a good job in predicting behavior in other fields, such as personality (e.g., Asendorpf, Banse, & Mücke, 2002; Egloff & Schmukle, 2002), social psychology (e.g.,

TABLE 15.1   Overview of Studies Comparing Explicit and Implicit Measures for Predicting Consumer Behavior

	Type of Implicit Measure	Type of Behavior	Incremental Predictive Validity of Implicit over Explicit Measures
Maison, Greenwald, & Bruin (2004, Study 1)	IAT	Self-reported brand preference (yogurt)	No
Maison, Greenwald, & Bruin (2004, Study 2)	IAT	Self-reported brand preference (restaurants)	No
Maison, Greenwald, & Bruin (2004, Study 3)	IAT	Self-reported brand preference (Coke vs. Pepsi)	Yes
Vantomme, Geuens, De Houwer, & De Pelsmacker (2006)	IAT	Self-reported buying of fair-trade products	Yes
Friese, Bluemke, & Wänke (2007)	SC-IATs	Self-reported voting behavior	Yes
Wänke, Plessner, De Houwer, Richter, & Gärtner (2006)	IAT	Observed preference for fair-trade products	Yes
Karpinski & Hilton (2001)	IAT	Observed choice between fruit and sweets	No
Spruyt, Hermans, De Houwer, Vandekerckhove, & Eelen (2007)	IAT	Observed choice between fruit and sweets	No
Spruyt, Hermans, De Houwer, Vandekerckhove, & Eelen (2007)	Affective priming	Observed choice between fruit and sweets	No
Spruyt, Hermans, De Houwer, Vandekerckhove, & Eelen (2007)	Picture–Picture Naming Task	Observed choice between fruit and sweets	Yes
Richetin, Perugini, Prestwich, & O´Gorman (2007)	IAT	Observed choice between fruit and sweets	Yes

Note. IAT: Implicit Association Test; SC-IAT: Single Category Implicit Association Test.

Dovidio, Kawakami, Johnson, Johnson, & Howard, 1997; Fazio et al., 1995), and clinical psychology (e.g., Wiers & Stacy, 2006), but their utility for research on consumer behavior is rather limited? On closer inspection, however, the mixed results reported in this section may not be all that surprising. The hypothesis of incremental predictive validity for implicit measures was based on current models in social psychology according to which human behavior is jointly influenced by reflective and impulsive processes. Inherent in this account is the possibility that some behaviors may be more strongly influenced by reflective rather than impulsive processes whereas for other behaviors it could be the other way around (e.g.,

Asendorpf et al., 2002; Dovidio et al., 1997). However, in the studies reviewed above, no attempt was made to directly manipulate the relative impact of reflective versus impulsive processes. The degree to which the dependent variables were influenced by one or the other kind of process is unknown. In the next section we will present a series of studies featuring experimental manipulations intended to foster either controlled or more automatic processes for behavior regulation. We will show how these manipulations affect the predictive validity of implicit and explicit measures.

CONTROL RESOURCES MODERATE THE PREDICTIVE VALIDITY OF IMPLICIT AND EXPLICIT MEASURES

Earlier, we referred to a number of contemporary dual-process and dual-system models in social psychology. These models suggest that behavior is a joint function of reflective and impulsive processes. Moreover, they specifically outline under which circumstances the influence of one or the other kind of process will be particularly dominant. We will briefly describe two of these models that are particularly influential in current social psychology, the Motivation and Opportunity as DEterminants model (MODE, Fazio & Towles-Schwen, 1999) and the Reflective-Impulsive Model (RIM, Strack & Deutsch, 2004).

The MODE model proposes that two kinds of processes influence how attitudes guide behavior, one spontaneous and the other deliberative. Spontaneous processes reflect the immediate, automatic perceptions of an attitude object in a given situation. In contrast, careful considerations about the pros and cons of a certain behavior represent deliberative processes. According to the model, a person will engage in such effortful processing only if she or he is sufficiently motivated and is also given the opportunity to do so. That is, resources such as time and cognitive capacity are needed for deliberation. If a person is not motivated and/ or does not have the resources to deliberate, spontaneous processes will be more influential in guiding behavior.

The RIM (Strack & Deutsch, 2004) proposes two interacting systems that jointly control behavior by means of reflective and impulsive processes. The reflective system relies on knowledge, goals, and standards. Its efficient operation depends on resources such as cognitive capacity. In contrast, the impulsive system works comparatively effortlessly. Upon encountering an attitude object, spreading activation in the associative network leads to the activation of a motivational approach or avoidance orientation toward the object (Chen & Bargh, 1999; Hofmann, Friese, & Gschwendner, in press), which then activates proper behavioral schemata that are associated with the object. The impulsive and the reflective system can often compete for the control of behavior, insofar as they can activate different behavioral schemata (e.g., a spontaneous approach toward a snack, but on second thought an avoidance orientation because of the caloric content). In the case of conflict between the systems, the reflective system can "overrule" the impulsive system, provided it has the necessary resources for its operation.

However, if these resources are not available, the behavioral schemata that are activated by the impulsive system will be executed.

A thorough discussion of the differences between the models is beyond the scope of this chapter. However, despite their differences the two models lead to similar predictions in many cases. In particular, both models predict that implicit measures should be particularly successful in predicting behavior in situations when impulsive processes are likely to guide behavior. These are situations, for instance, in which the person lacks the necessary resources to effortfully control behavior. Implicit measures should be less successful in predicting controlled behavior that is dominantly influenced by reflective processes. Given that implicit measures are assumed to tap into the processes that occur in the impulsive system while explicit measures should reflect deliberate evaluations and personal standards residing in the reflective system, the opposite pattern of predictive validity should result for explicit measures. Of course, a necessary prerequisite to observing this hypothesized pattern is that at least for some participants impulsive and reflective processes activate different behavioral schemata.

Preliminary evidence for this reasoning comes from research on condom use (Marsh, Johnson, & Scott-Sheldon, 2001). Similar to the behavior regarding fair-trade products discussed above, there is a noteworthy attitude–behavior gap with respect to condoms. Most people know about the indisputable advantages of condoms and they express distinctly positive attitudes toward them in opinion polls (Fisher, Fisher, & Rye, 1995). Unfortunately, despite these explicitly held positive attitudes very often people do not use condoms in situations when they should (Keller, 1993). Marsh and colleagues reasoned that situations of having sex with a *casual* partner are characterized by strong hedonic needs that can counteract the forming of deliberate intentions. In contrast, having sex with a *steady* partner should be more deliberate. It is beyond the scope of this chapter to elaborate on what exactly this is supposed to tell us about our steady relationships, but indeed, an IAT failed to predict condom use with steady partners. However, it predicted condom use with casual partners. The opposite pattern occurred for explicit attitude measures. These data support the notion that available control resources moderate the predictive validity of implicit and explicit measures. In the heat of the moment, when about to have sex with a casual partner, people may lack the cognitive resources to bring their behavior in line with their goals and standards. What is more, besides affecting available control resources, having sex with a casual partner may also undermine people's motivation to insist on adherence to standards that may be perceived as ruining the romantic and exceptional situation. Instead, people may follow their gut and waive their positive beliefs about condom use. In contrast, having sex with a steady partner may, we regret, not always be accompanied with as much excitement. This allows for more controlled behavior due to more available control resources and possibly more motivation to live up to one's standards.

Of course, situations of having sex with a casual versus a steady partner differ in many respects and it may be possible to come up with alternative explanations for this finding. In any case, these data point to the crucial role that characteristics of the situation in which the behavior occurs play in the predictive validity of implicit measures. In a series of studies we more closely investigated the role of situational characteristics. Specifically, we tested the hypothesis of differential predictive validity by manipulating the availability of control resources that are needed to deliberately guide a person's behavior.

Which kinds of resources can plausibly be assumed to moderate the impact of impulsive processes on the one hand and reflective processes on the other? The MODE model explicitly mentions processing time and cognitive capacity as necessary preconditions for deliberative processing. The RIM stresses the role of capacity as an operating condition of the reflective system. Therefore, we examined these two resources, processing time and cognitive capacity, in the first two studies. We then extended this approach to the ability to self-regulate and inhibit one's impulses after a temporary depletion of self-regulatory resources (Muraven & Baumeister, 2000). Finally, we reasoned that the consumption of alcohol should disrupt reflective processing and in turn increase the influence of impulsive processes. Importantly, despite several differences, we expected all of these manipulations to impair controlled processing and as a result lead to functionally equivalent effects across studies. Predictive validity of implicit measures should be high when control resources are scarce, but lower when control resources are plentiful. Table 15.2 gives a summary of the following studies.

Before we turn to the empirical evidence let us point out an important aspect regarding the methodology. Previous research that investigated the effects of

TABLE 15.2   Summary of Studies in Which Control Resources Moderate the Predictive Validity of an Implicit Measure for Consumer Behavior

	Type of Implicit Measure	Type of Behavior	Moderator of Predictive Validity of Implicit Measure
Friese, Wänke, & Plessner (2006)	IAT	Observed choice between generic and brand-name products	Processing time
Friese, Hofmann, & Wänke (2008, Study 1)	IAT	Observed choice between fruit and sweets	Cognitive capacity
Hofmann, Rauch, & Gawronski (2007)	SC-IAT	Observed amount of candy consumption	Self-regulatory resources
Friese, Hofmann, & Wänke (2008, Study 2)	SC-IAT	Observed amount of potato chip consumption	Self-regulatory resources
Friese, Hofmann, & Wänke (2008, Study 3)	SC-IAT	Observed amount of beer consumption	Self-regulatory resources
Friese & Hofmann (in press)	SC-IAT	Observed amount of chocolate consumption	Mortality salience
Hofmann & Friese (2008)	SC-IAT	Observed amount of candy consumption	Alcohol
Friese & Hofmann (2008)	SC-IAT	Observed amount of potato chip consumption	Trait self-control

Note. *IAT:* Implicit Association Test; *SC-IAT:* Single Category Implicit Association Test.

similar manipulations relied almost exclusively on mean differences between experimental conditions to examine the manipulations' effectiveness. For example, in a study by Shiv and Fedorikhin (1999), participants who were cognitively taxed during a choice task between a piece of cake and a fruit salad chose the (supposedly) affectively superior cake more often compared to participants who were not taxed. Had the number of people opting for cake not differed between conditions one would have had to conclude that cognitive load does not affect the cognitive processes leading to choice behavior. In contrast, in our studies we focused on varying predictive validities, not on mean differences. After all, a cake may be affectively superior for many, but probably not for all individuals. And even for those affectively preferring cake, the strength of this preference may vary. Although we expected that the predictive validity of implicit measures would improve under processing constraints because these constraints should lead to more impulsive choices of an individual, this would not necessarily have to be reflected in different choices between constrained and unconstrained groups. While constraints may increase choices of a given item among individuals with *positive* spontaneous reactions toward this item, constraints may decrease choices among individuals with *negative* spontaneous reactions. The shifts in opposite directions may cancel each other and thereby conceal the increased impact of spontaneous reactions on the level of mean differences between groups. Thus, a more detailed analysis is imperative to capture the full picture.

Processing Time

When people lack the time to carefully analyze their behavioral options they have to find a way to make a decision quickly. Research has shown that under such circumstances (obviously) less information can be considered. Usage of schemata, stereotypes, and heuristics is more frequent, and decision strategies are simpler than under unrestrained conditions. If time for behavior regulation is scarce, people have to rely more on easily available cues in judgments, decisions, and behavior (e.g., Dijker & Koomen, 1996; Kruglanski & Freund, 1983; Wright, 1974). We reasoned that an implicit measure should be able to capture such immediate preferences based on highly accessible cues.

In a marketing study we (Friese, Wänke, & Plessner, 2006; see also Perugini, 2005) investigated consumer behavior toward brand-name products and no-name (generic) products. Participants completed an IAT and explicit attitude measures pertaining to these product classes. As a reward for their participation, participants could choose between two sets of similar groceries. Both sets contained the same product categories (e.g., sweet corn, margarine) and were of equal monetary value. One set consisted entirely of brand-name products; the other contained only generic products. Importantly, we manipulated the time participants were allowed to take before choosing. Half of the participants could take as much time as they wanted to make their decision while the other group needed to make their decision in only 5 seconds with a time bar on the lower part of the screen indicating how much time was left.

For data analysis we divided the sample into those participants whose implicitly and explicitly measured preferences converged (i.e., preferred brand-name products on both measures or generic products on both measures) and those whose preferences diverged (i.e., implicitly measured preference for one but explicitly measured preference for the other). Participants with converging implicitly and explicitly measured preferences chose the product arrangement that corresponded to their preferences in more than 80% of the cases, independent of the manipulation of processing time. However, for participants with diverging implicitly and explicitly measured preferences the time manipulation made a big difference: When there was ample time to decide, almost all participants chose in accordance with their explicitly measured preferences. However, when processing time was scarce (i.e., when put under time pressure) more than 60% of participants with dissociated implicitly and explicitly measured preferences followed the preferences indicated by the *implicit* measure. These data suggest that when processing time is restricted reflective processes have a hard time unfolding. Consequently, impulsive processes that work effortlessly kick in more strongly.

Cognitive Capacity

In the study just described reflective processing was impeded because these kinds of processes need more time than do impulsive processes. Another important control resource—cognitive capacity—was left unchanged in both conditions. We next manipulated cognitive capacity (while leaving processing time up to participants' choice) and explored its effect on the predictive validity of implicit and explicit measures. Typically, capacity is manipulated by occupying participants with a second task that is unrelated to the action of primary interest (Baddeley, 1996). We assumed that this manipulation would impair deliberative reasoning but would leave impulsive processes intact. Hence, implicit measures should exhibit higher predictive validity under conditions of low cognitive capacity.

In a first session, explicit attitude measures toward chocolate and fruit were collected (Friese, Hofmann, & Wänke, 2008, Study 1). In a second session, participants completed an IAT and as reward they could pick five items out of a variety of fruit and chocolate bars. They could choose from apples, tangerines, small Snickers bars, and small Twix bars. Half of the participants had to keep in mind a one-digit number during the choice task (high-capacity condition). The other half was instructed to keep in mind an eight-digit number that they reported to the experimenter later on (low-capacity condition, Gilbert & Hixon, 1991). As expected, the implicit measure was a significant predictor of choice behavior for participants who were distracted by the secondary task but was unrelated to behavior when capacity was high. The opposite occurred for the explicit attitude measure. When participants were cognitively taxed, explicitly measured attitudes were remarkably unrelated to behavior. In other words, in this condition what participants reported about their liking had almost nothing to do with what they chose (see Figure 15.1). Thus, as hypothesized, cognitive capacity moderated the predictive validity of the implicit measure.

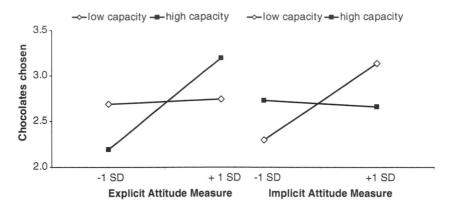

Figure 15.1 Number of Chocolates Chosen as a Function of Attitude Measure (Implicit vs. Explicit) and Capacity Manipulation (Low vs. High) in Friese et al. (2008, Study 1). Reproduced with permission from the British Journal of Social Psychology, The British Psychological Society.

Two further details are noteworthy in this data: First, participants who were distracted during the choice task did not take more time to make their decision than participants with ample capacity. Theoretically, these participants could have tried to make up for the lack of capacity by thinking longer about their choice. Second, the groups of high and low cognitive capacity did not differ in the number of chocolates chosen. As discussed earlier, most previous research relied on mean differences between groups on the dependent variable as evidence for an increased impact of impulsive versus reflective processing (e.g., Shiv & Fedorikhin, 1999). In our study the group means did not reveal that lack of cognitive capacity increases the influence of impulsive forces. However, by tapping into both impulsive and reflective behavioral precursors of behavior with the help of implicit and explicit measures, we were able to trace which of the two actually drove behavior under which condition.

Self-Regulatory Resources

Having shown the moderating role of processing time and cognitive capacity in the predictive validity of implicit measures, we turned to a third control resource, self-regulatory resources (Muraven & Baumeister, 2000). Furthermore, we wanted to expand the findings from product choices to actual consumption. Choosing a product in the supermarket is one important aspect of consumer behavior. Another intriguing facet is which factors influence *how much* people actually consume of the products they bring home. In contrast to single-act choice tasks, consumption is a continuous behavior that can stretch over several minutes, which makes it potentially even harder to control than single-act choices. It may be easier to choose the fruit salad over the cake at any moment than to have the cake in front of you and only taste it. To bypass the potato chip aisle in the supermarket and thus prevent one of the bags from mysteriously landing in the shopping cart takes only a moment of willpower. But picture yourself having just opened a bag of your favorite potato chips. You taste this delicious flavor and what always happens when you eat potato chips happens again: Once you start eating they are terribly hard to resist. In fact, whether you stop eating at all before the entire bag is gone is a question of self-control. For these matters actual consumption may be even more important than choice in many applied contexts such as health or clinical psychology, in addition to being of major importance for consumer researchers.

The model of self-regulation developed by Baumeister and colleagues proposes that self-control depends on a limited resource (e.g., Baumeister & Vohs, 2004; Muraven & Baumeister, 2000). Akin to a muscle, this resource can be depleted by exertion and it recovers after some time. Any act of self-control, independent of the behavioral domain, will draw on this resource and use up some of its precious capacity. Subsequent attempts at self-control will likely be less successful. Rather, impulsive action tendencies will gain more importance in the guidance of behavior. Although this model was introduced to the literature not even 10 years ago, a vast amount of research consistent with the muscle metaphor has been published in areas such as eating, drinking, and impulse buying (Muraven, Collins, & Nienhaus, 2002; Vohs & Faber, 2007; Vohs & Heatherton, 2000).

We reasoned that implicit measures should be better behavior predictors in situations in which self-regulatory resources are low compared to situations of full resources (and we expected the opposite for explicit measures).

We tested this assumption in several studies in which participants consumed various food products. In one study, participants first completed a categorization task about "a typical snack product" (i.e., a SC-IAT on potato chips), followed by explicit attitude measures and a short movie sequence (Friese et al., 2008, Study 2). One-half of participants were instructed to let their emotions flow during the film while the other half were instructed to suppress all emotions that came up in response to the clip. This emotion-suppression task is a standard procedure to deplete self-regulatory resources (e.g., Baumeister, Bratslavsky, Muraven, & Tice, 1998). Finally, participants took part in a taste-and-rate test of potato chips. They were asked several questions irrelevant to our hypotheses such as what they thought about the packaging and in which situations they would consider consuming the product. After the session we unobtrusively measured how much participants actually ate.

In line with previous research we found that participants who had exerted self-control during the emotion suppression task ate more potato chips than did participants in the control group. More importantly, self-regulatory resources moderated the predictive validity of implicit and explicit attitude measures. The implicit measure predicted potato chip consumption in the depletion condition, but not in the condition with full resources. The explicit attitude measure showed the reverse pattern. This study corroborates the assumption that self-regulatory resources constitute an important control resource that is needed to bring behavior in line with deliberate evaluations. If a person is depleted of these resources, more impulsive tendencies come through and influence behavior.

Another factor besides attitudes that should influence consumption is *restraint* (Carver, 2005). Importantly, in contrast to explicitly measured attitudes, restraint standards are nonevaluative. It is quite possible to like a certain product and yet to restrain oneself from consuming it (e.g., "I really like candy, but I restrain myself because I want to keep a slim figure"). That is, typical measures of dietary restraint do not ask how much one likes or dislikes certain foods. Rather, they investigate general nutrition strategies with questions about whether one occasionally stops eating despite still being hungry, or whether one intentionally avoids having a stock of certain tempting products at home (Stunkard & Messick, 1985; Pudel & Westenhöfer, 1989). Given these properties, restraint standards play an important role in food purchase and consumption. Of course, to live up to one's personal standards can be hard at times, for instance, when tempted by a delicious dessert or a bowl of candy. Depending on one's attraction to the tempting stimulus, much willpower is needed to resist and keep a clean record. Clearly, restraint standards depend on control resources to influence behavior, a property they share with explicitly measured attitudes. If the necessary preconditions for reflective action (e.g., available control resources) are not met, their controlling influence may go awry and impulsive precursors such as implicitly measured attitudes may take over.

This assumption was put to the test in a study in which participants completed an implicit measure related to candy, suppressed or did not suppress their emotions during a movie sequence, and subsequently engaged in a product test of candy (Hofmann, Rauch, & Gawronski, 2007). At the end of the session, participants completed a measure of dietary restraint standards. The results supported the expectations. The implicit measure predicted candy consumption for participants who were depleted of self-regulatory resources in the emotion suppression task but not for the control group with full resources. Importantly, dietary restraint standards showed the reverse pattern in that they inhibited consumption for participants with full resources but were ineffective when resources were low.

Finally, we sought to distinguish between explicitly measured attitudes and restraint standards not only on a theoretical but also on an empirical level. Additionally, we extended our approach to another behavioral domain, beer drinking. Participants were either depleted or not depleted of self-regulatory resources as described above. In a product test they sampled two different brands of beer and we unobtrusively measured how much they drank. Again, no significant mean differences in beer consumption emerged between conditions. However, in line with our reasoning we found all three individual difference measures to interact with the experimental condition. The implicit measure predicted beer consumption only for participants who were depleted of self-regulatory strength. In contrast, the explicit attitude measure correlated with consumption when beer drinkers had not been depleted. A measure of drinking restraint standards (Collins & Lapp, 1992; Cox et al., 2001) showed the same pattern as explicitly measured attitudes: a stronger impact under full as compared to depleted resources. Supporting our hypothesis, restraint standards contributed over and above implicitly and explicitly measured attitudes to the prediction of drinking behavior, indicating that restraint standards and explicitly measured attitudes are two distinct concepts. Both rely on higher order processes, but they control behavior independently from each other.

These data particularly highlight the dynamic and multifaceted nature of consumer behavior. Spontaneous evaluations of products, deliberate evaluations, and personal standards simultaneously compete for influence on behavioral control. What is more, their relative success is dependent on situational circumstances such as the availability of control resources.

A last study in this series on self-regulatory resources was concerned with the resource-consuming process of coping with being reminded of one's own mortality (Friese & Hofmann, in press, Study 2). Research on Terror Management Theory (TMT; for an overview see Arndt, Cook, & Routledge, 2004; Solomon, Greenberg, & Pyszczynski, 2004) has shown that thoughts about one's own death are experienced as aversive. Strategies to cope with the knowledge of one's mortality include the suppression of death-related thoughts or the redirection of thoughts to other topics (e.g., Greenberg, Pyszczynski, Solomon, Simon, & Breus, 1994). We reasoned that these effortful processes require self-regulatory resources and should lead to impaired self-control on subsequent tasks (Gailliot, Schmeichel, & Baumeister, 2006). In fact, thought suppression and redirection of thoughts are some of the standard manipulations to deplete self-regulatory resources (e.g., Muraven, Tice, & Baumeister, 1998). Consequently, we hypothesized that an implicit measure should predict the consumption of chocolate in a product test for participants whose mortality was made salient to them, but not for participants who had completed a control task.

Results were in line with the hypothesis: Participants' thoughts about their own death moderated the predictive validity of an implicit measure. An SC-IAT predicted the total amount of chocolate consumed. As expected, this predictive validity was limited to participants who had thought about their own death and was absent in the control condition. Presumably, the occupation with one's death consumed self-regulatory resources and led to more impulsive behavior afterward.

Unrelated to the predictive validity of implicit measures but not any less intriguing, the study found that mortality salience also influenced which brand of chocolate was eaten more, providing preliminary behavioral support for one of the central hypotheses of TMT. According to TMT people tend to defend the values of their own culture when faced with mortality as a means to underline belonging to this valuable and lasting group (e.g., Solomon et al., 2004). Previous applications of TMT to consumer behavior revealed that awareness of one's mortality boosts materialism (Kasser & Sheldon, 2000) and raises the attraction of high-status products that confer self-esteem, such as a Lexus automobile or a Rolex watch. In another study, American participants when reminded of their mortality put more blame for a car accident on the car manufacturer when they believed this manufacturer to be Japanese compared to American (Nelson, Moore, Olivetti, & Scott, 1997).

In our study we found not only that consumers who thought about their mortality evaluated domestic products better than foreign products, but also evidence for increased consumption. Relative to the German chocolate, our Swiss participants evaluated a Swiss chocolate as better than a German chocolate in the mortality salience condition than in the control condition. Moreover, relative to a German chocolate, they ate more of a Swiss chocolate in the mortality salience condition compared to participants in the control condition. These data provide preliminary evidence that the differential evaluation and also consumption of consumer goods can serve as a means to defend one's own culture when faced with reminders of death.

Having extensively studied the role of self-regulatory resources, we now turn to a final situational moderator of the predictive validity of implicit measures that we investigated in our laboratory: alcohol.

Alcohol

The effects of alcohol on the organism are manifold and despite huge amounts of research not yet fully understood (Hull & Slone, 2004). It is known that alcohol impairs executive functioning in a number of ways, for example, affecting attentional processes, abstract reasoning, self-monitoring, and working memory skills (Fillmore, Dixon, & Schweizer, 2000; Giancola, 2000; Hull & Slone, 2004). Interestingly, while it influences consciously controlled information processing in these diverse ways, automatic processes are less hindered (Fillmore, Vogel-Sprott, & Gavrilescu, 1999). This research is congruent with the notion proposed by alcohol myopia theory (Steele & Josephs, 1990) that alcohol leads people to perceive only salient and proximal cues in the environment. More abstract concepts such as goals and standards are less present. Obviously, to the extent that one's goals and standards escape attention they are less likely to influence behavior. This research leads to similar hypotheses to those we have discussed with regard to the other moderators. The predictive validity of implicit measures should be greater for participants who have consumed alcohol than for sober participants. At the same time, the predictive validity of higher order concepts such as restraint standards should suffer under the influence of alcohol.

We found evidence for this assumption (Hofmann & Friese, in press). Participants engaged in two product tests. The first concerned a drink that consisted of either orange juice with vodka or solely orange juice in the control condition. After some distraction tasks that gave the alcohol time to have an impact, the second product test concerning candy was administered. As expected, an implicit measure related to candy that was assessed at the beginning of the study predicted consumption for participants under the influence of alcohol, but not for sober participants. In contrast, dietary restraint standards limited consumption for sober participants but were ineffective when people had consumed alcohol. Apparently the intake of alcohol undermined the control of eating behavior by restraint standards and gave way to more impulsive preferences.

Are All Control Moderators Equal?

In this section we presented four different moderators of the predictive validity of implicit measures pertaining to different control resources: processing time, cognitive capacity, self-regulatory resources, and alcohol. We investigated several different types of behavior, such as product choice, eating, and drinking. One similarity of these studies strikes us as especially noteworthy: No matter which moderator we employed and which control resources were affected, our manipulations led to functionally equivalent results: The implicit measure was a good predictor of consumer behavior, be that choice or continuous consumption, when control resources were scarce, but failed to explain unique variance when resources were high. The opposite pattern occurred for higher order constructs such as explicitly measured attitudes or restraint standards. What, we should ask, are the differences and similarities between these manipulations? Do they share a common kernel that provokes analogous results despite their many differences?

Reduced cognitive capacity and processing time have been treated as interchangeable manipulations in much social psychological research. We argue that this was possible only because the two manipulations are *functionally equivalent*, but they reach their effects through different routes. In the case of cognitive load, capacity is actively curtailed, which impedes higher order thinking. In the case of time pressure, it is not capacity that is restrained. Rather, central executive functioning (Baddeley, 1990) is impaired because it simply needs time to unfold, even with full capacity.

The effects of both reduced cognitive capacity and processing time differ in at least two important ways from those of reduced self-regulatory resources. First, once working memory load or time pressure is removed, people are immediately able to engage in higher order reasoning again without any further impairment carried over from the manipulations. In contrast, depleted self-regulatory resources need some time to recover. A depleted person will show impaired self-control on any relevant task for quite some time. It is not fully clear yet how this replenishing process works or how long it takes, but sleep and glucose seem to help (Baumeister & Heatherton, 1996; Gailliot et al., 2007). A second difference relates to the extent to which increased motivation can counteract the effects of the reduced resources. We argue that in the cases of processing time and cognitive capacity even high motivation for accurate reasoning will not be of much help. If cognitive capacity is largely occupied by other things or if the time to deliberate is simply not available, there is no way to work around it, because higher order reasoning strictly depends on these resources, and the ability to stretch these resources by willpower is limited. In contrast, while it may be theoretically possible to completely deplete self-regulatory resources, in general people are capable of temporarily compensating for a shortage if they are really motivated to do so (Baumeister & Heatherton, 1996; Martijn, Tenbült, Merckelbach, Dreezens, & de Vries, 2002; Muraven & Slessareva, 2003; Webb & Sheeran, 2003). Accordingly, it may be easier to radically prevent higher order processes by taking away cognitive capacity or time to think than by depleting self-regulatory resources, which generally constitutes a relative rather than an absolute depletion. Thus, the depletion of self-regulatory resources reduces chances of but does not rule out effective self-regulation. This property is shared by moderate alcohol intoxication (Bailey, Leonard, Cranston, & Taylor, 1983; Hull, 1981; Hull & Reilly, 1983).

Despite these differences, questions arise about a common element between these manipulations that causes the functionally equivalent effects. The exact influences of the manipulations on the organism are complex and it may be too early to propose definite answers to this question. Future research could take a closer look at how the reviewed manipulations impair the efficient functioning of the central executive. The central executive is responsible for information processing and the distribution of attentional resources. To fulfill these functions it depends on controlled processes (Baddeley, 1990, 1996). Necessary preconditions are, for example, sufficient cognitive capacity and processing time (Baddeley, 1996). Also, the depletion of self-regulatory resources has been found to impair higher order executive functioning, but not automatic processing (Govorun & Payne, 2006; Schmeichel, Vohs, & Baumeister, 2003). Finally, various lines of research show that alcohol has negative consequences for central executive functioning (e.g., Giancola, 2000; Hull & Slone, 2004). To conclude, although the exact mechanisms differ, all of the described manipulations hinder the central executive in efficiently fulfilling its regulatory tasks. As a consequence, automatic processes gain in importance and implicit measures tapping into these processes gain in predictive validity under conditions of reduced control resources. This common aspect of the manipulations may be the Rosetta stone of the causes of their functional equivalence.

Situational and Dispositional Moderators

The moderators presented in this chapter all operate on the level of situational manipulations. For a limited time span, some participants had less control resources available than did others and this difference had an impact on the relative importance of reflective and impulsive processes in determining product choice or consumption. It stands to reason that dispositional differences between persons may also moderate the predictive validity of implicit measures. For example, people with low trait self-control have a chronically lower "ability to override or change [their] inner responses, as well as to interrupt undesired behavioral tendencies (such as impulses) and refrain from acting on them" (Tangney, Baumeister, & Boone, 2004, p. 274). As expected on the basis of studies on the situational depletion of self-regulatory resources described in previous sections, in one study an implicit measure predicted consumption of potato chips and alcohol better for participants low in self-regulatory resources than for those high in resources (Friese & Hofmann, 2008). Furthermore, working memory capacity may be a key moderator of impulsive and reflective influences on behavior. People high (compared to low) in working memory capacity are better able to keep relevant information in their focus of attention and shield this information from external or internal distractions such as impulses (Barrett, Tugade, & Engle, 2004; Engle, 2002). They are more successful in enacting controlled processing than individuals low in working memory capacity. Consistent with this view implicit measures were good predictors of viewing time behavior of erotic material and also of candy consumption in a product test, but only for participants with low, not with high working memory capacity. The opposite pattern occurred for explicit measures (Hofmann, Gschwendner, Friese, Wiers, & Schmitt, in press). Other personality characteristics such as chronic regulatory focus (Florack, Friese, & Scarabis, 2008; Higgins, 1997) or a preference for intuition (Betsch, 2004; Hofmann & Baumert, 2007) have also been found to exert similar moderating influences. Future research will likely be able to shed more light on personality traits that chronically affect the relative impact of reflective and impulsive processes in behavior determination with respective influences on the predictive validity of explicit and implicit measures.

Implications for Applied Contexts

We would like to stress the importance of the findings presented here especially for applied contexts. The situations that we created in our studies are not artificial, but very common in daily life. Consumers constantly make decisions and engage in consumption of various goods while being preoccupied with a secondary task, such as talking to an acquaintance, watching TV, writing notes, or thinking about the next meeting with a client. The same is true for time pressure. Just think about shopping right before closing time, or choosing from a menu with the waiter standing behind you. And concerning the depletion of self-regulatory resources, the literature suggests that demands in everyday life are even higher than those required by our emotion suppression tasks that lasted only a couple of minutes (Baumeister & Heatherton, 1996). In fact, resources vary over the course of a day and as a function of a variety of demands that occur frequently, such as resisting tempting foods or drinks, self-presentation in challenging situations, or self-control in response to disrespectful treatment by others (Baumeister & Heatherton, 1996; DeWall, Baumeister, Stillman, & Gailliot, 2007; Muraven et al., 2002; Vohs, Baumeister, & Ciarocco, 2005; Vohs & Heatherton, 2000). It is not necessary to highlight the array of times and social situations in which people consume alcohol with the respective consequences for the self-regulation of behavior. In any case, these frequently occurring situations lead to a specific mix of processes that drive behavior. What is more, we deem it likely that these conditions can also amplify or interact with each other, resulting in an even more complex regulation of behavior. For example, reflective processing may be even less likely if a person is depleted of self-regulatory resources not only after a tiring workday, but also if she has had a beer or two on the way home. In sum, a large amount, if not the majority, of consumer choices and actual consumption occurs when control resources are weaker than we would like and therefore promotes behavioral outcomes perhaps different from what we would like.

In a different vein, this research has implications for market research as well. Implicit measures may be useful to assess affective responses of consumers toward products, brands, and companies, especially in socially sensitive domains where consumers lack the ability and/or willingness to report their feelings. However, as pointed out in this chapter, implicit measures are not valuable in predicting consumer behavior per se. Market researchers should bear in mind the strengths and weaknesses of these instruments and the implications this has for practical purposes. We expect implicit measures to be of most value for the prediction of *impulsive* consumer behavior. To refer to our example at the outset of this chapter, an IAT on Mercedes and BMW may convey interesting information on consumers' spontaneous attraction to these car manufacturers. But although unconscious influences may play a role in the purchase of cars, these kinds of major purchases are characterized by considerable deliberation and conscious reasoning. Implicit measures are unlikely to explain a great deal of unique variance of such purchases. However, many purchasing situations do not promote and may even prevent deliberation and control. Implicit measures will be of particular value for predicting consumer behavior in these situations. Market research on brands and products that are often bought on impulse, that address hedonic needs, and that do not incur serious financial or other costs may profit most from the use of implicit measures.

CONCLUSIONS AND OUTLOOK

There is abundant evidence that impulsive, largely uncontrolled processes influence many consumer behaviors. We provided some brief examples in this chapter. Surprisingly, despite this evidence, the use of implicit measures for individual differences in impulsive processes is still rare in consumer behavior research. Compared to the range of possible applications in advertising and marketing, few studies have employed such measures for a better understanding of consumer information processing. In particular, there are no studies that take into account the particular strengths and weaknesses of the different measures.

The regulation of consumer behavior is an enormously complex and dynamic process. Manifold influences operate at the same time. Any sophisticated approach to predicting behavior will have to consider as many of these influences as possible. They include not only explicitly measured attitudes, as has been dominant in much of consumer research in the past, but also other higher order constructs such as personal (restraint) standards. Furthermore, implicitly measured attitudes can improve the prediction of behavior.

Based on current dual-process and dual-system models such as the MODE model or the RIM, we particularly stressed the role of control resources and their influence on the predictive validity of implicit and self-report measures. If control resources are low, implicit measures are particularly valuable in predicting behavior, but they are less valuable for the prediction of largely controlled behaviors. Explicit measures show the opposite pattern. In addition to control resources, various other situational or dispositional factors have been found to influence the predictive validity of implicit and explicit measures. For example, implicit measures predict behavior particularly well for people in a positive mood (Hermsen, Holland, & van Knippenberg, 2006) or for individuals who are low in need for cognition (Florack, Scarabis, & Bless, 2001). Elsewhere, we provide an overview of this literature (Friese, Hofmann, & Schmitt, 2008).

One limitation revealed in the reviewed literature is implicit measures' relatedness to specific objects. For example, in one of our studies on the moderating role of self-regulatory resources we assessed the spontaneous reactions of our participants toward potato chips. The measure predicted the consumption of potato chips quite well for participants whose self-control strength was weakened. This research provides valuable insights into the processes that drive behavior when people are depleted of self-control strength. However, in some contexts it may be more desirable to be able to more generally predict behavior, independent of a specific target product (e.g., potato chips). In this vein, Ferguson (2007) recently made an attempt to extend the predictive validity of implicit measures to nongraspable objects. Specifically, she assessed the spontaneous reaction toward the word *thin* in an affective priming task (Fazio et al., 1995), which she interpreted as an implicit measurement of the motivation to be thin. In several studies this measure predicted the consumption of different tempting foods over and above implicitly and explicitly measured attitudes toward those foods. From our perspective, Ferguson's research provides a valuable extension and fits nicely with the work presented in this chapter. The measurement of implicit motivations can potentially greatly broaden the possibilities for the prediction of consumer behavior. It will be interesting to disentangle the strengths and weaknesses of different implicit measures relating to specific objects on the one hand and goals on the other. What are the boundary conditions under which one will outperform the other? Will the predictive validity of implicit measures of goals also be dependent on control resources similar to the measures reviewed in this chapter? What are the assets and weaknesses of different implicit measurement procedures, such as evaluative priming or IAT-based measures? Research on the prediction of consumer behavior with the help of implicit measures has only just begun. Many forms of consumer behavior await further research. Many intriguing questions remain to be addressed. Hopefully, the research presented in this chapter will be a good place to start.

ACKNOWLEDGMENTS

We thank Marco Perugini for valuable comments on an earlier draft of this chapter.

ENDNOTES

1. This is not to say that direct measures cannot capture spontaneous responses as well under specific circumstances. Speeded direct measures may do so rather well (see Ranganath, Smith, & Nosek, 2008).
2. Interestingly, a similar claim can be made for implicit and explicit measures. While implicit measures primarily assess automatic processes, they are also influenced in part by controlled processes. The opposite holds for explicit measures (Payne, 2005).

REFERENCES

Ajzen, I., & Fishbein, M. (1977). Attitude-behavior relations: A theoretical analysis and review of empirical research. *Psychological Bulletin, 84*, 888–918.

Arndt, J., Cook, A., & Routledge, C. (2004). The blueprint of terror management. Understanding the cognitive architecture of psychological defense against the awareness of death. In J. Greenberg, S. Koole, & T. Pyszczynski (Eds.), *Handbook of experimental existential psychology* (pp. 35–53). New York: Guilford Press.

Asendorpf, J. B., Banse, R., & Mücke, D. (2002). Double discrimination between implicit and explicit personality self-concept: The case of shy behavior. *Journal of Personality and Social Psychology, 83*, 380–393.

Baddeley, A. (1990). *Human memory. Theory and practice*. Hove, England: Erlbaum.

Baddeley, A. (1996). Exploring the central executive. *The Quarterly Journal of Experimental Psychology, 49A*, 5–28.

Bailey, D. S., Leonard, K. E., Cranston, J. W., & Taylor, S. P. (1983). Effects of alcohol and self-awareness on human physical aggression. *Personality and Social Psychology Bulletin, 9*, 289–295.

Bargh, J. A. (2002). Losing consciousness: Automatic influences on consumer judgment, behavior, and motivation. *Journal of Consumer Research, 29*, 280–285.

Barrett, L., Tugade, M. M., & Engle, R. W. (2004). Individual differences in working memory capacity and dual-process theories of the mind. *Psychological Bulletin, 130*, 553–573.

Baumeister, R. F., Bratslavsky, E., Muraven, M., & Tice, D. M. (1998). Ego depletion: Is the active self a limited resource? *Journal of Personality and Social Psychology, 74*, 1252–1265.

Baumeister, R. F., & Heatherton, T. F. (1996). Self-regulation failure: An overview. *Psychological Inquiry, 7*, 1–15.

Baumeister, R. F., & Vohs, K. D. (2004). *Handbook of self-regulation: Research, theory, and applications*. New York: Guilford Press.

Betsch, C. (2004). Präferenz für Intuition und Deliberation (PID): Inventar zur Erfassung von affekt- und kognitionsbasiertem Entscheiden [Preference for intuition and deliberation (PID): An inventory for assessing affect- and cognition-based decision making]. *Zeitschrift für Differentielle und Diagnostische Psychologie, 25*, 179–197.

Blackwell, R. D., Miniard, P. W., & Engel, J. F. (2001). *Consumer behavior* (9th ed.). Orlando, FL: Harcourt.

Bluemke, M., & Friese, M. (2006). Do features of stimuli influence IAT effects? *Journal of Experimental Social Psychology, 42*, 163–176.

Bluemke, M., & Friese, M. (in press). Reliability and validity of the Single-Target IAT (ST-IAT): Assessing automatic affect toward multiple attitude objects. *European Journal of Social Psychology.*

Boulstridge, E., & Carrigan, M. (2000). Do consumers really care about corporate responsibility? Highlighting the attitude-behaviour gap. *Journal of Communication Management, 4*, 355–368.

Brendl, C. M., Chattopadhyay, A., Pelham, B. W., & Carvallo, M. (2005). Name letter branding: Valence transfers when product specific needs are active. *Journal of Consumer Research, 32*, 405–415.

Cacioppo, J. T., & Sandman, C. A. (1981). Psychophysiological functioning, cognitive responding, and attitudes. In R. E. Petty, T. M. Ostrom, & T. C. Brock (Eds.), *Cognitive responses in persuasion* (pp. 81–104). Hillsdale, NJ: Erlbaum.

Carrigan, M., & Attalla, A. (2001). The myth of the ethical consumer—Do ethics matter in purchase behaviour? *The Journal of Consumer Marketing, 18*, 560–577.

Carver, C. S. (2005). Impulse and constraint: Perspectives from personality psychology, convergence with theory in other areas, and potential for integration. *Personality and Social Psychology Review, 9*, 312–333.

Chartrand, T. L. (2005). The role of conscious awareness in consumer behavior. *Journal of Consumer Psychology, 15*, 203–210.

Chartrand, T. L., & Bargh, J. A. (1999). The chameleon effect: The perception-behavior link and social interaction. *Journal of Personality and Social Psychology, 76*, 893–910.

Chen, M., & Bargh, J. A. (1999). Consequences of automatic evaluation: Immediate behavioral predispositions to approach or avoid the stimulus. *Personality and Social Psychology Bulletin, 25*, 215–224.

Cobb, C. J., & Hoyer, W. D. (1986). Planned versus impulsive purchase behavior. *Journal of Retailing, 62*, 384–409.

Collins, R. L., & Lapp, W. M. (1992). The temptation and restraint inventory for measuring drinking restraint. *British Journal of Addiction, 87*, 625–633.

Conrey, F. R., Sherman, J. W., Gawronski, B., Hugenberg, K., & Groom, C. J. (2005). Separating multiple processes in implicit social cognition: The quad model of implicit task performance. *Journal of Personality and Social Psychology, 89*, 469–487.

Cox, W. M., Gutzler, M., Denzler, M., Melfsen, S., Florin, I., & Klinger, E. (2001). Temptation, restriction, and alcohol consumption among American and German college students. *Addictive Behaviors, 26*, 573–581.

De Houwer, J. (2003). The extrinsic affective Simon task. *Experimental Psychology, 50*, 77–85.

De Houwer, J. (2006). What are implicit measures and why are we using them? In R. W. Wiers & A. W. Stacy (Eds.), *Handbook of implicit cognition and addiction* (pp. 11–28). Thousand Oaks, CA: Sage.

DeWall, C. N., Baumeister, R. F., Stillman, T. F., & Gailliot, M. T. (2007). Violence restrained: Effects of self-regulation and its depletion on aggression. *Journal of Experimental Social Psychology, 43*, 62–76.

Dijker, A., & Koomen, W. (1996). Stereotyping and attitudinal effects under time pressure. *European Journal of Social Psychology, 26*, 61–74.

Dijksterhuis, A., Smith, P. K., van Baaren, R. B., & Wigboldus, D. H. J. (2005). The unconscious consumer: Effects of environment on consumer behavior. *Journal of Consumer Psychology, 15*, 193–202.

Dovidio, J. F., Kawakami, K., Johnson, C., Johnson, B., & Howard, A. (1997). On the nature of prejudice: Automatic and controlled processes. *Journal of Experimental Social Psychology, 33*, 510–540.

Egloff, B., & Schmukle, S. C. (2002). Predictive validity of an Implicit Association Test for assessing anxiety. *Journal of Personality and Social Psychology, 83*, 1441–1455.

Engle, R. W. (2002). Working memory capacity as executive attention. *Current Directions in Psychological Science, 11*, 19–23.

Epstein, S. (1994). Integration of the cognitive and the psychodynamic unconscious. *American Psychologist, 49*, 709–724.

Fazio, R. H., Jackson, J. R., Dunton, B. C., & Williams, C. J. (1995). Variability in automatic activation as an unobtrusive measure of racial attitudes: A bona fide pipeline? *Journal of Personality and Social Psychology, 69*, 1013–1027.

Fazio, R. H., & Olson, M. A. (2003). Implicit measures in social cognition research: Their meaning and use. *Annual Review of Psychology, 54*, 297–327.

Fazio, R. H., Sanbonmatsu, D. M., Powell, M. C., & Kardes, F. R. (1986). On the automatic activation of attitudes. *Journal of Personality and Social Psychology, 50*, 229–238.

Fazio, R. H., & Towles-Schwen, T. (1999). The MODE model of attitude-behavior processes. In S. Chaiken & Y. Trope (Eds.), *Dual-process theories in social psychology* (pp. 97–116). New York: Guilford Press.

Ferguson, M. J. (2007). On the automatic evaluation of end-states. *Journal of Personality and Social Psychology, 92*, 596–611.

Fiedler, K., Messner, C., & Bluemke, M. (2006). Unresolved problems with the "I," the "A," and the "T": A logical and psychometric critique of the Implicit Association Test (IAT). *European Review of Social Psychology, 17*, 74–147.

Fillmore, M. T., Dixon, M. J., & Schweizer, T. A. (2000). Alcohol affects processing of ignored stimuli in a negative priming paradigm. *Journal of Studies on Alcohol, 61*, 571–578.

Fillmore, M. T., Vogel-Sprott, M., & Gavrilescu, D. (1999). Alcohol effects on intentional behavior: Dissociating controlled and automatic influences. *Experimental and Clinical Psychopharmacology, 7*, 372–378.

Fisher, W. A., Fisher, J. D., & Rye, B. J. (1995). Understanding and promoting AIDS preventive behavior: Insights from the theory of reasoned action. *Health Psychology, 14*, 255–264.

Florack, A., Friese, M., & Scarabis, M. (2008). *Regulatory focus and reliance on automatic association in consumption contexts*. Manuscript in preparation.

Florack, A., Scarabis, M., & Bless, H. (2001). When do associations matter? The use of automatic associations toward ethnic group in person judgments. *Journal of Experimental Social Psychology, 37*, 518–524.

Friese, M., Bluemke, M., & Wänke, M. (2007). Predicting voting behavior with implicit attitude measures: The 2002 German parliamentary election. *Experimental Psychology, 54*, 247–255.

Friese, M., Hofmann, W., & Schmitt, M. (2008). *When and why do implicit reaction time measures predict behavior? Empirical evidence for the moderating role of motivation, opportunity, and process reliance.* Manuscript submitted for publication.

Friese, M., & Hofmann, W. (in press). What would you have as a last supper? Thoughts about death influence evaluation and consumption of food products. *Journal of Exprimental Social Psychology.*

Friese, M., & Hofmann, W. (2008). Trait self-control moderates the influence of impulsive precursors on eating and drinking behavior. Unpublished manuscript.

Friese, M., Hofmann, W., & Wänke, M. (2008). When impulses take over: Moderated predictive validity of explicit and implicit attitude measures in predicting food choice and consumption behaviour. *British Journal of Social Psychology, 47*, 397–419.

Friese, M., Wänke, M., & Plessner, H. (2006). Implicit consumer preferences and their influence on product choice. *Psychology & Marketing, 23*, 727–740.

Gailliot, M. T., Baumeister, R. F., DeWall, C. N., Maner, J. K., Plant, E. A., Tice, D. M., et al. (2007). Self-control relies on glucose as a limited energy source: Willpower is more than a metaphor. *Journal of Personality and Social Psychology, 92*, 325–336.

Gailliot, M. T., Schmeichel, B. J., & Baumeister, R. F. (2006). Self-regulatory processes defend against the threat of death: Effects of self-control depletion and trait self-control on thoughts and fears of dying. *Journal of Personality and Social Psychology, 91*, 49–62.

Gawronski, B., & Bodenhausen, G. V. (2006). Associative and propositional processes in evaluation: An integrative review of implicit and explicit attitude change. *Psychological Bulletin, 132*, 692–731.

Giancola, P. R. (2000). Executive functioning: A conceptual framework for alcohol-related aggression. *Experimental and Clinical Psychopharmacology, 8*, 576–597.

Gilbert, D. T., & Hixon, J. G. (1991). The trouble of thinking: Activation and application of stereotypic beliefs. *Journal of Personality and Social Psychology, 60*, 509–517.

Glasman, L. R., & Albarracín, D. (2006). Forming attitudes that predict future behavior: A meta-analysis of the attitude-behavior relation. *Psychological Bulletin, 132*, 778–822.

Govorun, O., & Payne, B. K. (2006). Ego-depletion and prejudice: Separating automatic and controlled components. *Social Cognition, 24*, 111–136.

Greenberg, J., Pyszczynski, T., Solomon, S., Simon, L., & Breus, M. (1994). Role of consciousness and accessibility of death-related thoughts in mortality salience effects. *Journal of Personality and Social Psychology, 67*, 627–637.

Greenwald, A. G., McGhee, D. E., & Schwartz, J. L. K. (1998). Measuring individual differences in implicit cognition: The Implicit Association Test. *Journal of Personality and Social Psychology, 74*, 1464–1480.

Greenwald, A. G., Nosek, B. A., & Banaji, M. R. (2003). Understanding and using the Implicit Association Test: I. An improved scoring algorithm. *Journal of Personality and Social Psychology, 85*, 197–216.

Greenwald, A. G., Poehlman, T. A., Uhlmann, E. L., & Banaji, M. R. (in press). Understanding and using the Implicit Association Test: III. Meta-analysis of predictive validity. *Journal of Personality and Social Psychology.*

Haire, M. (1950). Projective techniques in marketing research. *Journal of Marketing, 14*, 649–656.

Hammond, K. R. (1948). Measuring attitudes by error-choice: An indirect method. *Journal of Abnormal and Social Psychology, 43*, 38–48.

Hermsen, B., Holland, R. W., & van Knippenberg, A. (2006). *The happy act on impulse, the sad think twice: Mood as a moderator of the impact of implicit and explicit attitudes on behavior.* Manuscript submitted for publication.

Higgins, E. T. (1997). Beyond pleasure and pain. *American Psychologist, 52*, 1280–1300.

Hofmann, W., & Baumert, A. (2007). *Immediate affect as a basis for moral judgment: An adaptation of the affect misattribution procedure.* Manuscript submitted for publication.

Hofmann, W., & Friese, M. (2008). Impulses got the better of me: Alcohol moderates the influence of implicit attitudes toward food cues on eating behavior. *Journal of Abnormal Psychology, 117*, 420–427.

Hofmann, W., Friese, M., & Gschwendner, T. (in press). Men on the 'pull': Automatic approach-avoidance tendencies and sexual interest behavior. *Social Psychology.*

Hofmann, W., Gawronski, B., Gschwendner, T., Le, H., & Schmitt, M. (2005). A meta-analysis on the correlation between the Implicit Association Test and explicit self-report measures. *Personality and Social Psychology Bulletin, 31*, 1369–1385.

Hofmann, W., Gschwendner, T., Friese, M., Wiers, R., & Schmitt, M. (in press). Working memory capacity and self-regulatory behavior: Toward an individual differences perspective on behavior determination by automatic versus controlled processes. *Journal of Personality and Social Psychology.*

Hofmann, W., Rauch, W., & Gawronski, B. (2007). And deplete us not into temptation: Automatic attitudes, dietary restraint, and self-regulatory resources as determinants of eating behavior. *Journal of Experimental Social Psychology, 43*, 497–504.

Hull, J. G. (1981). A self-awareness model of the causes and effects of alcohol consumption. *Journal of Abnormal Psychology, 90*, 586–600.

Hull, J. G., & Reilly, N. P. (1983). Self-awareness, self-regulation, and alcohol consumption: A reply to Wilson. *Journal of Abnormal Psychology, 92*, 514–519.

Hull, J. G., & Slone, L. B. (2004). Alcohol and self-regulation. In R. F. Baumeister & K. D. Vohs (Eds.), *Handbook of self-regulation: Research, theory, and applications* (pp. 466–491). New York: Guilford Press.

Kardes, F. R. (2002). *Consumer behavior and managerial decision making* (2nd ed.). Upper Saddle River, NJ: Prentice Hall.

Karpinski, A., & Hilton, J. L. (2001). Attitudes and the Implicit Association Test. *Journal of Personality and Social Psychology, 81*, 774–788.

Karpinski, A., & Steinman, R. B. (2006). The Single Category Implicit Association Test as a measure of implicit social cognition. *Journal of Personality and Social Psychology, 91*, 16–32.

Kasser, T., & Sheldon, K. M. (2000). Of wealth and death: Materialism, mortality salience, and consumption behavior. *Psychological Science, 11*, 348–351.

Keller, M. L. (1993). Why don't young adults protect themselves against sexual transmission of HIV? Possible answers to a complex question. *AIDS Education and Prevention, 5*, 220–233.

Kihlstrom, J. F. (2004). Implicit methods in social psychology. In C. Sansone, C. C. Morf, & A. T. Panter (Eds.), *The SAGE handbook of methods in social psychology* (pp. 195–212). Thousand Oaks, CA: Sage.

Kruglanski, A., & Freund, T. (1983). The freezing and unfreezing of lay-inferences: Effects on impressional primacy, ethnic stereotyping, and numerical anchoring. *Journal of Experimental Social Psychology, 19*, 448–468.

Lane, K. A., Banaji, M. R., Nosek, B. A., & Greenwald, A. G. (2007). Understanding and using the Implicit Association Test: What we know (so far) about the method. In B. Wittenbrink & N. Schwarz (Eds.), *Implicit measures of attitudes* (pp. 59–102). New York: Guilford Press.

Maison, D., Greenwald, A. G., & Bruin, R. H. (2004). Predictive validity of the Implicit Association Test in studies of brands, consumer attitudes, and behavior. *Journal of Consumer Psychology, 14*, 405–415.

Marsh, K. L., Johnson, B. T., & Scott-Sheldon, L. A. J. (2001). Heart versus reason in condom use: Implicit versus explicit attitudinal predictors of sexual behavior. *Zeitschrift für Experimentelle Psychologie, 48*, 161–175.

Martijn, C., Tenbült, P., Merckelbach, H., Dreezens, E., & de Vries, N. K. (2002). Getting a grip on ourselves: Challenging expectancies about loss of energy after self-control. *Social Cognition, 20*, 441–460.

Mierke, J., & Klauer, K. C. (2003). Method-specific variance in the Implicit Association Test. *Journal of Personality and Social Psychology, 85*, 1180–1192.

Muraven, M., & Baumeister, R. F. (2000). Self-regulation and depletion of limited resources: Does self-control resemble a muscle? *Psychological Bulletin, 126*, 247–259.

Muraven, M., Collins, R. L., & Nienhaus, K. (2002). Self-control and alcohol restraint: An initial application of the self-control strength model. *Journal of Addictive Behaviors, 16*, 113–120.

Muraven, M., & Slessareva, E. (2003). Mechanisms of self-control failure: Motivation and limited resources. *Personality and Social Psychology Bulletin, 29*, 894–906.

Muraven, M., Tice, D. M., & Baumeister, R. F. (1998). Self-control as a limited resource: Regulatory depletion patterns. *Journal of Personality and Social Psychology, 74*, 774–789.

Nelson, L. J., Moore, D. L., Olivetti, J., & Scott, T. (1997). General and personal mortality salience and nationalistic bias. *Personality and Social Psychology Bulletin, 23*, 884–892.

North, A. C., Hargreaves, D. J., & McKendrick, J. (1997). In-store music affects product choice. *Nature, 390*, 132.

Nosek, B. A., & Banaji, M. R. (2001). The go/no-go association task. *Social Cognition, 19*, 625–664.

Nosek, B. A., Greenwald, A. G., & Banaji, M. R. (2006). The Implicit Association Test at age 7: A methodological and conceptual review. In J. A. Bargh (Ed.), *Social psychology and the unconscious: The automaticity of higher mental processes* (pp. 265–292). New York: Psychology Press.

Payne, B. K. (2005). Conceptualizing control in social cognition: How executive functioning modulates the expression of automatic stereotyping. *Journal of Personality and Social Psychology, 89*, 488–503.

Perugini, M. (2005). Predictive models of implicit and explicit attitudes. *British Journal of Social Psychology, 44*, 29–45.

Pudel, V., & Westenhöfer, J. (1989). *Fragebogen zum Essverhalten (FEV)*. Göttingen: Hogrefe.

Puri, R. (1996). Measuring and modifying consumer impulsiveness: A cost-benefit accessibility framework. *Journal of Consumer Psychology, 5*, 87–113.

Ranganath, K. A., Smith, C. T., & Nosek, B. A. (2008). Distinguishing automatic and controlled components of attitudes from direct and indirect measurement methods. *Journal of Experimental Social Psychology, 44*, 386–396.

Richetin, J., Perugini, M., Prestwich, A., & O'Gorman, R. (2007). The IAT as predictor of food choice: The case of fruits versus snacks. *International Journal of Psychology, 42*, 1–8.

Roediger, H. L. (1990). Implicit memory: Retention without remembering. *American Psychologist, 45*, 1043–1056.

Rook, D. (1987). The buying impulse. *Journal of Consumer Research, 22*, 305–313.

Rothermund, K., & Wentura, D. (2004). Underlying processes in the Implicit Association Test (IAT): Dissociating salience from associations. *Journal of Experimental Psychology: General, 133*, 139–165.

Salcher, E. F. (1995). *Psychologische Marktforschung* [Psychological market research]. Berlin: Walter de Gruyter.

Schmeichel, B. J., Vohs, K. D., & Baumeister, R. F. (2003). Intellectual performance and ego depletion: Role of the self in logical reasoning and other information processing. *Journal of Personality and Social Psychology, 85,* 33–46.

Shiv, B., & Fedorikhin, A. (1999). Heart and mind in conflict: The interplay of affect and cognition in consumer decision making. *Journal of Consumer Research, 26,* 278–292.

Solomon, S., Greenberg, J., & Pyszczynski, T. (2004). The cultural animal: Twenty years of terror management theory and research. In J. Greenberg, S. Koole, & T. Pyszczynski (Eds.), *Handbook of experimental existential psychology* (pp. 13–34). New York: Guilford Press.

Spruyt, A., Hermans, D., De Houwer, J., & Eelen, P. (2002). On the nature of the affective priming effect: Affective priming of naming responses. *Social Cognition, 20,* 227–256.

Spruyt, A., Hermans, D., De Houwer, J., Vandekerckhove, J., & Eelen, P. (2007). On the predictive validity of indirect attitude measures: Prediction of consumer choice behavior on the basis of affective priming in the picture-picture naming task. *Journal of Experimental Social Psychology, 43,* 599–610.

Steele, C. M., & Josephs, R. A. (1990). Alcohol myopia: Its prized and dangerous effects. *American Psychologist, 45,* 921–933.

Steffens, M. C. (2004). Is the Implicit Association Test immune to faking? *Experimental Psychology, 51,* 165–179.

Strack, F., & Deutsch, R. (2004). Reflective and impulsive determinants of social behavior. *Personality and Social Psychology Review, 8,* 220–247.

Stunkard, A. J., & Messick, S. (1985). The three-factor eating questionnaire to measure dietary restraint, disinhibition, and hunger. *Journal of Psychosomatic Research, 29,* 71–83.

Sudman, S., Bradburn, N. M., & Schwarz, N. (1996). *Thinking about answers. The application of cognitive processes to survey methodology.* San Francisco, CA: Jossey-Bass.

Tangney, J. P., Baumeister, R. F., & Boone, A. L. (2004). High self-control predicts good adjustment, less pathology, better grades, and interpersonal success. *Journal of Personality, 72,* 271–322.

Tanner, R. J., Ferraro, R., Chartrand, T. L., Bettman, J. R., & van Baaren, R. (2008). Of chameleons and consumption: The impact of mimicry on choice and preferences. *Journal of Consumer Research, 34,* 754–766.

Vantomme, D., Geuens, M., De Houwer, J., & De Pelsmacker, P. (2006). Explicit and implicit determinants of fair-trade buying behavior. *Advances in Consumer Research, 33,* 699–703.

Vargas, P. T. (2004). On the relationship between implicit attitudes and behaviour: Some lessons from the past, and directions for the future. In G. Haddock & G. R. O. Maio (Eds.), *Contemporary perspectives on the psychology of attitudes* (pp. 275–297). London: Psychology Press.

Vohs, K. D., Baumeister, R. F., & Ciarocco, N. J. (2005). Self-regulation and self-presentation: Regulatory resource depletion impairs impression management and effortful self-presentation depletes regulatory resources. *Journal of Personality and Social Psychology, 88,* 632–657.

Vohs, K. D., & Faber, R. J. (2007). Spent resources: Self-regulatory resource availability affects impulse buying. *Journal of Consumer Research, 33,* 537–547.

Vohs, K. D., & Heatherton, T. F. (2000). Self-regulation failure: A resource-depletion approach. *Psychological Science, 11,* 249–254.

Wänke, M., Plessner, H., De Houwer, J., Richter, L., & Gärtner, T. (2006). *Measuring attitude change and predicting brand choice with the IAT.* Unpublished manuscript.

Webb, E. J., Campbell, D. T., Schwartz, R. D., & Sechrest, L. (1966). *Unobtrusive measures: Nonreactive research in the social sciences*. Chicago: Rand McNally.

Webb, T. L., & Sheeran, P. (2003). Can implementation intentions help to overcome ego-depletion? *Journal of Experimental Social Psychology, 39*, 279–286.

Wiers, R. W., & Stacy, A. W. (2006). *Handbook of implicit cognition and addiction*. Thousand Oaks, CA: Sage Publications.

Wilson, T., Lindsey, S., & Schooler, T. Y. (2000). A model of dual attitudes. *Psychological Review, 107*, 101–126.

Wittenbrink, B., Judd, C. M., & Park, B. (1997). Evidence for racial prejudice at the implicit level and its relationship with questionnaire measures. *Journal of Personality and Social Psychology, 72*, 262–274.

Wittenbrink, B., & Schwarz, N. (2007). *Implicit measures of attitudes*. New York: Guilford Press.

Wright, P. (1974). The harassed decision maker: Time pressures, distractions, and the use of evidence. *Journal of Applied Psychology, 59*, 555–561.

16

The Dynamics of Self-Regulation
When Goals Commit versus Liberate

AYELET FISHBACH

University of Chicago

YING ZHANG

University of Texas

G oals are considered the building blocks of human motivation, and over the last century research in the social sciences has used the concept of goals to account for people's motivational responses, including evaluations, emotions, and behaviors (e.g., Ach, 1935; Atkinson, 1964; Austin & Vancouver, 1996; Bandura, 1986; Bargh, 1990; Carver & Scheier, 1998; Deci & Ryan, 1985; Fishbach & Ferguson, 2007; Gollwitzer, 1990; Higgins, 1997; James, 1890; Kruglanski, 1996; Lewin, 1926; Locke & Latham, 1990; Mischel, Cantor, & Feldman, 1996). Beginning with classic goal research, some of the field's important insights include identifying the criteria for goal selection (e.g., the expectancy-value model, Atkinson, 1974; Tolman, 1932), the motivational force of unfulfilled goals (Atkinson & Birch, 1970; Lewin, 1926; Zeigarnik, 1927), and the influence of goals on evaluation (James, 1890; Lewin, 1926, 1935) and information processing (Bruner, 1957). More recent goal research provides insights into the processes of goal setting and goal striving (Carver & Scheier, 1998; Förster, Liberman, & Higgins, 2005; Higgins, 1987, 1997; Gollwitzer, 1999; Kruglanski, 1996; Locke & Latham, 1990). And in line with the general theme of social psychology as the study of the situation, a large proportion of recent goal research concerns the situational variables that activate goals and govern goal pursuit, often outside of conscious awareness (e.g., Aarts & Dijksterhuis, 2000; Ferguson & Bargh, 2004; Chartrand & Bargh, 1996; Moskowitz, 2002; Shah, 2003).

A common theme running through both classic and recent goal research is the focus on a single goal and the initiation of a single goal-congruent action. That is, the unit of observation has usually been a single action or evaluation that was made with regard to a single activated goal. For example, research on goal priming has shown that the elicitation of goal states such as "achievement," "cooperation," and "seeking intimacy" (e.g., as a result of reading these words) increased people's likelihood of engaging in actions that pursue them. Thus, people primed with achievement invested more effort on a test, those primed with cooperation claimed less for themselves in a social dilemma game, and those primed with seeking intimacy expressed greater interest in an opposite-sex experimenter (Aarts, Gollwitzer, & Hassin, 2004; Bargh, Gollwitzer, Lee-Chai, Barndollar, & Troetschel, 2001; Shah & Kruglanski, 2003).

Our own research diverges from previous goal research in two ways. First, we assume that in many real-life situations, people hold more than one goal at a time. For example, in a social dilemma people may wish to achieve and cooperate at the same time. Our research aims to address the simultaneous consideration of multiple and frequently inconsistent goals (see also Cantor & Langston, 1989; Emmons & King, 1988; Higgins, 1997; Kruglanski et al., 2002; Markus & Ruvolo, 1989). Second, we assume that goal-directed actions are rarely chosen and pursued in isolation. Therefore, our research aims to address the influence of prior as well as planned future actions on people's choice of actions in the present (see also, Read, Loewenstein, & Rabin, 1999; Simonson, 1990). For example, walking into a restaurant simultaneously evokes multiple goals if a person wishes to select food items that are tasty, healthful, and inexpensive. In addition, the person usually makes successive choices from the menu (e.g., choice of an appetizer, an entrée, and a dessert), and these successive choices can potentially create a balance among the simultaneously activated goals, or they can emphasize one goal over the others. Similarly, students may hold simultaneous goals when selecting courses for the upcoming term, hoping to find classes that are interesting, easy, and useful. They can then select a schedule of classes that balances these goals or that highlights the most important one.

In general, when several goals are at stake and people see an opportunity to select several goal-related actions in a sequence, their choice pattern can either balance among the underlying goals or highlight the most important one. Our research addresses the question of what determines whether people highlight a single goal or balance among several goals across actions? A related question is what increases the motivation to work on a focal goal: the accomplishment of other goal actions, which reinforces congruent present action through highlighting, or the lack of accomplishment of other goal actions, which reinforces present action through balancing?

To address these questions, we conducted a research program on the dynamics of self-regulation (Fishbach & Dhar, 2005; Fishbach & Zhang, 2008; Fishbach, Dhar, & Zhang, 2006; Koo & Fishbach, 2008; Zhang, Fishbach, & Dhar, 2007). This research addresses the simultaneous pursuit of multiple goals via a sequence of actions that evolves over time and that can either balance among these multiple underlying goals or highlight the single most important one. Our basic premise is that people represent goal actions either in terms of progress toward a desired end state or in terms of commitment to a desirable end state. People then either balance among goals toward which they experience progress or highlight goals to which they feel committed.

In what follows, we discuss our theoretical framework in more detail. We divide our discussion into three parts. The first part addresses the self-regulatory process in each of the two dynamics: progress-based balancing versus commitment-based highlighting. The second part addresses the sources of feedback that affect self-regulation and promote one dynamic or the other. Finally, the third part addresses the determinants of the specific dynamic that individuals choose to follow.

THE DYNAMICS OF SELF-REGULATION

We propose that goal actions can be represented in terms of either progress toward a desirable end state or commitment to this end state. In a *progress* representation of goals, people feel motivated to choose actions that reduce the discrepancy between the existing undesirable state and a desirable end state. This framing of goals is assumed in the cybernetic models of self-regulation (Carver & Scheier, 1998; Locke & Latham, 1990; Miller, Galanter, & Pribram, 1960; Powers, 1973). According to these models, progress toward the end state elicits a sense of partial goal attainment, signaling that less effort is needed to accomplish the goal. For example, a dieter may set a goal to lose some weight, or a student may plan to earn an "A" in class. These goals direct the dieter's and the student's respective action choices, such as ordering a light dinner and studying on weekends. In turn, pursuing these actions signals that progress is being made and the goal is being partially attained.

Alternatively, people can represent goal actions in terms of commitment to the desirable end state. In a *commitment* representation of goals, people interpret their pursuit of congruent actions as signaling commitment to the goal, including an increased sense that the goal is valuable and that the expectancy of attainment is high (Atkinson & Birch, 1970; Atkinson & Raynor, 1978; Bem, 1972; Cialdini, Trost, & Newsom, 1995; Feather, 1990). This representation of goals is less concerned with the reduction of discrepancy between current state and desired end state, or the partial attainment of the goal that is being pursued. For example, a dieter may experience greater commitment to healthful eating when he or she has a light meal, and a student may experience greater commitment to academic success when he or she studies on the weekend. In these cases, the dieter and the student feel that their goals are more valuable and attainable following their pursuit.

These two mental representations of goals—progress versus commitment—have opposite consequences for the pattern of self-regulation when people simultaneously hold multiple goals that they want to pursue. In what follows, we address these behavioral patterns.

Progress-Based Balancing

The representation of goals in terms of progress implies that an initial goal-congruent action reduces the discrepancy between the present state and the attainment of the desirable end state (Carver & Scheier, 1998; Miller et al., 1960; Powers, 1973). As a result, a person may feel justified in relaxing and may consequently withdraw his or her efforts toward this particular end state and instead attend to other goals that are assumed to be neglected in a multiple goal environment. A progress representation of goals could thus result in balancing: a dynamic of self-regulation in which pursuing one goal motivates a person to pursue other goals at the next opportunity because he or she feels it is justified to disengage temporarily from a goal toward which progress has been made.

Previous goal research has documented a balancing dynamic in situations where people infer progress has been made toward a goal. For example, research on moral licensing (Monin & Miller, 2001) found less egalitarian behavior after participants were given an opportunity to express their egalitarian attitudes, compared with when participants were not given this opportunity. In this and similar studies, the perception of progress on the egalitarian goal liberated participants to temporarily abandon it to pursue other goals such as forming a quick and intuitive judgment of a target person. The result of the perceived progress was a pattern of balancing between being egalitarian and relying on intuitive judgment.

Commitment-Based Highlighting

The representation of goals in terms of commitment implies that an initial action that is congruent with a goal is indicative of a strong commitment to that goal. We define commitment as an increased sense that the goal is valuable and likelihood of attainment is high. A commitment interpretation increases a person's motivation to take similar, complementary actions and to inhibit any competing goals (Shah, Friedman, & Kruglanski, 2002) to ensure the attainment of this highly committed goal. The subsequent self-regulatory process would be highlighting: a dynamic of self-regulation in which pursuing one goal motivates a person to pursue other congruent actions that facilitate the same goal because the person is prioritizing this particular goal over others.

Previous goal research documented highlighting when people held a single focal goal and worked harder toward that goal after experiencing some initial goal accomplishment (Dreze & Nunes, 2005; Kivetz, Urminsky, & Zheng, 2006). For example, Kivetz and his colleagues found that shoppers were more likely to use a frequent-buyer card if the card endowed them with some illusionary accomplishment. In their study, shoppers that received a card that included two of 12 stamps required for a free coffee gift were more likely to use the coffee card than were others who had received a free coffee gift card that included zero of 10 required stamps. Although the objective effort that was needed to accomplish the goal was identical across conditions (10 purchases for a free coffee), the perception of initial accomplishment motivated shoppers to use the coffee card by increasing their sense of goal commitment.

Figure 16.1 illustrates these basic dynamics of self-regulation. The representation of goals in terms of progress toward a desirable end state increases the tendency to "juggle" between that goal and other simultaneously activated goals through balancing. Conversely, the representation of goals in terms of commitment

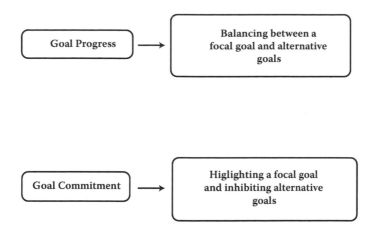

Figure 16.1   Dynamics of Self-Regulation.

to a desirable end state leads people to emphasize one goal over others through highlighting. It follows that in successive choice situations, after a person pursues an initial action, inferences of progress decrease his or her interest in similar, complementary actions, whereas inferences of commitment increase his or her interest in such actions.

Fishbach and Dhar (2005) conducted a series of studies to test whether the same action can both decrease and increase the motivation to choose another goal-congruent action depending on the representation of goals. In one study, these researchers manipulated the representation of goals by asking participants questions that focused their attention on the commitment to or progress toward a particular goal after they pursued congruent actions. Participants then indicated their motivation to choose actions that serve alternative, competing goals. For example, with regard to academic goals, student participants indicated whether, whenever they studied, they felt committed to academic tasks or whether they felt they made progress on their academic tasks. Those who considered their sense of commitment as a result of their actions indicated that they would be unlikely to socialize at night (an incongruent activity with studying) if they had studied during the day, whereas those who considered their sense of progress as a result of their actions indicated that they would be interested in socializing at night if they had studied during the day. These effects were replicated across several goal domains (Fishbach & Dhar, 2005, Study 3). It appears that the focus on commitment versus progress promoted a subsequent choice of actions that either highlighted the focal goal or balanced between that goal and an alternative one.

The model illustrated in Figure 16.1 has further implications for the behavioral consequences of failing to pursue a goal. After people fail to act on a goal, a progress frame motivates them to choose goal-congruent actions because they infer a lack of goal progress and thus feel that more actions are necessary to make up for the failure (Carver & Scheier, 1998). Alternatively, a commitment frame undermines the motivation to choose congruent actions after an initial failure because people infer low commitment and thus tend to disengage from the goal completely (Soman & Cheema, 2004).

In summary, we propose two factors that increase people's motivation to work on a goal: a lack of goal progress, which is based on low performance, and the presence of goal commitment, which is based on high performance. We also propose two factors that undermine people's motivation to work on a goal: low commitment, which is based on low performance, and sufficient progress, which is based on high performance. Goal progress and goal commitment are competing representations of goals; therefore, an action that signals progress toward a goal is less likely to signal goal commitment, and vice versa.

SOURCES OF FEEDBACK FOR SELF-REGULATION

One source of feedback for self-regulation is completed goal actions. Completed goal actions and past successes can provide feedback on goal progress or commitment, which affects subsequent self-regulation. However, there are other sources of feedback for self-regulation, which we explore in this section. We propose that plans for future actions provide a similar type of feedback to the extent that people believe that their plans will materialize and consider them to be accomplished actions. In this case, future plans can signal commitment or progress and can affect subsequent self-regulation. In addition, people's feelings and moods can provide feedback on their level of goal progress or commitment, which then affects self-regulation.

Future Plans as Feedback for Self-Regulation

There is some evidence in previous goal research that people infer either goal commitment or goal progress on the basis of actions they plan to pursue in the future. In this regard, research on self-efficacy (Bandura, 1997) and positive illusions (Taylor & Brown, 1988) finds that beliefs about future actions increase one's confidence in one's ability to pursue the related goals in the present; hence, it is possible these expectations increase goal commitment (see also Atkinson, 1964; Weiner, 1979). As an example, Oettingen and Mayer (2002) found that positive career expectations increased graduating students' motivation to search for a job. As a result of their favorable expectations, these students received more job offers and higher salaries. But future plans can also signal goal progress. For instance, Oettingen and Mayer (2002) also found that fantasies (unlike expectations) about the transition into professional life decreased the motivation to work toward that goal in the present and were associated with fewer job offers and lower salaries. Based on these findings, it is possible that fantasies, unlike expectations, are experienced as goal progress, and therefore they substitute for actual goal actions.

In a recent series of studies, Zhang, Fishbach, and Dhar (2007) tested for the effect of future plans on present actions, as a function of whether expectations were being indicative of goal progress or goal commitment. These researchers hypothesized that the direction of the impact of future plans depends on the representation of goal actions (commitment or progress), whereas the magnitude of the impact depends on people's degree of optimism about their future achievements.

That is, more optimistic individuals expect more goal pursuit will take place in the future, and they subsequently show a stronger tendency to either highlight or balance in the present, depending on whether they frame goal pursuits as goal commitment or goal progress. It further follows that the impact of plans is in direct proportion to the amount of goal pursuit considered: When people are optimistic that they will achieve more in the future than in the past (Buehler, Griffin, & Ross, 1994; Weinstein, 1989; Zauberman & Lynch, 2005), future plans should have an even greater impact on immediate goal pursuits than retrospection of actual past goal pursuits.

To support this prediction, Zhang and colleagues (2007, Study 1) approached gym members at the beginning of the year—a time when people typically make New Year's resolutions—and asked them to estimate either the frequency of their workouts in the coming year or the frequency of their actual workouts in the previous year. Not surprisingly, around the New Year, gym members planned to exercise more frequently in the upcoming year than they did in the past year; that is, those in the future condition of the study were optimistic. Further, the researchers asked all the gym members to rate their agreement with one of two sets of statements, which emphasized either their progress toward the goal of being healthy (e.g., do they feel that they are getting closer to their workout objectives?) or their commitment to this goal (e.g., do they feel committed to their workout objectives?). Finally, to measure their interest in another goal-congruent activity, the gym members were asked to choose between a healthful and an unhealthful drink—bottled water or sugared soda—as a parting gift. The researchers found that those who rated the extent to which they expressed their commitment to the health goal by exercising were more likely to select a healthful drink if they envisioned a future workout than a past workout. Conversely, those who rated the extent to which they were progressing toward their health goal by exercising were less likely to choose healthful drinks if they envisioned a future workout than a past workout. These findings suggest that future exercise plans impact present choice of goal-congruent actions as a function of goal framing, and even more so than past actions.

Another study of the impact of future plans found that the degree of optimism in future goal attainment moderated the effect of expectations on present self-regulation, again, as a function of the representation of goals as expressions of commitment rather than as an accumulation of progress (Zhang et al., 2007, Study 2). That study manipulated the degree of optimism by asking gym members to describe the process of working out (low optimism) versus the completion of a workout (high optimism; see Taylor, Pham, Rivkin, & Armor, 1998) before predicting their amount of future working out. Inducing high (vs. low) optimism about the amount of future working out had opposite effects on gym users' interest in congruent action— healthful eating—in the present: Those who focused on the progress made from exercising became less interested in healthful eating, whereas those who focused on goal commitment on the basis of exercising became more interested.

Mood as Feedback for Self-Regulation

Feelings and moods provide feedback about the progress toward a goal and the size of the discrepancy between the present state and goal attainment (Bandura, 1991; Carver & Scheier, 1990; Clore, 1994; Frijda, 1996; Higgins, 1997). But in addition, feelings and moods also signal whether a person should adopt or reject a goal and, this way, they provide feedback on goal commitment (Fishbach & Labroo, 2007; Gray, 1994; Schwarz & Clore, 1984, 1996; for a review see Pham, this volume). Specifically, a positive mood can signal to people that progress has been made or, alternatively, that they are committed to a goal, whereas a negative mood can signal a lack of goal progress or, alternatively, that goal commitment is relatively low. Whether one's mood provides feedback on progress or commitment can then depend on the representation of goal actions in terms of progress or commitment. In addition, the signal from mood depends on the attribution of the mood to the goal as opposed to an unrelated source.

In terms of attribution, people can attribute their mood either to goal performance or to an alternative source. When a positive mood is attributed to goal performance, it signals that progress is satisfactory, whereas a negative mood that is attributed to goal performance signals a lack of goal progress. As a result, a negative mood motivates goal adherence more than a positive mood because it signals a larger discrepancy (Carver & Scheier, 1990). When, however, mood is attributed to an unrelated source rather than to performance on a goal, a positive mood signals adoption of the goal and a negative mood signals rejection of the goal. By signaling the adoption of a goal, or goal commitment, a positive mood motivates goal adherence more than a negative mood does (Fishbach & Labroo, 2007; see also Gray, 1994).

In a study that supports this analysis, Eyal, Fishbach, and Labroo (2008) first induced a positive or negative mood by asking participants to generate creative associations for positive versus negative words (e.g., *healthy, beautiful* vs. *ugly, vomit*; see Isen, Johnson, Mertz, & Robinson, 1985), supposedly to assess their creativity. Then, half of the participants in a mood-related condition were (mis) informed that their feelings after completing the creativity task were indicative of their level of task performance, which was unknown to them. These participants interpreted their positive or negative feelings as indicative of high versus low performance, respectively. As a result of the misattribution, those who experienced a positive mood exhibited lower performance on a subsequent, related word-generation task than those who experienced a negative mood. This pattern is congruent with a progress representation of goals, because negative feelings suggested a large discrepancy between the current state and the desirable end state, and thus increased the motivation to adhere to the goal. In contrast, the participants in the mood-unrelated condition had no reason to associate their mood with task performance and, among them, those who experienced a positive mood worked harder on the word-generation task than those who experienced a negative mood. This pattern is congruent with a commitment representation of goals, in which positive feelings signal commitment to a goal more than negative feelings do, thus increasing adherence to the goal. This and other studies demonstrate that both a negative mood that is attributed to goal performance and a positive mood that is attributed to an alternative source increase goal adherence by signaling either low goal progress or high goal commitment. But a negative mood that is attributed to an alternative source and a positive mood that is attributed to goal performance decrease goal adherence.

THE DETERMINANT OF THE DYNAMIC OF SELF-REGULATION

In the previous section we reviewed several sources of feedback for self-regulation, including past achievements, future plans, and moods. The feedback on goal pursuit influences people's motivation for choosing actions that highlight a single goal under a commitment frame and for choosing actions that balance between different goals under a progress frame. In what follows we address the question of what makes people represent goals in terms of commitment or progress, which promotes the dynamics of highlighting or balancing, respectively. We propose that the representation of goals and the resultant dynamic of self-regulation can depend on the information the person seeks, either in terms of establishing commitment or ensuring sufficient progress is being made, as well as on the information that is in the presentation of action alternatives. For example, if a person asks about his or her level of commitment, and as a result follows a pattern of highlighting, the information that the perceiver seeks determines the self-regulatory dynamic. If however, two goal actions, such as eating healthy or unhealthy food, appear in competition with each other, and, consequently, a person makes a sequence of choices that highlights the pursuit of the highly committed goal, the information that is in the choice context determines the self-regulatory dynamic.

The Information That the Perceiver Seeks

Framing Cues   The tendency to represent goals in terms of commitment or progress is partially determined by framing cues, which direct a person to ask about the commitment or progress that results from his or her actions. For example, asking gym members whether they were getting healthier as a result of exercising induced a progress representation of working out, which decreased their subsequent interest in congruent actions (e.g., healthful eating). Asking gym members whether they were expressing their commitment to being healthy by exercising induced a commitment representation of working out, which increased their subsequent interest in congruent actions (Fishbach & Dhar, 2005; Zhang et al., 2007). In this and other studies, the framing questions led participants to ask themselves about commitment or progress. They then inferred either goal commitment or goal progress from their successful actions and, correspondingly, inferred either low commitment or lack of progress from unsuccessful actions. In other words, the questions that participants were led to ask themselves and then answer influenced the dynamic of self-regulation that they follow.

Committed versus Uncommitted Individuals People vary in whether they seek information about their level of commitment or about the remaining progress needed for goal attainment. In particular, when the commitment to a goal is uncertain, people ask themselves whether the goal is important, attainable, or worth pursuing further. For example, a person's assessment of his or her commitment level influences the decision to make a first-time contribution to a charity or to study for a relatively unimportant course. In such situations, a person's assessment of whether the cause of the charity is valuable or whether it is worth studying for a course determines his or her motivation to work on these goals. In contrast, when commitment is certain and known to be high, people are less concerned with evaluating the commitment to the goal and instead focus on evaluating the level of progress toward the goal and the remaining efforts to accomplish the goal. For example, estimates of progress toward goal completion increase a person's motivation to make a repeated contribution to a familiar and valuable charity or to study for a highly important course. In such situations, where goal commitment is already high, people are more likely to donate or to study if they experience a lack of progress on the goal.

We have proposed that accomplished actions increase motivation to adhere to a goal when they signal commitment and unaccomplished actions increase motivation to adhere to a goal when they signal lack of goal progress. It follows that when commitment is uncertain and people ask whether the goal is important, they will adhere to a goal if they consider their accomplished actions (vs. unaccomplished actions), which suggest higher commitment to the goal. But committed self-regulators, who ask about their level of progress, will be more likely to adhere to a goal if they consider their unaccomplished actions (vs. accomplished actions), which suggest more distance to goal attainment.

In studies that tested these predictions, Koo and Fishbach (2008) used goals with a clear end state and examined how the focus on either the accumulated amount of progress to date or the remaining amount of progress to go influences goal adherence. In one study, participants rated their motivation to study for a core course, to which their commitment was certain, or an elective course, to which their commitment was uncertain, as a function of the information they received: Either that they had accomplished 50% of the coursework to date, or they had another 50% of their coursework to go. Although the objective level of accomplishment was identical (50%), emphasizing the amount of completed (vs. remaining) coursework increased students' motivation to study for an elective course because it implied that studying for the exam was valuable. Conversely, emphasizing the remaining coursework to be completed (vs. completed coursework) increased students' motivation to study for a core class because it implied lack of progress (Koo & Fishbach, 2008, Study 1).

Individuals not only regulate their own personal goals, but at times, they jointly invest efforts with other members of their group toward a common social goal, such as when making contributions to a charity. The pursuit of group goals may then follow dynamics similar to those at work in the pursuit of personal goals; that is, a person may want to evaluate either whether the group goal is worth supporting (i.e., commitment) or whether additional efforts are needed to accomplish the goal (i.e., lack of progress). People infer goal commitment on the basis of others' accomplished actions or present contributions, which increase goal adherence through highlighting; and they infer lack of goal progress on the basis of others' unaccomplished actions or lack of contributions, which increase goal adherence through balancing.

A field study that demonstrated these effects used an actual fundraising campaign conducted by Compassion Korea, a charity organization dedicated to helping children in developing countries. With the cooperation of the South Korean office of Compassion International, Koo and Fishbach (2008; Study 4) created a campaign to support AIDS orphans in Africa. The solicited population included people who had never made contributions to Compassion (uncertain commitment) and regular donors who were making monthly donations of $35 to this charity (certain commitment). All those solicited learned that the campaign goal was to raise 10 million won (about US$10,000) to help AIDS orphans in Africa and that approximately half the money had already been raised through various channels. Half of the participants received a solicitation letter that emphasized accomplished actions, that is, how much had been donated, and the other half received a letter that emphasized unaccomplished actions, that is, how much was still required to achieve the campaign goal. As predicted, among first-time donors (uncertain commitment), an emphasis on accomplished actions (50% to date) increased the frequency and the average amount of donations more than an emphasis on unaccomplished actions (50% to go) did. However, among regular donors (certain commitment), an emphasis on unaccomplished actions (50% to go) increased the frequency and the average amount of donations more than an emphasis on accomplished actions (50% to date) did.

It appears that regardless of the goal type, personal or social, whether people's motivation is driven by commitment or by lack of progress depends on the information they seek as a function of their a priori level of commitment. Those who wish to evaluate their level of commitment are more likely to adhere to a goal if they consider accomplished actions, which establish goal commitment; thus, they follow a pattern of highlighting the pursuit of the focal goal. Those who wish to evaluate their level of progress are more likely to adhere to a goal if they consider unaccomplished actions, which suggest distance needs to be covered; thus, they follow a pattern of balancing between past goal actions and present ones.

The Information in the Goal Actions

The previous section addressed the perceiver's influence on the representation of goals and the resultant dynamic of self-regulation. We proposed that whether people ask about goal commitment or goal progress influences their pattern of self-regulation. This section addresses how the characteristics of choice sets can influence the dynamic of self-regulation that people follow. We propose that the dynamic of self-regulation depends on the relative salience of the overall goal versus that of specific actions, and the presentation of goal actions as either competing with or complementing each other.

Overall Goal Accessibility   People often break an overall goal into specific actions or subgoals as an adaptive self-regulatory response (Carver & Scheier, 1990; Gollwitzer, 1999; Shah & Kruglanski, 2003). In the course of self-regulation, they can then focus on the abstract, overall goal that initiated the action or on the concrete action that was initiated (Trope & Liberman, 2003; Vallacher & Wegner, 1987; see also Eyal, Liberman, & Trope, this volume). When people focus on attainment of the concrete action itself, they experience some of the benefits associated with goal fulfillment, which elicits a sense of progress or partial goal attainment. This can motivate them to move temporarily away from the goal and to attend to other neglected goals that have not progressed as much, through the dynamic of balancing. However, when the focus is on a more abstract, overall goal, this same level of successful attainment does not elicit the same sense of partial fulfillment but instead indicates a person's higher commitment to the goal that initiated the action, and thus promotes reinforcement of this goal through the dynamic of highlighting.

Fishbach and colleagues (2006, Study 3) tested this idea by giving participants an opportunity to work on two independent scrambled-sentence tasks that represented two subgoals toward an academic achievement goal. After completing the first task, participants received bogus feedback on their low or high success and were then asked to complete a second task, which was unsolvable. Participants' persistence on the second task indicated their performance motivation on this unsolvable task (Muraven, Tice, & Baumeister, 1998). In itself, high-success (vs. low-success) feedback on one task reduced the motivation to persist on a similar task. Quitting earlier after high (vs. low) success reflects the dynamic of balancing, a pattern that further replicates previous findings on means substitution (e.g., Shah & Kruglanski, 2002). However, in another experimental condition, the first scrambled-sentence task activated participants' abstract achievement goal outside their conscious awareness by including words such as *succeed*, *master*, and *accomplished* (see Bargh & Chartrand, 2000; Srull & Wyer, 1979). For these participants, high-success (vs. low-success) feedback on the first task elicited greater motivation to persist on the second, unsolvable task, a pattern that reflects the dynamic of highlighting.

In addition to the accessibility of an overall goal, any other variable that influences the relative focus on concrete goal-related actions versus abstract overall goals could influence the dynamic of self-regulation. For example, because actions that are temporally distant are represented in terms of more abstract goals than are actions that are temporally proximal (e.g., Trope & Liberman, 2003; see also Eyal et al., this volume), temporal distance could determine the relative focus on goal progress, for proximal actions, versus goal commitment, for distant actions. Accordingly, Fishbach and colleagues (2006; Study 4; see also Zhang et al., 2007, Study 4) found that actions scheduled for the near future signaled partial attainment, thus leading to more goal-incongruent actions in the present. Conversely, the same actions, when scheduled for the distant future, signaled commitment to an overall goal, thus leading to more goal-congruent actions in the present. For example, students represented studying for an exam in the near future (tomorrow) as accomplishment of an academic task, but studying for an exam in the distant future (next month) as commitment to an academic goal. In turn, thinking about studying in the distant future (vs. near future) increased the amount of time participants intended to spend studying for another exam, which is another means to the same overall goal of academic success.

Recall that, whereas initial success motivates a choice of similar actions when it signals goal commitment, when a failure to pursue certain goals is indicative of low goal commitment, it decreases the motivation to work on a goal. In addition, whereas initial success undermines one's motivation when it signals progress, when failure signals lack of progress, it increases the motivation to work harder toward the goal to make it up. It follows that success motivates more goal-congruent actions if a person focuses on the abstract goal, whereas failure motivates more goal-congruent actions if a person focuses on concrete actions. In support of this hypothesis, Fishbach and colleagues (2006, Study 2) gave gym users positive versus negative feedback on their workout frequency and then measured their interest in the congruent action of healthful eating. The feedback was manipulated by asking gym users to list the amount of time they exercised over the previous week on a survey form that had been previously filled out (presumably by another participant) and partially erased, but still legible. In this partially completed survey (e.g., Simonson, Nowlis, & Simonson, 1993), a fictitious gym user listed either a small or a large amount of time he or she had exercised, which made participants feel that they were doing relatively well or not so well, compared with that person. In addition, half of the participants were primed with the abstract goal of keeping in shape—they were given a hardcover book on health to use as their clipboard to complete the survey. The rest of the participants used a phonebook as their clipboard (control condition). This study found that positive (vs. negative) feedback increased participants' interest in healthful eating when the abstract goal of keeping in shape was primed. However, negative (vs. positive) feedback increased participants' interest in healthful food when they focused on the action itself in the no-priming, control condition.

In the studies reviewed thus far, initial actions (or expected actions) influenced people's subsequent choices of actions that pursued the same goal. We now turn to research that illustrates these dynamics of self-regulation in situations in which there is no initial action. In this case, the representation of goals in terms of commitment or progress and the resultant tendency to highlight versus balance are influenced by the arrangement of the action alternatives and do not require an initial action and action framing.

When Goal Actions Complement versus Compete

People often make selections from choice sets that include options that serve multiple underlying goals. For example, people browse a television guide that includes educational shows and funny sitcoms, they go through high-brow news magazines and low-brow fashion magazines on a newsstand, and they order dinner from a menu that has both healthful and unhealthful courses. In such situations, the presence of the choice alternatives simultaneously activates multiple goals (Shah & Kruglanski, 2003), and the arrangement of the choice alternatives influences the dynamics of self-regulation (Fishbach & Zhang, in press). Specifically, choice alternatives that are presented together, as part of a unified choice set, seem to complement each other and promote the dynamic of balancing among the underlying goals. Choice alternatives that are presented apart, in two separate choice sets that are organized by the underlying goals, seem to compete against each other and promote the dynamic of highlighting the more important goal.

The perception of goals as complementing or competing has unique implications for how people resolve self-control conflicts between high-order goals and low-order temptations (Baumeister, Heatherton, & Tice, 1994; Kuhl & Beckmann, 1985; Loewenstein, 1996; Metcalfe & Mischel, 1999; Rachlin, 1997; Trope & Fishbach, 2000). When choice alternatives that represent goals and temptations appear together and seem to complement each other, a person favors the immediately gratifying temptation, because the complementary relationship promotes the dynamic of balancing both pursuits. In such a sequence, a person could maximize the attainment by showing an immediate preference for the tempting option, which has higher value in the present, while holding an intention to choose a goal item with the delayed value at the next opportunity. As a result of this balancing pattern—first temptation, then goal—people assign a greater value to tempting alternatives than to goal alternatives and prefer these tempting alternatives for immediate consumption. For example, in this situation, people would prefer watching sitcoms or reading low-brow fashion magazines.

But if the choice alternatives that represent goals and temptations are presented separately and against each other, they foster a sense of competition and promote the dynamic of highlighting the more important goal. In these situations, people believe that one goal will be attained only at the cost of the other, and they expect to maximize the attainment by highlighting the higher order goal across several choices. As a result, people assign a greater value to goal alternatives than to tempting alternatives and prefer these goal alternatives for immediate consumption. For example, in this situation, people would prefer watching educational shows or reading news magazines.

In support of these predictions, Fishbach and Zhang (2008, Study 1) found that when healthful and unhealthful (yet tasty) food items appeared together in one image (e.g., a photo of a burger among tomatoes; a can of Coke among berries), they seemed to complement each other and primed balancing. As a result, participants evaluated the unhealthful items (e.g., burger, Coke) more positively than the healthful items (tomatoes, berries). However, when the same items were shown apart, in two separate images next to each other, they seemed to compete against each other and primed highlighting. As a result, participants evaluated the healthful items more positively than the unhealthful items. Follow-up studies assessed people's choices among these alternatives, which were depicted either together in one set or apart in two sets. These studies found that when healthful and unhealthful menu courses were presented together on a menu, the majority of the participants preferred to order an unhealthful entrée for immediate consumption and a more healthful dessert for delayed consumption; this choice sequence represents balancing. However, when the same food options were depicted in two separate parts of the menu—one exclusively for healthful and the other exclusively for unhealthful courses—the majority of the participants preferred to order the healthful entrée and dessert, thus choosing to highlight the more important health goal (Fishbach & Zhang, 2008, Study 4).

It appears that the presentation of choice alternatives can directly prime a tendency to balance among underlying goals or to highlight the most important one over successive choices. Notably, in self-control situations, balancing may imply that a person is more likely to resolve the conflict in favor of the temptation in the present. Then, to the extent that a person's choices for the future are not binding, the dynamic of balancing may potentially result in a repeated choice of tempting alternatives while repeatedly postponing the goal alternatives to the future. For example, a dieter may plan to balance between weight loss and food enjoyment but end up always planning to start the diet tomorrow. As this example illustrates, balancing can be less adaptive in self-control dilemmas, since individuals might not actually balance but rather postpone the goal. In these situations, a dynamic of highlighting the overall goal would be more adaptive since it requires exercising self-control in the present and adhering to the goal across successive choice.

CONCLUSIONS

This chapter considered the theory and research on the dynamics of self-regulation (e.g., Fishbach & Dhar, 2005; Fishbach et al., 2006; Fishbach & Zhang, 2008; Koo & Fishbach, 2008; Zhang et al., 2007). We explored two basic dynamics of self-regulation when people hold multiple goals: the dynamic of highlighting a single goal, which is based on a commitment representation of goals, and the dynamic of balancing among multiple goals, which is based on a progress representation of goals. We further identified two distinct factors that increase the motivation to adhere to a goal: a motivation that is based on the experience of goal commitment and a motivation that is based on the experience of lack of goal progress or a discrepancy between the present and desired states.

Several predictions follow from our theory, and goal research has consistently supported them. First, perceiving an initial action as indicative of commitment promotes the choice of similar subsequent actions and inhibits the choice of actions that serve other goals (e.g., Shah et al., 2002). Perceiving the same initial action as being indicative of progress promotes the subsequent choice of actions that pursue other goals (e.g., Monin & Miller, 2001; Kahn & Dhar, 2006). These different representations of goals can account for the discrepancy in the literature between goal pursuits that commit one to pursue congruent actions and goal pursuits that liberate one to pursue incongruent actions. Second, planned actions for the future (e.g., planned workouts) exert a similar impact as accomplished actions (e.g., past workouts), and both of them influence present actions that either emphasize the same focal goal or balance between this focal goal and alternative ones. Moreover, because the amount of the goal pursuit under consideration determines the magnitude of its impact on the motivation to pursue the goal in the present, optimistic plans for future can have a greater impact than less optimistic plans or recollection of past accomplishments can have. Third, people's feelings provide information for self-regulation. Negative feelings motivate goal adherence when they signal a lack of progress, whereas positive feelings motivate goal-congruent actions when they signal high commitment.

We further proposed several variables that influence whether initial goal-congruent actions increase the commitment to or liberate from the overall goal. First, the dynamic of self-regulation depends on the information that the perceiver seeks: whether he or she asks about commitment to the goal or progress needed for goal attainment. Accomplished actions or successes motivate people who seek information on goal commitment (see also Bem, 1972; Cialdini, Trost, & Newsom, 1995), but they undermine the motivation of people who seek information on their level of progress. Unaccomplished actions or failures motivate committed people who seek information on goal progress (e.g., Bandura, 1991; Carver & Scheier, 1998; Higgins, 1987, 1997; Locke & Latham, 1990; Miller, Galanter, & Pribram, 1960), but they undermine the motivation of those who seek information on their level of commitment. Therefore, the degree of certainty in one's commitment determines whether accomplished or unaccomplished actions are more effective in motivating more actions.

Second, the dynamics of self-regulation depend on the information that is in the choice alternatives. Thus, when people focus on the abstract goal, completed actions signal commitment and increase the likelihood of choosing complementary actions that serve the same goal. When people focus on the specific action, completed actions signal progress; thus, they decrease the likelihood of choosing complementary actions. One conclusion is that setting specific action plans or subgoals may secure the attainment of these subgoals (see Gollwitzer, 1999) but can potentially hinder other subgoals that serve the same overall goal. This undermining effect is more likely if people focus too much on their specific plans and substitute their initial accomplishment for overall goal attainment (e.g., Byrne & Bovair, 1997).

In addition, the dynamic of self-regulation depends on the representation of choice alternatives that serve different goals (e.g., healthful and unhealthful menu courses) as competing against each other or complementing each other. Presenting choice alternatives together in a unified choice set fosters the perception that these options complement each other and thus promotes the dynamic of balancing among the underlying goals. In self-control situations, this dynamic increases the preference for tempting alternatives. Presenting choice alternatives apart, in separate sets that are organized by the underlying goals, elicits the perception that these options compete against each other and thus promotes the dynamic of highlighting the more important goal. This dynamic increases the preference for alternatives that serve high-order goals.

There are likely to be other variables that influence the representation of goals and the dynamic of self-regulation. For example, it is possible that people's implicit theories (Schwarz, 2004; Wyer, 2004) influence the chronic activation of certain goal representations. As initial support for this idea, a recent study has found that gym users vary in the extent to which they represent working out as expressing commitment to or making progress toward a health goal (Zhang et al., 2007). Moreover, these dynamics of self-regulation have implications for variables beyond the current scope of this chapter. For example, the relative focus on commitment versus progress may have implications for people's levels of aspiration with regard to a single goal (Lewin, Dembo, Festinger, & Sears, 1944). People who focus on the progress that results from their actions and view goal pursuit as a continuous movement are more likely to set high aspiration levels and continue to escalate them than are those who focus on the commitment that results from their actions and view goals as a state of preference or value.

It is further possible that, whereas a commitment representation of goals dominates the initiation of goal-related actions, a progress representation of goals dominates its subsequent pursuit. The result is that for many goals, the initial pursuit is motivated by accomplished actions and inferences of commitment, whereas subsequent pursuits are motivated by unaccomplished actions and inferences of a lack of progress. For example, an amateur pianist may practice piano because he or she has already mastered a particular musical piece, and the initial success establishes commitment to this skill. However, an experienced pianist may practice mainly because he or she has not yet mastered a particular piece and would like to continue to improve.

Finally, social agents, such as educators, managers, and marketers, may benefit from considering the information that people derive from goal-related actions—commitment or progress—and the implications of goal representations for subsequent self-regulation. For example, it is possible that mandatory goal pursuits or imposed choice, such as banning unhealthful products, signals to people that they have made progress toward a goal without them experiencing the corresponding boost in goal commitment because the goal actions were not voluntarily selected. In such situations, imposed choices may be effective in the short run but will promote balancing between the goal that was progressed toward and alternative goals and eventually may decrease the likelihood of making complementary, voluntary choices. This may undermine the pursuit of the intended goal by promoting unhealthful behaviors. However, when people work on a goal without making any progress, for example, when they invest effort in a futile cause, in sunk-cost situations (Arkes & Ayton, 1999; Arkes & Blumer, 1985), they may experience commitment without progress. Such an experience should be effective in increasing commitment and motivating the voluntary choice of similar complementary actions that pursue the same goal.

REFERENCES

Aarts, H., & Dijksterhuis, A. (2000). Habits as knowledge structures: Automaticity in goal-directed behavior. *Journal of Personality & Social Psychology, 78*(1), 53–63.

Aarts, H., Gollwitzer, P. M., & Hassin, R. R. (2004). Goal contagion: Perceiving is for pursuing. *Journal of Personality and Social Psychology, 87*(1), 23–37.

Ach, N. (1935). Analyse des willens [Analysis of the will]. In E. Abderhalden (Ed.), *Handbuch der biolagishen arbeitsmethoden* (Vol. 6, Part E). Berlin: Urban & Schwarzenberg.

Arkes, H. R., & Ayton, P. (1999). The sunk cost and Concorde effects: Are humans less rational than lower animals? *Psychological Bulletin, 125*(5), 591–600.

Arkes, H. R., & Blumer, C. (1985). The psychology of sunk cost. *Organizational Behavior and Human Decision Processes, 35*(1), 124–140.

Atkinson, J. W. (1964). *An introduction to motivation*. Oxford, England: Van Nostrand.

Atkinson, J. W. (1974). Strength and motivation and efficiency of performance. In J. W. Atkinson & J. O. Raynor (Eds.), *Motivation and achievement* (pp. 193–218). New York: Wiley.

Atkinson, J. W., & Birch, D. (1970). *The dynamics of action*: New York: Wiley.

Atkinson, J. W., & Raynor, J. O. (1978). *Personality, motivation, and achievement*. New York: Halsted Press.

Austin, J. T., & Vancouver, J. B. (1996). Goal constructs in psychology: Structure, process, and content. *Psychological Bulletin, 120*(3), 338–375.

Bandura, A. (1986). *Social foundations of thought and action: A social cognitive theory*. Upper Saddle River, NJ: Prentice-Hall.

Bandura, A. (1991). Social cognitive theory of self-regulation. *Organizational Behavior and Human Decision Processes, 50,* 248–287.

Bandura, A. (1997). *Self-efficacy: The exercise of control*. New York: W. H. Freeman/Times Books/Henry Holt & Co.

Bargh, J. A. (1990). Auto-motives: Preconscious determinants of social interaction. In E. T. Higgins & R. M. Sorrentino (Eds.), *Handbook of motivation and cognition: Foundations of social behavior* (Vol. 2, pp. 93–130). New York: Guilford Press.

Bargh, J. A., & Chartrand, T. L. (2000). The mind in the middle: A practical guide to priming and automaticity research. In H. T. Reis & C. M. Judd (Eds.), *Handbook of research methods in social and personality psychology* (pp. 253–285). New York: Cambridge University Press.

Bargh, J. A., Gollwitzer, P. M., Lee-Chai, A., Barndollar, K., & Troetschel, R. (2001). The automated will: Nonconscious activation and pursuit of behavioral goals. *Journal of Personality and Social Psychology, 81*(6), 1014–1027.

Baumeister, R. F., Heatherton, T. F., & Tice, D. M. (1994). *Losing control: How and why people fail at self-regulation*. San Diego: Academic.

Bem, D. J. (1972). Self-perception theory. In L. Berkowitz (Ed.), *Advances in experimental social psychology* (Vol. 6, pp. 1–62). New York: Academic Press.

Bruner, J. S. (1957). On perceptual readiness. *Psychological Review, 64*(2), 123–152.

Brunstein, J. C., & Gollwitzer, P. M. (1996). Effects of failure on subsequent performance: The importance of self-defining goals. *Journal of Personality & Social Psychology, 70*(2), 395–407.

Buehler, R., Griffin, D., & Ross, M. (1994). Exploring the "planning fallacy": Why people underestimate their task completion times. *Journal of Personality & Social Psychology, 67*(3), 366–381.

Byrne, M. D., & Bovair, S. (1997). A working memory model of a common procedural error. *Cognitive Science, 21*(1), 31–61.

Cantor, N., & Langston, C. A. (1989). Ups and downs of life tasks in a life transition. In L. A. Pervin (Ed.), *Goal concepts in personality and social psychology* (pp. 127–167). Hillsdale: Erlbaum.

Carver, C. S., & Scheier, M. F. (1990). Principles of self-regulation: Action and emotion. In E. T. Higgins & R. M. Sorrentino (Eds.), *Handbook of motivation and cognition: Foundations of social behavior* (Vol. 2, pp. 3–52). New York: Guilford Press.

Carver, C. S., & Scheier, M. F. (1998). *On the self-regulation of behavior*. New York: Cambridge University Press.

Chartrand, T. L., & Bargh, J. A. (1996). Automatic activation of impression formation and memorization goals: Nonconscious goal priming reproduces the effects of explicit task instructions. *Journal of Personality and Social Psychology, 71,* 464–478.

Cialdini, R. B., Trost, M. R., & Newsom, J. T. (1995). Preference for consistency: The development of a valid measure and the discovery of surprising behavioral implications. *Journal of Personality and Social Psychology, 69*(2), 318–328.

Clore, G. L. (1994). Why emotions are never unconscious. In P. Ekman & R. J. Davidson (Eds.), *The nature of emotion: Fundamental questions* (pp. 285–290). New York: Oxford University Press.

Deci, E. L., & Ryan, R. (1985). *Intrinsic motivation and self-determination in human behavior*. New York: Plenum.

Dreze, X., & Nunes, J. C. (2006). The endowed progress effect: How unwarranted advancement increases future effort. *Journal of Consumer Research, 32*, 504–512.

Emmons, R. A., & King, L. A. (1988). Conflict among personal strivings: Immediate and longterm implications for psychological and physical well-being. *Journal of Personality and Social Psychology, 54*(6), 1040–1048.

Eyal, T., Fishbach, A., & Labroo, A. (2008). *When mood cues goal progress versus goal adoption: A matter of (mis)attribution*. Unpublished manuscript, University of Chicago.

Feather, N. T. (1990). Bridging the gap between values and actions: Recent applications of the expectancy-value model. In E. T. Higgins & R. M. Sorrentino (Eds.), *Handbook of motivation and cognition: Foundations of social behavior* (Vol. 2, pp. 151–192). New York: Guilford Press.

Ferguson, M. J., & Bargh, J. A. (2004). Liking is for doing: The effects of goal pursuit on automatic evaluation. *Journal of Personality and Social Psychology, 87*(5), 557–572.

Förster, J., Liberman, N., & Higgins, E. (2005). Accessibility from active and fulfilled goals. *Journal of Experimental Social Psychology, 41*(3), 220–239.

Fishbach, A., & Dhar, R. (2005). Goals as excuses or guides: The liberating effect of perceived goal progress on choice. *Journal of Consumer Research, 32*, 370–377.

Fishbach, A., & Dhar, R. (2006). Dynamics of goal-based choice. In C. P. Haugtvedt, P. M. Herr, & F. R. Kardes (Eds.), *Handbook of Consumer Psychology*. Hillsdale, NJ: Erlbaum Press.

Fishbach, A., Dhar, R., & Zhang, Y. (2006). Subgoals as substitutes or complements: The role of goal accessibility. *Journal of Personality and Social Psychology, 91*, 232–242.

Fishbach, A., & Ferguson, M. F. (2007). The goal construct in social psychology. In A. W. Kruglanski & T. E. Higgins (Eds.) *Social psychology: Handbook of basic principles* (pp. 490–515). New York: Guilford.

Fishbach, A., & Labroo, A. (2007). Be better or be merry: How mood affects self-control. *Journal of Personality and Social Psychology, 93*(2), 158–173.

Fishbach, A., & Zhang, Y. (2008). Together or apart: When goals and temptations complement versus compete. *Journal of Personality and Social Psychology, 94*, 547–559.

Frijda, N. (1996). Passions: Emotion and socially consequential behavior. In R. Kavanaugh, B. Zimmerbag, & S. Fein (Eds.), *Emotion: Interdisciplinary perspectives*. Hillsdale, NJ: Lawrence Erlbaum.

Gollwitzer, P. M. (1990). Action phases and mind-sets. In E. T. Higgins & R. M. Sorrentino (Eds.), *Handbook of motivation and cognition: Foundations of social behavior* (Vol. 2, pp. 53–92). New York: Guilford Press.

Gollwitzer, P. M. (1999). Implementation intentions: Strong effects of simple plans. *American Psychologist, 54*(7), 493–503.

Gray, J. A. (1994). Personality dimensions and emotion systems. In P. Ekman & R. J. Davidson (Eds.), *The nature of emotion: Fundamental questions* (pp. 329–331). New York: Oxford University Press.

Higgins, E. T. (1987). Self-discrepancy: A theory relating self and affect. *Psychological Review, 94*, 319–340.

Higgins, T. E. (1997). Beyond pleasure and pain. *American Psychologist, 52*(12), 1280–1300.

Isen, A. M., Johnson, M., Mertz, E. & Robinson, G. (1985). Positive affect and the uniqueness of word association. *Journal of Personality and Social Psychology, 48*, 1413–1426.

James, W. (1890). *The principles of psychology* (Vol. 2). New York: Holt.

Kahn, U. & Dhar, R. (2006). Licensing effect in consumer choice. *Journal of Marketing Research, 43*(2), 259–266.

Kivetz, R., Urminsky, O., & Zheng, Y. (2006). The goal-gradient hypothesis resurrected: Purchase acceleration, illusionary goal progress, and customer retention. *Journal of Marketing Research, 43*(1), 39–58.

Koo, M., & Fishbach, A. (2008). Dynamics of self-regulation: How (un)accomplished goal actions affect motivation. *Journal of Personality and Social Psychology, 94*, 183–195.

Kruglanski, A. W. (1996). Goals as knowledge structures. In P. M. Gollwitzer & J. A. Bargh (Eds.), *The psychology of action: Linking cognition and motivation to behavior* (pp. 599–618). New York: Guilford Press.

Kruglanski, A. W., Shah, J. Y., Fishbach, A., Friedman, R., Chun, W. Y., & Sleeth-Keppler, D. (2002). A theory of goal systems. In M. P. Zanna (Ed.), *Advances in experimental social psychology* (Vol. 34, pp. 331–378). City: Publisher.

Kuhl, J., & Beckmann, J. (1985). *Action control from cognition to behavior.* New York: Academic Press.

Lewin, K. (1926). Vorsatz, Wille, und Bedürfnis [Intention, will, and need]. *Psychologische Forschung, 7*, 330–385.

Lewin, K. (1935). *A dynamic theory of personality.* New York: McGraw-Hill.

Lewin, K., Dembo, T., Festinger, L., & Sears, P. S. (1944). Level of aspiration. In J. M. Hunt (Ed.), *Personality and the behavior disorders* (Vol. 1, pp. 333–378). New York: Ronald Press.

Locke, E. A., & Latham, G. P. (1990). *A theory of goal setting & task performance.* Upper Saddle River, NJ: Prentice-Hall.

Loewenstein, G. (1996). Out of control: Visceral influences on behavior. *Organizational Behavior & Human Decision Processes, 65*(3), 272–292.

Markus, H., & Ruvolo, A. (1989). Possible selves: Personalized representations of goals. In L. A. Pervin (Ed.), *Goal concepts in personality and social psychology* (pp. 211–241). Hillsdale, NJ: Lawrence Erlbaum.

Metcalfe, J., & Mischel, W. (1999). A hot/cool-system analysis of delay of gratification: Dynamics of willpower. *Psychological Review, 106*(1), 3–19.

Miller, G. A., Galanter, E., & Pribram, K. H. (1960). *Plans and the structure of behavior.* New York: Henry Holt and Co, Inc.

Mischel, W., Cantor, N., & Feldman, S. (1996). Principles of self-regulation: The nature of willpower and self-control. In E. T. Higgins & A. W. Kruglanski (Eds.), *Social psychology: Handbook of basic principles* (pp. 329–360). New York: Guilford Press.

Monin, B., & Miller, D. T. (2001). Moral credentials and the expression of prejudice. *Journal of Personality and Social Psychology, 81*(1), 33–43.

Moskowitz, G. B. (2002). Preconscious effects of temporary goals on attention. *Journal of Experimental Social Psychology, 38*(4), 397–404.

Muraven, M., Tice, D. M., & Baumeister, R. F. (1998). Self-control as a limited resource: Regulatory depletion patterns. *Journal of Personality and Social Psychology, 74*(3), 774–789.

Oettingen, G., & Mayer, D. (2002). The motivating function of thinking about the future: Expectations versus fantasies. *Journal of Personality & Social Psychology, 83*(5), 1198–1212.

Powers, W. T. (1973). *Behavior: The control of perception.* Oxford, England: Aldine.

Rachlin, H. (1997). Self and self-control. In J. G. Snodgrass & R. L. Thompson (Eds.), *The self across psychology: Self-recognition, self-awareness, and the self concept annals of the New York Academy of Sciences* (Vol. 818, pp. 85–97). New York: New York Academy of Sciences.

Read, D., Loewenstein, G., & Rabin, M. (1999). Choice bracketing. *Journal of Risk and Uncertainty, 19*(1), 171–197.

Schwarz, N. (2004). Metacognitive experiences in consumer judgment and decision making. *Journal of Consumer Psychology, 14*(4), 332–348.

Schwarz, N., & Clore, G. L. (1984). Mood, misattribution, and judgments of well-being: Informative and directive functions of affective states. *Journal of Personality and Social Psychology, 45*, 513–523.

Schwarz, N., & Clore, G. L. (1996). Feelings and phenomenal experiences. In E. T. Higgins & A. W. Kruglanski (Eds.), *Social psychology: Handbook of basic principles* (pp. 433–465). New York: Guilford.

Shah, J. (2003). The motivational looking glass: How significant others implicitly affect goal appraisals. *Journal of Personality and Social Psychology, 85*(3), 424–439.

Shah, J. Y., Friedman, R., & Kruglanski, A. W. (2002). Forgetting all else: On the antecedents and consequences of goal shielding. *Journal of Personality and Social Psychology, 83*(6), 1261–1280.

Shah, J. Y., & Kruglanski, A. W. (2002). Priming against your will: How accessible alternatives affect goal pursuit. *Journal of Experimental Social Psychology, 38*(4), 368–383.

Shah, J. Y., & Kruglanski, A. W. (2003). When opportunity knocks: Bottom-up priming of goals by means and its effects on self-regulation. *Journal of Personality and Social Psychology, 84*(6), 1109–1122.

Simonson, I. (1990). The effect of purchase quantity and timing on variety-seeking behavior. *Journal of Marketing Research, 27*(2), 150–162.

Simonson, I., Nowlis, S. M., & Simonson, Y. (1993). The effect of irrelevant preference arguments on consumer choice. *Journal of Consumer Psychology, 2*(3), 287–306.

Soman, D., & Cheema, A. (2004). When goals are counter-productive: The effects of violation of a behavioral goal on subsequent performance. *Journal of Consumer Research, 31*(1), 52–62.

Srull, T. K., & Wyer, R. S. (1979). The role of category accessibility in the interpretation of information about persons: Some determinants and implications. *Journal of Personality and Social Psychology, 37*(10), 1660–1672.

Steele, C. M. (1988). The psychology of self-affirmation: Sustaining the integrity of the self. In L. Berkowitz (Ed.), *Advances in experimental social psychology* (Vol. 21, pp. 261–302). New York: Academic Press.

Taylor, S. E., & Brown, J. D. (1988). Illusion and well-being: A social psychological perspective on mental health. *Psychological Bulletin, 103*(2), 193–210.

Taylor, S. E., Pham, L. B., Rivkin, I. D., & Armor, D. A. (1998). Harnessing the imagination: Mental stimulation, self-regulation, and coping. *American Psychologist, 53*(4), 429–439.

Tolman, E. C. (1932). *Purposive behavior in animals and men.* New York: Appleton-Century-Crofts.

Trope, Y., & Fishbach, A. (2000). Counteractive self-control in overcoming temptation. *Journal of Personality and Social Psychology, 79*, 493–506.

Trope, Y., & Liberman, N. (2003). Temporal construal. *Psychological Review, 110*(3), 403–421.

Vallacher, R. R., & Wegner, D. M. (1987). *A theory of action identification.* Hillsdale, NJ: Erlbaum.

Weiner, B. (1979). A theory of motivation for some classroom experiences. *Journal of Educational Psychology, 71*(1), 3–25.

Weinstein, N. D. (1989). Optimistic biases about personal risks. *Science, 246*, 1232–1233.

Wicklund, R. A., & Gollwitzer, P. M. (1982). *Symbolic self-completion.* Hillsdale, NJ: Erlbaum.

Wyer, R. S., Jr. (2004). *Social comprehension and judgment: The role of situation models, narratives, and implicit theories.* Mahwah, NJ: Lawrence Erlbaum.

Zauberman, G., & Lynch, J. G., Jr. (2005). Resource slack and propensity to discount delayed investments of time versus money. *Journal of Experimental Psychology: General, 134*(1), 23–37.

Zeigarnik, B. (1927). Das Behalten erledigter und unerledigter Handlungen [The memory of completed and uncompleted actions]. *Psychologische Forschung, 9,* 1–85.

Zhang, Y., Fishbach, A., & Dhar, R. (2007). When thinking beats doing: The role of optimistic expectations in goal-based choice. *Journal of Consumer Research, 34,* 567–578.

Index